# APPROACHES
# TO ENGLISH
# HISTORICAL
# LINGUISTICS

## AN ANTHOLOGY

### ROGER LASS
*Indiana University*

HOLT, RINEHART AND WINSTON, INC.
*New York   Chicago   San Francisco   Atlanta*
*Dallas   Montreal   Toronto   London   Sydney*

# FOREWORD

It seems to me that the essential contribution of this collection of essays on the history of English is to make the teaching of the subject *possible* in a way that it has not been previously. For many years general linguistics has had a vitality, an energy, an excitement about it that was, with few exceptions, simply not present in historical linguistics. This excitement emerged quite directly from the feeling that new discoveries about the nature of language were being made all the time, and perhaps even more from the feeling that there were readily definable areas where it was obvious that much remained to be discovered—the feeling that the subject was alive, changing, growing, and above all, capable of providing genuine *explanations* of the phenomena of human language. On the other hand, one got the feeling from much historical linguistics that explanations of phenomena were not sought, only systematic accounts of the existence of phenomena. This distinction—between explanations and systematic accounts of putative facts—is, as John R. Ross has pointed out in the introduction of his brilliant M.I.T. dissertation on "Constraints on Variables in Syntax" (1967), the most fundamental distinction in science.

It is not yet true that a new paradigm (in the sense of Kuhn, *The Structure of Scientific Revolutions*, 1962) has arisen for historical linguistics, as one clearly has arisen for general and descriptive linguistics through the work of Chomsky, Halle, and their associates. But at least the need for one is apparent, and the general directions in which it will shape up are available in hazy outline. Many of the papers in this collection suggest these directions and outline the beginnings of them: that they are often wrong in detail or unable yet to cut cleanly through the haze is a consequence of the incredible complexity of the problem and the inadequacy of our present methodological and theoretical equipment, rather than failure to seek real explanations. The failings of much of historical linguistics are different in kind from whatever failings are to be found here, by and large: the former are, like those of evolutionary theory, failings to seek serious answers to questions. To say that one form evolved from another, or that one form is genetically related to

227416    *iii*

another, falls distressingly short of the interesting goal of explaining why the evolution went in one direction rather than another. Historical linguistics offers certain kinds of weakly explanatory hypotheses: articulatory ease, for example, is repeatedly suggested or implied as a mechanism of change; but pushed to its logical conclusion, articulatory ease would result in the total demolition of distinctions. Counteracting articulatory ease, we find the suggestion of functional necessity, such that if too many distinctions merge, communication collapses. To explain directions of change, we find suggestions about prestige dialects: but of course there is change within prestige dialects, and plenty of change that rises from below though resisted from above. It became a battle cry of a certain kind of linguistics that the only kinds of proper explanations were historical ones: you could say what was, and what it had become, and there explanation must stop. But this is only to say that the present has a history: history is interesting, really, only when it succeeds in explaining *why* the facts now are not the same as they once were.

It seems to me that virtually all of historical linguistics needs, and indeed is in for, careful reanalysis along lines that are beginning to emerge [for example in Chapter 6 of Chomsky and Halle's *Sound Pattern of English*, or in Paul Kiparsky's M.I.T. dissertation on "Phonological Change" (1965)]. I find myself little satisfied by the quality of explanation offered for historical change by the familiar tradition of scholarship. If Chomsky's hypotheses about the rule-governed nature of linguistic behavior are correct, it is time to begin the serious formulation of a theory of linguistic development which will provide a set of formal constraints on what kinds of change are possible, at what point restructuring in a set of rules becomes likely, what the possible types of restructuring are, and so on—in short, a theory which has a range of the same kinds of formal properties that we now have in some detail for the notion "possible grammatical or phonological rule in a language."

I think that, as in general linguistics, the rich documentation and the many generations of meticulous scholarship on English almost dictate that the beginnings of a new theory may have to be worked out through the study of data drawn from the history of English. These essays constitute not so much the beginnings of such a theory, as clear evidence of the ways in which the tradition is unsatisfactory and the problems that a theory must account for. The collection brings together essays that focus on crucial problems that require theoretical explanation, and thus makes a significant contribution toward the broader goals I have outlined, above and beyond the great convenience it brings to the scholar who wishes to bring himself or his students quickly into some of the central theoretical problems posed by English historical linguistics.

ROBERT P. STOCKWELL

*Los Angeles, California*
*March 1969*

# PREFACE

I have had two major concerns in mind in collecting the papers reprinted here. First, I have tried to gather in one place, for the convenience of students of the history of the English language and related disciplines, a number of important but not easily obtainable papers, which embody the results of significant studies which have not got into the standard handbooks and histories—either because they are too recent and specialized, or just too specialized. Second, I wanted to make available to students important recent works in English diachronic linguistics "in the original." By this, I mean as written by professional scholars for an audience of professional scholars, not as mediated to students by writers of textbooks. A collection of this sort should make available not only the work itself, but some of the excitement that characterizes original exploration in historical linguistics—as well as the crusty and polemical liveliness generated by major debates.

For a long portion of its complex history, diachronic linguistics was more or less a separate discipline from general linguistics; especially when, after the striking birth of structural linguistics in this century, a dichotomy developed between the "philologists" and the "linguists"—a dichotomy which characterized my own early training in the field, since I began as a "philologist," with all the traditional accouterments, and did not really discover what the "linguists" had to say until I was out of graduate school. This book, containing as it does examples of some of the best works of both kinds of practitioners, may be in a sense a small contribution toward healing that breach—by the expedient of making available to the student papers representing the excellences of both traditions.

This book is by no means intended to be the sole text—or even the major one—for a course in the history of English. It makes no attempt to furnish a "complete" or unified history. In fact, one of its primary assumptions is that the history of English has not in any real sense been written, but is constantly being discovered, and will probably continue to be so in the imaginable future.

For this reason I have tried where possible to present instances of the ongoing labor of discovery, especially where it becomes clear that the main issue is not the evidence itself, but various styles of interpretation: for example, the growing concern with the nature of analytical constructs such as the phoneme, and the increasing interest in theoretical well-formedness. Thus, I have included papers in which equally respectable scholars take opposed positions on a given question: A case in point is Stockwell and Barritt (1961) vs. Hockett (1959) on the problem of the Old English "short diagraphs."

I have attempted to keep away from any formal or theoretical bias in my choice of articles: The collection as a whole does not represent any particular "school" or metatheory. A major aim, in fact, has been to represent the varied excellences of as many styles of inquiry as possible, to give the student a chance to explore a wide range of techniques and theoretical concerns. This collection therefore contains examples of traditional "philological" inquiry (Kökeritz, Dobson, Bliss), various outgrowths of "classical" structural linguistics (Hockett, Fries, Stockwell), investigation oriented toward information theory (Sigurd), dialect geography (DeCamp), and generative-transformational analysis (Traugott, Stockwell). The student will be able to weigh for himself the viability and intrinsic interest of a number of different approaches to a set of common problems.

The weight is, however, strongly post-Bloomfieldian; mainly because the results of the earlier generations of inquiry into the history of English are already entrenched in the standard handbooks and histories (Luick, Sweet, Jespersen, Wyld, Kökeritz, Baugh, Robertson and Cassidy, and Pyles). Any student learning the history of English from, for example, Baugh or Pyles, is likely to be familiar to some extent with the work of Jespersen, Luick, and Sweet; but (unless he is primarily interested in and trained in linguistics), not so likely to know of the contributions of Hockett, Stockwell, Fries, Lehmann, or McIntosh. This accounts for the heavy emphasis on "modern" pieces—but is in no sense to be taken as a repudiation of older work. However differently any of us happen to approach our material from the way Luick or Sweet did, our labors still rest on what Sievers called the "bahnbrechenden Arbeiten" of those pioneers: there were indeed giants in the earth in those days.

We may quarrel, for example, with the way the older philologists interpreted the ME lengthening in open syllables, or with Sweet's interpretation of OE "breaking"—we may even wish to revise the whole notion of "length" as it has been handed down by scholars since Jacob Grimm—but we still deal with bodies of material excogitated and given form by these men, and our work rests firmly on the foundations they laid.

The criteria for inclusion have been relatively simple: Though I have aimed where possible at variety and "coverage," I have been more concerned with quality. There is not one piece in this book that does not seem interesting (at the very least) to me, nor one whose reading is likely to prove valueless to the serious student who has not already read it.

There are, however, three notable disproportions in the structure of the collection which I should like to mention briefly and defend: (1) it is heavily weighted toward papers concerned with methodology and theory; (2) it is weighted toward Old English, and particularly toward phonology; and (3) it stops short (except for occasional mention in some of the papers) at Early Modern English, and does not concern itself much with later developments, or with American English.

I defend these disproportions as follows: (1) methodology is one of the most vital concerns in diachronic linguistics, which like any historical discipline is essentially speculative—though no less bound to rigor for that. My own emphasis in teaching the history of the language has always been more on the development of theories of maximal explanatory power, and on the methodology of diachronic investigation, than on the collection of "facts"; and this emphasis has carried over into my choice of papers. I have been more eager to present the student with several accounts of the same thing from different points of view (for example, the problem of the OE phonemes), and to let him wrestle with the arguments, than to present what I may see as "God's truth" on any particular matter; (2) the further back we go, the more we have to speculate; and Old English has in the past generated richer speculation than the later stages of the language. Further, as Robert Stockwell eloquently points out in "Mirrors in the History of English Pronunciation," there is a great need for explicit statements of aim and method in phonological (and other) reconstruction; and the papers collected here are particularly rich in such statements. And finally, diachronic phonology requires more reconstructive effort, it seems, than the study of morphology and syntax, and the number of good papers available is larger. (3) This last qualification carries over: there are fewer really good papers on the later stages of English. And further, limitations of space have led me to establish this cut-off point. One of the basic problems in selecting papers dealing with Early Modern English is that the greater part of the good material is to be found in the standard monographs (for example, Kökeritz' *Shakespeare's Pronunciation*, Dobson's *English Pronunciation, 1500–1700*), which do not bear excerpting, and besides are readily available—or scattered throughout articles on other subjects. Thus Stockwell ("Mirrors," "Overall Pattern"), Traugott, Fries, and Samuels ("Functional Selection") all treat aspects of Early Modern English in papers covering much wider territory.

A word about the level of preparation this collection requires of the student: some of the pieces are likely to be quite difficult for one who is untrained in descriptive linguistics and generative grammar. As many of the difficulties as possible are taken care of in the glossary at the end and in occasional editorial notes; most of the others, with some help from the teacher, should not be beyond the reach of the serious graduate student in English who has read and asked questions about the more theoretical sections of a book like Bloomfield and Newmark's *Linguistic Introduction to the History of English.* In my own experience, I have been able to give my students without linguistic background enough theory in three weeks or so of lectures to enable most of them to handle the material here—even if with something less than consummate ease. The mediation of a skilled teacher will be invaluable here; but I don't think that the difficulties will be insuperable. And, of course, the collection will certainly be useful in contexts other than the usual history of the language course; it might profitably be used in advanced courses in English diachronic linguistics for the specialist, and perhaps in general courses in diachronic and comparative linguistics, since much of the material deals with the wider provinces of linguistic theory and general Indo-European and Germanic linguistics.

Ideally, in a history of language course, this book should I think be used along with a more-or-less "standard" history of English, and of course a collection of illustrative texts. Its main purposes, as I have said above, are to present recent work in the history of English and some related disciplines directly to the student, and to open up for him the exciting possibilities of diachronic investigation.

ROGER LASS

*Bloomington, Indiana*
*March 1969*

# TEXTUAL NOTE

All papers here are reprinted in their original form, with the following exceptions: (a) in some cases, as will be noted in the credits, the authors have kindly supplied me with corrections and revisions; (b) the text and notes have been restyled in accordance with the publisher's uniform practice; (c) passages in foreign languages have been translated; (d) bibliographical references have where advisable been brought up to date, and some explanatory footnotes have been added for the student's convenience.

All editorial material interpolated is set off from the text in square brackets; editorial notes are marked [—Ed.], and translations are bracketed but not marked.

# ACKNOWLEDGMENTS

I am grateful of course to the authors and publishers who have kindly given me permission to reprint, and in many cases furnished me with corrections and revisions. These acknowledgments will be found appended to the papers themselves. I am also deeply indebted to my colleagues Robert P. Stockwell, Bengt Sigurd, Wolfgang Wölck, and Owen Thomas for their suggestions, for reading parts of the manuscript, and correction of various errors. Those that remain are of course my responsibility. And finally, I would like to thank Samuel R. Levin for his encouragement, and the staff of Holt, Rinehart and Winston for their cooperation and help in preparing this manuscript for publication: especially Jere Calmes, Kenney Withers, and Jane Ross for their patience in answering my endless questions.

# CONTENTS

# METHODS AND MATERIALS IN DIACHRONIC INVESTIGATION

# Introduction

There are many ways of investigating the historical processes of language change; the essays in this collection will probably be seen ultimately to reveal almost as many styles of investigation and presentation as there are authors. But this does not by any means imply that diachronic linguistics is a nonrigorous or fanciful pursuit; far from it. Rigor and consistency are of course vital in all forms of investigation, but perhaps nowhere so much as in historical study, which because it tries to *reconstruct* processes and states that no longer exist must be especially careful to base its procedures solidly. As Robert Stockwell writes in a paper reprinted later in this volume ("Mirrors in the history of English pronunciation"):

History is not an account of facts but of relations that are inferred to have existed between supposed facts. It is not at all easy to make a crucial observation as to what a particular fact is, or to discriminate between facts and inferences. The "facts" of historical scholarship are often simply useful hypotheses that in turn relate, by rough rules of inference, a variety of secondary "facts" to each other. The most insightful accounts of historical events often turn out to be intricate webs of suppositions and inferences removed at many steps from the citable data on which the conclusions ultimately rest.

That is, it is quite possible that the value of an historical statement may turn out to be directly proportional, not to the "accuracy" with which it reports the "facts" (which are probably not in an absolute sense recoverable), but to the strength and consistency of its framework, and the explanatory power of the inferential network it has set up.

The purpose of this introductory group of papers is to provide some examples of the kinds of theories and inferential structures that historical linguists make use of. With one exception, these papers are not directly related to the history of English (though they may use English examples from time to time): they are concerned with general problems, with ways of stating them, with the kinds of evidence that may profitably be used in diachronic study, and the kinds of analytical techniques that can be applied to the evidence in order to produce insightful statements.

The two papers by Roman Jakobson deal with some of the most basic issues in the field: especially the importance of an over-all, structural, systematic approach to the (apparently) isolated data of language change.

Jakobson is especially concerned with the notion of *system*, with the implications of the dichotomy, first classically formulated by the Swiss linguist F. de Saussure, between "language" and "speech" (*langue* and *parole*).

*Language* is the underlying, abstract system or matrix; *speech* is the infinite and variable set of realizations of this underlying structure. For example, the phoneme /aw/ in English (as in the syllabic of *mouse*) is an element of *langue*; the realizations in *parole*, in individual utterances, may be as widely different as [au], [æu], [ɑu], [ɪu], or [əu]. What really matters from the systematic point of view (Jakobson's "system of oppositions") is not the phonetic nature of /aw/; that is, the noises that implement it; what matters from the point of view of the system (and indeed what makes it possible for us to understand any speaker of our language other than ourselves) is the fact that whatever noise /aw/ comes out as, it is in contrast to the /ay/ of *mice*, the /uw/ of *moose*, the /e/ of *mess*, etc. It is this kind of system that historical linguists have become increasingly concerned with discovering and analyzing in past stages of languages.

It has become clear, in fact, that systems and the oppositions and relationships within them are really the only linguistic elements that are historically recoverable with any degree of certainty; how a dead language *sounded* (any aspect of its *parole*) is forever lost to us—though we can on the basis of various kinds of knowledge make some sharp guesses. We can, however, reconstruct, often with considerable rigor, the relations of systemic elements one to another.

The change from the older, "atomistic" or prestructural approach to the description of data from early stages of a language to a systematic approach can be shown briefly with an example from the phonology of Old English. Here is a description from Henry Sweet's *Anglo-Saxon primer* (9th ed., Oxford, 1957, 3), first published in 1882:

> ...*f* and *s*, in addition to their modern values, could represent respectively the sounds of *v* and *z*, letters which were not normally used in O.E. These three letters, *f*, *s*, *þ*, had the sounds of *f*, *s*, and *th* in thin ... initially and finally in accented words; next to "voiceless" consonants (such as *p*, *t*); and when double: *full* "full" ... *wearþ* "became" ... *sippan* "after." They had the sounds of *v*, *z*, and *th* in *then* ... when single between vowels, or between a vowel and another "voiced" sound (such as *l*, *r*, *m*, *n*): *lufian* "love," *cēosan* "choose" ... *māþm* "treasure"....

Now this statement, thorough as it is, does not indicate one very important fact about the OE spirant system: that the sound "of *f*" and the sound "of *v*," for example, are *not* members of a "distinctive opposition": the data themselves indicate that there could not in OE be any pair of words (a "minimal pair") distinguished solely by the difference between these two sounds, as, for example, MnE *fat* and *vat*. The occurrence of the voiced and voiceless sounds is totally *conditioned* by the environments in which they occur.

If we were to describe this set of data from a structural viewpoint, keeping in mind the total system of which the sounds in question are members, we should now say that OE had a phoneme /f/, with probable allophones [f] initially, finally and medially when double, and [v] between voiced elements.

That is, [f] and [v] are manifestations of *one* unit in the *langue* (opposed to /s/, /þ/ and so forth), as shown by the fact that they are in *complementary distribution*: the occurrences of each are mutually exclusive and predictable by environment. Or we might further, using a more recent set of conventions, sum this up economically in the form of a rule such as:

$$/f/ \rightarrow [v] \: / \: V\_\_\_V$$

That is, "(the phoneme) /f/ is realized as (its allophone) [v] when it is in an environment such that voiced elements both precede and follow it."

The concepts somewhat lengthily set out above will be seen to animate, in one sense or another, the following papers in this section—and indeed the majority of the papers in this whole collection. In the general papers immediately following this introduction, the writers deal with some of the basic problems raised by a structural approach, some of the methods that can be used in historical investigation, and the all-important question, which will be seen to arise again and again, of evidence and its uses.

Herbert Penzl, in "The evidence for phonemic change," considers, with special reference to the Germanic languages, just what sorts of phonemic changes ("splits," "mergers," and so on) occur historically, and the kinds of evidence linguists use in establishing and describing them: orthographic, orthoëpic (that is, statements made in the past by writers on language), metrical evidence, evidence from language comparison, and evidence from language contact (the behavior of borrowed items).

The important conception of language as a "code" is the basis for Bengt Sigurd's study of certain sound changes in Old Norse. Here, language and its changes are examined according to the framework of information theory, and various statistical techniques are used to study the changes in communicational "efficiency" undergone by a language in the process of historical change.

Angus McIntosh's paper on "The analysis of written Middle English" is an important document in diachronic linguistics: McIntosh is concerned here with the peculiar properties of writing systems, and the degree to which they reflect (or fail to reflect) the phonemic and phonetic realities of the speech forms they represent. He makes a strong case for the diachronic (and synchronic) study of written language as a valuable and legitimate procedure in itself, not merely as a window into the spoken language.

And finally, Einar Haugen, in a very important paper, sets up terminology and procedure for both the synchronic and diachronic study of language contact: how morphemes, phonemes, words, are borrowed from one language to another, how such items behave in the languages into which they are imported, and so on. The framework set up by Haugen is of particular importance in the study of the history of English, as there were at least two very important episodes involving language contact which have left their mark on its subsequent development—the English-Scandinavian contact dating from the Old English period, and the English-French contact beginning with the Norman Conquest.

# ROMAN JAKOBSON

## Phoneme and Phonology*

PHONEME is the basic concept of phonology. By this term we designate a set of those concurrent sound properties which are used in a given language to distinguish words of unlike meaning. In speech, diverse sounds can implement one and the same phoneme. This variety depends on the style of speech and/or on the phonetic environment in which that phoneme occurs. The difference between such sounds is determined by external factors and hence cannot serve to distinguish word meanings. Such sounds are labeled variants of the given phoneme. Thus, in Czech, the velar [ŋ], e.g., in [veŋku], and the dental [n], e.g., in [venek], are variants of one and the same phoneme /n/; the first variant appears before /k/ and /g/, the second in all other positions. In English, however, the dental nasal /n/ and the velar nasal (spelled ng) may occur in identical positions and thus serve to differentiate meanings (e.g., sin, sing); they are, then, two different phonemes. The concept of the phoneme was first outlined in the works of Baudouin de Courtenay and F. de Saussure,[1] but has received a wider and more precise utilization in modern phonological research. See Travaux du Cercle linguistique de Prague, IV.

PHONOLOGY is a part of linguistics dealing with speech sounds with regard to the functions which they fulfill in a given language, whereas phonetics has for its task the investigation of speech sounds from a purely physiological, physical, and psycho-acoustical point of view. Along with the term "phonology," we encounter such equivalent designations as phonematics, phonemics, and functional phonetics. The basic linguistic function of sound differences is the distinction of meanings. A sound difference which, in a given language, can be used to distinguish meanings is viewed as a phonological opposition. The inventory of phonological oppositions proper to a given language constitutes its phonological system. Certain structural laws of universal validity underlie the composition of any phonological system and limit the variety of systems, so that a phonological typology of the languages of the entire world is quite feasible.

Word phonology inventories the phonemes peculiar to a given language, their interrelations and possible combinations. It uses statistics to determine the functional load of these phonemes and their combinations, as well as their frequency in the vocabulary and in current speech. A special branch of

* From Roman Jakobson, Selected Writings, I (The Hague, 1961), 231–33. Reprinted by permission of the author and Mouton and Co. (First published in the Second Supplementary Volume to the Czech Encyclopedia—Ottův slovník naučný [Prague, 1932].)

word phonology is *morphological phonology* or *morpho(pho)nology*, which analyzes the phonological structure of the various morphological components of the word. While word phonology deals with those sound distinctions which are able to differentiate word meanings, *syntactical phonology* studies phonic differences capable of delimiting a word within a word group or of differentiating the meanings of word groups as wholes.

A second task of phonology, along with the synchronic description of individual phonological systems, is the characterization of their development. In contradistinction to traditional historical phonetics, *historical phonology* is based on the following principles: a) no sound change can be comprehended without reference to the system which undergoes that change; b) each change in a phonological system is purposeful. Historical phonology extends the application of the comparative method to genetically unrelated languages and in this way arrives at a typology of the phonological evolution of languages, whereas synchronic phonology works toward a typology of the systems themselves. Similarly, the study of the geographic distribution of different phonological types is not confined to cognate dialects or languages, but ascertains that the boundaries between different phonological features often do not coincide with the boundaries between languages or language families.

The phonological approach has proven to be particularly fruitful in respect to poetic language, standard language or writing, whereas a complete failure marked the attempts of older linguistics to treat these domains. The problem of the relation between the phonological system and writing is of theoretical and practical significance: it makes possible the solution of such questions as spelling and shorthand reform, the creation of alphabets for peoples without a written literature, etc.

The first foundations of phonology were laid by Baudouin de Courtenay, F. de Saussure, and their disciples. The systematic elaboration of phonology began only after the First World War when: a) there was posed the problem of the phonological system as a lawful structural whole, b) the psychological notion of phonological elements (the so-called psycho-phonetics) was replaced by a sociological approach, and c) synchronic phonology was supplemented by historical phonology. The Prague Linguistic Circle, which called the First International Phonological Conference (Prague, 1930), has become the organizational center of modern phonology. Cf. *Travaux du Cercle linguistique de Prague*, I ff., with further bibliography.

## FOOTNOTES

1. [For accounts of the lives and works of these two men, see Thomas Sebeok, ed., *Portaits of linguists* (Bloomington, 1966), I, 533 ff., II, 87 ff. Saussure's major work is available in English in *A course in general linguistics*, tr. Wade Baskin (New York, 1959). See also Rulon S. Wells, "De Saussure's system of linguistics," *Word* 3.1–31 (1947).—Ed.]

## ROMAN JAKOBSON

# The Concept of the Sound Law
# and the Teleological Criterion*

The basic assumption of the neo-grammarian linguistic methodology, that of the sound law operating without exceptions in a given language at a given time, has, up till recently, repeatedly met with negative criticism, since the neo-grammarians have not been able to give a theoretical foundation for this working hypothesis. The revision of the traditional tenet leads to the recognition of the fact that language (and in particular its sound system) cannot be analyzed without taking into account the purpose which that system serves. Once this amendment is made, the objections to the doctrine of the sound law lose their validity.

1) The idea of a sound law operating without exceptions in a given language must be limited to a linguistic system characterized by one and the same function, i.e., to linguistic entities which are functionally equivalent.

2) The neo-grammarians did not succeed in explaining the social character of sound changes (why a speech community accepts and sanctions individual slips), but this problem too finds its solution once it is posed teleologically. The same requirement applies if one attributes the decisive role in sound changes to the succession of generations.

3) The overlapping between territorially, socially or functionally distinct linguistic patterns can be fully comprehended only from a teleological point of view, since every transition from one system to another necessarily bears a linguistic function.

The first attempts at a goal-directed interpretation of sound changes, in particular their explanation with reference to the law of the economy of energy or to fashion and esthetic factors, are one-sided and greatly over-simplify the problem. It is impossible to deal with the sounds of a given language without regard to its phonological system, i.e., to the repertory of meaningful distinctions among the acoustico-motor images proper to the given language.

F. de Saussure and his school broke a new trail in static linguistics, but as to the field of language history they remained in the neo-grammarian rut. Saussure's teaching that sound changes are destructive factors, fortuitous and

* From Roman Jakobson, *Selected Writings*, I (The Hague, 1961), 1–2. Reprinted by permission of the author and Mouton and Co. (First published in Czech in *Časopis pro moderni filologii*, XIV [Prague, March, 1928], as a "brief extract" from a paper delivered in the Prague Linguistic Circle, January 13, 1927.)

blind, limits the active role of the speech community to sensing each given stage of deviations from the customary linguistic pattern as an orderly system. This antinomy between synchronic and diachronic linguistic studies should be overcome by a transformation of historical phonetics into the history of the phonemic system. In other words, phonetic changes must be analyzed in relation to the phonemic system which undergoes these mutations. For instance, if the order within a linguistic system is disturbed, there follows a cycle of sound changes aiming at its renewed stabilization (like in a game of chess).

The comparison of phonemic systems (both from the diachronic and from the synchronic points of view) enables us to lay down certain universally valid sound laws, e.g., laws which state the incompatibility of a dynamic accent with quantitative vocalic distinctions and with a pitch accent in one phonemic system; the incompatibility of a pitch accent with some tonality distinctions in consonants; the co-occurrence of quantitative vocalic distinctions and distinctive intonational varieties of accent in those phonological systems which include a pitch accent.

The surmounting of the neo-grammarian tradition does not imply a refutal of the sound law concept, but, on the contrary, it means a reinforcement of this notion by the substitution of a teleological approach for the mechanical view. And since not the motor but the acoustical aspect of speech sounds, aimed at by the speaker, has a social value, the teleological conception of sound problems increases the relevance of acoustical analysis in comparison with the physiology of speech.

HERBERT PENZL

# The Evidence
# for Phonemic Changes*

## I. Types of Phonemic Change

In diachronic linguistics a great variety of phonetic changes can be observed. Scholars seem to be agreed, however, that there are only very few types of phonemic change. Prehistorical, i.e., reconstructed changes, cannot be treated in the same manner as historically attested changes. Only a careful consideration of historical changes enables us to draw any conclusions regarding prehistorical changes. The problems of reconstruction should not be prematurely linked and added to the specific problems of diachronic phonemics.

§ 1.1 *Phonemic Change.* A number of changes affect only the shape of certain morphemes but not the phonemic stock. Among them we notice the loss or replacement of certain phonemes in morphemes (assimilation, dissimilation), e.g., *Tölpel* "bumpkin" (MHG *dörpære, dörper > dörpel*); *Pfennig* (OHG *pfenning*); *Welt* (MHG *werlt, welt*); *Hoffart* "arrogance" (MHG *hochvart*); *Elle* (OHG *elina*). The sequence of phonemes in a morpheme can be reversed (metathesis): *Wespe* (MHG *wefse, webse, wespe*), *Erle* "alder" (OHG *erila, elira*). A phoneme can be added to a morpheme: *Obst* "fruit" (MHG *obez*), *Habicht* "hawk" (MHG *habech*), *albern* "foolish" (MHG *alwære*), *niemand* (MHG *nieman*). All these changes could be called distributional; they do not constitute sound-change in the regular sense. Some of them may occur almost with the regularity of a sound-change at a given time in a given language, but they are not gradual, even if possibly produced unconsciously. They seem often sporadic, involving some morphemes but not others with the same structure. Analogical remodeling is a common factor in their occurrence. They may be a factor leading to a phonemic change, however, since any change in incidence or distribution may also result in a change in pattern and stock. The evidence for such distributional changes is usually plentiful and unambiguous; it does not differ from the evidence for phonemic changes which we will consider here. All observable phonetic changes in the history of a language may have some phonemic significance.[1] Thus a phonemic change is any sound-change that gradually affects the contrastive features of the phonemes, their general incidence and patterning, or their allophonic variation.

* From Ernst Pulgram, ed., *Studies Presented to Joshua Whatmough on His Sixtieth Birthday* (The Hague, 1957), 193–208. Reprinted by permission of the author and Mouton and Co.

The phonemic principle makes it necessary for us to view each and every change from the point of view of the entire pattern. This is perhaps the most important new methodological demand in historical linguistics that at the same time presents a distinct advance over an earlier approach that appears too atomistic now. If we thus isolate in this paper certain phonemic changes and do not analyze their pattern impact in detail, we are aware that we are not offering an adequate description of the change. After all, we do not indicate its absolute and relative chronology, its regional origin and spread, and its probable causes either. We are concerned here with its typological classification and the evidence for its occurrence, not with any other pertinent factors.

§ 1.2 *The Phonemic Shift.* All phonemic changes may either occur in all positions or only in specific ones; the latter changes are usually called "conditioned," the former "unconditioned." What is conditioned change diachronically, corresponds synchronically to conditioned allophonic variation.[2] André Martinet[3] subdivides phonemic changes into (1) those that do not affect the number of distinctive features within the language, (2) those that reduce them, (3) those that increase them. Daniel Jones' 29 types of phonemic change are partly based on phonetic criteria.[4] Among attested phonemic changes we distinguish six different types: shifts, mergers (§ 1.3), splits (§ 1.4), monophonemization (§ 1.5), diphonemization (§ 1.6), phonemic loss (§ 1.7). The phonemic shift consists of the change of a phoneme of one sound-type to a phoneme of another sound-type. Any such shift may result in a whole series of interconnected changes, but the pattern adjustment may also not exceed some allophonic variation which is not recoverable historically. The change from the high back-rounded vowel phoneme /u/ to a high front-rounded vowel phoneme /ü/ in French, *tu, dur, duc,* is an example of a shift. Another example is the change from an apical lenis spirant /þ/ to an apical lenis stop /d/ in Old High German: *ther* or *dher,* later *der; thing,* later *ding.* In both cases the "terminal" phoneme is of a different type than the "initial" one and not identical with any phoneme already in the language: neither /ü/ in French (Latin) nor /d/ in most Middle and Upper German dialects of Old High German existed before the phonemic change. In a shift the number of phonemes remains the same, since the loss of one or more units of the initial pattern seems compensated by the addition of one or more units in the terminal pattern. The formula to express a phonemic shift is: $/A/ > /x/$.[5] A. Martinet considers all phonemic changes that affect the pattern as part of a chain, which, from the point of view of the change in question, would either seem to be a "drag-chain" or a "push-chain."[6] Most shifts represent what R. Jakobson called "Umphonologisierung," i.e., a change from one phonemic distinction between two phonemes to another phonemic distinction between them.[7]

§ 1.3 *The Phonemic Merger.* Another important and most frequent type of phonemic change is the merger, the coalescence of two phonemes. This can either occur in all positions (unconditioned change) or only in some special phonetic environment (conditioned change). The result of the merger may be the exclusive occurrence of either one of the two contrasting units or the emergence of a new, possibly intermediate type. Two well-known examples for merger in the history of German are the medial and final coalescence of the two sibilants /s/ and /z/ in late Middle High German, e.g., *es* from earlier *ez* "it" and *es* "of it, of him," and the coalescence of the allophones of /a/ and /e/ before *i*-sounds in Old High German (primary umlaut of /a/), e.g., OHG *gesti*, plural of *gast*. The phonetic identification of the initial sibilant phonemes /s/ and /z/ has been a moot question, but at any rate a single terminal phoneme /s/ results, in contrast with the other new sibilant /š/ which developed from the cluster /sk/ in Middle High German (see below § 1.5). The Old High German [e] allophones of /a/ before *i*-sounds and the [e] allophones of /e/ in its rare occurrences before *i*-sounds, e.g., in *felis* (NHG *Fels*) "rock," *krebiz* (NHG *Krebs*) "crab," *pelliz* (NHG *Pelz*) "fur," merged; thus a suspension of the contrast between /a/ and /e/, in the terminology of the Prague school a "neutralization," resulted in that position. The /e/ phoneme prevailed however. Our formulas for merger will have to be:

$$\frac{/A/}{/B/} \quad > \quad /A/; \qquad \frac{/A/}{/B/} \quad > \quad /B/; \qquad \frac{/A/}{/B/} \quad > \quad /x/$$

This indicates that the terminal phoneme may be either one of the two initial phonemes or a phoneme that is different from them.[8] Partial or limited merger (neutralization), e.g., before a phoneme /X/, we can express as follows:

$$/AX/ \quad > \quad /BX/; \qquad /BX/ \quad > \quad /AX/$$

This indicates the merger of /A/ and /B/ only before /X/ with the terminal prevalence of /B/ or /A/, respectively. Most mergers represent what R. Jakobson called an "Entphonologisierung" of some distinctive feature.[9]

§ 1.4 *The Phonemic Split.* A third most important type of phonemic change is the split, a bifurcation of two phonemes out of the allophones of one initial phoneme. Striking examples are provided by the results of umlaut in late Old High German, when all rounded back vowel phonemes developed rounded front vowel phonemes from their allophones before former *i*-sounds:[10] /a/ and /ä/, /ā/ and /ā̈/, /ō/ and /ȫ/, /o/ and /ö/, /ū/ and /ǖ/, /u/ and /ü/, /au/ and /eu/, also /ē̆/ and /e/, e.g., MHG *maht*, pl. *mähte* (OHG *mahti*), *nāmen* (OHG *nāmun*) "they took," *næmen* subj. (OHG *nāmin*), *schōne* adv. "beautifully" (OHG *scōno*), *schoene* adj. "beautiful" (OHG *scōni*), *hūt* "skin," pl. *hiute* (OHG *hūti*), *übel* (OHG *ubil*) "evil." Our formula for a phonemic split is as follows:

$$/A/ \quad > \quad \frac{/A/}{/x/}$$

/x/ in this formula designates the new phoneme, which is often /A'/ from an allophone [A'] of /A/. All splits represent what R. Jakobson (see footnote 9) calls a "Phonologisierung" (a phonemization or phonemicization).

§ 1.5 *Monophonemization.* Another phonemic change consists of the change from a cluster to a single phoneme. This often resembles a phonemic shift (§ 1.2). As examples we quote the development of a groove sibilant /š/ from an earlier cluster consisting of a slit sibilant and a velar stop (/sk/) in Middle High German and in Middle English: MHG *visch* (OHG *fisk*), ME *fish, fissh* (OE *fisc*) (see § 3.4). In English and in German the cluster /ng/ developed into a single velar nasal phoneme /ŋ/: *singen, to sing*. The formula for such a change is as follows:

$$/AB/ \quad > \quad /x/$$

The new phoneme /x/ may represent /A'/ or /B'/, i.e., be the reflex of allophones [A'] or [B'] appearing in the initial cluster: e.g., /ɲ/ developed from the allophone [ŋ] of /n/ appearing before /g/ (or /k/); thus /ng/ ([ŋg]) > /ŋ/ is an example for /AB/ > /A'/.

§ 1.6 *Diphonemization.* A single phoneme can develop into a cluster of two phonemes: /A/ > /XY/. Also this change resembles a phonemic shift (§ 1.2). The terminal cluster can contain two phonemes already found in the pattern. An example for this change is the New High German diphthongization where Middle High German /ī/ became /ai/, /ū/ became /au/, /ǖ/ became /oi/: *Wein* (MHG *wīn*), *Haus* (MHG *hūs*), *Leute* (MHG *liute*) (§ 3.4).

§ 1.7 *The Phonemic Loss.* Another phonemic change is the loss of a phoneme either in some positions only or everywhere: /A/ > 0. It could be labeled "merger with zero."[11] As examples we can cite the Old High German loss of the phoneme /h/ in clusters as /hl/ /hr/ /hw/ /hn/, e.g., *laut* (OHG *hlūt*), *Ross* (OHG *hros*), *wer* (OHG *hwer*), *neigen* (OHG *hnīgan*), or the loss of /h/ in intervocalic position in late Middle High German: e.g., in *sehen* (§ 3.5).

The rise of a new phoneme by borrowing, e.g., the appearance of nasalized vowels in French loan-words in German (*Cousin, Bonbon*), or the adoption of /f/ in Russian, cannot be considered a counterpart to phonemic loss because the borrowing of foreign phonemes is not a sound-change from initial zero.[12]

## II. Evidence for Synchronic and Diachronic Analysis

§ 2.1 *Orthographic Evidence.* In historical linguistics diachronic analysis must be preceded by synchronic analysis. The former can only be based on the comparison between two or more successive stages of a language that have been analyzed synchronically. The evidence for the synchronic and diachronic analysis is the same. There are several types of such evidence. Their careful consideration, which seems to have been somewhat neglected, is of great importance for the methodology of historical linguistics.

Orthographic evidence (§ 3) must be mentioned first. The relationship between symbol and sound, between the graphemic and the phonemic system is a basic problem in historical linguistics. Alphabetic writing itself in its inception used to involve a certain "phonemic" interpretation of the sounds on the part of scribes and authors, particularly if they wrote their own native language or dialect, when they would attempt to render the essential units of their phonemic system and would not be aware of allophones. Thus the use and distribution of graphemes is important evidence in synchronic analysis. The known derivation of the symbols and their original values can be used for general phonetic identifications (§ 2.5). Occasionally recorded transliterations into another alphabet, e.g., into the Cyrillic, Arabic, or some phonetic alphabet, may be helpful. Diachronic interpretations are facilitated by the observation of changes in the orthographic system, of internal orthographic fluctuation or of a modern discrepancy between symbol and pronunciation.[13] Not every change in spelling implies a change in pronunciation; e.g., the Middle English use of "ou" for Old English "u" is simply due to the different spelling practice of the Anglo-Norman scribes. Not only the analysis of orthographic systems, but also the study of all deviations from them, namely of occasional spellings ("naive spellings"), provides evidence. Their synchronic analysis reveals the discrepancy between the traditional orthography and the phonemic system of its user.

The term "occasional spellings" suggest a minority-type of orthography which occurs together with the majority-type in identical or contemporaneous texts. Occasional spellings may represent just graphical errors, e.g., dittography, mistakes in copying, or only graphical variants, which are determined by the orthographic system with which the scribe or naive writer is familiar. They may reveal historical or dialectal variants for individual words: e.g., *jest* "just," *gould* beside *gold*, *loom* beside *loam*. Synchronic analysis has to screen these spellings carefully within a given text and separate them from spellings that reveal the writer's or scribe's phonemic distribution or phonemic changes (see below § 4).[14] Diachronic analysis centers on the relevant differences between the conventional orthography and the observed individual deviations.

§ 2.2 *Orthoëpic Evidence.* Statements by grammarians at different times offer one type of evidence to the synchronic and diachronic analyst that orthography itself cannot supply (§ 5): phonetic identifications of the values designated by the symbols. Certain characteristics of Latin, Greek, Sanskrit sounds can be ascertained from the descriptions of native grammarians.[15] With the notable exception of the First Grammatical Treatise written about Old Icelandic phonemes in the middle of the twelfth century,[16] evidence of this kind is not found for the Germanic languages until we reach early modern times. Then grammarians describe foreign sounds in terms of their native language; they describe the correct pronunciation and dialectal usage as to spelling and pronunciation; they describe the correlation sound: symbol to facilitate the teaching of reading and spelling. They are often interested in normalizing or reforming the orthographic evidence mentioned above (§ 2.1). They are usually themselves decisively influenced by the orthography.

Occasional and systematic representations of speech or dialect characteristics by deviant spelling in literary works can provide evidence equivalent to the observations of grammarians, e.g., the rendering of rustic American English in Lowell's *Biglow Papers*. The German schoolmasters' transcriptions of German dialects in conventional orthography for the Deutscher Sprachatlas as well as scholars' phonetic or phonemic field-notes or the phonetic recordings of a speech-atlas can also be interpreted by what Charles F. Hockett[17] called the analyst's "philological method."

§ 2.3 *Metrical Evidence.* Evidence is supplied by the structure of lines of poetry, either by the appearance of stressed or quantitatively marked syllables in a determined sequence, by the pattern of alliteration, or by the demands of assonance and rime (§ 6). Synchronic analysis of texts provides a description of these metrical patterns; diachronic analysis compares their observed differences at different times.

Similar to the evidence of alliteration, assonance, and rime is that furnished by puns in literary works. Puns may be homonymic or only show a partial correspondence in pronunciation.[18]

§ 2.4 *Comparative Evidence.* Comparative data provide important evidence for the analyst. Internal comparison considers distributional and structural facts, or other parallel sound-changes of the language itself. We often assume a symmetrical structure of the phonemic pattern and draw inferences from correlated features.[19]

The comparison may also concern the corresponding historical values of other dialects of the same language or of related languages within the same branch or within the same language family. We can call this "syncomparative" analysis. The comparison may involve a contrastive treatment of later attested stages of the same or related languages; this constitutes "diacomparative" evidence. It may pertain to the values that could have developed out of a reconstructed system of protophonemes and thus be "protocomparative," which is actually COMPARATIVE in the narrowest sense. Also all modern dialectal values in their present areal distribution can be interpreted diachronically as "neocomparative" material. Significant alternations at a later stage will often provide comparative evidence for an earlier stage of the same language or dialect. All diachronic interpretation implies a comparison, of course. The comparative evidence reveals that diachronic considerations can be fruitful also for supplementing or revising synchronic analyses. The terminal value can be used to determine the initial values. All historical comparative data consist in turn of orthographic, orthoëpic, metrical, and contact material. The method of direct contact or field-work can only be applied to neocomparative data.

§ 2.5 *Contact Evidence.* While syncomparative evidence concerns simultaneous or roughly simultaneous correspondences in related languages, further data for analysis are provided by the actual interchange, the loan and borrowing of words from one language to the other. The adoption of the alphabet or single letters of another language yields important evidence for the initial values linked to the letters. Accurate transliterations of words or sentences into different writing systems provide a welcome key to the corresponding values of the symbols (see above § 2.1). Loans based partly or totally on the written form or presumably provided by a third language as an intermediary must, of course, be interpreted differently from direct borrowings based on the spoken form in the contact between speakers of the two languages. The actual borrowing of foreign phonemes is a rare occurrence (§ 1.7). Ordinarily, we can observe in such direct loans the rendering of the foreign phoneme by corresponding native phonemes. In historical linguistics, of course, the graphic reflexes of the correspondences have to be subjected to synchronic analysis. Under favorable circumstances both the initial and the terminal values of phonemic changes that are involved in the borrowings can be isolated by diachronic interpretation of such reflexes in a foreign pattern.

## III. Orthographic Evidence and Phonemic Changes

§ 3.1 *Orthography and Shifts.* The orthographic system expresses all distributional changes, since they concern the incidence of phonemes, for which symbols are available (§ 1.1). It often indicates phonemic shifts (§ 1.2). The Old High German change from /þ/ to /d/ is clearly rendered, particularly in initial position, by the replacement of "th" or "dh" by the letter "d": *der* for earlier *ther* or *dher*. Originally the digraph which Latin scribes used to transliterate the Greek theta was employed to render the OHG apical spirant unknown to Latin; the prompt rendering of the new OHG value may be due to the convenient availability of the symbol "d" which agrees more or less with its Latin value. The French phonemic shift from /u/ to /ü/ in *tu, dur*[20] is not reflected by any orthographic change: the initial symbol "u" remains constant.

§ 3.2 *Orthography and Mergers.* Orthography indicates phonemic mergers and their results, e.g., by noncontrastive use of two formerly contrasting symbols or by the use of one symbol instead of two initial ones. The terminal use of one symbol only indicates the prevalence of the phoneme initially designated by it. The OHG spellings *gesti* "guests" (sing. *gast*), *eltir* "older" (*alt* "old") with the "e" symbol as found in *herza* "heart," *helfan* "help" indicate the merger of /e/ and /a/ before *i* and the replacement of /a/ in that position. The merger of /s/ and /z/ in medial and final positions in late MHG was first shown by the indiscriminate use of "s" and "z" and their graphic variants.[21] Reverse or inverse spellings ("umgekehrte Schreibungen") always indicate a phonemic coalescence (see § 4.2).

§ 3.3 *Orthography and Splits.* Orthography gives often belated recognition to a phonemic split (§ 1.4) by the creation of new symbols derived from the old ones or by consistently contrastive use of two available symbols. In

Middle High German most scribes use special diacritics or digraphs to render the new umlaut phonemes: e.g., *ä æ oe ü* in *mähte, næmen, schoene, übel*. The late OHG merger of the diphthong /iu/ and the umlaut of /ū/ provided a digraph symbol "iu" for /ü/: *hiute* (OHG *hūti*) "skins" like *hiute* (OHG *hiutu*) "today." This practice is already found in the orthographic system of Notker III. The phonemic split of Old English *k* was expressed by a contrastive use of the two available symbols "k" and "c" in some manuscripts, e.g., in that of the Rushworth glosses to the gospel of St. Matthew; *kining, cild*, since 1200 by the symbols "k (c)" and "ch," respectively: *king, child*.[22]

§ 3.4 *Orthography and Cluster Changes.* The development of clusters into single phonemes and of single phonemes into clusters is often indicated by a change in orthographic practice. Middle English spellings *s ss sch sh ssh* for historical /sk/ indicate its change to a single phoneme, similarly such Middle High German spellings as *sch sg sh ss (s)*: e.g., *sharp (sarp, ssarp, scharp), fissh*, MHG *scharpf* (OHG *scarpf*).[23] The change from /ng/ to /ŋ/ is not expressed by the orthography; the digraph "ng" remains in German and in English. The New High German diphthongization is indicated by the replacement of "i" "u" "iu" symbols from the twelfth century on by the digraphs "ei," "ou (au)," "eu," respectively:[24] *wein* (HMG *wīn*), *hous, haws, hauss* (MHG *hūs*), *leute* (MHG *liute*) (§ 1.6). A similar development in Early Modern English is not reflected by any change of the orthography: *wine* (ME *wīn*), *house* (ME *hous, hūs*). The French change from clusters of vowel plus nasal to nasalized vowel phonemes is not shown by the orthography, which still retains the digraph spelling: e.g., *danser, pain, bon*.

§ 3.5 *Orthography and Phonemic Loss.* The orthography usually reflects the loss of a phoneme. The OHG loss of initial /h/ is indicated by spellings without "h" (§ 1.7): *nigan, lut, ros, wer*.[25] The MHG phonemic loss of inter-vocalic /h/ is not reflected by a regular orthographic loss, only by occasional spellings (§ 4): *sehen* (MHG *sehen*), *Vieh* (MHG *vihe*), *Stahl* (MHG *stahel*).[26] But the Modern German "h" with the value zero signifying vowel-length, e.g., in *gehen* (MHG *gēn*), *mahlen* (MHG *maln*) "grind," indicates this post-vocalic "merger with zero" orthographically. It constitutes a reverse spelling (§ 3.2). The Late Latin loss of /h/ in all positions is also reflected by the alternation of the symbol "h" and zero: e.g., *onurem, hedernam*.[27]

The borrowing of foreign phonemes is usually accompanied by the adoption of foreign orthographic symbols: e.g., *Cousin, Bonbon* in Modern German with French orthography.

## IV. Occasional Spellings and Phonemic Changes

§ 4.1 *Occasional Spellings and Shifts.* Occasional or naive spellings (§ 2.1) render most readily all distributional changes found in colloquial speech: e.g., such Early Modern English and American English spellings as *nex* "next," *husbon* "husband," *myssomer* "midsummer," *wrytyn* "writing," *orphants* "orphans," *meten* "meeting," *of* "have."[28] Some of these spellings show loss (or addition) of phonemes in fast, unstressed forms. The *-en, -yn* spellings indicate the change of /ŋ/ (/ng/?) to /n/ in the suffix *-ing*. The traditional orthography usually reflects the forms of slow, careful speech.

Medieval scribes or copyists sometimes unintentionally, sometimes intentionally but inconsistently, substitute symbols either representing their own phonemes or at least their usual orthographic practice for those found in the original text. We find substitutions of the symbol "d" for a presumable "th" or "dh" in the OHG Monsee Fragments, the Freising MS. of Otfrid, in the MS of "Christ and the Samaritan Woman." This reveals the diffusion of the phonemic shift from /þ/ to /d/ in OHG dialects: e.g., *thaz, ther* and *daz, der* (Christ and the Samaritan Woman); *dhuo* and *duo*, "da" (Monsee).

§ 4.2 *Occasional Spellings and Mergers.* Occasional spellings indicate general (unconditioned) or limited (conditioned) phonemic merger. They may do this preceding a general orthographic change. They may reveal the phonemic change the orthography does not show through any adjustment. They may reveal a dialectal change that is not reflected by the established spelling, which rather shows the phonemic pattern of another dialect or of the standard language. Graphic confusion of the symbols "s" and "z" in late Middle High German and Early New High German manuscripts preceded the orthographic readjustment by the general adoption of "s" symbols (§ 3.2). All reverse spellings are really occasional at first (§ 3.5). Such spellings as OHG "hr" for /r/ indicate the loss of the /h/: e.g., *hrinnit* for *rinnit* "flows."[29] Occasional spellings readily show the merger with already existing phonemes: e.g., the merger of /sj/ and /š/ in Modern English is shown by such fifteenth century spellings as *conschens* "conscience," *ishu* "issue," *condishon* "condition," *pashens* "patience."[30] Such first century forms in inscriptions indicate an early substandard merger of *ae* and *e* in the Latin of Rome and Pompey: *etati* "aetati," *maeae* "meae," *saenatus* "senatus," *Clarie* "Clariae" (dat.).[31] Numerous occasional spellings indicate the merger of the rounded front vowels /ö/ /ü/ and their unrounded counterparts /e/ /i/ in High German dialects since the middle of the twelfth century. "e" "i" are written for the historical umlauts: *werter* "Wörter," *gresser* "grösser," *yber* "über," *vnglick* "Unglück," *anzinden* "anzünden." Also reverse spellings are numerous: *bösser* "besser," *moer* "Meer," *schüff* "Schiff," *kürche* "Kirche"; some of the "ö" and "ü" spellings may indicate new roundings or hyperforms.[32]

Phonemic splits are not as readily reflected by occasional spellings, since no contrastive symbols are ordinarily available, but they must have preceded a general orthographic adjustment wherever it took place (§ 3.3).

## V. Orthoëpic Evidence

Certain morpheme-bound (distributional) changes such as additions, omissions, or substitutions of phonemes are described in the statements of grammarians, and illustrative forms are often quoted as vulgarisms or dialectal. Elphinston (1765, 1787), e.g., "generally" heard *Lunnon* for *London*; he called *proddestant* "protestant," *pardner* "partner" London vulgarisms. Noah Webster in *Dissertations on the English Language* (1789) attacked the New England pronunciation *kiow* for *cow*.[33]

Orthoëpic evidence reveals the occurrence of the various types of phonemic changes. The statements of grammarians in the Early New High German period reveal that the Middle High German contrast between /s/ and /z/ has survived medially after long vowels and diphthongs in some dialects as one between a lenis written "s" and a fortis written "ss" "sz": e.g., Standard German *reisen* "travel," *reissen* "tear."[34] The phonemic development of the cluster /ng/ into a velar nasal /ŋ/ is confirmed by Valentin Ickelsamer in his *Teutsche Grammatica* (1537), who deplores the orthography "ng," since neither sound is completely heard in *Engel angel franck* but rather a fusion ("zusammen schmeltzung").[35] Orthoëpic evidence is obviously of particular importance, whenever the orthography fails to indicate a phonemic change. The Early Modern English change of Middle English /ī/ and /ū/ into diphthongs is also not expressed by the orthography but attested by descriptions of British grammarians like Salisbury (1547, 1567), Hart (1569), Gill (1621), and of French grammarians like Bellot (1580), Mason (1622), Festeau (1693).[36] Some of the latter sources clearly indicate a merger of Middle English /ī/ and Middle English /oi/ during their time (see below § 6).

## VI. Metrical Evidence

The synchronic analysis of the distribution of stress and quantity is aided by the rigid pattern of some verse lines (§ 2.3). For the recognition of phonemic changes the analysis of rime is of particular importance. Even assonances may yield some phonemic information. Such Otfrid rimes as *quad* : *sprah* anp *ward* : *tharf* have been interpreted as indicating that his final "d" still represents a spirant rather than a stop; thus the shift from /þ/ to /d/ has not been completed finally in spite of the misleading orthography.[37] The impure rime *hart* : *anbracht* of the Nürnberg poet Jakob Ayrer (1543–1605)[38] probably indicates a uvular *r*. The rime *zit* : *geleit* by Heinrich von dem Türlin (1215) may still be impure but it reveals the diphthongization of /ī/.[39]

On the whole, only poetry with predominantly pure rimes can reveal phonemic shifts, mergers, and splits, since only their occurrence or non-occurrence in rime position can indicate sameness or difference. The non-occurrence of certain types of rimes indicates, if statistics make mere chance unlikely, a phonemic split or a phonemic distinction; the occurrence of rimes indicates phonemic merger. Rimes may not always reflect the pattern of the poet's own dialect. Isolated rime-words may represent historical variants. Some rimes may reflect an earlier phonemic stage of the language (traditional rimes), particularly if the orthography still provides rimes for the eye: e.g., Modern English *hand* : *wand*. The results of more recent splits or coalescences may be rarely reflected by rimes if the orthography seems to disagree: such French rimes as *nous* : *loup, talent* : *grands* are considered incorrect; rimes of the *water* : *quarter* type are very infrequent in Modern British English.[40] Another type of rime may reflect the phonemic pattern of another, presumably more prestigious dialect or the standard language (literary rimes). The analyst will have to decide whether any given rimes of a poet are genuinely dialectal or just traditional or literary. Middle High German rimes of the classical period reveal what the orthography with its uniform symbol "e" does not indicate: there are two short *e* phonemes in the language which do not rime. Only in certain dialects and in certain positions, e.g., in Bavarian before *b d g t*, do /e/, the result of the historical umlaut, and /ẽ/, the old Germanic *e* sound, merge, as rimes show: *heben* "lift ": *lëben* "live"; *stete* "place": *bëte* "prayer, request."[41] Classical Middle High German shows no rimes of final *-z* and *-s*; they appear in the thirteenth century, e.g., Meier Helmbrecht shows *hūs* "house": *ūz* "out."[42] This indicates the merger of the two sibilants in final position. Rimes confirm the orthographic and orthoëpic evidence for a merger of the reflexes of ME /ī/ and ME /oi/ since the sixteenth century: *swine* : *groin* (Shakespeare); *smile* : *coil* (Suckling); *toil* : *isle* (Waller); *join* : *divine* : *line* (Pope).[43]

## VII. Comparative Evidence

§ 7.1 *Proto-Comparative Data.* All prehistoric reconstructed phonemic changes are exclusively based on proto-comparative evidence, e.g., the Germanic Consonant Shift or the Old High German Consonant Shift. The initial values of a phonemic change, e.g., of "th" in Old High German (which became /d/), can sometimes be established by comparative evidence. Syn-comparative evaluation reveals the existence of an interdental or postdental, nonsibilant, voiceless spirant in cognate morphemes in Old Icelandic, Gothic, Old English, Old Frisian, Old Saxon, Old High German: e.g., OIc. *þjófr*, Go, *þiubs*, OE *þēof*, OFrs. *thiāf*, OS *thiof*, OHG (Franc.) *thiob* "thief." This evidence can be used for the reconstruction of a proto-phoneme *þ, a voiceless, nonsibilant, interdental or postdental spirant. The umlaut variation of velar vowels in the Germanic languages can be compared, and postulated for the prehistoric stage. The feasibility of such a reconstruction confirms by its consistency the assumption of initial palatal allophones of long or short *a o u* before *i*-sounds in the Germanic languages. Reconstructed proto-phonemes can support the results of historical synchronic and diachronic analyses.

§ 7.2 *Diacomparative and Neocomparative Data.* Diachronic analysis pre-supposes "diacomparative" data from different periods, preferably within the same dialect or language but by no means excluding available allotopic evidence. Other phonemic changes can furnish evidence. The common dialectal change of *-ing* to *-in* makes the initial value [ŋ] more likely than [ŋg], thus provides evidence for the change from the cluster to a single nasal phoneme.

Evidence from modern dialectal conditions and from modern areal distribution, i.e., "neocomparative" material (§ 2.4), is of special importance, since it can be directly observed in the field, not only through its written reflexes. We can compare the modern sounds and their relation to modern orthographic symbols to the earlier symbols and their presumable sound-values. We find, e.g., that Modern French orthography still has the symbol "u" in *tu dur*, which is pronounced as [ü]: this definitely proves the completion of the phonemic shift from /u/ to /ü/. The fact that Modern German "s" is pronounced like a dorsal or like an apical sibilant at the present time has been used for phonetic identification attempts of the respective values of OHG and MHG "z" and "s." Modern German and Modern English "ng" are pronounced like a single velar nasal in final position: *sing*. But English shows a morphophonemic variation between the single sound and the cluster in such sets as *long* [ŋ], *longer* [ŋg], and it contrasts *finger* with the cluster and *singer* from *sing* with the simple nasal. Thus modern pronunciations confirm the assumed terminal values of phonemic changes, while sometimes their relation to the modern orthographic symbols or an internal phonemic alternation throws light on earlier or initial values. Neocomparative evidence can show the completion of phonemic shifts, splits, and mergers, also the presence of foreign phonemes of marginal status (§ 1.7). The modern areal distribution can also sometimes indicate which values are terminal and which initial or, as it is usually stated, which are archaic and which innovations. This modern dialectal diffusion and differentiation has been used to postulate intermediate stages of a sound-change, but this seems more of a problem of historical reconstruction, which we shall not take up here.

## VIII. Evidence from Contact between Languages

It is tempting to look for proof of a completed shift of French /u/ to /ü/ among French loan-words in Middle High German and Middle English, since the orthography does not indicate the phonemic shift. MHG forms like *natiure* (OF *nature*), *aventiure* (OF *aventure*), *creatiure* (OF *creature*), *hürten* (*hurten*) (OF *hurter*) "attack, push forward," *kabütze* (OF *capuce*) "monk's hood" reveal by the spellings "iu" (for /x/) and "ü" rounded palatal vowels. Only the western dialects of Middle English had a sound phonetically identical with the French sound. The diphthong /iu/ written "ew" "eu" renders French "u" in *glew, mewe, deuk*;[44] early ME *hurten, hirten, herten* renders French *hurter*, and Modern English /i/ is found in unstressed syllables in *minute, lettuce, conduit*, /ī/ in *pedigree* from *pied de grue*. Thus also the English evidence points to a rounded palatal vowel, and indicates the completion of the shift to /ü/ in French.

The adoption of certain orthographic symbols (§ 2.5) can throw light on the values in both languages. The use of the OHG symbol "z" to render the Old

Slovenian sibilants *s z*, but of the symbol "s" to render Old Slovenian sibilants *š ž* in the Freising documents[45] proves that the phonetic differences between the OHG sibilants /z/ and /s/ did not consist in voice participation or fortis and lenis articulation but rather in the manner and place of articulation. The MHG reflexes "s" and "z" of Old French *s* and *c* in loan-words reveal the phonemic contrast between the two sibilants but admit of no specific phonetic identifications or conclusions because of the ambiguity of the MHG "z" symbol: *birsen* (OF *berser*) "to hunt," *garzûn* (OF *garçon*) "page."

Sometimes we can be more specific in our synchronic and diachronic analyses. E. H. Sturtevant[46] has pointed out that OE *strǣt, strēt* from Latin (*uia*) *strāta* has preserved the dental stop *t* better than most Romance languages and reveals the long quantity of the Latin stem vowel. OHG *keisur* from Latin *caesar* suggests a late diphthongal pronunciation of "ae" as the basis for the OHG sound value. Thus, evidence through contact between languages can be valuable for phonetic identifications, which other evidence supplies even less readily.

## IX. Conclusions

The innumerable phonetic changes found in the history of languages represent not more than six types of phonemic change, which could even be further reduced to these three major types: phonemic shift (including cluster changes); phonemic merger (including phonemic loss); phonemic split. All reconstructed sound-changes and their special problems have been excluded from our consideration here, since we are at first concerned with methodological clarification, which must come from the synchronic analysis of both the initial and the terminal values of historical phonemic changes and their diachronic interpretation. Only one major aspect of phonemic change has been dealt with: its evidence. The various types of evidence have been analyzed as to how they can reveal the various types of phonemic change. Orthography and its deviations (the occasional spellings) reveal shifts and mergers but they indicate often only belatedly phonemic splits. Orthoëpic evidence is often tied to the orthography but can reveal all phonemic changes, even specific phonetic values. Evidence from rimes is sometimes particularly useful in detecting phonemic mergers and splits. Among the comparative evidence not proto-comparative reconstruction, but rather data from the structure of the language and from other sound-changes as well as from present-day dialects or the standard language (neocomparative data) throw light on historical shifts, mergers, and splits. The evidence from loan-words can sometimes reveal shifts where orthography and orthoëpic evidence fail to provide satisfactory data.

We cannot expect that all types of evidence can be found for each phonemic change within the history of a language. It is necessary, however, to make use of all available evidence and to correlate its data. Interpretation and even speculation has often taken the place of the missing data. It is imperative that the description of each assumed phonemic change should contain a discussion of the evidence, its type, scope, and conclusiveness.

## FOOTNOTES

1. R. Jakobson, "Prinzipien der historischen Phonologie," *TCLP* 4.247 ff. (1931) labeled sound-changes as "phonologisch" ["phonological" or "phonemic"] or as "ausserphonologisch" ["extra-phonological"]. N. van Wijk, *Mélanges van Ginneken* 94 ff., rejected this dichotomy.

2. Charles E. Osgood and T. E. Sebeok, *Psycholinguistics* 148 (1954).

3. *Économie des changements phonétiques* 175 (1955). Henry M. Hoenigswald, "Sound change and linguistic structure," *Language* 22.138 (1946), differentiated between: phonemic change without loss of contrast; unconditioned and conditioned mergers with loss of contrast; secondary rearrangements induced by a primary loss of contrast; borrowed contrasts.

4. D. Jones, *The phoneme: its nature and use*, chapter 32, pp. 233–52 (1950).

5. We use Roman capitals for the phoneme in the initial pattern (A B), Italic capitals for the corresponding more or less identical phonemes in the terminal pattern (*A B*), and lower case Italics (*x*) for a new terminal phoneme which is not identical with any initial phonemes.

6. A. Martinet, "Function, structure and sound change," *Word* 8.1 ff. (1952).

7. *TCLP* 4.255 ff.

8. See Osgood-Sebeok, *loc. cit.*, for factors determining the likelihood of merger between two phones.

9. *TCLP* 4.250 ff.

10. Herbert Penzl, "Umlaut and secondary umlaut in Old High German," *Language* 25.233 ff. (1949).

11. Hoenigswald, *Language* 22.139.

12. R. Jakobson, *TCLP* 4.254, 261; D. Jones, *The phoneme*, §§ 735–739.

13. C. L. Wrenn, "The value of spelling as evidence," *TPS* 1943, 14 ff., speaks of the "diachronicness" of English orthography (p. 16).

14. Herbert Penzl, *Language* 18.148–51 (1942). R. E. Zachrisson, *Pronunciation of English vowels 1400–1700* 52 ff. (1913) distinguished between "phonetic doublets" (historical variants), "irregular spellings due to miswriting, analogical transference, mechanical transference of symbols," and "phonetic spellings," which he defined as "deviations from the traditional spelling by which a sound-change is denoted."

15. E. H. Sturtevant, *The pronunciation of Greek and Latin*[2] § 5 (1940).

16. [Edited, with translation and commentary by Einar Haugen, *Language Monographs* 25, supplement to *Language* 26.4 (1950).—Ed.]

17. *Language* 24.119 f. (1948).

18. H. Kökeritz, *Shakespeare's pronunciation* 53–157 (1953); Sturtevant, *Pron.* § 10.

19. Sturtevant, *Pron.* § 11: "Having discovered, therefore, that Latin *ē* was closer than *ě*, we expect to find *ō* closer than *ŏ*."

20. A. G. Haudricourt and A. G. Juilland, *Essai pour une histoire structurale du phonétisme français* 100–13 (1949).

21. O. Behaghel, *Geschichte der deutschen Sprache*[5] § 380.7 (1928); V. Michels, *Mittelhochdeutsches Elementarbuch*[3,4] § 184 (1921); V. Moser, *Frühneuhochdeutsche*

*Grammatik* 3.3 § 146 (1951); Friedrich Kauffmann, *Geschichte der schwäbischen Mundart* 210 (1890).

22. Herbert Penzl, "The phonemic split of Germanic *k* in Old English," *Language* 23.34–42 (1947). (Reprinted here, pp. 97 ff.—Ed.)

23. R. Jordan, *Handbuch der mittelenglischen Grammatik* § 181 (1934); V. Michels 109; Karl Weinhold, *Mittelhochdeutche Grammatik*[2] §§ 206, 210 (1883).

24. K. Weinhold §§ 105 ff., 118; Michels § 91; Kauffmann §§ 76, 82.

25. W. Braune and W. Mitzka, *Althochdeutche Grammatik*[8] § 153 (1953).

26. Moser, *Frühnhd. Gramm.* 1.1 § 10 (1929).

27. R. L. Politzer, "The phonemic interpretation of Late Latin orthography," *Language* 27.151–4 (1951).

28. H. C. Wyld, *A history of modern colloquial English*[3] 69 f., 289 f. (1937); George Ph. Krapp, *The English language in America* 2.215, 232 (1925).

29. Braune-Mitzka § 153 Anm. 1.

30. H. C. Wyld, *HMCE*, pp. 69, 293.

31. Sturtevant §§ 4, 132; F. Sommer, *Handbuch der lat. Lautund Formenlehre* § 61 (1948); Max Niedermann, *Historische Lautlehre des Lateinischen*[3] §31 (1953).

32. V. Moser 1.1 § 65 f.; F. Kauffmann 79, 81; H. Penzl, *Language* 32.354 f. (1956).

33. Wyld, *HMCE* 302, 313; Krapp 2.210.

34. Moser 3.3 § 146, Anm. 9.

35. Johannes Müller, *Quellenschriften und Geschichte des deutschsprachlichen Unterrichts bis zur Mitte des 16. Jhd.* 139 (1882).

36. Zachrisson, *Pron. of Engl. vowels*, 129 ff., 205 ff.

37. Braune-Mitzka § 167, Anm. 4; J. Franck, *Altfränkische Grammatik* § 92 (1909); but see W. Wilmanns, *Deutsche Grammatik*[3] 1. § 83, Anm. 1 (1911).

38. Herbert Penzl, *Language* 18.299–302 (1942): review of W. A. Kozumplik, *The phonology of Jacob Ayrer's language based on his rhymes.*

39. Michels § 91.

40. O. Jespersen, *A Modern English grammar* 1.13.27 (1909); C. L. Wrenn, *TPS* 1943, 34–7; H. C. Wyld, *Short history of English*[3] § 214 (1927).

41. K. Zwierzina, *ZfdA* 44.249 ff. (1900).

42. A. Schirokauer, *PBB* 47.97–100 (1922).

43. Wyld, *SHE* § 270; *HMCE*, pp. 224, 249–51.

44. Karl Luick, *Historische Grammatik der englischen Sprache* § 412 (1921); Jespersen *MEG* 1.3.815; Karl Brunner, *Die englische Sprache* 1.146 f., 241 (1950).

45. W. Braune, *PBB* 1.527–34; also Primus Lessiak, *Beiträge zur Geschichte des deutschen Konsonantismus* 83 ff. (1933).

46. *Pronunc.* §§ 3c, 130e.

# BENGT SIGURD

# The Code Shift in Old Norse*

## Introduction

This paper[1] will not present any new data, nor make any attempt to alter the chronology or modify the almost generally accepted description of the details of the great changes that occurred in Old Norse during the period about 200–800 A.D. This paper aims at supplementing the earlier description with a new point of view. The important changes called syncope, mutation and breaking will be regarded here from the point of view of the linguistic code. Conceptions and terminology are taken from the theory of communication, which seems to be very valuable whenever the mechanism of language is studied. An account of this theory will be found in C. Shannon and W. Weaver, *The Mathematical Theory of Communication*, Urbana 1949, or the simpler adaptation for linguists in Gleason, *An Introduction to Descriptive Linguistics*, New York 1955. The data used in this paper are such as can be found in ordinary handbooks like Wessén, *Svensk språkhistoria* I (5 ed. 1958). Knowledge of the facts as they are presented in ordinary handbooks is presupposed.

## Two simple codes

We shall examine Old Norse against the background of two simple codes called *A* and *B*. Code *A* has two signals *a* and *b*. If we want to get bigger units by combining these two signals to form groups, here called words, we shall first get the group presented in Table 1. The words in this code will increase their length rapidly with increasing number. In order to get 15 different words one must have a word length of 4 signals, to get 31 different words 5 signals.[2]

Let us now look at *B* which has 10 signals that can be combined to form words, *a*, *b*, *c*, *d*, *e*, *f*, *g*, *h*, *i*, *j*. Table 1 shows the shortest words that can be formed by combining the ten signals into groups. It is obvious from the table that the words of code *B* need not be so long. In code *A* at least 4 signals must be used to form 15 different words, in code *B* 2 signals are sufficient to construct a vocabulary of 15 words. In code *B* 2 signals will be sufficient to construct 110 different words[3] (cf. binary and decimal numbers).

*A* can be called a low-number code, *B* a high-number code considering the number of signals in the two codes.

* From *Studia Linguistica* 15.10–21 (1961). Reprinted with corrections and revisions by permission of the author and the editors of *Studia Linguistica*.

TABLE 1 | *The table shows how, in order to construct words, a low-number code like A must use greater word length than a high-number code like B.*

|      | Code A (2 signals) | Code B (12 signals) |
|------|--------------------|---------------------|
| 1    | a                  | a                   |
| 2    | b                  | b                   |
| 3    | aa                 | c                   |
| 4    | ab                 | d                   |
| 5    | ba                 | e                   |
| 6    | bb                 | f                   |
| 7    | aaa                | g                   |
| 8    | aab                | h                   |
| 9    | aba                | i                   |
| 10   | abb                | j                   |
| 11   | baa                | aa                  |
| 12   | bab                | ab                  |
| 13   | bba                | ac                  |
| 14   | bbb                | ad                  |
| 15   | aaaa               | ae                  |

## Calculation of information

We shall here also use the special definition of information that has been introduced in the theory of communication. Information in this technical meaning is defined

$$I = log_2 a$$

where $I$ is amount of information in a signal of the code, $a$ is the number of different signals in this code. In calculations of the amount of information of a signal its frequency in the text should also be taken into account, but in this paper the calculations are made on the code with no considerations of frequency. For the purpose of this paper it is sufficient to know that the amount of information increases with the number of signals in the code; the further mathematical implications are here ignored. When evaluating codes one must also take time into account. A code that can communicate the same amount of information in shorter time than another is more effective and better. However, other factors must also be taken into consideration. Code *A* in our example has one advantage compared to *B* in that it is easier to handle. When code *A* is used the transmitter and the receiver have only two signals to remember, when code *B* is used there are ten different signals to remember and keep apart. As a practical example it might be useful to think of the two codes as flag codes. When code *A* is used only two signal flags are needed, which then can be chosen with well contrasting colours and designs. When code *B* is used quite a store of flags in many different colours and designs must be used. The possibility of making mistakes is evidently greater in code *B* both for the transmitter and the receiver of the message. It must be understood that information in this technical sense is not the same as meaning in ordinary usage. It is a purely statistical measure based on the occurrence of signals in messages.

The amount of information can also be calculated in the groups or words that are formed by the signals in the codes. The information is evenly distributed on the different positions of the words in both codes. In code *A* there can occur two different signals in any position, *a* or *b*. Hence any position of a word in code *A* carries the amount of information $log_2 2$. In code *B* accordingly any position carries the amount of information $log_2 10$. The amount of information can also be calculated on the groups of sounds that constitute syllables. This way of calculating is useful in some linguistic investigations. It is used below to show the transmission of information from unstressed syllables to stressed. A word in a language consists of one syllable or a chain of syllables. The various syllables that can alternate in the positions (in the first syllable position, in the second and so on) of the words can be determined by studying a dictionary and the amount of information in the different positions can be calculated. The amount of information in a syllable position will clearly be higher than the amount got when calculating in the phoneme positions. The sum of the figures for the different phoneme positions of a syllable should equal the figure for the amount of information in the whole syllable. The calculating on syllables presupposes the determination of the syllable frontier in every single case, but this problem can probably be solved for the immediate purpose by some simple arbitrary rule of division. Let us take as a simple example a language where the first syllable can be constructed in 495 different ways. It can consist of *a*) one of 5 different vowels alone (V = 5), *b*) combinations of these 5 vowels and 10 different preceding consonants (CV = 50), *c*) combinations of these 5 vowels and 8 different following consonants (VC = 40), *d*) combinations of the 10 consonants, the 5 vowels and the 8 consonants (CVC = 400). Since the number of alternatives was 495, the amount of information in this first syllable position of the words would be $log_2 495$. The second syllable in the words may be differently constructed and so carry a different amount of information. Other ways of calculating could also be attempted, e.g., calculating the primarily stressed syllables separately and the others according to degree of secondary stress. Having calculated the amount of information in the different syllables it is then possible to say something about the distribution of information over the different syllables of the words of the language. The distribution of information over the syllables will turn out to be different for different languages and during different periods of the same language. Some languages are characterized by even distribution, others by uneven, with most of the information placed at one syllable, as is the case in the Germanic languages.

The two codes described above are very simple and primitive compared to living languages. They differ from languages used by human beings, above all since the combination of signals is completely unrestricted. In living languages there are usually very rigid constraints on the combination of phonemes (letters) to syllables, morphemes, or words. This can easily be illustrated by making the experiment of regarding the words of code *A* as being written Swedish. According to well-known structural patterns the only possible words are *a, ab, ba, aba, abb, bab*. Out of these structurally possible words (those which do not violate any of the rules for combinations of letters in Swedish words) there is only one word utilized to carry meaning in Swedish, namely *a*, which is used to designate a letter and a sound.

Our examples *A* and *B* contain a rather small number of signals. Living languages generally utilize more signals. Many languages have a written form which uses about 25 letters. With such a large number of signals there is a good theoretical chance of keeping the word length small. If there were no limitations, 2 letters would be sufficient to give a vocabulary of 650 words, groups of three letters would give a total vocabulary of 16275 words. In living languages these theoretically possible vocabularies are not equivalent to the real ones. Only a fraction of the theoretically possible words are used. Phoneme (letter) constraints reduce the number considerably. Of those structurally possible only a fraction is utilized to carry meaning. The number of phonemes in the languages of the world is between 13 and 75 with an average number of 27 (cf. Hockett, *A Course in Modern Linguistics*, New York 1958, p. 93, and Sigurd, *A Note on Number of Phonemes, Statistical Methods in Linguists*, 2, Stockholm 1962). A linguistic code with such a great number of signals could have short words. If the code had 40 signals, the number of words would be 1640 even if only a word length of 2 phonemes is accepted. As far as is known no complete calculations have been made of the proportion of potential words actually used in various languages. Such a calculation is by no means easy. In a study of Swedish monosyllables it was found that in Swedish the 35 phonemes could give 1260 words with a length of one or two phonemes, but only about 250 of these were real words (20%).

## Old Norse

Let us now turn to Old Norse and look at the development with the two codes in mind. The following is a sentence found on the Gallehus horn from about 400 A.D.

> *Ek HlewagastiR holtijaR horna tawido*

If this sentence is rendered into Runic Swedish of about 900 A.D. it could be written:

> *Jak Hlägästr höltir horn tada.*

The number of syllables has decreased from 13 to 8. The number of sounds has decreased from 32 to 25. The syncope has caused elimination of the sounds -*wa*-, -*i*-, -*ja*-, -*a*, -*wi*, in *Hlägästr* and *tada* the vowels *e* and *a* probably became long (and *ē* > *ä*) as a consequence of the elimination of -*wa*- and -*wi*-, respectively, and breaking turned the short *e* of *ek* into a diphthong. Syncope causes a great decrease in the word length of Old Norse. There are two ways of determining the decrease of the number of syllables or phonemes; one is to determine the decrease in the text mass, one is to determine the decrease in the dictionary. The text sample on the Gallehus horn has been reduced by about 25% of its phonemes, if the later rendering given above is correct, but the overall figure is probably smaller. Sample tests with other material point to a figure around 10%.

A written form after the syncope period could obviously be made shorter than an earlier form. But we cannot jump to the conclusion that late Old Norse after syncope had taken place was pronounced more rapidly than earlier Norse. It is not absolutely certain that the same meaning or information could be given faster after syncope. As remarked above some of the sounds probably grew longer, and the *ia* was perhaps longer than the original *ĕ*, which balanced the loss of some sounds. It is also quite possible that the syllables left, which became the main carriers of information, acquired more energy and duration, as they were stressed in the pronunciation. If this is the case the "phonetic mass" might be about the same after as before the time of syncope. It is hard to see how this phonetic problem could be solved at the present time 1500 years later. It is however tempting to believe that the reduction was a reduction of pronunciation time and this seems to be the general view (cf. Skautrup, *Det Danske sprogs hist.* Kbnh 1944, I:44).

It is interesting to see how a similar reduction would influence a code like code *A*. Suppose that all final *a*'s in words of two or more signals were dropped. The result would be that the number of words in the table goes down from 15 to 11. The words *aa, ba, aba, bba* would coincide with *a, b, ab, bb*. In this code any change will cause coincidences. In a living language this is not the case since the groups used for carrying information are only a fraction of the possible groups. In a living language a reduction in word length does not have such strong and revolutionary consequences as in code *A*. The number of coincidences will not be so great, but the words will be separated by fewer elements and can be said to come closer to each other. The words in such a reduced code can be said to be solved with smaller intervals.

Even if word coincidence, homonymy, is not completely lacking in languages, it is certainly true that there is a fundamental tendency to avoid coincidences. Another similar factor must also be taken into account when linguistic change is studied, namely the redundancy of languages. It was mentioned above that the groups that could be constructed from the phoneme inventory were only to a small extent used in languages as carriers of meaning, the exact percentage (and the dispersion) is not known. This fact implies what is known as redundancy in communication theory. The existence of redundancy in the code is a guarantee of perfect communication free of distortion. The less redundancy the greater the chance of getting words confused. When the word length in a language is reduced, as resulted from the syncope in Old Norse, the redundancy is decreased and the possibilities of perfect communication also decreased.

If a reduction of the linguistic units in a code can be brought about without any adverse consequences, it shows that the earlier code was unnecessarily redundant. It can probably be proved by calculations of the redundancy in many languages that a certain degree of redundancy is needed and it will probably be found that there is a certain variation in different languages. Possibly some differences are due to differences in milieu, indoor variants spoken in ideal listening conditions seem to need less redundancy than outdoor variants which are more exposed to noise.

If, however, a certain limit is exceeded in a language, as a consequence of some linguistic change, there will be some other change in the code to restore the redundancy. Calculations that allow of predictions of this sort have, however, not yet been undertaken, but communication theory provides us with useful tools.

Changes like the syncope in Old Norse can evidently take place in a language without any compensation (see below), but in Old Norse there are certain processes that can be interpreted as an attempt to retain or restore the redundancy of the language and retain efficiency of communication. In Old Norse the syncope seems to have had some adverse consequences. The compensation needed has been given by an increase of the phoneme inventory caused by mutation and breaking.

An early stage of Old Norse had the following stressed vowels:

| | |
|---|---|
| ĭ | *þĭnga*, "*thing*" |
| ī | *līþan*, "*go*" |
| ĕ | *ĕtan*, "*eat*" |
| ē | *grēt*, "*cried*" |
| ă | *dăgaR*, "*day*" |
| ā | *lāsa*, "*lock*" |
| ō | *brōþer*, "*brother*" |
| ŭ | *sŭnuR*, "*son*" |
| ū | *sūraR*, "*sour*" |
| au | *augō*, "*eye*" |
| ai | *stainaR*, "*stone*" |
| eu | *beudan*, "*bid*" |

By mutation and breaking the following vowels were added:

| | | |
|---|---|---|
| ŏ | *hŏrn < hŭrna*, "*horn*" | *a*-mutation |
| ă | *gästR < gästiR*, "*guest*" | *i*-mutation |

| | | |
|---|---|---|
| ā̃ | *lägRe < lāgiRē*, "*lock*" | *i*-mutation |
| ö̃ | *ö̃fRe < ö̆biRe*, "*upper*" | *i*-mutation |
| ȫ | *fȫtR < fōtiR*, "*feet*" | *i*-mutation |
| y̆ | *sy̆niR < sŭniuR*, "*sons*" | *i*-mutation |
| ȳ | *knȳta < knūtian*, "*knit*" | *i*-mutation |
| ŏ | *ŏl < ălwa*, "*beer*" | *w*-mutation |
| ǭ | *hǭnom < hānum*, "*him*" | *u*-mutation |
| öy | *höyRa < hauRian*, "*hear*" | *i*-mutation |
| ia | *hiarta < hĕrtō*, "*heart*" | *a*-breaking |
| io | *iord < ĕrþu*, "*earth*" | *u*-breaking |

Some of the vowels can have been reached in other ways than shown here. East Scandinavian breaking has not been taken into account because of its geographically restricted extension.

At least for a time these sounds were probably kept apart (and had phonemic status), but later coincidences took place. Icelandic has retained the system best, in Swedish ĕ coincided early with ā, ē with ā̃ (geographically restricted). The mutated vowel ǫ is not retained in Swedish as an independent sound, it has coincided with one of the vowels ö, o, u. In Swedish the diphthongs became contracted. But these later changes as well as the details of the changes in Old Norse are here ignored (e.g., nasalization of vowels).

After the time of breaking and mutation Old Norse had an inventory of 24 vowels including diphthongs. During the time before breaking and mutation the number was 12. The inventory had thus been doubled.

Investigations in the other Germanic languages show that syncope can take place without any connected increase of the vowel inventory, but only Gothic shows no signs whatever of mutation and breaking of the type found in Old Norse. West Germanic has *a*- and *i*-mutation but not *u*-mutation and breaking of this kind. In this branch of Germanic the reduction by syncope has not been balanced so strongly as in Old Norse. East Germanic as represented by Gothic has had syncope of *a* and *i* (*dags < dagas*, "*day*," *gasts < gastis*, "*guest*") but has retained *u* (*sunus*, "*son*"). The lack of *i*-mutation in Gothic is particularly remarkable, and one is tempted to ask whether the Gothic writing conventions perhaps conceal mutated vowels heard in the pronunciation. As shown clearly by the Runic alphabet of 16 types it is quite possible to write texts with a number of signs that is much lower than the number of phonemes in the pronunciation.

After mutation, breaking and syncope the words of Old Norse were shorter but the variation in the stem syllable (the first syllable) had increased considerably. The two stages of Old Norse can be compared to the two codes above, *A* and *B*. *A* is characterized by few signals and, as a consequence, long words; *B* is characterized by a greater number of signals and shorter words. As pointed out above, living languages are different from the codes *A* and *B* in that they have a certain amount of redundancy, since only a fraction of the theoretically possible words is used. But since this fraction is probably fairly constant and does not vary too much from one language to another, the comparison with the codes *A* and *B* is relevant. Living languages are of the type *A* or *B*, but for the fact that a certain percentage of the words is eliminated. From this point of view the development in Old Norse can be described as a development from a code of the type *A* to a code of the type *B*, a development towards a code with a higher number of signals and shorter words.

If it is true that a certain message could be pronounced in a shorter time after the period of syncope, mutation and breaking, the average time of pronunciation of a signal would be shorter and as a consequence Old Norse must be said to have developed towards a better code if only these factors are considered. But the gain in information has not occurred without losses in other parts of the communication process. A greater phoneme inventory demands greater ability of the speaker to pronounce sounds and greater ability of the listener to discriminate sounds. When the number of phonemes is high, more subtle articulatory and acoustic differences must be used. The gain in information time is thus counterbalanced by the greater mental and physiological efforts needed for a code with many phonemes. This explains why languages do not use extremely large phoneme inventories. The number of phonemes in languages is always less than 75 (cf. p. 28). A language with an inventory of 1000 phonemes could easily construct short words and the amount of information per signal would be great. There is presumably an upper limit caused by limitations of our brains, by our articulatory ability to produce different sounds, and by our auditive ability to discriminate sounds. There is probably also a lower limit beyond which no languages go, since a small number of phonemes also has disadvantages. A small number of phonemes means long words with many of the sounds repeated one or more times, and just like tongue-twisters these words can be quite difficult to pronounce. Recognition of words constructed as long chains of a few phonemes can also be hard. Judging from the average number of phonemes in languages an optimal stage has been reached when the language has about 27 phonemes.

The stress is supposed to have been free during the Indoeuropean period, i.e., the stress could occur at any part of the word, stem or ending. The distribution of information in the word was probably rather even during that period. Of course the distribution was not as even as in the codes *A* or *B* above, but the number of different syllables that could alternate at different syllable positions was probably about the same. There were not many phonemes that were restricted only to special position as, e.g., the first syllable. In the Germanic languages the situation was changed. The distribution of information was distorted so that most of the information was concentrated on the first syllable of the word, the stem syllable. The amount of information carried by the other syllables was greatly decreased. The stem syllable became more varied by introducing new phonemes or phoneme combinations (diphthongs) in the vowel position.

Beside syncope there were other events that lowered the amount of information in the unstressed (later) syllables or parts of the words. The reduction of final consonants and vowels which started in Primitive Germanic continued in Old Norse. Final -*n* occurring in verbs (e.g., *valjan*, *"choose"*) and *n*-stems of nouns (e.g., *logæn*, *"flame"*) is dropped. In the final position only voiceless sounds become permitted (e.g., *band* > *bant*, *"bound"*). The neutralisation of the distinction *voiced* : *voiceless* also implies a loss of information in this position. Some of the distinctions between final vowels are also neutralized (cf. Iversen, *Norrøn gram.*, Oslo 1946, p. 26).

The cases when the "colouring" phoneme is not dropped (e.g., *sỹniR* < *sŭniuR*) increase the redundancy. This increase is however counterbalanced by the cases when phonemes are dropped with no consequences (*stainR* < *stainaR*).

Germanic languages are characterized by a strong dynamic stress placed on the stem syllable, which is almost always also the first syllable of the word. This fact is clearly connected with the special distribution of information in the words, and the strong stress has probably developed at the same time as the change of distribution of information. It is hardly feasible to find out whether the change of distribution has caused the strong stress or the strong stress has caused the change of distribution. The two things are closely interrelated and the development has probably been a process in which the two factors have repeatedly influenced each other. The process could have started with either. If one part of a word for some reason is the more essential carrier of information and thus more important, it seems natural to stress this part so that it stands out better and is better perceived by the listeners. This strong stress has the consequence that the other less stressed parts of the words tend to be dropped or slurred over. The information of these parts then decreases and as a consequence their relative degree of stress is reduced still further. Some of the information of the less stressed parts can be transferred, as in Old Norse when the *a*, *i* and *u* "colour" the stem vowel. Since the stem syllable grows still more important by this it will be still more stressed and so on.

It is of course natural to ask why this process began, but the answer is not easy to find. Even if the new code is better in some respects and is able to communicate more information in the same time (which is not absolutely certain), this is counterbalanced by the development of some new phonemes which demand greater efforts of the speaker and listener. The change is thus perhaps not a change for the better. It is perhaps a change of no real value, a change of almost the same kind as changes in dress fashions. We have no right to look upon the Germanic languages as being more effective than e.g., Finnish, which from many points of view has remained at a stage similar to that of Old Norse before syncope took place. Many of the linguistic changes in historic times are perhaps a matter of vogue rather than a step towards better communication. We have not yet methods, which would enable us to

evaluate changes from all points of view, even physiological and psychological, but communication theory is a great step in this direction.

*Summary*

Syncope, mutation and breaking in Old Norse should not be regarded as
isolated events that only lead to dropping of unstressed syllables and changes
of the stem vowels according to the quality of the following vowels respectively. Syncope, mutation and breaking together imply a change in the linguistic code, a change to a code with more signals and shorter groups, a
high-number code. This code allows of the transmission of more information
per unit of time, but this improvement is counterbalanced by the greater effort
demanded of the speaker and the listener since the new code includes a
number of new phonemes. The code shift is essentially brought about by
introducing new vowel phonemes in the stem syllable and thus in transferring
to this syllable the information of the syncopated phonemes. The trend, which
started in Primitive Germanic, towards a concentration of the information on
one syllable (the stem syllable) is closely tied up with the development of a
strong dynamic stress on that syllable.

## FOOTNOTES

1. This paper was first presented at the Symposium of Statistical linguistics at
Sundbyholm, Nov. 1960, and I have profited from the discussion there.
2. In code $A$ $2^x$ is the number of words with length $x$. Hence

$$n = 2 + 2^2 + \cdots + 2^x = 2^{x+1} - 2$$

is the number of words with length $\leqslant x$.
3. In code $B$ $10^x$ is the number of words with length $x$. Hence

$$n = 10 + 10^2 \cdots + 10^x = \frac{10(10^x - 1)}{9}$$

is the number of words with length $\leqslant x$.

*ANGUS McINTOSH*

# The Analysis
# of Written Middle English*

During the past few years, the writer of this paper has been making an examination of a large number of vernacular texts of the later Middle English period in order to establish an adequate set of criteria for distinguishing them dialectally.[1] Many questions have arisen during the planning of this task and in the process of assessing the material already assembled; they have led the writer to re-examine a number of common assumptions about the nature of the information which such texts offer to an investigator of dialectal problems, and to consider how it may most satisfactorily be handled. The present paper examines a matter of quite central importance to these enquiries: that of the linguistic status of written language (with special reference to later Middle English), and its relationship to spoken language. This leads on to an examination of current analytical approaches to written language and to a plea for their reorientation.[2]

## I

If we consider English as it was spoken in England around 1400 we may regard all its numerous forms as falling under the general description "Later Middle English." This term is an abstraction, embracing under one convenient heading a large number of interrelated sub-species or varieties of the spoken language, and no single variety is to be regarded as more strictly or fittingly described by the term than any other.[3] All evidently bore very marked resemblances; though the student of dialects will tend to be more concerned with the differences between them than with their resemblances, it should be noted that the exploitation and interpretation of these differences is only possible within some sort of controlling framework of similarity or relatedness.

Though we are justified in assuming the existence of spoken varieties of Later Middle English, and indeed in making certain statements about them, we have in fact no shred of direct information about any single feature in any of them. Whatever we may claim to know is derived indirectly; by making a study of written material and drawing certain conclusions from it, and by studying still surviving forms of spoken English and then drawing conclusions

* From *Transactions of the Philological Society* (1956), 26–55. Reprinted by permission of the author and the Philological Society.

about the earlier stages by a process of extrapolation. And there can be no doubt that it is written material of the late Middle English period itself which provides us with the bulk of what we believe we know about the spoken language of that time.[4] The fact that modern scholars feel able to speak with some confidence of various kinds of regional differences in the spoken language rests not merely on the circumstance that these once existed, but on the fact that there are regional differences in written Middle English. More important still, it rests on the making of far-reaching assumptions about the *correlation* which pertained between a given variety of the spoken language and the "equivalent" or "corresponding" variety of the written language; otherwise, it would be impossible to draw conclusions about the one from facts available only or mainly in extant specimens of the other.

It is unnecessary for the moment to question the existence, in some sense or other, of "equivalence" or "correspondence" of this kind. But there are good reasons for not taking for granted some of the accompanying assumptions which have been made about the nature of the correlation, especially since the principles on which they are founded seem never to have been critically propounded. It may be advisable therefore to consider this matter in some detail, and more particularly to examine the points at which the correlation would appear to fail, and the reasons for this failure. For only by understanding the limitations of the correlation can we, for one thing, make proper use of the available written material as evidence about the spoken language. Furthermore, if we do reach some such understanding we shall be much better equipped to make a critical assessment of those features in this or that variety of the written language which do *not* correlate, and to appreciate what special interest these very things have thereby in their own right.

It may be as well to begin by considering features in written Middle English which almost certainly do correlate with features in spoken Middle English. Certain variants appear in two or more varieties of the written language which may be assumed to testify to the parallel existence of variants in the corresponding varieties of the spoken language. Thus variant written forms like *swilk, swich, soche; -eþ, -es; þam, hom, hem*, will usually entitle us to assume that there existed a corresponding diversity in the spoken language, of which we may then say that we have evidence that it had (according to locality or other factors) three different words for "such," two different ways of forming "the third singular present indicative of the verb," and three different forms of "the objective case of the personal pronoun, third plural."

We should note however, that though they strongly suggest such diversity in the spoken language, the written forms offer us no very precise information about the way their equivalents sounded in the appropriate varieties of the spoken language.[5] For example, the exact phonetic value of letters is in doubt: a spelling *swilk* does not even enable us to say whether the pronunciation of the scribe who wrote it was, say, [swilk] or [swɪlk] or [swɪɫk],[6] all three of which spellings are in any case themselves phonetically imprecise, or whether *þam* represents, say, [ðam] or [ðæm]. Indeed, as we shall see, any such statement as "*swilk* and *þam* 'represent' or 'stand for' [swɪɫk] and [ðam]" runs a grave risk of lacking any meaning whatever.

It is true, of course, that when a certain northern scribe wrote *swilk*, it evidently carried for him an indication of the most unequivocal kind of his own pronunciation of the word. For any reader who belonged to the *swilk* area it would have equally unequivocal phonetic implications, but each would interpret it in the light of his own pronunciation of the word. Whenever a reader's pronunciation diverged from that of the scribe, say because of some local usage, the written word *swilk* would have correspondingly divergent phonetic implications. To one reader it might indicate [swilk], to another [swɪɫk] and so forth, and all we can safely say is that to any contemporary reader who used the word in his own speech, the sign *swilk* conveyed (among other things) exactly *that reader's* pronunciation of it.

Therefore in the general framework of the different spoken varieties of English in use in this or that part of the *swilk* area as a whole, the written form of the word is no precise visual equivalent of any particular pronunciation. *A fortiori*, it can in itself provide the modern student with only an approximate idea of the range of pronunciations it may have had in different varieties of spoken Middle English. At the same time there are signs of some sort of *systemic* correlation, the nature of which we must examine later; this does not however enable us to deduce full details about the pronunciation of a form in a given variety of spoken Middle English from the way its equivalent "looks" in the corresponding written variety. Scribes did not have at their disposal anything like enough symbols to indicate such nuances, and in any case they inherited a tradition which recognised that to attempt to do so was unnecessary and indeed undesirable.

If we move to a higher level of analysis we shall observe at once that different varieties of written Middle English do, nevertheless, show an evident readiness to diverge from one another in such a way as to reflect lexical variations (to take only one example) in their spoken equivalents. Because of this divergence, we may take it that though *swilk* might be multivalent in the special sense of being able to imply a large number of possible pronunciations like the three already given, it could not, however, imply, say, [switʃ] or [sɔtʃ]. It carries with it then certain definite reservations as to the legitimate phonetic range of spoken equivalents. The main reason for this is that any given letter has, in the majority of cases, similar (though not, as we have seen, identical) phonetic implications in each and every variety of the written language.[7] As a consequence of this, we can, except in relatively rare cases, make such statements as: "*sw-*, in the hands of no matter what scribe, irrespective of his locality or background, implies (among other things) under no circumstances [s]," or "*-k* (similarly) under no circumstances [tʃ]."

It would not be difficult of course to envisage an alternative convention whereby *swich*, let us say, was used universally in written Middle English to designate "the word for 'such'," irrespective of the spoken form of that word.[8] This too would constitute a very close relationship, though of a quite different kind, between all written varieties of the language; indeed, if a similar convention existed for all words, it would reduce these varieties, at any rate on the lexical level, to one homogeneous type. But a close relationship or ultimate identity of that kind would not be with respect to the functions of individual letters in the sense implied above; so long, for instance, as *sw-* implies "under no circumstances [s]," this other convention is ruled out.

The implication of *swilk* that its spoken equivalents are limited in range, that it implies for example, "not [switʃ]," "not [sɔtʃ]," raises the whole problem of the relationship between the functions of individual letters and of sounds. We may now therefore conveniently examine the statement made earlier that there is a systemic correlation between a written form (e.g., a word) and its spoken equivalent. The word *swilk* cannot imply merely "the word for 'such'" precisely because, letter by letter, it carries certain direct implications about the sound-*structure* of every one of the various possible phonetic forms of its opposite number in the spoken language. We may say in fact that *swilk* implies /swilk/ and not, phonemically, anything else. A scribe writing it cannot imply, or be taken by anyone else to imply, /sɔtʃ/ or /switʃ/ or /sik/; if he had such words in his vocabulary (whether with the meaning "such" or not does not matter) their differing structure would require and obtain different orthographic expression, say *soch* as the equivalent of /sɔtʃ/, and so forth.

In any spoken language there are phonic phenomena which have no relevance as criteria for phonemic units and which may be described as phonemically irrelevant. Any such phenomena which occurred in a given manifestation[9] of spoken Middle English are not normally reflected in its written equivalent. Hence, though we may have good orthographic grounds for believing that the vowel in the spoken equivalent of *swilk* always contrasts with that in *balk* and *folk* and *welk*, we can learn nothing from a text about the exact phonetic value (or the exact permitted range of values) of any example of a vowel of which the written equivalent is *i*. If we attempt the comparative study of phonemically irrelevant features in two or more varieties of spoken Middle English we are therefore likely to find that the appropriate written texts do not reflect these either.[10]

Here already then, we have some indications of the so-called "failure" of written varieties of Middle English to reflect certain differences between the corresponding spoken varieties.[11] It should be noted however that the main limitation so far considered has to do with a breakdown in correlation at the phonetic level; this, as we have already suggested, does not in itself upset what we have called the systemic correlation. But we must now note another kind of breakdown which arises for a very different kind of reason, in some cases at such a level as to affect the systemic correlation itself.

We have observed that written texts lack anything which reflects certain phonetic variants present in their spoken equivalents. But they also manifest other new distinctions of their own, distinctions which are in no sense a reflection of, or correlated with, anything in the spoken language. The spoken manifestations of Middle English have thus no monopoly in this matter; nor do they control, by the total extent of their own deviation one from the other, the extent to which corresponding written manifestations may deviate.

These other distinctions are of two kinds. First there is variation in handwriting, which will often enable us to notice a marked difference between the way two or more scribes *write* (as distinct from *spell*). This has nothing to do with whether their pronunciation is different or not; it is a question of "hand," which may for the moment be set apart as a (linguistically) non-systemic matter parallel to certain (linguistically) nonsignificant variations in pronunciation in spoken manifestations of the language.[12] Secondly, there is the possibility of differences in orthography as distinct from calligraphy, as a result of which we find such variants as *erþe, erthe* "earth"; *him, hym* "him"; *noȝt, noght* "not"; *up, vp* "up."[13] As far as can be seen, these reflect no variation in the spoken language either, standing in this respect in contrast to forms like *swilk, swich, soche*, which almost certainly do.[13] They have in fact no more direct correlation with anything in the spoken language than have the precise shapes of letters executed by this or that scribe, or—for that matter—than their size or the colour of ink they are written in.[14] But they certainly have a higher status within the written system than these other things, and because of this they affect in some sense the systemic correlation between written and spoken language.

The problem of orthographic variation in the work of different scribes and its possible correlation with places[15] is one which has scarcely attracted the attention it deserves. It is true that editors and others note such uses as the *-th* and *x-* of East Anglian *myth* "might" and *xal* "shall," the *qu-* found in certain areas in such words as *quen, quan* "when," and the *-tȝ* of *watȝ* "was" in MS. Cotton Nero A X. But orthographic variation rarely attracts much interest unless it offers at least the possibility of clues about phonetic variation or unless (as in the last example) some variant form is at once striking and rare. It is important here to stress the fact that there is a great deal to be learnt from a thorough examination of those numerous cases of orthographic variation which have no phonetic implications, such as the examples (*þ/th, i/y, ȝ/gh, u/v*) noted earlier. They can be plotted on maps like any other variants, and many of them turn out to be demonstrably regional with a distribution in some cases of quite extraordinary interest.

The very fact that such things cannot be correlated with anything in the spoken system gives them a special significance and importance. The regional distribution of *erþe* and *erthe*, for example—once it is perceived that it is not merely haphazard[16]—becomes as interesting a matter from the point of view of anyone studying varieties of the written language as are the distribution of *vche* and *eche* "each," or *mon* and *man* "man," for anyone studying regional variations in the Middle English sound-system.

There seems to be some doubt among students of dialects whether mere variation in the pronunciation of what we might call one and the same word (e.g., [mɔn] : [man]) should be regarded as constituting a dialectal difference. This is a question of terminology which need not be discussed fully at this point; the answer may well depend on the precise nature of the type or types of variation involved.[17] However we may decide to assess the status of such variations, we cannot for some purposes afford to ignore them, for they have an indubitable interest of their own. The same is true, in written manifestations of Middle English, of variant forms like *erþe* and *erthe*, which have a status there comparable to two such forms as /stɔːn/ and /staːn/ in spoken manifestations; the fact that they are independent of anything in the spoken language does not weaken their claim to that status in the slightest.[18] They are variations such as could theoretically have arisen even if later Middle English, no matter where spoken, had been entirely homogeneous; if they had originated in circumstances of that sort, they would without doubt be taken much more seriously than they are as it is.

## II

These preliminary observations about spoken and written Middle English raise questions concerning the relationship between the two mediums and the ways in which they may be subjected to linguistic analysis. It is necessary to say something about current attitudes to these matters.

There is beyond doubt at present a fairly prevalent feeling that the approach to spoken manifestations of language is in some fundamental sense a more linguistically rewarding—not to say reputable—pursuit than that to written texts. A spoken manifestation of language is felt to be "the real thing," a corresponding written manifestation is felt to be no more than a dim and distorted reflection or derivative. Among other things it is argued that this must be so because one can infer some but not all the facts about spoken language from written.[19] True though this may be, it is perhaps curious that little is ever said about the difficulties which confront a person who has only a speaking knowledge of a language, if he attempts from this to infer full details about its accepted written form.

It is not hard to understand this tendency to relegate what is in a sense rightly regarded as a derivative medium to a secondary and inferior position. For the majority of those who interest themselves linguistically in specimens of it are from the start preoccupied with the highly special task of extracting therefrom all possible clues about the spoken language to which they are constantly trying to work back.[20] Persons so engaged can hardly be expected to do justice to all those features in a written text which as it were compensate for its obvious shortcomings from their point of view, and give it such an interest in its own right. It is still more understandable that they should be reluctant to analyse it purely as a specimen of written language, and to deny themselves at that stage so much as a side-glance at anything in it which may throw light on its spoken equivalent.

Apart from this traditional preoccupation, there is evidently a very strong feeling that anything connected with utterance is in some way much more part and parcel of the "fabric of the language" than ink-marks on paper or parchment can ever be.[21] Phonetic features are felt to be peculiarly, almost mystically, bound up with the physiological and psychological make-up of a person; anything written is felt on the other hand to be much more "external" and artificial, presumably because it involves such extraneous and tangible and durable things as pens and ink and vellum instead of transitory mouth-positions and puffs of air. Nor is this feeling usually dispelled if it is pointed out that writing too is the product of physiological and psychological processes and that the two resultant products are hardly more discrepant than one would expect in view of the inevitable differences which in one way or another the very nature of the two mediums imposes.[22] Another curious objection often made is that a person's handling of written language is merely the result of imitating or learning from other people; it might be replied that the same is true of speaking except that here the process is often less regimented. In both speaking and writing there is much the same room for various idiosyncrasies, which cannot legitimately in either go beyond a certain point, but which inevitably assert themselves to some degree in each.

The extent to which the conventions of written language depend on those of spoken language is an interesting matter in itself. It cannot be ignored, for example, by anyone attempting to exploit these conventions in a way for which they were never intended, that is to reveal facts about its spoken equivalent to the uninitiated.[23] But preoccupations of this sort should in no way control or bias the organization of techniques for the analysis of written language. For if the existence of non-correlating features is at best grudgingly admitted, there is a considerable danger that the resultant analysis will fail to give these their due place in the system as a whole.

One cannot altogether avoid here the terminological question of whether such an analysis would be fundamentally less linguistic (or, for that matter, more so) than that normally applied to spoken language. This question has an importance far beyond that of a mere verbal quibble, because it relates to a subject where the ingrained use of certain words in habitual (and sometimes not very clear) senses has obscured and confused a major issue. It is one of the main purposes of this paper to suggest that no position is satisfactory which fails to accord equality of status to spoken and written language and that the analysis of one is neither more nor less linguistic than the other. Any statement to the contrary, we would maintain, is chiefly of interest as an attestation of a common restricted sense of the word "linguistic" itself.[24]

The claim of equality of linguistic status for written and spoken language has important implications. For if we accept it without reserve we should then see the need for the application to written language of techniques of analysis at least as rigorous as those at present applied to spoken language. Furthermore, though it is not intended in this paper to exaggerate the extent to which written and spoken English correlate, one may say that they do so sufficiently for such techniques as are applied to the spoken language to suggest interesting and fruitful approaches to at least some of the problems likely to be encountered in analysing the written. Besides, written texts will always be ransacked for information about spoken language and they can be the more fully exploited to this end the more carefully we explore the nature of their relationship to their spoken equivalents.

Something of the complexity and of the probable value of a full graphematic analysis of a text may be perceived by considering first what is involved in certain similar tasks of phonological analysis. One might consider a single problem of that sort, the question of what is involved in establishing the phoneme system of a spoken language.[25] In the process of carrying this out it becomes clear that certain differences of sound provide criteria for the distinction of terms in the system, whereas others do not; it is therefore necessary at some stage to sort out those which have no significance in this context from those which have.[26] Prior to that stage the investigator is necessarily involved in a scrutiny of phenomena by no means all of which are finally accepted as criteria for the establishment of the linguistic distinctions with which he is concerned. Those which are not may be termed "linguistically irrelevant."[27]

In the analysis of written language we are clearly confronted by a somewhat similar situation, for there is evidently some sort of relationship between the "letters"[28] of a text written according to an alphabetic system and the "sounds" of a stretch of utterance. The written system of any variety of Middle English, it need scarcely be said, involves far more than a set of graphemes, but the analysis of it must in part be concerned with the establishment of the distinctions implicit in that set. This necessarily involves the examination of visible graphic data, and (as with the examination of phonic data) phenomena must necessarily be considered not all of which will finally prove relevant for the establishment of linguistic distinctions on the graphematic level.[29] The process of "graphemicizing" can only come later; there is no trustworthy way of short-circuiting the procedure of having to make a general "impressionistic" examination of variants without a knowledge of their precise status or significance.

Even in comparatively familiar varieties of written language such as those represented by Middle English texts, it must not be supposed that our orientation is such as automatically to render this kind of examination in any way superfluous. To believe this would be as unrealistic as to credit a linguist with the power to excogitate the phoneme system of his own language without further ado. We are in fact more likely to be blinded to the true significance of the graphic data by our own particular kind of familiarity than to be enlightened about it in reference to the problem in question. Furthermore, such familiarity as there is tends to be somewhat impractically divided between the paleographer and the linguist, neither of whom is at present primarily interested in this problem in any case. It must therefore be regretted that there is not a closer liaison between those equipped to study letter-shapes and the like, and those who are best in a position to study written texts from a more centrally linguistic point of view. It is further to be deplored that there is not a clearer perception of the unity of principle underlying both studies from the point of view of graphematic analysis, to which both have a vital contribution to make.[30] Were there as little connection between the disciplines of phonetics and phonemics, techniques for the analysis of spoken language would be in a poor state indeed.

## III

It may perhaps at this stage be worth considering another matter with which we are confronted if we attempt to analyse written language as a co-equal of spoken language. It soon becomes obvious that the traditional Aristotelian attitude has endowed us with a terminology which does far less justice to written language than to spoken. Above a certain level of abstraction this deficiency is not very much in evidence; we begin to encounter it most obviously when we come to a point where, in one way or another, there begin to be marked differences between "what happens" according to whether we speak or write.

All such differences must be regarded as being bound up with what in glossematic terms would be described as the *substance*. According to whether our data are phonic or graphic, we are able to establish terms in the spoken or the written system. From these two abstractions we may in turn derive something which we can call "the language system." In that case "the spoken language system" and "the written language system" may be regarded as standing in some sort of filial relation to "the language system." So long as we speak in terms of the latter, we must leave open any matters concerning the alternative *expression-substances* or alternative kinds of medium in which it may be realized. Thus we may speak of "the system of modern English" and make statements about it which neither assume nor make any mention of "written forms" or "spoken forms." On this level, such terms as "adjective" or "the word for 'cat'" or "morphemes indicating plurality" can have meaning, whereas others, such as "/p/" or "grapheme" can have none. Certain terms therefore, if they are relevant at all, are equally so with whichever *expression-substance* we are dealing and it is at this level that the investigator of written language is at no serious disadvantage with respect to terminology.[31]

When we descend to the lower level of abstraction where we are considering "the spoken language system" and "the written language system" then at once terms like /p/ and "grapheme" can be meaningfully employed. It is at this stage that the terminology for the two must in some measure part company and that the deficiences begin to be serious; this is illustrated, as we have already suggested, by the looseness with which the word "letter" is frequently used, and by its inadequacy in the present context; "grapheme" and "allograph" are two examples of terms devised to supplement it. It would not be difficult to suggest other features of "the written system" for which at present there is no word at all.

Even when we have arrived at this level, it should be noted that we are still dealing with abstractions; the phonemes and graphemes and other terms to which we may wish to allot a role in a spoken and a written system are not themselves audible or visible. We are not therefore at the end of our terminological difficulties. For a given system of spoken or written language has this as one of its characteristics: that the criteria for distinguishing the several terms of that system (as opposed to the abstract relations between these terms) are ultimately derived from phonic or graphic material which is concretely describable. Any deviation of the criteria as thus constituted beyond some conventionally established range or "tolerance" would usually be considered to produce an unacceptable[32] manifestation of the system. Thus we may say that in modern English it is prescribed that the word *cat* must be pronounced "something like [kat]" and certainly not (let us say) [gid] or [ŋɯɸ]. And similarly that in modern written English the word *cat* must be written some-

thing like $cat$ and certainly not (let us say) $fim$ or $\partial\!\!\!\gamma\!\!\zeta$ .[33] At this point

therefore we are likely to be confronted, in analysing written language, with further problems of terminology. And since we are now at a level relating specifically to the written system, we should be ill-advised to attempt to build up our technical vocabulary on the pattern of that used in describing a spoken system; our terminology can only emerge as a product of the analysis itself. The main danger of the present deficiences in this vocabulary is that they might lead to the supposition that little new remains to be said.

The final stage of the descent in the scale of abstraction is only reached when we come to consider those concrete details which are connected merely with variations within the limit of "tolerance" or deviation which are allowed by convention in the actual realization in a spoken or written text of terms in the system. These are of different order from such matters as we have discussed above; in most, though not all, contexts they could be described, we have suggested, as "linguistically irrelevant."[34]

We have already observed that in the comparison of varieties of spoken language there is much to be learnt from the examination of such details. For it often happens that two dialects realize some term common to both in two phonetically different ways which turn out to be of great interest from various comparative points of view. The student of spoken dialects is therefore prepared to deal with such things, not merely with a view to discounting them, but as phenomena potentially important in themselves. The phrase "linguistically irrelevant" is a convenient distinguishing label, not a term of abuse.

There is every reason to treat similar details in written manifestations of language with equal seriousness and to be prepared once more for the consequent enlarging of our vocabulary to deal with them. These details are perhaps in greater danger of being neglected than anything else we have mentioned, except perhaps from the usually rather different point of view of the paleographer. One cogent argument for the studying of them, so far as Middle English is concerned, has already been presented: the probability that they can be shown to correlate much more closely than has been realized with geographical factors, and thus throw more light than has been thought possible hitherto on problems of provenance.[35] But there are other reasons. Language, whether written or spoken, varies not only between one place and another, but according to individual bent, social status, occupation, age and numerous other considerations. If we are to go very far towards a correlation of these factors with the great variety characteristic of extant specimens of written Middle English, we must clearly evolve a technique for their detailed description. This once more underlines the need for a much closer integration of the work of the paleographer and the linguist than is at present customary.

## IV

In the preceding pages, an attempt has been made to show that specimens of written Middle English offer opportunities for analytical study of great potential importance. It has also been suggested that the problems involved are not likely to be less complex than those which confront the student of a spoken language, but that, being in many respects very different, these problems of written language must be met with techniques specially devised to overcome them. We must now return to a matter which has been touched upon from time to time earlier; the nature of the somewhat complex relationships between a written manifestation of the language and its spoken equivalent.

A distinction has already been made between correlations and what we have referred to as mere parallels and analogies. It is important to stress the difference between these two types of resemblance. A correlation may be said to exist when there is underlying identity of what Hjelmslev calls the *linguistic schema*, the realization or substance of which differs only (as we have said before) in a manner dictated, or at least readily accounted for, by the conditions which the diverse nature of the two mediums imposes. Thus wherever there is a one-to-one relationship between the graphemes of a written system and the phonemes of a spoken system, it is legitimate to speak of a correlation between them in this respect.[36]

In the case of parallels and analogies, resemblances are not to be accounted for in the same way. For conditions pertain in the employment of the two mediums which in themselves often lead naturally to resemblances without there being any correlation between these, or without features in one medium being in any sense "taken over" from the other. Thus in a written manifestation of language, graphemically irrelevant variations in the shape of *p* are in a sense analogous to parallel variations in the realisation of /p/ in the spoken medium. But there is no correlation: the varieties of written *p* do not mirror the varieties of spoken *p*,[37] and the two are related only in the sense that they both spring from a psycho-physiological organization which tends to produce similar types of variation in parallel situations.

The existence of merely analogous resemblances of this kind suggests in itself that any analysis involving such things in a written manifestation can itself be no more than roughly similar to an analysis of their parallels in the corresponding spoken one; it must be devised specifically to handle the special characteristics which an understanding of the frequent absence of true correlation reveals. Even in considering features which might be said to correlate, problems calling for a separate assessment of the written language arise. This happens for example whenever that correlation is not a question of a one-to-one relationship. The widespread "scribal confusion" (as it is often called) of Middle English /eː/ and /ɛː/ would seem to be a good example of a correlation of this sort. So also is the "failure" of most texts to distinguish /θ/ and /ð/ or /u/ and /v/ or (quite often) long from short vowels. In such cases "confusion" and "failure" are misleading words which should have no place in the vocabulary describing the written language.[38]

The need for an independent assessment arises even in the case of straight correlation, because the analysis of written material must proceed according to the specific characteristics of the medium, with due regard to the exact role played therein by the correlating elements. Thus we must not be misled by the fact that there is evidently some sort of correlation in English between vowel phonemes and graphemes which—as it would be usual to put the matter— "represent" or "stand for" vowels. For it by no means follows that a graphematic analysis should therefore be under any compulsion to establish a category of "vowel-graphemes." If some such category is to be established (and it should in any case have some less tendentious name) it must be because the graphic data under examination seem to require it, and for no other reason.[39]

This same fundamental guiding principle for the establishment of terms proper to the written system is bound to lead to the serious examination of numerous features which have hitherto been regarded with little interest from the point of view of their relevance to the establishment of that system. It therefore gives a new significance to the study of punctuation, of abbreviations and capitals, of spaces between words, and other related matters, all of which become immediately relevant to the task of graphematic analysis. An investigation on these lines implies the sifting of all graphic data as a step towards the isolation of whatever is relevant to the system we are seeking to establish; it can scarcely be carried out unless we approach a Middle English (or any other) text as a manifestation of a system operating in its own right —a system specifically of written language such as we might envisage flourishing even if all its users were deaf and dumb.[40]

Both from a descriptive and from various comparative points of view, such an analysis would have certain clear advantages. It would above all take us out of the false position of continually regarding a written manifestation of language as in some sense inferior in status to, and functionally dependent on its spoken equivalent. It would also enable us to exploit, instead of merely deploring or at best tolerating, whatever does not correlate with anything in the spoken manifestation. This is particularly relevant to the task of comparing varieties of written language as such, not because these features have a special significance above that of the others but because—being to so large an extent unexplored in any systematic way—they are likely to throw more new light on the questions involved.

An analysis of this kind, taking full account of all aspects of the written language, would undoubtedly enable us in due course to decide far better than is possible at present just what we are entitled to deduce about spoken language from written remains.[41] But this would only be possible at a later stage; it would be no part of the task of the analysis itself, any more than the describing of a modern spoken dialect carries the obligation of looking into the question of how (if at all) it is traditionally written down. The study of the relationship between a written manifestation of language and its spoken equivalent is comparative and not descriptive.

On the higher levels of linguistic analysis there would not seem to be so great a need for any such basically separate kind of approach as characterizes that which we have described as graphematic.[42] The differences between "what happens" in spoken and written language, at any rate so far as Middle English is concerned, are not equally marked at each level of analysis. Since morphemes, words, phrases, clauses, etc. can all be handled in either medium, once we have reached the stage of talking about them at all, we can handle them on more or less parallel lines in each; the matter would of course be quite different if some physical or other reason made it impossible to write down plural endings of nouns, let us say, or personal pronouns, or adjectival clauses.[43] This is not to say that there is by any means complete correlation at such levels, but the fundamental differences of the kind encountered at the graphematic level are not in evidence to anything like the same extent. In any case such differences as exist are for the most part well recognized now.

Any attempt to demonstrate an analysis on the lines here suggested is beyond the scope of this paper. The case for a re-orientation of current approaches to written language has been presented in some detail because of a conviction that it opens up interesting new possibilities in the field of Middle

English studies. A new assessment on strictly descriptive principles of a small selection of the enormous number of available texts would put at our disposal a mass of information indispensable for the carrying out of comparative studies of various kinds. From these we should expect in turn to learn a great deal about the history of writing in the vernacular. And in the end, though seeming perhaps to recoil from the present deeply-rooted preoccupations with speech, this new approach would without doubt throw further light on many problems relating to the spoken language itself.

## FOOTNOTES

1. This work is being carried out in collaboration with Professor M. L. Samuels at the University of Glasgow.

2. The author wishes to express his thanks for much helpful discussion and criticism to Mr. David Abercrombie, Professors W. S. Allen and J. R. Firth, Mr. M. L. Samuels and Mr. H. J. Uldall.

3. Cf. E. J. Dobson, "Early Modern Standard English," *TPS*, 1955, p. 25, footnote. [In this collection footnote 1 in Dobson's paper, pp. 419 ff.—Ed.]

4. We may often, of course, draw with profit upon information gleaned from written material of other dates, earlier or later, and in other languages, e.g., Norse or French or Welsh, and use this as evidence by a different process of extrapolation.

5. Archbishop Trench noted this over a hundred years ago (*English Past and Present*, 1st. ed. 1855, p. 170): "Pronunciation . . . is far too fine and subtle a thing to be more than approximated to, and indicated in the written letter." Cf. also W. S. Allen, "Phonetics and Comparative Linguistics," *Archivum Linguisticum* 3, 1951, p. 133.

6. [The symbol [ɫ] represents a velarized [l], as in the common American pronunciation of *milk*.—Ed.]

7. This situation is not of course disturbed in cases where a particular letter, in one and the same text, has two or more very different phonetic implications (e.g., [v] and [u] in the case of initial *v*), provided that the use of both is normal or common practice. Nor, with the same provision, is it disturbed if two or more spelling devices have the same phonetic implications, e.g., *sch* and *sh*. It should be noted however that this general similarity of the phonetic implications of letters throughout all later Middle English writings does not always hold; it is usual and no more than that. A well-known exception is the common use, in texts of certain areas, of *qu* with the probable approximate implication [ʍ]; texts from other areas strictly avoid this and do not use *qu* except with the implication [kw]. [The symbol [ʍ] represents a voiceless [w], as in those dialects that "pronounce the *h*" in *which*.—Ed.]

8. For this type of convention, cf. Y. R. Chao, "The Logical Structure of Chinese Words," *Language*, 22, 1946, pp. 10–11.

9. Here and subsequently the word "manifestation" is used when the intention is to compare or contrast a spoken and written "realization" of a language; the word "variety" in comparing or contrasting different written (or different spoken) "realizations."

If we speak here and subsequently of a language or some term in a linguistic system being *realized*, this should not be taken to imply that it has an existence "behind" the visible or audible or other manifestations of it. It is merely a convenient way of expressing a relationship between the linguistic abstraction and the material which provides us with data for the formulation of that abstraction. The same qualification applies to the word "manifestation," though when I have used this the intention has been to emphasize the medium or mediums involved rather than the link between abstraction and material. Cf. H. C. Borgström, "The Technique of Linguistic Descriptions," *Acta Linguistica* v, 1945–9, p. 13.

10. This is by no means to say that they cannot be studied: a comparative approach, involving (among other things) the study of written texts of different dates and localities, may well enable us to draw conclusions about such things. Cf. footnote 4.

11. Because of this, it is necessary to be quite clear what we mean when we say of a specimen of written language that it has or had a spoken equivalent. For example, the autograph copy of the *Ayenbite of Inwyt* has excellent evidence associating the author with Canterbury in 1340, and we tend to speak, without reservations, as if the speech of Canterbury at that time (or at least the idiolect of Dan Michel himself) was the spoken equivalent of the written language exemplified in this text. It is true in the sense that we may well decide that there is nothing in the characteristics of the *Ayenbite* which is specifically at variance with the characteristics of this spoken dialect or idiolect. But the written text nevertheless has other characteristics (whether of equally local provenance makes no matter) which have no counterpart in the spoken dialect, just as some of the features of the spoken dialect (e.g., the intonation system) find little or no reflection in the written text. It is often highly convenient to speak of a variety of written language and a spoken equivalent; but we must be careful, in doing so, not to imply thereby a completely systematic correspondence between them at all levels.

To be clear about this is helpful in another way. We have from time to time encountered cases of two written texts which "look" different, not merely in handwriting, but in other details, e.g., of an orthographic kind. But they have this peculiarity: that when they are more closely examined, the evidence strongly suggests that they stem from the same, or almost the same, place. This, if correct, implies one of two things: either that those contrasting features (or at least, for each feature, the form used in one of the two texts, and perhaps in both) which make them "look" different, have no correlation with places; or else that the forms employed by both, though different, are each characteristic of written practice in one place. In either case, both texts may nevertheless be said to have the same spoken equivalent; they need not themselves be identical for this to be possible.

12. For a fuller discussion of this point, see footnote 34.

13. Such forms as *erþe* and *erthe* might be described as "orthographic variants," but this phrase, if applied to words as distinct from individual symbols, should be restricted to synonyms, so that, e.g., Modern English *two* : *too* would be excluded. On the other hand, the term should not be confined to homophones, and one must be careful, in dealing with written language from a descriptive point of view, about making any distinction of genre between the type *erþe* : *erthe* and the type *swilk* : *swich*. It is tempting to do so by appealing to the facts of the spoken language and saying that there *is* a distinction since the latter were "pronounced differently" whereas the former (so far as we know) were not. For it is certainly true that there are distinctions in the written language which are phonematically motivated and others which are not, and it is clearly desirable at some stage to attempt to discriminate between them on this basis. But to do so during the process of description is hardly legitimate or even practicable for there are many written forms of which it is difficult or impossible to say whether their peculiarity derives from something in the spoken language or not. For instance the variations *myȝt* :

*myght* "might" probably imply no distinction in the spoken language and on the other hand *myȝt* : *meȝt* most probably do. But of *myȝt* : *myth* it is somewhat difficult to decide whether they do or do not, so that if we made a distinction between the two types we should not know into which category to place this pair.

In any case a decision on this point is unnecessary for an analysis of written language. If a distinction is to be made between the type *erþe* : *erthe* and the type *swilk* : *swich* it should be on the basis of criteria established by observation of the written language only, and the possibility of criteria of commutability suggests itself. For example, if one observed examples of the alternance of *þ* : *th* in many different words and nothing parallel with *lk* : *ch*, one might feel justified in distinguishing the two type on this basis.

14. We are not thinking here, of course, of systematic variation of size or colour for some specific purpose, in which case these factors would take on a new significance.

15. The word "place" is used here and subsequently for the sake of brevity; more precisely we mean "the set of environmental conditions which leads a particular scribe to employ a certain variety of written Middle English." It may well be, of course, that this is in fact the product of experiences in more than one place (in the ordinary sense), but the same is often true of the variety of spoken language used by a particular speaker. In each case, such complexity of background may preclude us from associating the resultant language in its entirety with any one locality.

16. Nor is it by any means a question of date only; *erþ(e)* is still preserved with marked regularity in some areas after *erth(e)* has become fully established in others. The fact that many such orthographic variants have a significant distribution would lead one to predict that certain characteristics of hand (as distinct from spelling) are ultimately likely to prove to have the same.

17. One should distinguish at least three categories of variation, which may be listed in ascending order of status:—

(1) A difference between dialects A and B in the phonetic realization of phoneme systems identical as such, i.e., identical as abstract sets of relations.

(2) A difference in the distribution and incidence of a similarly identical set of phonemes, so that dialect A in certain situations manifests one phoneme where dialect B manifests another.

(3) A difference in the number of phonemes in the systems of A and B.

We should note that 2 may (and usually will) be accompanied by 1, and 3 by 1 and 2. The above, of course, takes no account of certain other variations, e.g., those of a prosodic character.

18. These and their kind are not the only variants for which we should wish to claim such a status. Despite their different motivation there is a good case for according a similar status, strictly from the point of view of the written language, to variants like *ston, stan*, or *vche, eche*. There are probably good reasons for ultimately devising a terminology which would make clear the difference of motivation but this has not been attempted in the present paper.

19. Cf. Shaw, Preface to *Pygmalion*, speaking about English: "no man can teach himself what it should sound like from reading it."

20. The history of such forms of linguistic study produces some curious ironies. Analysis of written language for the most part preceded that of spoken language but it was usually carried out with numerous side-glances at certain tempting aspects of the "underlying" spoken language. The result was a sort of compromise in which full justice was rarely done to the facts of the written language and in which special prominence was given to some aspects of spoken language and (necessarily) to some only; this has remained generally true ever since. When the

analysis of forms of spoken language came to be undertaken, its pattern tended to be modelled on this compromise. The resultant descriptions have therefore often ignored many important matters connected with spoken language which perforce lay outside the scope of the inherited type of analysis. Thus the very fault of the traditional approach to written language—that of concentrating unduly on the task of revealing facts about the spoken language—has had the unfortunate result of tending to inhibit progress in the development of techniques adequate for the description of spoken language.

This same tendency is also partly the consequence of a widespread interest specifically in problems of historical linguistics. Earlier stages of a language are attested only in written forms and (as we have noted) the written equivalents mask certain characteristics of the spoken. However important these characteristics may be in themselves, many scholars have seen little point in examining them in the contemporary language, for (unlike other things which are not entirely masked) they cannot be studied directly in earlier stages, and therefore suggest no alluring possibilities of diachronic investigation.

21. Cf. H. J. Uldall, "Speech and Writing," *Acta Linguistica*, vol. IV, fasc. I, 1944, pp. 12–13: "the substance of ink has not received the same attention on the part of linguists that they have so lavishly bestowed on the substance of air."

22. Or by insisting that it is quite possible to envisage a process of human development in which man devised written language first, and only learnt to "convert" this into a spoken form subsequently, see J. van Ginneken, "La réconstruction typologique des langues archaïques de l'humanité," *Verh. Kon. Ned. Akad. Wetensch., Afd. Lett.* 44, 1939. Cf. L. Hjelmslev, "Prolegomena to a Theory of Language," Supplement to *International Journal of American Linguistics*, Vol. 19, No. 1, January 1953, p. 67: "Bertrand Russell quite rightly calls attention to the fact that we have no means of deciding whether writing or speech is the older form of human expression (*An Outline of Philosophy*, London 1927, p. 47)." This would not be to deny of course that, as things are, many of the devices actually employed in a *given* written language can be accounted for by features in the (clearly anterior) spoken language. But we should note that many of these features belong to a *past* stage of the spoken language; as H. J. Uldall (*op. cit.* p. 14) says, "it is not true that the present sound pattern preceded the present orthography."

23. By "uninitiated" is meant a person not himself fully familiar with this spoken equivalent, either because of belonging to a different place or (like a modern scholar) to a different age, and therefore not in possession of certain kinds of information taken for granted by the writer in the reader or readers he had in mind. Being uninitiated in this sense need not of course result in a breakdown in communication but it inevitably debars writer and reader from complete *rapport*—if this can indeed ever be said to exist, even in the most favourable circumstances.

24. Cf. W. F. Edgerton, "Ideograms in English Writing," *Language*, 17, 1941, p. 148; the author points out that Bloomfield, "Linguistic Aspects of Science" (*International Encyclopædia of Unified Science*, 1.4, 1939, p. 6) distinguishes "language" from "substitutes such as writing or drum signals." For a similar attitude, see E. H. Sturtevant, *An Introduction to Linguistic Science*, 1947, p. 3, footnote 3. The first statement of it known to me is in Aristotle, *De Interpretatione* I (ed L. Minio-Paluello, p. 49): Ἔστι μὲν οὖν τὰ ἐν τῇ φωνῇ τῶν ἐν τῇ ψυχῇ παθημάτων σύμβολα, καὶ τὰ γραφόμενα τῶν ἐν τῇ φωνῇ. ["Spoken language symbolizes mental experience or things that go on in the mind and anything that is written symbolizes spoken language."] This same view is held by sixteenth-century English writers. Thus John Hart says: "even as the voices in speaking do make a word, so the letters *which ar their markes, and figures* [italics mine] shal doo the like in writing," and cites Quintillian: "Hic enim est usus litterarum ut custodiant voces et velut depositum

reddant legentibus" ["This trueli is the use of letters, that they shuld kepe the voices, and yeld yt unto the readers as a paune."] ("The Opening of the Unreasonable Writing of our English Tongue," 1551, ed. Bror Danielsson, *John Hart's Works on English Orthography and Pronunciation*, Part 1, 1955, pp. 118-9). So also Sir Thomas Smith: "Est autem scriptura, imitatio sermonis, ut pictura corporis." ["For writing is an imitation of speech, as a painting is of a body"] (*De recta et emendata Linguæ Anglicæ scriptione, Dialogus*, 1568, ed. Otto Deibel, *Neudrucke Frühneuenglischer Grammatiken*, Band 8, 1913). Later we find Bacon (*De Augmentis*, vi, i, ed. Ellis and Spalding, p. 439) quoting Aristotle (*loc. cit.*) with approval.

The seventeenth-century interest in universal language not unnaturally brought about some modification to this attitude; for (like Esperanto, etc.) the construction of a universal language began with the written form and its spoken manifestation came later if at all. Miss Margaret McIntosh has called my attention to two statements from the period bearing on this matter. The first is in a letter from John Wallis to Robert Boyle, March 14th 1661/2, printed in the Philosophical Transactions of the Royal Society for July 1670: "why should it be thought impossible, that the eye (though with some disadvantage) might as well apply such complications of letters or other characters to represent the various conceptions of the mind, as the ear a like conception of sounds? For though as things now are, it be very true that letters are, with us, the immediate characters of sounds, as those sounds are of conceptions: yet there is nothing in the nature of the thing itself why letters and characters might not as properly be applyed to represent immediately, as by the intervention of sounds, what our conceptions are." The other passage, which is found in John Wilkins, *An Essay towards a Real Character . . .* (1668), Part iv, chapter I, p. 385, is remarkably similar and adds nothing to the above.

I do not know how far this line of thought was followed up thereafter. Thomas Sheridan (*A Course of Lectures on Elocution*, 1762, pp. 250-1) described the language of hieroglyphics as having "ideas for its immediate object, without reference to sounds." In the nineteenth century, interest in comparative philology turned men's thoughts mainly in other directions; but J. R. Firth (*TPS*, 1935, p. 39, footnote) has cited Archbishop Trench: "a word exists as truly for the eye as for the ear," (*On the Study of Words*, 6th ed. 1855, p. 194: the 1st edition was published in 1850). Later (e.g., *English Past and Present*, 1st ed. 1855, p. 166) Trench seems to have withdrawn somewhat from this position. But he clearly foreshadows the views put forward in 1913 by Henry Bradley in his remarkable paper "On the relations between Spoken and Written Language with special reference to English," *Proceedings of the British Academy*, vol. vi. See especially p. 17: "Speech and writing are two organs for the expression of meaning, originally co-ordinate and mutually independent." This paper has been cited again and again (sometimes quite unfairly) as an argument against spelling reform; its profounder insights have scarcely met with the recognition they deserve.

The point of view maintained in this present paper is admirably put by Josef Vachek, "Some remarks on Writing and Phonetic Transcription," *Acta Linguistica* 5, 1945-9, p. 86 ff.; cf. especially: "whereas a transcribed text is to be regarded as a sign of the second order (i.e., the sign of a sign of the outside world . . .), the text recorded in writing is to be taken, at least in advanced cultural communities, as a sign of the first order (i.e., the sign of an outside world)." For other discussions of the problem of the status and analysis of written language, see references in Hjelmslev, *op. cit.* p. 46, footnote 3. To these may be added: R. H. Stetson, "The Phoneme and the Grapheme," *Mélanges . . . van Ginneken*, 1937, p. 353; D. Abercrombie, "The Visual Symbolization of Speech," *Proceedings International Shorthand Congress*, 1938; C. L. Wrenn, "The Value of Spelling as Evidence," *TPS*, 1943, p. 14; D. L. Bolinger, "Visual Morphemes," *Language* 22, 1946, p. 333

[now reprinted in *Forms of English: Accent, morpheme, order* (Cambridge, Mass., 1965), 267 ff.—Ed.]; J. Vachek, "Written Language and Printed Language," *Mélanges J. M. Kořínek*, Bratislava, 1949 [now reprinted in J. Vachek, ed., *A Prague school reader in linguistics* (Bloomington, 1964), 453 ff.—Ed.]; E. Pulgram, "Phoneme and Grapheme," *Word* 7, 1951, p. 15; I. J. Gelb, *A Study of Writing*, 1952, especially Chapter I.

25. We are not concerned here with the exact terms of reference or with details of the procedures which might be favoured by different linguists attacking such a problem, especially since we do not believe that it is safe for these to be in any sense adopted or taken over by anyone devising a technique for graphematic analysis. On the other hand there can be little doubt that he has much to learn from an understanding of the complexity of the factors with which the phonologist is involved.

26. Cf. W. S. Allen, *TPS*, 1953, p. 81, footnote 1.

27. The term is roughly equivalent to Bloomfield's *non-distinctive*. It should be noted that what is relevant will depend on the nature of the linguistic distinctions being established, and will vary according to the particular level of analysis with which the investigator is concerned. Thus we have spoken earlier (p. 38) of distinctions which are phonemically irrelevant. Failure to be precise about levels of analysis explains in part the confusion which often arises when an attempt is made to draw a hard and fast line between that which is "linguistic" and that which is "linguistically irrelevant" or "non-distinctive." Cf. footnote 34.

28. The word "letter" in everyday use is ambiguous. It may be employed in the sense of "grapheme," as when we say that the word *swilk* begins with "the letter *s*"; at other times it is used of the particular allographic form a grapheme may have in a given context, e.g., when we speak of "the *s* used in final position in Greek"; again it may be used of a single instance of an allograph, as when we say "that's a badly formed letter." It is preferable, except in cases where it would be mere pedantry to do so, to avoid the use of "letter" in a technical context and to speak in these three cases of "grapheme," "allograph," and "instance of an allograph." The use of these terms implies however that a certain stage of analysis has been reached; before this stage, or whenever one wishes not to commit oneself to statements in systemic terms, the word "graph" and (where necessary) the phrase "instance of a graph" may profitably be used.

29. Thus anyone attempting to establish the grapheme system of some variety of written language must solve, among other things, the problem of how many graphemes this system has. An initial inspection of the material may give the impression that the number is far larger than in fact it is, because of variations in letter-shapes which prove ultimately to be irrelevant to the establishment of the system, but which cannot be written off as such at the beginning. Conversely he may at first fail to perceive altogether certain other variations which prove ultimately to be significant.

30. Something of what might be achieved in this sphere of mediæval English studies may be seen from H. J. Lambert, *Introduction to the Devanagari Script*, 1953, and T. F. Mitchell, *Writing Arabic*, 1953.

31. There is however one general deficiency which simply arises from the habit of thinking mainly in terms of the spoken language. If the word "dialect" means "spoken dialect" (whether the data for its description exist in written or spoken form) it is mainly because of this habit and because no one has been greatly impressed with the need for a parallel word meaning "written dialect" or, alternatively, with the advantages of keeping "dialect" neutral in this respect, i.e., equally applicable, according to context, to either medium. The phrase "standard English" tends to be limited in the same way. In each case this restriction is as it were clinched

by the fact that the terms as normally used embrace matters which are systemically common to both mediums (e.g., morphological system, vocabulary) and matters which refer specifically to the spoken language (e.g., the "pronunciation" of the word *garage*); this being so, they cannot well be used in reference to written language at all. It might also be noted that even in reference to the spoken language they are open to the same sort of criticism as we have made in the case of the word *letter* (footnote 28). "Standard English," for instance, despite cogent objections (see A. McIntosh, *Introduction to a Survey of Scottish Dialects*, 1952, p. 29, and David Abercrombie, "English Accents," *English Language Teaching*, vol. VII, no. 4, 1953), is still frequently used as a kind of portmanteau term within which phenomena of various different levels of significance are needlessly confused.

32. "Unacceptable" is of course a somewhat dangerous term. Texts written in simple substitution cypher might for instance be a quite acceptable medium of communication for a group of schoolboys. But they would not constitute written English as we normally understand the term.

33. Some would claim that such statements are not part of the code of statutes of the spoken or the written system, and that they have relevance only at a lower level of abstraction; they would say that the system counts on the word for "cat" being kept distinct from the word for "dog," "cow," etc., but by what precise device is irrelevant. This being so, it is rather odd that the habit should be so widespread of designating the phonemes of a language by such signs as /p/, /i/ etc., which have a distinct phonetic coloration, rather than by numerals or some other neutral convention. For it is not possible to speak or write of the phoneme /p/ without giving the impression that it is not on the whole likely to turn out to be realized as [z] or [ɛː]. It would seem, therefore, that certain phonetic implications and hints about the approximate realization of phonemes are conveyed in statements which purport to be about the system, and this even by writers who hold the above-mentioned view.

The truth is that a statement about phonemes is apt to be ambivalent, to be in fact two statements telescoped into one. The two kinds of information conveyed may both be relevant, but they are not so at the same level. The exact status of each, the exact point in the scale of abstraction at which each is meaningful, is perhaps not usually of first importance, but we should be aware that there is sometimes a danger in putting things in this way. An example may be given here. It is customary to make statements of the kind: "the dialect employs the twenty phonemes /p/, /b/, /f/, /v/ ... /i/, /e/, /ɛ/." This is in effect two statements:—

1. "The spoken language operates with a system of twenty phonemes."
2. "The distinctions inherent in such a system are realized by using a number of consonants and vowels, and the phonemes in question may usefully be designated /p/, /b/ etc., since these symbols give convenient expression to the fact that these consonants and vowels generally sound something like [p], [b] etc."

1 is clearly a statement appropriate to a higher level of abstraction than 2. In much the same way, a statement about the quaternary system of contrasts used normally in traffic signals belongs to a higher level of abstraction than a statement about the red, green, amber and red plus amber colours by which it is "realized."

34. We have noted (footnote 27) that what may be classed as irrelevant depends on the nature of the linguistic distinctions being established or considered, and that failure to perceive this gives rise to much confusion. There is indeed some justification for the frequent tendency to class together as "linguistic" almost everything which happens to be involved in the process of writing or speaking; it is only the indiscriminate nature of the resultant statements which is open to real objection. It

is clear that some of the difficulty is due to a confusion of two meanings of the adjective "linguistic" which as Professor W. S. Allen (*TPS*, 1953, p. 52) puts it, "has been used to refer both to language and languages, and to the linguist's technical statements about language." But even when it is confined to the second of these two meanings, difficulties arise—as we have already suggested, p. 43 ff.—when the adjective is used of phenomena which belong properly under other headings, e.g., "spoken linguistic," "written linguistic," of a lower order of abstraction.

These difficulties, as we have already implied, are mainly due to a failure to distinguish (as Saussure did) form and substance; they are in a large measure resolved by Hjelmslev's and Uldall's development of Saussure's distinction. A further confusion is due to a common assumption that "meaning" of any sort must, if conveyed through speech or writing, be in some sense a direct product of a single underlying linguistic system. But meaning which is specifically the product of some non-accepted or even slightly abnormal use of spoken or written language (thereby producing such reactions as "he does not sound like a native speaker of English" or "the man was obviously drunk when he wrote this"), is not normally taken into account in the establishment of linguistic systems. We may well of course—though not usually till some later stage—attempt to establish further systems to handle the data available. Investigation of the "meaning" of voice quality or the use of purple ink or scented notepaper might well at this point become the legitimate concern of the linguist. But it is useful to distinguish such things from others, common to stretches of utterance produced in all kinds of voice, or to specimens of written language in all colours of ink and on all kinds of paper, which are likely to preoccupy him first.

35. See p. 39.

36. This relationship is not of course a *sine qua non*: correlation of a different kind would exist, for example, where pairs of phonemes had one graphemic equivalent, e.g., in a situation which might be traditionally expressed in some such statement as "long and short vowels are not distinguished orthographically."

37. It is worth noting that any such thing is specifically excluded by a fundamental factor in the relationship between the two manifestations. For (except in rare circumstances) the written manifestation specifically avoids giving expression to allophonic and other variations of similar or lower status in the spoken (see p. 38); it starts, so to speak, with a clean sheet in this matter. Such allographic and other variations of similar or lower status in the shapes of *p* as then show themselves are features peculiar to the written manifestation, depending on nothing in the spoken language. In a printed book these features are not usually in evidence; here all *p*s look alike, though there may be marked differences between the *p*s used in two different books. In one and the same book, of course, "*p*" may be found in Roman and Italic form, upper and lower case, but these four forms must be regarded as significantly different and therefore—however we may decide to order them—describable in systemic terms at some level.

38. The word "confusion" might of course be appropriately applied to certain usages of a writer or speaker which are not characteristic of the linguistic norm with which we are associating him. Thus some types of slovenly writing, for example where there is a regular or frequent "failure" to distinguish *u* and *n* or *r* and *v*, will probably lead to serious ambiguity sooner or later, though over large stretches of text the "correct" realization of a sufficiency of the rest of the system will be enough to carry the reader safely along. In the same way, an English speaker who habitually failed to distinguish /b/ and /p/ would at most points in his utterance be completely understandable; we should, however, be hard pressed to interpret him—in terms of the "normal" system—here and there, for example to decide whether his name was Bryce or Price. It is interesting to note how far the failure to distinguish what would

generally be regarded as indispensable terms of the appropriate system may extend with impunity in practice, e.g., in whistle talk and some examples of modern cursive writing. Other "confusions" may be of the much more occasional kind which are to be accounted for by what are usually described as slips of the pen or tongue; in these the resultant form is not characteristic even of the norm of the writer or speaker himself.

None of the above idiosyncratic or sporadic confusions, whether in written or spoken language, should be confounded with an amalgamation of originally distinct terms which has at some date or other become general practice and which thereafter must therefore be regarded as fully characteristic of the system. Thus modern English /iː/ might possibly be described as a large-scale confusion of Middle English /ɛː/ and /eː/, but only in a historical sense. Similarly the "*y*" grapheme manifested regularly in many later Middle English texts not only in words like *yede* "went," *yet* "yet," and *ye* "ye" but also in such words as *yink* "think," *oyer* "other" and *ye* "the," might be described as a confusion of earlier *y* and *þ*. But whenever such amalgamations have become accepted practice, the word "confusion" cannot be meaningfully applied to them except in a diachronic context.

It should be noted that certain structural distinctions which are not always explicit in the spoken language are so in the written. [dʒounəːtn] has an ambiguity in ordinary conversational English which would be absent in the alternative written equivalents *Joe Norton* and *Joan Orton*, not merely because of the "difference of spelling" but because of the observance of word division. Modern written English, of course, explicitly distinguishes many homophones, thus again as it were beating the spoken language at what some would regard as its own game.

39. A further point should be noted here. Even when there is a straight correlation in the sense that the distinctions in question are all found to be made both in speech and writing, we must use some caution in speaking of a one–to–one correspondence between the units in the two mediums. Thus *we* and *he* are graphematically distinguished by means different from those used to distinguish *we* and *she* or *he* and *she*. We may say that *w* correlates with /w/ and *h* with /h/, but if we say the same of *sh* and /ʃ/ then we must recognize the possibility of two graphemes correlating with one phoneme. To claim *sh* as a single grapheme would merely be to force the written data to square with a previously and independently established phoneme system and would lead to serious difficulties. And to assert that the co-existence of such pairs as Middle English *miʒt* and *might* supports this claim is no more reasonable than to set up a Modern English /ft/ phoneme because of the co-existence of /ɔfən/ and /ɔftən/ "often."

40. This is not to imply the absence of influence from the spoken language; there are obviously ceaseless repercussions in both directions. (In this connection the term "pronunciation spelling" might well take its place beside the familiar "spelling pronunciation" and be used to describe certain forms in the written language—no doubt always cropping up hesitantly and sporadically in the first instance—resulting from the influence of the spoken language.) But such repercussions in no way invalidate a strictly descriptive approach to written language any more than they do to spoken. Furthermore—at least in the context of any past period of English—they can scarcely be discussed adequately before the descriptive work has been carried out.

41. It might also help to show how tentative and subjective all recordings must be which attempt to reproduce the "pronunciation" of say Chaucer or Shakespeare. Evidence is wanting for so many of the phonetic phenomena relevant to a full reconstruction that the result is likely to tell us as much about the phonetic habits of the reciter as anything else. One is reminded of Bedier's famous comment on people who attempt to express the relationship between manuscripts in genealogical

terms (preface to *Le Lai de l'Ombre*): "on est en présence, non point de faits réels de l'histoire de la transmission des textes, mais à l'ordinaire de phénomènes qui se passent dans l'esprit des éditeurs de textes" ["One is in the presence not at all of real facts of the history of textual transmission, but as usual of phenomena that take place in the imaginations of textual editors"].

42. Cf. J. Vachek, *op. cit.*, *Acta Linguistica* 5, especially pp. 91–2.

43. The practice of putting a dash in place of a vulgar or profane word is a minor example of a situation of this sort.

## EINAR HAUGEN

# The Analysis
# of Linguistic Borrowing*

1. *Bilingualism and Borrowing.*   As early as 1886, Hermann Paul pointed
out that all borrowing by one language from another is predicated on some
minimum of bilingual mastery of the two languages.[1] For any large-scale
borrowing a considerable group of bilinguals has to be assumed. The analysis
of borrowing must therefore begin with an analysis of the behavior of bilingual
speakers. A vast literature has come into being on the subject of borrowing,
particularly in the historical studies of individual languages; but there is still
room for discussion of the relationship between the observed behavior of
bilingual speakers and the results of borrowing as detected by linguists. Any
light that can be thrown on the question by a study of bilingual speakers
should be welcome to all students interested in borrowing and in the general
linguistic problems associated with this process.[2] In the present article an
effort will be made to define more precisely the terminology used in the linguistic analysis of borrowing, and to set up certain hypotheses concerning
the process of borrowing. It should then be possible to test these by
their usefulness of application to particular studies of bilingualism and
borrowing.[3]

2. *Mixing the Languages.*   Perhaps the most widely understood term for
the phenomena we are here considering is based on the metaphor of "mixture." Among speakers of immigrant languages in America it is indeed a
popular term; cf. the practice of AmN speakers when they say *han mikser*
"he mixes" or the AmG book title *Gemixte Pickles*, in which the loanword
*mix* is at once a description and an example of the process. From popular
speech it has passed into the usage of linguists, especially of the older generations; Hermann Paul headed his chapter in the Prinzipien "Sprachmischung"
["speech-mixture"], and the term was regularly used by men like Whitney and
Schuchardt. As a description of the process it might seem to have a certain
vividness that justifies its use, but on closer inspection it shows disadvantages
which have apparently led later linguists, such as Sapir and Bloomfield, to
abandon it. Even Paul had to warn against the misunderstanding that it was
possible to mix languages "ungefähr in gleicher menge" ["casually in like
proportions"], as if they could be poured together into a cocktail shaker and
result in an entirely new concoction. Except in abnormal cases speakers have

* From *Language* 26. 210–31 (1950). Reprinted by permission of the author and the
Linguistic Society of America.

not been observed to draw freely from two languages at once. They may switch rapidly from one to the other, but at any given moment they are speaking only one, even when they resort to the other for assistance.[4] The introduction of elements from one language into the other means merely an alteration of the second language, not a mixture of the two. Mixture implies the creation of an entirely new entity and the disappearance of both constituents; it also suggests a jumbling of a more or less haphazard nature. But speakers of e.g., AmN continue to speak a recognizably Norwegian language distinct from their English down to the time when they switch to the latter for good.

So much for the process itself. A further inaccuracy is introduced if the resulting language is called "mixed" or "hybrid." It implies that there are other languages which are "pure," but these are scarcely any more observable than a "pure race" in ethnology. The term is ambiguous because it can mean either that the language has adopted elements of foreign origin at some time in the past, or that it shows mutually inconsistent elements in its present-day structure as a result of such adoption. Yet we know that great numbers of words in English which once were adopted are now quite indistinguishable from native words by any synchronic test. Schuchardt insisted that all languages were mixed, but in saying this he gave the word so wide an application that its value for characterizing individual languages would seem to be greatly reduced. In some circles the term "mixed" or "hybrid" has actually acquired a pejorative sense, so that reformers have set to work "purifying" the language without seeing clearly what they were about. For the reasons here given, the term "mixture" is not used in the present discussion. It may have its place in a popularized presentation of the problem, but in technical discussion it is more usefully replaced by the term "borrowing," which we shall now proceed to define.

3. *A Definition of Borrowing.* At first blush the term "borrowing" might seem to be almost as inept for the process we wish to analyze as "mixture." The metaphor implied is certainly absurd, since the borrowing takes place without the lender's consent or even awareness, and the borrower is under no obligation to repay the loan. One might as well call it stealing, were it not that the owner is deprived of nothing and feels no urge to recover his goods. The process might be called an adoption, for the speaker does adopt elements from a second language into his own. But what would one call a word that had been adopted—an adoptee? Anthropologists speak of "diffusion" in connection with a similar process in the spread of nonlinguistic cultural items. We might well speak of linguistic diffusion, though this would suggest the spread of the language itself rather than of elements from it. The real advantage of the term "borrowing" is the fact that it is not applied to language by laymen. It has therefore remained comparatively unambiguous in linguistic discussion, and no apter term has yet been invented. Once we have decided to retain this well-established linguistic term, we shall simply have to disregard its popular associations, and give it as precise a significance as we can.

(1) We shall assume it as axiomatic that EVERY SPEAKER ATTEMPTS TO REPRODUCE PREVIOUSLY LEARNED LINGUISTIC PATTERNS in an effort to cope with new linguistic situations. (2) AMONG THE NEW PATTERNS WHICH HE MAY LEARN ARE THOSE OF A LANGUAGE DIFFERENT FROM HIS OWN, and these too he may attempt to reproduce. (3) If he reproduces the new linguistic patterns, NOT IN THE CONTEXT OF THE LANGUAGE IN WHICH HE LEARNED THEM, but in the context of another, he may be said to have "borrowed" them from one language into another. The heart of our definition of borrowing is then THE ATTEMPTED REPRODUCTION IN ONE LANGUAGE OF PATTERNS PREVIOUSLY FOUND IN ANOTHER. We shall not here take up the question of what is meant by "another language"; Bloomfield has adequately pointed out the difficulties involved.[5] The term reproduction does not imply that a mechanical imitation has taken place; on the contrary, the nature of the reproduction may differ very widely from the original, as we shall see.

For our definition it does not matter why the speaker does it, nor whether he is conscious of what he is doing. We shall proceed to analyze what he does by comparing the pattern that he is reproducing with the results that he succeeds in turning out. While it is true that we shall rarely if ever be able to catch a speaker in the actual process of making an original borrowing, it is clear that every loan now current must at some time have appeared as an innovation. Only by isolating this initial leap of the pattern from one language to another can we clarify the process of borrowing.

4. *Types of Borrowing.*   Since borrowing has been defined as a process involving reproduction, any attempt to analyze its course must involve a comparison of the original pattern with its imitation. We shall call the original pattern the MODEL, and recognize that the loan may be more or less similar to it. It may vary all the way from an imitation satisfactory to a native speaker to one that the native speaker would not recognize at all. Where the loan is (to a native speaker) noticeably different from the model, we are faced with a case of partial learning due to the interference of other factors, as yet unnamed. If we assume, on the basis of common observation, that these factors are the previously established patterns of the speaker's language, we shall be able to separate out two distinct kinds of reproduction. If the loan is similar enough to the model so that a native speaker would accept it as his own, the borrowing speaker may be said to have IMPORTED the model into his language, provided it is an innovation in that language. But insofar as he has reproduced the model inadequately, he has normally SUBSTITUTED a similar pattern from his own language. This distinction between IMPORTATION and SUBSTITUTION applies not only to a given loan as a whole but to its constituent patterns as well, since different parts of the pattern may be treated differently. An AmN speaker who tries to reproduce AmE *whip* [hwɪp] will often come out with [hypp-]; he has imported the whole form itself with its meaning, but he has substituted his own high-front-round vowel for the E rounded glide plus lowered-front vowel. If the loan contains patterns that are not innovations in

the borrowing language, it becomes impossible to distinguish the two kinds of reproduction. Thus importation and substitution fall together in the initial consonant [h], which are not distinguishable in N and E.

A study of the way these two kinds of reproduction operate in speech suggests that whenever the patterns of the model are new to the borrowing language, a compromise is likely to take place between the two sets of patterns. Some kind of adjustment of habits occurs, whereby the speaker chooses one of his own patterns to stand for a similar one in the model. A study of the results of this normally unconscious procedure indicates that while there are many apparently capricious choices, the overall pattern is not unreasonable. The bilingual speakers who make the first substitutions are in a rough way carrying on an operation of comparative linguistics. That substitution is a common phenomenon under such circumstances has been recognized for phonetics, where the term is well established. That it also applies to elements of inflection, word formation, and syntax has not been so clearly recognized. Yet when an AmPort. speaker substitutes the agent suffix *-o* for English *-er* in *boarder*, producing *bordo*, he is giving evidence that he recognizes the equivalence between the two suffixes. He would not be able to formulate it, but his behavior is evidence of some kind of complex reaction which for brevity's sake we may as well call "mental," though it can hardly have been conscious. It is the linguist's task to make the speaker's procedures explicit, a task for which he has the advantage of a sophistication that comes from having a vocabulary with which to talk about linguistic behavior. Whether the distinction between importation and substitution can be shown to correspond to mental procedures is uncertain. But it is clear that it is used in describing the course of borrowing over a period of time, when there is a growing tendency to import rather than substitute as the bilingual command of the languages grows more adequate.

5. *The Terminology of Borrowing.* Borrowing as here defined is strictly a process and not a state, yet most of the terms used in discussing it are ordinarily descriptive of its results rather than of the process itself. We shall discuss later the question of the role which loans play within the structure of a language and the extent to which they can be identified without resort to comparative studies. We are here concerned with the fact that the classifications of borrowed patterns implied in such terms as "loanword," "hybrid," "loan translation," or "semantic loan" are not organically related to the borrowing process itself. They are merely tags which various writers have applied to the observed results of borrowing. We shall illustrate their usual meanings with examples and then try to relate them to the terminology so far proposed and defined.

LOANWORD is the vaguest of the group, since it may include practically any of the others. But it is ordinarily limited to such terms as AmE *shivaree* "an uninvited serenade of newlyweds" from Fr. *charivari*, in which speakers have imported not only the meaning of the form but also its phonemic shape, though with more or less complete substitution of native phonemes.[6] HYBRID is sometimes used to distinguish loanwords in which only a part of the phonemic shape of the word has been imported, while a native portion has been substituted for the rest. Thus PaG has adopted AmE *plum pie* as [blaʊməpaɪ], in which the morpheme [paɪ] has been imported, but the native [blaʊmə] has been substituted for *plum*.[7] In this case the borrowing speakers must have analyzed the compound into its component morphemes while they were borrowing it, or else they could not have made this partial substitution. This distinction puts the process on a different level from the merely phonemic substitution of the preceding type, so that we are required by the evidence to postulate a MORPHEMIC SUBSTITUTION which operates independently of the phonemic.

If we turn now to the LOAN TRANSLATION (known in French as a CALQUE), we encounter such examples as the French *presqu'île*, German *Halbinsel*, modeled on Latin *paenīnsula*; or German *Wolkenkratzer*, Fr. *gratte-ciel*, Sp. *rascacielos*, modeled on E *skyscraper*.[8] But are these anything more than an extension of the process observed in the preceding "hybrid" examples? Instead of substituting only one half of the word, the borrowers have here analyzed and substituted both halves. They have imported a particular structural pattern, viz. the combination of the two constituents into a compound expression with a new meaning of its own not derivable by a simple addition of the two parts.[9] Closely related to this is the SEMANTIC LOAN, which is exemplified by the AmPort. use of *humoroso* with the meaning of the AmE *humorous*, though it meant only "capricious" in Portugal.[10] Here no formal structural element whatever has been imported, only a meaning, and the substitution of phonemic shape is complete. To call this a "semantic loan" overlooks the fact that all the loans described above are semantic; it is merely that in this case the new meaning is the only visible evidence of the borrowing. The morphemic substitution is complete. This is true also of phrasal loans, in which syntactic patterns are involved, such as AmN *leggja av* "discharge," modeled on AmE *lay off*.

If we now try to sum up this discussion, we see that we have succeeded in establishing a division of loans according to their extent of morphemic substitution: none, partial, or complete. Complete morphemic substitution precludes phonemic substitution, but within the morphemic importation there may be a division into more or less phonemic substitution. We thus arrive at the following groupings, based primarily on the relationship between morphemic and phonemic substitution; the terms used to describe them are makeshift expressions, in lieu of an established terminology or better inventions:

(1) LOANWORDS show morphemic importation without substitution. Any morphemic importation can be further classified according to the degree of its phonemic substitution: none, partial, or complete.
(2) LOANBLENDS show morphemic substitution as well as importation. All substitution involves a certain degree of analysis by the speaker of the model that he is

imitating; only such "hybrids" as involve a discoverable foreign model are included here.

(3) LOANSHIFTS show morphemic substitution without importation. These include what are usually called "loan translations" and "semantic loans"; the term "shift" is suggested because they appear in the borrowing language only as functional shifts of native morphemes.

Separate sections will be devoted to the study of each of these types. For all of them it is taken for granted that semantic importation has taken place. It should be noted that the term "morpheme" does not here include inflectional modifications; when these are applied, they do not affect the grammatical function of the word, but are necessary and therefore non-distinctive accompaniments of its use in the sentence.

6. *Loanword Phonology.* The simplest and most common substitution is that which takes place when a native sound sequence is used to imitate a foreign one. Complete substitution is characteristic of naive language learners and is heard as a "foreign accent" by native speakers. However undesirable this may be when one is speaking a foreign language, it is normal when reproducing foreign materials in one's own. The results may be almost completely unrecognizable to the speakers of the model language, as when Spanish *virgen* is reproduced in the language of the Taos Indians as [mˡilxinạ] or English *spade* is introduced into AmPort. as [ʃiˡpeiro].[11] In many cases the speakers are completely unaware that they have changed the foreign word, as in the story told by Polivanov of the Japanese student who asked his teacher whether *dzurama* or *dorama* was the correct pronunciation of the European word *drama*. When the teacher answered that it was neither one, but *drama*, he nodded and said, "Ah yes, then it's *dorama*."[12] Hermann Paul and many writers after him have described this process as one in which the speaker substitutes "the most nearly related sounds" of his native tongue for those of the other language.[13] But neither the speaker himself nor the linguist who studies his behavior is always certain as to just what sound in his native tongue is most nearly related to the model. Only a complete analysis of the sound system and the sequences in which sounds appear could give us grounds for predicting which sounds a speaker would be likely to substitute in each given case. When the Yaqui Indians reproduce Sp. *estufa* as [ehtúpa], the [h] for [s] is a substitution that occurs only before [t] and [k], where [s] does not occur in their native language; elsewhere they have no trouble with [s]. Polivanov expressed it as follows:[14] "En entendant un mot inconnu étranger . . . nous tâchons d'y retrouver un complexe de *nos* représentations phonologiques, de les décomposer en des phonèmes propres à *notre* langue maternelle, et même en conformité à *nos* lois de groupement des phonèmes."[15] Speakers have been trained to react to certain features in the stream of speech and to reproduce these in their own; but they are also trained to reproduce them only in a limited number of combinations and sequences. Loanword phonology is the attempt to recapture the process of analysis that results in phonemic substitution.

7. *Phonological Importation.* The problem of description is greatly complicated by the fact that the process of learning changes the learner's view of the language. The more he acquires of the new language the less necessary it is for him to interpret its habits in terms of the old language. So he gradually begins to import into his own language those habits of the other which he has mastered and which are not too incompatible with his previously established habits. Linguists have generally assumed that a scale for the time of borrowing can be set up on the basis of phonological form. Early loans are assumed to be the more distorted words, while the late are more similar to their models. Thus Trager in his list of Spanish loans in Taos distinguishes between the "oldest," the "more recent," and the "most recent" largely on the basis of differences in loanword phonology.[16] In general the principle is sound, but we need to make certain reservations. First, there are some words that offer us no criteria, since they do not happen to contain the critical sounds. Second, the difference between the most and the least distorted depends not as much on time as on the degree of bilingualism. Bilingualism may come suddenly or slowly; it may persist over many generations, as among the PaG, and words may come in through various members of the community in several different forms. In AmN communities most loanwords may appear in various forms, with more or with less phonemic substitution; but some substitutions are so widespread that they can hardly have been borrowed recently. It is also possible for bilinguals to touch up the form of an older word and introduce a more "correct" form if they happen to know it.

Since we cannot follow the fate of individual words and expressions from their earliest introduction, we can only guess at the factors that have influenced the form of any given word. We are entitled, however, to make certain assumptions. First, that A BILINGUAL SPEAKER INTRODUCES A NEW LOANWORD IN A PHONETIC FORM AS NEAR THAT OF THE MODEL LANGUAGE AS HE CAN. Secondly, that IF HE HAS OCCASION TO REPEAT IT, OR IF OTHER SPEAKERS ALSO TAKE TO USING IT, A FURTHER SUBSTITUTION OF NATIVE ELEMENTS WILL TAKE PLACE. Thirdly, that IF MONOLINGUALS LEARN IT, A TOTAL OR PRACTICALLY TOTAL SUBSTITUTION WILL BE MADE.

In the case of AmN we are dealing very largely with bilinguals, most of whom learned E in childhood, so that many words may vary from a wholly adapted form to one that is almost wholly unadapted. We shall here reckon with certain characteristic stages, while realizing that these are not always chronological:

(1) A PRE-BILINGUAL period, in which the loans are made by a relatively small group of bilinguals and spread widely among the monolingual majority; the words show (almost) complete native substitution, with great irregularity in the phonetic results. Some phonemes and phoneme sequences will cause the speakers to vacillate, so that they choose now one, now another of their own as substitutes. In AmN the rhyming words *road* and *load* are reproduced with different N phonemes as /råd/ and /lod/.

Such behavior may be called ERRATIC SUBSTITUTION, and is comparable to the scattering of shots over the target of a novice marksman.
(2) A period of ADULT BILINGUALISM, when growing knowledge of E leads to a more SYSTEMATIC SUBSTITUTION, in which the same N phoneme is consistently employed for new E loans. This may often be accompanied by the use of familiar sounds in new positions where they were not found in the native tongue. Thus the initial *v* in E *very*, *vicious*, and other words of French origin must once have seemed strange to Englishmen who were used to pronouncing it only between vowels. In modern Czech *g* is found initially only in loanwords; elsewhere it is only an allophone of *k*.[17] We shall call this process PHONEMIC REDISTRIBUTION, since it affects the distribution of the phonemes.
(3) A period of CHILDHOOD BILINGUALISM, in which the characteristic process is one of PHONEMIC IMPORTATION, i.e., completely new sound types are introduced. The Yaqui whose first-generation speakers had to substitute *p* for *f* in Spanish *estufa* "stove," saying [ehtúpa], are by now sufficiently bilingual to produce [fonografo] "phonograph" without difficulty. AmN speakers acquired E *whip* as /ˈˈhyppa/ in the first generation, but as /ˈˈwippa/ in the second.

8. *The Grammar of Loanwords.* If loanwords are to be incorporated into the utterances of a new language, they must be fitted into its grammatical structure. This means that they must be assigned by the borrower to the various grammatical classes which are distinguished by his own language. Insofar as these are different from those of the model language, an analysis and adjustment will be necessary here as in the case of phonology, and we observe the same predominance of substitution in the early phases, which later yields to a certain degree of importation. The broadest kind of form classes are those that are traditionally known as the "parts of speech." In the case of E and N there is no problem at this level, since their structures are closely parallel: E nouns are adopted as AmN nouns, and so forth. It is reported from Chiricahau, an Athabaskan language, that the Spanish adjectives *loco* "crazy" and *rico* "rich" are borrowed as verbs.[18] But within the form classes (at least those that have inflections), there are problems for AmN also. N nouns belong to one of three classes known traditionally as masculine, feminine, and neuter, which differ from each other in inflection and syntactical environment. Since E has no corresponding division, an E noun must be assigned to one of these classes on the basis of analogies which are often difficult to discover both for the speakers and for the analyst. In most languages for which the phenomenon has been studied a clear tendency is seen to assign loanwords to one particular gender unless specific analogies intervene to draw them into other classes. This is even more marked in AmN verbs, where practically every loanword falls into the first class of weak verbs. Such grammatical categories as definiteness, possession, and plurality correspond with sufficient closeness so that little more is involved than a substitution of N forms for E. Again, this would not be true in languages less closely related; the Yaqui have given many loanwords a suffix *-um* with a singular sense though the suffix is plural in Yaqui.[19]

But even in the relation of E and N there are many cases of erroneous analysis, based on special situations, so that e.g., E -*s* (plural) may be borrowed with its stem and treated as if it were part of a singular noun. An example is *kars* "car," plural *karser*; similarly in AmItalian *pinozzi* "peanuts." But the next step, correlated to a bilingual stage of learning, is to import the plural suffix for E loanwords. This becomes such a common thing that the N suffixed article may be added to it, producing a hybrid inflection -*s*- + -*a* "the," e.g., *kisa* "the keys." Adjectives and adverbs may also receive N suffixes, but to a much lesser extent. Here the E influence has frequently led to an importation of zero suffixes, i.e., the abandonment of inflection. Aasta Stene has pointed out that this is promoted by the fact that N also has zero suffixes in some positions.[20] The verbs, on the other hand, have invariably a complete N inflection, with practically no substitution from E. This phenomenon has been noted for several languages, and is sufficiently striking to merit some consideration.[21] Miss Stene stresses the opportunity available to nouns and adjectives of appearing in positions where inflection can be avoided, which is not possible for verbs. While this is true, it should not be overlooked that the function of verb inflections is somewhat different from that of the rest. Tense is a necessary feature of every N (and E) sentence in a way that plurality is not; verbs have no inflectional form with the kind of generalized function that the noun singular has. The noun singular not only refers to individuals of the species, but also to the species itself, and in many cases this is quite sufficient (e.g., *rabbit* as a loanword may refer either to a single rabbit or to rabbits in general). The adjective inflections are even more secondary, since they have no independent meaning but are dependent on the nouns which they modify. Thus the importation of the E lack of inflection is facilitated by the relative unimportance of the corresponding N inflections and we need not assume any deliberate "avoidance of inflection," at least by the unsophisticated speakers dealt with in this study.

9. *Loanblends.* In reproducing the forms of another language speakers will frequently go farther in their adaptation than merely to substitute native sounds and inflections for the foreign ones. They may actually slip in part or all of a native morpheme for some part of the foreign, as in AmPort. *alvachus* "overshoes," *alvarozes* "overalls," where the native prefix *al*- has been substituted for the E *o*-.[22] Such substitutions are only discernible when the phonetic results differ from those that derive from phonological substitution. Thus E -*er* is reproduced as AmN /-ər/; only when it is not, can one be sure of a suffix substitution, as in /ˡˡkårrna/ "corner" (by blending with N *hyrrna* "corner"). The same would not be true in AmPort., where Eastern AmE -*er* [-ə] is normally reproduced as /-a/. Suffix substitution is obvious in such a word as /ˡbordo/ "boarder," since /-o/ is a regular agent suffix.[23] The /-a/ is actually ambiguous, since it not only reproduces E -*er*, but is added as a regular suffix to many words which in E end in consonants.[24] In cases like AmN /ˡˡkårrna/, where the suffix is itself meaningless, hardly more than a

gender marker, we are dealing with a BLENDED STEM. Nearest to this is the BLENDED DERIVATIVE, in which native suffixes are substituted for the foreign. Thus in PaG *-ig* is often substituted for E *-y*, e.g., *bassig* "bossy," *fonnig* "funny," *tricksig* "tricky."[25] In AmN it is often hard to distinguish E from N suffixes, since many of them are phonologically equivalent; e.g., E *-y* [-i] is homophonous to N /-i/. BLENDED COMPOUNDS constitute the largest class of blends in AmN. Compounds may be borrowed about as freely as simple stems, since the two languages have parallel structures in compounding. But about half of the compounds show substitution of one or both parts. It is conspicuous that in practically every case the substitute closely resembles the foreign term in sound and has a meaning not too remote from it. An example from PaG is *bockabuch* "pocketbook," where *buch* was substituted for E *book*. The force of the compounding pattern was such that even some phrases which were not compounds in E became so in AmN, e.g., *black walnut* > /ˈblakkvalˌnot/. Only such terms as had direct E models have here been considered loanblends. Independent AmN formations involving E morphemes are here regarded as creations which fall outside the process of borrowing.

10. *Loanshifts.* Some foreign loans appear in the language only as changes in the usage of native words. Such changes will here be classed as "shifts," which will be made to include all changes that are not strictly phonological and grammatical. Complete substitution of native morphemes has taken place. When this occurs in simple stems, two possibilities result according to the degree of similarity between the new and the old meanings of the word. If the new meaning has nothing in common with the old, it may be described as a LOAN HOMONYM. This is the situation when AmPort. has substituted its word *grosseria* "a rude remark" for E *grocery*; the result is that the word *grosseria* has two homonymous meanings. In a dictionary they would presumably be listed as two distinct words. When there is a certain amount of semantic overlapping between the new and old meanings, one may speak of a LOAN SYNONYM, which only adds a new shade of meaning to the native morpheme. These can in turn be distinguished into SEMANTIC DISPLACEMENTS, in which native terms are applied to novel cultural phenomena that are roughly similar to something in the old culture, and SEMANTIC CONFUSIONS, in which native distinctions are obliterated through the influence of partial interlingual synonymity. It is a semantic displacement when AmPort. uses *pêso* "weight" (from Span. *peso*) to mean "dollar"; but it is a semantic confusion when they substitute the native *livraria* "bookstore, home library" for E *library* instead of using the Port. *biblioteca*.[26] This process may be symbolized as follows: if language $A$ has two words $a_1$ and $a_2$ which both overlap some meanings of word $b$ in language $B$, pressure of $B$ on $A$ will often lead to confusion of $a_1$ and $a_2$; if $a_1$ resembles $b$ phonetically, it may even displace $a_2$ entirely.

The lack of any satisfactory method of classifying degrees of semantic similarity means that it is not always possible to make the distinctions here suggested. Thus it would be possible to disagree on the classification of AmPort. *crismas* "Christmas." It is similar enough to the AmE model so that one might at first imagine it to be a loanword with phonemic substitution; only the fact that a word with exactly this phonemic form already exists in Port. requires us to class it as a loanshift. But is it a loan homonym or a loan synonym? Pap regards its native meaning, "oil of sacrament," as sufficiently similar to the new meaning to call it the latter ("semantic loan" in his terminology); but one might well feel that there is no common "area of synonymity" between them, so that it should rather be called a loan homonym.[27] Compounds may also show complete native substitution, as when N *korn* "grain" + *krubba* "fodder-rack" are substituted for *corncrib* in the sense of a building for storing unshelled maize. These are the so-called LOAN TRANSLATIONS, which have played a great role in the development of many languages. Thus Gk. *sympátheia*, which was reproduced in E by importation, was reproduced by morpheme substitution in Lat. *compassiō*, G *Mitleid*, Dan. *Medlidenhed*, and Russ. *soboléžnovanie*.[28] Substitution may equally well extend to complete phrases, whose parts are reproduced as native words; we may call these SYNTACTIC SUBSTITUTIONS, and include such expressions as AmPort. *responder para tras* "to talk back."[29]

Loanshifts in general occur most readily when there is both phonetic and semantic resemblance between foreign and native terms. Terms that are interlingually similar will be called ANALOGUES; if the similarity is purely phonetic, they will be called HOMOPHONES, and if it is purely semantic, HOMOLOGUES. All three kinds can become starting-points for a morphemic substitution; in the case of AmN it is noteworthy how strong the force of pure homophony is. The similarity of E and N makes it easy to pour new wine into old bottles—for the old bottles are scarcely distinguishable from the new.

11. *Creation.* Loanword lists are often made to include a number of terms whose existence may ultimately be due to contact with a second culture and its language, but which are not strictly loans at all. These did not come into being as direct imitations of a foreign model, but were secondarily created within the borrowing language. An example is the Yaqui term *liósnóoka* "pray," composed of the loanword *liós* "God" (from Sp. *dios*) and the native *nóoka* "speak."[30] Such formations are sometimes confused with loanblends, since they resemble these in being "hybrid." But seen in the light of the borrowing process as here defined, they cannot have come into being as imitations of a foreign model, for there is no Spanish word of the shape *godspeak* meaning "pray." A parallel from AmN is *sjærbrukar* "one who operates a farm for a share of the profits," a technical term used in the tobacco-raising districts of Wisconsin. The first part is a loanword *sjær* (from AmE *share*), the second is a N *brukar* "farmer, tenant." The AmE *sharecropper* is not in use in these districts; a word *shareman* is sometimes heard in English. But neither of these can have suggested the AmN word; its origin must be sought

in the N word *gardbrukar* "farmer (lit. farm-user)," in which the loanword *sjær* was substituted for the native *gard*. This kind of REVERSE SUBSTITUTION, in which loan morphemes are filled into native models, is clearly different from the borrowings previously described and should be distinguished from them. PaG has an interesting series of terms of the type *Gekick* "habitual kicking or objecting" (e.g., *Gekooks* "coaxing," *Gepeddel* "peddling," *Getschäbber* "jabbering").[31] When classified without regard to the borrowing process, they appear as "hybrids"; but their starting point is different from such loanblends as *blaumepai* "plum pie" previously cited. These do not have a specific E model, for English has no words of this type, implying a habitual or even annoying activity. They appear to be secondary derivatives from the borrowed verbs (e.g., *kicken*), and are filled into the pattern of the native words of the type *Gejämmer* "incessant moaning or lamenting." The only criterion available for deciding whether a term belongs to this class of native creation is that no model exists in the other language. This may be difficult to ascertain without a rather complete knowledge of the language in question. A doubtful case is raised in the AmIt. word *sciainatore* "boot-black," apparently formed by substituting the loanword *sciainare* "shine (shoes)" in a native pattern of the type represented by *trovatore* "troubadour." But if, as the Italian scholar A. Menarini supposes, there is an AmE word *shiner* meaning "boot-black," it could be a loanblend, in which the native *-tore* was simply substituted for AmE *-er*.[32] This writer has never heard or seen such a word (except in the sense of a black eye), the usual word being *boot-black*, but he recognizes that it does exist in the compound *shoe-shiner* (also and more commonly *shoe-shine*).

Since the type of creation here discussed needs a name to distinguish it from the kind of creation that consists entirely of native material we might dub it HYBRID CREATION, thus emphasizing its bilingual nature. But it must be recognized that it is not a part of the borrowing process, rather does it give evidence of an intimate fusion into the language of the borrowed material, since it has become productive in the new language. The number of hybrid creations seems to vary markedly according to circumstances. PaG appears to have great numbers of them, involving such highly productive suffixes as *-erei, -es, -sel, -keet, -meesig, -voll, -weis* and the verbal prefix *var-*.[33] AmN, on the other hand, has relatively few, which may be due to the comparative lack of productive affixes in Norwegian, but also to the briefer period of residence in America. Most hybrid creations are of the type in which loan morphemes have been substituted in the nucleus, while the marginal parts (the affixes) are native. The opposite kind, showing marginal substitution (exemplified by E *talkative*), is not found at all in the AmN materials.

Occasionally one finds reference in loanword studies to a completely native kind of creation, when this has occurred in response to stimuli from another culture. Examples from the Pima Indians have been presented by George Herzog of such newly created descriptive terms as "having downward tassels" (oats), "wrinkled buttocks" (elephants), "dry grapes" (raisins), "lightning box" (battery), etc.[34] A solitary example from AmN is the word *kubberulla* "oxcart," from N *kubbe* "chunk of wood" and *rulla* "cart" (the wheels were made of slabs of wood).

12. *Cross-currents of Borrowing.* We may assume that unless a number of individuals borrow a word, it is not likely to attain great currency. If they learn it from the same source, and speak the same dialect and have the same degree of bilingualism, the effect will merely be one of reinforcement of the original form. But the situation is rarely, if ever, as simple as this. The speaker of AmPort. in New Bedford, Mass., is not exposed to the same English as the speaker of the same language in California. More important within any one community is the fact that in a bilingual group the same word is liable to variations in reproduction because of the varying degree of bilingualism. The loan is subject to continual interference from the model in the other language, a process which will here be called REBORROWING. It is a commonplace among immigrant groups in America that younger and older speakers will use different forms of the same loanwords. The difference usually consists in the extent of phonological and morphological importation. Some examples from AmN are the following:

| MODEL: | whip | tavern | surveyor | Trempealeau | crackers | mocassin | lake |
|---|---|---|---|---|---|---|---|
| OLDER: | hyppa | tavan | saver | tromlo | krækkis | maggis | lek |
| YOUNGER: | wippa | tævərn | sørveiər | trempəlo | krækərs | magəsin | leik |

The forms acquired will also be differently reproduced when speakers of different dialects attempt them. This follows from our previous definition of borrowing; but the situation becomes almost hopelessly confused when speakers of different dialects live together in the same community, as is the case among immigrants, and the form is passed from speaker to speaker, many of whom may be monolingual at the beginning. It has been possible in the case of AmN dialects to isolate a few instances that seem reasonably certain evidence for the transmission of loanwords within the dialects. At least it is simpler to account for them as INTERDIALECTAL loans than as directly derived from E models. They are listed in the following tabulation:

|  | | Original | Interdialectally transmitted |
|---|---|---|---|
| *English model* | | *borrowing* | *form* |
| (1) E [dl] > WN [dl] > EN [ll] | | | |
| cradle (grain harvester) | .... | krɪdl | krill |
| middling (coarse flour) | .... | mɪddlɪng | milling |
| peddler | | peddlar | pellar (1 inf.) |
| (2) E [eɪ] > EN [ei] > WN [ai] | | | |
| lake | | leik | laik |
| pail | | peil | pail |
| jail | | jeil | jail |
| frame | | freim | fraim |

(3) E [ɔu] > EN [å] > WN [ao]
hoe . . . . . . . . . . . . . . . . . . . . . hå . . . . . . . . . . . . . . . . . hao
(4) E [au] > EN [æu] > Solør [əy]
> Røros [ö]
flour . . . . . . . . . . . . . . . . . . . . flæur . . . . . . . . . . . . . . . fləyr, flör
(5) E [ə] > EN [å] > Gbr. [öu]
log . . . . . . . . . . . . . . . . . . . . . lågg . . . . . . . . . . . . . . . . löugg

In each of these cases the variations within the loanword forms correspond to different reflexes from the same Old Norw. originals, found in a considerable number of native words also. But other loanwords with the same E phonemes have different forms, e.g., *mail* has not become [mail] in the dialects referred to above, but [meil].

A further source of interference with the process of borrowing is the influence of SPELLING. Spelling pronunciations may be suspected wherever the reproduction varies from normal in the direction of a pronunciation traditionally given to a letter in the borrowing language. In any literate community such influence is likely to be present in a number of words which have been brought to the community in writing. Among immigrants this is not true to any considerable extent, but at least in AmN there is a marked tendency to pronounce AmE [æ] as /a/ and [a] as /å/, spelled respectively *a* and *o*.

| | *bran* | *alfalfa* | *saloon* | *tavern* | *lot* | *gallon* | *battery* |
|---|---|---|---|---|---|---|---|
| Eng. model | [bræn] | [ælˈfælfə] | [səˈlun] | [ˈtævərn] | [lat] | [ˈgælən] | [ˈbæt(ə)ri] |
| Oral reprod. | *bræn | *ælˈfælfa | *saˈlun | ˈtævərn | latt | *gælən | ˈbætri |
| Spelling pron. | brann | ˈˈalfalfa | ˈˈsalon | ˈˈtavan | lått | ˈˈgallan<br>ˈˈgallon | ˈˈbattəri |

Such words as *lot* probably come from official documents, *bran* and *alfalfa* from sacks, *saloon* and *tavern* from signs, *gallon* and *battery* from advertisements. The striking part of it is that the spelling pronunciation does not usually affect the entire word, where a choice is possible, so that e.g., *gallon* may have an /a/ in the second syllable, corresponding to the [ə] of the original. A comparison with the E loanwords adopted in N, as reported by Aasta Stene, shows a much higher proportion of spelling pronunciations in the latter, e.g., *buss* "bus" for AmN *båss*, *kutte* "cut" for AmN *katta*, *hikkori* "hickory" for AmN *hekkri* (or even *hikkrill*). As one AmN informant commented, when asked for the word for "battery": "They just give Norwegian sounds to the English letters."

13. *Structural Resistance to Borrowing*. It has long been known that some kinds of linguistic patterns are more likely to be borrowed than others. As long ago as 1881 William Dwight Whitney set up a scale on which he ranged the various patterns according to the freedom with which they are borrowed.[35] Nouns are most easily borrowed, then the various other parts of speech, then suffixes, then inflections, then sounds. He did not deny the possibility of borrowing even members of the last two classes, but contended that they are

unusual and generally secondary to the borrowing of vocabulary items. "The exemption of 'grammar' from mixture is no isolated fact; the grammatical apparatus merely resists intrusion most successfully, in virtue of its being the least material and the most formal part of language. In a scale of constantly increasing difficulty it occupies the extreme place."[36] Emphasis should be laid on Whitney's explanation, viz. that "whatever is more formal or structural in character remains in that degree free from the intrusion of foreign material." The same view is expressed by Lucien Tesnière in 1939, apparently without awareness of Whitney's earlier formulation: "La miscibilité d'une langue est fonction inverse de sa systematisation."[37]

Whatever the explanation, the facts are abundantly supported by the available lists of loanwords, e.g., for AmN and American Swedish. The following figures show the percentage of each of the traditional parts of speech in the total number of loanwords listed:

|  | Nouns | Verbs | Adj's | Adv.-prep. | Interj. |
|---|---|---|---|---|---|
| AmN (author's word list) | 75.5 | 18.4 | 3.4 | 1.2 | 1.4 |
| AmN (Flom, Koshkonong Sogning) | 71.7 | 23.0 | 4.2 | 0.8 | 0.5 |
| AmSw. (Johnson, Chisago Lake Småland) | 72.2 | 23.2 | 3.3 | 0.4 | 0.8 |

It is conspicuous that articles and pronouns do not appear in the lists, though again it would be foolish to deny that they can be borrowed (e.g., English *they* from Scandinavian). All linguistic features can be borrowed, but they are distributed along a SCALE OF ADOPTABILITY which somehow is correlated to the structural organization. This is most easily understood in the light of the distinction made earlier between importation and substitution. Importation is a process affecting the individual item needed at a given moment; its effects are partly neutralized by the opposing force of entrenched habits, which substitute themselves for whatever can be replaced in the imported item. Structural features are correspondences which are frequently repeated. Furthermore, they are established in early childhood, whereas the items of vocabulary are gradually added to in later years. This is a matter of the fundamental patterning of language: the more habitual and subconscious a feature of language is, the harder it will be to change.

This discussion raises the further question whether there is a corresponding difference between languages with respect to borrowing. It would seem that if internal differences exist within a language, similar differences might exist between languages, insofar as these are structurally different. This has frequently been asserted, on the basis of the greater homogeneity of vocabulary in some languages than in others. Typical is the treatment by Otakar Vočadlo, who set up what might be called a SCALE OF RECEPTIVITY among languages, dividing them into the major groups of homogeneous, amalgamate, and heterogeneous.[38] Unfortunately Vočadlo excludes in his definition of "receptivity" the words borrowed from other languages of the same stock, so that he regards e.g., Danish as a "homogeneous" language. He is also more concerned with practical problems of linguistic purification, so that the basic question of whether structural or social forces are more important does not emerge too clearly. Kiparsky, in commenting on Vočadlo's paper, declared flatly, "die Fähigkeit der sog. 'homogenen' Sprachen, Entlehnungen aufzunehmen, hängt *nicht* von der linguistischen Struktur der Sprache, sondern von der politisch-sozialen Einstellung der Sprecher ab."[39]

Perhaps one of the most hopeful fields for finding an answer to this question is the situation in the United States. Here a relatively uniform language and culture has exerted a similar pressure on a large number of different languages; much could be learned by comparing the borrowings of immigrant languages of different structures, and by then comparing these with the borrowings of Indian languages, whose structures are even more different than the immigrant languages among themselves. Most of the differences brought out by Vočadlo are not differences in actual borrowing, but in the relationship between importation and substitution, as here defined. Some languages import the whole morpheme, others substitute their own morphemes; but all borrow if there is any social reason for doing so, such as the existence of a group of bilinguals with linguistic prestige.

14. *Structural Effects of Borrowing.* Closely related to the preceding is the problem of what borrowing does to a language. The classic instance of English (with which may also be compared Danish) leads one to believe that borrowing is at least a contributory cause of structural reorientation (we avoid as scientifically questionable the term "simplification"). But if it is true, as pointed out earlier, that the more structural a feature is, the less likely it is to be borrowed, it will be evident that a corollary is that the effects of borrowing on structure are likely to be small. The instances of new inflections actually introduced into wide use in the language are few, cf. the uncertain fate of classical plurals in E words like *phenomena, indices,* etc. In the lexicon the foreign patterns may actually predominate over the native, but the structural elements tend to persist. The chief danger represented by loanwords is the instability of classification which they bring in. They have been shown to vacillate to a statistically higher degree than native words, since they often fail to show criteria that make it possible to classify them immediately in one or another category of gender, number, or the like.[40] The fact that they tend to fall into only one class where there is a choice of several, will strengthen that class at the expense of others. They will often introduce affixes or other bound morphemes that stand in a different relation to their stems from that of affixes in native words. While some of these will not be discovered by the borrowing speakers, others will, and may even, as we have seen, become productive.

In phonology the effects may consist exclusively of the filling up of gaps in the native utilization of possible phoneme sequences. Thus when AmN acquires E *street* in the form /strit/, no new phoneme sequence is added: words like *stri* "stubborn" and *krit* "chalk" exhibit the same types. But sooner or later loanwords introduce sequences not previously utilized, as when AmFinnish adopted the word *skeptikko* "sceptic," which then became the only word with *s* before a stop; words like *stove* were reproduced as *touvi*.[41] This type of change has here been called PHONEMIC REDISTRIBUTION, since it will require a different statement concerning the distribution of phonemes and their allophones. There is also the possibility of PHONEMIC IMPORTATION, though the usual rule is that this does not extend beyond bilingual speakers. In English the last sound of *rouge* is limited to words of French origin, but its importation is hardly thinkable if English had not already had it as a "bound" phoneme occurring after *d* in words like *edge*.

Very little thoroughgoing study has been given so far to the structural effects of borrowing on the phonemic systems, so that we are still uncertain just how to evaluate contentions like those of Pike and Fries concerning the existence of "conflicting coexistent systems."[42] Pike's studies of Mazateco have shown that in this language [d] occurs only after nasals and may there be regarded as an allophone of *t*. But the Spanish loanword *siento* "hundred" is one of a small number of loans in which [t] occurs after nasals, thus setting up a contrast of *t* and *d* not found elsewhere in the language. Yet, as Pike has shown, it contradicts the "sprachgefühl" ["language-feeling"] of the natives to recognize [d] after nasals as a separate phoneme for this reason. It seems probable, however, that this is a temporary and marginal situation in the language; for according to his own evidence, monolingual speakers tend to nasalize the preceding vowel and drop the *n*, thus restoring the more common native situation. Meanwhile, it is hardly more than a phonemic redistribution which permits voiceless *t* to occur in a position that is otherwise not known in the language, parallel in effect to that which occurred in English when medial *v* was introduced in initial position by the entry of French loanwords. As pointed out by Paul Garvin in commenting on a similar situation in Zoque, no new features of articulation are introduced; but it may happen that they are combined in a new way.[43]

15. *The Identification of Loans.* So far the identification of loans has been taken for granted, but it must not be inferred from the confidence with which such lists are put forward that it is always possible to isolate loan material in each given case. The difficulty, as elsewhere, is that the historical and the synchronic problem have not been clearly distinguished by those who have written about it. Nonscientific writers or speakers show an interesting tendency: if they are monolinguals, they are quite unaware of loans; if they are polylinguals, they suspect them everywhere.

(1) *The Historical Problem.* As here defined, borrowing is a historical process and therefore to be identified only by historical methods. This means a comparison between earlier and later states of a given language, to detect

possible innovations; and thereupon a comparison of the innovations discovered with possible models in other languages. This double comparison is a corollary of our definition of borrowing; its application requires a knowledge of earlier states of the language, as well as of whatever languages may conceivably have exerted the influences in question. As applied specifically to immigrant speech in America, this means a comparison of present-day speech with the speech brought to these shores, and then a comparison of the innovations with AmE as spoken within the areas inhabited by the immigrants. The complete success of this venture depends on a number of factors which will be obvious to the reader, such as the existence of studies of the language in its homeland describing it at the time of immigration. Certain more special problems which the writer has encountered in treating AmN may be less obvious.

(a) *Pre-immigration Loans.* Some E loanwords penetrated into N speech, even the more remote rural dialects, before immigration. Trade, shipping, and the tourist traffic had led to contacts with the English-speaking world even in those classes that lacked the educational opportunities of acquiring the English language. Some immigrants may even have picked up their first E loanwords from N sailors on board the immigrant ships, not to mention the fact that there were many sailors among the immigrants themselves.[44] An example of a pre-immigration loan is the word *træn* "train," apparently introduced by the English builders of Norway's first railroad in 1855. In cultivated N usage it was soon replaced by *tog* (a loanshift modeled on G *Zug*), but it is still widely known among dialect speakers.[45] A further complication is introduced by the fact that returning immigrants brought English words back to the homeland.[46]

(b) *International Words.* A special category of words is made up of those that are sufficiently common to most west European languages to have a similar spelling and meaning, in spite of widely differing pronunciations. Cultivated people in Norway certainly knew such words as *cigar, district, section* at the time of emigration, so that it becomes uncertain whether they should be regarded as loans even in the rural dialects when they turn up in forms not markedly different from that of the spelling. It is not always possible to say whether given words were current in the dialects; and the spelling pronunciations which they have in AmN might as well have arisen in America as in Norway. This was certainly true of *alfalfa* and *timothy*, which must have been learned in this country since they were the names of American products first met with over here. On the other hand, such words as *music, museum,* and *university* reveal by a highly Americanized pronunciation that the words were not in common use among the immigrants in their Norwegian forms at the time of immigration; yet they can hardly have failed to have heard them in Norway.

(c) *Interlingual Coincidences.* Where semantic-phonetic similarities exist between two words in different languages, it may be quite impossible to be

certain whether borrowing has taken place. Such similarities are of un-
questionable importance in causing confusion between two languages spoken
by bilinguals. Typical AmN wordshifts are the substitutions of the N *korn*
"grain" for E *corn* "maize," *grøn* "food prepared from grain" for E *grain*
"grain other than maize," *brusk* "tuft of straw" for E *brush* "thicket." In
each of these cases the fact that we are dealing with the N word in question is
confirmed by the variation in phonetic form from dialect to dialect, even
though the limited distribution might speak against it in some cases. But
when E *crew* is reproduced as N *kru*, we have very little to help us decide
whether this is a loanword or a loanshift. The N form is identical with a
dialect word *kru* "crowd, household, multitude." The AmN word has been
identified with this by an AmN writer, Jon Norstog, who asserted that *kru*
was not an English word at all, but a Telemark word which he had known
from his childhood. The claim must be disallowed, however; for the N word
is highly limited in its occurrence and is always neuter in gender, while the
AmN word is widespread in all dialects, is mostly feminine, and has nowhere
been recorded over here in its N meaning. Similarly with the AmN *travla*
"walk," a widely used word. There is a N dialect term *travla* "struggle, labor,
slave," found only in remote sections of the country; nowhere does it have the
meaning of the AmN word. Yet since its meaning is not identical with that of
AmE *travel*, one might be in doubt whether it is a loan at all, were it not for
the existence of an English dialect meaning of *travel* "to walk" (very widespread according to Wright's EDD). Even though this is not at present
recorded from Wisconsin, it seems most probable that it was used there and
acquired by the N settlers in that state. The E word *cold* with the double
meaning of "a cold spell" and "an infection" has influenced the meaning of
the corresponding N words, which usually meant only "a cold spell"; yet we
find that in some N dialects the N word already had the double meaning.[47]
In such cases it has been necessary to weigh the probabilities in the light of
our knowledge of the state of the dialects at the time of immigration.

(2) *The Synchronic Problem.* It appears to be taken for granted, even by
some linguists, that a borrowed word somehow occupies a special status
within a language. The acute consciousness of the loanword as a "problem"
in certain modern cultures has led to some confusion in the question of what
the loanword is and how it is to be regarded in a description of a language at
a given time. The rise of synchronic linguistic studies (also called "descriptive") has led to a renewed consideration of the question whether loanwords can be identified without the kind of double comparison described in
the preceding section. Can loanwords be identified by a student who knows
nothing of the previous stages of a language?[48] Such a technique, if there is
one, would seem to be most useful in dealing with previously unwritten
languages; indeed it would be the only one available.

The analyses made so far, however, have applied to languages where the
historical facts were at least partially known, and the lists of loanwords to be

analyzed have first been determined by historical means. This is true even of Miss Stene's list of E loanwords in modern Norwegian, though she has included in her final list only those words that could be identified by some synchronic criterion as "not in complete agreement with the linguistic system of Norwegian." These represent, she believes, the words that "are felt by the language-conscious speaker to be 'foreign'."[49] She sets up a series of formal characteristics "by which they reveal the fact that they are aliens in the system." These are: non-Norwegian orthography, pronunciation, correspondence between spelling and pronunciation, musical accent, dynamic accent, morphology, word-formation, and meaning. Unfortunately no one of these is absolutely decisive (except perhaps the foreign spelling, which is not strictly a linguistic matter), since many of them occur also in words of native origin; and some are so common that it seems very doubtful if they are felt as "foreign" by anyone except the professional linguist.[50] Furthermore, the criteria fail to include some quite obvious loans, such as *drible* "dribble," *start* "start," and *streik* "strike": these have in every respect been assimilated to a common pattern.

Now it would be impossible to deny that, as we have shown in a preceding section, many loanwords have introduced features of arrangement which are numerically less common than certain other features and which sometimes stand in other relationships to the rest of the language than the previously existent patterns. But to identify the results of a historical process like borrowing is simply not possible by a purely synchronic study. What we find when we study a structure without reference to its history is not borrowing or loans, but something that might rather be described as "structural irregularity." This is not an absolute thing: word counts have shown that patterns vary in frequency from the extremely common to the extremely rare, with no absolute boundary between the two. Patterns of high frequency are certain not to sound "queer" to native speakers; just how infrequent must a pattern be before it begins to "feel foreign"? Very few studies have so far been made in which structural analysis is combined with frequency determinations.[51] Until a language is thus analyzed, any statement about the "aberrations" of loanwords must remain open to question. Even so it is evident that no synchronic analysis can discover such loanwords as *priest*, *due*, *law*, or *skirt* in English. If other words contain sequences that are less common and are found by synchronic analysis to have a different status, they will not thereby be revealed as loanwords, but as something else to which a different name should be given. If confusion is not to be further confounded, the term "borrowing" and its kinsmen should be limited to the uses of historical linguistics.

This is apparently the conclusion also of Pike and Fries when they state that "in a purely descriptive analysis of the dialect of a monolingual speaker there are no loans discoverable or describable."[52] The Germans here make a distinction between the Lehnwort, a historical fact, and the Fremdwort, a contemporary fact.[53] But it does not appear just how the line is to be drawn.

None of the languages of modern civilization are so simple in their structure that a single set of categories will exhaustively describe them. Along with their high-frequency habits they exhibit a great number of "marginal" habits which come into play in given circumstances, perhaps only in given words. Current phonemic theory seems to assume that the only description of distribution that is relevant in phonology is the phonetic environment. But it seems impossible to get away from the fact that individual words and word groups may have habits of their own, which can only be described in terms of lexical distribution. This does not surprise anyone when speaking of morphological characteristics: thus the first person singular of the verb occurs only in one word in English, viz. *am*. The problem in phonology is not different in kind, only in extent. Rather than to regard such complications as "coexistent systems," it will probably be best to treat them as systemic fragments occurring under given circumstances—items of LIMITED LEXICAL DISTRIBUTION.

*Summary.* An attempt has been made in this article to establish a precise definition for the term "borrowing" by describing it as the process that takes place when bilinguals reproduce a pattern from one language in another. Two kinds of activity which enter into borrowing are distinguished, viz. substitution and importation, which are defined in terms of a comparison between the model and the reproduction. By distinguishing morphemic and phonemic substitution it becomes possible to set up classes of loans: (1) loanwords, without morphemic substitution; (2) loanblends, with partial morphemic substitution; and (3) loanshifts, with complete morphemic substitution. The second of these includes what are more commonly known as "hybrids," the third the "loan translations" and "semantic loans." Various periods of bilingualism are described, involving erratic and systematic substitution, or importation of phonemes. Loanblends are classified into blended stems, derivatives, and compounds, while loanshifts are divided into loan homonyms and loan synonyms. The process of hybrid creation is so defined as to distinguish if from borrowing, being a reverse substitution, in which the model is to be found in the borrowing language. Among the crosscurrents of borrowing, which sometimes confuse the picture, are the procedures called reborrowing, interdialectal loans, and the influence of spelling. The question of structural resistance to borrowing is discussed, and a scale of adoptability is set up, which is shown to have a correlation to the structural organization of the borrowing language. It is shown that the scale of receptivity assumed by some writers is really a difference in the relationship between importation and substitution. The structural effect of borrowing is found to be largely a certain instability in the categories; in phonology it may produce extensive phonemic redistribution, but little phonemic importation. The question of identification of loans is shown to be primarily a historical question, not susceptible to the methods of synchronic analysis. So far as loans are discovered by the latter method, it is not as loans, but as residual structural irregularities, which might rather be called "systemic fragments" than "coexistent systems." The historical problem is difficult enough, fraught as it is with the problems of distinguishing loans made before immigration, international words, and interlingual coincidences from bona-fide loans made during the period of inter-language contact. But the synchronic problem is insoluble without complete analyses of structure which also take into account the relative frequencies of the elements analyzed.

## FOOTNOTES

1. *Prinzipien der Sprachgeschichte*[2], Chap. 22 (Halle a. S., 1886).
2. See the writer's article, "Problems of bilingualism" (to appear in *Lingua*, Vol. 2), for a discussion of the social pressures that lead to bilingualism, and for some recent studies of the problem.
3. Languages frequently referred to are abbreviated as follows: E English; N Norwegian; PaG Pennsylvania German; AmG American German; AmN American Norwegian; AmPort. American Portuguese. Other abbreviations are standard or obvious.

Examples from AmN are taken from the writer's own materials, collected chiefly in Wisconsin, under research grants from the Research Committee of the University of Wisconsin (1936, 1937), the Guggenheim Foundation (1942), and the Rockefeller Foundation (1949). The substance of the article was presented to students attending the writer's course Problems and Methods of Research in Bilingualism at the Linguistic Institute (University of Michigan, 1949), and to his colleagues of the Linguistic Circle at the University of Wisconsin; the paper has profited from valuable suggestions made by both groups.

The examples from AmPort. are taken from Leo Pap, *Portuguese-American Speech* (New York, 1949).

4. Paul, *Prinzipien* 338; Meillet, *La méthode comparative* 82 (Oslo, 1925); Meillet, *Linguistique historique et linguistique générale* 76 (Paris, 1921).
5. *Language* 445 (New York, 1933).
6. On *shivaree* see Alva L. Davis and Raven I. McDavid Jr. in *American Speech* 24.249–55 (1949).
7. Paul Schach, "Hybrid compounds in Pennsylvania German," *American Speech* 23.121–34 (1948).
8. Kr. Sandfeld-Jensen, *Die Sprachwissenschaft* 69 (Leipzig and Berlin, 1915).
9. Cf. the apt criticism of the term in Pap 176–7, note 58.
10. Pap 87–8.
11. George L. Trager, *IJAL* 10.146 (1944); Pap 94.
12. *TCLP* 4.79–96 (1931).
13. Paul, *Prinzipien* 340–1; George Hempl, *TAPA* 29.37; Bloomfield, *Language* 446.
14. *TCLP* 4.80 (1931).
15. ["Upon hearing an unknown foreign word . . . we try to find in it a complex of *our own* phonological representations, to decompose them into phonemes proper to *our own* maternal language, and even in conformity with *our own* laws of phoneme grouping."]
16. *IJAL* 10.145 (1944).
17. V. Mathesius, *Englische Studien* 70.23 (1935–6).

18. Harry Hoijer, *Lg.* 15.110–5 (1939).

19. Spicer, *Am. Anthr.* 45.410–26 (1943).

20. *English Loan-words in Modern Norwegian* 164 (London and Oslo, 1945).

21. Stene 163 (her opinion that borrowed verbs are for this reason fewer than nouns seems insufficiently founded); Pap 106.

22. Pap 96.

23. Pap 97.

24. Pap 101.

25. Paul Schach, *Symposium* 3.120 (1949).

26. Pap 79, 88.

27. Pap 87.

28. Sandfeld-Jensen 69.

29. Pap 89.

30. Spicer, *Am. Anthr.* 45.210–26.

31. Schach, *Symposium* 3.115.

32. A. Menarini, *Ai margini della lingua* 145–208 (Firenze, 1947); reviewed by Robert A. Hall, Jr. in *Lg.* 24.239–41 (1948).

33. Schach, *Symposium* 3.115.

34. *Language, culture, and personality* (Essays in memory of Edward Sapir) 66–74 (Menasha, Wis., 1941).

35. W. D. Whitney, "On mixture in language," *TAPA* 12.5–26 (1881).

36. Whitney's statement in *Language and the study of language* 199 (New York, 1867) to the effect that "a mixed grammatical apparatus" is a "monstrosity" and an "impossibility" has often been quoted, while his later, more considered, statement has been overlooked, e.g., by Otto Jespersen in *Language* 213 (New York, 1922) and by Alf Sommerfelt, *Un cas de mélange de grammaires* 5 (Oslo, 1926).

37. *TCLP* 8.85 (1939). ["The miscibility of a language is an inverse function of its systematization."]

38. Otakar Vočadlo, *Some observations on mixed languages, Actes du IV<sup>e</sup> congrès internationale de linguistes* 169–76 (Copenhagen, 1938).

39. *Op. cit.* 176. ["The ability of a so-called 'homogeneous' language to take in loans is not dependent on the linguistic structure of the language, but on the socio-political environment of the speaker."]

40. Cf. Stene 5.

41. J. I. Kolehmainen, *Am. Soc. Rev.* 2.62–6 (1907).

42. Fries and Pike, *Lg.* 25.29–50 (1949).

43. Paul Garvin, "Distinctive features in Zoque phonemic acculturation," *SIL* 5.13–20 (1947); cf. William Wonderly, *IJAL* 12.92–5 (1947).

44. Unfortunately no study has been made of E words in the N dialects, parallel to Aasta Stene's for the standard language; anyone who has ever heard Norwegian sailors speak is aware that they have borrowed heavily from English. Cf. Ivar Alnæs, *Bidrag til en ordsamling over sjømandssproget* (Christiania, 1902); R. Iversen, *Lånord og lønnord hos folk og fant* (Trondheim, 1939); A. Larsen and G. Stoltz, *Bergens bymål* (Christiania, 1912).

45. Evidence on this point was gathered for the writer from the N dialect archives in Oslo by Magne Oftedal and in Bergen by Olai Skulerud. The related term *rells* "rails," on the other hand, does not seem to have been known in Norway, though it took root in Sweden; cf. G. Langenfeldt, *Språk och Stil* 15.88–110 (1915).

46. The words *river, ticket, coat, surveyor, courthouse,* and *table-knife* are reported from Tinn, Norway, as characteristic of returned emigrants by Skulerud, *Telemaalet* 73 (Christiania, 1918), and *Tinnsmaalet* (Halle a. S., 1922); cf. similar reports from Sweden and Swedish Finland in *Folkmålsstudier* 2.137–40 (1934) and *Svenskbygden* 1932.3–5.

47. Cf. Aasen NO² s.v. *kjøld* "Sogn og fler," but not under *kulde* and the other words.

48. Cf. V. Mathesius, "Zur synchronischen analyse fremden sprachguts," *Englische Studien* 70.21–35 (1935–6); B. Trnka, *Phonological analysis of present-day standard English* 49–53 (Prague, 1935); Stene, *op. cit.*

49. Stene 5.

50. Cf. the writer's review, *Lg.* 25.63–8 (1949).

51. Cf. W. F. Twaddell, *A phonological analysis of inter-vocalic consonant clusters in German*, *Actes du IVᵉ congrès internationale de linguistes* 218–25 (Copenhagen, 1938); Hans Vogt, "Structure of Norwegian monosyllables," *NTS* 12. 5–29 (1940).

52. *Lg.* 25.31 (1949).

53. Cf. Eugen Kaufman, "Der Fragenkreis ums Fremdwort," *JEGP* 38.42–63 (1939). Kaufman wishes to eliminate Fremdwörter from German, but not Lehnwörter.

# PERSPECTIVES ON ENGLISH PHONOLOGY

# Introduction

The study of sound change has been central to diachronic linguistics since the beginning of the discipline: to many students in the past, it has seemed to be the only content of the study. Part of this emphasis is due, I think, to the fact that the phonology of a dead language is at first glance its least available aspect: the morphology and syntax, however one may interpret them, are at least there, on the surface—but certainly the phonetics, and to a large part the phonemics, are hidden in the writing systems in which our data have come down to us.

Nineteenth-century historical linguistics devoted the greater part of its energy to establishing viable and rigorous methods for studying phonology; and the most striking early steps in the structural linguistics were precisely in the field of phonemics. It might not be going too far, in fact, to say that the phoneme principle was the foundation and underpinning for most important work in linguistics until the nineteen-fifties. There has not been, in fact, until recently (in the syntax-centered work of the transformationalists) any serious challenge to the centrality of phonology in linguistic description. Most of the "classic" linguistic descriptions of the structural schools (for example, Smith and Trager's *Outline of English structure* [Washington, D.C., 1957]) have been cast in a fairly standard form, with phonology first, followed by morphology and then syntax. In the above-mentioned book, just to give an example, 52 pages are devoted to phonology, 13 to morphology, and 10 to syntax.

The reasons for this are complex. Part of the emphasis is due to the fact that the number of phonemes in a language is invariably smaller than the number of morphemes or syntactic combinations; part is also due to the fact that the units of phonology are smaller and more easily subject to rigorous and quantifiable analysis; and in diachronic work, a large part of the emphasis stems from the fact that phonologies *must be reconstructed*, and therefore present a greater challenge to linguistic method and historical technique. Further, since phonological interpretations of historical data are usually based on written materials which are often susceptible of more than one interpretation, there are strong possibilities for disagreement; and the papers in this section are characterized to some extent by the polemical flavor that such disagreements generate.

Because the tools for phonological analysis had been developed first, and because the outstanding work of the great nineteenth-century scholars had been phonological, it was natural that structural linguists, many of whom had been trained first as Indo-Europeanists or Germanists, should begin early to turn the tools of their new discipline on the great classic syntheses. Beginning roughly with W. Freeman Twaddell's important paper of 1938 ("A note on Old High German umlaut," *Monatshefte für deutschen Unterricht* 30.177–81, reprinted in M. Joos, *Readings in linguistics* I⁴ [Chicago, 1966], 85–87), linguists have devoted much time to reinterpreting and restating the conclusions of the earlier philologists, applying such tools as phonemic analysis to data that had previously been differently organized. Aside from attacks on relatively limited problems, like Twaddell's paper, there have also been attempts to deal phonemically with issues of greater scope, for example, William Moulton's important "The stops and spirants of early Germanic," *Lg.* 30.1–42 (1954), and Winifred P. Lehmann's *Proto-Indo-European phonology* (Austin, 1955).

The papers collected here deal with both general approaches and specific problems. In his first of three articles, Robert P. Stockwell comes to grips with a vital problem in the history of English: the apparent typological break that came somewhere between EMnE and MnE, whereby the distinctive opposition of long to short vowels seems to have disappeared, and been replaced by the present opposition of simple vowel to vowel-plus-offglide (simple nucleus vs. complex nucleus). Stockwell argues in detail here, as he does also in "The Middle English 'long close' and 'long open' mid vowels," that this kind of assumption is uneconomical, and that one would do better by assuming a single typology or "over-all" pattern for all periods. In this first article, he treats various problems, including the Great Vowel Shift; in his ME paper, he treats in detail one item, the so-called lengthening in open syllables, which he reinterprets by positing the same kind of phonemic structure for ME as has been posited for MnE.

In "The phonemic split of Germanic *k* in Old English," Herbert Penzl studies the effect of the i-Umlaut in changing the structure of the Germanic /k/ phoneme: this had, in early OE, two allophones, a palatal and a velar, each of which was conditioned by its environment: the velar allophone before back vowels, the palatal before front. But with the i-Umlaut, and the development of "secondary" front vowels (for example, $\bar{e} < \bar{o}/i$), the velar allophone came also to stand before front vowels; the two phones were no longer in complementary distribution, but had split into two phonemes. This paper is a richly detailed study, utilizing the kind of techniques Penzl discusses in an earlier paper in this collection, for the solution of a specific problem.

The two following articles are part of a long controversy about the nature and status of the so-called OE "short digraphs," *ea* and *eo*. The dispute revolves around their phonemic status, and covers such important areas as the nature of the OE system of vowel phonemes, the nature of "length," the techniques of using written records as evidence for phonemic structure, and the role that our assumptions about scribal practice must play in this kind of study. Basically, Hockett and Stockwell-Barritt represent two positions in the complex debate; the latter is an answer to the former. Perhaps the most essential difference between the two accounts of the structure of the system is that Hockett considers *ea* to represent a phoneme, while Stockwell-Barritt see it as an allophone of /æ/. Both papers show an ingenious and delicate handling of exceedingly complicated material, and while neither party (at least to my mind) "wins," it becomes quite clear that the traditional accounts of the entities represented by *ea* and *eo* (the "short diphthongs") stand in need of revision.

Hans Kurath's paper on the "long consonants" in ME is also phonemically oriented, and deals with the fate of the OE geminate consonants in ME, and the relation of this fate to the loss of the "final -*e*" resulting from the weakening of unstressed final vowels. Again, a structural approach is used to obtain more elegant results from material that had been worked over by an earlier generation of scholars.

The next two papers, by Bliss and Kökeritz, are examples of the non-structural, prephonemic approach to historical data. Bliss' study of Anglo-Norman borrowings into ME is really a monograph, and one of the reasons for including it here is the vast amount of sheer factual data that it contains, which is elsewhere unavailable. Bliss has gathered together much scattered material, and organized it brilliantly and with great learning. Kökeritz' paper represents the work of a man who was probably one of the two greatest authorities on early MnE of our times—the other being E. J. Dobson, one of whose papers appears in a later section of this book. Kökeritz is concerned here with historical phonology as an adjunct to literary study, and examines Elizabethan prosodic practice in the light of what is known about the way in which English was pronounced at the time. This paper is of greatest importance to anyone concerned at all with Shakespeare—as well as being of interest to students of the history of English.

And finally, Robert Stockwell closes this section with an astute revaluation of previous directions in the study of diachronic phonology, and some suggestions as to directions the discipline is likely to take in the future. Stockwell analyzes both the "philological" and structural positions in terms of their implicit theoretical and methodological assumptions, and then goes on to suggest some of the exciting possibilities of recent developments in generative phonology—a movement "beyond the phoneme," as it were, or at least beyond the kind of "autonomous" or "taxonomic" phonemic approach which figures in so many of the papers here. The fullest accounts of this exciting new field are Paul M. Postal's *Aspects of Phonological Theory* (New York, 1968) and Noam Chomsky and Morris Halle's *The Sound Pattern of English* (New York, 1968).

## ROBERT P. STOCKWELL

# On the Utility of an Overall Pattern
# in Historical English Phonology*

The overall pattern concept[1] has met with a variety of responses.[2] I will try first to clarify what its characteristics are, and then try to see whether it provides anything useful to the investigator who wishes to introduce a degree of reason and pattern into the story of how English pronunciation came to its present state.

The strongest form of the concept holds that there exists in a language an inventory of phonemes from which speakers select a subset in producing utterances. It asserts that mutual intelligibility between dialects results from an awareness of the system as a whole on the part of speakers who themselves utilize one subset but are capable of interacting with speakers who utilize another subset. The pattern is assumed to be implicit within the linguistic awareness of any speaker of the language, whether or not he himself in fact utilizes more than some indeterminate fraction of the system. This strong form of the concept is untenable, asserting that because there are dialects of English in which a centralizing glide **ɪ͡ə** phonemic (*can* /kéǝn/ "container" vs. *can* /kǽn/ "be able"), then all dialects must have such a glide transcribed phonemically wherever it occurs phonetically, even if it is never contrastive (i.e., even if it is always predictable). It is useful to compare two dialects and to find, for example, that one of them *has* such a contrast and the other does not; to discover that in spite of this difference, and presumably others, speakers of the two dialects communicate with each other efficiently; to seek to explain *why* the difference in structure does not inhibit such communication. But the explanation is to be found in such facts as syntactic coincidence, lexical coincidence, contextual probability, and the practice that speakers have had in making appropriate adjustments. Of the many hypotheses that might explain why the gap is easy to bridge, surely the least verifiable is the speculation that the speakers share an awareness of the entire phonological pattern, in terms of which each can place the other's phonological habits appropriately.[3] There is a weaker form of the concept[4] which does not make the mistake of treating the units in the pattern as indivisible particles (phonemes), from which inventory a selection is made in each dialect. The weaker form instead views the units of the pattern as convenient labels for intersecting categories of distinctive features. In this view, one aspect of the vowel system which is

* From *Proceedings of the Ninth International Congress of Linguists* (The Hague, 1962), 663–71. Reprinted by permission of the author and Mouton and Co.

"overall" for English is merely a set of features—*high, mid, low* intersecting with *front, central, back*—assuming that no dialect of English has a vowel system that is adequately characterizable by fewer than these six features. The features may be labeled in other ways, as with terms which are applicable to the feature analysis of consonants also. The other aspect of the system which is "overall" for English is that three of the categories of the system of simple nuclei—*front, central, back*—are distinctive features among the glides also. One of the most debated properties of the system has been the insistence on three such glides, since it is demonstrable that only two of them are distinctive in numerous dialects. But there is no *need* to insist on this: some dialects exploit the set of six features more fully than others, and whereas *central* is distinctive among the simple nuclei of all dialects, it is not distinctive among the glides in all dialects.

In this weaker form, it may be argued that nothing has been gained; we must still examine an adequate sample of tokens from each dialect and demonstrate what the system of contrasts and their distribution is. It may turn out that all English dialects, shorn of phonetic differences and reduced to a set of minimal feature oppositions, in fact are not reducible below this particular set of features—even though some exploit the set more fully than others. But we have gained nothing in explicitness, which resides in the detailed sub-rules that describe the phonetic exponents of the feature bundles, and in the differentiation of the bundling habits of different dialects. We have not gained any power to describe the phonological system of English as a whole until we have seen the results of several linguistic atlases now in progress to determine whether the feature analysis has any general validity. Dialect geographers have attacked the system in its stronger form, but they have not considered it in its weaker, but testable and more general, form.

So it is not immediately clear that for purely synchronic purposes anything has been gained. But I should like to remain cautious: it is generally the case that an analysis which appeals to so many linguists has elements of truth, though they may await correct formalization.

For diachronic purposes a good deal more has been gained. For one thing, only sets of oppositions are recoverable from historical documentation; there is no way at all to test the physical realization of these oppositions in the speech of any individual; there is no way to defend historically the assertion, common in synchronic discussion, that John has a contrast that James lacks. Documents from one area may consistently distinguish two items that are not distinguished in documents from another area or another period. But there is very little chance, except with an Orrm or a Wilkins, that such distinctions are assignable to a single individual's awareness of his own speech habits. A very considerable degree of generalization about what oppositions were consistently maintained over a wide range of documents is required. Furthermore, the internal symmetry of alternative formulations of these oppositions counts for vastly more than it does in synchronic description.

And finally, descriptions of phonological change cannot rest merely on synchronic descriptions of periodic slices through the time continuum, since the synchronic descriptions of historical systems depend not only on documents (a description of graphic contrasts is not a phonological description but the starting point for one), but also on the internal consistency of the transitional rules that link one slice with the next.

I hold that the laws of sound change are the simplest set of general rules, plus exceptions, which with earlier forms as input yield later forms as output; the most insightful analysis of the structure of the most investigable state of the language—contemporary speech—is evidence of a high order for the structure of earlier states. This does not mean that the phonological structure of OE or ME was identical with that of MnE. A simple untenable form of this assumption was made by R. F. Weymouth in his long forgotten dispute with A. J. Ellis.[5] He assumed there had been no change at all from OE vowels to MnE vowels, that the graph ⟨ii⟩ or ⟨ī⟩ was as reasonable a way to write [ai] or [əi] then as now.

The assumption as I wish to state it is not that the vowels remained unchanged, but that the *system* did; I believe this assumption should be overruled by only the most convincing evidence of systemic change, as, e.g., between IE and Gmc. By the *system* I mean the set of features and their bundling potential; even more generally, I mean the *types* of features and the *types* of bundles. I would differentiate four types:

(1) Vowel plus length (i.e., oppositions of short vs. long vowels): a/ā, e/ē, i/ī, etc. This system also requires a small number of diphthongs: ai/au/ɔi. [Jones, Kökeritz, Dobson, etc.]

(2) Vowel plus vowel (where, to be justifiable, a significant variety of the potential clusters must be shown to occur): a/aa, e/ee, i/ii, a/ai, a/ae, e/ea, etc. [Sledd, Jakobson, Lamberts.]

(3) Vowel plus glide (where only direction of glide is significant, with a range of variation as to the extent of the glide): a/ay, e/ey, i/iy, a/aə, i/iə, a/aw, u/uw, u/uə, etc. [Trager, Smith, Hill, Bloomfield, Sweet, etc.]

(4) Vowel quality (where such features as height, tenseness, and off-glides are considered to be inherent in the qualitative distinction): i/ɪ, e/ɛ, u/ʊ, etc. Like (1), this system requires additionally ai/au/ɔi. [Pike, Kurath, Kenyon, etc.]

Within each of these types, certain features are taken as distinctive and others as redundant. All of them agree, for English, that at least three grades on the vertical axis (height) are distinctive, and three grades on the horizontal axis. But no two agree as to what *other* features are distinctive. For (1), length is distinctive, but off-glides (except in ai/au/ɔi) and tenseness are redundant. For (2), nothing is distinctive but vertical-horizontal categories and clustering. For (3), off-glides are distinctive, but length, tenseness, and grades of height beyond three are redundant. For (4), at least five grades of height are distinctive, but length, off-glides (except in ai/au/ɔi), and tenseness are redundant. (1) is the least realistic in terms of the phonetic facts of MnE, since length need not occur acoustically in the instances where it would have to be transcribed as distinctive, and it does occur acoustically across a spectrum of conditioning environments. (2) is the most economical of symbols but it provides for far more contrasts than can be shown to occur, and at the same time requires drastic *ad hoc* adjustments to account for noncontrastive variation in the system (such as the variability of the extent of the glides in *bite*, *boat*, *bout*, etc.). (3) requires that two symbols (*y* and *w*) be utilized which are not required by (2), but it allows for variation in extent of glide, and it is just as economical in terms of the features required for its specification. (4) is, in my view, the most acceptable competition for (3), though it is the most wasteful of symbols and of features required for specification. Synchronically, I view (3) and (4) as about equally defensible in terms of dialect studies, psychological validity, pedagogical application, and so on. Diachronically, I think the case for (3) is much stronger.

In historical studies of English it has always been assumed that (1) is the strongest of the four types.[6] If it could be demonstrated that (1) is best for MnE, then, since it certainly corresponds best, on the surface, with OE and ME spelling practices, I should be less inclined to question the traditional analysis of English historical phonology.[7] But (1) is not considered the best analysis for MnE by most investigators.[8] The assumption that it is best for OE and ME must therefore be put aside until it can be shown that there is no reasonable alternative to the conclusion that OE-ME were type (1) and that they changed, not only in details within the type, but changed from type (1) to some other type altogether. We *must* seek alternatives to this conclusion, since it is inherently more complex than an analysis which shows changes within a system, but no change of systemic type.

(2) is the type that has been proposed for MnE by James Sledd,[9] and for the history of English phonology in a still unpublished account of the great vowel shift by J. J. Lamberts. Since Lamberts' work is not generally accessible, I cannot properly comment on it here beyond observing that on certain essential points he and I are evidently in agreement, though having arrived at them independently.[10] The only advantage of (2) over (3) is that it provides for an enormously larger inventory of potential contrasts, at the cost of complicating allophonic statements and of having no dialect whatever realize more than a tiny fraction of the potential. It is less a systemic analysis than a grid for transcription of data to be systematized.

(4), while very popular as an analysis of MnE, has been proposed by no one that I know of as the basic type from OE down. Whatever the "long/short" contrasts of earlier English were, evidently no one thinks they were distinctively qualitative.

What, then, are the strengths of (3) as a type of phonological structure within which not only is MnE reasonably describable but also as a type within which the diachronic changes may be simply accounted for?

(a) In the OE spelling *-ig* (in *bodiġ*, *stiġ*, etc.[11]), *ġ* is generally assumed to have represented a voiced palatal fricative, roughly a front-gliding [i] plus friction. In ME -*ig* falls in with the reflexes of inherited *ī*. If *ī* by this time represented /iy/, the collapse of *ī*/*iġ* is fully accounted for merely by loss of friction in -*ġ*. In this way it appears to be precisely parallel with such developments as *hægl → hail*, *dæg → day*, *weg → way*, etc., where the assumption that -*ġ* → /-y/ is fully borne out by ME spelling and MnE pronunciation.

(b) In the OE spelling -*ug* (in *fugol, sugu, bugan*, etc.), *g* is generally assumed to have represented a voiced velar fricative with strong lip rounding (by assimilation to the preceding rounded vowel). In ME -*ug* falls in with the reflexes of inherited *ū*. If *ū* by this time represented /uw/, then the collapse of *ū*/-*ug* is fully accounted for merely by loss of friction and velarity—the voiced lip rounding components remaining as /-w/. The /-w/ which is present in *fowl, sow*, etc. now may thus be traced in a direct line to -*g*, without the complication of -*ug* → *ū* → /aw/, which posits total assimilation of -*g* to *ū* and then generation of a new /-w/ subsequently.

(c) The assumption that one of the three types of "long" vowel was V + /ə/ (or simply /ə/, or even /h/) makes at least reasonable an account of the phenomenon known as lengthening in the tenth century before certain clusters (liquids or nasals plus homorganic voiced consonants, shown consistently in Orrm, but more generally restricted to the groups -*ild*, -*eld*, -*uld*, -*old*, -*ald*, -*ind*, -*und*, -*imb*, and -*omb*). The mid-central resonance of /l/ in English is well known. I know of no contemporary instances where a simple vowel falls in with a complex nucleus under this influence, probably because MnE complex nuclei are predominantly out-gliding, whereas those of OE were predominantly in-gliding. Instances of analogous phenomena in MnE include the influence of velar stops in Southeast Midland American where e/ey have coalesced in *leg, egg, beg*, etc., or of palatal fricatives in Southwest Midland American where ə/əy have coalesced in *wash*, u/uy in *push, bush*.

(d) The curious relation of ME *ē* to *ĭ*, and of *ō* to *ŭ*, such that thirteenth century "lengthening" of *ĭ* yields *ē*, *ŭ* yields *ō*, is readily accounted for without special *ad hoc* sound laws. The change OE → ME includes the series given below. Since I have presented elsewhere[12] the argument for this interpretation, I will omit further details of it here.

| | OE | | ME | | | OE | | ME | |
|---|---|---|---|---|---|---|---|---|---|
| ⟨*ig*⟩ | iġ | → | iy | ⟨*ī*⟩ | ⟨*ug*⟩ | ug | → | uw | ⟨*ū*⟩, ⟨*ou*⟩ |
| ⟨*ī*⟩ | iə | ↗ | iə | ⟨*ē̜*⟩ | ⟨*ū*⟩ | uə | ↗ | uə | ⟨*ō̜*⟩ |
| ⟨*ē*⟩ | eə | ↗ | eə | ⟨*ē̜*⟩ | ⟨*ō*⟩ | oə | ↗ | oə | ⟨*ǭ*⟩ |
| ⟨*ēa*⟩, ⟨*ǣ₂*⟩ | æə | ↗ | | | ⟨*ā*⟩ | ɔə | ↗ | | |

(e) The "first step" in the Great Vowel Shift, which has been the subject of arguments through hundreds of pages of the journals since the time of Ellis, becomes reasonably clear—at least as to *what* it must have been, if not why. Leaving the question of dating aside for the moment, we ask where ME *ī* /iy/ might "go," so to speak, without intersecting and coalescing with other units with which it was in opposition.[13] For the vocalic element to lower, yielding /ey/, was impossible without coalescence (which did not occur) with the existing /ey/ from a variety of sources, including Norse loans (*they*, etc.). For the glide to become centralizing or backing rather than fronting, yielding /iə/ or /iw/, would result in coalescence with the existing /iə/ (long close *ē*) or /iw/ (from such sources as OE *-īew*), and would be unlikely in any case since the glide is still /-y/. The only possible change that would maintain the oppositions already in existence was for the vocalic element to centralize, yielding /iy/, subsequently /əy/ and finally /ay/. The widespread present-day alternation between /iy/ and /ɨy/ (Cockney, Philadelphia, etc.) gives dialectal support to this suggestion. Support for the parallel series /uw/ → /ɨw/ → /əw/ → /aw/ is even stronger: all four stages still exist, in the same words, in present-day dialects (Scots /huws/; Tidewater Virginia /hɨws/; Piedmont Virginia and Eastern Canada /həws/; /haws/ ~ /hæws/ elsewhere).

(f) The OE features distinctive in the vowel system were *high, mid, low* and *front, round,* and *back.* Loss of the front rounded vowels (which were, in any case, structurally *central* as between front and back) left a gap which was filled by the splitting off of the central allophones of high and mid front vowels (i.e., the OE system /i e æ ü ö u o ɔ/ had become /i e æ ɨ ə u o/ by ME). In some dialects (Southwestern), the front round vowels fell in with the new central vowels rather than with front unround. The assumption of a high central vowel is more defensible in late ME than is the assumption of a high front rounded vowel at that time.

(g) Finally, the question of chronology. By some investigators the GVS has been assigned an almost cataclysmic timing (roughly 1400–1500), and a more generous spread by others (roughly 1350–1650). It is my contention that the series of changes of which the GVS is a part have been going on at a remarkably steady rate for more than 1500 years, and that the GVS part of that series was in no way more abrupt or sudden than the rest of the changes—which, one can demonstrate, are still going on in the same pattern. The pattern consists in two main types of change: (1) raising of the vocalic element in complex nuclei toward the extremes, and centralizing followed by lowering of the extremes; (2) alternation between out-glides and in-glides. Thus:

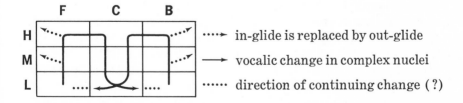

····▸ in-glide is replaced by out-glide

⟶ vocalic change in complex nuclei

······ direction of continuing change ( ? )

Limitations of space do not permit me to fill in the details of this chart, nor to list the pre-GVS and post-GVS changes that belong in the same series.[14] I have tried only to show that the notion "overall pattern" is a useful and stimulating one in diachronic phonology.

*University of California,*
*Los Angeles*

## Discussion

ROBSON:

1. Overall pattern has long been taken into account in linguistic reconstruction, in the attempt to attribute substantial phonetic values to the asterisked allophone categories set up by comparison: "substantial identifications have ultimately to be made *via* the individual languages, with some selection where they are not in agreement," W. S. Allen, *TPS*, 1953, 82. The selection may involve favoritism, and depends in any case on the range of investigable languages available to the historical grammarian. Thus, the seven-vowel system postulated for VL and ME (four grades of height with front-back contrast for all but the lowest) appears to be extrapolated from Modern Italian and Modern Dutch (on the low degree of stability of the system in the former cf. Malmberg, above, p. 80). [Page reference is to the original source—Ed.]

2. This method was often coupled with a monolithic *simplicity* as regards the phonology of synchronic stages, which did not allow for co-existent phonologies within a single koinè language or under the surface of a single set of graphic and grammatical conventions, and an undue *complexity* in the postulation of successive systemic changes.

3. That the Great Vowel Shift is best regarded as part and parcel of long-term changes between two major linguistic stages, OE and ME, is a conclusion suggested to me independently by Romance historic phonology. In each case we have two successive stages and a postulated intermediary:

|         | *a* | *b*  | *c*  |
|---------|-----|------|------|
|         | CL  | *VL  | OF   |
|         | OE  | *ME  | MnE  |
| systems | (1) | (4)  | (3)  |

Here system (1), length distinction with a small number of diphthongs, is attributed to CL on the unanimous evidence of ancient tradition; type (3) is a favorite analysis of MnE dialects and is a *prima facie* interpretation of classical OF spelling (glides represented by *-i, -e* and *-u*, alternating with zero, e.g., *ui/u, ie/i, ou/o*). While I hesitate, on account of its superior graphic tradition, to place an asterisk against OE, all systems of ME phonology must be regarded as purely hypothetical.

4. Stockwell and I appear to be in agreement in tending to eliminate the intermediary stages in our respective fields; for I hold that OF diphthongs can be explained in neo-Diezian terms as reflexes of the free-blocked allophonic contrast and of cl. length, without reference to the *VL stage extrapolated

from modern Italian, see *TPS*, 1955, 172–80. On the traditional hypothesis CL diphthongs and length contrasts merged into a system of simple vowels distinguished by quality only, and diphthongs reappeared from "secondary length" in the VL stage; explanations of the GVS seem to proceed from related concepts current in the 1870's and '80's. It is possible however to suppose that when CL *oe* merges with *ē* both the diphthongal and the non-diphthongal interpretation of the result are valid from the outset, the simple vowel being preserved in Italian *pena* and the diphthong in dial. OF *poine* (cf. Stockwell on the merger of OE long vowels with -*ig* and -*ug*).

5. Here again one can envisage a "strong" version ("stage *a* is already best interpreted in terms of system (3)") and a "weak" version of the doctrine ("stages *a* and *c* are in direct contact, with both systems (1) and (3) interpretatively valid from an early stage").

To defend even the latter will require an examination of the credentials of *ME as excogitated by Sweet, Sievers, Luick and others, and a study of the geographic distribution of overall patterns in NW Europe today with a view to a probable reconstruction of their distribution in medieval times.

LEHMANN:

Commending Professor Stockwell for his lack of dogmatism in presenting various analyses of the Old English vowel system I would like to point out that the balancing of vowels in the late Middle English period favors the assumption of vowel plus length. In closed syllables, for example, OE *cēpte*, NE *kept*, long vowels were shortened; in open syllables, for example, OE *stelan*, NE *steal*, short vowels were lengthened. Consideration of the entire phonological system may therefore indicate the make-up of some of its members better than does examination of sound changes which they have undergone.

# FOOTNOTES

1. G. L. Trager and H. L. Smith, Jr., *Outline of English Structure* (= *Occasional Papers No. 3 of Studies in Linguistics*) (1951).
2. For reasonably full bibliographical notes, see my "Structural Dialectology: A Proposal," *American Speech* 34.4 (1959), 258–68, or James Sledd's review of Trager and Smith in *Language*, 31.3 (1955), 312–45.
3. This is not to suggest that I disapprove of the notion that grammar is a kind of Platonic ideal lying behind actual instances of speech, in terms of which slips of the tongue, grammatical deviation, reduced constructions, etc., can reasonably be explicated. On the contrary, I see no very satisfactory approach to the characterization of utterance tokens other than in terms of underlying abstract rules to which the tokens conform in varying degrees and manners. But this notion, and the over-all pattern notion, though in some surface ways similar, are notions sharing nothing that is really distinctive. Abstract rules of the types found in a transformational grammar or a stratificational grammar are quite explicit about the structure of the sentences they characterize; an overall pattern of vowel phonemes is explicit only

about potential contrasts—not about the system of contrasts that characterizes a set of utterance tokens from a single dialect.

4. Found in A. A. Hill's exposition of the Trager-Smith nine vowels (*Introduction to Linguistic Structures*, New York, 1958), and in my "Structural Dialectology: A Proposal" (*loc. cit.*).

5. R. F. W., *On Early English Pronunciation* (London, 1874); A. J. E., *On Early English Pronunciation*, EETS 1867–89.

6. I believe we can reject quite flatly, however, Sherman Kuhn's assertion ("On the Syllabic Phonemes of Old English," *Language* 37.4, 522–38) that in OE "Length was clearly phonemic, as Reszkiewicz has demonstrated by means of minimal pairs" (528). What R. demonstrated was only that there was a contrast, of undetermined nature, between two types of vowels. The contrast may equally well have been of any one of the four types, or perhaps of some combination of two or more types.

7. There would still remain certain exceedingly perplexing aspects to the Great Vowel Shift, such as [ī] → [ai], aspects that do not seem so perplexing within an analysis of type (3).

8. Key references basic to documentation are the following: Einar Haugen and W. F. Twaddell, "Facts and Phonemes," *Lang.* 18.3 (1942), 228–37; R. M. S. Heffner, "Notes on the Length of Vowels," *Am. Sp.*, 12.2 (1937), 128–34, with continued study through six parts up to 1943.

9. *A Short Introduction to English Grammar* (Chicago, 1959).

10. Particularly we agree on setting up, instead of length, three kinds of "length" (i.e., three kinds of nonsimple nuclei), which he writes /-i/, /-ɨ/, /-u/, which I have elsewhere written /-y/, /-h/, and /-w/. We agree on positing stages /iy/ and /iw/ as the first steps in the changes $i →$ [ai] and $\bar{u} →$ [au].

11. I use the dot over the *g*, as is the practice of modern editors, to distinguish the palatal fricative from the velar.

12. "The Middle English 'Long Close' and 'Long Open' Mid Vowels," *U. of Texas St. in Lit. and Lang.*, 2 (1961), 529–38. [Reprinted in this collection, pp. 154–163—Ed.]

13. I take *i* simply for exemplification; *ū* would do as well, since it is completely parallel.

14. I hope to complete a monograph, *Structural History of English Phonology*, giving such details, within the near future.

HERBERT PENZL

# The Phonemic Split
# of Germanic *k* in Old English*

[Two allophones of Germanic *k* became separate phonemes after the *i*-umlaut had changed the distribution of palatal vowels in Proto-Old-English. Not the phonetic development of palatal [k′], but the distributional change involving velar [k] caused the completion of the phonemic split.]

Changes in the phonemic system of a language, e.g., the development of new distinctive units or the coalescence of old ones, are the most important events in its history. It is often difficult to interpret the evidence for such phonemic changes in the older stages of languages, because it consists exclusively of indications in orthography and spellings. It is still harder to interpret such evidence if the phonemic change in question preceded our earliest written sources in the language. Fortunately, orthographic evidence and occasional naive spellings lend themselves primarily to phonemic, hardly ever to a purely phonetic interpretation,[1] because they show essential sound-contrasts and distinctions but never specific sound-values. We shall deal here with the circumstances of the phonemic split of Germanic *k*, of which we find the results now in such Modern English word pairs as *chin* and *kin*, *chill* and *kill*, *batch* and *back*. First, we shall take up the evidence for the split in Old English and Middle English.

## 1. Old English Evidence
## for the Phonemic Split

1.1. All words with initial *c* alliterate with one another in Old English poetry. This fact is not conclusive evidence against a phonemic split, because it may have been due to a poetic tradition of the kind that is responsible for Modern English "eye-rhymes."[2]

1.2. *c* is the almost universal spelling for Germanic *k* in Old English manuscripts. But a second symbol, *k*, is occasionally used. Such *k* spellings appear e.g., in the Cotton and Hatton manuscripts of the Cura Pastoralis: *kyninȝ*, *kyþan*, *kynn*, *kenninȝ*, *markien*. *k* spellings occur frequently in the Rushworth glosses to the Gospel of St. Matthew: *kasere*, *unklene*, *Krist*, *kneu*, *kempe*, *kennisse*, *kyninȝ*, *bokere*, *ȝebroken*, *ek*, *eknisse*, *ciken*, *kælic*, *kæȝen*.[3]

* From *Language* 23.34–42 (1947). Reprinted by permission of the author and The Linguistic Society of America.

1.3. Germanic *k* is rendered by the so called cēn-rune in Old English runic inscriptions: it appears e.g., on the cross of Lancaster in *Cuþbereh(t)*, *Cynibal(þ)*.[4] The poet Cynewulf writes his name with the cēn-rune. The Old English alphabet shows several adjustments to phonemic changes;[5] thus a second symbol for Germanic *k*, the so called calc-rune, was formed from the cēn-rune.[6] The calc-rune in its simplest form is nothing but a cēn-rune symmetrically supplemented. The cross of Bewcastle shows a slightly varying form. The cross of Ruthwell has a sign consisting of the ʒār-rune with a vertical shaft through it for the sound of the calc-rune. The cēn-rune appears on the cross of Ruthwell in *ic, kyniqc, licæs, riicnæ*; probably on the cross of Bewcastle in *Alcfriþu*. The calc-rune appears at Ruthwell in *Crist, cwomu*, at Bewcastle in *Cyniburug, Cristtus*, on the third stone of Thornhill in *becun*. The ʒār-rune with the shaft, which Viëtor transliterates by *k*, appears at Ruthwell in *kyniqc, uqket*; at Bewcastle perhaps in *kyniq*.[7]

1.4. In some Old English manuscripts *e* or *i* is written after *c*, mostly before velar vowels. We find the spellings *ce* for *c* in *ciricean, tæcean, streccean*; *ci* for *c* in *drencium, ecium, birciae, ciae*.[8] Spellings with this intrusive *e* are particularly common, also initially, after *c* in the cluster *sc*: *sceacan, sceomu, sceond, sceop, sceoh* occur beside *scacan, scomu, scond, scop, scoh*. In late West Saxon, spellings like *sceucca, sceocca* are found beside *scucca*; *sceufan, sceofan* beside *scufan*; *sceap* beside *scæp*.[9]

1.5. *cea*- and *cie*-spellings in West Saxon have been interpreted to indicate a special change of the palatal vowels *æ, e* after the palatal *c* sound: *ceaf* (\**æ* > *ea*) "chaff," *sceap* (\**ǣ* > *ēa*) "sheep," *scield* (\**e* > *ie*) "shield." Some scholars—e.g., ten Brink,[10] Kluge,[11] Dieter,[12] V. Rehm, and E. Prokosch[13]— assumed this apparent "diphthongization" to be merely orthographic, only an expression of the palatal quality of the preceding *c*, as in the forms *ciricean, sceacan* quoted above: *e* or *i* after *c* was to them just a diacritical mark on the line, a "Palatalzeichen"[14] ["palatalization–sign"]. Already Sievers[15] pointed out that *ea* and *ie* written after *c* seem, on the whole, to follow the development of the diphthongs *ea, ie* in the dialect: instead of *ea* we find later the spelling *e* (*scep* "sheep," *cerf* "carved"); instead of *ie* we find the spellings *i, y* (*cyse* "cheese"). Whether we are dealing with actual changes of palatal vowels or merely with spelling variation, in either case we have evidence for the palatal quality of sounds written *c*.

1.6. Certain naive spellings reveal a phonetic change involving *c*. The spelling *orceard* for *ortʒeard* appears in the Cura Pastoralis, *feccan* for *fetian* in Alfred's writings. Other spellings include *wicca* for *witʒa, witeʒa*; *cræftca* for *cræftʒa, cræfteʒa*.[16] The use of the symbol *c* for a cluster of dental plus palatal consonants indicates a frequent similar sound-value of *c* elsewhere. Sievers[17] quotes an Old English loan-word where *c* corresponds to Old French *ch*, a sibilant: *kæcepol* "catchpoll," from Old Northern French *cachepol*. This indicates a sound-value for *c* resembling that of Old French *ch*.

1.7. Like all *c*'s, all *ʒ*'s alliterate together in most of Old English poetry.[18]

Germanic *g* is almost exclusively rendered by *ʒ*. But in runic writing a special velar ʒár-rune was developed from the ʒifu-rune. The latter appears e.g., on the cross of Ruthwell in *gistoddun, gidrefid*; the former occurs in *galgu, god*. There is ample evidence that the reflex of the palatal [g']-allophone merged with the reflex of Germanic *j*.[19] *ʒea-* and *ʒie*-spellings have been interpreted exactly like the cases of *ea, ie* after *c* discussed in § 1.5, as diphthongizations of palatal vowels or as orthographic variation.[20] A special development of the cluster *g'g'* < *gj, gi*, and of *ŋg'* < *ŋgj* in Old English is indicated by the use of the symbols *cʒ*. The writing of *e* after *c, cʒ* as in *lecʒean, secʒean, strenʒeo, ʒemenʒean* resembles the *ce*-spellings for *c*.[21] Occasional spellings show *cʒ* instead of *dʒ*, e.g., *micʒern* for *\*midʒern, Muncʒiu* for *Muntʒiof*;[22] they provide more evidence for a sound-value of *c* that resembles that of a cluster of dental plus palatal.

1.8. The Old English use of a second symbol *k* in manuscripts, as well as the development of the calc-rune out of the cēn-rune in runic inscriptions, is evidence for a phonemic split of Germanic *k*. The variations *cea/ca* and *cie/ce* provide additional evidence for the split, whether they indicate an actual change of palatal vowels or are only orthographic. The appearance of *c, cʒ* instead of *tʒ, dʒ* in naive spellings, and the substitution of *c* for Old French *ch* in a loan-word reveal that *c* sometimes has a sound-value far removed from original [k] or [k'], probably close to [tj] or [tš]. The evidence for a phonemic split of Germanic *g* partly parallels and confirms the evidence for the split of Germanic *k*. But initially, this split of *g* led to a phonemic merger, since the reflex of the palatal allophone [g'] coalesced with Germanic *j*. The phonetic development of the allophone [g'] in medial clusters to the sibilant [dž] offers a parallel to the phonetic change of the allophone [k'] to [tš].

## 2. Middle English and Modern English Evidence for the Phonemic Split

2.1. Middle English orthography, with its departure from the Anglo-Saxon scribal tradition, indicates the phonemic split of Germanic *k* even more clearly. The symbols *ch* on the one hand, and *c k* on the other hand came to be generally used for the two phonemes. *ch* has the value [k] only in some texts of the late Old English and earliest Middle English period.[23] Its normal Middle English sound-value is based on the Anglo-Norman value of *ch*, which is [tš]. *ch* is in general use around 1200;[24] *tch* does not occur with great frequency even in the fifteenth century.[25] Both *c*[26] and *k*[27] are used with the value [k]; *k* becomes frequent before *e, i* in the eleventh and twelfth centuries: *kepen, kei*. It is common before *n*: *knee, knowen*; before unstressed *e*: *maken, drinken*. *c* is common before velar vowels: *can, corn*; before consonants other than *n*: *clene, crepen*. In final position, *c* is used until the fourteenth century, then *k* becomes more common: *bok, folk*.[28]

2.2. Middle English orthography not only indicates the split of Germanic *k*; it also reveals the change of the Old English cluster /sk′/ into the unit phoneme /š/, with the spellings *s*, *ss*, *sch*, later *sh*: *scharp*, *ship*. The phonemic split of Germanic *g* into /j/ and /g/ is indicated by the use of spellings with *ʒ* (later *y*) and with *g* respectively: *ʒellen*, *yellen*, *girden*, *gilden*. The change of [g′] in the clusters *g′g′* and *ŋg′* to [dž], however, is not clearly expressed by Middle English orthography: *egge* "edge," *sengen* "singe." *dg* is very rare before the fifteenth century.[29]

2.3. Spelling and pronunciation of words with initial *ch* and with initial *c* or *k* in Modern English throw light on the corresponding forms in Middle English and Old English: we pronounce [tš] in *child*, *cheese*, *cheer*, [k] in *can*, *cool*, *clean*, *kill*, *ken*. Phonemicists are still debating whether [tš] in *child* should be considered a unit-phoneme /č/ or a cluster of /t/ and /š/;[30] but this descriptive problem of Modern English phonemics has no immediate bearing on our historical study. As for the split of Germanic *g*, Modern English spelling and pronunciation clearly confirm the values of Middle English *y* and *g*: *yell*, *yolk*, *gird*, *gild*.

## 3. The Distribution of Velar and Palatal Allophone Reflexes

3.1. We must assume that Proto-Old-English /k/ had two main types of positional variants: a palatal allophone [k′] before palatal vowels, and a velar allophone [k] before velar vowels. The occurrence and distribution of the derivatives of these two allophones in Old English is important for the understanding of the phonemic split of Germanic *k*. The symbol *k* in Old English manuscripts expresses everywhere the reflex of the velar allophone. There is, however, not a single document where *k* is used exclusively for the derivatives of the velar, and *c* exclusively for the derivatives of the palatal allophone. Farman in his Rushworth glosses uses *c* more often than *k* before velar vowels, before consonants, and even before *y*. He differentiates, however, almost without exception between initial *ce* and *ke*, *ci* and *ki* where the distinction is really important: *ceke*, *kempe*, *cild*, *kininʒ*.[31] *c* appears before Germanic *e* and *i*; *k* appears before *e* and *i* that originated through the *i*-umlaut of Germanic velar vowels.

3.2. The calc-rune is found in runic inscriptions before consonants (*r*, *w*) and velar vowels (*u*); the modified ʒār-rune, that is assumed to be identical with the calc-rune, appears after a nasal and before *y*, the *i*-umlaut of *u*. The cēn-rune, however, mostly appears after Germanic *i* (see above § 1.3). The runic texts have no example of Germanic *k* before Germanic palatal vowels.[32] But the cēn-rune does not exclusively indicate the reflexes of the palatal allophone [k′]; it occurs also before Germanic *u* and its umlaut *y*, e.g., in *Cuþbereh(t)*, *Cynewulf*. The calc-rune indicates only reflexes of the velar allophone [k].

3.3. After *s* or medially before original *i*, spellings with *ce* and *ci* are frequent. In words like *ceaf, sceap, scield*, original palatal vowels are written *ea* and *ie*. These *c*'s represent reflexes of the palatal allophone [k']. No such spellings with *ce* and *ci* for *c* ever occur before velar vowels (as in *calan, corn, cuþ*) or palatal vowels that originated through the *i*-umlaut of velar ones (as in *cepan, cynn*).

3.4. Middle English orthography reveals velar /k/ in the following positions: initially before the Old English velar vowels *a ā o ō u ū* and their umlauts *æ ǣ e ē (oe) y ȳ (i)*, and before consonants, e.g., *care, corn, cocc, cu (ku, kow), kennen, kempe, keie* (Old English *cæȝe*), *kissen* (Old English *cyssan*), *clene, knee, knowen*; in medial position before original velar vowels, e.g., *maken, token, naked*; in final position after Old English velar vowels, e.g., *bok, milk*. The Middle English spelling *ch* and the Modern English pronunciation [tš] indicate that the descendant of the palatal allophone [k'] of Germanic *k* occurs in the following positions:[33] initially before the Proto-Old-English palatal vowels *æ ǣ e ē ī i ea ēa eo (io)*, e.g., *chaff* (OE *cealf*), *chest* (OE *cest*), *chep* (OE *ceap*), *cheke* (OE *ceace*), *chesen* (OE *ceosan*), *chin* (OE *cinn*), *chiden* (OE *cidan*); in medial position before original *i ī j* or after original *i*, if not followed by velar vowels, e.g., *beche* (OE *bece*), *eche* (OE *cee*), *techen* (OE *tæcan*), *strecchen* (OE *streccan*), *wicche* (OE *wicce*); in final position after *i ī* or before original *i*,[34] e.g., *picche* (OE *pic*), *hwich* (OE *hwelc, hwilc, hwylc*), *bench* (OE *benc* < *\*banki*).

3.5. The Middle English spellings *s, ss, sch, sh*, which indicate /š/ for the Old English cluster /sk'/, occur initially before all vowels; medially before palatal vowels; finally after palatal vowels. The spellings *sc* and *sk*, which indicate /sk/, appear medially before originally velar, also finally after velar vowels: *asken, tusk*.[35] Middle English *g*, indicating /g/, the reflex of the velar allophone [g] of Germanic *g*, occurs before the Old English velar vowels *a ā o ō u ū* and their umlauts, e.g., *galwes* (OE *ȝalȝa*), *gyrden, girden* (OE *ȝyrdan*), *gilden* (OE *ȝyldan*). The spelling *ȝ* or *y*, indicating /j/, the reflex of the palatal allophone [g'] of Germanic *g*, appear before Proto-Old-English palatal vowels, e.g., *ȝellen, yellen* (OE *ȝellen*), *ȝolke, yolke* (OE *ȝeolca*). The distribution of the derivatives of the velar and palatal allophones of Germanic *g* thus corresponds to that of the derivatives of the allophones of Germanic *k*.

3.6. The description in § 3.4 of the distribution of /k/ and /tš/ does not take into account the results of analogical transfer. Variation between /k/ and /tš/ even within the forms of one paradigm would have to be expected, because the inflectional endings contained both velar and palatal vowels or had lost their vowels at an early date. Within the nominal declension the plural endings *-as, -a, -u, -um*, and the weak ending *-an* contrasted with the singular endings *-es, -e*, e.g., *ȝelic, ȝelices, ȝelice*, but *ȝelica, ȝelicum*: the singular forms must originally have contained the palatal allophone [k'], the plural forms the velar allophone [k]. Middle English actually has both *liche* and *like*, of which the latter prevailed in Modern English.[36] The first, second, and third classes of the strong verbs must originally have had a [k']/[k] variation according to the vowel in the stem, e.g., *cīnan* [k'], *cinon* [k'], *cinen* [k'], but *cān* [k]; *cēosan* [k'], *cēas* [k'], but *curon* [k], *coren* [k]; *ceorfan* [k'], *cearf* [k'], but *curfon* [k], *corfen* [k]. Later, analogical leveling of this variation took place.[37] Such leveling would bring reflexes of the palatal allophone [k'] into positions where only derivatives of the velar allophone formerly occurred (*chosen*), and the velar allophone [k] into positions where only the palatal allophone formerly occurred (ME *kerven*). The /k/ of such forms as *secst, secþ, þyncst, recþ, wyrcþ*, where a velar [k] had developed before the consonants after an early loss of *i*, was transferred to the infinitives in Middle English *seken, þinken, rekken, wirken*.[38]

3.7. The assumption that the phonemic split of Germanic *k* had not taken place in the North and the Northeastern Midland turned out to be false. It is a general English development.[39] Since there are dialectal differences in the analogical transfer of /k/ or /tš/ to the various forms, Middle English as well as Modern English dialects often show a double development, e.g., *teken* and *techen, benk* and *bench, birk* and *birch*, Modern English *dike* and *ditch*. A number of the /k/ forms are probably due to Scandinavian influence: *kirk* "church"; *casten, kesten; ketel*. Some may be forms directly borrowed from Scandinavian, some may be hyperforms due to false analogy.[40] Romance loan-words also introduced forms with /k/ and /tš/ in positions that differed from the native development: *chasen, chaumbre, chalengen, escapen*.

## 4. The Phonetic Change of the Palatal Allophone

4. The phonetic development of the palatal allophone [k] to [tš] and the intermediate stages of this change were formerly widely discussed by scholars. It seemed the most important problem in regard to the development of Germanic *k*. Hempl[41] assumed a development from velar stop to palatal stop to palatal affricate to dental affricate; Jordan[42] and Luick[43] assumed a development from [k] to [kχ] to [tχ] to [tš]. Some scholars asserted that the [tš] stage had been reached in Old English, e.g., Bülbring[44] and Sievers.[45] Sweet[46] assumed the [tj] stage for Old English; H. C. Wyld[47] agreed, and thought that [tš] had been reached in the middle of the thirteenth century. The phonetic development of palatal [g'] in the clusters *g'g'* and *ŋg* to [dž] was assumed to have been parallel to and simultaneous with the change of palatal [k'] to [tš].[48] Orthographic evidence in support of either [tš] or [tj] for Old English is inconclusive, of course, because orthography never lends itself to detailed phonetic interpretation: such spellings as *orceard, feccan* do not prove any specific sound-value;[49] *micȝern* does not prove [dž];[50] *c* in *kæcepol* does not necessarily indicate [tš] simply because it corresponds to Old French *ch*. However, the specific phonetic values at any particular time are not as important as the distinctive sound units and their contrasts. Old

English has satisfactory evidence for the phonemic split of Germanic *k* itself, but only the general sound-types of the historical phonemes can be ascertained on the basis of the available evidence.

## 5. The Completion of the Phonemic Split

5.1. We have assumed the existence of velar and palatal allophones of Germanic /k/. Positional variation within the /k/ phoneme, i.e., the fact that a palatal [k'] is pronounced before front vowels like [e] and [i], and a velar [k] before back vowels like [o] and [u], cannot by itself lead to a phonemic split, even if the difference between the allophones comes to be phonetically quite large. As long as the phonetic quality of the allophones is determined by their phonetic surroundings, we are not yet dealing with two distinctive sound units, two phonemes. But the moment that we find two different sounds in the same phonetic position with a difference in meaning, we can tell that the phonemic split has been completed and that two phonemes have developed out of allophones of one. Old English orthography already indicates the split; Middle English orthography and Modern English pronunciation confirm it. We find clear indications in Middle English inflectional paradigms of transfers of /k/ forms into original /tš/ positions and conversely, through the working of analogy. Scandinavian and Romance loan-words introduced /k/ and /tš/ into positions where the sounds were not found in their regular native development. But all this has nothing to do with the change of two allophones into separate phonemes. No analogical transfer took place; no foreign loan-words introduced /k/ and /tš/ into unusual positions before the two allophones had reached phonemic status. Transfers and loans only affected the internal distribution of the phonemes; they did not create the contrastive units.

5.2. Scholars have noticed, in the historical distribution of forms with /k/ and with /tš/, that these sounds developed differently before Germanic palatal vowels (Sievers' and Luick's "primäre Palatalvokale") and before palatal vowels developed by Proto-Old English *i*-umlaut from velar vowels ("sekundäre Palatalvokale"). A typical explanation is that "the process of palatalization had ceased" by the time of the *i*-umlaut, so that the velar allophone [k] was no longer affected by the new palatal vowels.[51] No further inferences were ever drawn from this striking distribution. Actually, the phonemization of [k] and [k'] is a direct result of the Proto-Old-English *i*-umlaut. Twaddell[52] has shown that the *i*-umlaut in the Germanic languages presupposes the existence of positional variants of velar vowels before *i ū j* in a following unstressed syllable. We must assume, therefore, that certain Proto-Old-English vowels had special allophones before unstressed *i ī j*; these are listed here, with an indication of the probable phonetic values of the allophones: /a/: [æ], /æ/: [e], /ā/: [ǣ] or [ē], /ea, eo/: [ie] or [ē], /u/: [ü], /ū/: [ū],

/o/: [ö], /ō/: [ȫ].[53] For example, the variation between the allophones [o] and
[ȫ] in Proto-Old-English *fōtu-* and *fōti-* was determined simply by the
following unstressed vowels *u* and *i* respectively. When final *u* and *i* were lost,
the vowels /ō/ and /ȫ/ in *fōt* and *fȫt* (later *fēt*) were brought into contrast as
two separate phonemes. Thus, the two allophones of original /ō/ at first
created new independent contrastive values. The /ö/ sounds that were written
*oe* in the oldest Old English documents (e.g., Cod. Epinal *coempa*) soon
developed into /e/, except in the Northumbrian dialect, where [ö] was preserved until the eleventh century. The /ü/ sounds were written *y* in Old
English (e.g., *cyþan, ʒylden, cyninʒ*), but later Old English sources frequently
write *i*, indicating the value /i/ (e.g., *cininʒ, cinn*).[54] Proto-Old-English velar
[k] was not affected by this *i*-umlaut. If all the new palatal vowels had remained phonetically distinct from the old palatal vowels, the velar allophone
[k] and the palatal allophone [k'] would not have been brought into contrast,
because they would have continued to occur only in complementary, mutually
exclusive positions. But since the new palatal vowels merged with the old
ones—since for example the new allophones [e] and [æ] merged with the old
phonemes /e/ and /æ/ respectively—both the velar and the palatal allophones
came to stand before identical palatal vowels: the sounds [k] and [k'],
formerly mere variants of a single phoneme /k/, were now in contrast, and had
thus become separate phonemes. The phonemic split was complete.

The phonemic status of /k/ and /k'/ can be understood without knowing
exactly how the two sounds differed phonetically at the time that they were
brought into contrast. We have no evidence to determine whether /k'/ had
the sound-value [kj] or [tj] or [tš] or something intermediate.

5.3. The great and exclusive interest hitherto shown in the change [k] >
[tš] has probably prevented the recognition of the fact that it was the velar,
not the palatal allophone of Germanic *k* that was responsible for the phonemic split. The crucial innovation was the appearance of a velar [k] before
the new palatal vowels developed through *i*-umlaut. All the Old English
evidence points clearly in that direction: the special *k* symbol is used for the
velar sound, while *c* indicates the reflexes of Germanic *k* in general, not merely
the palatal ones; the calc-rune was created specially for the velar sound, while
the cēn-rune often represents Germanic *k* in general.

It was not the phonetic change of the palatal allophone [k'], but the persistence of the velar allophone [k] in a changing environment that caused the
phonemic split of Germanic *k* to be completed.


## FOOTNOTES

1. See *LANG*. 20.84 ff.
Abbreviations: AB = *Anglia Beiblatt*; Bülbring = K. D. Bülbring, *Altenglisches
Elementarbuch* (Heidelberg, 1902); Bülbring II = K. D. Bülbring, "Was lässt sich
aus dem gebrauch der buchstaben *k* und *c* im Matthäus-Evangelium des Rushworth-

Manuscripts folgern?," *Anglia Beiblatt* 9.289–300 (1899); Dieter = F. Dieter, *Laut- und Formenlehre der altgermanischen Dialekte* (Leipzig, 1898); Jordan = Richard Jordan, *Handbuch der mittelenglischen Grammatik*² (Heidelberg, 1934); Kluge = F. Kluge, "Geschichte der englischen Sprache," *Paul's Grundriss*² 1.926–1151 (Strassburg, 1900 sqq.); Ley = Hermann Ley, *Der Lautwert des altenglischen* c (Diss. Marburg 1914); Luick = Karl Luick, *Historische Grammatik der englischen Sprache* (Leipzig, 1914 sqq.); Sievers = E. Sievers, *Angelsächsische Grammatik*³ (1898); Viëtor = W. Viëtor, *Die northumbrischen Runensteine* (Marburg, 1895); Wyld = H. C. Wyld, "Contributions to the history of the guttural sounds in English," *Transactions of the Philological Society* 1899.129–260.

2. Cf. G. Hempl in *Anglia* 22.382; Bülbring, AB 9.102 ff.; Ley 64; A. Pogatscher, *Zur Lautlehre der griechischen, lateinischen, und romanischen Lehnwörter im Altenglischen* 185 ff. (Strassburg, 1888). As to the alliteration of ȝ see fn. 18.

3. Cf. Wyld 138–41; Kluge 990 (§ 65b); Bülbring II.

4. Viëtor § 33, *Anm.* 1; also § 73, where he states that the cēn-rune "offenbar den gutturalen Laut mitbezeichnet" ["clearly indicates the guttural sound"]; Bülbring, AB 9.77 f.

5. Out of the original a-rune were created signs for /æ/ (the æsk-rune), for /a/ (the āc-rune) and for /o/ (the ōs-rune). This happened after the allophones of original /a/ had developed into distinctive sound units (phonemes). The original symbol for /o/ became the symbol for the umlauted sound /ö/, later of /e/. A runic sign for /ü/ was formed by combining the characters for /u/ and /i/. Cf. Helmut Arntz, *Handbuch der Runenkunde* 146 ff. (1935); O. von Friesen, *Runorna* 55 ff. (1933).

6. Friesen 58; Th. v. Grienberger, *Arkiv för Nordisk Filologi* 15.22 (1899).

7. See Viëtor; A. B. Webster in G. Baldwin Brown, *Arts in Early England* 5.21, 2, 5.264 ff.; Zupitza-Schipper, *Alt- und mittelenglisches Übungsbuch*⁶ 3 ff. (1902). [For illustrations of and further commentary on the Ruthwell and Bewcastle runes, see Bruce Dickins and A. S. C. Ross, eds., *The dream of the rood*⁴ (London, 1954), 1–19.—Ed.]

8. Sievers § 206.3b; Bülbring § 499, *Anm.* 4.

9. See Kluge 993 f. (§ 66); Sievers § 76.2; V. Rehm, *Die Palatalisierung der Gruppe* sc *im Altenglischen* (Heidelberg, 1901). Luick, § 254, thinks of genuine diphthongs but assumes a "flüchtige erste Komponente" ["unstable first component"]; cf. also § 691.

10. Anglia 1.518 ff.

11. Anglia 5, Anzeiger 83.

12. § 57.

13. Rehm 53; E. Prokosch, *A Comparative Germanic Grammar* 77, § 148 (Baltimore, 1939).

14. Kluge, 990 (§ 65b), suggests in a footnote "eine eingehende Geschichte des e als Palatalzeichen" ["an exhaustive history of e as a palatalization symbol"]. This remark inspired V. Rehm's study. Ley, 39 ff., assumes the Palatalzeichen to indicate the assibilation of c—[kx] or [kj].

15. § 75 f. and Anm. 5; Dieter § 57; Luick §§ 171 ff., 263, 279; Bülbring § 315.

16. See Luick § 667, *Anm.* 2 and 4; Kluge 993 (§ 65g); Sievers §§ 196.3, 416, *Anm.* 15b; G. Hempl, *Anglia* 22.376 f.

17. *Anglia* 13.314.

18. But see Kluge 1000 (§ 68); R. Loewe, *Germanische Sprachwissenschaft* 73 (1933); Luick §§ 633, 696 and *Anm.* 1; Prokosch 76 f. Alliteration offers no evidence for such specific sound-values as Prokosch's [g] for ȝ before velar vowels, Luick's [gj] for ȝ before palatal vowels.

19. See Viëtor; A. B. Webster, *loc. cit.* 5.213 f.; Sievers § 212, *Anm.* 2; Bülbring § 492 and *Anm.* 1.

20. Sievers §§ 74 ff.; see also fn. 15.

21. Hempl, *Anglia* 22.375 ff.; Bülbring § 499, *Anm.* 4.

22. Sievers §§ 192.2, 196.3, 216.1, *Anm.* 2.

23. See Wyld 140; Jordan § 178, *Anm.* 1; Bülbring, AB 9.75; E. Ekwall, AB 32.157 f.; W. Schlemilch, *Beiträge zur Sprache und Orthographie spätaltenglischer Sprachdenkmäler der Ubergangszeit* 48 (1914).

24. Wyld 142; Kluge 990.

25. Jordan § 179; Wyld 146.

26. *c* beside *ch* with the sound-value [tš] is found in some texts of the early twelfth century. *c* was also used in French loan-words with the sound-value [ts], which became [s] in the twelfth century. In the latter part of this century, marks in Old English mss. show that *c* was ambiguous: a *k* is written over the *c* in *swylce*, *stearce*, *ceas*, an *h* over the *c* in *rica*, *ceald*, *wyrcan*. See S. J. Crawford, "The Worcester Marks and Glosses of the Old English Manuscripts in the Bodleian," *Anglia* 52.1 ff.

27. After 1135, *k* is used more frequently in the Peterborough Chronicle. See Wyld 140 f.; Jordan § 178, *Anm.* 1.

28. Jordan § 178.

29. Jordan §§ 192, 194; Kluge 998; Wyld 154 ff.

30. N. S. Trubetzkoy, *Grundzüge der Phonologie* 50 ff. (1939), discusses "monophonematische Wertung" and "polyphonematische Wertung" ["monophonemic value"... "polyphonemic value"]. See also L. Bloomfield, *Language* 120 (1933) and *LANG.* 11.98, fn. 3 (1935); Bloch and Trager, *LANG.* 17.229 (1941) and *Outline of Linguistic Analysis* 49 (1942). Phonetic differences between the cluster [t] plus [š] as in *courtship* and the cluster [tš] as in *child* have often been pointed out, e.g., by W. L. Thompson, *Le Maître Phonétique* 1914.46 ff.; Daniel Jones, id. 1931.64 and *Outline of English Phonetics* § 608 (1932). Cf. also J. S. Kenyon, *American Pronunciation*[8] § 207.4 (1940).

31. See Bülbring II.

32. Viëtor § 73, *Anm.* 1. On *c* in *kyniqc* see Bülbring, AB 9.74.

33. Jordan § 179; Kluge 991 ff.

34. Luick says § 685.3: "Ob auch nach anderen hellen Vokalen, etwa auf kleinerem Gebiet, ähnliches eintreten konnte, ist zweifelhaft." ["It is doubtful whether after other front vowels, perhaps in more limited environments, it can stand for the same thing."] See also Jordan § 179, *Anm.* 2; Kluge 992; E. Ekwall, AB 32.160 ff.

35. Luick § 691; Jordan § 181; H. Weyhe, *Englische Studien* 39.161 ff.; Kluge 993 f. (§ 66); V. Royce West, *Der etymologische Ursprung der neuenglischen Lautgruppe* [sk] (Heidelberg, 1936).

36. Luick § 688; Sievers § 240, *Anm.* 3.

37. Luick § 637, *Anm.* 6. On the leveling of a variation between [sk] and [sk'] in paradigms like that of Old English *fisc*, see Luick § 691.2; Weyhe *loc. cit.*; Jordan § 181.

38. Jordan § 179; Luick § 689.

39. Wyld 142 f.; A. Ritter, *Die Verteilung der* ch- *und* k- *formen im Mittelenglischen* (Diss. Marburg 1904); O. Gevenich, *Die englische Palatalisierung von k zu č im Lichte der englischen Ortsnamen* 159 (Halle, 1918). Jordan, § 179, *Anm.* 1, calls the change "lautgesetzlich gemeinenglisch" ["a general English phonetic law"].

40. See Gevenich, *op. cit.* 15; Jordan § 179; Erik Björkman, *Scandinavian Loan-Words in Middle English* 139 ff. (1900); Luick §§ 687, 701. On the dialectal variation between forms with /g/ and /dž/ see Jordan § 192; Luick § 690 and *Anm.* 1.

41. *Anglia* 22.376.

42. § 177.
43. § 685, also § 687; Max Förster, *Idg. Forschungen, Anz.* 12.105 ff.
44. AB 9.102; § 493.
45. § 206.4; *Anglia* 13.312 ff.
46. *History of English Sounds* §§ 496, 737; *An Anglo-Saxon Primer*[8] 3 (1905).
47. 136 f. See also Kluge 993 (§ 65g). Joseph and Elizabeth Wright, *An Old English Grammar* § 309 (1908), call [tš] for Old English "an assumption which cannot be proved."
48. Jordan §§ 192, 194; Luick § 685, on an assumed change from [g′] to [gj] to [dj] to [dž]; Hempl., *loc. cit.*
49. See Luick § 687; Ley 49 ff. (§ 44).
50. Wyld 149.
51. Ley states (31), "die Vermutung läge nicht fern, dass eine richtige Erkenntnis des Wesens des i-Umlauts mit seiner Wirkung und Gegenwirkung auch die hier bestehenden Schwierigkeiten aufhellen würde" ["it is not improbable that an accurate understanding of the nature of the i-Umlaut, and its effects and countereffects, might clear up the problems that exist here."]
52. "A note on Old High German Umlaut," *Monatshefte für deutschen Unterricht* 30.177–81 (1938). [Reprinted in Martin Joos, ed., *Readings in Linguistics* (Chicago, 1966), 85–7.—Ed.]
53. See Luick §§ 182 ff.; Bülbring §§ 158 ff.
54. Luick § 281; Bülbring § 307.

## CHARLES F. HOCKETT

# The Stressed Syllabics
of Old English*

In recent years, a number of scholars have expressed dissatisfaction with the traditional view of the Old English vowel system, particularly with the customary interpretation of the OE spellings *ea*, *eo*, *io*, and *ie*, and have presented more or less coherent alternative theories.[1] The arguments of the malcontents have received an excellent critical review by Kuhn and Quirk,[2] who, however, give no new analysis of their own, seeming rather to suggest that the traditional view is essentially correct.

The present paper is an attempt at an exploration of the problem de novo. Although I shall occasionally cite forms from other sources, my focus is on the testimony of the Old English in the Vespasian Psalter and Hymns, officially Cottonian MS. Vespasian A.1. I have seen neither the original manuscript nor a facsimile, but have worked exclusively with Henry Sweet's careful rendition in his *Oldest English texts* 183–420 (London, 1885). Sweet's meticulous fidelity in editing is well known, as is his disgust (often strongly expressed) for the thoughtless normalizations indulged in by some of his predecessors and contemporaries, especially in Germany.

Cottonian MS. Vespasian A.1 is a Latin Psalter of uncertain age to which an interlinear OE gloss has been added. On the basis of the hand and the language, the gloss is ascribed by Sweet to approximately the first half of the ninth century. The dialectal provenience is apparently more doubtful. It is most certainly not West Saxon, and almost certainly not Northumbrian. The external evidence points to Mercian. Sweet at one time suspected that it might be Kentish (*OET* 184), but was later not so sure. In this paper I have, perhaps rather glibly, called it "Midlands" or "Anglian"; but I believe that no part of my argument really rests on that assignment.

Concerning the Old English recorded in this source—but only this variety—I shall argue four propositions.

(1) The spellings *ea*, *eo*, and *io* represent, among other things, short syllabics phonemically distinct from those represented by *ae*, *e*, and *i* (or any other one-letter spelling)—the so-called "short diphthongs." This is the traditional view, contested by Stockwell and Barritt.

(2) The short syllabics so represented were, in the early Anglian dialect of the time, structurally on a par with the so-called "short vowels," and there

* From *Language* 35.575–97 (1959). Reprinted by permission of the author and the Linguistic Society of America.

is good reason to believe that they were monophthongs. Whether they were monophthongal or diphthongal in an absolute phonetic sense (whatever that may mean), they are to be taken as part of the stock of (short) vowel phonemes of the dialect, yielding a vowel system that can be charted as follows:

| | Front | | Back | |
|---|---|---|---|---|
| | *Spread* | *Rounded* | *Spread* | *Rounded* |
| *High* | /i/ *i* | /y/ *y* | /ɨ/ *io* | /u/ *u* |
| *Mid* | /e/ *e* | /ø/ *oe* | /ə/ *eo* | /o/ *o* |
| *Low* | /æ/ *ae, æ, ę, e* | (none) | /a/ *ea, æa* | /ɑ/ *a* |

My argument does not insist that the vowel written *a*, and here transcribed as /ɑ/, was necessarily rounded in the physiological sense, as /u o/ certainly were. The main reason for suspecting that it was rounded, at least during some periods, is that its principal source, Proto-Gmc. *a*, was structurally the low back member of a two-by-two vowel system, in turn the result of the falling-together of Proto-IE *a* and *o*, the latter certainly rounded. But a structurally low back "rounded" vowel is often, phonetically, simply more retracted than the other low vowels of the same system.[3] The important point, on which my argument does insist, is that *a* /ɑ/ occupied the structural position indicated on the chart.

The proposed monophthongal interpretation of *io, eo, ea* is the independent suggestion of Mossé, of Daunt, and of Stockwell and Barritt, but only the latter specifically suggest that these were central or back spread vowels. (As already implied, I consider their view that these retracted spread vowels were allophones of /i e æ/ to be in error.)

The selection of symbols for the phonemic notation has involved several problems, to which I have found no neat joint solution. The symbols flanked by slant lines are of course phonemic, not phonetic; and thus they must be understood throughout in terms of the table of three intersecting oppositions given above, rather than in terms of would-be absolute articulatory definitions. My /a/ is not the vowel usually written *a* by the scribes. My /ə/ is not necessarily phonetically like the English and German unstressed vowel (*bottom, beissen*) often so transcribed in IPA notation.

(3) The so-called "long vowels" written with the symbols *i, e, ae, oe, y, u, o, a* were, in early Anglian, clusters of the respective vowel phonemes /i e æ ø y u o ɑ/ and a phoneme of length which I shall transcribe as /·/. It is possible that this postvocalic /·/ was phonemically the same as the Old English syllable-initial aspiration written *h* by the scribes, which seems to have been in complementation both with /·/ and with the dorsovelar spirant which they wrote *h* and *g*.[4] But the investigation of this problem is beyond the scope of the paper.

(4) The so-called "long diphthongs" written *ea, eo*, and *io* were certainly diphthongs of the type [æw ew iw] at some early stage, but this stage may have

been pre-English. By the period of the Vespasian glosses, the first of these was /aˑ/, pairing the short /a/ also written as *ea*; the other two were either /əw ɨw/ or /əˑ ɨˑ/. If they were still the former, then not long after Vespasian times they became the latter.

I shall say nothing of the later West Saxon results of the front-umlauting of *ea, ēa, io, īo*. The problem is very difficult; also, this local change does not seem to have affected the main stream of English (Anglian Old English, Midland Middle English, "standard" New English), save by way of loans.

As illustrated in the foregoing, supposedly phonemicized forms appear between slant lines, transliterated Old English spellings in italics. Occasionally, when I wish to emphasize the actual shape of a letter, I place it between double quotes.

Since the proposals made in this paper are so at variance with tradition, it may be well to insert here an extremely brief survey of the development of the tradition. For early modern Old English scholars, such as Hickes, a language was a phenomenon to be analyzed in terms of letters and spellings. The more recent insistence on the distinction between writing and language was not yet part of the scholarly climate of opinion. Consequently, the term "diphthong" was used in a purely graphic sense: OE *ae, oe, ea, io, eo, ie* were all equally diphthongs, since each consisted of two successive vowel letters. As late as Bosworth, one finds passages such as the following[5] (I simplify capitalized ligatures): "Where we now use A or E, the diphthongs AE, OE, and Ea continually occur in Anglo-Saxon . . ."

The comparative Germanic scholarship of the nineteenth century brought about some radical changes in point of view; the exact sequence of events can be traced in the literature.[5a] I do not know who first recognized that the Old English syllabics written *ae* and *oe* were monophthongs; presumably it was a scholar who discerned that these syllabics had arisen in pre-English, at least in part, by a process of umlauting comparable to that operative in early German and Scandinavian. As a consequence, the term "diphthong" was abandoned for *ae* and *oe*; but the other digraphs, *ea, io, eo, ie*, continued to be called "diphthongs" as in Hickes's day. The term "diphthong" itself, however, had acquired a new meaning: the word had come to refer to a sequence of two vowel-sounds within a single syllable. Since *ea, io, eo, ie* were "diphthongs," and since a "diphthong" was a sequence of two vowel-sounds, it followed that OE *ea, io, eo, ie* must represent something like [ea̯, io̯, eo̯, ie̯]. Of course this is a non sequitur, but the logical invalidity of the conclusion was not noticed. I suspect that just such a sequence of historical accidents is responsible for the continuing gratuitous assertion in our Old English manuals that *ea, io, eo, ie* were phonetically diphthongs.

1. *Assumptions about Scribal Practice.*   Our primary source of information about Old English is of course the surviving documentary record. While we can also learn much through indirect methods—the later history of the

language, comparison with the other old Germanic languages and with Indo-European as a whole, and loanwords—any formulation of the Old English phonological pattern must be based fundamentally on the written documents, and must account realistically for Old English scribal habits. For this reason, it is imperative to approach the analysis of Old English with an overtly formulated hypothesis as to why scribes spell as they do.

I shall assume that when a native speaker of a language writes a word in an alphabetical writing system,[6] his spelling of the word is determined by one or both of the following factors: (1) the word has a culturally prescribed spelling which the scribe has learned from others; (2) the spelling of the word is worked out, however quickly and unconsciously, in terms of established associations between certain letters or combinations of letters and certain phonemes or sequences of phonemes. When a writing system has been in use for a long time, the first of these factors may loom large—obviously, for example, in modern English or French. But when a writing system is new, and particularly if there has not yet arisen any strong doctrine of "correctness," the second factor will carry more weight.

Furthermore, even when the first factor is responsible for a given spelling in a given manuscript, in the early days of a writing system the line of transmission of this prescribed spelling from some earlier scribe, who invented it under the influence of the second, cannot be very long. Therefore, though a regularly maintained graphic distinction may in some cases indicate nothing about the phonological system of the scribe who wrote a particular manuscript, we can still use the distinction as evidence pointing towards a phonological state of affairs for speakers of a slightly earlier form of the language.

The factor of prescribed spellings for given words (or stems, or endings) may operate to maintain distinctions in spelling which reflect no distinction at all in pronunciation: e.g., NE *ee* versus *ea* in *meet, beet, reed, feed*:*meat, beat, read, lead*. It should be noted that NE /ij/ does not have two distinct allophones, which are kept apart by the spelling difference between *ee* and *ea* (nor does English /t/, for example, have two allophones distinguished by the choice of spelling for the preceding vowel in *meet* and *meat*): indeed, if *ee* and *ea* in any way reflected two allophones, we would be able to hear the difference between *meet* and *meat*, and the two allophones would by definition belong to different phonemes. While I must admit that even in the early days of an alphabetical writing system a scribe may inherit two or more notations for a single phoneme or cluster of phonemes, I hold that any fairly regularly maintained distinction of spelling either shows (1) no difference at all in the pronunciation of the scribe, who remembers the proper spellings in terms of MORPHEME identity, or (2) a PHONEMIC contrast in his pronunciation. That is, I reject the notion that a difference in spelling can correlate with a merely ALLOPHONIC difference in pronunciation.

The hypothesis just formulated could not have been proposed by the Junggrammatiker of the late nineteenth century who established most of the traditions of our manuals. They could not have formulated the hypothesis because their terminology of "speech sounds" did not distinguish between allophone and phoneme: rather precisely, a neogrammarian "speech sound" is an allophone, regardless of its phonemic affiliation. Typical of the neogrammarian assumption about spelling in its relationship to pronunciation is the following passage from Thurneysen,[7] where I have italicized the key phrase:

Where a stressed syllable ends in a palatal consonant or group of consonants, *i* is inserted as a glide after vowels or diphthongs other than . . . *It must have been quite audible, since it is rarely omitted in writing.* It was not a full vowel, however, for it did not combine with a preceding short vowel to form a diphthong, and the syllable remained short.

The more exegetically one works on this passage, the more obscure it becomes in modern terms. The clue is the word "audible": we now realize that "audibility" is a very different matter to a trained phonetician, to a speaker of a specific language, and to a speaker of some other language. That which is "audible" to a monolingual native speaker of a language is precisely that which he has been trained to hear because of the phonemic system of his language, and it is this that he will reflect in his use of an alphabetical writing system.

This brings us, however, to a consideration of certain rare circumstances under which my generalization does not hold. The Spanish conquistador Sahagún trained speakers of Nahuatl to write their own language in Latin letters; in the spelling which he gave to them, he provided for some distinctions which were phonemic in Spanish, though not in Nahuatl; and it would seem that he virtually stood behind his scribes with a whip to enforce the maintenance of these distinctions.[8] Latin-alphabet literacy was brought to England during the late sixth or early seventh century, by missionaries of whom all spoke Latin, and some certainly spoke Old Irish. It is not at all unlikely that these culture-bearers taught their English-speaking converts to write on Sahagún's principle, introducing graphic provision for distinctions subphonemic in English though phonemic in Old Irish. But a considerable period of time intervened between this introduction of the Latin alphabet and the earliest of our surviving documents—at least a century before the writing of the Glossaries, and perhaps two before the Vespasian records. In the meantime, the scribal tradition had become naturalized. Knowledge of Latin as a second language was maintained; knowledge of Old Irish seems less likely. It is reasonable to suppose, therefore, that any initial Sahagún effects would have been smoothed out by the period of the records with which I propose to deal.

The Old English notation for consonants supports the validity of my assumption about scribal practice. In the earliest stages, /b/ had both stop and spirant allophones (all voiced); later, the spirant allophone fell together with the voiced allophone of /f/, and thereafter only *f* is written where this allophone of /f/ is expected. It would have been perfectly feasible for the scribes to write intervocalic *b* for [v], initial and final *f* for [f]; but they did not do so. There were two handy symbols for the spirant /θ/: "þ" and "ð." It would have been easy to specialize one of these symbols for the voiceless allophone of /θ/, the other for the voiced allophone; but this, also, they did not do: the two were used interchangeably for both allophones, some scribes showing a preference for the one or the other, other scribes choosing between them randomly. There is no reason to believe that a habit of allophonic writing would be maintained for vowels when it was not maintained for consonants even where symbols were at hand.

In short, regularly maintained graphic distinctions correlated with phonemic contrasts in the speech of the scribes or of their immediate predecessors. The converse of this, of course, does not hold: there were phonemic contrasts in Old English (particularly quantitative) which never found systematic expression in the spelling.

All of the above applies to the scribe's "intention" as he sets pen to vellum, but between this and the marks that philologists can see in the surviving manuscripts there are other sources of variation. Setting aside the ravages of time, weather, and later human agencies, there are "slips of the pen." Some unusual spellings in the manuscripts represent a deviation towards some other word, orthographically, phonemically, or semantically similar to the intended one, also in some ways fit for the context, but for some reason less appropriate. We cannot always know what the disturbing word was; but the mechanism itself is familiar enough to anyone who writes. This and other minor factors mean that we must make due allowance for a small percentage of radical spelling deviations as irrelevant to our concern.

The assumptions just outlined will not be acceptable to everyone, and the discussion which follows has no validity unless the assumptions are correct. Presumably Stockwell and Barritt examined the same evidence in reaching conclusions diametrically opposed to mine; hence their unstated assumptions about scribal practice must have been different.[9]

2. *Evidence for the Distinctiveness of io, eo, and ea.* I shall begin with an examination of the Vespasian evidence which, in my opinion, points to the separate phonemic status (at or shortly before Vespasian times) of units represented by the spellings *io, eo,* and *ea;* for the moment, I am not concerned with the precise phonetic nature of these units.[10]

2.1. *The Spellings eo and e.* Here I confine myself to the digraph *eo,* in those environments in which it has traditionally been interpreted as representing a "short diphthong" and in which one might also expect, but for certain sound shifts specific to English, short *e.*

In the Vespasian documents there is a strong tendency towards complementation of *e* and *eo* (as limited in the preceding paragraph). In monosyllables checked by a single consonant, or by a cluster other than *r* or *l* plus consonant (including another *r* or *l*), *e* predominates. In stressed syllables followed by a single intervocalic consonant, *eo* is much the more common when the following unstressed vowel is back, but *e* predominates if the next vowel is front. Before *r* or *l* plus consonant, *eo* predominates; before other clusters of two consonants, in polysyllables as well as monosyllables, *e* predominates.

But this is only a tendency, not an absolute rule. Thus we find, from *wer* "man," the expected *wer*, *were*, *weres*, *weoras*, and *weorum*, but *werlice* rather than *\*weorlice*. From *\*beran* "to bear" we find the expected *forðberen* "they bring forth," *beorað*, but unexpected *eo* in *beorende* (twice), *unbeorende* (once), and *unbeore[n]dnisse* (*n* omitted by scribe; once). *Wel* appears only so spelled; derivatives from it all have *eo*, whether according to the tendency towards complementation or not: expected *weolan*, *weolum*, *weolga*, *ge-weolgian*, but also *weolena*, *weolig*, *weoligum*, *weolie*. In the last two, the spellings may represent postvocalic clusters /lj/, but/ no such factor can be evoked for the others.

Other instances of *eo* where *e* would be expected are *weolere* (3 times), *weolerum* (3), *weolera* (2); *cweoðende* (3), *hearmcweoðendra*, *wer[g]cweoðende*; *geofe* (5); *spreocende* (3), *spreocendra*, *yfelspreocende*, *wiðspreocen*; *wreocende* (3); *gebreocendes*; *eotenne*, *eotendes*; *ofergeoteliu* (2); *wergcweodelade*; *fortreodendes*; *hehseotle*; *ongeotende* (2), *ofergeotele*; *heoretas*, *heoretes*; *heofen*, *heofene*, *heofenes*, *heofenas*, *heofenum* (all many times); *heofenlic*, *heofenlican*; *seofen*, *hundseofentigum*.

Spellings other than *e* and *eo* appear occasionally in the family of words here under consideration, but are extremely rare. Thus, *fiolu* appears once, as against three occurrences of *feolu*; *hiofene* and *hiefene* once each, otherwise (many times) with *eo*; *hionan*, occurring once, is the only occurrence of this particle with any spelling; *eatað* twice, the only spelling for this inflected form, while all other forms of this verb appear only with *eo*, except for one occurrence of *eten*; *afearra* once, otherwise always *eo*; *ætfealan* once and *fele* once.

For the moment, I set aside these spellings with other than *e* and *eo*: see § 2.4 below. By my assumptions about scribal practice, in order to prove that *e* and *eo* must have represented phonemically distinct syllabics, it is not necessary to adduce absolute minimal pairs: it suffices to show that both occurred in largely analogous environments. The examples cited so far show many occurrences of the spelling *eo* before a single consonant followed by a front vowel.[11] But there are also many instances of *e* in the same general situation: *were*, *weres*, *forðberen*, as mentioned earlier; *cweðe* (many times, and never *\*cweoðe*); *geefenlican*; *efenisse* (several times); *agefe*, *agefen*; *sprece* (2), *sprecen*, *gesprece* (2), *gespreces* (several times); *wegw*, *weges*; *eten*; *cweden* (4); *wiðcwedenisse* (6); *gebede*, *gebedes*; *efenameten*, *efenmeten*; *ongete*.

If *e* and *eo* had not represented phonemically distinct units for the scribe who produced the Vespasian glosses, we should expect one of two things: (1) some clear graphemic basis for the choice, in each instance, of one spelling or the other—comparable, let us say, to the principle in late Greek orthography by which sigma was written one way in word-final, another way in other positions; or (2) a completely random distribution of the two spellings. We find neither.

2.2. *The Spelling io.* The evidence for *io* is not so clear-cut, and must be presented in greater detail. Some stems (or roots) appear with both *i* and *io*, others with *i*, *io*, and *eo*, still others with still other spellings.

(1) Spelling *io* only. Only one stem, occurring in only one form in one place: *liomu* "limb" (VH 12/2).

(2) Spelling *i ~ io*.
    (a) Stem *niðer-*: *niðerlican, niðeriað, geniderað, geniðerad*; but *nioðerran* (3), *nioðerrum*.
    (b) Stem *bid-* (preterit): *abiden* and *abiodun*, each once.

(3) Spelling *i ~ io ~ eo*.
    (a) Stem *nim-* "take": *nimeð* (3), *genimes*; *niomu, niomað, geniomað, genioman, daelniomend, daelniomenis*; *neomendum*.
    (b) Stem *wit-* "know": *wite* (3), *witen* (2), *gewite*; *uðwiotan*; *weotað, weotun, weotendum, geweotun, uðweotan, geweotan, geweot, weotudlice* (3).

(4) Spelling *i ~ eo*.
    (a) The proximal demonstrative: *ðis, ðissum, ðisses, ðisse*, all common; *ðeossu[m]* once, *ðeosne* common.
    (b) *beswic-* "deceived": *biswicen* once, *bisweocun* once.
    (c) *stig-* "climbed": *upstige* (2); *asteogun* (2), *ofdunesteogun*.
    (d) *besmit-* "defiled": *bismite, besmiten, bismiton, unbesmiten*; *bismeotun* (2), *bisme[o]ton*.
    (e) *writ-*: *awriten* (4), *awritenne*; *gewreotum*.
    (f) *flit-*: *geflite*; *fleotun*.

(5) Spelling *i ~ io ~ eo ~ ea*.
    (a) *wlite* "beauty": *wlite* (4), *wlites, ondwlitan* (5), *wlitig, wlitige*; *ondwliotan* (4); *ondwleota, ondwleotan* (many times); *ondwleatan* (2).
    (b) *libb-, lif-* "live": *lifgu* (3), *lifgað* (2), *lifge* (3), *lifgan, lifgende* (7), *lifgendan, lifgendra* (7), *lifgen, bið lifd*; *liofað* (2); *leofað* (4); *leafað* (once).

(6) Spelling *io ~ eo ~ ea*. *\*irre* "angry": *iorre* corrected to *eorre* (once); *eorre* (many times), *eorres* (2), *eorru*; *earres* (2), misspelled *eare* once. *\*irsian* "be angry": *eo* in all cases.

(7) Spelling *eo* only: *heorda*; *teolunge* (2), *teolungum*; *seoðan* "since"; *geostran* "yesterday"; *reopan* (2), *winreopad*; *sceopu* (2), *sceopum*.

(8) Spelling *eo ~ ea*; only in forms of *\*clipian* "call" and its derivatives: *eo* common; *ea* only once each in *cleapede* and *cleapade*, as over against four occurrences each of *cleopede* and *cleopade*.

For the moment I shall lump together the three non-*i* spellings *io*, *eo*, and *ea*. The cited material then shows some reason to assume a contrast between /i/ and something other than /i/, though even with the three digraph spellings grouped together the evidence is not as clear-cut as for the set *e ~ eo*. The spelling *i* is common before single consonant plus front vowel, but we also find, in that environment, the following few digraph spellings: *nioðerran, nioðerrum, daelniomend, daelniomenis, neomendum, weotendum, cleopede, cleapede*. Before two consonants, we find *ðissum* and the like, but *ðeossu[m]* once, *ðeosne*, and forms of *lif-* where the spelling shows *-fg-* with preceding *i*. Surely the contrast, whatever its phonetic nature, could not have been of any great statistical importance,[12] but the phonemic status of a phonetic difference depends only on the EXISTENCE of contrast, not on the number and frequency of the forms which the contrast serves to distinguish. I cannot convince myself that the range of spelling, from *i* through *io*, *eo*, and *ea*, reflects only a single phoneme in all pronunciations of all the forms involved: there must have been at least two different phonemes.

The fluctuations among the three different digraph spellings can be taken up only after we have looked at the next body of evidence.

2.3. *The Spelling ea.* Here I am concerned with those words which, etymologically, would be expected to show a short low vowel. The spellings which must be considered are *a*, *ea*, *ae*, the ligatured form *æ* of the last, and a rapid cursive form of the ligature which it is customary to print as *ę*.[13] But we also often find simple *e* where one would expect *ę* (if not *æ* or *ae*), and it is not certain in this context that we can regard all such instances of *e* as a mere "forgetting" to include the bottom stroke. (By way of contrast, the letter now usually printed as "ð" was written as a *d* with a stroke through it, and it is pretty obvious that a good number of *d*'s for expected *ð* are due merely to forgetting, and some *ð*'s for expected *d* to an absent-minded complementary overcorrection.)

The justification for the reservation about *e* and *ę* is found in the Vespasian scribe's habits of use of these same letters for long syllabics. I assume here, without detailed examination of the evidence, that, where long syllabics are expected, the spellings *e*, *e*/*ę*/*ae*, *ea*, and *a* represent four phonemically distinct syllabics. Expected *ā* is almost invariably written *a*; expected *ǣ* in the word family which includes *sǣ* "sea," *rǣran* "to raise," *lǣran* "to teach" is quite usually written *ae*, *æ*, or *ę*, though with apparently random selection among these three; the other word family which appears in West Saxon with *ǣ* (*hǣr* "hair," *tǣlan* "blame," *ǣfen* "evening," etc.) is quite regularly written *e*; expected *ē* also appears regularly as *e*; and expected *ēa* most often appears as *ea*, save before *c*, *h*, *g*, where the regular spelling with *e* certainly indicated a special phonemic shift.[14] Most of the exceptions to the statements just made appear in atonic words, where unstressing and restressing had doubtless produced a wider variety of phonemically distinct shapes. I conclude that the written symbols *ae*, *æ*, and *ę* were not graphemically distinct, but that as a set they contrasted with *e*, *ea*, and *a*; for the longs, the interchange of *e* and *ę* was quite rare and probably accidental.

Against this background, the distribution of occurrences of the same letters and ligatures for short syllabics is significantly different. The frequency of *e* is relatively so great that we must assume /e/ as a common pronunciation in at least many forms where a lower front vowel would be expected. Before a nasal, we find only *o*, except in the Latin loan word *plant* and its native derivatives *plantian* and *geplantian*, where the spelling (eleven occurrences) is always *a*. This loan word is especially valuable in that we can conclude that earlier /a/ (Gmc. /a/) had not merely been rounded before nasals in some subphonemic nondistinctive way, but had, in the Old English dialects in question, fallen completely together with /o/ prior to the importation of the Latin word.[15] The rest of the evidence can largely be summarized in a table: the columns show the commonest spellings (with *ae* serving also for *æ* and *ę*) in the environments sketched at the left; I omit those environments in which there are extremely few cases or no evidence at all pointing to contrast; the particular ordering of the columns is intentional.

| | | | | | |
|---|---|---|---|---|---|
| (a) | $\acute{V}\eth V$: | *e* | | *ea* | |
| (b) | $\acute{V}tV$: | *e* | | *ea* | |
| (c) | $\acute{V}dV$: | *e* | | *ea* | |
| (d) | $\acute{V}t$: | *e* | | *ea* | |
| (e) | $\acute{V}dr$: | *e* | | *ea* | |
| (f) | $\acute{V}rc$: | *e* | | | *a* |
| (g) | $\acute{V}rn$: | *e* | | | *a* |
| (h) | $\acute{V}l$: | *e* | | | *a* |
| (i) | $\acute{V}lf$: | | *ae* | | *a* |
| (j) | $\acute{V}h$: | | *ae* | | *a* |
| (k) | $\acute{V}fV$: | *e* | | *ea* | *a* |
| (l) | $\acute{V}cV$: | *e* | *ae* | *(ea)* | *a* |
| (m) | $\acute{V}gV$: | *e* | *ae* | | *a* |

The contrast between *e* and *ea* is clearly attested in environments a–e and k. That between *e* and *a* appears in environments f–h and k–m. That between *ae* and *a* is obvious from environments i, j, l, and m. Without further discussion we can conclude:

$$e \neq ea$$
$$e \neq a$$
$$ae \neq a$$

Graphic contrast between *e* and *ae* appears only in l and m, between *ae* and *ea* only in environment l, and between *ea* and *a* only in k and l. These three therefore need further consideration.

Before *f* plus vowel (environment k), the evidence is as follows: The stem "raise" appears only with *e*: *upahefen* once, *upahefenisse* twice, and *uphefenis* once. The stem "have" appears only with *a*: *hafast* once, *hafað* twice, *bihafað* once. With *ea* there is greater variety, though hardly more occurrences: *heafuces* once; *gedeafien* once and *gedeafunge* twice (all with *d* for *ð*); *gedeafenað* once, *gedeafineað* once—and, with *eo*, one occurrence of *gedeofenað*. *Ea* occurs with both front and back vowels in the next syllable, while *e* occurs only with a front vowel following, and *a* only with a back vowel. Whatever is represented by *ea* is therefore in close-to-minimal contrast with whatever is represented by *e* and by *a*.

To the three sure contrasts already listed we might thus add the assertion that *ea* ≠ *a*. Yet this conclusion is not really safe on just the evidence so far considered, at least not for the dialect of the Vespasian scribe himself. The apparent evidence could be explained away if we assumed that a contrast between *ea* and *a* had been operative earlier but had disappeared by Vespasian times. The argument would be that the Vespasian scribe inherited a spelling with *a* for the stem *haf-*, to which he adhered, in the few occurrences of that stem, even though there was no longer an *ea–a* contrast in his own speech. The *a*-spelling would be reinforced by the association between the stem shapes of "have" with *-f-* and with *-bb-*: *habbað* occurs a number of times, and the negative *nabbende* once. (These are, incidentally, the only instances of *-bb-* after any of the vowel spellings which concern us here.) We should also have to assume that the stem "have," in either shape, was much more common both in the scribe's speech and in his writing in general than is reflected by its frequency in the surviving document. We would have to believe this last assumption in order to have any confidence in the inherited-spelling theory: a socially prescribed spelling for a rarer word would be much more easily forgotten. But these ancillary assumptions are not contrary to good sense, and therefore this possible way of explaining away the *ea–a* contrast cannot be lightly put aside.

Before *c*, the record is more complex, partly because *c* represented both /ċ/ and /k/, and it is not always possible to know which stop was used at the time in a given form of a given stem. I take it that the OE stems "shake," "quake," and "ax" had only /k/: the forms are *tos[c]aecendes* once, *ascecen* twice; *cwęcede* twice, *cwaecade* twice, *cwaecian* once, *cwaecunge* once, *cwaecung* five times; *ęcesum* once. The Latin loan for "priest" appears only with *a*: *sacerd* once, *sacerdas* twice; considering the Latin pronunciation of the time and place, the *c* here probably represents /ċ/.[16] The Latin loan for "dragon" appears as follows: *dracena* once, *draecena* once; *dracan* twice, *draecan* once; *draca*. In this instance, Latin points to /k/. For "watch," I would assume /ċ/, but Kuhn informs me that /k/ is more likely: *waecio* once, *waecade* once, *węciað* once, and *waecene* once. "Revenge, punishment" involved either just /k/ or an alternation between /k/ and /ċ/: *wręca* once, *wrece* four times, and *wreca* once. "Throat" may also have had the consonantal alternation: *hraece* once, *hraecae* once, *hracan* once, and *hreacan* once. If we assume that the scribe wrote what he meant to write—that is, in particular, that he did not intend *ę* for any actually written *e*—then the distribution seems to have been as follows, where /F/ means an unstressed front vowel and /B/ an unstressed back vowel:

$$
\begin{array}{ccc}
e/kF/ & e/kB/ & e/ċF/ \\
ae/kF/ & ae/kB/ & ae/ċB/ \\
 & ea/kB/ & \\
a/kF/ & a/kB/ & a/ċF/
\end{array}
$$

Note that in order to achieve this portrayal of apparent contrast, we must assume that different spellings of the stressed vowels of stems reflect different pronunciations of those stems. Thus, "revenge" and "shake" seem to show pronunciations with both *ae* and *e*; "dragon" with both *ae* and *a*; "throat" with *ae*, *ea*, and *a*. If we assume that *e* for expected *ę* is in some cases a scribal error, then the first row of the table is to be deleted, and we have no grounds for positing a contrast between *e* and any of the other three spellings before *c*. If we consider less common spellings to be slips for more common ones, then, at the very least, the single occurrence of *ea* is thrown into doubt, and we have no evidence for the contrast between *ea* or between *ea* and *a*. Thus, none of the more tentative earlier assumptions of difference are greatly strengthened.

The position before graphic *g* requires a comparable refinement: *g* represented a voiced spirant /j/ and a voiced allophone of the /x/ phoneme, as well as a stop /g/ and a stop /ġ/ in environments that do not here concern us. Before *g* representing /j/, we find only *e*: "hail" *hegel* three times; "struck" *slegen* (1), *ofslegendra* (1), *ofslegen* (1), *ofslegenisse* (1); "beauty" *fegernis* (1), *fegernisse* (2); "can" once as *mege*. Setting the word "day" aside for the moment, the other evidence is *magun* (1), *maegon* (1), and *asagas* (1), in all of which *g* is /x/: the first two may well reflect genuine doublets with fronter and backer low vowels. "Day" shows the most varied spellings. The stem obviously had shapes with two different final consonants, /j/ and /x/, originally in complementation, but with the complementation analogically lost by Vespasian times in this extremely common word. The forms are:

| *deg* | (often) | *dęg* | (1) | | |
|-------|---------|-------|-----|--|--|
| *dege* | (3) | | | | |
| *deges* | (5) | | | | |
| *degas* | (1) | *dęgas* | (often) | | |
| | | *dægas* | (often) | | |
| | | *daegas* | (often) | | |
| *dega* | (1) | *dęga* | (3) | | |
| | | *dæga* | (3) | | |
| | | *daega* | (1) | | |
| *degum* (1) | | *dęgum* | (1) | *dagum* (1) | |
| | | *dægum* | (often) | | |
| | | *daegum* | (1) | | |

To these must be added, for the first line, one occurrence of *dig* and one of *dig* corrected to *deg*.

Apart from *i* for *e*, I see no reason for any assumption other than that the variety of spellings for the stressed syllabic of "day" reflects a corresponding variety of contrasting (i.e., phonemically distinct) pronunciations. The known prehistory of English would give us two stem shapes for the form at some pre-Vespasian period: /dǽj-/, with a fronter vowel and a fronter voiced spirant, when no inflectional ending follows or when the inflectional ending contains a front vowel, and /dáx-/, with a backer vowel and a backer voiced spirant, when the inflectional ending contains a back vowel. A regular Anglian change would then raise /æ/ to /e/ before word-final /j/,[17] just as before other word-final consonants (cf. *fer, aber, hel, cweð, wes, sprec, bec, gebrec, sec, meg, set, geset, oset, fet, beget/biget, onget, get, fortred, bed, gebed*). Then the forms with all three vowels, as well as those with the two different final consonants, would be analogically extended, in this extremely common word, to give just the variety of alternative phonemic shapes which the scribal record seems to imply.

If so, then to our three firm conclusions of contrast we can now add a fourth:

$$e \neq ae$$

To summarize: the spellings examined in this section (2.3) show clearly a three-way contrast between *e*, *ae*, and *a*. They do not attest the existence of a fourth unit, although the spelling *ea* is fairly common. It is rather clear that *ea* is not to be identified with *e*, and it is reasonably clear that—if not for the Vespasian scribe himself, then for a slightly earlier variety of Anglian Old English—*ea* cannot be identified with *a*. But the only direct graphic evidence for a separation of *ea* and *ae* is too limited to bear any weight.

However, before we can abandon the hypothesis that the spelling *ea*, at least in some occurrences, represented a phonemically separate unit, we must bring together all the evidence examined in § 2.1, § 2.2, and so far in § 2.3. The most striking point to be observed about the spelling *ea* is that it is never the only one found for a form:

*ea* alternates with *eo, io*, and *i* in *ondwleatan* (2), *ondwleotan* (many times), *ondwliotan* (4), *ondwlitan* (5);
*ea* alternates with *eo* and *io* in *leafað* (1), *leofað* (4), *liofað* (2); *eare* (1), *eorre* (many times), *iorre* corrected to *eorre* (1);
*ea* alternates with *eo* in *earres* (2), *eorres* (2); *cleapede* (1), *cleopede* (4); *cleapede* (1), *cleopade* (4); *gedeafenað* (1), *gedeafineað* (1), *gedeofenað* (1).
*ea* alternates with *a* in *hreacan* (1), *hracan* (1).

Yet, with all this graphic instability, the spelling *ea* never alternates, in any form, with *ae*. What are we to make of this? By my basic assumption about scribal habits, *ae* and *ea* cannot represent two phonetically different but phonemically identical vowels. Either they represent exactly the same allophone, with some purely graphic basis for the distribution of the two spellings (as for the two cursive shapes of late Greek sigma), or else they represent two phonemically distinct vowels—two points in the pattern. There seems to be no obvious graphic basis for the distribution. Therefore, by my assumptions, I am forced to conclude that *ae* and *ea* were phonemically distinct, even if never (or virtually never) in minimal contrast.

Before the reader rejects this conclusion as unrealistic, let him consider the following two points.

(1) In the first place, the functional status suggested for a separate phoneme *ea* in Vespasian or pre-Vespasian Old English should be compared with that

of certain phonemes in languages known to us through direct observation. New English will do quite well. In my own dialect, as in many, no word exists which has only a single pronunciation with stressed /i/. *Just*, for me, has /i/ or /ə/; *good* has /i/ or /u/; *little* has /i/ or /i/; and so on. Only a very unrealistic and oversimplified variety of phonemic philosophy allows one to conclude, from such a distribution as this, that NE /i/ is not a separate phoneme. But this is my own view; in fairness, I must add that a reader who is able to explain away NE /i/ in a dialect such as mine can equally well explain away the proposed phonemically separate Vespasian *ea*. Such a rejection will do no violence to my assumptions about scribal habits, since the sort of phonemics I mean to involve in those assumptions is the sort which forces recognition of NE /i/ as a phoneme. Anyone whose professional conscience will let him recognize a single phone as an allophone of several different phonemes can easily conclude that Vespasian *ea* represented an allophone that belonged with *a* in some forms, with *eo* in others, and so on.

(2) There seems to have been a fairly extensive parallelism in early Old English between short and long syllabics. I have shown earlier in § 2.3 that the spellings *e*, *ae*, *ea*, and *a* for long syllabics clearly reflect four different longs. I shall later argue that by the time of the Vespasian documents all four of these long nuclei were monophthongal: that is, that each consisted of a short-vowel phoneme plus a phoneme of length /·/.

But this would mean that the proposed four vowel phonemes were indeed in functional contrast in at least one position, namely, before the length phoneme /·/. In all other environments, there was almost complete complementation between *e* and *ae*, between *ea* and *a*, and (even more nearly complete) between *ae* and *ea*. The functional load carried by these three contrasts (among the four vowels when not accompanied by /·/) was reduced even more by the fact that a great many stems had alternate shapes differing only as to the syllabic, with only a tendency towards complementary distribution in terms of inflectional and derivational suffixes.

Consider, now, the scribe's problem in writing. He was not trained to pay attention to quantitative differences in syllabics as he wrote. The QUALITATIVE difference between, say, long *e* and long *ae* not only was phonemic but carried a fair load, and he wrote the difference. The essentially identical qualitative difference between short *e* and short *ae* would therefore also be written, most of the time, despite its very low functional load.

2.4. *Summary.* § 2.1 musters evidence which attests, I believe, to a phonemic difference between a short syllabic regularly written *e* and one regularly written *eo*. In § 2.2 the evidence is less convincing, but seems to point to a phonemic difference between a short syllabic regularly written as *i* and at least one short syllabic reflected by spellings with *io*, *eo*, or (rarely) *ea*. In § 2.3, the evidence points towards an extremely low functional load for contrasts in the low and low-front region; yet I am unable to account realistically for the spellings unless I posit *a*, *ea*, *ae*, and *e* all as different "points in the pattern."

Two questions remain: (1) Do the *e* spellings of § 2.1 and those of § 2.3 all represent a single short syllabic phoneme, or must we assume a phonemic difference not reflected in the spelling habits? (2) Do the three spellings *io*, *eo*, and *ea* point to three different phonemes, all three different from *i*, *e*, *ae*, and *a*, or to only two or only one?

The first of these questions needs to be considered together with the problem of the scribe's use of *o* for short vowels. The scribe wrote merely *e*, in words like *deg*, *hegel*, *wrece*, *upahefen* as in words like *wer*, *cweðe*, *wel*. Similarly, he wrote merely *o* both for historic *o* and for historic *a* before a nasal (*mon*, *orn*, *born*). This means that, in using the Vespasian glosses as evidence for the structure and history of Old English as a whole, it is absolutely forbidden to introduce a two-way distinction in either the short-*e* area or the short-*o* area. My main purpose here, however, is different: I wish to describe as accurately as possible the dialect of the Vespasian scribe himself, or of his predecessors who transmitted his spelling habits to him. And here I reach an impasse. The scribe's use of *e* and *o* may reflect a single short vowel in each case, or it may conceal a two-way phonemic distinction in either case or in both cases. My hypothesis insists that a writer will not maintain a sub-phonemic distinction; but it allows, of course, that he may conceal a distinction that is phonemic. We cannot argue from later linguistic history, since subsequent documentary evidence, as well as New English, may reflect Anglian dialects other than that of the Vespasian scribe, and certainly reflects constant and extensive dialect mixture.

Nor can we reach any safe conclusion from consideration of "neatness of pattern." It is true that symmetrical patterns are more common, as languages go, than skew ones. But skew patterns do exist. Therefore I have no alternative but to grant that the vowel system sketched in paragraph (2) of my introduction may undercut the actual (but indeterminable) situation by the omission of a contrast /e/–/ɛ/ or a contrast /o/–/ɔ/ or both.

The other question allows a more nearly determinate answer. Note, first, the sharp difference between the *eo* spellings of § 2.1 and those of § 2.2 and § 2.3. The *eo* spellings of § 2.1 are very stable (except so far as they alternate with *e* spellings): instances of *io* or *ea* in place of *eo* are exceedingly rare. In § 2.2 and § 2.3, on the other hand, *eo* spellings are sporadic and unstable, alternating with *io*, *i*, and *ea*. The few instances of apparent stability of *eo* in § 2.2 are doubtless due to the very low frequency with which the forms concerned occur in the Vespasian glosses.

From this evidence and my assumptions, the only realistic conclusions seem to me the following. (1) Vespasian spellings reflect a somewhat earlier stage in which the spellings *io*, *eo*, and *ea* correlated with three short syllabics phonemically distinct both from one another and from all others—yielding the eleven-vowel system tabulated near the beginning of this article. At this earlier stage, words with *io* may have also shown *i*, but did not show variants with *eo* (or *ea*); words with *ea* showed comparable stability. (2) The dialect of the Vespasian scribe himself still included all eleven short vowels, but with major shifts in functional load. Sound change and dialect mixture had probably led to a state of affairs in which every form pronounced with *io* had a by-form pronounced with *eo* (though not conversely), and in which every form pronounced with *ea* had a by-form pronounced with *a* or with *eo* (though again not conversely). These conclusions account both for the spelling habits which the Vespasian scribe inherited, and for the particular way in which he modified and varied those habits.

3. *Evidence for the Phonetic Interpretation of io, eo, ea.* In the preceding section, I used my assumptions and the testimony of the spellings to show the phonemic distinctiveness of certain stressed vowels, but without guessing at their phonetic characteristics. In the present section I turn to the latter issue.

The scribes who first attempted to write Old English with Latin letters faced various problems. The Latin alphabet offered only five different vowel letters, plus *y* (to be discussed in a moment) and at least two digraphs, *ae* and *oe* (perhaps sometimes ligatured), which by these times had monophthongal pronunciations in Latin. The number of short-vowel phonemes in the Old English of the time was unquestionably greater than five—though the exact number is just the problem here.

The assignment of the five Latin letters *a, e, i, o, u* to Old English short vowels was easy. All but *a* were assigned to the short vowels which I transcribe phonemically with the same letters; *a* was assigned to the most common nonfront low vowel (or to the only nonfront low vowel, if there was but one), which I have chosen, for typographical convenience, to transcribe as /ɑ/. With these five conventions established, the scribes had to develop some way to represent the remaining short vowels of their language, as well as the various long nuclei. From our vantage point we ask instead, in what realistic ways might various sequences of two vowel letters, ligatured or not, be used in trying to apply the Latin alphabet to a language hitherto but seldom written? For Old English there are five possibilities.

(1) The digraph XY (where X and Y are any two single vowel letters) may represent two successive syllable nuclei, with no intervening consonant, or no intervening consonant which it is the scribes' habit to represent by a separate letter. This is obviously what happened in the postradical syllables of verb forms like *ðeowiað, wynsumiað, lufiað, eorsiað, syngian, bodiende, cleopiu* (all these examples from the first few pages of the Vespasian Psalter). It is also what happened when a prefix like *be-* or *ge* preceded a root written with an initial vowel letter: *geecna, geeaðmodað*.

(2) In the digraph XY, X may be a diacritic marking the pronunciation of a preceding *c* or *g* as palatal rather than velar: *gearwað, geondgað*. In these cases, X is almost always *e*, but sometimes *i*. We must allow for the possibility

that a digraph like *ea* may represent a syllable nucleus distinct from *e* or *a* and at the same time mark the palatal nature of the preceding *c* or *g*.

(3) The digraph XY may represent a syllable nucleus Y preceded by a consonant X. So in Cp. 122: *huitfoot* (Latin *albipedius*), presumably /hwíˑt fòˑt/.[18] In these cases, X is always *u*, and the proper interpretation is almost always clear either through comparative evidence or because the same words also occur spelled with the borrowed rune which it is nowadays customary to transcribe as *w*.

(4) The digraph XY may represent a falling diphthong, beginning with vowel X and gliding in the direction roughly indicated by Y. This is most strongly suspected in words like *ceosan*, *deop*, *leof*, *deor*, *beod*, *beor*, where the testimony of the other old Germanic languages supports a reconstructed Proto-Gmc. /ew/ or /iw/.

(5) The digraph XY may represent a monophthongal vowel something like the vowels written respectively with X and with Y, but distinctively different from both.

It has not, for a long time, been denied that this last principle was actually followed in the formation of the Old English spelling system; but the amount of evidence for it is somewhat larger than has been recognized. The two obvious digraphs of Latin, *ae* and *oe*, were used in this way, in values probably different from their Latin values at the time—unless those involved spoke Latin with an Old English accent. But the Old English use of what has been taken as "the letter *y*" also follows principle 5, as I shall now show.

3.1. *The Letter y.*   The alphabet of the International Phonetic Association assigns the letter *y* to the range of high front rounded vowels. This is one of a number of features adopted by the founders of the IPA from the earlier usage of Henry Sweet, who, in his turn, had selected this particular symbol for the sound type on the basis of Scandinavian and Old English orthographic habits. The Scandinavian use of *y* for [y, yˑ] also traces back to Old English, since it was Anglo-Saxon culture-bearers who taught the Norsemen to write. But where did our early English forebears get this particular association between sound and symbols? Sweet writes as follows:[19]

In determining the values of the letters in Old English we must be guided by the traditional pronunciation of Latin, remembering, however, that the pronunciation heard by the Anglo-Saxons was more archaic than that of the continent. The evidence of such Welsh loan-words as *cwyr* from Lt *cēra* shows that the Celts pronounced Lt *c* as [k] everywhere, and it is to Celtic tradition we must ascribe such Old English spellings as *Cent* = our *Kent*, while in the OHG of the eighth century *c* before front vowels was used to express [ts], as in *cit* = *zīt*. . . . Old English spelling is also very archaic in its retention of *y* in its original value of Greek *u*, while in OHG it had been confounded with *i*, and almost entirely disused.

Both of Sweet's examples in support of his theory must be questioned. It is more likely that the Celts borrowed *c* only for [k] because they did not have, and did not hear, the velar-palatal difference which had arisen in Latin by this time, and that the Anglo-Saxons borrowed it for their distinct pair of stops because they heard both stops in Latin in different words with the spelling *c*. It was natural to obscure in Old English writing a distinction that was obscured in Latin writing. As to "y," Sweet's theory is that the Anglo-Saxons were familiar with the letter "y" in Latin words of Greek origin; that they pronounced such words with [y]; and that they adopted *y* to represent their own high front rounded vowels quite as naturally as they borrowed *i* for their high front unrounded vowels and *u* for their high back rounded vowels.

This theory is not impossible, but it is improbable. There is no evidence—except, circularly, the Old English orthographic use of *y*—to support the belief that Latin as pronounced in Saxon England distinguished in pronunciation between *i* and *y*. In Roman times, when many Greek words were being borrowed into Latin and many educated Romans were learning Greek, there was no doubt a prevalent foreignism of pronouncing Greek loanwords containing an upsilon as the Greeks then did—with [y]. In exactly the same way, some more or less educated speakers of English currently use the French pronunciation of *u* in a certain number of half-assimilated French loans. This is no part of the fabric of English, and is not likely to have any noticeable consequences a few centuries from now; the same sort of comment applies to the Graeco-Roman situation. The upsilon of Greek loanwords in Latin that have survived into Romance shows exactly the same reflexes as Latin *i*.

Bearing more directly on Sweet's theory are the Latin writing habits of the Saxons themselves. Whoever wrote the surviving manuscripts of the Epinal and Second Corpus glossaries certainly knew Latin, since any literate Englishman of that day must have known it. In the Latin words of these two glossaries, there are not many occurrences of *y*, but there are some—and there are some words not spelled with *y* which in classical or post-classical times would have been. Here is the evidence;[20] the correct Graeco-Latin forms are given in a column at the right.

| | |
|---|---|
| Cp 468 *cinoglossa* | *cynoglossos* |
| Cp 540 *corimbos* | *corymbos* |
| Cp 757 *ependiten*, Ep 390 *efetidem* | *ependytes* |
| Cp 759 *erenis*, Cp 771 *eurynis* | *erinnys* |
| Cp 1221 *limphaticus* | *lymphaticus* |
| (Cp 1263 and Ep 575 both correctly *lymphatico*) | |
| Cp 1315 *mirifillo*, Ep 623 *mirifillon* | *myriophyllon* |
| Cp 1487 *papiliuus*, Ep 781 *papiluus* | *papyrus* |
| Cp 1873 and Ep 919 *simbulum* | *symbolum* |
| (Cp 1971 correctly *symbulum*) | |
| Cp 1869 and Ep 975 *sinfoniaca* | *symphoniaca* |
| Cp 1826 and Ep 965 *scifus* | *scyphus* |
| Cp 2006 and Ep 1042 *termofilas* | *thermopylas* |

| | |
|---|---|
| Cp 2037 and Ep 1045 *tipo* | *typhon* |
| Cp 1264 *lymbo* | *limbo* |
| Cp 1378 *nimbus* "corrected" to *nymbus* | *nimbus* |
| Cp 1677 *ptysones* | *ptisanas* |

In the two glossaries, then, there are 22 occurrences of *i* for expected *y*, and 3 of *y* for *i*. In addition, the two glossaries include about a score of occurrences of correct *y* (not listed above) and numberless instances of correct *i*.

There can be no doubt but that the native Old English of the scribes responsible for the glossaries included a phonemic contrast between something like [y] and something like [i]. We cannot absolutely date the pre-English development of this contrast, but it was certainly in existence before the introduction of Christianity, and thus of the use of Latin. If the Latin pronunciation learned by the scribes had included a phonemic contrast between [y] and [i], the scribes would have transferred their English speech habits to their Latin, and hence would have kept the two Latin spellings apart. But they did not.

Old Irish affords no basis for the use of *y* for [y]: the letter occurs only randomly in unassimilated loans.[21]

The origin of the Old English use must thus be sought elsewhere.

The actual shape of the Old English letter which we call *y* was not far from the shapes "Y" and "y" that we use today. The shape "Y" can easily be interpreted as composed of two parts, an upper part like "U" or "V" and a lower part like "I." The graphic distinction between "U" and "V" is, of course, very late, so that the difference between the pointed bottom of "V" or of the upper half of "Y" and the curved bottom of "U" is for our purposes irrelevant. Certainly the earliest English scribes were familiar with the letter "Y" of the Latin alphabet; but I suggest that in their actual use of this letter they took it as a ligatured digraph of "U" and "I," just as they took the Latin digraphs "AE" and "OE," ligatured or not, as in some sense composite letters.

In immediate support of this proposition, note that in the short First Corpus glossary there occurs one spelling, *buiris* (Latin *foratorium*), where the digraph *ui* certainly represents [y]. Sievers (*Angelsächsische Grammatik*[3] 6 Anm. 1) states that *ui* was an occasional Northumbrian spelling for [y], and cites a form *suinnig* for ordinary *synnig* "sinful," but does not give his source.

The occurrence of an equivalent unligatured digraph of the two letters that I interpret as ligatured in *y* is important, because no other ligatures used by the Old English scribes are without such parallels. The earliest surviving manuscripts show *ae* almost to the exclusion of *æ*; only later does *æ*, along with its abbreviated cursive alternant *ę*, come into frequent use. But *y* is very early, and *ui* with the value [y] extremely rare, so that we need further support.

One possible factor is that in the earliest Latin-alphabet documents, the rune for [w] had not yet been added to the stock of Latin letters; instead, [w] was written with *u* or in some cases (initially and intervocalically) with *uu*. The letter sequence *ui* was thus ambiguous for [wi, wiˑ] and [y, yˑ]. There is perhaps no special reason why this ambiguity should have been eliminated, by regular use of the ligature *y*, when so many other ambiguities were allowed to remain, except that in this instance the ligature was a shape already familiar in the Latin alphabet. Furthermore, Runic spelling in England afforded a basis for an analogical transfer of the habit.

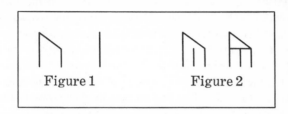

Figure 1          Figure 2

Our scant supply of surviving English Runic inscriptions contains 11 occurrences of a special rune for [y]. The runes for [u] and for [i], both on the Continent and in Britain, are of approximately the shapes shown in Fig. 1. The rune for [y], which seems to have been devised in England, has the shape shown in Fig. 2. Obviously, the [y] rune was made by placing the rune for [i] below (and within) that for [u], sometimes with an extra stroke.[22] Nothing could be more obvious than the parallelism between this Runic ligature and the adoption of the shape of the Latin letter *y* as an equivalent ligature with equivalent value.

3.2. *Digraphs for Monophthongs.* In three relatively clear-cut instances, the earliest Old English scribes followed principle 5 (§ 3 above) in assigning vowel-letter digraphs to monophthongs. (1) They had a vowel phoneme with the lip position of /u/, which they were writing *u*, but the tongue advancement of /i/, which they were writing *i*: for this they adopted the unligatured digraph *ui* and the ligatured form *y*. (2) They had a vowel phoneme with the lip position of /o/, which they were writing *o*, but the tongue advancement of /e/, which they were writing *e*: for this they adopted the unligatured digraph *oe*. (3) They had a vowel phoneme of the height of /ɑ/, which they were writing *a*, but the tongue advancement of /e/, which they were writing *e*: for this they adopted the Latin digraph *ae*, *æ*.

It is not unrealistic to attribute to the scribes the degree of sophistication implied by their assumed use of this principle. We have no records of their orthographic speculations, but they were intelligent men; we must remember the direct evidence of penetrating brilliance in First Grammarian, who, though later, lived in somewhat the same intellectual climate.[23]

We may reasonably ask why the digraphs in question should have been written, at least when unligatured, in the order *ae oe ui* rather than the reverse (*ea eo iu*). Latin *ae* and *oe* furnished a model. In addition, there were living morphophonemic relations between /u/ and /y/, /o/ and /ø/, /ɑ/ and /æ/, but none to speak of between /y/ and /i/ or between /ø/ and /e/, and only a rather different sort between /æ/ and /e/. Presumably the first position in such a digraph is more prominent than the second.

Turning now to *io*, *eo*, *ea*, we first observe that the traditional interpretation—supported by the known etymology of the "long" diphthongs—has turned entirely on principle 4 (§ 3). I think it at least equally likely that these digraphs were introduced on the basis of principle 5, as a continuation of the practice established with *ae*, *oe*, and *y*. (4) *io*, which in the earliest records appears also occasionally as *iu*, was chosen to represent a vowel of the height and lip position of /i/, written *i*, but with the retracted tongue position of /u/ and /o/: thus a high unrounded central-to-back vowel /ɨ/. (5) *eo* similarly implies a vowel of the height and the lip position of /e/, written *e*, but with the retracted tongue position of /o/, written *o*: thus a mid unrounded central-to-back vowel /ə/. (6) *ea* would at first seem to imply a vowel of the height and the lip position of /e/ (*e*) but of the retracted tongue position of /ɑ/ (*a*). The earliest manuscripts, however, sometimes show *æa*, and even in the Vespasian documents we find a few occurrences: 9/30 *geræafie*, 118/122 *hæarmcweodelien*. Therefore I assume the height of *æ* and *a*, yielding /a/, distinct from the /ə/ written *eo*.

The order for the vowel letters used in these digraphs is determined not only because of the assignments already made of the same letters in opposite order, but also because of living morphophonemic relations, at least between /i/ and /ɨ/, /e/ and /ə/.

From the point of view of realism in phonetic change, particularly in assimilations, it is certainly as likely that a back-umlauting of front unrounded vowels should produce unrounded back vowels as it is that a front-umlauting of back rounded vowels should produce rounded front vowels. The same applies to the modification of vowel color by a following consonant: "breaking" is a loaded term stemming from the habit of talking about letters instead of sounds, and prejudices reinterpretation.

3.3. *The "Long Diphthongs."*   Early in the history of Old English writing, halfhearted attempts were made to distinguish graphically between what seem to have been short and long monophthongal syllable nuclei. The first Corpus Glossary shows *flood*, *boor*, *hornnaap*, *saa*, *fylledflood*, *specfaag*, but also *nepflod*; the second shows, on the first few pages of Sweet's edition, *piic*, *gaarleec*, *waar*, *huitfoot*, *meeli*, *streamraad*, *wiingeardes*, *boog*, *scaan*, *beer*. Later this habit of doubling was lost; the habit of marking "long" nuclei with what the modern editions reproduce as an acute accent never gained much ground, and the actual occurrences of this mark do not wholly correlate with the incidence of what we should expect, on a historical basis, to be "long" syllabics.[24] Yet the existence of quantitative contrasts is indisputable. We must assume that the functional load carried by quantitative contrasts was sufficiently slight that the literate speaker of Old English was not inconvenienced in reading a text in which these contrasts were not indicated. The many clear instances of minimal pairs (e.g., *god* "God," *gōd* "good") do not alter this conclusion. We must also assume, however, that at least in most instances a "short" syllabic and a "long" syllabic with the same graphic representation were qualitatively similar to each other. For this reason, I conclude that the "long" syllabics written *i, e, ae, y, oe, u, o, a* were qualitatively much like the shorts written the same way. I tentatively phonemicize the eight "longs" as involving a recurrent length phoneme /·/.

It is also clear that the short syllabics written *ea, eo, io* were matched by longer or more complex syllabics written with the same three digraphs; but in these three cases it is by no means so certain that the more complex syllabics consisted merely of the shorts plus a phoneme of length. The long *ea* is cognate to a diphthong of the [aw] type in the other old Germanic languages, and the long *eo* and *io* are cognate to diphthongs of the types [ew, iw]. In the earliest Old English texts, long *ea* occasionally appears rather as *æo, eo,* or *æa,* and long *eo* as *eu*: Cp *genæot,* Ep *eorisc,* BH *Æodbald, Æanfled*; Ep *treuteru, steupfædær.* The cognation and some of these early spellings point towards a late pre-English and very early Old English triad of the type [æw, ew, iw], with front unrounded vowels and a glide to high back rounded tongue and lip position. From this as point of departure, the likely general course of events in Anglian down to late Old English or early Middle English times can be sketched as follows:

| | | |
|---|---|---|
| (1) | [æw, ew, iw] | /æw, ew, iw/ |
| (2) | [æɯ, eɯ, iɯ] | /æw, ew, iw/ |
| (3) | [aɯ, əɯ, iɯ] | /aw, əw, ɨw/ |
| (4) | [a·, əɯ, iɯ] | /a·, əw, ɨw/ |
| (5) | [a·, ə·, (i·)] | /a·, ə·, (i·)/ |
| (6) | [æ·, e·, (i·)] | /æ·, e·, (i·)/ |

At stage 1, the phonemic contrast between (short) [æ e i] and [a ə ɨ] has not yet developed. /æ e i/ may already have begun to develop retracted allophones in some positions, perhaps in part in the position before /w/.

Between stages 1 and 2, there is only a subphonemic change: /w/ after unrounded vowel develops an unrounded allophone [ɯ].

Between stages 2 and 3, the contrast between front unrounded and retracted unrounded is phonologized, by both morphemic and allophonic analogy. The first elements of the three diphthongs have by this time come to be retracted rather than front. Thus, as soon as the contrast develops, the first elements of the diphthongs are phonemically /a ə ɨ/.

Between stages 3 and 4, the second element in /aw/ becomes a less and less noticeable glide (towards high back UNROUNDED, it must be remembered), and when the glide is altogether gone the diphthong has become phonemically /a·/. The spellings *æa* and *ea* mark this change: when, in any particular dialect area, it has been completed, *ea* (rarely *æa*) has come to spell paired short and long monophthongs /a/ and /a·/, just as *e* spells paired /e/ and /e·/, *i* spells paired /i/ and /i·/, and so on.

Between stages 4 and 5, a similar change happens to the second element of /əw/ and /ɨw/, to eliminate these two syllabics and to add /ə·/ and /ɨ·/, completing the pairing of shorts and longs. However, something else has been happening during the same period: the contrast between /ə/ and /ɨ/ has been diminishing in functional load, through sound change in some dialects (lowering of /ɨ/ for the most part) and subsequent dialect mixture, so that it is by no means clear whether any instances of /ɨ·/ remain.

Between stages 5 and 6, the retracted unrounded vowels are altogether eliminated from the system, through coalescences with various other syllabics in various environments (with no guarantee of uniformity from one dialect to another). In particular, /ə·/ and /e·/ largely fall together, which means also that most (or all) instances of earlier /ɨ·/ or /ɨw/ are carried into the resulting /e·/; and /a·/ and /æ·/ fall together as /æ·/. The NE words *creep, knee, flee, freeze, thief, seethe, see, priest, fee, cleave* ("split"), *cleat, be, beer, friend, breast, thigh* were all at one time /ə·/ words; *queen, wheeze, weep, keep, meet, (be)seech, green, sweet, seek, feet, meed, here* all had /e·/; and *three, cheese, beetle, free, dear, devil* all at one time had /ɨ·/ (or /ɨw/, if there was no /ɨ·/ stage). The multiple results in each case reflect later vicissitudes of dialect borrowing or of conditioned sound changes; the original three-way contrasts of the syllabics cannot be inferred from the later history. Similarly, NE *flea, sheaf, beat, leap, beacon, ear, ear* (corn), *near, flay, slay, great, head, deaf, eye, nigh, high,* once with /a·/, and NE *sleep, needle, lead, reach, teach, mead, clean, even*(*ing*), *either, eel, each, bleach, breech, dread, let, flesh, ever, empty, any, meadow, ready,* once with /æ·/, imply a complete coalescence of /a·/ and /æ·/ in very late Anglian Old English or very early Middle English. Yet the stated coalescences certainly had some exceptions. The word *ceosan* points to one: certainly this was at the earliest stage/ céwsan/, yielding later, in different dialects, both /ćó·san/ and /ćɔ́·san/; dialect mixture put these alternants into competition; the former survives in NE *choose,* the latter in later Midlands speech became /ćé·san/ and survived into Middle English as *chesen, chese,* now obsolete.

Thus we have an obvious diphthongal point d'appui, and a well-attested monophthongal outcome in late Old English or early Middle English, at least in the Midlands. The remaining problem is the approximate timetable. Can we decide just what stage in this sequence had been reached by the period reflected in the Vespasian glosses? Indeed we can, though with certain remaining indeterminacies.

To begin with, my discussion of the historically low vowels in § 2.3 implies that the four shorts /e æ a ɑ/ stood in phonetically parallel relationship to the four longs /e· æ· a· ɑ·/: that is, for each pair the difference was basically one of quantity with little difference in quality. Unless we can assume this, the argument of § 2.3 falls to the ground, but the graphic evidence points to this part of the interpretation as well as to the rest. Even the predominant spelling *ea* supports the monophthongal theory, as I have pointed out.

Vespasian spellings show a considerable confusion of expected "long" *io* and "long" *eo*, mainly with *io* for expected *eo*. This is the reverse of the balance for the "shorts"; there *eo* appears for expected "short" *io* much more often than the reverse. This is all evidence for the falling-together of /i/ and /ə/, in the diphthongs /iw əw/ (or the longs /i· ə·/) as well as elsewhere.

What is clear from this is that the dialect reflected by Vespasian spellings was somewhere in the vicinity of stage 4 or 5 of the table. What remains indeterminable, so far as I can see, is whether "long" *io* and *eo* were still phonemically /iw əw/ or had become /i· ə·/. The spellings are appropriate for either stage.

## FOOTNOTES

1. Robert P. Stockwell and C. Westbrook Barritt, *Some Old English graphemic-phonemic correspondences*, (*SIL* Occasional Papers, No. 4; 1951); Fernand Mossé, *Manuel de l'anglais du moyen âge* (1945); M. Daunt, Old English sound-changes reconsidered in relation to scribal tradition and practice, *Transactions of the Philological Society* 1939.108–37 (1939).

I wish to express my thanks to Sherman M. Kuhn, who graciously read an earlier version of this paper and gave me the benefit of his broad scholarship in Old English. His help does not constitute endorsement of my conclusions, about which he has some serious doubts. As a result of his criticism I have been enabled to eliminate a number of obvious errors, and have tried to clarify several points on which my earlier discussion impressed him as obscure.

2. Sherman M. Kuhn and Randolph Quirk, *Lg.* 29.143–56 (1953); see now also the same authors in *Lg.* 31.390–401 (1955), replying to Stockwell and Barritt, *Lg.* 31.372–89 (1955).

3. See my *Manual of phonology*, esp. § 244 (1955).

4. For Old English consonantism I find the arguments of William G. Moulton in *Lg.* 30.1–42 (1954) entirely convincing. In particular, his insistence on the phonetic (and possibly phonemic) distinction between syllable-initial [h] and postvocalic [x], in all the old Germanic languages and thus in reconstructible Proto-Germanic, is much to be preferred to Stockwell and Barritt's assumption (stated without evidence) that even in Old English *h-* was something like [x].

The consonant system of Midlands Old English by the time of the Vespasian document was then as follows: four voiceless stops /p t ċ k/, spelled *p, t, c, c*; four voiced stops /b d ġ g/ of limited distribution, written *b, d, g, g*; four spirants /f þ s x/, written *f, ð ~ þ, s, h ~ g*, voiced or voiceless depending on environment; one spirant /j/ (not a semivowel!), always voiced, also spelled *g*; and /m n r l w h/, spelled *m, n, r, l, w, h*.

5. J. Bosworth, *The elements of Anglo-Saxon grammar* 51 (London, 1823).

Since I have not been able to undertake this task, the following outline may be partly wrong.

6. The restriction "alphabetical" is essential: obviously one's assumptions must be different for a morphemic writing system such as that of Chinese, and doubtless in part different for a nonalphabetical but basically phonemic writing system such as some of those of the ancient Near East.

7. Rudolf Thurneysen, *A grammar of Old Irish*, translated from the German by D. A. Binchy and Osborn Bergin (Dublin, 1946). The passage is from § 86, corresponding to § 82 of the original: "Schliesst ein palataler Konsonant oder eine palatale Konsonantengruppe eine haupttonige Silbe, so tritt hinter jeden Vokal oder Diftong ausser ĭ . . . ein Übergangs- oder Gleitelaut *i*. Er muss sehr hörbar gewesen sein, da er in der Schrift selten unbezeichnet bleibt. Aber er war kein voller Vokal; er bildete mit einem vorhergehenden kurzen Vokal zusammen keine Länge (keinen eigentlichen Diftong), sondern die Silbe blieb kurz." Thurneysen's *Handbuch des Alt-Irischen* is dated 1909; it is firmly in the prephonemic neogrammarian tradition.

8. Fide Norman A. McQuown.

9. [See the following paper by Stockwell and Barritt, in which they state their assumptions.—Ed.]

10. For both the Vespasian records and the Glossaries, as already noted in the second paragraph of this paper, I have relied on Henry Sweet, *Oldest English texts*, *EETS* (1885).

11. It is highly unlikely that posttonic unstressed *e* had by these times been retracted to anything like [ə]; but if it had been, the argument still applies, for we still find both writings for the stressed syllabic before identical vocalism in following syllables.

12. That is, in Martinet's sense of "functional load"; see his *Économie des changements phonétiques: Traité de phonologie diachronique* (Berne, 1955). The contrast between /š/ and /ž/ in New English is not rendered nonphonemic by the existence of at most a handful of minimal pairs in any one person's speech; but this contrast does less of the work of keeping utterances apart than does, say, that between NE /p/ and /b/ or between /p/ and /t/.

13. This is Sweet's view of the symbol *ę*; see his *History of English sounds*[2] 102 (1888). Kuhn tells me that the symbol was borrowed from Latin writing habits and thus, for Old English, should probably not be described as a cursive form of *æ*. I believe that the difference does not bear integrally on the line of argument in the text.

14. [The so-called "Anglian Smoothing." See A. Campbell, *Old English grammar*[2] (Oxford, 1961), §§ 222–33.—Ed.]

15. The coalescence also preceded *r*-metathesis: The Vespasian glosses consistently show forms like *orn* "ran," *born* "burned." Later developments, all the way to New English, attest to the simultaneous existence of dialects—even in the Midlands—in which the coalescence did not occur (*man, hand, lamb* alongside *long, strong*). The commonest alternative hypothesis proposes an additional separate lower-mid back rounded vowel phoneme from earlier *a* before nasals. I see no justification for this alternative, but discuss it briefly in § 2.4 below.

16. In *sacerd* the *a* may have been long: see Alois Pogatscher, *Zur Lautlehre der griechischen, lateinischen, und romanischen Lehnworte im Altenglischen* 31 ff., 42, 116–7 (1888).

17. [The so-called "Second Fronting." See Campbell, §§ 164–9.—Ed.]

18. For these earlier forms from the Corpus glossary, I again rely on Sweet's *OET*, cited in footnote 10.

19. Sweet, *History of English sounds*[2] 101.

20. Taken from the Latin forms in Sweet's reordering of the Glossaries, in his *Oldest English texts*.

21. Thurneysen, *op. cit.* 23.

22. Sweet, *History of English sounds*[2] 97.

23. Einar Haugen, *First grammatical treatise*, *Language monograph no. 25*, Supplement to *Lg.* 26.4 (1950).

24. Sweet, *History of English sounds*[2], especially 108–9.

# ROBERT P. STOCKWELL and C. W. BARRITT

## Scribal Practice: Some Assumptions*

In a recent article in *Language*,[1] Charles F. Hockett has presented an analysis of the stressed syllabics of the Vespasian Psalter and Hymns.[2] Hockett opposes the traditional view which interprets *ea*, *eo*, *io*, and *ie* as short diphthongs, and offers a solution of his own which within the limitations of one MS is in part convincing. In general, he equates each vowel letter or digraph with a phoneme. In agreement with us, with Mossé, and with Daunt, but in contradiction of the established tradition, he regards the digraphs *ea*, *eo*, *io*, and *ie* as spellings for monophthongs; he believes, however, that these short digraphs represent separate short vowel phonemes; we believe that in early OE they represented allophones of the front vowels /i/, /e/, and /æ/; we believe that *eo*, *io*, and *ie* represented allophones ONLY in the earlier period. These allophones later became phonemes, whereas the allophone represented by *ea* did not. Hockett's speculations about the motivations of the scribes who first selected these particular digraphs in these particular values are appealing. Especially ingenious is his theory about the origin of the letter *y* in OE, which he considers to have been originally a digraph (591–4).

Although we agree to a limited extent with the conclusions of Hockett's article (which might better be entitled The Stressed Syllabics of the Vespasian Psalter and Hymns), we wish to reaffirm the stand taken in our monograph and our subsequent article,[3] in particular with regard to *æ–ea*, but also with regard to the structure of OE vowels in general. Concerning the long diphthongs and long vowels we are more nearly in agreement with the position Hockett took in the book that appeared before this article:[4] "there were complex nuclei consisting of one or another of the eleven vowels [we do not think there were as many as eleven vowels] plus a glide element. The details are not clear." There are, however, other basic, more axiomatic assumptions with which we do not agree at all. They are discussed below.

1. As Hockett points out, the documentary record is the primary source of information. Assumptions about scribal practice are axioms in the study of the phonemic nature of the entities represented by the spellings.

An axiom which Hockett wishes to propose is that a distinction in spelling never correlates exclusively with an allophonic difference. He is only partially correct when he says that our "unstated assumptions about scribal practice must have been different" (580) from the ones he based his conclusions on.

* From *Language* 37.75–82 (1961). Reprinted by permission of the authors and the Linguistic Society of America.

Our assumptions were different, but they certainly were not unstated. In essence we wrote that native speakers would spell only phonemes except under specific conditions: (1) when foreigners introduced the system, and (2) when there was a careful system through which new generations of scribes learned the spellings.[5]

An alphabet is nearly always a gift from one people to another. For a variety of possible reasons, religious reasons typically, emissaries from one culture, speaking their own language, enter another culture and attempt to reduce the foreign language to writing. They tend to overwrite and underwrite the language which they learn as foreigners. Hockett himself has mentioned one example, Nahuatl, in which allophones were spelled, but we are skeptical whether it was necessary for Sahagún to stand "behind his scribes with a whip to enforce the maintenance of these distinctions" (579), or, if it was, whether this is sufficient basis for so powerful a generalization. Many modern languages maintain more unreasonable orthographic features than the writing of allophones. Castilian maintains a similar scribal practice today (though for different reasons historically), as between *z* representing /θ/ before /a/, /o/, and /u/, and *c* representing /θ/ before /e/ and /i/. In English in most positions we write *k* or *c* for /k/, but before /w/ spelled *u* we regularly write *q*; but in English we learn a host of more difficult orthographic tricks. Perhaps it was necessary for someone to whip us in grammar school; this is a matter of personality. Most youngsters learning to write take the word of their teacher as if it were handed to them from Mount Sinai; the teacher's authority is accepted with little question. Indeed, the student who insists on writing "phonetically" is probably of the rarest intelligence and is certainly more analytical than the majority who find memorizing much easier than analyzing. Of course a child misspells, but his misspellings are often NOT in the direction of phonemic writing, but are analogies with other sequences of letters.

Hockett could have offered other examples besides Nahuatl. A few are listed in our study with appropriate references: Cakchiquel, Tarascan, Quechua (35). In Quechua, for example, /i/ and /u/ have two allophones each: they are [e] and [o] always when adjacent to /q, qʰ, q'/ and optionally elsewhere, and [i] and [u] optionally everywhere except adjacent to /q, qʰ, q'/. The orthography calls for *e* and *o* next to /q, qʰ, q'/, *i* and *u* elsewhere.[6] Pike, following a lesson learned in some instances the hard way, recommends the above device so as not to antagonize Spanish sensibilities.[7] Another example can be found in the American Bible Society's edition of the New Testament in Mexican (Aztec) of the Sierra of Puebla, where /k/ before /i/ and /e/ is spelled *qu*, elsewhere *c*.

Scribes following Sahagún in writing Nahuatl used *hu* for voiced [w] and *uh* for voiceless [W]. In Tamil /n/ has two allophones: a dental [n] when stem-initial (perhaps after juncture) and before dental /t, d/, alveolar [ṇ] elsewhere; the orthography distinguishes them.[8] Tagalog has lowered allophones of

/i/ and /u/ under weak stress before juncture; these are written *e* and *o*, elsewhere *i* and *u*. They can only be called allophones, of course, in an analysis
which establishes two quite separate vowel systems for stressed and unstressed
syllabics—/i, e, a, o, u/ under strong stress, /i, a, u/ under weak stress. To use
an argument of Hockett's to which we will return, those whose "professional
conscience" insists that similar phonetic qualities must be identified with a
single phoneme regardless of distributional facts, cannot accept the notion
that [e] under weak stress can be assigned to /i/, while [e] under strong stress
is assigned to /e/.

Hockett can hardly quarrel with at least some of these examples, since he
lists two factors which govern the native who is writing a word in his own
language and using an alphabetical writing system. They are: "(1) the word
has a culturally prescribed spelling which the scribe has learned from others;
(2) the spelling of the word is worked out, however quickly and unconsciously,
in terms of established associations between letters or combinations of letters
and certain phonemes or sequences of phonemes" (578). The second of these
principles, Hockett maintains, takes precedence, at least after a certain lapse
of time, over the first: "It is not at all unlikely that these culture-bearers
[Irish missionaries] taught their English speaking converts to write on
Sahagún's principle, introducing graphic provision for distinctions subphonemic in English though phonemic in Old Irish" (579). Up to this point,
then, we seem to be in agreement; but Hockett argues that the passage of time
would smooth out this overwriting through the operation of the second
factor. We cannot, of course, deny that the second factor is operative.
Indeed, we pointed out the tendency to write phonemically when we found *æ*
being written on occasion for *ea* in the "breaking" environments, and *ea*
being written for *æ* occasionally in nonbreaking environments. This alternation of spellings is one of several motivations for arguing that *æ* and *ea*
represent allophones.

The problem then seems to be this: how much time is necessary to smooth
out a writing system to the point where all subphonemic writing has been
eliminated? While there was no Académie ancien-anglaise to regulate these
matters, the power of tradition must not be discounted. Modern English
would seem to show that spellings never get smoothed out completely, whatever may have been the original cause of the roughness. The more thorough
the educational system, the less chance a phonemic system of spelling has of
remaining phonemic (as the language changes) or of becoming phonemic if it
was not in the first place. We maintain that the England of the eighth through
the tenth centuries, the England which developed one of the earliest literatures
after the fall of Rome, the England which sent scholars to help Charlemagne
in his scholastic efforts, could not have had anything but a reasonably
thorough system of instruction for its scribes. We realize that there must have
been variations from area to area, from monastery to monastery, and from
personality to personality, yet we believe that there were scribal traditions

which were adhered to with a substantial degree of rigidity. Hockett appears to assume the contrary.

The evidence to support our belief is in a certain sense negative, for other than *Aelfric's Colloquy*, in which the students accept the rod as a necessary part of their education, there is little direct evidence that academic discipline was firm and that orthography was taught according to traditional rules. Nevertheless it is wrong to assume that this education was haphazard. Schools were established for children who might enter holy orders; therefore schools and education and of course scribal work were all under the control of the church. In the church, tradition and obedience to rule were and are a way of life. A firm discipline and a reasonably abundant library must have been necessary to produce a Bede or an Alcuin. A firm discipline probably included castigation for misspelling. Training was of course primarily in Latin, but scribal apprentices must certainly have followed the spelling habits of their masters, whether in Latin or in English.

The sheer mass of the intellectual effort in early England leads us to suppose that education was widespread. Learning developed rapidly: within a hundred years of the overthrow of Penda in 654, "England had become the home of a Christian culture which influenced the whole development of letters and learning in western Europe."[9] Many centers of learning developed, libraries were assembled, and the names of great teachers appear—Theodore, Hadrian, Aldhelm, Bede.[10]

To support his argument Hockett cites what at first blush is a convincing parallel. /b/ had both stop and spirant allophones, yet later when the spirant allophone fell together with the voiced allophone of /f/ we have only *f* written. But this is not in fact parallel to the *æ–ea* problem, for we do not maintain that any allophones of any other phoneme fell in with either allophone of /æ/, though of course later when secondary influences operated ("lengthening"), the allophone represented by *ea* in some environments fell in with other phonemes. Furthermore Hockett may not have found any alternations between *f* and *b* in the *Vespasian Psalter*, but they existed in OE. Bosworth and Toller have *hæbern* vs. *hæfern*; *nabo-gar* vs. *nafo-gar*; but this information is beside the point. There were two phonemes /f/ and /b/; they were usually written *f* and *b*, which is to be expected.

Hockett also uses *þ* vs. *ð* as a case in point. "It would have been easy to specialize one of these symbols for the voiceless allophone of /θ/, the other for the voiced; but this, also, they did not do; the two were used interchangeably for both allophones, some scribes showing a preference for the one or the other, other scribes choosing between them randomly" (580). The same statement might apply to *æ* and *ea*, though there is clearly less random choice between the two symbols; *æ* appears much more consistently in one set of environments and *ea* in the others. There is nonetheless some random variation, and we should expect some when separate graphs are used for allophones of a single phoneme. In *OP* 4.10 we stated that "within either environment both *ea* and *æ* may occur in free variation," though this fact was offered as negative evidence. We should point out now that the distribution of *þ* and *ð* is perhaps not as random as Hockett maintains; at least not in one manuscript. In the first nine pages of Earle and Plummer's diplomatic rendition of the *AS Chronicle* (the Laud MS E printed on odd-numbered pages 2–19) we find the following situation; numbers indicate occurrences.

| | |
|---|---|
| word-initial | *þ* approximately 90 |
| | *ð* 22 |
| between vowels | *þ* 3 |
| | *ð* 28 |
| word-final | *þ* 6 |
| | *ð* 23 |
| between C and V | *þ* 4 |
| | *ð* 6 |
| between consonants | *þ* 2 |
| | *ð* 5 |

(The five interconsonantal occurrences of *ð* include several cases of *forðferde*. Perhaps these should be classed as word-final *ð*.) It really does not matter what we assume about the nature of the allophone represented by *þ* or by *ð* as far as the present discussion is concerned; but if we assume that *þ* had some notion of voicelessness attributed to it originally and *ð* some notion of voice, we might then infer that this notion is further borne out by the above distribution in initial and medial positions. The least we can say is that in this MS one graph predominates in one environment and the other in another.

It is more than a little difficult to understand how Hockett, given his assumptions about scribal practice, can so readily conclude that the spelling *h* represented two phonemes, /h/ and /x/. He perhaps can justify the assumption that /x/ is in contrast with /h/ on the evidence that /x/ alternates (morphophonemically) with /g/, so that /x/ is often spelled *g* rather than *h* in the forms where the morphophonemic alternation is regular. Nonetheless, his assertion (fn. 4) that there were two phonemes /h/ and /x/, simply because he is convinced that syllable-initial *h-* was phonetically smooth whereas postvocalic *-h* had considerable velar friction, is gratuitous as a linguistic argument. The logic of his assertion should be viewed closely. He finds Moulton's "insistence on the phonetic (and possibly phonemic) distinction between syllable-initial [h] and postvocalic [x] . . . much to be preferred" to our assumptions that OE *h-* represented the phoneme /x/. Then, without further evidence, having acknowledged that even Moulton would describe the [h]–[x] phonetic difference as only "possibly" phonemic, he proceeds to assign phonemic status to the difference—an assignment which contradicts every principle of phonemic assignment from documentary evidence that he has enumerated: the two "phonemes" are consistently spelled alike except in environments where morphophonemic alternation with /g/ readily explains the use of *g*, they are in complementary distribution, and, to the extent that we know what their phonetic shape was at all, they were certainly phonetically similar. Nor is this the entire story. In the very article by Moulton[11] to which Hockett assigns a heavy measure of agreement, we find a description of the following curious orthographic situation (27): the structure of the velars is analyzed as (k:g) : x, with [g] assigned as an allophone of /x/, not of /g/. Yet,

The stop [g] was written quite consistently with the letter *g*, but the spirants [g] and [x] were written with both *g* and *h*. For a while *g* predominates for [g], and the choice of *h* or *g* for [x] was governed largely by morphophonemic convenience . . . Later on the scribes began to write [x] more or less consistently with *h*, regardless of morphophonemics, and continued the use of *g* for [g] and [g].

Clearly, if [g] is assigned to /x/, this is an instance in which an allophone was written with remarkable consistency. Of course, if [g] is assigned to /g/, as we believe it should be in spite of the failure of parallelism with the dentals (like Hockett, we trust the scribes further than we trust internal symmetry within the consonantal oppositions), this is not an instance in which allophones are written.

2. The speculation that *ð* and *þ* are allographs of the same grapheme (a notion which Hockett accepts) seems to be based on the same sort of evidence from which we deduced the allographic nature of *æ* and *ea*, that is, actual distribution of the graphs and historical evidence.

It is remarkable that Hockett admits virtually no *æ–ea* contrast (587), yet sets up a phonemic distinction anyway, arguing only on the basis of "professional conscience" and the remarkably loose analogy of /ɨ/. While it may be true that in certain dialects (such as Hockett's) there is no word which has only a single pronunciation with stressed /ɨ/, it hardly follows that a scribe would ever write such a phone consistently or be such an expert phonetician that he would indicate the difference in pronunciation each time he happened to pronounce the word with one of the alternates of this phoneme. This is to attribute to the scribe a sophistication that not many people have, including a good many of Hockett's own critics (reviewers of his *Manual of phonology*), who are not by any means convinced that his criteria for phonemic solutions of phonetic data are satisfactory. It has been our experience that there are many trained linguists who have a good deal of trouble accepting /ɨ/ as a phoneme in American English or even in their own dialects, lumping it with /ə/ or giving it status only in the system of vowels under weak stress. It is true that many English words have alternate pronunciations, and since this was no doubt true in OE, it must in part account for the alternate spellings of a single word; but to say that this principle accounts for all the variants of spelling in OE of a single form is to assert more than we can accept.

The following statement (588) requires comment: "Anyone whose professional conscience will let him recognize a single phone as an allophone of several different phonemes can easily conclude that Vespasian *ea* represented

an allophone that belonged with *a* in some forms, with *eo* in others, and so on."
We cannot escape the necessity of assuming that Hockett is here confused
between orthography and speech. Some linguists are convinced that a single
phone-type cannot be assigned to several different phonemes. We do not
happen to accept this version of the bi-uniqueness principle, as Hockett
apparently does; but even if one believes this, it is still true that a single
graph can represent several different phonemes. An example from modern
English is *th*. We see no reason why Vespasian *ea* could not represent an
allophone that belonged to the phoneme /a/ in some few forms, even though
in most instances it belonged to /æ/.

The most crucial argument against the position that *æ* and *ea* represent
different phonemes is that the contrast is totally unproductive in subsequent
history. This was the first argument developed in *OP* 4, where we state that
the allophones cease to be distinguished in Middle English, and that the result
of either allophone in Modern English is /æ/ unless secondary developments
intervene. They started as allophones in early or pre-OE; at no date did they
split and have independent reflexes; and they finally came back together
graphically in Middle English, even though there was still a wide range
within the single low vowel of Middle English.

It is conceivable of course that *æ* and *ea* represented phonemes in OE or in
the *Vespasian Psalter* and that they later fell together into one phoneme—
just as OE *a* and OE *æ* fell together. On the other hand, *æ* and *ea* clearly
emerged from a single phonemic entity; and since the subsequent history
shows one phoneme, our argument is in part nothing more than that of
parsimony.

In our still unpublished discussion of *i* vs. *io* and *e* vs. *eo* (Stockwell's
dissertation, University of Virginia, and a paper by Barritt at the 1955 Linguistic Society meeting), we do not maintain that these did not become
phonemic sets. Stockwell argued in his dissertation that these oppositions
became phonemic by early Middle English. Surveying some of the earliest
glosses, the *Epinal*, the *Erfurt*, and the *Corpus*, Barritt demonstrated a distribution which suggests the allophonic status of *eo* and *io* with *e* and *i*
respectively in early OE; however, in later documents (the *Orosius*, Aelfric's
*Colloquy*, and some Kentish Charters) the distribution is not clearly complementary (though is it also not unarguably contrastive) and seems to indicate
a split of the allophones into separate phonemes. At any rate, it becomes
merely a matter of agreeing on the date of the separation, a date which
Hockett indicates as earlier than we had thought. Neither Hockett's work nor
our own has shown the conditions that produced the split in the high and mid
front short vowels. This, of course, is the really critical issue. We, Hockett,
and the established tradition all agree that the short digraphs arose from
conditions which phonetically split the three short front vowels. Whatever
the graphic evidence, the reflexes of *æ–ea* do not indicate two phonemes,
whereas the later graphic evidence and a rather small number of reflexes do

appear to indicate two phonemes each from *i–ie* and *e–eo io* (especially in the southwestern dialects of Middle English). This is a problem really worth the sound and fury heretofore generated by *æ–ea*.

The stressed long syllabics of OE are quite a different problem. We hope to say more about them at a later date; here we point out only that Hockètt's handling of them has a good deal less to be said for it than his handling of the short digraphs. He is much concerned with the assumptions that can properly be made about graphic evidence, yet without stating his assumptions about the nature of the Great Vowel Shift, he asserts that "the existence of quantitative contrasts in OE is indisputable" (595), and that the scribe "was not trained to pay attention to quantitative differences" (588). No assumption of quantitative contrasts in OE can be properly validated, in our estimation, without close attention to the mechanism by which this quantitative system shifted to one which is clearly not quantitative. The assumption about the OE vowel system which is indisputable is that there were contrasts between syllabic nuclei of two types; but whether these types were differentiated by the presence vs. the absence of quantity, by the presence vs. the absence of glides, or (conceivably) by differences in height or tenseness or the like, is certainly open to considerable dispute.[12]

## FOOTNOTES

1. Charles F. Hockett, "The stressed syllabics of Old English," *Lg*. 35.575–97 (1959). [Reprinted here, pp. 108 ff.—Ed.]

2. Cottonian MS Vespasian A. 1, published under the directions of Henry Sweet, *Oldest English texts* 183–420 (London, 1885).

3. Stockwell and Barritt, *Some Old English graphemic-phonemic correspondences* (SIL, Occasional papers, No. 4; 1951), hereafter referred to as *OP* 4; "The Old English short digraphs: Some considerations," *Lg*. 31.372–89 (1955).

4. Hockett, *A course in modern linguistics* 375 (New York, 1958).

5. Stockwell and Barritt, *OP* 4.34–55.

6. For this information and for the information on Tamil and Nahuatl we are indebted to William Bright.

7. Kenneth L. Pike, *Phonemics: A technique for reducing languages to writing* 225 (Ann Arbor, 1947).

8. See Murray Fowler, "The segmental phonemes of Sanskritized Tamil," *Lg*. 30.362–3 (1954).

9. F. M. Stenton, *Anglo-Saxon England* 177 (Oxford, 1950).

10. See Stenton 177–90; P. H. Blair, *An introduction to Anglo-Saxon England* 311–29 (Cambridge, 1956). Stenton discusses in considerable detail the influence of Ireland and of the Continent on English letters, and mentions the "half uncial" script (178–9) as being of Irish origin. This script was still in use—along with the Continental style—until the tenth century. We offer this merely as one detail showing the power of tradition: even after the troubles of the ninth century, which destroyed most of the ancient Irish culture in England, this form of writing was maintained.

11. *Lg*. 30.1–42 (1954).

12. See Stockwell, "The ME 'long close' and 'long open' mid vowels," *Texas Studies in Literature and Language* 2.530–8 (1961). [For further reading on the vexing problem of the OE "short" digraphs, the most important sources are probably the following: Sherman M. Kuhn and Randolph Quirk, "Some recent interpretations of Old English digraph spellings," *Lg.* 29.143–56 (1953); Stockwell and Barritt, "The Old English short digraphs: Some considerations," *Lg.* 31.372–89 (1955); Kuhn and Quirk, "The Old English short digraphs: A reply," *Lg.* 31.390–401 (1955); Stockwell, "The phonology of Old English: A structural sketch," *SIL* 13.13–24 (1958); Stockwell and Rudolph Willard, "Further notes on Old English phonology," *SIL* 14.10–13 (1959); and Sherman M. Kuhn, "On the syllabic phonemes of Old English," *Lg.* 37.522–38 (1961).—Ed.]

## HANS KURATH

# The Loss of Long Consonants
# and the Rise of Voiced Fricatives
# in Middle English*

1. In OE,[1] long consonants are fully established in one and only one position: between a fully stressed or a half-stressed SHORT vowel (or diphthong) and a following unstressed vowel, as in *clyppan, settan, reccan, ebba, middel, hycgan, frogga, fremman, spinnan, spillan, steorra, sibban, missan, hliehhan* (*hlæhhan*), and (after a half-stressed short vowel) in *bliccettan* "glitter," *oretta* "challenger," *faranne* (inf.), *wēstenne* "wilderness."[2]

In MSS of the tenth century, double letters are written with great consistency in such words, whereas in other words single letters appear with equal consistency in the same position, e.g., in *witan* "know," *sunu* "son," *stelan* "steal." The consistent writing of double letters in some of these words and of single letters in others makes it clear that between a short stressed or half-stressed vowel and a following unstressed vowel long and short consonants are in phonemic contrast in OE. To support this inference from the spelling, one may cite such minimally differentiated pairs as *sittan* "sit" : *witan* "know," *sellan* "sell" : *stelan* "steal."

In OE, double consonants are also written at the end of stressed monosyllables whose dissyllabic forms have long consonants after short vowels, as in *bed(d), cyn(n), eal(l)*, infl. *beddes, cynnes, ealle*, but without consistency. From this inconsistency in spelling we may safely draw the inference that long consonants were no longer phonemic in this position; for if OE had preserved long consonant phonemes at the end of words, they would be written with the same consistency as long consonants between vowels. We must therefore regard such spellings as *bedd, cynn, eall*, beside *bed, cyn, eal* as analogical to the spellings of the inflected forms, i.e., as instances of standardized spellings of the morphemes in question, each of which had two stem variants (allomorphs) in the paradigm.

Double writing, of stops and fricatives only, occurs furthermore between a short stressed vowel and a following sonorant, as (1) in *ap(p)las* "apples," *bet(t)ra* "better," *bit(t)re* (infl.), *offrian* "sacrifice" (from Latin), and (2) in *at(t)re* (dat.) "poison," *æt(t)rig* "poisonous," *æd(d)re* "vein," *næd(d)re* "adder," *mab(b)um* "treasure." All native words in these two groups had stem variants (allomorphs): in group (1) e.g., *æpel/æppel/æp(p)l-/ap(p)l-*,

* From *Language* 32.435–45 (1956). Reprinted by permission of the author and the Linguistic Society of America.

*biter/bitter/bit(t)r-*; in group (2) e.g., *nædr-/næder-/næd(d)r-/nædder-, māþm-/ maþþum.*[3]

It is generally assumed, and properly so, that in such words stops and fricatives were lengthened in those forms in which they were immediately followed by a sonorant, e.g., in dat. pl. *applum < \*aplo-miz*, but not in nom. and acc. sg. *æpel < \*apl < \*apla-z, \*apla-m*, whereupon either stem variant could be extended to the entire paradigm.[4]

Apparent inconsistencies in the OE spelling should, I believe, be interpreted as follows. (1) Since consonant length in other historical types was unquestionably phonemic between vowels, we must take the spelling variants *biter ~ bitter, æpel ~ æppel, māþm ~ maþþum* at face value and admit the existence of variations (unsettled or regional usage) in this position. (2) On the other hand, the variation in the spelling of the consonants between a SHORT vowel and a following sonorant, as in *bittre/bitre, æppla/æpla, nædre/ næddre*, should be taken as reflecting the phonemically ambiguous status of phonically long stops and fricatives in a position in which phonically short consonants did not occur.

This interpretation is not in conflict with the historical observation that long stops and fricatives actually developed before sonorants in prehistoric Old English (West Germanic) and were secondarily extended to the intervocalic position, e.g., from pl. *æppla* to sg. *æppel*, which occurs in historic Old English alongside the old sg. *æpel*. The shape of the older sg. form, it may be noted, survives in ME *āker* (OE *acer*), whereas all other words in this group have short vowels in ME in accordance with the normal development of OE short vowels before long consonants and before consonant groups, as in *appel, ap(p)les* from OE *æppel, æp(p)la(s)*.

In summary we may say that c1000 Old English had contrastive long consonant phonemes only in the sequence /v́ccv/, i.e., between a stressed or half-stressed short vowel and a following unstressed vowel, as in *settan, hycgan, spinnan*, etc. and in *bitter, æppel*.[5]

Before turning to ME, brief comments on relevant aspects of OE spelling will be appropriate. (1) In accordance with Latin spelling, phonemically long and short vowels are not identified in OE, but phonemically long and short consonants are. (2) Although double consonant symbols stand for long consonants, they also indicate indirectly the quantity of the preceding vowel, which is always short in this position. (3) We may therefore expect, especially in view of the defective spelling of phonemically long and short vowels, that the double writing of consonants will be retained as a diacritic of vowel quantity after its primary function is lost with the loss of phonemically long consonants. It is this adaptation of double consonant symbols to a new function—the retention of the old spelling for a new purpose—that conceals from us the sweeping changes in the consonant system of Middle English. Hence, spelling alone will be of little help in our problem. We must look to other clues.

2. The most important lead for tracing the history of the long consonants comes from a consideration of the structure of sound sequences and the development of the sounds in these sequences in ME. Since the long consonants of OE occur only between vowels, we shall consider those sequences of OE in which a single consonant, long or short, is flanked by vowels. These sequences are three in number:

(1) /v́ccv/, as in *sittan, sunna, tellan, frogga, bannan*;
(2) /v́cv/, as in *witan, sunu, brecan, brocen, bana*;
(3) /v́vcv/, as in *wītan, brūcan, blēdan, sōna, stānas*.[6]

It should be clear that here both vowels and consonants have functional (phonemic) length, since any SHORT consonant can be preceded by either a short or a long vowel (e.g., *wītan* "blame" but *witan* "know"), and any short vowel can be followed by either a short or a long consonant (e.g., *witan* "know" but *sittan* "sit"). It must further be granted that both vowels and consonants will retain phonemic length as long as these three sequences are preserved, whereas the coalescence of any two of the sequences would result in complementary distribution of long and short vowels, long and short consonants, or both. In either event contrastive quantity would be lost either in the vowel system or in the consonant system.

From these preliminary observations we shall now turn to a consideration of the history of long consonants in Middle English, which in the transition period from OE to ME occurred unambiguously only in the sequence /v́ccə/.

There is general agreement among scholars that in the Northeast Midland and in parts of the North, apparently from Norfolk northward to Yorkshire (or beyond), the sequence /v́cə/ changed to /v́vcə/ in words of two syllables, through the lengthening of ALL short stressed vowels in this position, some time before 1200. Thus OE *talu, brecan, (ge)brocen, witan, sunu* became ME *tāle, bręken, brǫken, wįten > węten, sųne > sǫne*, coalescing in type with ME *bǫnes, ręden*, etc. from OE *bānes, rēdan* (Anglian), etc.

The elimination of the sequence /v́cə/ in these dialects of the East Midland left only two sequences, in which PHONICALLY long and short consonants as well as PHONICALLY long and short vowels were in complementary distribution. How are the two PHONIC sequences [v́vcə] and [v́ccə] to be interpreted in phonemic terms? Are both the vowels and the consonants PHONEMICALLY long?

The answer, it seems to me, is perfectly clear. (1) Since phonic vowel length is phonemic in the sequences /v́vc/ versus /v́c/, as in *bǫk, fīn* vs. *buk, fin*, it is also phonemic in the sequences [v́vcə] vs. [v́ccə] despite complementary distribution. (2) On the other hand, since contrastive phonemically long consonants are restricted to the sequence /v́ccə/ before the coalescence of /v́cə/ with /v́vcə/, the resulting complementary distribution of phonically long and short consonants in the two remaining sequences, [v́ccə] and [v́vcə], deprives the long consonants of their phonemic function; that is, the phonic sequences [v́ccə] and [v́vcə] have become /v́cə/ and /v́vcə/, in which only vowel length is phonemic (functional).

The changes brought about by the lengthening of all short vowels in the sequence /v́cə/ in these Northeast Midland and Northern dialects of ME can be conveniently summarized as follows:

|  | 1000 | a1200 |
| --- | --- | --- |
| (1) | /v́vcv/ | phonically [v́vcə], phonemically /v́vcə/ |
| (2) | /v́cv/ | falls together with (1) |
| (3) | /v́ccv/ | phonically [v́ccə], phonemically /v́cə/ |

This loss of phonemically long consonants in intervocalic position inevitably entailed the loss of phonemically long consonants before sonorants, as in *apples, bittre, offren*, whose phonemic status depended upon the contrastive consonant length in the sequences /v́cv/:/v́ccv/. Remaining phonically long, stops and fricatives in this position became allophonic.

It is interesting to observe that a PHONIC change in the vowels of the sequence /v́cə/ subverts the PHONEMIC status of the long consonants in the sequences /v́ccə/ and /v́ccr, v́ccl/ without changing them phonically, and thus eliminates phonemic length from the consonant system of these dialects of ME.

The loss of phonemic length in the consonant system of the dialects of the Northeast Midland and parts of the North resulted (1) in the elimination of the long sonorants /mm, nn, ll, rr/ and the long stops /pp, bb, tt, dd, čč, ǰǰ, kk, gg/ of older English as separate phonemic entities, and (2) in the regrouping of the voiced and the voiceless allophones of the fricatives /f, þ, s/.

Since in older English the long sonorants and stops contrasted with their short counterparts only in length, the long and the short simply coalesce into one set of sonorants and stops, namely /m, n, l, r/ and /p, b, t, d, č, ǰ, k, g/, all of which occur before, after, and between vowels.

The development of the fricatives is more complicated. The older English short fricative phonemes /f, þ, s/ had voiced allophones [v, ð, z] between vowels, and contrasted in this position with the voiceless long fricatives /ff, þþ, ss/ both in quantity and in vocalization. Since quantity was the sole distinctive feature between the short and the long sonorants and stops, the quantitative difference between short and long fricatives of OE must be regarded, from the point of view of the system, as their primary distinctive feature, and the difference in vocalization as a secondary, concomitant feature. With the loss of quantity as a distinctive feature in the stops and the sonorants, and hence also in the fricatives, voicing becomes the distinctive feature of the fricatives in intervocalic position. Thus, although between vowels the phonemes /f, þ, s/ and /ff, þþ, ss/ of older English continue to be pronounced as [v, ð, z] and [ff, þþ, ss] respectively, undergoing no PHONIC change, they now contrast PHONEMICALLY as /v, ð, z/ vs. /f, þ, s/.

The shift from length to vocalization as the distinctive feature entailed a regrouping of the allophones of the fricatives. Intervocalic [ff, þþ, ss], derived from the older phonemes /ff, þþ, ss/, join the initial and final allophones [f, þ, s] of the older phonemes /f, þ, s/ to constitute the new phonemes /f, þ, s/, while the intervocalic allophones [v, ð, z] of the phonemes /f, þ, s/ of older English come to function as the separate phonemes /v, ð, z/.

At this stage in the development of the English consonant system the voiced fricatives /v, ð, z/ occurred only between vowels, as in *liven, bathen, risen*. Initial /v/ became established later through the adoption of French words, such as *veile, venim, vertu*; intial /z/, through the slow adoption of such words as *zele* "zeal," *zodiac* (usually *sodiac* and always *senith, cenith* "zenith"). Initial /ð/ arises at a later date from a native development in such normally (or frequently) unstressed words as *the, there, than*, starting as a prosodic allophone.

Not until final /ə/ was lost, beginning c1300 in the North Midland and the North, did the voiced fricatives /v, ð, z/ also occur in final position, e.g., *live, bathe, rise*.

The fricative /š/, as in *ship, fish, fishes*, has no voiced counterpart in ME. It is derived from the OE cluster *sc*, which yielded long /šš/ between a short stressed vowel and a following unstressed vowel, and a short /š/ in all other positions—in accordance with the restrictions governing the occurrence of long consonants in late OE. Evidence for this development is scant, but quite unambiguous. OE *flǣsces* (gen.) appears in ME either as *flęshes* /vvcə/, with shortening of the consonant, or as *flesshes* /vccə/, presumably in regional distribution. Southwestern ME *eschen* "ask" /vccə/, from OE *āscian*, clearly shows the shortening of *ā* to *a* > *e* before the rounding of *ā* to *ō*. For examples see Kurath and Kuhn, *Middle Engl. dict.* under *flesh* and *asken*.

A voiced partner of /š/ arises in MnE through the assimilation of medial /zj/ to /ž/, as in *measure, azure*.

From this brief sketch it should be clear that the fricatives of English have a rather complicated history in ME. As has been pointed out above, the contrast between voiceless and voiced fricatives arose in medial position before 1200 through a native development in the dialects here discussed. This development must have facilitated the acceptance of this contrast in initial position in French and Latin loanwords during the thirteenth century. When, with the loss of final /ə/ during the fourteenth century, the voiced fricatives came to stand also in final position, the voiced–voiceless contrast had been extended to all positions, a situation that has persisted to this day.[7]

The loss of long consonants as phonemic entities in the Middle English dialects of the Northeast Midlands and the Northern areas as a consequence of the lengthening of all short vowels in the sequence /v́cə/ before 1200 is only sporadically reflected in the spelling of the manuscripts, since the double writing of the formerly long consonant phonemes is retained to indicate short vowels.

Clear evidence for the changes in the consonant system may be expected only in unconventional spelling systems, such as that of Orm, who uses

double consonant letters with remarkable consistency to indicate that a preceding vowel, stressed or unstressed, is short. He does this not only where
older English had long consonants but also where it had short consonants.
Thus Orm writes *mann, forr, þatt; fissk, rihht; manness, fillenn*, etc.; *bedd,
beddess*, but *bede; wittness*, but *witen; summ*, but *sume; godd, staff*, but *godes,
stafes; little*, but *litell*, etc. On this interpretation of Orm's use of double
consonant letters scholars are in complete agreement; but no one appears to
have drawn from his practice the conclusion that Orm would not have used
this spelling device if long consonants had still been phonemic in his dialect
(Lincolnshire, a1200). It is, however, quite certain that in his dialect Orm has
only the two phonemic sequences /v́cə/, as in *mannes, wittes, sunne*, and
/v́vcə/, as in *godes, witenn, sune*.

It should be pointed out that the adoption of this spelling device did not
remove the ambiguity of the vowel letters in Orm's orthography, but it reduced their burden from three phonemes to two, by identifying the short
vowels.[8] Also, it leaves the quantity of word-final vowels unmarked, as in
*clene, temmple*, which end in /ə/; in *se, be* (sbj. of *sen, ben*), which have /ẹ̄/; in
the pronouns *he, we*, and the preconsonantal variants of the prepositions *i*
"in" and *o* "on," which probably had two allomorphs each, ending in a long
and a short vowel respectively. Of more serious consequence is the resulting
ambiguity of the spellings *ff* and *ss*, which in Orm's system represent both
/f, s/ and /v, z/, as in *offrenn, blisse* and in *heffne, grissli* respectively. Since,
however, *ff* and *ss* between vowels always stand for voiceless fricatives in
Orm's spelling, the ambiguity is confined to the relatively few words in which
the fricative is followed by a sonorant, as in *offrenn* /ofrən/ and *heffne*
/hevnə/.

3. It has been shown above that the loss of long consonant phonemes in
the Northeast Midland and parts of the North resulted from the elimination
of the sequence /v́cə/, which, on the evidence of Orm's spelling, occurred no
later than 1200. This theory implies that long consonant phonemes would
persist as such in dialects of Middle English that preserve the sequence /v́cə/
along with the sequence /v́ccə/, the only sequences in which /cc/ contrasts with
/c/.

Such a situation is generally assumed, though not presented in these terms,
for the South Midland dialect and for Southern. In these dialects the mid
vowels /e, o/ and the low vowel /a/ were lengthened in the sequence /v́cə/, as
in the North Midland and the North, but the high vowels /i, u/ remained
short. Since, as a result of this change, the sequences /ecə, ocə, acə/ became
/ẹ̄cə, ọ̄cə, ācə/, falling in with the old sequence /v́vcə/, the sequence /v́cə/ came
to be restricted to /icə/ and /ucə/.

Henceforth the sequences /eccə, occə, accə/ contrast only with /ẹ̄cə, ọ̄cə,
ācə/; but /iccə, uccə/ contrasts both with /icə, ucə/ and with /īcə, ūcə/. That is
to say, after the low vowels /a, ā/ and the mid vowels /e, ẹ̄, ẹ̄; o, ọ, ọ̄/, long and

short consonants occur in complementary distribution (a long consonant only after a short vowel, a short consonant only after a long vowel), and might therefore be regarded as positional allophones rather than as separate phonemes. However, since both long and short consonants occur in these dialects after short /i, u/, as in *sittan* "sit," *sŏnne* "sun" vs. *witan* "know," *sŏne* "son," long consonants clearly remain phonemic in the sequences /iccə, uccə/ vs. /icə, ucə/. Hence the phonetically long consonants after short /a, e, o/ must be taken as phonemically long also, though they never contrast with short consonants in these positions.

How long do phonemically long consonants persist in these dialects, including the literary dialect of the London area? The generally accepted view is, that phonemically long consonants disappeared c1400, with the loss of final /ə/ in the sequence /vccə/; but that is only part of a rather complicated story, which is initiated by the loss of final /ə/.

The loss of long consonants in these dialects, we may feel sure, occurred in three or four stages:

(1) The word-final sequence /vccə/ became /vc/, as in *sitten, frogge, sunne, tellen, missen, laughen > sit, frog, sun, tel, mis, laugh*. At this stage, the inflected forms *sitteth, frogges*, etc. still had long consonants, so that such words had variant allomorphs, e.g., /sit/ ~ /sitt-/, /frog/ ~ /frogg-/.

(2) Some word-final sequences of the type of /vcc-əc/ became /vc-c/, as in *sittes* (replacing *sitteth*), *frogges > sits, frogs*; but others retained /ə/, and hence also the long consonants, as *misses, wasshes*. At this stage, such inflected words as *sit : sitting, mis : misses, missing* still had allomorphs with phonemically short and long consonants respectively. Variant allomorphs occurred at this time also in the dissyllabics *bitter ~ bit(t)r-e, appel ~ ap(p)l-es, adder ~ ad(d)r-es, letter ~ let(t)r-es*.

(3) The allomorphs with phonemically long consonants were eliminated within the paradigms of inflected words and in derivational sets, under pressure of the great majority of words that had no such allomorphs.

(4) At this stage, these dialects of English had given up contrastive length in the consonants, except for a residue of plurisyllabics, such as *shilling, fissūre*, in which only long consonants occurred within the paradigm. Here the phonically long intervocalic consonants after a short vowel are interpreted as consonants pure and simple, since the phonic length of consonants had become allophonic in the vast majority of words current in English— short consonants after long vowels, long consonants after short vowels.

Steps (1) and (2) in the history of the long consonants are the result of a well documented phonemic change, the loss of /ə/; step (3) is an instance of stem-leveling, a common process in Middle English and in early Modern English (cf. *dai ~ dau-es > dai, dai-es; liğğ-en ~ lī-eth > lī-en, lī-eth; whīt ~ whīt-re > whīt, whīt-er*); step (4) results from the pressure of the dominant pattern (Systemzwang)—here the lack of contrastive consonant length in the bulk of the English vocabulary.

Between steps (2) and (3) the phonemic status of phonically long consonants must have fluctuated, as the extreme instability of their spelling c1400 betrays. A language cannot pass from one system to another without temporary disorganization.[9]

4. In what precedes we have undertaken to show (1) that phonically long consonants had lost their phonemic status by 1200 in the dialects of the Northeast Midland and parts of the North, as the result of the lengthening of ALL short vowels, including /i, u/, in the sequence /v́cə/; (2) that phonically long consonants retained their phonemic status until c1400 in the Southeast Midland dialect, and in all other dialects in which the sequences /ícə, úcə/ survived unaltered and thus contrasted with the sequences /íccə, úccə/; and (3) that the elimination of the long consonant phonemes in these dialects was initiated by the loss of /ə/ in the sequence /v́ccə/, which was thus reduced to /v́c/.

In Chaucer's London the Southeast Midland type predominated; but it seems safe to assume that the Northeast Midland type was also current to some extent. Other Northeast Midland features, such as the leveled stem of the ablaut preterit, the extension of the *s*-plural in nouns, the regularized forms of the 2nd and 3rd singular of the present, the *n*-plural of the present, and the pronoun *thei*, were widely current in London in Chaucer's time. Still other features, such as *theim* and the 3rd sg. in -(*e*)*s*, intruded later from the same direction. Whatever the explanation in terms of economic, social, and cultural history for this persistent intrusion of North Midland features in the London area may be, its reality cannot be doubted.[10]

In view of this dominant trend, the currency in Chaucer's London of the North Midland derivatives /ḝcə, ǭcə/ from earlier /icə, ucə/ can hardly be questioned. (1) Spellings such as *reden* "ridden," *to wete* "to wit," *dede* "did," *stodes* "studs," *sholen* "shall" are not uncommon in the Brewers' Records (1422–5).[11] (2) The Midland type became established in Standard English *beetle* (OE *bitela*), *creek* (cf. OIcel. *criki*), *week* (OE *wicu*), *weevil* (OE *wifel*), *wood* (OE *wudu*), and must therefore have been current in London at a rather early date. (3) The common spellings *rody* (OE *rudig*, MnE *ruddy*), *rode* (OE *rudu*), *wouke* (OE *wucu*, from *wicu*) in early-fifteenth-century MSS also point to the currency of the North Midland type in London English at the turn of the century.

In view of the great probability that alongside the South Midland type the North Midland type of the features under discussion had some currency in London during the latter part of the fourteenth century, Chaucer's rime practice, and the reasons for it, call for reconsideration.

Chaucer keeps the ME derivatives of the OE contrastive sequences /íccv: ícv:ḝcv/ and /úccv:úcv:ǭcv/ strictly apart. He never rimes /icə/, as in the ppls. *riden, writen*, with /iccə/, as in the infs. *bidden, sitten*, or with /ḝcə/, as in *fḝden, grḝten*. Correspondingly, /ucə/, as in *sŏne* "son," never rimes with

/uccə/, as in *sŏnne* "sun," or with /ǭcə/, as in *sǭne* "soon." This rime practice mirrors the phonemic features of the South Midland dialect to perfection: both vowels and consonants have phonemic length.[12]

Although Chaucer's rime practice clearly conforms to the South Midland dialect of the latter part of the fourteenth century, must we assume that he was unfamiliar with the divergent situation in the North Midland type? Should we not consider an alternative motivation for his deliberate practice? I think we should. If words like the ppls. of *rīden* and *wrīten* had two different pronunciations in London, rimming with *fę̄den* and *grę̄ten* in the speech of some of his contemporaries but not in that of others, Chaucer might well avoid such rimes for that very reason. For the same reason he would forgo riming *sone* (OE *sunu*) with *sone* (OE *sōna*). Moreover, he would then also avoid riming *riden, writen, sŏne*, etc., with *bidden, sitten, sŏnne*, etc., whether the latter still had PHONEMICALLY long consonants or not. By adhering to self-rime he could satisfy all of his readers, whatever their dialect.

5. The brief comments offered below on several texts representing different literary dialects written in rather consistent and largely unique orthographies should serve to point up the types of evidence that are relevant to the problem under discussion, and to illustrate the types of analogical and phonic changes that resulted in eliminating long consonants in certain words or positions prior to the loss of phonemically long consonants, or on the other hand, in introducing them on such models as *bed*:*beddes*. When the evidence of rimes is not available, a systematic analysis of spelling habits and a tabulation of consistent vs. sporadic deviations from the "historically" normal spelling offer the only hope for tenable inferences. Since the double writing of originally long consonants—which occurred only short vowels even in the oldest English known to us—remained orthographically functional after the loss of long consonant phonemes, serving as an indicator (diacritic) of short vowels, the spelling evidence, scant as it is, demands extremely cautious handling.

*Ancrene Riwle.*   A rapid reading of pp. 101–26 of Mabel Day's edition of the Nero MS of the *Ancrene Riwle* (London, 1952), written in an orthography devised to render a Southwestern (Southwest Midland) literary dialect of c1225, and rather consistently applied, leaves no doubt that between a stressed short vowel and /ə/, contrastive long and short consonants of older English are preserved. The only clear deviations observed in a rather cursory reading of the 25 pages are these: (1) *dredfule, gledfule, seoruhfule, wunderfule* (but *fulle*); *leofmone* (also 47/34 *leofmones*); (2) ჳ*ichinge* (cf. OE *giččan*), *grime* (also *grimme*); (3) *summe, summe-cherre* (3 ×); *schullen, schallen*; *troddeþ*; (4) *luddere* "louder," *schennure* "brighter," *woddre* "angrier"; *sliddrie* "slippery"; (5) *nammore* (2 ×) "no more."

In group 1 the originally long consonants are shortened under weak stress, a purely phonetic process that occurred also in other dialects. In group 2 we may simply have aberrant spellings. In group 3 long consonants may have been introduced on the model of such sets of all omorphsas *bed* : *bedd-es*, unless the doubled letters merely indicate that the preceding vowel is short. In group 4 the double letters probably show that the preceding vowel is short, though *d* (hardly *n*) may actually have been lengthened phonically before *r*, as in *woddre* (< *wod-re* < OE *wōd-re*). *Nammóre*, stressed on the second syllable, may have a spelling patterned on Old French, a spelling that appears in many words taken into Middle English, such as *af(f)órcen*, *al(l)óuen*, *as(s)ígnen*, in which the spelling of the consonant BEFORE the stressed vowel varies in English as well as in French.

*Ayenbite of Inwit.* Even a casual sampling of short passages (150–4, 172–83) of the *Ayenbite*, written in 1340 in a fairly consistent orthography created to render a Southeastern (Kentish) literary dialect, makes it perfectly clear that long consonants between vowels are kept apart from short consonants, for example in *habbeþ*, *nette*, *zeþþe*, *nesssse* ( : *ulesse*), *beginne*, *conne*, *alle*, *uolle*, as opposed to *betere*, *biter*, *nime*, *siker*, *loue*, *ynome*, *come*, *zome*, *wones*.

But there are some troublesome problems. (1) Under secondary stress, long consonants seem to have been sometimes shortened, as in *to comene*, from OE *cumanne* (with which compare the inconsistent treatment in *to done*, *to zyenne*), sometimes preserved, as in the suffix *-nesse*. (2) *Eddre*, *little* ( : *litel*), *gratter* "greater" (beside *grater*) pose the same problem as in the *Ancrene Riwle* above. (3) the spelling of *onneaþe* (7 ×), with *nn* preceding the stressed vowel, seems to be modeled on that of words taken from Latin or OF, such as *commun* (6 ×). (4) the *tt* in *abbotte(s)* (3 ×) is puzzling. Obviously, a systematic study of the spelling of this important MS is needed to deal with such peculiarities.

*The Gawain Poet.* The rime practice of the *Gawain* poet largely agrees with Chaucer's, which is not surprising in the literary dialect of a contemporary of Chaucer. Nevertheless, there are several interrimes in the *Pearl* that point to an infusion from the Northeast Midland dialect: *gome*, *com*, *innome* (OE *u*) in lines 697–703 rime with *dome* (OE *ō*), and *won* (OE *u*) in line 918 rimes with *done*, *mone* (OE *ō*), the vowel being /ǭ/. Though there is no rime evidence for [ę̄] from OE *i*, the spelling *e* in *smeten* (ppl. of *smīten*) in *Gawain* 1763, and *glede* "kite" in *Cleanness* 1696 may be taken to represent /ę̄/.[13]


6. My object has been to sketch in outline the history of phonemically long consonants from OE to late ME times, from a structural point of view. I hope to have shown (1) that the loss of functionally long consonants occurred in some dialects of ME before 1200, in others not until c1400; (2) that in these two dialectal types the loss of phonemically long consonants resulted from very different causes; and (3) that the loss of phonemic length in consonants entailed the rise of voicing as a distinctive feature of intervocalic fricatives. These developments have not been treated adequately, if at all, by earlier students of English, although they produce rather revolutionary changes in the English consonant system.[14]

## FOOTNOTES

1. The substance of this paper was presented in the Linguistic Forum at the University of Michigan in the summer of 1953. The results are briefly stated in H. Kurath and S. M. Kuhn, *Middle English dictionary: Plan and bibliography* 6 (Ann Arbor, 1954).

2. Most long consonants in this position result from the assimilation of /j/ to the preceding consonant, as in *settan* < *\*satja-nam*; a few are inherited from Proto-Germanic, in as *fulle* < *\*fullai*. Since /j/ was assimilated to a consonant without lengthening it if the consonant was preceded by a long vowel, a diphthong, or a short vowel plus consonant (as in *sēcan* "seek," *hwǣte* "wheat," *sendan* < *\*sōkja-*, *\*hwaitja-*, *\*sandja-*), long consonants occur only after short vowels in OE (as also in continental West Germanic; NHG *weizen* has /ts/ from /t/ in syllable-initial position, as in *wälzen*.).

3. Since in one and the same morpheme OE did not have long vowels before long consonants in other positions, it must certainly be assumed that long vowels were shortened when a following consonant before a sonorant was lengthened.

4. Corresponding developments occurred in the other West Germanic languages, which display similar variation; e.g., OHG *affal* beside *apfal* "apple," *ahhar* beside *ackar* "field." See K. Luick, *Hist. Gram.* § 631.3 and *Anm.* 7; W. Wilmanns, *Deutsche Gram.* 1.192 (1911).

5. It should be noted that this statement refers only to the occurrence of /v́cc-v/, in which both consonants belong to the same morpheme. Complex forms such as the preterits *rǣd-de* "advised," *mēt-te* "met," do not have long consonants, but sequences of identical short consonants, i.e., such forms must be taken as /v́vc-cv/. Here OE retains long vowels, which in late OE or early ME are shortened before these consonant clusters. The derivative ME *red-de*, *met-te*, /vc-cə/, are also complex; they become *red*, *met* in late ME.

6. For convenience, long vowel phonemes are represented by /vv/, long consonant phonemes by /cc/.

7. In the Southern dialects of ME, which had only [v, ð, z] in initial position, the introduction of /f, s/ in French and Latin loan words created the contrast in this position.

8. In Orm's spelling of the long vowels (identified as long by a following single consonant letter) only *æ* is unambiguous, as in *hæte* (OE*ǣ* < *\*ai/j*), *dæp* (OE *ēa*), *ærd* (OE *eard*). *e* and *o* represent both close /ē, ọ/ and open /ę, ǫ/; *i* and *u* stand for close /ī, ụ/ and for open /ị, ụ/ (later /ē, ọ/), as in *min* (OE *ī*), *fir* (OE *ȳ*), *hus* (OE *ū*), and in *witen* (OE *i*), *sune* (OE *u*), respectively; *a* spells a low back vowel /ā/ (later /ǫ/) in *stan* (OE *ā*) and a low front vowel /ā/ in *name* (OE *a*). The open high vowels of this dialect later coalesced with the close mid vowels, the low back vowel with the open mid back vowel, as in *wę̄ten*, *sǫne*, and in *stǫn* respectively. It should also be pointed out that the letter *e* has a third value, standing for /ə/ in unstressed syllables.

9. Some American structuralists are reluctant to admit this obvious fact. The aim of the structural analysis is, after all, to discover the extent of the systematization in a language at a given time, not to impose a system on it.

10. For an important recent statement concerning the influx, beginning c1300, prominent merchant families from Norfolk, Lincolnshire, and other East Midland counties into London, see Eilert Eckwall, *Two early London subsidy rolls* 69–70 (*Skrifter utgivna av Kungl. Humanistiska Vetenskapssamfundet i Lund*, Vol. 48; 1953).

11. R. W. Chambers and Majorie Daunt, *A book of London English, 1384–1425* 140–91 (Oxford, 1931).

12. Since the sequences /icə/ and /ucə/ occur only in a small number of words, Chaucer's ingenuity in finding suitable rimes for such words was severely taxed. For instance, *love* (n. and v.) occurs more than 700 times in verse, but only 44 times in rime (38 times with *abŏve*, 3 times with the ppl. *shŏve*, and once with *Lŏve*); *sŏme* occurs more than 300 times, but only 13 times in rime (12 times with *cŏme*); *sŏne* occurs about 120 times, but only 8 times in rime (invariably with *wŏne* n. and v.); *wŏde* "wood" occurs 21 times, but never in rime; *dide* "did" occurs about 180 times, but only once in rime. On the other hand, the ppl. (*i*)*nŏme* occurs only in rime (8 times with *cŏme*, once with *sŏme*). Here Chaucer uses the "Southern" verb, which had been replaced by *taken* in contemporary London speech, for the sake of the rime. There could be no clearer evidence for his determination to use only self-rime. [The diacritic ˘ above an *o* indicates that it is a spelling for *u*.—Ed.]

13. Mabel Day and Mary S. Serjeantson, p. xlvi of their edition of *Gawain* (London, 1940) regard this as "unlikely"; and R. Menner, p. lx of his edition of *Cleanness* (New Haven, 1920) points out that the spelling *e*, which occurs in *þeder* (64, 461) beside *i* (45, 61) also turns up along with *i* in *wekked* (855), *wykked* (570), where the vowel is certainly short. However, the clear rime evidence for /ǭ/ from OE *u*, supports the view that /ē/ from OE *i*, a parallel feature of the Northeast Midland dialects, had a degree of currency in this literary dialect.

14. The only fairly detailed treatment of long consonants in Old English is given in Karl Luick, *Historische Grammatik der englischen Sprache* 797–932, edited from Luick's notes by F. Wild and H. Koziol. Although the structural point of view (analogous patterning) was not at all foreign to Luick—witness his treatment of the sweeping quantitative changes in the vowels of late OE and early ME (§§ 203–6, 352) and his presentation of the Great Vowel Shift of late ME and early MnE (§§ 479 ff.), his treatment of the long consonants is plainly nonstructural. Hence my interpretation of double consonant letters written at the ends of words and before sonorants differs sharply from that of Luick and his editors.

*ROBERT P. STOCKWELL*

# The Middle English "Long Close" and "Long Open" Mid Vowels*

The relation between a linguistic structure at a given date and a derived linguistic structure at a later date can be stated as a series of rules by which the later structure can be generated from the earlier, plus exceptions. The generating rules are called sound laws, but exceptions do not invalidate laws of this type: they merely require that stronger generalizations be sought that will permit a shorter list of exceptions.

One of the strong generating rules of traditional historical English phonology is that short vowels, when lengthened, appear in the quality of the matching long vowels, and that long vowels, when shortened, appear in the quality of the matching short vowels.[1] The rule may be written in some such form as this:[2]

$$
\text{OE} \left\{ \begin{array}{c} \breve{\imath} \\ \breve{e} \\ \breve{æ} \\ \breve{a} \\ \breve{o} \\ \breve{u} \end{array} \right\} \text{ plus length} \rightarrow \text{LOE} \left\{ \begin{array}{c} \bar{\imath} \\ \bar{e} \\ \bar{æ} \\ \bar{a} \\ \bar{o} \\ \bar{u} \end{array} \right.
$$

$$
\text{OE} \left\{ \begin{array}{c} \bar{\imath} \\ \bar{e} \\ \bar{æ} \\ \bar{a} \\ \bar{o} \\ \bar{u} \end{array} \right\} \text{ minus length} \rightarrow \text{LOE} \left\{ \begin{array}{c} \breve{\imath} \\ \breve{e} \\ \breve{æ} \\ \breve{a} \\ \breve{o} \\ \breve{u} \end{array} \right.
$$

Examples to prove that lengthened vowels (lengthened, for instance, before certain clusters in the tenth century) behaved just like the inherited long vowels may be cited at greater length for some vowels than for others. One of each will serve:

| OE *wĭlde* | like | OE *wīs* |
|------------|------|----------|
| OE *fĕld* | like | OE *grēne* |
| OE *ǽ* | like | (see discussion below) |

---

* From *Texas Studies in Literature and Language* 2.259–68 (1961). Reprinted by permission of the author and the University of Texas Press.

OE (Ang.) *ăld*    like    OE *stān*

OE *gŏld*    like    OE *fōd* (i.e., → *Gould*)

OE *grŭnd*    like    OE *hūs*

/ǣ/ had earlier broken in many of the environments which later caused lengthening. In the remaining environments that later caused lengthening (i.e., those that consisted of nasal plus voiced stop), the following nasal had maintained the quality of WGmc /ă/ as low central or back in opposition with the shift to low front that otherwise occurred under Frisian influence.[3] It is therefore difficult, perhaps impossible, to cite examples of /ǣ/ vs. /ǣ/ which are revealing in their subsequent history in the same way that examples from the other five vowels are. No problem exists in establishing the essential validity of the generalization, however; we merely reverse it, and examples are numerous. /ǣ/, with shortening, has the subsequent history that the generalization predicts: OE *blǣdre*, shortened, is *blǽddre*, becoming MnE *bladder*, with the normal history of any OE /ǽ/. Similarly for the other five vowels: *hid* (OE *hȳdde*), *kept* (OE *cēpte*), *soft* (OE *sōfte*), *hussy* (OE *hūswīf*), *lamb* (OE *lāmbru*).

This generalization, then, is one of very considerable power, and any apparent exceptions to it should be studied carefully before either throwing it out (which, as far as I know, no one has suggested) or setting up additional subsidiary generalizations for data that are thought to be unaccountable under the primary one. It is on a generalization of precisely the latter type that I wish to focus our attention, one that is to be found in every standard reference book on the subject of historical English phonology.

This subsidiary generalization can be stated as follows: /ē/ (long close *e*) and /ō/ (long close *o*) when shortened during ME times fell in with /ĭ/ and /ŭ/, and, conversely, /ĭ/ and /ŭ/ when lengthened during ME times fell in with /ē/ and /ō/.[4] Examples:

*Shortening*[5]

OE *rēdels*    → ME, MnE *riddle*

OE *sēc, sēoc*    → ME, MnE *sick*

OE *hrēc*    → ME, MnE (*hay*) *rick*

OE *brēc*    → ME, MnE *breeches*

OE *sēlig*    → ME, MnE *silly*

OE *blōd*    → LME *blŭd*, MnE *blood*

OE *flōd*    → LME *flŭd*, MnE *flood*

*Lengthening*

OE *wicu*    → ME *wēke*, MnE *week*

OE *bitel*(*a*)    → ME *bētel*, MnE *beetle*

OE *wifel*    → ME *wēvel*, MnE *weevil*

OE *yfel*    → EME *ivel*    → ME *ēvel*, MnE *evil*

OE *wudu*        → ME *wōde*, MnE *wood*
OE *duru*        → ME *dōre*, MnE *door*
OE *lufu*        → ME *lōve*, MnE *love*

Examples of shortening in the above pattern are a good deal scarcer than examples of lengthening, since lengthening in the open syllable is a regular occurrence in the thirteenth century. The lengthening occurred after OE /ē/ and /ō/ had become what are ordinarily called "long close *e* and *o*," i.e., ME /ē/ and /ō/, in contrast with "long open *e* and *o*," i.e., ME /ę̄/ and /ǭ/. The long open vowels are never the reflexes of OE /ē/ and /ō/. They come from ME /ĕ/ and /ŏ/ lengthened in the open syllable, or from OE *ēa* and *ā* (examples: ME *mę̄te* from OE *mĕte*, ME *stę̄len* from OE *stĕlan*, ME *smǭke* from OE *smŏca*, ME *hǭpe* from OE *hŏpa*, ME *dę̄th* from OE *dēað*, ME *stǭn* from OE *stān*). But whereas lengthening in the open syllable was a regular occurrence, there was no comparable regular and widespread pattern of shortening at the same date: shortening before two syllables under weak stress, and before certain consonant clusters, was earlier, whereas that before dentals was later. If this chronology did not hold, then forms like ME *wĕpte* (OE *wēpte*), ME *frĕndschip* (OE *frēondscipe*), ME *gŏsling* (OE *gōsling*), ME *sŏfte* (OE *sōfte*) would be inexplicable counter-examples to the pattern seen above. So long as these shortenings occur at a time *before* the open-close contrast arises, however, they present no problem (since they follow the primary generalization about the matching of vowel quality in long vs. short sets).[6]

Since we seek always the simplest set of rules that will generate later forms from earlier ones, we are faced with the question of just what is the simplest way to account for this breakdown in our fundamental—and I think both powerful and necessary—generalization about the matching of vowel quality in long vs. short sets.

The solution offered by Luick and now, as far as I can determine, the only solution widely accepted by scholars in the history of English, is as described above, namely to write in an exception to the otherwise powerful generalization about the matching of long vs. short vowels as to quality. The phonetic logic that justifies the exceptional rule is solid but not inescapable. Since /ē/ is phonetically intermediate between /ī/ and /ę̄/, and since there existed only *two* short vowels in the same range, a shortening of /ē/ must necessarily fall in either with the higher quality or with the lower—if, of course, it did not generate a third short phoneme, for which there is no evidence at all.

But suppose we have a different hypothesis about the structure of long vowels. Instead of assuming that they were structured as short vowel plus a phonemically relevant element of length, suppose we assume that length was a property of glide vowels (i.e., semivowels) of two or even three types. It makes no difference what symbols are attached to phonemic length in the traditional view: length may about equally well be viewed (1) as vowel clustering (so that /ī/ would be transcribed as /ii/), (2) as a unit phoneme that can occur after any segment, vowel, or consonant (so that /ī/ would be transcribed /iː/), or (3) as a set of long vowels in opposition with a set of short vowels (the length being viewed as inherent in the vowel itself). Nor does it make any difference what symbols are attached to the interpretation of length as being a property of a cluster made up of a vowel plus a semivowel. A front glide may, for purposes of this argument, equally well be written with /y/ or /i/; a back glide with /w/ or /u/; and a central glide with /h/ or /ə/ or /ˈ/ or /ˇ/ or /H/ or whatever suits the convenience of one's typewriter and the conditioning of his theoretical training or disposition. In short, I am not discussing symbols but structure.

If we assume that length was a post-nuclear glide of any one of three kinds, front /y/, back-round /w/, or relaxed central /h/ (which should not be confused with the OE and ME fricative /x/, spelled *h*, *ʒ*, and later *gh*), we have a good deal of evidence immediately in our favor. For instance, OE *-ig* comes to be spelled *i*, *y*, and *ii*, i.e., /ī/—a spelling which is entirely reasonable if the palatal fricative originally symbolized by *g* had lost its friction, thus falling in with /y/: OE *stig* becomes ME *stye*. Likewise OE *-ug* comes to be spelled *u*, *ou*, *ow*, i.e., /ū/—reasonable if the velar fricative had lost its friction, thus falling in with /w/: OE *sugu* becomes ME *sow*. That is, if /ī/ and /ū/ were structurally /iy/ and /uw/, then a sequence like OE /ij/ (in which /j/ represents the voiced palatal fricative written *ġ* by modern editors) easily becomes /iy/ merely by loss of friction, and OE /uʒ/ (in which /ʒ/ represents the voiced velar fricative) easily becomes /uw/ in the same way. There is a good deal more evidence that falls into place in this hypothesis: without detailed specification, we may mention that tenth-century lengthening before certain clusters is readily interpretable as the achieving of phonemic status of a previously allophonic centralizing glide toward the dark-vowel coloration of /LC$_v$/ and /NC$_v$/ (L for /l/ and /r/, C$_v$ for voiced consonant, N for nasal); that the long-term stability of a vowel like OE /ō/ before /w/ as in OE *grōwan* is easily explained if /ō/ was assimilated from an earlier /oh/ to /ow/ in the environment of a following /w/ in *-wan*; and that the perplexing problem of the so-called great vowel shift, in which the crucial change is the diphthongization of the high front and high back vowels /ī/ and /ū/ to MnE /ay/ and /aw/, is much more readily formulated as

$$
\begin{array}{cccc}
\text{iy} \rightarrow \text{ɨy} & & \text{ɨw} \leftarrow \text{uw} \\
\downarrow & & \downarrow & \\
\text{əy} & & \text{əw} & \\
\uparrow \quad \downarrow & & \downarrow \quad \uparrow \\
\vdots \quad \text{ay} & & \text{aw} \quad \vdots
\end{array}
$$

All this is only to say that the glide-vowel interpretation of length is not *ad hoc*, not limited to the explanatory power it has for the phenomena of the long close and long open mid vowels of ME, even though the detailed discussion of this paper is limited to an explication of the latter.

Turning back now to the evidence that shows /ĭ/ and /ē/, /ŭ/ and /ō/ to behave in ME as though paired with respect to quality, but seeking to re-analyze their structure in such a way as to eliminate an exception from the primary generalization about the matching of paired long and short vowels, we find that the crux of the problem is that there were three long vowels in front and three in back, but only two short vowels:

$$\left.\begin{matrix}/\bar{\imath}/ \\ /\bar{e}/\end{matrix}\right\} \quad /\breve{\imath}/ \qquad /\breve{u}/ \qquad \left\{\begin{matrix}/\bar{u}/ \\ /\bar{o}/\end{matrix}\right.$$
$$/\bar{\epsilon}/ \qquad /\breve{e}/ \qquad /\breve{o}/ \qquad /\bar{\varrho}/$$

But if "length" is of more than one type, then two short vowels in front and two in back are quite enough counters to account for all the contrasts:

$$\left.\begin{matrix}/\,iy/ \\ /\,ih/\end{matrix}\right\} \quad /i/ \qquad /u/ \qquad \left\{\begin{matrix}/uw/ \\ /\hat{u}h/\end{matrix}\right.$$
$$/eh/ \qquad /e/ \qquad /o/ \qquad /oh/$$

Indeed, we have one counter left over in each area: /ey/ and /ow/. Both left-over slots are, so to speak, already occupied: /ey/ from the inherited /æj/ and /ej/ with loss of the friction in /j/, and /ow/ by assimilation from /oww/. The remaining unused combinations—/iw/, /ew/, /uy/, and /oy/—are taken up in French loan words and a few inherited forms (OE *fēawe* becomes ME /few/, /fiw/). So while the analysis of ME /ē/ and /ō/ as /ih/ and /uh/ is offhand some-what startling, we are in fact forced to it by our primary hypothesis. We must then look again at the evidence to see whether we have been forced into a corner that we might well wish to be out of.

We saw earlier that /ē/, when shortened, gave /ĭ/. Now if we rewrite /ē/ as /ih/, when it is shortened it must yield /i/—and no exception to our primary generalization is needed to explain why it does. Similarly /ō/, if it is /uh/, must give /u/ when shortened—as it does. Conversely, if an /i/ is lengthened, it must fall in with /ih/, and /u/ with /uh/—as they do. That is, by formulating the structure of Old and Middle English vocalism in different terms, we do not at all require that the most powerful generalizations about the history be re-vised, but we *do* eliminate a difficult set of exceptions and show that they in fact behave exactly as the primary generalizations predict they ought to behave. The fact that they do behave in conformity with the most general rules is very strong corroboration of the revised formulation of Old and Middle English vocalism: so strong that it then becomes necessary for an alternate interpretation, no matter how well established by tradition and usage, either to demonstrate that the revised formulation is not in fact simpler or, if it fails, then to accept this formulation.

The examples cited earlier may be briefly recapitulated in the revised formulation:

### Shortening

| | | |
|---|---|---|
| OE *rēdels*: | OE /réhdel(s)/ | → ME /ríhdəl/, |
| | | shortened /rídəl/, *riddle* |
| OE *sēc*: | OE /séhk/ | → ME /síhk/, |
| | | shortened /sík/, *sick* |
| OE *hrēc*: | OE /xréhk/ | → ME /xríhk/, |
| | | shortened /(x)rík/,—*rick* |
| OE *brēc*: | OE /bréhkj/ | → ME /bríhč(əs)/, |
| | | shortened /bríčəs/, *breeches* |

[/kj/ is one possible phonemicization of the OE palatal /k/, written ċ by modern editors].

| | | |
|---|---|---|
| OE *sēlig*: | OE /séhlij/ | → ME /síhliy/, |
| | | shortened /síliy/, *silly* |
| OE *blōd*: | OE /blóhd/ | → ME /blúhd/, |
| | | shortened /blúd/, *blood* |
| OE *flōd*: | OE /flóhd/ | → ME /flúhd/, |
| | | shortened /flúd/, *flood* |

### Lengthening

| | | |
|---|---|---|
| OE *wicu*: | OE /wíku/ | → ME /wíhkə/, *week* |
| OE *bitel*: | OE /bítel/ | → ME /bíhtəl/, *beetle* |
| OE *wifel*: | OE /wífel/ | → ME /wíhvəl/, *weevil* |
| OE *yfel*: | LOE /ífel/ | → ME /íhvəl/, *evil* |
| OE *wudu*: | OE /wúdu/ | → ME /wúhdə/, *wood* |
| OE *duru*: | OE /dúru/ | → ME /dúhrə/, *door* |
| OE *lufu*: | OE /lúfu/ | → ME /lúhvə/, *love* |

It is clear that all other shortenings and lengthenings, both later and earlier, are in the same pattern, but they have never required a revision in formulation because they could, in each instance, readily be paired with a matching vowel in the appropriate quality. Thus OE *wēpte* /wéhpte/ → ME /wéptə/, OE *sōfte* /sóhfte/ → ME /sóftə/, because such shortenings occurred before OE /eh/ → /ih/, /oh/ → /uh/.

The spellings of ME /ih/ and /uh/ as *e, ee* and *o, oo* remain to be accounted for. The dilemma facing the scribe was simply that he had only two symbols for front vowels and two for back: *i, e* and *u, o*. Given three front vowels of the long variety, he had little choice but to write two of them alike. Similarly in the back. That he should file /ih/ and /eh/ in the same folder, leaving /iy/ in a separate one, suggests that /ih/ and /eh/ seemed more nearly alike than /ih/ and /iy/. Similarly /uh/ and /oh/ vs. /uw/. It is of course always difficult to account for spelling practices, but lest anyone should feel that this particular difficulty is damaging to the case, I must emphasize that no account of ME vowel structure has any *less* difficulty in explaining the fact that ē and ę̄ were spelled alike but have consistently different subsequent histories. Similarly ō and ǭ. The tradition which writes both the higher and the lower entities with the same letter modified by different diacritics perhaps makes it appear to be less of a problem by using the same letters, but it does not thereby escape the problem. Any phonemicization must presumably postulate phonetic shapes for ē and ō that are nearer to ę̄ and ǭ than they are to ī and ū, respectively. I offer the following suggestions:

$$[\text{i}^{\times}\ \text{i̯}]\ /\text{iy}/\ \text{ī};\ [\text{i̯}^{\vee}\ \text{ə̯}]\ /\text{ih}/\ \bar{\text{e}};\ [\text{e}^{\wedge}\ \text{ə̯}]\ /\text{eh}/\ \bar{\text{ę}};$$
$$[\text{u}^{\times}\ \text{u̯}]\ /\text{uw}/\ \bar{\text{u}};\ [\text{u̯}^{\vee}\ \text{ə̯}]\ /\text{uh}/\ \bar{\text{o}};\ [\text{o}^{\wedge}\ \text{ə̯}]\ /\text{oh}/\ \bar{\text{ǫ}}.$$

Whatever the phonetic facts may have been (they are, after all, unrecoverable: only contrasts and cognate relationships are recoverable, so that those rules that generate the latter two most simply must be assumed to provide the soundest basis for speculating about phonetic shape), we are not wholly without evidence that long close e /ih/ and long close o /uh/ were in fact often identified with *i* and *u* rather than e and o. There are many instances from the fourteenth and fifteenth[7] centuries of spellings of /ih/ and /uh/ words with *i, y* and *u, ou* rather than e and o. These spellings have previously been taken[8] as evidence that, among some speakers, that part of the great vowel shift in which the OE mid vowels were raised to their modern quality occurred quite early. I see no reason why they cannot equally well be taken as instances where /ih/ and /uh/ were heard as closer to /iy/ and /uw/, respectively, than to /eh/ and /oh/. In this way, the early spellings that appear to wreck any general chronology for the details of change in the great vowel shift can be viewed simply as additional corroboration for this revised formulation.

To sum up, then: viewed through the traditional phonological frame of reference, the relationship between ME short *i* and long close *e*, and that between ME short *u* and long close *o*, requires that a special rule be written which contradicts a much more general rule about the phonetic quality of long vs. short pairs. Viewed through a different formulation of the structure of long vs. short vowels, in which length is assigned to one of three glide phonemes, the general rule is seen to hold without exception.[9] In addition, it is apparent that certain related rules imposed by the traditional analysis can either be eliminated or stated more simply within the revised formulation.

## FOOTNOTES

1. This rule is implicit not only in modern grammars and phonologies, from Luick to Brunner to Quirk and Wrenn, but also in all earlier grammars of OE and of comparative Gmc, back at least to the first quarter of the nineteenth century. I have not been able to determine who first stated it as an explicit assumption. It is, in fact, rarely made explicit down to the present day, since the traditional interpretation of OE phonology adheres so closely to OE spelling that this crucial assumption is not often described for what it is, namely a hypothesis that has great explanatory power, in that without further specification it will generate many later forms of English from earlier forms.

2. I leave the front-round vowels /ü/ and /ö/ unlisted, since they unrounded and fell in with /i/ and /e/. The fact that the latter coalescence (/e/ and /ö/) occurred relatively early, and the former (/i/ and /ü/) relatively late, is irrelevant to the present argument, though it is significant indeed in a more inclusive statement of English vocalic history. I also ignore, for this purpose, the graphic diphthongs, short and long, since a one-to-one relationship of nucleus vs. nucleus-plus-length clearly does not hold between the short and long members of the class.

3. David DeCamp, in "The Genesis of the Old English Dialects: A New Hypothesis" in *Language*, XXXIV (1958), 232–44, has so convincingly argued the role played by Frisian in the initiation and spread of certain key dialectal features of Old English that I have here adopted a manner of speaking that implies my confidence in DeCamp's arguments, whatever doubts others may still have. [DeCamp's paper is reprinted in this collection, pp. 355–368—Ed.]

4. As far as I can determine, the earliest statement *in essentially this form* is Luick's, in his *Untersuchungen Z. Engl. Lautgesch.*, 1896 (pp. 209 ff.). Earlier discussions of the same material are cited by Luick and hence need not be cited here.

5. The problem of what forms to cite in lists like these two is acute. Wyld (*Short Hist. Eng.*, § 174) and Brunner (*Die Eng. Spr.*, p. 221) cite OE *bitul, wifol* instead of *bitela, wifel*. Bosworth and Toller cite *bītela, wifel*, and Toller's supplement cites *bitela* with short *i*. Luick (*Hist. Gram.*, § 393) cites instances of regular morphophonemic alternation between long and short vowels: *sun—sōnes, gum—gōmes, dur—dōres, wud—wōdes, cum—cōmes, gif—gēves, lif—lēves, wit—wētand, crik—crēkes*, and others like these in which one form would normally be lengthened, the other would not. Similar pairs, arising from the fact that one form has three syllables so that the first remains short (or if originally long, becomes short), but the other form has only two syllables and so may have a long vowel in the first, include *sōmer—sumeres, thōner—thuneres, ēvel—iveles, crēpel—cripeles, wēdow—widowes, bēsi—bisily*, and others like these. It is obvious that in the subsequent history of such pairs EITHER form may be analogically extended throughout the paradigm, so that a list which shows a late ME singular with /ē/ may, in fact, have the length from analogical extension of the plural. These morphophonemic alternations can be cited at much greater length than can the direct-derivation type shown above. Even if every example of the type of *wifel → wēvel (weevil)* could somehow be accounted for without assuming that /ī/ plus length became /ē/, the morphophonemic alternants cited by Luick would still have to be explained by some such assumption. That is, Luick's hypothesis that /ī/ and /ē/, /ū/ and /ō/ are related as long and short matched pairs would stand unaltered by the loss of any examples in the cited lists.

6. Alan S. C. Ross, in *Etymology* (London, 1958), is the most recent of several scholars who would reverse the whole direction of English sound change by assuming that OE /ĕ/ and /ŏ/ were close vowels that became open vowels at the beginning of the thirteenth century, so that when lengthened after that date they gave /ę̄/ and /ǭ/ (p. 125), though they had earlier given /ē/ and /ō/. Thus, whereas in the Luick tradition—with which I agree on this detail—it was necessary to assume a *raising* of OE long mid vowels, resulting in a contrast between the raised inherited long mid vowels and the newly generated long mid vowels, Ross assumes a *lowering* of OE short mid vowels, resulting, by a different route, in the same contrast, but describable rather as between the inherited long mid vowels and the long mid vowels newly generated from *lowered* short mid vowels.

7. Wyld, *Hist. Mod. Coll. Eng.* (p. 67), cites *myte* "meet," *dyme* "deem," *agryed* "agreed," *wyping* "weeping," *slyves* "sleeves," *stypylle* "steeple." He also cites *must* for ME *mōste, Munday, suthly* "truly," *forsuk, stude*. Unhappily, Professor C. E. Bazell writes me that in his experience of checking the spellings cited by Wyld, he has found little reason to have confidence in their reliability. I have no

independent evidence on this matter, and I must leave the validation or invalidation to later study. It would be surprising if study of informally written documents of the fourteenth and fifteenth centuries did not turn up a small but significant number of items with /ē/ spelled *i*, *y*, and of items with /ō/ spelled with *u*, *ou*. The doubt that Bazell casts on Wyld leaves me temporarily without convincing examples, nonetheless. I am not sure that such spellings are a *necessary* consequence of my hypothesis, but they are probably a likely one. The reason why they may not be necessary is that by the beginning of the fifteenth century ME /iy/ was almost certainly well on its way to becoming MnE /ay/. That is, it was perhaps /iy/ by this date. If so, then the identification of the letters *i*, *y* with a diphthong approximating /iy/ would make it unlikely that /ih/ could be spelled with the same symbols. The same argument of course holds for the high back area.

8. Wyld concludes from the *y*-spellings cited in the preceding footnote that they "show that the Mod. sound had already developed out of the old ē . . ." (67). From the *u*-spellings he concluded that they "show that [ū], or this sound shortened, was already pronounced." (67) Kökeritz states flatly (*Shakeapeare's Pron.*, p. 190) that "The raising of ME *ē* in *he*, *see*, etc., to [iː] occurred at least as early as the beginning of the fifteenth century, and the new vowel has remained virtually unchanged in an independent position ever since." Since this is the starting point of his discussion of *ē*, one cannot object that he finds no evidence to contradict it. Yet, as I see it, every citation (the most striking one: *miter* for *meter*) can equally well be explained by /ih/, without having to push the chronology of the great vowel shift back to an unreasonably early date.

9. One objection has already been raised to the views I have presented here, and since it is important, it must be dealt with. Professor C. A. Bazell, in personal correspondence about this problem, has pointed out that it is easier to formulate rules which will generate a later phonological structure from an earlier one, if the later structure is, as it were, built into the earlier one. The point is a strong one, and amounts to an accusation of circularity. Yet I think it is possible to avoid both the accusation and the danger, if the position I have been developing is a little clarified. There are two theories of the nature of "long vowels" in Modern English: that they are to be analyzed as vowel and length, or as vowel and semivowel. The same two theories exist for Old English. It would be wasteful to say that English had developed from a language with vowels and length to one with vowels and semivowels. It would be equally wasteful to assume that vowels and semivowels had become vowels and length. Either assumption would involve a theory of maximum rather than minimum change, and no one seriously proposes either theory. The assumption of this paper is that both Old English and Modern English are characterized by vowel and semivowel sequences. The alternate hypothesis is that both are characterized by vowel and length. What I have done is test which of these two alternate hypotheses gives a simpler and more powerful statement for dealing with changes in vowel quantity. Since the traditional view requires a set of exceptions, whereas the revision suggested here does not, it would seem that there is some gain in revision.

If, then, I am right in assuming that such a simplification represents a genuine gain, the result is one of the reasons for carrying on what Voegelin has called "structural-restatement linguistics" (Review of Bloomfield-Hockett's *Eastern Ojibwa*, in *Language*, XXXV [1959], 109–25). From this kind of activity we expect to reach insights that we did not possess before the restatements, and we expect insights to emerge from the statements, rather than to be built into them. The test which was applied suggested that Old English was like Modern English in the structure of its vowel nuclei. If this is a reasonable conclusion, it carries with it a further suggestion which certainly was not visible at the start of the investigation. Since some stage of pre-Modern English must have been more like the structure of the other Indo-European languages than Modern English is, there must have been a change. Reorganization of vowel structure is shown to have required vastly more time than has elapsed since the reign of Alfred. The reorganization of vowels could very well have been a change of the order of magnitude and time depth represented by Grimm's law, which separates the Germanic from the Indo-European line.

## A. J. BLISS

# Vowel-Quantity in Middle English
# Borrowings from Anglo-Norman*

### Introductory

1. In subjecting to a systematic and exhaustive examination the vexed question of vowel-quantity in ME[1] borrowings from AN I have had to assume certain axioms which do not seem to me capable of proof;[2] some of these are so fundamental that my investigation has little value if they are not acceptable, and they must therefore be stated at once.

(1) That the pronunciation of a loanword in ME corresponded to its pronunciation in AN as closely as the phonetic structure of native words allowed.

(2) Hence, that an AN sound underwent no alteration if the same sound occurred in the same type of context in native words.[3]

(3) That, if an AN sound did not occur in the same type of context in native words, it was replaced by the most closely related sound which did occur in the same type of context in native words.

(4) Hence, that where the exact nature of an AN sound is in doubt, the equivalent sound in the ME borrowing is likely to have existed already in AN, unless one of the other possible sounds does not occur in the same type of context in native words.

* From *Archivum Linguisticum* 4.121–47 (1952), 5.22–47 (1953). Reprinted by permission of the author and the editors of *Archivum Linguisticum*.

(5) That once the pronunciation of a loanword had been fully adapted to the phonetic structure of native words, its component sounds underwent the same sound-changes as those of native words, unless it was subsequently influenced by continental OF.

2. If these axioms are applied to the vowels of ME borrowings from AN there can be no doubt that long vowels existed already in AN. In the loanwords, for instance, *i* and *u* are usually long in an open syllable; but in native words *i* and *u* may be either short or long in an open syllable, the distribution depending entirely on the original Germanic quantities, not on the context in ME. Further, if short *ĭ* and *ŭ* in native words are lengthened in an open syllable they become, not *ī* and *ū*, but *ę̄* and *ǭ*: compare AN *chīve* with native *lĭve*, northern *lę̄ve*, or AN *ȯure*[4] "hour" with native *dŭre* "door," northern *dǭre*. Again, in the loanwords *u* is long before *m* or *n* final, or followed by any consonant; but in native words *u* is long only before the groups *mb* and *nd*. OE *munt* "mount" could not by any native sound-change have developed into ME *mȯunt*, MnE [maʊnt],[5] which must therefore be a reborrowing from AN. These instances could easily be multiplied almost indefinitely. Yet the obvious conclusion that the vowels of *chīve*, *ȯure*, *mȯunt*, and all the other words in which the vowel-quantity cannot be explained in terms of the phonetic structure of native words, were long already in AN is frustrated by an unexpected obstacle: none of the OF grammars admits that long vowels existed at all in OF, with the possible exception of *ę̄* from VL *ā*.

3. Since "no direct evidence of differentiation of quantity in vowels is afforded by the rhymes in Old and Middle French,"[6] and since the quantity of a vowel in MnF depends entirely on its context, not on its origin, this attitude involves no practical difficulties; but the logical objections to it are considerable. It is admitted by the very scholars who deny the existence of long vowels in OF that long vowels existed in VL; unless these long vowels were shortened at some stage in the development of French, they must still have existed in OF; yet no such shortening is even mentioned—there is a conspiracy of silence about quantity. The solitary exception already mentioned only aggravates the inconsistency. OF *e* < VL *ā*, as in *cler* "clear" < *clārum*, assonates neither with *ę* as in *cręste* "crest" < *crĭsta* nor with *ę* as in *fęste* "feast" < *fĕsta*; most scholars therefore assume that it was distinguished from them in quantity, and was in fact a long close *ę̄*. Few would dispute this conclusion; but it would seem necessary to explain why this alone among OF vowels retained its VL length, and at what period it lost it—for in MnF it is often short; but the conspiracy of silence continues, and these questions remain unanswered. As long ago as 1879 this inconsistency was pointed out by ten Brink in his valuable study of vowel-quantity in OF:[7] "der Zweck dieser Skizze wird erreicht sein, sobald ein Berufener dadurch angeregt wird, die hier angedeutete Lücke der romanischen Grammatik auszufüllen"; and again,[8] "doch ich lasse hier den Faden fallen—in der Hoffnung, dass der eine

oder andere Fachmann ihn wieder aufnehmen werde." This pious wish has remained unfulfilled for over seventy years.

4. It is interesting to observe how the ME grammars deal with this difficulty. Luick, quite uncharacteristically, hedges.[9] "Mannigfach gestalteten sich auch die Quantitätsverhältnisse, da das Altfranzösische nicht so fest ausgeprägte und also gegensätzlich empfundene Quantitätstypen besass wie das Englische und ausserdem die Vokaldauer im Satzzusammenhang vermutlich starken Schwankungen unterlag. Die englischen Entsprechungen lehnten sich vor allem an die heimischen Typen der Silbenquantität an, wie sie in Wörtern entsprechenden Baues galten." As I have shown, this last statement is untrue, and Luick hastens to modify it in a note.[10] "Diese Quantitierungen bewegen sich innerhalb der Grenzen, die die heimischen Quantitätsverhältnisse boten, nur die Längen vor *r* + Kons. gehen über sie hinaus, vielleicht in Zusammenhang mit zweigipfligem Akzent. Die Quantität der Quellsprache scheint aus den Fällen unter 4 und 2 durchzuschimmern [*i.e.* before a single consonant and in an open syllable]: sie scheint im ganzen der englischen Länge näher gestanden zu haben als der Kürze." Jordan goes further than Luick; following Keller, he sees the difficulties involved in Luick's explanation, and attributes distinctions of quantity to OF.[11] "Als die Hauptmasse der französischen Lehnworte aufgenommen wurde, hatte das Altfranzösische den Unterschied von Länge und Kürze der Vokale noch nicht verwischt. Die französischen Worte im Mittelenglischen lassen eine Regelung der Quantitäten erkennen, welche vielfach nicht zu den einheimisch-englischen Verhältnissen stimmt, also auf die altfranzösischen zurückgehen muss." But after this promising beginning Jordan's courage fails: instead of attempting to determine the nature and distribution of AN vowel-quantity, he proceeds, like Luick, to list the various contexts in which each vowel appears short, and those in which it appears long. This procedure makes no distinction between ME and OF sound-changes, and obscures the regularity which lies behind the apparent disorder.

5. I have here attempted a double task, not only to determine which vowels were long in AN, but also to explain why they were long. Since, for the sake of brevity and clarity of exposition, I have preferred to describe my results systematically, I must here explain concisely how they were obtained. First of all I compiled a list, short enough to be manageable, yet long enough to be representative, of AN loanwords in ME and MnE. The original list was based on those of such earlier writers as Behrens, Skeat, Sturmfels and Serjeantson;[12] but I omitted many of their words, either because the etymology is uncertain, or because their early obsolescence makes it difficult to ascertain the vowel-quantity in ME; on the other hand, I added many words from my own reading. I have not omitted any words because they do not suit my theory; on the contrary, I have taken some pains to mention all important exceptions to my rules. From the completed list I first of all eliminated all those words whose stem-vowel is regularly short in ME. Next

I eliminated all those words whose long vowel can be explained in terms of the phonetic structure of native words, and those whose long vowel may be due to ME sound-changes. According to the axioms stated in § 1 the vowels of the remaining words must have been long already in AN;[13] and thus the first part of my task was completed.

6. The next stage of the investigation involved three more axioms:

(6) That any vowel which was once long is still long unless there is clear evidence that it has been shortened.
(7) That any vowel resulting from the smoothing[14] of a diphthong or triphthong is long unless there is clear evidence that it has been shortened.
(8) That any vowel resulting from the juxtaposition of a short vowel and a glide-vowel of the same quality is long unless there is clear evidence that it has been shortened.

In accordance with these axioms I next eliminated from the list all those words whose long vowel was derived either from a VL long vowel or from an earlier diphthong or triphthong, or from the juxtaposition of a short vowel and a glide-vowel of the same quality; these I took to be sufficiently explained. The vowels of the remaining words were presumably originally short, and must have been lengthened by sound-changes which occurred before the date of their adoption into English, possibly in all OF dialects, possibly in AN only. These I examined carefully to see whether there were any common factors which might explain the lengthening, and it proved possible to formulate a few simple rules which included all but a very small number of words. Finally I re-examined in the light of these rules all the words whose stem-vowel is generally short in ME, to see whether any vowels which ought to be long were in fact short; and it was gratifying to discover that all but a very few short vowels in words of this type could be explained in terms of well-established ME sound-changes. In practice, of course, the investigation was not as simple as it sounds; tentative conclusions often had to be revised in the light of later results. But the system outlined here provides a simple and logical explanation of the vowel-quantity in the large majority of ME borrowings from AN.

7. I have made no attempt to offer a systematic picture of vowel-quantity in OF, and it is important to realise that I have included in my discussion only those aspects of OF phonology which are relevant to the loanwords in ME; thus, I have deliberately refrained from distinguishing various dialect types within AN. Nor is it generally relevant to my purpose to discuss any changes which took place in OF after the thirteenth century; but, whenever there is any evidence in OF dialects other than AN, in MF or in MnF, which supports my conclusions about sound-changes in AN, I have very briefly cited it.

8. OF contains both popular and learned words. Popular words were derived from VL, that is, from Latin as it was spoken, not only in Rome but also in the provinces; learned words were derived partly from spoken and partly from written Latin. The phonetic development of learned words shows

marked variation, and cannot be reduced to any simple system of rules. Not only were words borrowed at different periods—sometimes the same word was borrowed more than once—but a learned word was constantly subjected to the influence of its etymon, which in contemporary Latin was pronounced in a popular or semi-popular way. Here I am concerned only with vowels, and it is possible to divide learned words quite arbitrarily into two types, according to the treatment of the vowels. In the first type the vowels developed in the same way as the vowels of popular words; here belong the early borrowings and those which early ceased to be associated with their Latin etyma. In the second type the vowels had their own special developments, often quite different from those of the vowels of popular words; here belong the later borrowings and those which were most influenced by their Latin etyma. I have made no attempt to distinguish learned words of the first type from popular words; but I have devoted a special paragraph (§ 25) to learned words of the second type, because vowel-quantity in these words is governed by rules quite different from those which affect popular words.

## AN Tonic Vowels in ME

### VL long vowels

9. In early VL, as in CL, vowels were distinguished by quantity but not by quality; that is to say, each vowel could occur both short and long, but the short and long varieties had the same quality. In course of time a qualitative distinction came to be associated with the quantitative distinction, and all long vowels became relatively close while all short vowels became relatively open; next, the original quantitative distinction was completely lost, and open $i$ and $u$ from earlier $\breve{\imath}$ and $\breve{u}$ became identical with $\rho$ and $\varrho$ from earlier $\bar{e}$ and $\bar{o}$.[15] The whole process can be simply represented in tabular form:

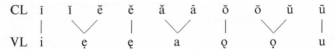

Finally a new quantitative distinction developed, whereby all tonic vowels became short in a closed syllable, and all tonic vowels became long in an open syllable.[16] This tendency continued to operate over a long period of time, and vowels were shortened in syllables closed by secondary consonant groups formed by the syncopation of unstressed vowels.[17] Groups consisting of stop consonant $+r$ did not close the syllable and a preceding vowel was consequently lengthened.[18] Only one of these VL long vowels remained unchanged into OF; the others were either changed in quality or diphthongised, according to the context in which they occurred. Some of the diphthongs thus developed were later smoothed, and these smoothings are discussed in §§ 17–22. In ME the long vowels of AN generally remained long unless the stress was shifted to another syllable; in this case they were normally shortened and often later obscured; but the original length is frequently attested by spelling and rhyme in earlier ME.

10. VL *ī* remained unchanged in OF. When the stress was not shifted in ME the vowel remained long:[19]

| VL | | ME | | |
|----|----|----|----|----|
| | *advīsum | ME | avīs | "advice" |
| | *arrīpa-nt | | arīve | "arrive" |
| | compīla-nt | | còmpīle | |
| | crīmen | | crīme | |
| | quĭrīta-nt | | crīe | "cry" |
| | dēclīna-nt | | declīne | |
| | *disfīda-nt | | defīe | "defy" |
| | dēscrību-nt | | descrīve | "describe" |
| | *dēvīsa-nt | | devīse | |
| | *dēvīna-nt | | devīne | "divine" |
| | fīnem | | fīne | |
| | frīgu-nt | | frīe | "fry" |
| | *wīla | | guīle | |
| | *wīsa | | guīse | |
| | *wīða[20] | | guīve | "gyve(s)" |
| | inclīna-nt | | enclīne | "incline" |
| | īra | | īre | |
| | prīma | | prīme | |
| | *slīza | | slīce | |
| | spīna | | spīne | |
| | *strīða-nt | | strīve | |
| | vīlem | | vīl | "vile" |
| | vīpĕra | | wīvre | "wyver, viper" |

When the stress was shifted in ME the long vowel was shortened and later obscured:

| VL | | ME | | |
|----|----|----|----|----|
| | *baccīnum | ME | bacĭn | "basin" |
| | cortīna | | curtīne | "curtain" |
| | *cŏxīnum | | cuischĭn | "cushion" |
| | gentīlem | | gentĭl | "gentle" |
| | Lătīnum | | Latĭn | |
| | nūtrĭcĭa | | nurĭce | "nurse" |
| | *trīlicĭum | | trelĭz | "trellice" |

11. VL *ū* remained a simple vowel, but was fronted in OF to *ü*; the symbol *u* remained in ME orthography, but when the stress was not shifted the unfamiliar sound was replaced in popular speech by the diphthong [iu],[21] in educated speech the sound [y:] may have remained until the seventeenth century.[22]

| VL | | ME | | |
|---|---|---|---|---|
| cūra | | cūre | | |
| *dēbūtum | | dū | "due" | |
| dūra-nt | | dūre | "(en)dure" | |
| flūmen | | flūm | "flum, river" | |
| glūtem | | glū | "glue" | |
| mūta-nt | | mūe | "mew" | |
| mūla | | mūle | | |
| pūrum | | pūr | "pure" | |
| rūta | | rūe | | |
| exclūsa | | slūse | "sluice" | |
| sēcūrum | | sūr | "sure" | |
| *ūsa-nt | | ūse | | |
| *vĭdūta | | vūe | "view" | |

When the stress was shifted in ME the long vowel was generally shortened and unrounded in popular speech to *ĭ*:

| VL | ăvis strūthĭo | ME | ostrĭche | "ostrich" |
|---|---|---|---|---|

But before a nasal *m* or *n* the long vowel was shortened and retracted to *ŭ*:

| VL | ălūmen | ME | alŭm | |
|---|---|---|---|---|
| | commūnem | | comòn | "common" |
| | *costūmen | | custòme | "custom" |

In educated speech, however, a long vowel or diphthong was retained into MnE:

| VL | ăcūta | ME | agūe | |
|---|---|---|---|---|
| | conjūra-nt | | cònjūre | |
| | festūca | | festūe | "fescue" |
| | virtūtem | | vertū | "virtue" |
| | vŏlūmen | | volūm | "volume" |

Here belong a large number of words in *-ūra, -ātūra*: *fētūre* "feature," *aventūre* "adventure," *mesūre* "measure," *wageūre* "wager."

12. VL *ę̄* was normally diphthongised to *ęi*; but when it was preceded by a palatal consonant it was raised to *ī*, which remained in OF.[23] When the stress was not shifted in ME the vowel remained long:

| VL | cēpa | ME | chīve | |
|---|---|---|---|---|

When the stress was shifted in ME the long vowel was shortened and later obscured:

| VL | lĭcēre | ME | lę̄sĭr | "leisure" |
|---|---|---|---|---|
| | mercēdem | | mercĭ | "mercy" |
| | plăcēre | | plę̄sĭr | "pleasure" |
| | răcēmum | | raisĭn | |

In *lḗsĭr* and *plḗsĭr* the final syllable was ultimately altered to *-ūre* by false analogy with the variation between *ĭ* and *ū* in words which originally had *-ūre* (§ 11).

13. VL *ā* became *ẹ̄* in OF before all oral consonants;[24] in AN this *ẹ̄* was lowered to *ę̄*, at first only before *l*, but later also before *r*; the loanwords in ME were borrowed after the lowering before *l*, but before the lowering before *r*. When the stress was not shifted in ME, OF *ẹ̄* remained:

| VL | | ME | | |
|----|--------|------|-------|----------|
|    | clārum | ME   | clẹ̄r  | "clear"  |
|    | dātum  |      | dẹ̄    | "die"    |
|    | frātrem|      | frẹ̄re | "friar"  |
|    | grātum |      | grẹ̄   | "gree"   |
|    | părem  |      | pẹ̄r   | "peer"   |
|    | rĕpăra-nt |   | repẹ̄re| "repair" |

When the stress was shifted in ME the long *ẹ̄* was shortened and later obscured. Here belong a large number of words in *-āre, -ārem, -ātum* and *-ĭtātem* : *autĕr* "altar," *pilĕr* "pillar"; *aischelĕr* "ashlar"; *maundĕ* "maundy," *privĕ* "privy"; *beutĕ* "beauty," *bóuntĕ* "bounty," *citĕ* "city," *plentĕ* "plenty," *povertĕ* "poverty."[25] When the stress was not shifted in ME, OF *ę̄* before *l* remained:

| VL | | ME | | |
|----|------|----|------|--------|
|    | āla  | ME | ę̄le  | "aisle" |
|    | pāla |    | pę̄le | "peal" |

When the stress was shifted in ME the long *ę̄* was shortened and later obscured. Here belong a large number of words in *-ālem*: *catĕl* "cattle," *chanĕl* "channel," *charnĕl, chatĕl* "chattel," *ostĕl* "hostel." Before nasal consonants VL *ā* was diphthongised to *ai*.

14. VL *ǭ* was normally diphthongised to *ǫu*, but before nasal consonants it became *ū*, usually written *ou*, in OF. When the stress was not shifted in ME the long vowel remained, and was usually written *ou* as in OF:

| VL | | ME | | |
|----|--------|----|--------|---------|
|    | cŏrōna | ME | cróune | "crown" |
|    | nōmen  |    | nóun   |         |
|    | sōnum  |    | sóun   | "sound" |

When the stress was shifted in ME the long vowel was shortened and later obscured. Here belong a very large number of words in *-ōnem*: *(a)bandón, achesón* "occasion," *arsón* "saddlebow," *bacón, barón, burdón, capón, dragón, dónjón* "dungeon," *faucón* "falcon," *fació́n* "fashion," *felón, foisón, galón* "gallon," *glutón* "glutton," *gujón* "gudgeon," *lessón, masón, mutón* "mutton," *ónión, oreisón* "orison," *penón* "pennon," *póisón, prisón, ransón* "ransom," *rę̄són, sermón, sturjón* "sturgeon," *talón, trę̄són* "treason," The remaining VL long vowels *ę̄* and *ǭ* became *ie* and *ue* respectively; these diphthongs were later smoothed, and are discussed in §§ 17–18.

## The smoothing of diphthongs

15. At various periods during the long development of VL into AN, diphthongs and triphthongs were smoothed to simple vowels, which were presumably long (axiom 7, § 6). The CL diphthongs *oe* and *ae* were smoothed to *ē* and *ę̄* respectively, early enough to undergo the redistribution of quantity described in § 9; that is, the new long vowels remained long in an open syllable, but were shortened in a closed syllable. It is, therefore unnecessary to distinguish this *ę*, *ę* from VL *ę*, *ę* from other sources. The smoothing of VL *au* to *ǭ* occurred much later, after the diphthongisation of VL *ǭ* to *ue* had ceased to operate: *clausum* becomes *clǭs*, not *\*clues*. None the less, the re-distribution of quantity according to the context must have been still in progress,[26] since in a closed syllable *ǫ* from VL *au* is affected by a sound-change which only affects short vowels—the raising of short *ǫ̆* to *ŭ* before a nasal: *ăvuncŭlum* > *\*aunclu* > *\*ǫncle* > *uncle*, just as *mǫntem* > *munt*. This con-clusion is confirmed by the evidence of the loanwords in ME. VL *au* in an open syllable gives ME *ǭ*:

|     | VL          | ME  |                |                   |
| --- | ----------- | --- | -------------- | ----------------- |
|     | allauda-nt  | ME  | alǭe           | "allow"           |
|     | clausum     |     | clǭs           | "close"           |
|     | laus        |     | lǭs            | "los, praise"     |
|     | paupĕrem    |     | pǭvre[27]      | "poor"            |
|     | restaura-nt |     | restǭre        |                   |
|     | *rauba      |     | rǭbe           |                   |

In *rǭste* "roast" < *\*hraustu-nt*, *fǭrǧe* < *\*faurga* < *fabrĭca*, and *lǭǧe* "lodge" < *\*laubja*, the vowel was originally short, but was lengthened for various reasons in AN (see §§ 38, 41, 45). In all smoothings later than that of *au* to *ǭ* the length of the resulting vowel seems not to have been affected by the nature of the syllable in which it occurred.

16. Primitive OF *\*iei* from VL *ę*, *ę̄* + *i̯* and VL palatal + *ā* + *i̯* was smoothed to *ī* in OF. When the stress was not shifted in ME the long vowel remained. Thus, with VL *ę*, *ę̄* + *i̯*:

|     | VL        |        |             |
| --- | --------- | ------ | ----------- |
|     | dēlĕctum  | delīt  | "delight"   |
|     | dēnĕga-nt | denīe  | "deny"      |
|     | dēspĕctum | despīt | "despite"   |
|     | intĕgrum  | entīr  | "entire"    |
|     | nĕscĭum   | nīce   |             |
|     | prĕtĭum   | prīs   | "price"     |
|     | *sĕjor    | sīre   |             |
|     | *spĕcĭa   | spīce  |             |

There is only one example in ME of VL palatal + *ā* + *i̯*, *ǧīste* "joist" on the stem of OF *gīse-nt* < *iăce-nt*. When the stress was shifted in ME the long vowel was shortened:

| VL | confĕctum | ME | cònfĭt | "comfit" |
| | *cĕrĕsĭa | | cherĭse | "cherries" |
| | convĕnĭum | | còvĭn | "coven" |
| | ingĕnĭum | | engĭn | "engine" |
| | prōfĕctum | | profĭt | |
| | rĕspĕctum | | respĭt | "respite" |

17. The development of OF *ue* in AN and ME is not free from difficulty. In most dialects of OF, *ue* was smoothed to [øː]; but in the western dialects the stress was shifted from the first element of the diphthong to the second, and the first was consonantalised, so that the result was *u̯e*; the consonantal element was often lost, giving a simple vowel *e*. ME borrowings sometimes have spellings *ue, eo, o*, which indicate the pronunciation [øː], but more often simply *e*, which is found also in AN, doubtless through English influence. The development to [øː] is clearly a genuine smoothing, so that the quantity is not in doubt; but the *e*-forms may be due either to the unrounding of earlier [øː] or to the adoption of western OF *e*. Since the western OF reduction is not a genuine smoothing, the resulting vowel cannot be considered long without further proof. In fact, it is unlikely that ME *e* represents the western OF development, since it is all but universal in the north and east Midlands, precisely those areas in which earlier [øː] from OE *ēo* had been unrounded to *ę̄*; while the west Midlands and south-west, in which a rounded vowel was retained for OE *ēo*, generally retain a rounded vowel for OF *ue*. But even if ME *e* does represent the western OF reduction, it is likely that the vowel was long, for where the consonantal element was retained after a velar, as in ME *quę̄r* "choir" < *cuer* < *chŏrum*, the ME borrowings always have a long vowel.[28] Whatever the process involved, OF *ue* from VL *ǭ* appears as *ę̄* in all dialects of ME except the western and south-western. When the stress was not shifted in ME the vowel remained long:

| VL | bŏvem | OF | buef | ME | bę̄f | "beef" |
| | *ăb ŏcŭlo | | avuegle | | *avę̄gle | "enveigle" |
| | mŏve-nt | | mueve-nt | | mę̄ve | "move" |
| | pŏpŭlum | | pueple | | pę̄ple | "people" |
| | prŏba-nt | | prueve-nt | | prę̄ve | "prove" |

When the stress was shifted in ME the long vowel was shortened and later obscured:

| VL | *scūrĭŏlum | OF | escüiruel | ME | squirĕl | "squirrel" |

18. The development of OF *ie* in AN and ME is also somewhat doubtful. In most dialects of OF the stress was shifted from the first element of the diphthong to the second, and the first was consonantalised, so that the result was *i̯e*; but in the northern dialects the falling diphthong was smoothed directly to *ī*. In AN and ME *ie* is regularly appears as *ę̄*. If this *ę̄* is to be interpreted as the result of a genuine smoothing it is necessary to postulate

an entirely unrecognised sound-change, a north-western smoothing to ę̄
beside the northern smoothing to ī. While there is nothing intrinsically improbable in such a change, it seems better to avoid the multiplication of
hypotheses by assuming that AN and ME ę̄ is a development of OF *ie* with
loss of the consonantal element; the regular appearance of a long vowel in
ME suggests that the consonantalisation of the first element of the diphthong
was accompanied by a compensatory lengthening of the second. Whatever
the process involved, OF *ie* from VL ę̄, VL palatal + ā and VL ę + palatal
appears in AN and ME as ę̄. When the stress was not shifted in ME the vowel
remained long. Thus, with VL ę̄:

| VL | | OF | | ME | | |
|----|----------|----|-----------|----|-------|------------|
| | *ad rētro | | ariere | | arę̄re | "arrear(s)" |
| | brĕvem | | brief | | brę̄f | "brief" |
| | fĕrus | | fiers | | fę̄rs | "fierce" |
| | *grĕvum | | grief | | grę̄f | "grief" |
| | *lĕdĭgum | | liege | | lę̄ğe | "liege" |
| | pĕtra | | piere | | pę̄re | "pier" |
| | rĕlĕva-nt | | relieve-nt | | relę̄ve | "relieve" |
| | *sĕdĭcum | | siege | | sę̄ğe | "siege" |

With VL palatal + ā:

| VL | | OF | | ME | | |
|----|--------|----|--------|----|-------|---------|
| | *căra | | chiere | | chę̄re | "cheer" |
| | *căpum | | chief | | chę̄f | "chief" |

With VL ę + palatal:

| VL | | OF | | ME | | |
|----|----------|----|-------|----|------|---------|
| | *nĕptĭa | | niece | | nę̄ce | "niece" |
| | *pĕttĭa | | piece | | pę̄ce | "piece" |

When the stress was shifted in ME the long vowel was shortened and later
obscured. Here belong a large number of words in *-ę̄ru, *-ę̄ra by mutation
from -ārĭum, -ārĭa, and a large number in -ātum and ĭtātem when the stem
ended in a palatal: *erbĕr* "arbour," *celĕr* "cellar," *chancelĕr* "chancellor,"
*colĕr* "collar," *dangĕr, drapĕr, lavendĕr, medlĕr* "medlar," *mercĕr, mortĕr*
"mortar," *sautĕr* "psalter"; *banĕre* "banner," *cornĕre* "corner," *gutĕre*
"gutter," *manĕre* "manner," *rivĕre* "river"; *clergĕ* "clergy," *trę̄tĕ* "treaty";
*deintĕ* "dainty," *pitĕ* "pity."

19. OF *ǫu* from VL ǭ was smoothed in AN, as in the western dialects of
OF, to ū, usually written *ou*. When the stress was not shifted in ME the long
vowel remained, and was usually written *ou* as in AN:

| VL | | OF | | ME | | |
|----|-----------|----|---------|----|-------|-----------|
| | *advōta-nt | | avoue-nt | | avóue | "avow" |
| | flōrem | | flour | | flóur | "flower" |
| | hōra | | oure | | òure | "hour" |
| | *prōdem | | prou | | pròu | "prow" |
| | vōtum | | vou | | vòu | "vow" |

ME *recóvere* "recover" is only an apparent exception to the rule: the normal development of VL *rĕcŭpĕra-nt*, OF *recouvre-nt*, is ME *recóuvre*; but a parasite vowel develops between *v* and *r*, and then the long vowel is regularly shortened in a proparoxytone. When the stress was shifted in ME the long vowel was shortened and later obscured. Here belong a large number of words in *-ōrem, -ātōrem* and *-ōsum*: *clamór* "clamour," *cólór* "colour," *favór* "favour," *flavór* "flavour," *genchór* "ginger(ly)," *onór* "honour," *labór* "labour," *odór* "odour," *savór* "savour," *tenór*, *valór* "valour," *vapór* "vapour"; *brocór* "broker," *creatór*, *emperór*, *flatór* "flatter," *lechór* "lecher," *levór* "lever," *rasór* "razor"; *famós* "famous," *gloriós* "glorious," *graciós* "gracious," *jelós* "jealous," *preciós* "precious."

20. OF *üi* from VL *u, ū + i̯* and VL *ǫ, ǭ + i̯* was smoothed in AN to *ǖ*; the symbol *u* remained in ME orthography, but the unfamiliar sound was replaced in popular speech by the diphthong [iu]; see § 11. When the stress was not shifted in ME the long vowel remained. Thus, with VL *u, ū + i̯*:

| | | | | | | | |
|---|---|---|---|---|---|---|---|
| VL | frūctum | OF | früit | ME | frŭt | "fruit" |
| | Jūnĭum | | Jüin | | Jŭn | "June" |

With VL *ǫ, ǭ + i̯*:

| | | | | | | | |
|---|---|---|---|---|---|---|---|
| VL | *lǭþrĭa-nt[29] | OF | lüire-nt | ME | lŭre | |
| | *pŏdĭa | | püie | | pŭe | "pew" |

Examples of the development of VL *ǫ, ǭ + i̯* to ME *ǖ* are few, because in many words the OF diphthong *üi* has undergone a shift of stress after a velar (§ 17): VL *cŏxa > cüisse > quisse*, VL *\*kŏkrum > cüivre > quivre* "quiver." In the word *queint* "quaint" < *cŏgnĭtum* prehistoric *\*uei* from which OF *üi* developed seems to have been preserved.

21. OF *ai* from VL *a, ā + i̯* was smoothed in AN to *ę̄* with some regularity before *t, d* and *s*, and sometimes also before *g*. When the stress was not shifted in ME the long vowel remained:

| | | | | | | | |
|---|---|---|---|---|---|---|---|
| VL | *disfactum | OF | desfait | ME | defę̄t | "defeat" |
| | ācrem | | aigre | | ę̄gre | "eager" |
| | ăquĭla | | aigle | | ę̄gle | "eagle" |
| | *adjăce | | aise | | ę̄se | "ease" |
| | factum | | fait | | fę̄t | "feat" |
| | *crassĭa-nt | | graisse-nt | | grę̄se | "grease" |
| | măcrum | | maigre | | mę̄gre | "meagre" |
| | pāx | | pais | | pę̄s | "peace" |
| | rĕlăxa-nt | | relaisse-nt | | relę̄se | "release" |
| | *sātĭa-nt | | saise-nt | | sę̄se | "seize" |
| | tracta-nt | | traite-nt | | trę̄te | "treat" |

When the stress was shifted in ME the long vowel was shortened and later obscured:

| VL | fornācem | OF | furnais | ME | furněs | "furnace" |
|----|----------|----|---------|----|--------|-----------|
|    | pălātĭum |    | palais  |    | palěs  | "palace"  |

22. OF *ei* from VL *ę̄* and VL *ę*, *ę̄* + *i̯* was also occasionally smoothed to *ę̄* before dentals in AN, but much less regularly than *ai*. The immediate antecedent of the simple vowel *ę* must have been a diphthong *ęi* and it is probable that the change *ai* > *ęi* was earlier than the change *ęi* > *ęi*; the smoothing of *ęi* before dentals may have occurred mainly in the interval between these two changes, so that it rarely affected *ęi* < *ęi*. When the stress was not shifted in ME the long vowel remained. Thus, with VL *ę̄*:

| VL | pĭsum | OF | peis | ME | pę̄s | "pease" |
|----|-------|----|------|----|------|---------|

With VL *ę*, *ę̄* + *i̯*:

| VL | dĭscum    | OF | deis        | ME | dę̄s    | "dais"     |
|----|-----------|----|-------------|----|--------|------------|
|    | incrēscu-nt |    | encreisse-nt |    | encrę̄se | "increase" |
|    | plĭcĭtum  |    | pleit       |    | plę̄t   | "pleat"    |

When the stress was shifted in ME the long vowel was shortened and later obscured. Thus, with VL *ę̄*:

| VL | *burgensem  | OF | burgeis | ME | burgěs | "burgess"   |
|----|-------------|----|---------|----|--------|-------------|
|    | *cŏhortensem |    | curteis |    | curtěs | "courteous" |

## The absorption of glide-vowels

23. There are only two long vowels in the ME borrowings from AN which have resulted from the juxtaposition of a short vowel and a glide-vowel of the same quality, *ī* < *ĭ* + *i̯* and *ū* < *ŭ* + *u̯*. Long *ī* < *ĭ* + *i̯* was formed partly in OF and partly in ME itself. When the stress was not shifted in ME, OF *ī* < VL *ĭ* + *i̯* remained:

| VL | běnĭgnum  | ME | benīn  | "benign" |
|----|-----------|----|--------|----------|
|    | *indĭcta-nt |    | endīte | "indict" |
|    | mălĭgnum  |    | malīn  | "malign" |
|    | *pĭncta[30] |    | pīnte  | "pint"   |

When the stress was shifted in ME the long vowel was shortened. Here belong a number of verbs in *-īscu-nt*: *abolĭsche, banĭsche, burnĭsche, finĭsche, polĭsche, ravĭsche, vanĭsche*. Another *ī* arose in ME from the juxtaposition of *ĭ* and epenthetic *i̯* produced by the depalatalisation of the unfamiliar sounds [ɲ] and [ʎ]:

| VL | rěsīgna-nt | OF | resigne-nt | ME | resīne | "resign" |
|----|-----------|----|-----------|----|--------|----------|
|    | sīgnum    |    | signe     |    | sīne   | "sign"   |
|    | vīnĕa     |    | vigne     |    | vīne   |          |

When the stress was shifted in ME the long vowel was shortened. Here belong a number of words in *-ĭcŭlum*: *cŏnĭl* "cony,"[31] *lentĭl, perĭl*.

24. OF *ū* from earlier *ŭ* + *ṷ* remained in ME, and was usually written *ou*; there appear to be no instances in which the stress was shifted.

| VL | | ME | | |
|----|----|----|----|----|
| ădŭlter | | avòutre | "adulterer" |
| pŭlvĕrem | | pòudre | "powder" |
| *ascŭlta-nt | | ascòute | "scout" |
| *sŭlza | | sòuce | "souse" |
| stŭltum[32] | | stòut | |

Probably ME *pŭsche* "push" belongs here, if it is indeed from VL *pŭlsa-nt*; but its development is obscure, and its etymology must therefore remain uncertain. VL *pŭlsa-nt* should normally give ME *pòusse*, and the occurrence of *sch* instead of the expected *ss* is difficult to explain; but the same substitution occurs in ME *rusche*, probably from VL *\*rursa-nt* and it may be due to analogy with northern OF [ʃ] for OF [s] in such a word as *anguische* "anguish." The short vowel of *pŭsche* has been levelled from the proparoxytone past tense *pŭschede* in which shortening is regular; see § 27.

## Learned words

25. As I have already explained in § 8, learned words in OF may be quite arbitrarily divided into two types, according to the treatment of the vowels: in the first type the vowels developed in the same way as the vowels of popular words; in the second type the vowels had their own special developments, often quite different from those of the vowels of popular words. In these words the CL vowels developed according to the following scheme:

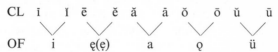

The CL distinctions of quantity were not preserved, and in OF all vowels were long in an open syllable and short in a closed syllable; here we are concerned only with the long vowels which appear in an open syllable. Words borrowed into ME show no peculiarities, except that the quality of long *ē* in words of this type seems to diverge from the OF quality: in OF this *ē* was apparently always open,[33] except finally, when it was closed;[34] in ME, on the other hand, some words have close *ẹ̄*, others open *ę̄*, irrespective of the context; according to Luick,[35] early borrowings had *ẹ̄*, later borrowings *ę̄*, but this distinction does not seem entirely reliable. As with other words, the vowel remained long when the stress was not shifted in ME, but was shortened and later obscured when the stress was shifted. Thus, with ME *ī*: *bīble, desīre, discīple, entīce, tīgre* "tiger," *tītle, vīce*, and, with shift of stress, *anĭs, chapĭtre* "chapter," *cofĭn* "coffin," *habĭt, offĭce*; in longer words such as *exercīce* "exercise,"

*sacrifīce*, where the originally tonic syllable retained a secondary stress, the vowel remained long. With ME *ẹ̄*: *decrẹ̄* "decree," *discrẹ̄t* "discreet," *procẹ̄de, succẹ̄de* "succeed," and, with shift of stress, *anĕt, poĕte* "poet," *profĕte* "prophet." With ME *ę̄*: *complę̄t* "complete," *extrę̄me, repę̄te* "repeat," *sevę̄re, suprę̄me, thę̄me*.[36] With ME *ā*: *cās* "case," *cāve, declāre, estāt* "estate," *grāce, lāc* "lake," *spāce*, and, with shift of stress, *curăt, legăt, palăt, prelăt, senăt, solăz* "solace." With ME *ǭ*: *devǭt* "devote," *dispǭse, glǭrie* "glory," *nǭble, sǭbre* "sober," *stǭrie* "story," *suppǭse*. With ME *ū*: *crūde, dūc* "duke," *refūse*, and, with shift of stress, *refŭge*. The word *delŭge* < *dīlŭvĭum* is anomalous, for it shows the learned development of the stem vowel, and the popular development of the consonant group *vĭ*. Many of the words listed above may in fact have been adopted directly from Latin into English; but since the pronunciation of such direct loanwords was certainly adapted to conform with the French pronunciation the distinction is of no importance for our present purpose.

## The absorption of vowels in hiatus

26. All the long vowels that I have discussed so far have been long by origin; the remaining tonic vowels were originally short, and were lengthened by sound-changes which occurred within AN (and possibly in other dialects of OF). The least controversial of these lengthenings is that whereby a short vowel acquires additional length through the absorption of a preceding unstressed vowel in hiatus with it; the preceding vowel is usually an obscure vowel, but it sometimes has the same quality as the stressed vowel which absorbs it. There are very few certain instances of this sound-change: in nearly every case the length of the stem-vowel can be explained in some other way. Thus, in *dū* "due" < *deŭ* < *\*dēbūtum, sŭr* "sure" < *seŭr* < *sēcūrum, vŭe* "view" < *veŭe* < *\*vĭdūta* the stem vowel is long by origin (§ 11), and so with a very large number of words in *-ātōrem, -ātūra*, such as *emperòr, lechòr* "lecher," *levòr* "lever," *armŭre* "armour," *wağeŭre* "wager," in all of which the stress was shifted in ME; in *round* < *reund* (*ruund*) < *rŏtundum* the vowel might have been lengthened before the following *n* (§ 33); in *gòurde* "gourd" < *guurde* < *cŭcurbĭta* the vowel might have been lengthened before the following *r* (§ 41); in *āğe* < *aage* (*eage*) < *\*aetātĭcum* the vowel might have been lengthened in an open syllable (§ 35). The only unambiguous examples of this sound-change seem to be *sę̄l* "seal" < *seęl* < *sĭgillum* and *vę̄l* "veal" < *veęl* < *vĭtellum*.[37]

## Lengthening before certain consonants

27. The next lengthenings to be discussed—those produced by a following consonant—are more controversial. It must be admitted that the results of these changes have very often been obscured by later shortenings; many of

these shortenings are regular in their occurrence, but others are sporadic and unpredictable. Among the regular shortenings two main types may be distinguished, shortening before three consonants and shortening in a proparoxytone. Already in early OE long vowels were shortened before groups of three consonants,[38] and the results of the OE lengthening before certain consonant groups cannot be discerned when a third consonant followed the lengthening group:[39] either the lengthening did not occur, or the lengthened vowel was shortened again. So among the loanwords: AN *nūmbre* > ME *nómbre* "number." In early ME long vowels were shortened in proparoxytones, even before consonant groups which normally caused lengthening.[40] Since the only proparoxytones among the loanwords are those in which an originally countertonic vowel has been stressed in ME, and since countertonic vowels in AN are usually short (§ 48), this shortening primarily affects the past tense of verbs: thus, AN *plūngēr* "plunge" gives a past tense *plóngede* in ME. From the past tense the short vowel is often levelled into the infinitive, and thence into the related noun: thus, the noun *gĕste* "jest" owes its short vowel to the verb *gĕste*, which in turn owes its short vowel to the past tense *gĕstede*. This kind of levelling gives rise to many double forms which are often attested in early MnE by the orthoepists.

28. Sporadic shortenings sometimes occurred in ME before some of the groups which had caused lengthening in late OE: thus, the long vowels which had developed before *rd* and *ng* were shortened again during the ME period with hardly any exceptions. The effect of this native tendency was enhanced in the loanwords by the existence of consonant groups which occurred not at all or only very rarely in native words. By axiom 2 in § 1 "an AN sound underwent no alteration if the same sound occurred in the same type of context in native words"; since "the same type of context" cannot be precisely defined, it is to be expected that variation will occur before an unfamiliar consonant group. For instance, long vowels are frequent before the group *nd* in native words; does this fact justify the retention of long vowels before *n* + any consonant, or only before *nd*? Individual speakers would doubtless have given different answers, and this uncertainty is reflected in the numerous double forms attested in ME or early MnE. It is scarcely an exaggeration to say that there are few words which in MnE have a long vowel before a consonant group which are not also attested with a short vowel in early MnE, and few which in MnE have a short vowel before an AN lengthening group which are not also attested with a long vowel in early MnE. Where an AN lengthening seemed insufficiently attested by MnE forms I have often quoted evidence from early MnE, but I have seldom had room to quote evidence for a short vowel where MnE has a long vowel.

29. Perhaps the most important sound-change in AN is the lengthening of the two back vowels *a*[41] and *u* before nasal *m* and *n*—but not, apparently, before the velar nasal [ŋ]. The lengthening of *u* is very widely accepted: it is

fully attested by the spelling *ou* which becomes all but universal in words of this type by the end of the thirteenth century. On the other hand, there is no agreement among scholars about the development of *a* before a nasal. In the early thirteenth century the spelling *au* began to replace *a* before a nasal in both AN and ME manuscripts; during the fourteenth century the *au* spelling predominated, though an alternative spelling *o* is sometimes found; in many words, such as *aunt, haunt, launch*, the *au* spelling has survived into MnE, though the pronunciation varies; in other words *au* has been replaced by *a*, again with varying pronunciation. Authorities disagree about the significance of the *au* spelling: Miss Pope and Wyld, for instance, assume that it represents a simple vowel, but Luick and Jordan assume a diphthongal pronunciation. In these circumstances it is clearly necessary to examine the evidence for each assumption.

30. Evidence for a simple vowel:

(1) The digraph *au* is often used in later AN to represent a lengthened and retracted *a* before *s*: *chaustel, tauster*. See Pope, *op. cit.*, § 1153.

(2) The symbol *o* is occasionally used as an alternative to *au* both in AN and ME: *quinoncie* (Bozon), *chonge* "charge," *penonce* "penance," *marchont* "merchant" (Dan Michel). On this spelling see further § 32.

(3) Before a group of three consonants AN *au* is often replaced in ME by *ă*, just as a long vowel is shortened in the same circumstances: *aumble-nt > ămble, scaundle > scăndle* "scandal," just as *nūmbre > nòmbre* "number," *encūmbre-nt > encòmbre* "encumber."

Evidence for a diphthong:[42]

(1) The digraph *au* is normally used to represent a diphthong [au] both in OF and ME.

(2) Before a labial *m* or the affricate group *nğ*, ME *au* from *a* + nasal is smoothed to *ā*, just as the genuine diphthong *au* is smoothed to *ā* before a labial *v* or the affricate *ğ*: *chaumber > chāmber, straunğe > strānğe*, just as *sauve > sāve, sauğe > sāğe*.

(3) A diphthongal pronunciation for *au* from this source is implied in the Welsh *Hymn to the Virgin* and recorded by the orthoepists Salesbury, Hart, Bullokar, Mulcaster, Gil and Butler.

31. None of this evidence can very easily be explained away, and it seems to follow that both types of pronunciation must have existed in AN and ME. But they need not necessarily have coexisted: a simple vowel may have anteceded a diphthong, or a diphthong may have anteceded a simple vowel. In default of clear external evidence we shall have to rely on intrinsic phonetic probability to decide between the two possibilities. There are two main ways in which a diphthong can be formed: it can result from the coalescence of two originally distinct vowels, one of which is often a glide or epenthetic vowel; or it can result from the "breaking" of a single vowel, either because of an isolative tendency towards breaking, or because of the influence of a neighbouring sound. In the first case the original stressed vowel may be either long or short: OE *o, ō* + *u̯* from the vocalisation of *w* both give ME *ǫu*; VL *u, ū* + epenthetic *i̯* both give OF *üi*. In the second case the original vowel is always

long: ME *ī*, *ū* give MnE [aɪ, aʊ] because of an isolative tendency towards breaking; VL *ā* + nasal gives OF *ai*. There can be no question of a glide or epenthetic vowel before a nasal: hence it follows that the diphthong *au* belongs to the second type, and therefore that the vowel from which it developed was originally long.[43] If this conclusion is accepted, it is easier to assume that the simple vowel whose existence is proved by the evidence listed above anteceded the diphthong, rather than the contrary; furthermore, the evidence of the orthoepists supports this order, since otherwise it would be necessary to assume either that all the orthoepists were mistaken, or that a simple vowel derived from an earlier diphthong *au* was re-diphthongised to *au* in early MnE.

32. It is now possible to present an orderly and consistent picture of the development of OF *a* before a nasal. Short *a*, originally the front vowel [a], was retracted in AN to the back vowel [ɑ] when it was followed by a nasal. This [ɑ], like the only other back vowel *u*, was lengthened in AN when it was followed by nasal *m* or *n*: the resulting long [ɑː] was at first represented by the symbol *a* both in AN and in ME. Long [ɑː] was adopted as such into ME, and underwent shortening in those circumstances in which other long vowels were shortened; the resulting short [ɑ] was usually fronted again to conform with the normal ME [a], but occasionally, and particularly in Kentish, it was further retracted to conform with ME short *o*.[44] In the early thirteenth century long [ɑː] wherever it survived began to be broken under the influence of the following nasal to [ɑu], which may have been modified to [au] to conform with the normal ME *au* from other sources. The breaking of [ɑː] to [ɑu] is exactly parallel to the earlier breaking of VL *ā* to *ai* by a following nasal: in each case the latter part of the long vowel was raised, either to front *i* or back *u* according to the quality of the original vowel. The raising influence of a following nasal is too well known to require illustration. It is impossible to determine how regularly the breaking occurred, or whether it occurred at the same time in all dialects: the spelling *au* may sometimes be no more than a graphy for a simple vowel [ɑː]; in later AN it is written for a lengthened and retracted *a* before *s*, where it is extremely improbable that a diphthong could have developed. But there can be little doubt that the simple vowel had become obsolete before the end of the ME period, since none of the four MnE pronunciations illustrated by the words *aunt*, *haunt*, *scandal*, *strange* can be traced back with any plausibility to a ME [ɑː]. In the present discussion I am, of course, concerned only with the lengthening of *a* before a nasal; but in the word-list in § 34 the ME forms are those with *au*-spellings, since the occurrence of a diphthong presupposes a long vowel.

33. OF *u* from VL *ǫ* and *ọ* before a nasal was lengthened to *ū* in AN before a following *m* or *n* (not [ŋ]). When the stress was not shifted in ME the long vowel generally remained and was usually written *ou*; but it often underwent

regular or sporadic shortening, and variant forms are often found in early MnE. With VL ǫ:

| VL | | OF | | ME | | |
|----|----|----|----|----|----|----|
| cŏmĭtem | | cunte | | cȯunte | "count" |
| cŏmpŭta-nt | | cunte-nt | | cȯunte | "count" |
| fŏntem | | funt | | fȯunt | |
| mŏntem | | munt | | mȯunt | |

With VL ọ:

| VL | | OF | | ME | | |
|----|----|----|----|----|----|----|
| ăbŭnda-nt | | abunde-nt | | abȯunde | "abound" |
| annŭntĭa-nt | | anunce-nt | | anȯunce | "announce" |
| confŭnda-nt | | confunde-nt | | cȯnfȯunde | "confound" |
| expōnĕre | | espundre | | espȯunde | "expound" |
| fŭnda-nt | | funde-nt | | fȯunde | "found" |
| ŭncĭa | | unce | | ȯunce | |
| *pŭmĭcem | | punce | | pȯunce | |
| prŏfŭndum | | profund | | profȯund | |
| prŏnŭntĭa-nt | | pronunce-nt | | pronȯunce | |
| tŭmba | | tumbe | | tȯumbe | "tomb" |

In ME *nȯmbre* "number" < *nŭmĕrum* and *encȯmbre* "encumber" < *incŏmbra-nt* the long vowel has been regularly shortened before a group of three consonants. In ME *encȯuntre* "encounter" < *incŏntra-nt*, on the other hand, the expected shortening has not occurred: the reason seems to be that a parasite vowel sometimes developed in words of this type, so that *encȯntre* > *encȯuntere* > *encȯunter*: in this case, of course, no shortening is to be expected. Sporadic shortening has occurred in *frȯnt* < *frŏntem* and *spȯngĕ* < *spŏngĭa*. When the stress was shifted in ME the long vowel was shortened and later obscured. Thus, with VL ǫ:

| VL | | OF | | ME | | |
|----|----|----|----|----|----|----|
| *submŏnĕre | | sumundre | | sȯmȯnde | "summon" |
| *submŏnsa | | sumunse | | sȯmȯnse | "summons" |

34. OF *a* from VL *a* + nasal and VL *ę* + *m* was lengthened in AN before a following *m* or *n* (not [ŋ]). The lengthened vowel was subsequently broken to *au*, and this is the most usual form when the stress was not shifted. Thus, with VL *a* + nasal:

| VL | | OF | | ME | | |
|----|----|----|----|----|----|----|
| *abantĕa-nt | | avance-nt | | avaunce | "advance" |
| ămĭta | | ante | | aunte | "aunt" |
| *blanka | | blanche | | blaunche | "blanch" |
| *branka | | branche | | braunche | "branch" |
| *cambĭa-nt | | change-nt | | chaungĕ | "change" |
| canta-nt | | chante-nt | | chaunte | "chant" |
| *commanda-nt | | comande-nt | | comaunde | "command" |
| *dansa-nt | | danse-nt | | daunse | "dance" |

| *dămĭta-nt | dante-nt | daunte | "daunt" |
| *grānĭca | grange | graunğe | "grange" |
| *hanka | hanche | haunche | "haunch" |
| lancĕa | lance | launce | "lance" |
| lancĕa-nt | lanche-nt | launche | "launch" |
| *landa | lande | launde | "lawn" |
| pantĭcem | panche | paunche | "paunch" |
| expandu-nt | espande-nt | spaunde | "spawn" |
| extrānĕum | estrange | straunğe | "strange" |
| tantum | tant | taunt | |
| *vānĭta-nt | vante-nt | vaunte | "vaunt" |

In ME *amble* < *ambŭla-nt* and *scandle* "scandal" < *scandălum* the long vowel has been regularly shortened before a group of three consonants. In ME *chaumbre* "chamber" < *cămĕra, sclaundre* "slander" < *scandălum* and (with VL *ę* + *m*) *ensaumple* "example" < *exemplum*, on the other hand, the expected shortening has not occurred, probably because of the development of a parasite vowel. Sporadic shortening has occurred in *lampe* "lamp" < *lampăda*, and perhaps in *scampe* "scamp" < **excampa-nt*; but the latter may owe its short vowel to the proparoxytone past tense *scămpede*. Although all the MnE forms listed above presuppose ME *au*, many show sporadic shortening in the dialects. When the stress was shifted in ME the long vowel was shortened and later obscured; the most usual spelling is *a*, but *au* is not uncommon.

| VL | gĭgantem | ME | giant | |
| | *mercantem | | merchant | |
| | sĭmŭlantem | | semblant | |
| | *servĭantem | | serjant | "sergeant" |

Here belong a large number of words in *-antĭa*: *importance, nüisance, penance, pitance* "pittance."

35. Another important AN sound-change is the lengthening of short vowels before tautosyllabic *s* or [z] (not necessarily *s* or [z] + consonant). Lengthening before [z] later effaced is scarcely controversial:

| VL | *blastĭma-nt | OF | blasme-nt | ME | blāme | |
| | chrĭsma | | cresme | | crẽme[45] | "cream" |
| | insŭla | | isle | | īle | "isle" |
| | mascŭlum | | masle | | māle | |

In ME *medle* "meddle" < **miscŭla-nt* and *medler* "medlar" < **mespĭ-lārĭum* [z] had been dentalised to [ð] before the lengthening occurred. Lengthening before *s* is practically restricted to lengthening before *st*, for the number of instances of a short vowel followed by *s* final or *s* + any consonant other than *t* is very small indeed: examples of *s* final are *ās* "ace" < *as* < *ăs* and *pās* "pace" < *pas* < *passum*; an example of *s* + *k* is *taske* "task" < *\*tasca*, in which sporadic shortening has occurred. I shall here limit my discussion to the question of lengthening before *st*, since there are many examples of this change. This lengthening is usually treated[46] as a special instance of the ME lengthening in an open syllable, and this view is at first sight the more plausible since the ME lengthening in an open syllable does in fact occur before *st* in the inflected forms of such native words as *ȝest* "yeast," *post* and *wast* "waist"; however, it is not difficult to prove from the most varied evidence that the long vowel existed already in AN, and that it is due to the following consonant, not to an open syllable.

36. The evidence is as follows:

(1) As early as the beginning of the twelfth century AN *ę* before *st* was rhymed with *ẹ̄* from *ai*. Ten Brink quotes the following rhymes from Philippe de Thaün[47]: *Silvestre: maistre, beste: paistre, beste: maistre, tempestes: maistres, estre: maistre*.
(2) In the north-eastern dialects of OF, *ę* and *ǫ* were broken to *ie* and *ue* respectively before *r* and *s*[48]: *fier* < *ferrum, iestre* < *\*essĕre, muert* < *mortem, tuest* < *\*tostum*. In these dialects the tendency to diphthongise long vowels must have lasted longer than elsewhere, for long *ẹ̄* from VL *ā* is broken to *ei*,[49] just like original VL *ę̄*; the most probable explanation of the breaking of *ę* and *ǫ* before *r* and *s* is that these vowels had first been lengthened to *ę̄* and *ǭ*, and were then broken just like original VL *ę̄* and *ǭ*. Although the late breaking was restricted to the north-eastern dialects, there is no reason to suppose that the lengthening before *r* and *s* was similarly restricted.
(3) Lengthening occurs as regularly in forms such as ME *ǭst* "host" < *hostem*, in which the *st* is final, as in forms such as ME *ǭste* "host" < *hospĭtem*, in which the *st* is followed by a vowel. It should further be noticed that final *-e* was effaced earlier in the loanwords than in native words; it had often disappeared before the date of the ME lengthening in an open syllable.
(4) Forms such as ME *jòuste*[50] < *juste-nt* < *\*juxta-nt* cannot be due to the ME lengthening in an open syllable, since when *ŭ* was lengthened at all it became, not *ū*, but *ǭ*.
(5) In those dialects of the north Midlands in which a distinction is still preserved between [ɪə] from OE *ǣ, ēa* (i.e., originally long vowels) and [eɪ] from OE *ĕ* in an open syllable, the words *beast* and *feast* always have [ɪə].[51]

In view of this diverse evidence I shall here assume that lengthening took place in AN before tautosyllabic *s*.[52]

37. There are no clear examples of the lengthening of the close front vowels *i* and *ü* before *st*: *Crīst* is probably from OE rather than from AN; the short vowel of the verb *resĭste* is inconclusive, since it may be either original or levelled from the proparoxytone past tense *resĭstede*; the vowel *ü* seems never to occur before *st*. There are only two examples of the lengthening of *e* before *st*:

| VL | *bę̄sta* | OF | beste | ME | bę̄ste | "beast" |
|----|---------|----|-------|----|-------|---------|
|    | fę̄sta   |    | feste |    | fę̄ste | "feast" |

The verbs *arĕste* "arrest," *gĕste* "jest" and *tĕste* "test" have levelled the shortened vowel of the past tense into the present, and the nouns *gĕste* and *tĕste* have adopted the short vowel of the verb. Examples of the lengthening of *a* before *st* are more numerous:

| VL | | OF | | ME | | |
|----|----|----|----|----|----|----|
| | castum | | chast | | chāst | "chaste" |
| | *haifsta | | haste | | hāste | |
| | pasta | | paste | | pāste | |
| | *taxĭta-nt | | taste-nt | | tāste | |
| | vastum | | wast | | wāst | "waste" |

However, variant forms with a short vowel are frequent in early MnE. It is possible that *ā* was often shortened in ME before *st*, and that a long vowel was sometimes reintroduced by the ME lengthening in an open syllable; there is a close parallelism between the early MnE forms of *wāst* "waste" and those of the native *wāst* "waist."

38. Examples of the lengthening of *o* before *st* are again fairly numerous:

| VL | | OF | | ME | | |
|----|----|----|----|----|----|----|
| | costa | | coste | | cǭste | "coast" |
| | hostem | | ost | | ǭst | "host" |
| | hospĭtem | | oste | | ǭste | "host" |
| | posĭta | | poste | | pǭste | "post" |
| | *hraustu-nt | | roste-nt | | rǭste | "roast" |
| | *tosta-nt | | toste-nt | | tǭste | "toast" |

Variant forms with a short vowel are sometimes found in early MnE. The verb *coste* "cost" is anomalous, since both the strong and the weak forms should normally have *u*, not *o*, in OF: *constant > custent, constāre > custēr*; compare MnF *coûter*. The *o* must be due to the analogy of the frequent vocalic alternation *o–u*: *obstant > ostent, obstāre > ustēr*. The short vowel of MnE *cost* has been levelled from the proparoxytone past tense; a long *o* is recorded by some of the orthoepists.[53] The only clear example of the lengthening of *u* before *st* is *jǒuste* "jouste" < *juxta-nt* (§ 36.4). The verb *ǒuste* "oust" may be derived from the OF weak form *ustēr* < *obstāre* with lengthening in a countertonic syllable (§ 52), but it is more probably derived from the strong form *oste-nt* by the south-western OF sound-change of lengthened *ǭ* to *ū*,[54] which has to be invoked to explain the *ǒu* of ME *pǒuche* "pouch," *tǒuche* "touch" and *vǒuche* "vouch" (§ 42(2)).

39. A further important AN sound-change is the lengthening of short vowels before tautosyllabic *r* (not necessarily *r* + consonant). The evidence that this change had taken place in AN is as follows:

(1) As early as the beginning of the twelfth century AN *ę* before *r* was rhymed with *ē̢* from *ai*. Ten Brink quotes the rhyme *termes* : *lermes* from *The Voyage of St. Brendan*.[55]

(2) An OF lengthening before *r* is presupposed by the northeastern sound-change discussed in § 36(2).

(3) The occurrence in early MnE of such forms as *fǫrce*, *fǭrǧe* and *pǭrche* (§ 41) proves that the lengthening of *o* before *r* antedated the AN raising of *ǭ* to *ǭ* after labial *p*, *b* and *f*; for proof that this change took place in AN see § 42(1).

(4) Such a form as ME *tóur* "tower" cannot owe its long vowel to the influence of the ME lengthening in an open syllable in the inflected cases, since when *ŭ* was lengthened at all it became, not *ū*, but *ǭ*.

In view of this evidence I shall here assume that lengthening took place in AN before tautosyllabic *r*[56]; but it must be admitted that its results have very often been obscured by sporadic shortening. The MnE pronunciation is nearly always derived from a ME or early MnE variant with a short vowel; but fortunately a long vowel is often attested either by the evidence of the ortho-epists or by the MnE spelling.

40. There seem to be no examples of the close front vowels *i* and *ü* before *r*. No example of the lengthening of *e* before *r* seems to have survived into MnE, but early MnE evidence proves that in ME the following words had a long vowel, at least as a variant:

| VL | | OF | | ME | | |
|----|----|----|----|----|----|----|
| *herpĭcem | | herce | | hęrce | | "hearse" |
| *perla | | perle | | pęrle | | "pearl" |
| pertĭca | | perche | | pęrche | | "perch" |
| *circa-nt | | cerche-nt | | cęrche[57] | | "search" |
| termĭnum | | terme | | tęrme | | "term" |

In the words *hearse*, *pearl* and *search* the long vowel is attested by the MnE spelling. On ME *pęrce* "pierce," see § 53. Only one word in MnE preserves *ā* from the lengthening of *a* before *r*:

| VL | | OF | | ME | | |
|----|----|----|----|----|----|----|
| *excarpsum | | escars | | scårs | | "scarce" |

But early MnE evidence proves that in ME the following words had a long vowel, at least as a variant:

| VL | | OF | | ME | | |
|----|----|----|----|----|----|----|
| artem | | art | | årt | | |
| charta | | carte | | cårde | | "card" |
| *warda-nt | | guarde-nt | | gårde | | "guard" |
| lārĭdum | | lard | | lård | | |
| *larga | | large | | lårǧe | | |
| *margĭla | | marle | | mårle | | "marl" |
| partem | | part | | pårt | | |

This long *ā* has survived more regularly in modern Scots than in Standard English, witness such forms as *pairt*, *lairge*.

41. Lengthening of *o* before *r* cannot be proved from MnE pronunciations, since ME *ŏr* and *ǭr* are both pronounced [ɔː], but early MnE evidence proves that in ME the following words had a long vowel, at least as a variant:

| VL | | OF | | ME | | |
|---|---|---|---|---|---|---|
| chorda | | corde | | cǭrde | "cord" |
| corpus | | cors | | cǭrs | "corpse" |
| *disporta-nt | | desporte-nt | | despǭrte | "disport" |
| *fortĭa | | force | | fǭrce | |
| fabrĭca | | forge | | fǭrǧe | |
| forma | | forme | | fǭrme | "form" |
| fortem | | fort | | fǭrt | |
| ordĭnem | | ordre | | ǭrdre | "order" |
| portĭcum | | porche | | pǭrche | "porch" |
| porcum | | porc | | pǭrk | |
| portum | | port | | pǭrt | |
| *excorna-nt | | escorne-nt | | scǭrne | "scorn" |
| sortem | | sort | | sǭrt | |

There are alternative forms *fǫrce*, *fǫrǧe* and *pǫrche* with close *ǫ* due to the AN raising of *ǭ* to *ǫ* after labial *p, b* and *f*; see § 42(1). The lengthening of *u* before *r* is regularly attested by the MnE pronunciation in the following words:

| VL | | OF | | ME | | |
|---|---|---|---|---|---|---|
| cursum | | curs | | coúrs | "course" |
| cŏhortem | | curt | | coúrt | |
| sursum | | surs | | soúrs | "source" |
| turrim | | tur | | toúr | "tower" |

## Lengthening in an open syllable

42. There remains still a further lengthening which must have occurred in AN, a limited lengthening of short vowels in an open syllable. The evidence for this sound-change is as follows:

(1) The MnE pronunciation of *boot* and *fool* proves that the ME forms must have been *bōte* and *fōl* with close *ō*. In OF *bote* and *fol* the vowel was short; if the long vowel had been due to the ME lengthening in an open syllable it would have had open quality; the raising of *ǭ* to *ǫ* after labial *p, b,* and *f* cannot be a ME change, since it does not affect such a word as ME *fǭle* "foal" < OE *fŏla*. Hence it follows that the raising of *ǭ* to *ǫ* is an AN change; and, since this raising affects only long *ǭ* (either original, as in *pǫvre* "poor," or due to lengthening, as in *fǫrce, fǫrǧe, pǫrche* "porch"), the vowel of *bote* and *fol* must have been long already in AN. Since there is no other common feature in these two words the vowel must have been lengthened because it stood in an open syllable.

(2) The long *ou* of ME *poúche* "pouch" < *pocca*, *toúche* "touch" < *tocca-nt* and *voúche* "vouch" < *vocca-nt* can only be due to the south-western OF raising of *ǭ* to *ū*,[58] which also affects lengthened *ǭ* before *s* (§ 38); hence it follows that the vowel of these words must have been long already in AN.

(3) Such forms as *dŏute* "doubt," *gŏute* "gout," *rŏute* "rout" and *gŏuğe* cannot owe their long vowels to the ME lengthening in an open syllable, since when *ŭ* was lengthened at all it became, not *ū*, but *ŏ*.

This evidence is sufficient to prove that lengthening in an open syllable could take place in AN; but it is by no means sufficient to delimit the circumstances in which it actually did take place. The only details which can be admitted at this stage are that *o* could be lengthened in an open syllable before *t*, *l*, and *ch*, and *u* before *t* and *ğ*. This information is quite insufficient, and it is therefore necessary to have recourse to the evidence offered by the ME gemination of certain consonants in borrowings from AN.

43. All OF double consonants except *rr* had been simplified before the Norman Conquest[59]; but in circumstances which have never yet been clearly defined simple consonants were sometimes geminated in the ME borrowings. If the numerous instances of this gemination are examined in the light of the laws of vowel-quantity I have here formulated, a simple rule can be discerned: simple consonants may be geminated after a short vowel, but they are never geminated after a long vowel or after a diphthong. The voiced affricate *ğ*, for instance, is regularly geminated in *abrĕğğe* "abridge" < *abbrĕvĭa-nt*, *alĕğğe* "allege" < *allĕvĭa-nt*, *alĕğğe* "allege" < *\*exlītĭga-nt* and *plĕğğe* "pledge" < *\*plĕvĭum*, where the vowel is short, but never in *lēğe* "liege" < *\*lēdĭgum* nor *sēğe* "siege" < *\*sēdĭcum*, where the vowel is long, nor in *sauğe* "sage" < *salvĭa* after a diphthong.[60] The reason for this gemination is not far to seek: in native words, for various reasons, a short vowel was very frequently followed by a double consonant, and a long vowel was never followed by a double consonant.[61] The main source of double consonants in native words was the West Germanic gemination by *j*, which took place only after short vowels; and in late OE all original long vowels were shortened before a double consonant of any other origin. The gemination can occasionally be observed even in native words: when dental *t* or *d* was palatalised and affricated by a following [j] in such words as *fetian*, *\*midgern*, the resulting forms *fecc(e)an*, *micgern* had geminated consonants; similarly, when the vowel of *\*rēc(e)an* was shortened for unknown reasons, the result was *recc(e)an* with a geminated consonant. The value of this gemination for our purpose is obvious: if the consonant is never geminated after a vowel which should by origin be short, there is a strong presumption that the vowel had been lengthened already in AN; and evidence of this kind enables us to delimit the AN lengthening in an open syllable with considerable accuracy.

44. The evidence of this gemination shows that in AN only the vowels *a*, *o*, and *u* were lengthened in an open syllable, and these only before the dental consonants *t*,[62] *ch*, *ğ*, *c*,[63] *l*, and *n*. There are no instances of the consistent absence of gemination of any consonant after *i*, *e*, or *ü*, nor of any consonant other than those listed above after *a*, *o*, or *u*, unless the vowel is already

known to be long. It must be admitted that certain consonants, particularly the labials *p*, *b*, and *f*, are very rarely attested in my word-list; but the fact that all the consonants before which lengthening can be proved to occur are dentals is suggestive. It will be noticed that all the instances of lengthening quoted in § 42 are included in this larger statement.

45. AN *a* was lengthened before *t* in *abāte, debāte, plāte*; before *ch* in *nāche* "aitch(-bone)"; before *ǧ* in *cāǧe, pāǧe, rāǧe, sāǧe, wāǧe*; before *c* in *brāce, chāce*, "chase," *fāce, māce, plāce, trāce*. The short vowel attested by the gemination in *căcche* "catch" is due partly to levelling from the proparoxytone past tense *căcchede*, recorded in early ME beside the more usual *cauȝte*, and partly to analogy with the native *lăcche* "latch." AN *o* was lengthened before *t* in *bǭte* "boot," *cǭte* "coat"; before *ch* in *aprǭche* "approach," *brǭche* "brooch," *encrǭche* "encroach," *reprǭche* "reproach," *rǭche* "rock," and in *póuche, tóuche, vóuche*, see § 42 (2); before *ǧ* in *lǭǧe* "lodge"; before *l* in *fǭl* "fool." The short vowel attested by the gemination in the alternative form *lŏǧǧe* is borrowed from the related verb, in which it is due to levelling from the proparoxytone past tense; the short vowel of the alternative form *rŏcche* may be borrowed from the variant *rŏkke*, in which the short vowel is regular before a velar. AN *u* was lengthened before *t* in *dóute* "doubt," *góute* "gout," *róute* "route"; before *ch* in *gróuche* "grouch"; before *ǧ* in *góuǧe*; before *n* in *góune* "gown." The short vowel of the alternative form *grŭcche* "grudge" is due to levelling from the proparoxytone past tense.

46. It is no part of my present plan to discuss in full the AN vowels which remained short, or those which were lengthened by native English soundchanges; but for the sake of completeness I have added a few notes on the fate of AN short vowels in an open syllable. AN *i* always remains short, since it is affected by neither the AN nor the ME lengthening in an open syllable; it occurs only in a few such words as *trĭcche* "trick," *atĭffe*. AN *e* usually remains short, since it is not affected by the AN lengthening, and is usually protected from the ME lengthening by the gemination: *abrĕǧǧe* "abridge," *alĕǧǧe* "allege" < *allĕvĭa-nt*, *alĕǧǧe* "allege" < *exlītĭga-nt*, *cĕlle* "cell," *chĕkke* "check," *confĕsse* "confess," *crĕcche, dĕtte* "debt," *destrĕsse* "distress," *drĕsse* "dress," *plĕǧǧe* "pledge," *spĕlle* "spell," *vĕcche* "vetch." But occasionally the gemination fails, and then *e* is lengthened to *ę̄* by the ME lengthening: *apę̄le* "appeal," *cę̄se* "cease" beside *cĕsse, nę̄t* "neat" (by levelling from inflected cases), *prę̄se* beside *prĕsse* "press." AN *a* does not occur short before dentals, but before labials it sometimes undergoes lengthening in ME: *escāpe*, and, before labial + liquid, where no gemination is possible, *āble, cāble, fāble, stāble* < *stābĭlem, stāble* < *stăbŭlum, tāble*. AN *o* does not occur short before dentals, but before velars it sometimes undergoes lengthening in ME: *clǭke* "cloak."

## AN Countertonic Vowels
## in ME

### The shift of stress

47. All OF words were stressed either on the final syllable, or, if the word
ended in obscure -*e*, on the penultimate syllable. In ME, on the other hand, all
native words were stressed either on the first syllable, or, if the word began
with one of a limited number of prefixes, on the second syllable. Always in
monosyllabic loanwords, and sometimes in disyllabic and trisyllabic ones
the OF and the native stress coincided; but often the native stress clashed
with the OF stress. Generally when this happened the OF stress sooner or
later gave way to the native stress; that is to say, sooner or later the stress
was transferred either to the first syllable, or, if the word began with a
recognisable prefix, to the second syllable. It is difficult to define so subjective
an element as a "recognisable prefix"; but in general a prefix may be considered recognisable if the stem of the word in which it occurs can also be
found in other words; thus, *contẹ̄ne* "contain" and *detẹ̄ne* "detain" are both
stressed on the second syllable, but *contreie* "country" and *desert* are stressed
on the first syllable. Frequent prefixes like *de-* and *re-* are often recognised
even when this rule does not apply; and a prefix which is not recognised in a
noun may be recognised in the related verb, since in native words prefixes are
far more frequent among verbs than among nouns. The date of the shift of
stress is necessarily uncertain: probably as many as three variant forms of
some words co-existed, one in which the stress was fully accommodated to the
native pattern, a second in which the OF tonic syllable retained a secondary
stress, and a third in which the OF stress remained unchanged; the third
form is frequent in poetry for the sake of rhyme or metre, but it is unlikely
to have survived long in colloquial speech.[64] Since the effect of the shift of
stress was to stress an originally countertonic syllable, we must proceed to
discuss the quantity of countertonic vowels in AN.

### The smoothing of diphthongs

48. There can be no doubt at all that countertonic vowels were short in VL,
for the characteristic breaking of long $\bar{ẹ}$, $\bar{ę}$, $\bar{ǫ}$ and $\bar{ǫ}$ never occurs in a countertonic syllable. It can easily be shown that the long vowels resulting from the
earlier smoothings were shortened in countertonic syllables. The vowels
resulting from the smoothing of CL *oe* and *ae* cannot be distinguished from
*ẹ* and *ę* of other origins, and must have been short, since they do not undergo
breaking. The vowel resulting from the smoothing of VL *au* cannot be distinguished from *ǫ* of other origins, and must have been short, since not only
does it not undergo breaking, but it is raised to *u* before a nasal—a change
which only affects short vowels: \**sagmārĭum* > \**saumārĭum* > *sumier*
"summer," \**sagmātārĭum* > \**saumātārĭum* > *sumetier* "sumpter." On the

other hand, $\bar{e}$ from the later smoothing of countertonic *ai, ei*[65] seems to have remained long, judging by ME borrowings[66]:

| VL | | OF | | ME | | |
|---|---|---|---|---|---|---|
| factūra | | faitūre | | fẹ̄tūre | | "feature" |
| lĭcēre | | leisīr | | lẹ̄sĭr | | "leisure" |
| phāsĭānum | | faisān | | fẹ̄sănt | | "pheasant" |
| plăcēre | | plaisīr | | plẹ̄sĭr | | "pleasure" |
| rătĭōnem | | raisūn | | rẹ̄sȯn | | "reason" |
| sătĭōnem | | saisūn | | sẹ̄sȯn | | "season" |
| tractātum | | traitie | | trẹ̄tĕ | | "treaty" |

The words *leisure, pheasant* and *pleasure* have undergone shortening in MnE; these together with *hĕrȯn* < *\*hăgĭrōnem* and *vĕssel* < *vascellum*, in which the shortening took place already in ME, are discussed in § 61.

## The absorption of glide-vowels

49. Long $\bar{\imath}$ from VL $\bar{\imath}$ + $\underset{\cdot}{\imath}$ and long $\bar{u}$ from earlier $\ddot{u}$ + $\underset{\cdot}{u}$ are not treated alike in countertonic syllables: long $\bar{\imath}$ seems to have been shortened, but long $\bar{u}$, developed much later than long $\bar{\imath}$, seems to have retained its length. Short $\ddot{\imath}$ is attested for ME *pĭtĕ* "pity" < *\*pĭịtātem* < *pĭĕtātem* by the occasional northern lengthening to *pētĕ*, and for ME *quĭtte* "quit" < *\*quĭịtāre* < *quĭētāre* by the gemination of the consonant (§ 43). But long *ȯu* is attested for ME *cȯuche* "couch" < *collŏcāre* by the MnE pronunciation [kaʊtʃ].[67] Forms which show shortening, such as *mŭtȯn* "mutton" < *\*multōnem*, are discussed in § 61.

## The absorption of vowels in hiatus

50. A countertonic short vowel was sometimes lengthened through the absorption of a following unstressed vowel in hiatus with it—that is to say, an intertonic obscure vowel. Here belong the following words:

| VL | | OF | | ME | | |
|---|---|---|---|---|---|---|
| impĕdĭcāre | | empeechier | | empẹ̄che | | "impeach" |
| praedĭcāre | | preechier | | prẹ̄che | | "preach" |

ME *vĕlĭn* "vellum" < *veelin* < *\*vĭtellīnum*, in which the long vowel has been shortened, is discussed in § 61. After the shift of stress in ME the originally tonic vowel was sometimes absorbed by the newly-stressed vowel in hiatus with it; but in this case the newly-stressed vowel is always long.[68] In every instance in my word-list the newly-stressed vowel is $\bar{e}$ from the smoothing of *ai, ei*:

| VL | | OF | | ME | | ME | | |
|---|---|---|---|---|---|---|---|---|
| dĕcānum | | deiien | | dẹ̄en | | dẹn | | "dean" |
| găgātem | | jaiiete | | jẹ̄ete | | jẹ̄te | | "jet" |
| mĕdĭānum | | meiien | | mẹ̄en | | mẹ̄n | | "mean" |

MnE *jet* is from a variant form with sporadic shortening.

*Lengthenings before certain consonants*

51. Lengthening of the back vowels *u* and *a* before nasal *m* and *n* (not [ŋ)]
seems to have occurred as regularly in countertonic as in tonic syllables.
Examples of the lengthening of *u* are the following:

| VL | *bŏnĭtātem | OF | buntē | ME | bóuntĕ | "bounty" |
|----|-----------|----|-------|----|--------|----------|
|    | concĭlĭum |    | cuncilie |  | cóuncil |          |
|    | consĭlĭum |    | cunseil |   | cóunsel |          |
|    | *cŏmĭtissa |   | cuntesse |  | cóuntesse | "countess" |
|    | fontāna |     | funtaine |  | fóuntaine | "fountain" |
|    | *montānĕa |   | muntagne |  | móuntaine | "mountain" |

Shortening has taken place before three consonants in *còntreie* "country"
< *contrāta* and in a proparoxytone in *abòndance* "abundance" < *ăbund-
antĭa; plònğe* "plunge" < *plumbĭcāre* owes its short vowel to the proparoxytone past tense *plònğede*; in *còuntesse, fòuntaine* and *mòuntaine* above the long
vowel is preserved in a proparoxytone by analogy with *còunte, fòunt,
mòunt.* Examples of the lengthening of *a* are the following:

| VL | mandūca-nt | OF | manjŭe-nt[69] | ME | maunjŭe | "mange" |
|----|-----------|----|--------------|----|---------|---------|
|    | mandātum |   | mandē |     | maundĕ | "maundy" |

Shortening has taken place before three consonants in *lămpreie* "lamprey"
< *lamprēda* and in a proparoxytone in *ăncestre* "ancestor" < *antĕcessor.*

52. Lengthening before *s* has been largely obscured by later shortening,
and only one certain example has survived in MnE pronunciation: ME
*pǭsterne* "postern" < *posterne* < *postĕrŭla.* Another possible example is
ME *óuste* "oust," which may be from the OF weak form *ustēr < obstāre*;
but see § 38. Shortening has occurred before three consonants in *ŏstrĭche*
"ostrich" < *ăvis strūthĭo,* and in a proparoxytone in *ŏstage* "hostage"
< *obstātĭcum.* Apart from these regular shortenings sporadic shortening
is very frequent, as in *ŏstĕl < hospĭtālem* and *căstel* "castle" < *castellum,*
among very many others.

53. Lengthening before *r* has also been largely obscured by later shortening,
and only one example survives in MnE pronunciation; but the evidence
of MnE spelling and the statements of the orthoepists make it clear that it
was once widespread. There are no examples of the lengthening of *i* or *ü.*
The only clear example of the lengthening of *e* is ME *pęrce* "pierce" <
*percier < *pertūsĭāre,* and this word presents an interesting phonological
problem, since the result of the lengthening of tonic *e* is always open *ę,*
not close *ẹ* as here. According to the OF grammars[70] countertonic *ę* was
raised to *ẹ* in all contexts except before tautosyllabic *r* and *l*; in fact the
inclusion of *l* must be considered dubious, since the only example of *ę*
before tautosyllabic *l* seems to be *bęautē < *bellĭtātem,* in which the influence

of *bẹaus* < *bellus* is naturally paramount. ME *pẹrce* suggests that countertonic *ę* was raised to *ẹ* in all contexts, and that the occurrence of *ę* before
*r* in OF is due to a later sound-change. I have already pointed out in § 13
that OF tonic *ẹ̄* was lowered to *ę̄* before *r*, but that this change occurred too
late to affect the ME borrowings; if, therefore, countertonic *ę* before *r*
had been lengthened to *ẹ̄* before the lowering of *ẹ̄* to *ę̄*, we should expect to
find exactly what we do find, *ẹ̄* in ME but *ę̄* in OF. However, this may
seem too elaborate a hypothesis to build upon a single word. No examples
of the lengthening of *a* before *r* survive in MnE, but early MnE evidence
attests a long vowel in ME *chārğe* < *\*carrĭcāre* and *gārdĭn* "garden" <
*\*gardīnum*. Lengthening of *o* before *r* is attested by early MnE evidence
in *bǫrdĕr* < *\*bordārĭum*. Lengthening of *u* before *r* is attested by the MnE
spelling in *cóurteis* "courteous" < *\*cŏhortensem*, *jóurneie* "journey" <
*\*dĭurnāta*, *scóurğe* < *excŏrĭāre* and *tóurneie* "tourney" < *\*tornĭzāre*; the
MnE pronunciation of *tourney* with [ɔ:] beside [ɜ:] presupposes a long
vowel.[71]

## Lengthening in hiatus

54. It is not to be expected that short countertonic vowels should be
lengthened in an open syllable in AN, nor is there any evidence that they were;
as we shall see, *e*, *a*, and *o* were sometimes lengthened in ME after the shift
of stress; *i* and *u* were usually not lengthened, and if they were they became
*ẹ̄* and *ǭ*, not *ī* and *ū*. But there is an AN sound-change which may perhaps
be considered parallel to the lengthening of tonic vowels in an open syllable,
the lengthening of certain countertonic vowels in hiatus with a following
tonic vowel. This lengthening affects only the close vowels *i*, *ü*, and *u*,[72]
and is quite regular in its operation. Examples of the lengthening of countertonic *i*:

| | VL | | OF | | ME | |
|---|---|---|---|---|---|---|
| | gĭgantem | | giant | | gīant | |
| | lĕōnem | | liun | | līon | |

Examples of the lengthening of countertonic *ü*:

| | VL | | OF | | ME | |
|---|---|---|---|---|---|---|
| | *crūdālem | | crüẹ̄l | | crüĕ̄l | |
| | *grūtellum | | grüel | | grüel | |

Examples of the lengthening of countertonic *u*:

| | VL | | OF | | ME | |
|---|---|---|---|---|---|---|
| | allŏcāre | | aluẹ̄r | | alȯwe | "allow" |
| | advŏcātum | | avuē | | avȯwĕ | "avow" |
| | bŏtellum | | buel | | bȯwel | |
| | pŏtēre | | pueir | | pȯwer | |
| | *prōdĭcĭa | | pruece | | prȯwece | "prowess" |
| | *trŭella | | truele | | trȯwele | "trowel" |

ME *jewĕl* < *\*jŏcāle* and *fewaile* "fuel" < *\*fŏcālĭa* show the influence of OF *jeu* < *jŏcum* and *feu* < *fŏcum*.

## Lengthening in an open syllable

55. One of the main problems in the phonology of borrowings from AN is the frequent absence of lengthening in words whose structure presents the necessary conditions for the ME lengthening in an open syllable: words, that is to say, in which the newly-stressed vowel is followed by a single consonant. After the shift of stress all the conditions for lengthening were present,[73] but in well over half of this type no lengthening in fact occurred. At least four quite distinct explanations of this curious phenomenon have been offered at various times. According to Wright,[74] early borrowings underwent the lengthening, but later borrowings did not. This will not do, for many of the words which do not show lengthening are recorded in ME well before 1250, the approximate date of the lengthening: *băret* (1230),[75] *bărŏn* (1200), *cătel* "cattle" (1205), *cĕler* "cellar" (1225), *chătel* "chattel" (1225), *dĕsert* (1225), *drăgŏn* (1220), *ŏnŏr* "honour" (1200), *Lătin* (950), *lĕgat* "legate" (1154), *lĕssŏn* (1225), *prĕlat* "prelate" (1205), *prĕsent* (1225), *vĕnim* "venom" (1220). Luick, followed in the main by Jordan,[76] offers two distinct explanations. According to him all words of this type were adopted into English with a secondary stress on the second vowel and the first vowel long, because all native words with a secondary stress had a long first syllable. Later the vowel was shortened in many words, after the loss of secondary stress, either through a desire for a closer approximation to the continental pronunciation, or through the influence of proparoxytone inflected forms. In the first case, it was naturally those words most used by the educated classes which underwent shortening, and those most used by the lower classes which retained the long vowel; but it is hard to see why such words as *băril* "barrel," *cătel, cĕlar, chătel, gălŏn* "gallon," *mĕtal, pŏtel* "pottle," should be used chiefly by cultivated speakers, or such words as *blāsŏn* "blazon," *fāvŏr* "favour," *ǭdor* "odour," *sāvŏr* "savour," *vācant, vāpŏr* "vapour," by the illiterate. Luick's second explanation is no explanation at all; it merely removes the question a stage further, and leaves us to wonder why the short vowel of the inflected forms should be levelled in some cases and not in others. Still a further explanation has been given by Eckhardt, and, with some variation, by Eliason.[77] According to these writers, lengthening was inhibited by the survival of some degree of stress on the final syllable—according to Eckhardt, half stress, but according to Eliason "weak stress," an intermediate degree between half stress and complete lack of stress. This again is no explanation at all: at best it elucidates only the process by which the lengthening was inhibited, and leaves us wondering why some words retained a greater degree of stress than others; in fact, it is far from clear that there is any connection between stress and

quantity in words of this type. None of these various explanations can be considered at all satisfactory.

56. It is important to realise that words of this type could not have been affected by the ME lengthening in an open syllable until after the shift of stress—that is, until their pronunciation had been fully accommodated to the native pattern. It follows that the factor which dictates the difference of quantity in the loanwords must have affected native words also; and in fact an examination of native words of similar form reveals just the same kind of variation as we find in the loanwords. For purposes of comparison I have prepared two lists, one of loanwords and one of native words. The list of loanwords includes only those words which the *NED* records in or before 1400; it does not include words such as *lẹ̄sir* "leisure," *plẹ̄sir* "pleasure," *rẹ̄sòn* "reason," *sẹ̄sòn* "season," in which the vowel was long by origin; these are discussed in § 61; nor does it include words whose first vowel was *i* or *u*, since these vowels are not normally affected by the ME lengthening.[78] Of 111 words, only 26 have undergone lengthening: *bācòn*, *bāsin*, *blāsòn* "blazon," *brọ̄còr* "broker," *cāpòn*, *dẹ̄ver* "(en)deavour," *drāper*, *fāmòs* "famous," *fāvòr* "favour," *flāvòr*, "flavour," *jẹ̄lòs* "jealous," *lābel*, *lābòr* "labour," *lẹ̄vòr* "lever," *māsòn*, *mọ̄ment*, *ọ̄dòr* "odour," *pāper*, *pātent*, *prọ̄ces* "process," *rāsòr* "razor," *sāvòr* "savour," *tābòr*, *trẹ̄sor* "treasure," *vācant, vāpòr* "vapour."[79] The remaining 85 show no lengthening: *ălum, ănet, ănis, ăzūr* "azure," *băròn, bărain* "barren," *băret* "barrat," *băril* "barrel," *bĕril* "beryl," *bĕsant* "bezant," *bŏnet* "bonnet," *brĕvet*, *cătel* "cattle," *cĕler* "cellar," *chănel* "channel," *chătel* "chattel," *clămòr* "clamour," *clăret, clŏset, cŏfin* "coffin," *cŏler* "collar," *cŏmòn* "common," *cŏral, crŏchet* "crotchet," *dămask, dĕsert, drăgòn, făgot* "faggot," *fĕlòn, flătŏr* "flatter," *flŏrin, fŏrain* "foreign," *fŏrest, gălòn* "gallon," *hăbit, hăsard* "hazard," *hĕraud* "herald," *ŏnòr* "honour," *jŏlif* "jolly," *kĕnil* "kennel," *lăchet* "latchet," *Lătin, lătòn* "latten," *lĕchòr* "lecher," *lĕgat* "legate," *lĕssòn, mălard,* "mallard," *măneir* "manor," *măreis* "marish," *mĕtal, mŏral, pălais* "palace," *pălat* "palate," *pănel, pĕnòn* "pennon," *pĕril, pŏtel* "pottle," *prĕlat* "prelate," *prĕsent, prŏfit, rĕcord, rĕvel, rŏchet, rŏket* "rocket," *săchel* "satchel," *sătin, sĕcònd, sĕnat* "senate," *sŏket* "socket," *sŏlaz* "solace," *stătūt* "statute," *tăbard, tălent, tălòn, tăssel, tĕnant, tĕnòr, trăvel, trĕliz* "trellice," *trĕmòr, vălòr* "valour," *văssal, vĕnim* "venom," *vŏlūm* "volume," *wărant* "warrant." My list of native words, which, for reasons which will become obvious, I print in their OE form, contains 57 words.[80] Of these, 22 show lengthening: *æcer* "acre," *beofor* "beaver," *(be)neopan* "(be)neath," *bræsen* "brazen," *ceafor* "chafer," *cradol* "cradle," *efes* "eaves," *efen* "even," *feþer* "feather," *hæsel* "hazel," *heofon* "heaven," *hlædel* "ladle," *leþer* "leather," *\*mapul* "maple," *nacod* "naked," *ofer* "over," *open, hræfn* "raven," *stapol* "staple," *tapor* "taper," *tredel* "treadle," *weder* "weather."[81] The remaining 35 show no lengthening: *botm* "bottom," *copor* "copper,"

*alor* "elder," *eln* "ell," *fæder* "father," *fæþm* "fathom," *fetor* "fetter," *fetel* "fettle," *ganot* "gannet," *hamor* "hammer," *heorot* "hart," *hænep* "hemp," *holegn* "holly," *cetel* "kettle," *lator* "latter," *merisc* "marsh," *neoþor* "nether," *oter* "otter," *ofen* "oven," *hraþor* "rather," *sadol* "saddle," *seofon* "seven," *setl* "settle," *sc(e)acol* "shackle," *sc(e)amol* "shamble(s)," *sc(e)ofl* "shovel," *sweþel* "swaddle," *teter* "tetter," *waroþ* "warth," *wæter* "water," *watol* "wattle," *welisc* "Welsh," *weþer* "wether," *weoloc* "whelk," *hwæþer* "whether."

57. The most cursory examination of these lists reveals that a large number of the words which do not show lengthening contain a medial liquid or nasal. Thus with medial *l*: *alum, celer, coler, felón, galón, jolif, malard, palais, palat, prelat, solaz, talent, talón, treliz, valór, volūm; alor, eln, holegn, welisc, weoloc.* With medial *r*: *barón, barain, baret, baril, beril, claret, coral, florin, forain, forest, heraud, mareis, moral, peril, warant; heorot, merisc, waroþ.* With medial *m*: *clamór, comón, damask, tremór; hamor, sc(e)amol.* With medial *n*: *anet, anis, bonet, chanel, onór, kenil, maneir, panel, penón, senat, tenant, tenór, venim; ganot, hænep.* One of the words which do show lengthening—*jēlós*—has medial *l*, and in this the vowel is short in MnE; two words—*fāmós* and *mōment*—have medial *m*; there are no exceptions among the native words. A study of these native words suggests a reason why no lengthening has occurred. Out of the twelve words listed above, seven are monosyllabic in MnE: *ell, Welsh, whelk, hart, marsh, warth, hemp.* Two others have developed a glide consonant, a development which presupposes the syncopation of the second vowel: *elder, shamble(s).* The *Promptorium Parvulorum*[82] includes two more words, *gante* and *hambyr*, in forms which presuppose the syncopation of the second vowel. It is irrelevant to my purpose to discuss whether the syncopation occurred directly in the uninflected forms of these words, or was levelled into them from the inflected forms: the important point is that syncopated forms do occur beside unsyncopated forms; that no lengthening would occur in the syncopated forms; and that short vowels would naturally be levelled from the syncopated into the unsyncopated forms. It is not necessary to suppose that syncopation actually occurred in the loanwords as well as in native words—such a supposition would require a very early and complete loss of stress in the final syllable—since the prevalence of short vowels in native words of the same type would be sufficient to inhibit lengthening. The feeling that a medial liquid or nasal requires a short preceding vowel can be observed in the pronunciation of such recent borrowings as *helot, melon,* and *zealot*; the last example is particularly striking, since the simplex *zeal* would suggest a pronunciation [ziːlət].

58. An examination of the remaining words reveals that a further large proportion of those which do not show lengthening end with a liquid or nasal or liquid or nasal + consonant. Thus, with final *l*: *catel, chatel, metal, potel, revel, sachel, tassel, travel, vassal; fetel, cetel, sadol, setl, sc(e)acol,*

*sc(e)ofl, swepel, watol*. With final *r* or *r* + consonant: *azūr, desert, flatòr, hasard, lechòr, record, tabard; copor, fæder, fetor, lator, neopor, oter, hrapor, teter, wæter, weper, hwæper*. With final *m*: *botm, fæpm*. With final *n* or *n* + consonant: *besant, cofin, dragòn, Latin, latòn, lessòn, present, satin, secònd; ofen, seofon*. But many of the words which do show lengthening in ME or MnE also have these endings. Thus, with final *l*: *lābel; cradol, hæsel, hlædel, *mapul, stapol, tredel*. With final *r*: *brǫcòr, drāper, dęver, fāvòr, flāvòr, lābòr, lęvòr, ǫdòr, pāper, rāsòr, sāvòr, tābòr, tręsor, vāpòr; æcer, beofor, ceafor, feper, leper, ofer, tapor, weder*; in MnE *azūr* has a by-form with [eɪ], while *fæder* and *hrapor* often had a long vowel in early MnE. With *n* or *n* + consonant: *bācòn, bāsin, blāsòn, cāpòn, māsòn, pātent, vācant; (be)neo-pan, bræsen, efen, heofon, open, hræfn*. On the other hand, in a considerable number of these words the MnE pronunciation is from a ME variant form with a short vowel: *(en)deavour, treasure* and sometimes *patent; treadle, feather, leather, weather, heaven*. None the less it is clear that a final liquid or nasal does not inhibit lengthening as regularly as a medical liquid or nasal.

59. A study of the exceptions—words, that is, in which a final liquid or nasal does not inhibit lengthening—is helpful in determining the exact process by which lengthening was inhibited. A large number of these exceptions, both loanwords and native words, have a medial labial: mostly *v* but also *p* and *b*. Thus, with medial *v*: *dęver, fāvòr, flāvòr, lęvòr, sāvòr; beofor, ceafor, efen, heofon, ofer, hræfn*. With medial *p*: *cāpòn, drāper, pāper, vāpòr; *mapul, open, stapol, tapor*. With medial *b*: *lābel, lābòr, tābòr*. Now, it is well known that the group *vr* was eliminated in ME, both from native words and from loanwords, by the insertion of a glide-vowel between the two consonants[83]: thus, OE *æfre* > ME *evere* and OF *recouvre-nt* > ME *recòvere*. Other groups consisting of labial + liquid or nasal are much less frequent, but there is some evidence that they also were avoided. The supposition that lengthening of the stem-vowel was inhibited by the syncopation of the second vowel before a final liquid or nasal would explain the exceptions listed above, since syncopation would naturally not occur if the result were an objectionable consonant group. Syncopation must have occurred in uninflected rather than in inflected forms, for two reasons: firstly, the group consonant + liquid does not constitute a closed syllable in ME[84]; secondly, borrowings from AN usually form their plural in -*s* rather than -*es* in ME. However, it would not be difficult to assume that the group consonant + syllabic liquid or nasal, final or before a consonant, did constitute a closed syllable in ME, and this assumption is sufficient to explain the quantity of the vowel in all but a few of the words listed in the last paragraph. Of course, it is not necessary to suppose that syncopation actually occurred in the loanwords before the date of the lengthening; the prevalence of short vowels in native words of the same type would be sufficient to inhibit lengthening.

60. All but one of the loanwords that I have not yet discussed end in *t*, and these all have a short vowel: *brevet, closet, crochet, fagot, habit, lachet, legat, profit, rochet, roket, soket, statüt*. It would seem that final *t* tends to inhibit lengthening, but I have found no plausible reason why this should be so. The remaining word—*prǫces*—has a long vowel. The conclusions of the last three paragraphs can be summed up in the following simple rule: lengthening is inhibited by

(1) a medial liquid or nasal;
(2) a final liquid or nasal, unless the medial consonant is a labial;
(3) a final *t*.
Of the 111 loanwords in my list, only 13 have in late ME quantities contrary to those to be expected from the operation of these factors: *bācòn, bāsin, blāsòn, brǭcòr, fāmòs, jēlòs, māsòn, mǫment, ǭdòr, rāsòr, rĕvel, trăvel, trēsor*.

61. The same factors which inhibit lengthening of an originally short vowel may also induce shortening of an originally long vowel: this is the probable explanation of the short vowel in a number of loanwords. With medial *l*: *vĕlin* "vellum" (§ 50). With medial *r*: *hĕròn* (§ 48). With final *l*: *vĕssel* (§ 48). With final *r*: *lĕsir* "leisure," *plĕsir* "pleasure" (§ 48). With final *n* or *n* + consonant: *mŭtón* "mutton" (§ 49), *fĕsant* "pheasant" (§ 48). But shortening has not occurred in *rēsòn* "reason," *sēsòn* "season." There is an alternative explanation of these words: possibly the long vowels resulting from the smoothing of all diphthongs were shortened already in AN; in this case these words are not to be distinguished from the words discussed in §§ 56–60. But the smoothing of *ai, ei* occurred later than the development of long *ū* from *ŭ* + *u̯*; since the latter remained long it seems likely that *ē* from *ai, ei* also remained long.[85]

## Index Verborum

Current words are listed in their MnE forms, obsolete words in their ME forms. Native words are italicised. References are to paragraphs.

seize, 21
semblant, 34
senate, 25, 56, 57
sergeant, 34
sermon, 14
*settle*, 56 & n., 58
*seven*, 56, 58
severe, 25
*shackle*, 56, 58
*shamble*(*s*), 56, 57
*shovel*, 56 & n., 58
siege, 18, 43
sign, 23
sire, 16
slander, 34
slice, 10
sluice, 11
sober, 25
socket, 56, 60
solace, 25, 56, 57
sort, 41
sound, 14
source, 41
souse, 24
space, 25
spawn, 34
spell, 46
spice, 16
spine, 10
sponge, 33
squirrel, 17
stable [stăbŭlum], 9n., 46
stable [stābĭlem], 46
*staple*, 56, 58, 59
statute, 56, 60
story, 25
stout, 24 & n.
strange, 30, 32, 34
strive, 10
sturgeon, 14
succeed, 25
summer, 48

summon, 33
summons, 33
sumpter, 48
suppose, 25
supreme, 25
sure, 11, 26
*swaddle*, 56, 58

tabard, 56, 58
table, 46
tabor, 56, 58, 59
talent, 56, 57
talon, 14, 56, 57
*taper*, 56, 58, 59
task, 35
tassel, 56, 58
taste, 37
taunt, 34
tenant, 56, 57
tenor, 19, 56, 57
term, 40
test, 37
*tetter*, 56, 58
theme, 25
tiger, 25
title, 25
toast, 38
tomb, 33
touch, 38, 42, 45
tourney, 53
tower, 39, 41
trace, 45
travel, 56, 58, 60
*treadle*, 56 & n., 58
treason, 14
treasure, 56 & n., 58, 60
treat, 21
treaty, 18, 48
trellice, 10, 56, 57
tremor, 56, 57
trick, 46

trowel, 54
truss, 44n.

uncle, 15
use, 11

vacant, 55, 56, 58
valour, 19, 56, 57
vanish, 23
vapour, 19, 55, 56, 58, 59
vassal, 56, 58
vaunt, 34
veal, 26
vellum, 50, 61
venom, 55, 56, 57
vessel, 48, 61
vetch, 46
vice, 25
view, 11, 26
vile, 10
vine, 23
virtue, 11
volume, 11, 56, 57
vouch, 38, 42, 45
vow, 19

wage, 45
wager, 11, 26
*waist*, 35, 37
warrant, 56, 57
*warth*, 56, 57
waste, 37
*water*, 56, 58
*wattle*, 56, 58
*weather*, 56 & n., 58
*Welsh*, 56, 57
*wether*, 56, 58
*whelk*, 56, 57
*whether*, 56, 58
wyver, 10

*yeast*, 35

zealot, 57

## FOOTNOTES

[Note: Modern English pronunciations referred to are in every case those of "British" English—Ed.]

1. The following abbreviations are used: AN—Anglo-Norman; CF—Central French; CL—Classical Latin; ME—Middle English; MF—Middle French; MnE—Modern English; MnF—Modern French; OE—Old English; OF—Old French; VL—Vulgar Latin.

2. These axioms do not seem to have been clearly stated before, but they are implicit in the pioneer work of W. Keller, "Mittelenglische lange Vokale und die altfranzösische Quantität," *Englische Studien*, LIV, pp. 111 ff., and in a recent article by H. Flasdieck, "Ne. *pint*," *Anglia*, LXIX, pp. 398 ff.

3. For a discussion of the ambiguity of this axiom, see § 28.

4. The symbol *ȯ* indicates that *o* is written in AN or ME for *ŭ*; the digraph *ȯu* indicates that *ou* is written in AN or ME for *ū*. Other diacritics are those in common use and need no explanation.

5. The phonetic symbols used are those of the International Phonetic Association.

6. M. K. Pope, *From Latin to Modern French*, § 558. This statement requires some modification; see §§ 36 (1), 39 (1).

7. B. ten Brink, *Dauer und Klang*, p. iii. ["The purpose of this outline will have been achieved as soon as some scholar is prompted by it to fill the gaps in Romance grammar to which it draws attention."]

8. *Ibid.*, p. 50. ["but I let the thread drop here—in the hope that some specialist or other will take it up again."]

9. K. Luick, *Historische Grammatik der englischen Sprache*, § 413. ["The distribution of quantities was also very complicated, since OF did not have such clearcut and strongly contrasted differences of quantity as English has; moreover, the length of vowels was probably subject to great variation according to the syntactical context. The English reflexes were based primarily on the native types of syllable-quantity which prevailed in words of similar structure."]

10. *Ibid.*, § 413, Anm. 1. ["These quantities fluctuate within the limits imposed by the distribution of native quantities; only the long vowels before *r* + consonant transgress these limits, perhaps as a result of complex stress. The quantity of the language of origin seems to be reflected in cases 4 and 2 [*that is* before a single consonant and in an open syllable]: this quantity seems in general to have been closer to the English 'long' than to the English 'short.'"]

11. Jordan-Matthes, *Handbuch der mittelenglischen Grammatik*, § 219. ["When the bulk of the French loanwords were borrowed, OF had still not effaced the distinction between long and short vowels. The French words in ME reveal a distribution of quantities which often does not correspond to conditions in native English words, and which must therefore go back to OF."]

12. See D. Behrens, "Französische Elemente im Englischen," in Paul's *Grundriss*, I, pp. 950 ff.; W. W. Skeat, *Principles of English Etymology*, Part II; A. Sturmfels, "Der altfranzösische Vokalismus im Mittelenglischen bis zum Jahre 1400," *Anglia*, VIII, pp. 201 ff.; IX, pp. 551 ff.; M. S. Serjeantson, *Foreign Words in English*.

13. It does not follow that *only* these vowels were long in AN; some vowels which might be explained by ME sound-changes may have been long already in AN.

14. By "smoothing" I mean the reduction of a diphthong or a triphthong to a monophthong by mutual assimilation of its elements; see §§ 17–18.

15. In Sardinian *ĭ* and *ŭ*, and in Roumanian *ŭ*, remained distinct; see Meyer-Lübke, *Einführung*, §§ 113, 119.

16. It should be noted that Romanic scholars rarely distinguish the vowels of VL as "short" and "long," but prefer to use the terms "blocked" and "free"; but the more recent grammars recognise that the distinction between "blocked" and "free" vowels is one of quantity.

17. For a discussion of the period during which this redistribution of quantity continued, see § 15.

18. It remains doubtful whether vowels were lengthened before stop + *l*. In some words lengthening seems to have occurred: the diphthong in *fieble* < *\*flēbĭlem*, for instance, presupposes a long vowel; but in many words there is no lengthening, and it seems unlikely that *fable* < *fābŭla*, *estable* < *stăbŭlum*, and the many adjectives in -*able* < -*ābĭlem* can all be learned words.

19. In this and other similar lists, the MnE form is intended only to assist identification, not to explain the ME meaning; but when the word is practically

obsolete I have often added the MnE equivalent. I have given the VL etymon in its written or CL form, which is more easily recognized than the phonetic form; and I have included Germanic roots without special distinction. The root form of a noun is generally derived from the accusative case of the etymon, except in the first declension, where the early effacement of final -*m* obliterated the distinction between the nominative and the accusative. The root form of a verb is usually derived from the strong or stem-stressed form of the etymon, and in these cases I have given the third person plural present indicative as the most characteristic form; in the rare cases where the root form of a verb is derived from the weak form of the etymon I have given the infinitive.

20. For the etymologies of *gyves* and *strive*, see *English and Germanic Studies*, IV, pp. 29–30.

21. In the more northerly dialects of OF the vowel was not fully fronted, and traces of this pronunciation can be observed in such ME spellings as *auentour* "adventure."

22. Luick, *op. cit.*, § 412. 2.

23. Some scholars prefer to assume that $\bar{e}$ was diphthongised to $ei$ as usual, that an epenthetic $i$ developed after the palatal consonant, and that the resulting triphthong *iei*, like *iei* from VL $e, \bar{e} + i$ (§ 16), developed into $i$. My argument would not be affected by this assumption.

24. Except when preceded by a palatal (§ 18).

25. The frequent ending -*āta* became -$\bar{e}e$ in OF, but in AN a glide-vowel developed and -$\bar{e}e$ became -*eie*, so that words of this type are not relevant to my present purpose.

26. There is nothing surprising about this; the tendency is a very natural one, and can be observed in most of the Germanic as well as the Romance languages.

27. The word $p\bar{\varrho}vre$ usually appears in ME as $p\bar{\varrho}vre$, with the AN raising of $\bar{\varrho}$ to $\bar{\varrho}$ after labial *p*, *b*, and *f*; for a discussion of this sound-change, see § 42 (1).

28. Probably the consonantalisation of the first element of the diphthong was accompanied by a compensatory lengthening of the second. The treatment of the diphthongs *üi* and *ui* is not comparable; here, apparently, the shift of stress occurred only after a velar and the second element remained short. Thus, ME *quívre* < *cüivre* < \**kǒkrum*, and ME *quíssin* < *cuissin* < \**cǒxīnum* both have short vowels.

29. For the etymology of *lure* see *English and Germanic Studies*, IV, pp. 20–22.

30. For the etymology of *pint*, see H. Flasdieck, *op. cit.*

31. MnE *cony* may go back to the OF plural *cuniz*; in this case the long vowel was formed in OF, not in ME.

32. VL *stultum* probably entered OF with changed meaning through one of the Germanic languages; but the phonological development is perfectly regular.

33. Schwan-Behrens-Bloch, *Grammaire de l'Ancien Français*, § 39, Remarque.

34. W. Meyer-Lübke, *Historische Grammatik der französischen Sprache*, § 62.

35. Luick, *op. cit.*, § 424.

36. Dr. Dobson points out that the MnE pronunciation of these words may go back to ME variants with $\bar{e}$ instead of $\bar{\varrho}$.

37. This change did not take place until after $\varrho$ had been lowered to $\varrho$, since the resulting long vowel always has an open quality, irrespective of the quality of the original short vowel. Pope, *op. cit.*, §§ 242–4, 269, places it in MF, but this is clearly far too late.

38. Sievers-Brunner, *Altenglische Grammatik*, § 138.1; Jordan-Matthes, *op. cit.*, § 23.

39. Sievers-Brunner, *op. cit.*, § 137.3; Jordan-Matthes, *op. cit.*, § 22.

40. Jordan-Matthes, *op. cit.*, § 24.

41. OF *a* was generally the front vowel [a]; but in AN it had been retracted to [ɑ] before a nasal; see Pope, *op. cit.*, § 1152, and *Kastner Miscellany*, pp. 401 ff. Short *ǫ* had been raised and rounded to *u* before a nasal, so that *a* and *u* were the only short back vowels which could occur before a nasal.

42. It might appear at first sight that the *au* in such words as *braun* "brawn" < *\*brādōnem, flaun* "flan" < *\*flădōnem, paun* "pawn" < *pedōnem, faun* < *fētōnem*, is a genuine diphthong formed from two vowels in hiatus, and that the identity of the subsequent development of *au* from this source with that of *au* from *a* + nasal is evidence in favour of a diphthongal pronunciation for the latter; but in fact *au* + nasal had become *a* + nasal already in OF (Pope, *op. cit.*, § 242).

43. It should be noticed that there is no doubt that OF *a* was *eventually* lengthened before a nasal: "The merging of prae-consonantal *n* in the preceding nasal vowel induced the lengthening of that vowel" (Pope, *op. cit.*, § 563). Miss Pope places this lengthening in MF. There can be no doubt that it had been completed in 1584, since it is noticed in that year by Théodore Bèze: "Every syllable ending in the letter *m* or *n* that is not double but precedes another consonant is long by nature" (Bèze, *De Francicæ linguæ recta pronuntiatione*, reprint 1868, p. 88, quoted and translated by Pope, *ibid.*). The point at issue is whether or not this lengthening is required to explain the AN loanwords in ME. It is interesting to note that if the early date of the lengthening can be proved by a consideration of the loanwords, Miss Pope's phonetic explanation of it is wrong, since the lengthening must have antedated and may in OF have provoked the effacement of the nasal consonant, which in every case survives in ME.

44. This is the most probable explanation of Dan Michel's *o*- spellings: they occur chiefly in syllables which lost the stress in ME, where shortening was regular, and also before the doubtful consonant groups discussed in § 28.

45. This change did not take place until after the lowering of *ę* to *ę*, so that the lengthened vowel is always *ē̜*.

46. E.g., by Jordan-Matthes, *op. cit.*, § 220.

47. Ten Brink, *op. cit.*, p. 32. Ten Brink interprets these rhymes as showing the shortening of *ē̜* from *ai* before a group of three consonants; but it can hardly be a coincidence that in each case the vowel is followed by *st*.

48. Pope, *op. cit.*, §§ 225, 1321. iii. OF *ę* was also broken before other consonants, particularly *l*, but this development is not relevant to the present discussion.

49. Pope, *op. cit.*, §§ 232, 1321. iv.

50. The form *jóuste* is extremely rare in ME, but its existence is presupposed by the MnE pronunciation [dʒaʊst].

51. Wright, *Elementary Middle English Grammar*, § 78; *English Dialect Grammar*, § 220. These words sometimes occur with [eɪ], but not in the dialects in which the distinction is maintained.

52. Once again there can be no doubt that this lengthening occurred at some time during the history of French. In MnF all vowels are long before *s* now effaced: "lang ist ein Vokal . . . nach welchem einst ein silbenschliessendes *s* gestanden hat, das verstummt ist" ["a vowel . . . after which there once stood a pre-consonantal *s*, now mute, is long."] (Meyer-Lübke, *op. cit.*, § 108). This statement was already true in the sixteenth century: "when *s* is elided before a consonant, as in *est*, they sound a double or triple sound *eee*" (Erasmus, *De recta latini græcique sermonis pronuntiatione*, 1528. Translated and quoted by Pope, *op. cit.*, § 564). "Every *s* mute before a consonant . . . lengthens the preceding vowel" (Bèze, *op. cit.*, p. 90; Pope, *ibid.*). And once again Miss Pope's phonetic explanation of the change must be considered erroneous, for she says: "The effacement of prae-consonantal *z* and *s* in later Old French was accompanied by compensatory lengthening of the preceding

vowel"; but the invariable survival of pre-consonantal *s* in MnE proves that the lengthening must have anteceded and may have provoked the effacement of *s* in French.

53. Fox and Hookes, 1673, *Writing Scholar's Companion*, 1695.

54. Pope, *op. cit.*, §§ 581, 1144, 1325. xiv.

55. Ten Brink, *op. cit.*, p. 32. See § 36 (1) note.

56. Yet again there can be no doubt that this lengthening took place at some time in the history of French. In MnF all stressed vowels are long before *r*: "mann kann im allgemeinen sagen, dass jeder Vokal lang ist, wenn ihm ein stimmhafter Reibelaut oder *r* folgt, sofern das Wort am Gruppenende steht" ["in general one can say that any vowel is long when followed by a voiced fricative or *r*, as long as the word is at the end of a phrase."] (Meyer-Lübke, *op. cit.*, § 108). But Bèze notices a long vowel only before *rr*, not before *r*: "every syllable is lengthened by *rr* as *catairre, guerre, pourrir, enterrer*" (Bèze, *op. cit.*, p. 90. Translated and quoted by Pope, *op. cit.*, § 569).

57. This change did not take place until after the lowering of $\rho$ to $\varrho$, so that the lengthened vowel is always $\bar{\varrho}$.

58. Pope, *op. cit.*, §§ 581, 1144, 1325. xiv.

59. Pope, *op. cit.*, § 366. Original *rr* from VL *rr* was never simplified in OF; but the group [ðr] sometimes became *rr*, sometimes *r*. (Pope, *op. cit.*, § 372).

60. It is important to note that the consonant may, but need not necessarily, be geminated after a short vowel; some ME forms presuppose a simple consonant after a short vowel. Even the occasional occurrence of gemination indicates a short vowel; only its complete absence indicates a long vowel. The position is somewhat complicated when both a short and a long vowel exist in variant forms of the same word.

61. [See Hans Kurath, "The Loss of Long Consonants and the Rise of Voiced Fricatives in Middle English," reprinted in this volume, pp. 142 ff.—Ed.]

62. There is no instance in my word-list of a vowel in an open syllable followed by *d*; analogy would suggest that the lengthening would also occur before *d*, but I cannot prove it.

63. The original value of AN *c* was [ts], but it was early simplified to [s]; probably the lengthening occurred before the simplification, since the geminated consonant in such a word as *trusse* "truss" implies that no lengthening occurred before *s*.

64. In the rare cases in which the weak form of a verb was adopted into ME an immediate shift of stress was unavoidable, since the weak forms are stressed on the ending which was dropped in ME; thus the strong form *múevent* retains its stress in ME *mę̄ve* "move," but the weak form *muvéir* can only become *móve* with a shift of stress. The pronunciation [mʌv] is widely attested in the modern dialects (Wright, *English Dialect Grammar*, § 215); MnE *move* [muːv] shows lengthening of *u* to $\bar{\varrho}$ in an open syllable.

65. Countertonic *ai, ei*, unlike tonic *ai, ei*, are smoothed in hiatus as well as before certain consonants; see § 50.

66. This point cannot be proved, for alternative hypotheses are available; see the discussion in § 61.

67. The strong form *çouche-nt* < *collŏca-nt* would have given ME *çouche*, MnE [koʊtʃ].

68. Necessarily so, since of the five countertonic short vowels *e* and *a* were absorbed by the tonic vowel (§ 26), and *i, ü*, and *u* were lengthened (§ 54).

69. VL *mandūcant* should give *\*mandǖent*; *manjǖent* owes its consonant to the weak form *mangier* < *mandūcāre*.

70. E.g., Pope, *op. cit.*, § 234.

71. The most frequent pronunciation, with [ʊə], is probably a pseudo-French pronunciation of a non-colloquial word.

72. Necessarily so, since the only other countertonic vowels, *e* and *a*, had already been absorbed by a following tonic vowel in hiatus with them (§ 26).

73. The lengthening of originally tonic vowels was usually inhibited by the gemination of consonants (§ 43); but the gemination must have ceased before the shift of stress, for there is no trace of it after originally countertonic vowels.

74. Wright, *Elementary Middle English Grammar* § 215.

75. Dates from the *NED*.

76. Luick, *op. cit.*, § 422.1; Jordan-Matthes, *op. cit.*, § 224.

77. E. Eckhardt, "Die Quantität einfacher Tonvokale in offener Silbe bei zwei- oder dreisilbigen Wörtern französischer Herkunft im heutigen Englisch," *Anglia*, LX, pp. 49 ff.; N. E. Eliason, "The Short Vowels in French Loan Words like *City*, etc.," *Anglia*, LXIII, pp. 73 ff.

78. I have, of course, excluded proparoxytones such as *banere* "banner," *bataile* "battle," *chapele* "chapel," *manere* "manner"; in many cases the final vowel had been lost before the date of the lengthening, but the short stem-vowel always might be due to its survival.

79. In MnE three of these words—(*en*)*deavour, jealous* and *treasure*—have short vowels, but an original long vowel is attested by the spelling.

80. I have made no attempt to distinguish words in which the second vowel is original from those in which it is a glide-vowel; and I have included words such as *botm, eln, fæþm, hræfn, sc(e)ofl, setl*, in which the glide-vowel is not normally written in OE.

81. In MnE five of these words—*feather, heaven, leather, treadle*, and *weather*—have short vowels, but an original long vowel is attested by the spelling.

82. [A Latin-English dictionary of "hard" words, from the fifteenth century.—Ed.]

83. Jordan-Matthes, *op. cit.*, § 147, Anm. 2.

84. Jordan-Matthes, *op. cit.*, § 25, Anm. 2.

85. My thanks are due to Dr. E. J. Dobson of Jesus College and Professor A. Ewert of Trinity College, who have helped me with criticism and advice, and to Mr. R. Shackleton of Brasenose College, who has read the proofs. [For some of Professor Bliss' later thoughts on this material, see his "Quantity in Old French and Middle English," *Archivum Linguisticum* 7.71–86 (1955).—Ed.]

## HELGE KÖKERITZ

## Elizabethan Prosody
## and Historical Phonology*

The great American lexicographer Noah Webster, whose surname has become almost synonymous with dictionary, held very decided views on the structure of the iambic pentameter line. He voices them in his *Dissertations on the English Language* (Boston, 1789), pp. 297 ff., where he complains that the trisyllabic feet (tribrach, dactyl, and anapaest) "have suffered most by the general ignorance of critics; most of them have been mutilated by apostrophes, in order to reduce them to the Iambic measure. Thus in the line before repeated,

"*Murmuring*, and with him fled the shades of night,"

we find the word in the copy reduced to two syllables, *murm'ring*, and the beauty of the Dactyl is destroyed." The same sentiment, namely the beauty of trisyllabic substitution, had previously been expressed by Thomas Sheridan in his *Lectures on the Art of Reading* (1775), p. 344, which also analyses the above line (p. 126) and like Webster blames Pope and other poets for syncopating the middle syllable of such words as *am'rous, hum'rous, glitt'ring*, "though all the world, in reading the verse, pronounce the three syllables of the word glittering" (p. 221). Webster, with his usual self-assurance, observes that "it requires but little judgement and an ear indifferently accurate, to distinguish the contractions which are necessary, from those which are needless and injurious to the versification." As an apt illustration he cites ll. 14–22 of Pope's "Epistle to Miss Blount, on her leaving the Town, after the Coronation," which has *op'ra, pray'rs, 'twixt, o'er, 'squire, sev'n, heav'n*, and comments: "Here *e* in *opera* ought not to be apostrophized, for such a contraction reduces an Amphibrachic foot to an Iambic. The words *prayers, seven* and *heaven* need not the apostrophe of *e*; for it makes no difference in the pronunciation. But the contraction of *over* and *betwixt* is necessary; for without it the measure would be imperfect." We cannot now tell if Webster pronounced *prayer, seven* and *heaven* as monosyllables or disyllables, but his strictures on Pope and his predecessors suggest that the three words were disyllabic with him. However that may be, in view of his dictum that the trisyllabic feet "are the most flowing and melodious of any in the language" and that anapaests are "admissible into every place of the line," we must concede that only a

* From *Annales Academiae Regiae Scientiarum Upsaliensis* 5.79–102 (1961). Reprinted by permission of Almqvist and Wiksell, Uppsala; Kungl. Vetenskapssamhället, Uppsala; and Mrs. Signe Östlink.

person endowed with Webster's ear and judgment would have been able to determine why *over* and *betwixt* made the measure "imperfect" but not *opera*.[1]

The Sheridan-Webster affection for trisyllabic feet is symptomatic of a new trend in prosodic theory, which was destined to become the dominant one down to the present day. As Fussell has shown,[2] the seeds of this revolutionary change in attitude were planted in the latter half of the seventeenth century, but the real break between "syllabism" and "accentualism" (to use Fussell's terms) did not come until after 1770 with the publication of treatises on versification by Allan Ramsay, Thomas Sheridan, and Joshua Steele. Since then accentual prosody has held unquestioned sway and, what is worse, has been unscrupulously applied to verse composed in a totally different prosodic tradition. Metrists like George Saintsbury, Matthew A. Bayfield, T. S. Omond, Sir George Young and their followers should indeed be pilloried for misleading students of early English prosody. That they may have acted in good faith, does not exonerate them from blame. Though expert phonological advice was readily available, they would apparently have none of it, preferring instead to let quasi-esthetical principles of versification determine their method of analysis. I am afraid it will be a long time before the damage they inflicted can be undone. Fortunately, however, a reaction to their unhistorical way of treating English prosody of the past is finally setting in and seems to be gaining momentum. "A multitude of modern errors in scansion and interpretation," says Fussell,[3] "have resulted from a failure to take into account the theory of prosody under which various poems were composed, and from a tendency to assume that one prosody governs English poetry of whatever period." And, he might well have added, from the implicit, naive assumption that twentieth-century spoken English was the idiom also of, say, the sixteenth and seventeenth centuries. Anyhow, it is a sad reflection on the actual state of modern metrical studies that Fussell should have to emphasize the necessity of an historical approach to the analysis of early English verse.

This lack of historical perspective, this failure on the part of most modern metrists to realize that the structure of sixteenth-century English verse might differ from that of the twentieth, stems ultimately, I am convinced, from the fact that they have been neither philologists nor phoneticians. They have been literary scholars and critics like Saintsbury and Young, poets like Robert Bridges and Sidney Lanier, classical scholars like Bayfield and E. A. Sonnenschein, and believe it or not, even a Scottish lawyer like Omond, but certainly not English philologists.[4] Not only did these men base their examination of Shakespeare's verse on doctored nineteenth-century editions of his works, but they had no conception at all of what spoken Elizabethan English was like phonologically, nor did they consider it worth their while to try to find out. So they turned up hosts of trisyllabic feet in the verse of Chaucer, Shakespeare, and Milton, to the delight no doubt of modern accentualists. As I have said elsewhere,[5] I think "it is an anomaly in Shakespearean scholarship that those who have written most extensively on Shakespeare's versification have been linguistically least qualified to express their views on the subtle problems involved." I then singled out Bayfield as the perpetrator of the worst prosodic absurdities, some of which I exemplified, but I might have added Omond, who in his *English Metrists* (p. 149) makes this categorical statement: "To me it seems clear that any word may be used which can be readily pronounced in the normal time of disyllabic feet, even quadrisyllables like *ministering* or *spiritual*, and that there is not the slightest reason to suppose that such words were pronounced by readers of our verse *m'nist'ring* or *sp'ritual*. A contrary opinion verges on paradox." Had Omond consulted OED (its M volume had appeared at that time), he would have discovered the doublet *minstryng* recorded as a separate entry with a reference to *ministering*, and he would not have propounded the monstrosity *m'nist'ring*; tetrasyllabic *ministering* formerly had two variants, trisyllabic *minist'ring* (still used) and disyllabic *minst'ring*, the form to be used at H 5.1.264 (both Q2 and F, however, print *ministring*). As for *spiritual* we may note that syncopated forms like *sprital* (a separate entry in OED), spelled *sprytwalle*, and *sprytrall*, *spirtuall* (both in Henslowe) are on record from the fifteenth and sixteenth centuries.[6] What verges on paradox, therefore, is not the undeniable fact that there once existed disyllabic forms like *minstring* and *sprital*, but that a Scottish lawyer was presumptuous enough to pose as an authority on Elizabethan pronunciation and, indeed, was able to get away with it.[7]

The historical approach recommended by Fussell cannot, however, be limited merely to the prosodies of the period in question. Its chief concern must be the salient phonological features of contemporary speech, with special attention to word shortening (aphaeresis, apocope, syncope, etc.), word fusion (e.g., synalepha), and stress deviations from modern usage. The awareness of these linguistic phenomena is absolutely essential to the understanding of syllabic prosody. Examples abound in early poetry, though poets are usually most inconsistent in indicating them. They knew, and their readers knew, that one generally wrote, e.g., *agree, desperate, amorous, the enemy, thou hast, in the*, but commonly said *'gree, desp'rate, am'rous, th'enemy, thou'st, i'th'*, and that the fuller forms were useful metrical variants when an extra syllable was needed. At times poets indicated the shorter form by writing *desprate, amrous, thenemy*, and so on, and so did contemporary prose writers—with equal inconsistency. What we must remember is that neither were all these contractions exclusively used in poetry nor did they originate in poetry. They arose in the spoken language at the beginning of the Middle English period, that is, from about 1100 on, at first in trisyllabic forms of native words, e.g., ME *laverke* > *lark*, and later increasingly in polysyllabic loan-words.[8] Hence we have *Monday* < OE *Mōnandæg, hawks* < OE *hafocas, lords* < ME *loverdes* < OE *hlāfweardas*, and *captain* < *capitain, apron* < *naperon, marshal* < *mareschal, damsel* < *dameisele, minstrel* < *ministral*, and such well-known English doubtlets as *courtesy–curtsy, fantasy–*

*fancy*, *poesy–posy*, *summoner–sumner*, *paralysis–palsy*, *procurator–proctor*, *corrosive–corsive*, etc., not to mention a staggering number of place-names like *Gloucester*, *Worcester*, *Salisbury*, *Birmingham* (< OE *Beornmundinga-hām*), *Cholmondeley*, pronounced [ˈtʃʌmlɪ], *Cambridge* (< OE *Grantabrycg*), *Oxford* (< OE *Oxenaford*), and so on. Sixteenth-century spellings like *amralte*, *tabret*, *denry*, *nunre* (Machyn's Diary), *entring*, *medsin*, *fiznamy* (Laneham), *altrynge*, *pastrall*, *repracyones* (Henslowe), and a wide variety of similar forms in Shakespeare[9] reveal that if written English had adjusted itself to the spoken language or if at any rate the latter had been able to with-stand the increasing pressure of the conservative spelling, metrists would have been deprived of at least 90 percent of their alleged instances of trisyllabic substitution—indeed, that phenomenon would probably have been reduced to a minor problem of caesural variation. As it is, most literary scholars and metrists seem to believe that a word always had as many syllables as its present lexical form. This fallacy is particularly widespread in the United States where spelling-pronunciation is rampant thanks to generations of zealous school-teachers. Not many Americans today dare to omit the medial vowel in *desperate*, *several* (some even say [ˈɛvəri] for *every*), *difference*, *medicine*, etc., though this is commonly done in Britain, the reason being an exaggerated consciousness of the written form inculcated through artificial and un-natural reading habits. This peculiar brand of *horror vacui* then prompts them to deny emphatically that the second *e* in *desperate* is ever completely lost, though some admit reluctantly that it may perhaps be slurred. No wonder that in their opinion Shakespeare's blank verse is full of anapaests.

As I have said before, a notable exception to this unrealistic attitude to the phonological problems of early prosody is Paul Fussell's valuable, perceptive study *Theory of Prosody in Eighteenth-Century England*.[10] Though he finds it "unpleasant ... to recognize the fact" [why?], he is nevertheless convinced that "almost all readers in the early eighteenth century both scanned and pronounced 'am'rous,' 'om'nous,' and 'del'cate' when such words con-fronted them in poetry" (p. 71). He rightly criticizes the naive dialectics of the prosodists who insist that eighteenth-century poets "could not have in-tended their verse to be thus read, since such reading erases much of the prosodic variety of the line," adding the pertinent observation: "The sup-position that prosodic variety of the nineteenth-century type is the goal of earlier poetries often sends modern scholars and critics into ambiguities on this matter, and some have sought to defend eighteenth-century poetry by explaining that the apostrophe was intended to be merely a 'fiction,' and by scanning as if the syllables so elided were read anyhow. But there is an over-whelming amount of contemporary evidence to the contrary." These words are equally true of the treatment accorded sixteenth- and seventeenth-century poetry by modern prosodists and editors. In *Shakespeare's Pronunciation* (p. 28) I have shown how metrically exact forms like *ventring* RL 148, *sclandrous* RL 161, and *desp'rate* RL 219 have usually been expanded to *venturing, slanderous, desperate* by modern editors, except by Kittredge who paid much greater heed to the text than most of his contemporaries and predecessors. Van Dam-Stoffel[11] adduce an even more drastic change from the Globe and Cambridge editions, which both print the rhyme *tempring*: *ventring* VA 565–7 as *tempering*:*venturing*, thereby "converting the lines into alexandrines and restricting the rhyme to the weak ending -*ing*." For a century at least Victorian ideas of linguistic propriety have been stamped not only on Shakespeare's text but also on his prosody, and anyone who attempts to sweep away the accumulated junk, the potted palms, the antimacassars, and the decorous fig-leaves, exposes himself to the reprimands and sneers of those who cherish the dust and cobwebs of the past. "Finger-counter" or "syllable-counter" is a condescending appellation often bestowed on the philologist who wants to make readers of Shakespeare's verse understand that the colloquial pronunciation of the period was the medium used by the Elizabethan poet and that this differed from its present-day descendant in sounds as well as in a powerful tendency, now regressive, to reduce the number of syllables of polysyllabic words or of common phrases. Shakespeare's pentameter line was syllabic and hence intrinsically regular, with the hypermetrical syllables occurring as a rule only in caesuras or at the end of a line. This was the opinion also of the great Danish philologist Otto Jespersen who apropos of modern metrists had this to say in his stimulating paper, "Notes on Metre":[12] "It is necessary to read these writers with a critical mind, for very often lines are given as containing such supernumerary syllables which are perfectly regular in Shakespeare's pronunciation, e.g., 'I am more an antique Roman than a Dane' (I am = I'm), 'The light and careless livery that it wears' (livery = livry)." Incidentally, Jespersen's paper is worth pondering by those who argue that by and large prosodic variety is synonymous with trisyllabic substitution: his keen-sighted analysis reveals that the essence of this variety is really the subtle relationship between verse stress and word or sentence stress.

What philologists have long known, the majority of prosodists have consequently chosen to ignore. Since in their opinion all English verse must have been accentual, they refuse to accept any phonological evidence to the contrary, no matter how conclusive, as prosodically valid. How can we persuade them not only that syncopation and other types of contraction were regular features of spoken English in the sixteenth and seventeenth centuries but above all that words and phrases that could be so curtailed were employed by Elizabethan and Jacobean poets as metrical variants whenever the rhythm of the line required the use of the shorter form, irrespective of whether or not such contraction was orthographically or typographically indicated? Obviously we must adduce corroborative evidence of a purely prosodic nature, statistically supported, in order to convince the doubters of the validity of our thesis, namely the interrelationship of phonology and prosody in the period under consideration. Indeed, such evidence does exist but it has apparently been overlooked in the prosodical controversy. It is as conclusive as any internal evidence at its best can be, and it confirms the phonological evidence which I consider fully conclusive in itself. Since there is a considerable body of the new evidence, an exhaustive treatment is out of the question here, though this ought to be undertaken not only for Shakespeare but for all major poets of his era. While the Shakespeare *Concordance* has greatly facilitated the necessary statistical investigations, the fact that the *Concordance* was prepared from the Globe edition makes it imperative to check each case against a more reliable text, preferably the Folio or a Quarto; this I have done throughout. Nevertheless many statistically significant words do not appear in the *Concordance* because of the compiler's policy of not including auxiliary verbs, pronouns, articles, many adverbs and prepositions; whenever these enter into my statistics, I have instead used Schmidt's *Shakespeare-Lexicon*, which lists a fairly representative number of the categories omitted from the *Concordance*. Even with these limitations the results arrived at are quite revealing and will, I trust, be accepted as valid criteria of the intrinsic syllabic regularity of Shakespeare's verse, and of all sixteenth- and seventeenth-century verse, barring, of course, experiments with classical metres.

Like other poets of his time, Shakespeare has a great many names, words, and phrases with alternate forms that differ in their number of syllables, e.g., *Helen–Helena, maid–maiden, broke–broken, which–the which*.[13] Now if it can be shown that he uses such alternate forms or doublets, as I shall call them hereafter, in strict conformity with the metre so that the longer variant never occurs where it would result in a trisyllabic foot, such regularity will entitle us to infer, I maintain, that the same metrical principle governs his use of phonological doublets like *desp'rate–desperate, I've–I have*, regardless of their printed form (the uncontracted variant quite often appears where the scansion requires the shorter form). The ideal would be a 100-percent agreement between word-form and scansion, but the nature of the text precludes this as does the relative frequency of a given variant, which may favour the use of, e.g., *spoken* as against *spoke* (both past participles). The Shakespearean scholar knows that in the transmission of the text from the author's foul papers to the printed pages of the Qq and the F there were abundant opportunities not only for textual revision but simply for errors of one sort or another, some of which may have resulted in seeming metrical irregularities. Moreover, who can tell whether Shakespeare himself was consistent when penning his lines—there is, indeed, every likelihood that he may inadvertently have written *spoken* instead of the less common *spoke*. We must consequently reckon with a margin of error but precisely how wide, it is hard to determine; though 2 percent seems to me a conservative estimate, I think it advisable to let the outcome of the statistical investigation supply the answer. I am confident that this will be considered both unequivocal and definitive.

Let me begin with the name doublets (*Helen–Helena, Pandar–Pandarus*, etc.), which constitute a characteristic, well-defined group; all of these alternate metrically—with one single exception (see fn. 15). Perhaps the most illuminating pair is *Desdemona* 26 × –*Desdemon* 7 × ,[14] because in seven cases the F corrects the obviously hypermetrical *Desdemona* of the Qq to its apocopated, affective variant *Desdemon*: 0 3.1.56, 3.3.55, 4.2.41, 5.2.25, 205, 281 (2 ×).[15] In the *Concordance*, which follows the Globe edition, the name is always rendered *Desdemona*. With regard to *Pandarus* 5 × and *Pandar* 5 × the situation is the reverse: at TC 3.2.14 (end of line) the F reads *Pandarus*, which results in an alexandrine, but Q more correctly *Pandar*. For the problem of trisyllabic substitution within the pentameter line such a final case is actually of little interest, since the use of the longer variant merely results in the addition of a sixth foot. This is true also of *Prospero* T 5.1.119 (end of line) and T 1.2.70 (first and second foot), whereas at T 2.1.271 *Prospero* ends the line in the F: "You did supplant your Brother *Prospero*," which is followed by "True" on a separate line; modern editions add *true* to line 271, thereby creating a hypermetrical caesura in the fifth foot, somewhat of an anomaly. Otherwise the occurrence of *Prospero* 9 × and *Prosper* 3 × is metrically exact, with two instances of *Prospero* in a caesura (T 1.2.20, 5.1.159) instead of the shorter form; this is a permissible variation in Shakespearean prosody.

There are several other names in Shakespeare with double forms. *Afric* occurs three times in verse, and *Africa* once (2H4 5.3.104): "I speake of Affrica and Golden joyes," where it is metrically regular. So are *Nile* 6 × and *Nilus* 5 ×, *Europe* 6 × and *Europa* 3 ×, *Collatine* 24 × and *Collatinus* 5 ×, *Helicane* 5 × and *Helicanus* 13 ×, and disyllabic *Priam* 37 × as against trisyllabic *Priamus* 2 × . With regard to *Philomela* 3 × and *Philomel* 6 × we note the significant omission of "why" from the F text at TA 2.4.38, where the Q reads: "Faire *Philomela* why she but lost her tongue" (with a hypermetrical caesura). *Cressida*, the normal form in prose, appears only four times in verse, including one instance of it in a caesura (TC 4.2.68): "The Lady *Cressida*. / Is it concluded so" (two short lines in F, for which Q has instead: "Is it so concluded," whose *is it* may of course be read *is't*). *Cressid* appears 33 times in verse without any metrical deviation, and in addition it is fairly common in prose passages. *Dian*, always disyllabic, is found 24 times in verse and once in prose, whereas *Diana*, always trisyllabic, occurs 16 times in verse and 3 in prose. There are at least 36 instances of disyllabic *Helen* in verse—it is also very common in prose, principally in TC—as against 21 cases of trisyllabic *Helena*: of these, one occurs in a caesura: "His folly Helena is no fault of mine" (MND 1.1.200 Q), which the F regularizes by printing "is none of mine," and another at the end of a line (MND 3.2.321), where I suspect that the text originally had *Helen* and that consequently *Helena* may be due to a copyist or the printer, unless an alexandrine was intended. An interesting name is *Isabella*, which has two variants, *Isbel*, found three times in prose and obviously the current colloquial form, and *Isabel*, the common variant in verse: it occurs 21 times as against 4 for

*Isabella*; three of these appear at the end of a line (MM 3.1.151 has actually 14 syllables) and only one medially: "I am that *Isabella*, and his Sister" (MM 1.4.23), which is metrically regular. Of the 21 instances of *Isabel* four appear hypermetrically in caesuras and four at the end of a line, where they should perhaps be read *Isbel*, e.g. MM 2.4.154: "What man thou art.—Who will beleeve thee *Isabell*?" *Abram* 2 × and its expanded variant *Abraham* 2 × are not clearly distinguished, probably because *Abraham* was normally pronounced *Abram* as J. Jones tells us in his *Practical Phonography* (1701), p. 22. A disyllabic form is metrically desirable at R3 4.5.38: "The Sonnes of Edward sleepe in *Abrahams* bosome," whereas the modern lineation of R2 4.1.103–4, which is that of Q1, "Sweet peace conduct his sweete soule to the bosome / Of good olde Abraham! Lords Appellants," is metrically ambiguous: if l. 104 has four feet, *Abraham* may be read *Abram* or as a trisyllable with a hypermetrical caesura, but if it is a pentameter line, then a pause is essential after trisyllabic *Abraham* ($\acute{-} - \acute{-}$). The F prints these lines: "Sweet peace conduct his sweet Soule / To the Bosome of good old *Abraham*. / Lords Appealants . . ." Only *Capulet* 17 × with its apocopated variant *Capel* 2 × causes some trouble. In Brooke's *Romeus and Juliet* the two forms *Capel* and *Capilet* alternate in strict conformity with the metre, and so do *Capel* and *Capolet* in Q1 of *Romeo and Juliet*, but in three instances Q2 and F have *Capulet* where *Capel* would be metrically preferable. Particularly interesting is the line, "Where be these Enemies? *Capulet, Mountague*"(5.3.291), which actually conflates two lines in Q1: "Come *Capolet*, and come olde *Mountagewe*. / Where are these enemies? see what hate hath done." Here *Capulet* may, of course, be considered a caesural case as also in 1.1.86 (that line is hypermetrical anyhow), but *Capulet* 4.1.112, "Where all the kindred of the *Capulets* lie," cannot be so explained, nor has the line a direct counterpart in Q1, where we find instead: "And when thou art laid in thy Kindreds Vault." Since elsewhere *Capels* appears in a similar context, namely "in *Capels* Monument" (5.1.18) and "in the *Capels* Monument" (5.3.127),[16] the probability of miswriting or a printer's error in Q2, the basis of F, is very strong. We may compare the Q1 line, "The day is hot, the *Capels* are abroad," whose rhythm Q2 ruins by omitting *are*: "the *Capels* abroad," and the F restores as "the *Capulets* abroad" (3.1.2), a syntactically less satisfactory version than that of Q1.

The preceding analysis has consequently established that with one highly dubious exception, *Capulet* RJ 4.1.112, these name doublets are used in conformity with the metre and further that there is no case of trisyllabic substitution involving the longer variants, except of course occasionally in caesuras. The relatively small number of such names has made it possible to give full statistics, but such completeness cannot be expected when I now proceed to examine the far more common word doublets of several categories, including synonyms, and the many syntactical or phrasal doublets, which likewise alternate metrically. Here I shall have to be selective in the hope that my findings will encourage further study of such rhythmical variation in Renaissance verse.[17]

Among the multifarious word-doublets that an Elizabethan poet could draw on for metrical purposes, it is possible to distinguish at least four principal types. They may be classified as (1) etymological doublets, e.g., *mount* (< OE *munt*)–*mountain* (< OFr *montaigne*); (2) morphological doublets, e.g., *mead* (< OE *mǣd*, nominative)–*meadow* (< the corresponding oblique cases *mǣdwe*) or such past participles as *trod–trodden*; (3) derivational doublets, e.g., *pale–paly*; and (4) analogical doublets, e.g., *fount–fountain* (the former developed from the latter on the analogy of *mount–mountain*) or verbs with or without the ending -*en* like *haste–hasten*. In the following analysis of the more important of these doublets I will take them in that order but shall feel free to treat related cases together whenever convenient.

Etymological doublets are not very common, a typical example being *mount* 4× –*mountain* 48 × (once, RJ 3.4.177, hypermetrically in a caesura).[18] For the analogical pair *fount–fountain* the figures are respectively 5 and 18. We find further *vale* 10× –*valley* 8×, *debitor* (0 1.1.31)–*debtor* 12×, *empery* 2× (in the sense of "empire")–*empire* 16× and *sully, sullied* 3× (+ *sullies* sb. 1×)–*soil(ed)* 8×. *Greek*, both adjective and noun, which is used about 5 times, has two metrical variants, both disyllabic, *Grecian* 28× (once, TC 4.4.57, in a caesura) and *Greekish* 8× ; TC 4.5.124–25 clearly show the metrical variation: "Were thy commixion, Greeke and Troian so, / That thou could'st say, this hand is Grecian all." Of interest, stylistically no less than metrically, is also the single occurrence of *Danskers* H 2.1.7: "Enquire me first what Danskers are in Paris," instead of the usual *Dane* 7×. To this group may be added a few doublets which though they cannot precisely be classified as etymological, nevertheless have something in common—at least superficially —with the preceding cases. The most important are *maid–maiden*, *morn– morning*, and *hate–hated*. *Maid*, a shortened form of *maiden*, occurs over 200 times in Shakespeare, whereas *maiden* as a noun appears 25 times, with an additional 36 cases of it as an adjective; moreover, we find *maidhood* 2× and *maidenhood* 2× as well as *maidenhead* 8× ; two of the latter, WT 4.4.116: "Your Maiden-heads growing: O Proserpina," and H8 2.3.25: "And venture Maidenhead for't, and so would you," are hard to scan, not because of tri-syllabic *maidenhead*, which seems to be metrically exact, but owing to the heavy syllables following it. *Morn* 45× and its analogical extension *morning* 91× are kept strictly apart metrically, and so are the two compounds *morn-dew* AC 3.12.9 and *morning dew* MND 4.1.126, TA 2.3.201. Disyllabic *morrow* is used mainly in the phrase *good morrow* and in rhymes with *sorrow*; in addition there are about 200 instances of the adverb *to-morrow*. *Hate* as a noun appears at least 85 times but *hatred* only 15, without any metrical deviation. And finally we may mention here *noon* 13× –*noon-day* 1× –*noontide* 5×, *canstick* 1× –*candlestick* 1×, *childness* 1× –*childishness* 3×, and *bride-bed* 2× –*bridal bed* 3×.

The morphological group is somewhat larger, with *mead* 9 × –*meadow* 3 × as a representative pair of doublets. More significant, however, are the many past participles with or without final -*en*, e.g., *chose* 7 × –*chosen* 12 × (plus *well-chosen* 1 ×), one of these with trisyllabic substitution, apparently in a caesura, "Be chosen with proclamations to day" (TA 1.1.190); further *froze* 1 × –*frozen* 10 ×, *broke* 45 × (plus *unbroke* 1 ×)–*broken* 40 ×, including one hypermetrical case, "Has broken a staff or so; so let it pass" (P 2.3.35), *spoke* 88 × –*spoken* 33 ×, including two instances of trisyllabic substitution in caesuras (RJ 1.1.13, AC 2.2.102) and two elsewhere: "You might have spoken a thousand things, that would" (WT 5.1.21), and "'Twere good she were spoken with, for she may strew" (H 4.5.15 Q2—but F prints this: "'Twere good she were spoken with, / For she may strew . . ."), *unspoke* 1 × –*unspoken* 1 ×, and *well-spoken* 3 ×. The three hypermetrical cases, *broken* and *spoken* (2 ×), may well be due to the printer, who simply set the more common variant by mistake, but since *broken* and the first example of *spoken* are followed by *a*, it is possible for -*en* [ŋ] to be non-syllabic [n], thus *broke-na*; in the H 4.5.14 instance the scansion actually requires *she were* to be one syllable, perhaps *sh'were* or *s'here*.[19] Other participial doublets are *beat* 9 × –*beaten* 22 × –*beated* 1 ×, *chid* 9 × –*chidden* 3 ×, *drunk* 19 × –*drunken* 14 ×, *eat* 5 × –*eaten* 6 ×, *forbid* 11 × –*forbidden* 5 ×, *hid* 35 × –*hidden* 6 ×, and *writ* 55 × –*wrote* 2 × –*written* 24 ×. *Struck* 39 ×, usually spelled *strook(e)* and even *stroke*, alternates both with *strucken* 6 ×, spelled *stro(o)ken*, and *stricken* 3 ×. For *get* and its derivatives the figures are as follows: *got* 49 × –*gotten* 4 ×, *begot* 14 × –*begotten* 2 × –*misbegot* 1 × –*misbegotten* 3 ×, *forgot* 75 × –*forgotten* 12 ×, *ungot* 1 × –*ungotten* 1 × (plus *unbegotten* 1 ×). Similarly we find *trod* 5 × –*trodden* 5 ×, *untrod* 1 × –*untrodden* 1 × –, *downtrod* 1 × (1H4 1.3.135 Q1— F *downfall* must be an error for disyllabic *downfalne*)–*downtrodden* 1 ×, *forsook* 8 × –*forsaken* 5 ×, *shook* 10 × –*shak'd* 4 × –*shaken* 5 ×, *unshak'd* 2 × – *unshaken* 2 ×, and *unshap'd* 1 × –*unshapen* 1 ×. It is a noteworthy fact that the very common verb *takes* strictly differentiates metrically between monosyllabic *took* 23 × and *tane* 80 × on one hand and disyllabic *taken* 54 × (twice in hypermetrical caesuras, H5 4.8.80 and L 1.4.353) on the other; this is true also of *mistook* 12 × and *mistane* 2 × versus *mistaken* 6 ×.

Derivatives, whether original or analogical, provide a goodly number of metrical doublets. By the side of *babe* 65 × we find *baby* 14 ×, and as variants of adjectival *brass* 2 × both *brassy* 1 × ("From brassie bosomes, and rough hearts of flint" MV 4.1.31) and *brazen* 11 × (cf. *Brasse Cannon* H5 3.1.11, *Brasse voyce* TC 1.3.257, and *Brazon Cannon* H 1.1.73, *Brazen Trumpet* R2 3.3.33, *brazen dinne* AC 4.8.36), while *grasse-plot* T 4.1.73 is paralleled by *Grassie Carpet* R2 3.3.50. *Count* 15 × alternates with *county* 12 ×, a back-formation from disyllabic *count's* or *counts* [ˈkəʊntɪz].[20] Metrically import-ant are what we may call double adjectives, that is to say, new, derivative adjectives formed by the addition of the adjectival suffix -*y* to existing mono-syllabic adjectives like *paly* from *pale*. As I have pointed out elsewhere,[21] such formations are on record from about 1400 but are doubtless older; they originated in the spoken language on the pattern of adjectives like *icy, happy, dirty,* etc., which were far more common than monosyllables like *cool, lean, pale,* etc., and found their way into verse as convenient metrical doublets. Both Spenser and Shakespeare employ them a few times; thus Shakespeare has *brisky* MND 3.1.97, *paly* H5 4.pr.8, 2H6 3.2.141, RJ 4.1.100, *plumpy* AC 2.7.119, *primy* H 1.3.7, *steepy* TmA 1.1.75, S 63.5, and *vasty* MV 2.7.41 Q (F misprints *vaste*), 1H4 3.1.52, H5 pr. 12, 2.2.123, 2.4.105. The corresponding figures for the simple adjectives are: *brisk* 3 ×, *plump* 1 ×, *prime* 6 ×, *steep* 5 ×, *vast* 13 ×, and *pale* over 150 ×. Three other adjectival pairs may be listed here, *eterne* 2 × (both at the end of the line)–*eternal* 36 ×, *majestic* 3 ×–*majestical* 6 ×, and *magic* 3 ×–hypermetrical *magical* 1 × ("That magicall word of Warre we have effected" AC 3.1.31), which may well have been *magic* in Shakespeare's manuscript.

Ancient verb doublets like *threat* < OE *þrēatan* and *threaten* < OE *þrēatnian* gave rise to analogical doublets like *hap–happen, haste–hasten,* and *ope–open* (*ope* is a back-formation from *open*). The Shakespearean figures for these doublets are: *threat* 17 ×–*threaten* 17 ×, *haste* 27 × (including 6 cases of the reflexive verb, e.g., *haste me*)–*hasten* 6 ×, and *ope* 32 ×–*open* 111 ×, plus *op'd* 4 ×–*open'd* or *op'ned* 10 × ; since both *ope* and *open* may be adjectives or adverbs as well as verbs, the following breakdown of their totals are illuminating: *ope,* verb, 24 ×–*open,* verb, 46 ×, the rest adjectives or adverbs, with no less than 34 instances of the attributive adjective *open.* Only one hypermetrical case has turned up, "Then let my Fathers blood open it againe" (3H6 1.3.23), where, however, an enclitic *it,* that is *'t* (of common occurrence in Shakespeare), will restore the syllabic regularity. Of a similar type is the adverb *often,* which is an analogical extension of original *oft.* The two forms are carefully differentiated: *oft* 46 ×–*often* 36 ×. Their metrical distribution is clearly illustrated by the following two quotations: "Oft have you (often have you thanks therefore)" TC 3.3.20, and "So oft as that shall be, / So often shall the knot of us be call'd" JC 3.1.116–17. And as a metrical variant of *seldom* 28 × we find the probably archaic *seld* 2 × (a back-formation—TC 4.5.150, PP 175) and *seld-shown* C 2.1.229.

In Shakespeare's usage *defensible* 2 × (2H4 2.3.38, H5 3.3.50) and *defensive* 2 × (R2 2.1.48, 1H6 2.1.49) had the same meaning and consequently alternated metrically. This is true also of *plausive* 2 × (AW 1.2.53, H 1.4.30), which means "plausible," and of *plausibly* RL 1854, which stands for "plausively." The reason for this confusion of the two suffixes *-ive* and *-ible/-able* is first of all the fact that earlier *-ible/-able* had active sense, so that *defensible* could mean "able to defend," and probably also the close phonetic similarity of adverbs like *plausibly–plausively.* In my paper "Shakespeare's Language" (pp. 46 ff.) I pointed out that this confusion is not restricted to Shakespeare but is evidenced from such fine Latinists as Mulcaster and Milton. Like Shakespeare, Milton uses *unexpressive* for "inexpressible" in the "Hymn on the Morning of Christ's Nativity" (1. 11): "Harping in loud and solemn quire, / With unexpressive notes to Heav'n's new-born Heir," and in "Lycidas" (1. 176): "And hears the unexpressive nuptial Song"—cf. "The faire, the chaste, and unexpressive shee" AYL 3.2.11; Mulcaster of St. Paul's School wrote *plausibly* for "plausively" in 1581: "His judgement is so often and so plausibly vouched by the curteouse maister Askam" (OED).[22] Shakespeare has other cases of the same kind: *insuppressive* JC 2.1.134 meaning "insuppressible," *directive* "directable" TC 1.3.357, *respective* "respectable" TGV 4.4.200, and *uncomprehensive* "incomprehensible" TC 3.3.198. Of the same type is the use of *deceivable* TN 4.3.21, R2 2.3.84 as a semantic and metrical variant of *deceitful* 7×.

We may pause here for a moment to glance at a small group of derivatives of interest both metrically and in terms of word-formation. A few of them are uniquely Shakespearean though this fact may not necessarily mean that they were coined by Shakespeare. He has at least seven noteworthy derivatives in *-ment*, namely *blastments* H 1.3.42, *controlment* 3×, a common sixteenth–seventeenth-century term (OED), versus *control* 4× (cf. *without controlment* TA 2.1.68, *without control* R3 3.5.84), *designment* 2×, *encompassment* H 2.1.10, *engrossment* 2H4 4.5.80, *strewments* H 5.1.256, and *supplyment* Cy 3.4.182. Another suffix employed to add an extra syllable to a word is *-(t)ure* in *climatures* H 1.1.125, *composture* TmA 4.3.444 (but *compost* H 3.4.151), *discomfiture* 1H6 1.1.59 (cf. *discomfit* 2H6 5.2.86), *distemperature* 5× (all four syllables, with syncopation of the second *e*), and the strange *embrasure* TC 4.4.39. Instead of the noun *transport*, first recorded by Florio in 1611 (OED), or *transportation*, both of which would have been metrically inexact, Shakespeare has *transportance* TC 3.2.12. And once he uses *cloistress* TN 1.1.28 instead of *nun*. According to the precepts of Tudor rhetoric nonce-formations like *climature, embrasure, blastment,* and *transportance* should probably be classified as cases of proparalepsis (the addition of a syllable at the end of a word). If the syllable was added medially, the device was termed epenthesis. As a matter of fact we seem to have at least three instances of this in Shakespeare, all metrically justified: *cursorary* H5 5.2.77, *intrinsicate* AC 5.2.307, though this may be an adoption from Italian (see OED), and *vastidity* MM 3.1.69.

Genuine cases of what Tudor rhetoricians called prothesis, the addition of a prefix to the beginning of a word, are actually rare, if we look for nonce-formations, but to judge from their examples of this scheme, they classified as prothesis well-established derivatives like *embolden, endanger, ymade*. Shakespeare has a great many words beginning with *em-, en* or *in-*, some of which are obviously metrical variants of the corresponding words without these prefixes and hence should all be examined, but this is impossible here; I must confine myself to mentioning only the following which generally make their first or unique appearance in Shakespeare: *embounded* J 4.3.137, *enclog* O 2.1.70 F ("Traitors ensteep'd, to enclogge the guiltlesse Keele," where *to* should be read *t'*—note that Qq have instead *clog*), *endart* RJ 1.3.98, *enfree* TC 4.1.38 (also pre-Shakespeare), *enfreedom* LLL 3.1.130, *enlink* H5 3.3.18 (also pre-Shakespeare), *enpierced* RJ 1.4.19, *enrank* 1H6 1.1.115, *enrooted* 2H4 4.1.207, *enscheduled* H5 5.2.73, *ensear* TmA 4.3.188, *enskied* MM 1.4.34, *ensteeped* O 2.1.70, H5 4.6.12, *entame* AYL 3.5.48, *enwheel* O 2.1.87. Let me also cite *confix* MM 5.1.232, *commingled* H 3.2.74, and *commix* Cy 4.2.55, LC 28. The opposite tendency, aphaeresis, or the dropping of an initial syllable from a polysyllabic word, which has been a common feature of the spoken language for centuries, is likewise a useful metrical device. Unfortunately complete statistics cannot be given for the probably most illuminating instance of aphaeresis, *'gainst*, and its fuller form *against*, but on the basis of examples listed in Schmidt's *Lexicon* the following figures are nevertheless significant: *'gainst* 61 × – *against* 62 ×. Four of the 61 cases of *'gainst* reveal a difference between F and Q: twice Q has correctly *'gainst* (R2 5.2.46, MV 4.1.451), F incorrectly *against*, and twice F correctly *'gainst* (2H4 1.3.84, TA 5.2.206), Q incorrectly *against*; once (MM 5.1.244) F has hypermetrical *against* which F2 corrects to *gainst*. There are however other interesting doublets of this type. *Alarum* 13 × has two metrical variants, *'larum* 4 × and *alarm* 5 ×; the latter form may actually have been intended at C 2.2.80, "When the Alarum were strucke, then idly sit," where otherwise we have a case of trisyllabic substitution as, permissibly, in a caesura at 2H6 2.3.95. For *leopard* 2 × (once trisyllabic but metrically exact, 1H6 1.5.31) we find *'pard* 4 ×, for *apparel* 13 × *'parel* 1 × (L 4.1.51), for *apparitor* (not in Shakespeare) *'paritor* LLL 3.1.188, and for *apothecary* 4 × *'pothecary* 2 ×. *Entice* 5 × appears as *'tice* 1 × (TA 2.3.92). The best examples I have come across so far are *escape* 16 ×, *escap'd* 5 × (plus one case of *escapëd*) versus *'scape* 32 × and *'scap'd* 9 × (note 3H6 2.1.6–7: "Or had he scap't, we should have heard the newes: / The happy tidings of his good escape"), *behaviour* 23 × – *'haviour* 5 ×, and *espy*, *espies*, *espied* 10 × – *spy*, *spies(t)*, *spied* 16 ×. As a case of aphaeresis we should, in my opinion, interpret *cital* 1H4 5.2.61: "He made a blushing cital of himself," which I take to be *recital* "account, description" with omission of initial *re-* as in Spenser's *hersall* "rehearsal" FQ 3.11.18—cf. also *cernes* "concerns" TS 5.1.77 (prose). Dr. Johnson's interpretation "reproof, impeachment," tentatively quoted in OED and strangely enough accepted by Onions, *Shakespeare Glossary*, is nothing but a conjecture.

Regardless of whether we believe that there are no true synonyms, not even such well-defined terms as the numerals of different languages, e.g., *three*, *drei*, *trois*, or we take a more common-sense attitude to semantic problems and admit, for practical purposes at any rate, the existence of synonyms and near-synonyms in any language,[23] the fact remains that for centuries synonyms and synonymic expressions have been one of the staples of the poet's craft. It matters very little if to a sensitive modern reader the associations evoked, say, by *forest* differ from those called up by *wood*, since it cannot be proved that the poet's associations were the same, nor that his choice of a particular synonym was determined by these associations rather than by metrical considerations. What matters is the occurrence in his poetry of two semantically identical or related words whose distribution is clearly predicated on their respective number of syllables. This is precisely what those semantic doublets in Shakespeare reveal that I have been able to examine. Thus *forest* appears 24 times, once hypermetrically in *Forest of Arden* AYL 1.3.109, while *wood* is used 44 times. Similarly *billow(s)* and *wave(s)* alternate, the former being used 8 times, the latter 12. The corresponding figures for *welkin* and *sky* are 14 and 49 respectively;[24] *heaven(s)* cannot be used statistically because it was both monosyllabic and disyllabic in this period, depending on its metrical occurrence. Instead of *face* or *look* (hundreds of examples in the *Concordance*) we find *visage* 36× as well as *countenance* which, however, cannot be used here since it is often syncopated to *count'nance*. *Confine(s)* and *bound(s)*, too, alternate, the former occurring 12 times, the latter 24, and similarly *confineless* 1× and *boundless* 8×. The adjective *dark* 55× has at least two metrical variants, *darksome* 1× and *dusky* 6×, and *hard* (probably over 100×) both *flinty* 11× and *stony* 7×; cf. *hard heart* 5× (plus 3 in prose) and *flinty heart* 1× (plus *flinty bosom, ribs*, etc.), *stony heart* 1× as well as *stony-hearted* 1×–*hard-hearted* 5×—note 3H6 2.1.202: "Were thy heart as hard as Steele, / As thou hast shewne it flintie by thy deeds." Statistically important are further *isle* 36×–*island* 25× (once in a hypermetrical caesura) and *country* 140×–*land* over 250×. Though I am fully aware that in certain locutions *town* and *city* are not interchangeable, the fact is that in Shakespeare the vast majority of *town* and *city* do interchange, both occurring 113 times if my calculations are correct; cf. e.g., these two quotations from CE (1.2.12 and 1.2.31): "Ile view the manners of the towne"—"And wander up and downe to view the Citie." We may note further that York and Leicester are each twice referred to as *town*, and that *city* is three times directly followed by the name of the city without the connecting preposition *of*: *city Tours* 2× and *city Rome* 1×.

Strictly speaking these last three instances of *city* plus name belong to a different category of metrical variants, which we may call syntactical doublets. Here Shakespeare exploits two parallel constructions, both time-honored, one representing the common usage of the day (and of today) as in *the city of London* 1H6 3.1.77, the other a more learned and probably obsolescent practice;[25] he does so, too, in *the Country Maine and Anjou* 1H6 5.3.154 and in *the river Sala* H5 1.2.63 versus *the river of Cydnus* AC 2.2.191 (prose). This group of doublets covers many syntactical phenomena, some of which can easily be exemplified but are nevertheless hard to get at statistically without time-consuming excerption of the whole text. Thus the use and non-use of the definite article depends on the metre in *the Lady Blanch* J 2.1.443–*Lady Blanch* J 2.1.431, *the Prince Florizel* WT 4.2.29 (prose)–*Prince Florizel* WT 5.1.85, *the Tarquin* JC 2.1.54—*Tarquin* JC 2.2.92, and *o'th' Nile* AC 2.7.20—*Nile* AC 5.2.356; further in "So *longest* Way shall have *the longest* Moanes"

R2 5.1.90, *best safety* H 1.3.43, *at mercy of* TC 4.4.116, "More tuneable than *Larke* to *shepheards* eare" MND 1.1.184, *at very heart* Cy 1.1.10, *at very root on's heart* C 2.1.176, *by help of* T 1.2.275—*with the help of* T ep. 10, *at the last* C 5.6.37, etc.—*at last* VA 566, etc., *at the least* RL 1654, etc.—*at least* RL 1053, etc., and many other such expressions.[26]

Continuing this sketch of syntactical doublets in Shakespeare, we note for instance the variation between the personal pronouns used reflexively and the corresponding forms in -*self*, which arose in ME times; a good example is "I will discase *me*, and *my selfe* present" T 5.1.85, another is "Therefore prepare *you*" H 3.3.2 (plural), which should be compared with "Therefore prepare *thy selfe*" H 4.3.45. The colloquial practice of repeating a substantival subject by an immediately following personal pronoun is sometimes resorted to, e.g., *God he knows* CE 5.1.229, J 5.7.60, etc. (but *God knows* MA 5.1.87, J 2.1.549, etc.), *King Richard, he* R2 3.4.83, and so on. The subject pronoun sometimes appears redundantly after imperatives, e.g., *Wipe thou thine eyes* T 1.2.25, *take you this* TGV 2.2.6. On the other hand, a subject pronoun is often omitted altogether, e.g., *prithee* T 2.1.9, 228, etc., but *I prithee* T 1.2.245, MM 1.2.181, etc., *Why speak'st not* C 4.5.59, *Wilt break my heart* L 3.4.4., etc. The relative *which* has a common variant *the which*, found e.g., at T 1.2.137 " *Which* now's upon's: without *the which*, this Story," and CE 5.1.229 " *Which* God he knowes, I saw not. For *the which*." Schmidt's *Lexicon* lists 45 instances of *the which* in poetry, probably only a fraction of the total number.

Double comparatives and superlatives occur both in prose and verse and, to judge from the characters employing them, they were fully acceptable in fashionable speech; thus Prospero and Bottom both say *more better* (T 1.2.19, MND 3.1.21) and Hamlet *more nearer, more richer*, and *more raver* (H 2.1.11, 3.2.316, 5.2.129). Since these double comparatives and superlatives frequently appear in verse, one cannot escape the conclusion that they were felt to be convenient metrical variants whenever an extra syllable was needed to fill the syllabic measure. The following comparatives occur once each in verse: *more better, more braver, more corrupter, more elder, more fairer, more fitter, more harder, more kinder, more larger, more mightier, more proudlier, more richer, more sharper, more stronger, more worse*, and the following twice: *more nearer* (the F version of O 5.2.110 has "more neerer Earth," the Qq instead "more near the Earth"), *more wider* and *more worthier*. All of the analogous superlatives occur once: *most best, most boldest, most bravest, most dear'st, most dearest* (L 1.1.219, in a caesura, where *dearest* may be either monosyllabic or disyllabic), *most heaviest, most poorest, most stillest, most unkindest, most worst, most worthiest*. In addition we find *worser* 18 ×, *lesser* 28 ×, and *nearer* 8 × as against *worse* over 150 ×, *less* about 250 × (cf. "No, nor a man that feares you *lesse* than he, / That's *lesser* then a little," C 1.4.14–15) and the original comparative *near* 3 × as in M 2.3.146–7, "The *neere* in blood, the *neerer* bloody." As a double superlative may further be regarded *chiefest*, which occurs 13 × in contrast to *chief* 24 × (adjective and adverb).

Though in Shakespeare's time adverbs in *-ly* preponderate over those without this suffix, the latter were still a feature of colloquial syntax and as such potential metrical variants. There are a number of these adverbial doublets in Shakespeare but I have been able to check only a few of them e.g., *exceeding* 6 × *exceedingly* 2 ×, *grievous* 2 × *–grievously* 3 ×. Particularly significant is the metrical variation between monosyllabic and disyllabic forms like *swift* 9 ×– *swiftly* 6 × (note also the adverbial comparative *swifter* 5 ×), *scarce* 54 ×– *scarcely* 15 ×, *quick* 2 × *–quickly* 73 ×, and *sweet* 5 × *–sweetly* 21 × ; in the line "All which secure, and sweetly he enjoyes" (3H6 2.5.50) *-ly* belongs as much to *secure* as to *sweet*—had Shakespeare not bothered about syllabic regularity he would certainly have written *securely and sweetly*.

There are many other syntactical and phrasal doublets in Shakespeare which should be statistically investigated, but unfortunately, for most of them the *Concordance* is of little or no help. Reliable figures can be obtained only by excerpting all the plays and poems. A case in point is pleonastic *do*, which is often used in positive statements with an infinitive as a substitute for a single finite verb, e.g., "The sunne *doth* burne my face" VA 186, "The Countrey Cocks *doe* crowe, the Clocks *doe* towle" H5 4.pr.15, "Horses *did* (F do) neigh, and dying men *did* grone" JC 2.2.23; usually *do/did* then appears in a thesis, but it may just as well stand in an arsis without being emphatic, e.g., "Here *doe* I choose" MV 2.7.60 (cf. "And here choose I" MV 3.2.107), "Wherein it *doth* impaire the seeing sense, / It pais the hearing double recompence" MND 3.2.179–80 (note the shift from the periphrastic to the simple form in conformity with the metre), "I *did* upbraid her and fall out with her" MND 4.1.53. I am convinced that a statistical investigation of this pleonastic *do* would reveal complete agreement between syntax and verse rhythm. This is moreover likely to happen in respect of *for to–to* (cf. H 1.2.175 F "Wee'l teach you to drinke deepe," with the Q2 version "Weele teach you for to drinke"), and several other phrasal doublets such as *after that–after*; *ere that–ere*; *if that–if*; *lest that–lest*; *when that, whenas–when*; *while that–while*; *the whilst, whilst as–whilst*; *for why, for that–for*; *like as–as*; *like to–like*; *an(d) if–if*; and many more.

The foregoing statistical survey, though not complete, has consequently established the almost absolute metrical regularity of these three types of Shakespearean doublets. Only eight cases of seeming trisyllabic substitution have been found: *Capulet, broken, spoken* (2 ×), *magical, open, alarum, Forest of Arden*. All of these are easily accounted for and may, if we desire, be explained away as orthographical or typographical errors, with the exception of *Forest of Arden*; though this may be a metrical makeshift or a poetic license of sorts, it would not be impossible to suggest a monosyllabic variant of *forest* (unrecorded, so far as I know) with the same omission of *e* as in superlatives like *dear'st* and related to the well-documented syncopated form *forster* (also found in the surname *Foster*) < *forester*. Even if we accept these eight cases at their face value, their number is insignificant compared to a total of 1929 instances of the longer variants (not counting the ambiguous *Abraham* and many of the phrasal doublets) and about 3090 of the shorter ones (excluding all the instances of *face* and *look*), if my calculations have been correct. This is 0.41 percent of the former total and precisely 0.16 of the combined totals of about 5000. Either figure is considerably below the tentative limit suggested above, and both promise even lower percentages when more complete data are made available than I have been able to present here.

Though not unexpected, the metrical regularity of the non-phonological doublets carries with it important implications not only for Shakespearean prosody but also for Elizabethan prosody in general. It means first of all that the same regularity must be reckoned with in the case of all phonological doublets that may arise through syncopation and other forms of contraction or elision; it therefore confirms my theory of the interrelationship of prosody and phonology in this period. It means further that any lexically polysyllabic word or phrase with a potential phonological doublet of fewer syllables cannot possibly be adduced as evidence of trisyllabic substitution even if the text prints the longer variant; only the scansion will determine whether a line containing, e.g., *perilous, ministering, I am, many a*, should or should not be regularized by reading *parlous, ministring* or *minstring, I'm, man-ya*, since both the spoken language and the prosody of the period sanction such contractions. From a statistical point of view therefore such words and phrases are of no value whatever to those who wish to prove the accentual character of Shakespeare's verse. Only when a line cannot be made to scan by the application of all known devices of word reduction are we entitled to consider the possibility of trisyllabic substitution. But even so each emergent case of apparent metrical irregularity must be scrutinized in relationship to the caesural pattern and as much to the problem of textual transmission in so far as this has any bearing on the poem or play under study. The fact is that at least in Shakespearean prosody the residual cases that cannot be accounted for as caesural may well be due to the mistakes of a copyist, printers' errors, mislineation and careless cutting or reshuffling of speeches. Some of them may even have been caused by the greater metrical freedom which is believed to characterize Shakespeare's mature years.[27] Only a thorough statistical analysis of Shakespeare's verse on the lines employed in this paper may help to prove or disprove this challenging hypothesis. But reducible polysyllables, what I call phonological doublets, can never be cited in support of it.

## FOOTNOTES

1. Pope's *op'ra* occurs in a caesura, where trisyllabic *opera* would have been permissible. In accentual verse the fuller forms *over* and *betwixt* should really not disrupt the metre, and I therefore suspect that despite his avowed love for trisyllabic feet, Webster was at heart a syllable-counter.—Here are the twelve lines from Pope:

> She went, to plain-work, and to purling books,
> Old-fashion'd halls, dull aunts, and croaking rooks,

She went from Op'ra, park, assembly, play,
To morning walks, and pray'rs three hours a day;
To pass her time 'twixt reading and Bohea,
To muse, and spill her solitary tea,
Or o'er cold coffee trifle with the spoon,
Count her slow clock, and dine exact at noon;
Divert her eyes with pictures in the fire,
Hum half a tune, tell stories to the squire;
Up to her godly garret after sev'n,
There starve and pray, for that's the way to heav'n.

2. Paul Fussell, Jr., *Theory of Prosody in Eighteenth-Century England* (New London, Conn., 1954), pp. 104 ff. and 133 ff.

3. *Op. cit.*, p. 157.

4. Recently some structural linguists have turned their attention to metrics and as is usual with missionaries or converts they make the most extravagant claims for the blessings of the new faith; see especially *The Kenyon Review*, 18 (1956), pp. 411 ff. Like young ambition they scorn the base degrees by which they did ascend. Indeed, it now appears to have become good form in linguistic circles to belittle what philologists have contributed in the past and are still contributing to the scientific study of language and to the elucidation of older literatures. Yet without the pioneering work of generations of philologists there would probably have been no structural linguistics and we should then have been spared such shocking manifestations of it as the analysis of Proto-Germanic, Old and Middle English in Charles F. Hockett's *A Course in Modern Linguistics* (New York, 1958), pp. 372 ff., and the same author's article, "The Stressed Syllabics of Old English," *Language* 35 (1959), pp. 575–97. [Reprinted in this volume, pp. 108 ff.—Ed.]

5. *Shakespeare's Pronunciation* (New Haven, Conn., 1953), p. 26.

6. For the pronunciation of *-ual* see *ibid.*, p. 288, as well as the above spelling *sprytwalle* and the OED entry *spiral*.

7. Osmond's passing reference to the time element in verse betrays his dependence on those metrists who mistakenly equate verse rhythm and musical rhythm. This is a common fallacy which stems from a lack of phonetic insight on the part of its advocates. The infinitely variable syllable quantities of spoken English depending on position in a word or phrase, on emphasis, intonation, and meaning, cannot be rendered in mechanical musical notation which arbitrarily assigns, say, an eighth or a sixteenth to one syllable, a quarter note or even a half-note to another as the scanner deems appropriate. A phonetician knows for instance that before a pause the final syllable of *pity* is actually longer than the first, but that in a phrase like *the pity of it* the first syllable is considerably longer than the second. What is important in verse is the relationship of stresses in a line and to the underlying metrical pattern, not the syllabic quantities of individual words, and speech stress has no equivalent in music. For some cogent remarks on this important question see René Wellek and Austin Warren, *Theory of Literature* (New York, 1949), pp. 168 ff.—also W. K. Wimsatt, Jr., and Monroe C. Beardsley, "The Concept of Meter: An Exercise in Abstraction," *PMLA* 74 (1959), pp. 585 ff. [See further the papers in Part Two ("Metrics") of Seymour Chatman and Samuel R. Levin, eds., *Essays on the language of literature* (Boston, 1967). The Wimsatt-Beardsley paper is reprinted there, along with others by Jespersen, Chatman, Wells, *et al.*—Ed.]

8. See Jordan-Matthes, *Handbuch der mittelenglischen Grammatik* (Heidelberg, 1934), §§ 142, 248, and Luick, *Historische Grammatik der englischen Sprache* (Leipzig, 1921–40), §§ 456, 462.

9. *Shakespeare's Pronunciation*, pp. 283 ff.

10. My only quarrel with it concerns Fussell's unrealistic attitude to the relationship of poetic and colloquial contractions (pp. 96 ff.). He takes exception to Culler for asserting "that the poetic contractions . . . are simply reproductions of the ubiquitous colloquial contractions," and even criticizes Otto Jespersen for saying that the poetic contractions represent "a natural everyday pronunciation" (*Linguistica*, pp. 273 f.). He then expounds his own unhistorical views, basing his arguments mainly on what in his opinion might have been considered linguistically proper in the eighteenth century, apparently confusing colloquial and low (p. 97), and certainly ignoring all the irrefutable evidence presented in handbooks like Jordan and Luick (cf. n. 8 above).

11. *William Shakespeare, Prosody and Text* (Leyden, 1900), p. 215.

12. *Linguistica* (Copenhagen, 1933), p. 265. [Reprinted in Chatman and Levin, *op. cit.*, 71–90.—Ed.]

13. Compare, e.g., "Sees *Helens* beauty in a brow of Egipt" MND 5.1.11—"And *Helena* of Athens looke thou finde" MND 3.2.95; "To conjure teares up in a poore *maids* eyes" MND 3.2.158—"That frights the *maidens* of the Villagree" MND 2.1.35; "If *broken* then, It is no fault of mine: / If by me *broke*, What foole is not so wise" LLL 4.3.71–72; "*Which* now's upon's; without *the which*, this Story" T 1.2.137.

14. This means "*Desdemona* 26 times—*Desdemon* 7 times"—always in verse. Play titles have been abbreviated in the same way as in my *Shakespeare's pronunciation*.

15. Note also O 3.4.35, where the Q reading "How do you do, Desdemona" becomes metrically satisfactory in F: "How do you, Desdemona." This significant variation has not been noted in the new Arden Ed. of *Othello*, p. 125.

16. Modern editions print the first form *Capel's* and the second *Capels'*, but since Shakespeare tends to omit the definite article for metrical reasons (see Wilhelm Franz, *Die Sprache Shakespeares in Vers und Prosa*, Halle, 1939, § 267, and my discussion below), both instances of *Capels* should probably be analysed as the genitive plural, *Capels'*. Perhaps we have an analogous case in "At this same auncient Feast of *Capulets*" (1.2.87), where *Capulets* need not, so far as I can see, be interpreted as *Capulet's* (an appositional genitive, to use Jespersen's terminology) as is regularly done, but may well stand for *the Capulets*.

17. The influence of verse rhythm on the language of Chaucer, Gower, Marlowe, and Kyd has been examined by J. Bihl, *Die Wirkungen des Rhythmus in der Sprache von Chaucer und Gower* (Heidelberg, 1916), and F. Stroheker, *Doppelformen und Rhythmus bei Marlowe und Kyd* (Heidelberg, 1913), but not as a criterion of metrical regularity.

18. The corresponding figures for Spenser are 2 and 33, respectively.

19. Shakespeare has *you're best, thou'rt best*, with *'re, 'rt* standing for *were, wert*—see *Shakespeare's Pronunciation*, p. 277.

20. See *Shakespeare's Pronunciation*, p. 265, n. 8.

21. In "Shakespeare's Language," *Shakespeare: Of an Age and for all Time*, The Yale Shakespeare Festival Lectures, ed. Charles T. Prouty (New Haven, Conn., 1954), pp. 48 ff.

22. Ben Jonson has *responsible* in the sense of "responsive" in *The Case is Alterd* 1.6.45.

23. On this see, e.g., Björn Collinder, *Språket, Inledning till det vetenskapliga språkstudiet* (Stockholm, 1959), pp. 90 ff.

24. Apropos of Gordon's characterization (in *Shakespeare's English*, S.P.E. Tract No. XXIX, Oxford, 1928, p. 274) of *starry welkin* as a strange misalliance between rustic *starry* and "the archaic and ludicrous *welkin*" I pointed out in "Shakespeare's Language," pp. 49 f., that *starry* was certainly not rustic, nor was

*welkin* archaic and ludicrous in the sixteenth century, and I expressed the conviction that *welkin* was probably a literary word rather than a colloquialism and that *starry welkin* was a poetic cliché of the same kind as *wormy bed* in Shakespeare and Milton.

25. See, e.g., Wilhelm Franz, *op. cit.*, § 521.

26. In Thomas Preston's *Cambises* (1569) the metrical use of the article is very conspicuous, e.g., *then deed of happy prince* (1. 28), *go into the Egypt land* (1. 95), *To Egypt land* (1. 110), *when deede is doone* (1. 436), *to pass from worlds delight* (1. 520).

27. A rapid reading of *Antony and Cleopatra* has yielded the following cases of trisyllabic substitution which appear to be conclusive (the relevant word is italicized here): "Like to a *Vagabond* Flagge upon the Streame" 1.4.45; "That *magicall* word of Warre we have effected" 3.1.31 (cf. p. 218 above); "'Tis done already, and the *Messenger* gone" 3.6.31; "And we in *negligent* danger: cheere your heart" 3.6.81; "Where death is sure. Yon *ribaudred* Nagge of Egypt" 3.10.10—note the many contractions in the following line: "(Whom Leprosie o're-take) i'th' midst o'th' fight"—"Which *promises* Royall perill. Trumpetters" 4.8.35. But *opulent* 1.5.46, *penitent* 2.2.92, and *fugitive* 3.1.7 may have had disyllabic variants through syncopation of the medial syllable. For *seven-fold* 4.14.38 (also TmA 1.1.289) we may compare Pope's disyllabic *sev'nfold* in *The Dunciad* 1.244 as well as dialectal [sem] *seven* (Wiltshire). Hypermetrical caesuras are very common in this play; see, e.g., 2.2.148, 3.2.57, 5.2.321.

## ROBERT P. STOCKWELL

# Mirrors in the History
# of English Pronunciation*

History is not an account of facts but of relations that are inferred to have existed between supposed facts. It is not at all easy to make a crucial observation as to what a particular fact is, or to discriminate between facts and inferences. The "facts" of historical scholarship are often simply useful hypotheses that in turn relate, by rough rules of inference, a variety of secondary "facts" to each other. The most insightful accounts of historical events turn out to be intricate webs of suppositions and inferences removed at many steps from the citable data on which the conclusions ultimately rest.

In no area of historical research is this spidery network of inference more apparent than in the attempt to reconstruct what English has sounded like at various periods of its history. It is so apparent, indeed, that remarkably few people have bothered to comment on it: there is obviously no other way of working, and the intricate chains of inference have come, through generations of scholarship, to be felt to be as strong as the steel cables of the Bay Bridge. At least, this is one of the two extremes of reaction to a standard history of English phonology—i.e., that the subject is nicely wrapped up in steel bonds. At the other extreme is the reaction that the whole study is mushy, lacking any firm foundation whatever. This reaction is a consequence of the difficulty of discovering the assumptions about the nature of sound change which are presumably imposed by the historian on his data. The historian clearly assumes, in practice, that only certain kinds of changes are possible in, for instance, vowel systems. He would not suggest that OE *ī* came to its MnE pronunciation [aⁱ] by way of [ʊᵘ] as an intermediate stage. The fact that [ʊᵘ] is not attested as an intermediate stage is surely not what deters him: in dozens of other instances he unhesitatingly sets up unattested intermediate stages (as, for example, in the standard reconstruction of the history of the OE vowel in *cȳse* "cheese"[1]). What is more interesting, he not infrequently sets up intermediate stages in the face of primary data where the latter may contradict his theory-based inferences. About a dozen of the early English orthoepists represent the reflexes of ME *ī* with *ei*, and identify it with Latin *ei* or Greek *ει* or Dutch *ij* or *ey*.[2] But Dobson, quite rightly in my view, rejects this evidence because [ɛⁱ] as an intermediate stage between ME *ī* and MnE

* This selection will also appear in E. Bagby Atwood and Archibald A. Hill, eds., *Studies in the language, literature and culture of the Middle Ages and later* (University of Texas Press, 1968). Printed here by permission of the author.

[a$^i$] would intersect reflexes of ME *ai*. His own solution, [iː] to [i$^i$] to [ə$^i$], creates certain new problems. I have proposed a stage [ɪ$^i$] between [i$^i$] and [ə$^i$].[3] But since it is not entirely clear what Dobson means by [ə$^i$] (or [əi]), since he has also an [ʌi] (or [ʌ$^i$]) of a difference "so slight that it is not of great importance which sound they actually used,"[4] it may be that our actual views on this detail are not in conflict. In any case, there must be *reasons* for such reconstructions, and these reasons are to be found not in data-based inferences, but in theory-based inferences: a theory, that is, of the nature of sound change. The sense of mushiness that one may get from a history of English phonology comes from one's inability to discover what the historian's particular theory is, or the extent to which his reconstructions depend on it.

With respect to vowels in the history of English there appear to be two distinct theories. One is oriented to the physiological facts of articulation, to speech, parôle, in a concrete form. Something like the vowel chart of D. Jones, or even more precisely his X-ray plotting of tongue height in vowel production (the chart which looks roughly like an egg with the small end up and tilted to the left), seems—with trivial variations—to underlie the phonetic reconstructions (which themselves may differ widely in detail) of lost stages in sound change that are to be found in the works of Jespersen, Wyld, Luick, Ellis, Zachrisson, Dobson, Kökeritz, Orton, Kurath, and other scholars who belong to what may be labelled the philological tradition. This is a great tradition: we owe nearly all of what we know about the marks in manuscripts, the orthoepical commentaries, the rimes and puns, etc., to this group of scholars.

The other theory is oriented to the structure, the system, langue, of speech production and perception. The notion that the stream of speech can be analyzed as a sequence of bundles of a small number of recurrent features seems—again with trivial variations—to underlie the phonetic reconstructions of Trnka, Vachek, Martinet, Lamberts, Reszkiewicz, and most recently Halle and Keyser. These scholars represent a part of what may be labeled the structural tradition. I do not wish to oppose the labels "philological" and "structural" in any sense other than the one under discussion: namely, with respect to the assumptions made in the theory-based inferences upon which unattested or contradictorily attested intermediate stages of vowel reconstruction rest. In this particular respect there are distinct traditions of scholarship which correspond with fairly distinct theories. We might, to give them unprejudicial labels, call them the "concrete" theory and the "abstract" theory.

# I

We can characterize the two theories by listing in parallel form some of their respective axioms. C is for Concrete, A for Abstract. A subdivision is made in the abstract column between P, the theories that are oriented toward phonemes as units, analyzable into subphonemic features, though not necessarily the features of a particular prespecified universal set; and F, those that are oriented toward the distinctive features of such a set, with the phoneme playing no more than a convenient typographical role.

1C. Vowel variation is infinitely graded on a continuum.

1APF. Vowel variation is discrete (i.e., in steps), each step corresponding to a feature in the system.

2C. The mechanism of variation is unconscious phonetic drift, probably caused by faulty imitation between generations of speakers.

2AP. The mechanism of variation is conscious (at least partly) selection of alternates that have equal linguistic, though not social, status within the system.

2AF. The mechanism of variation is the construction of simpler rule systems (in general eliminating anomalies) whose output is similar to, but different in small ways from, the output of the rule systems of the model.

3C. Living dialects preserve archaic pronunciations, and illustrate the process of change by providing instances of intermediate vowels.

3AP. Living dialects illustrate the kinds of alternates and selectional processes that have probably been around for hundreds of years, certainly further back than any explicit documentation.

3AF. Living dialects illustrate how rules may be alike at the more abstract levels but diverge at the lowest phonetic level (i.e., earlier vs. later rules).

4AF. The internal synchronic ordering of generative rules may recapitulate the order of historical sound change. [There seems to be no corresponding *4C or *4AP.]

Unless one has recently been working through the literature on English sound change, these generalizations must mean very little. They are illustrated below in some detail, the paragraphs labeled in accord with the numbering of the generalizations above.

*1C.* That vowel variation is infinitely graded on a continuum is, in one sense, not to be doubted. But the standard use of the Jones vowel chart (and derivatives thereof) consists in placing dots on the chart at the point of maximum tongue constriction in accordance with the phonetician's perception of the corresponding vowel quality: this implies, surely, that the phonetician is capable of differentiating infinitely many vowel qualities consistently. In working with Jones-trained (1st or 2nd generation) phoneticians I have become convinced that they are, almost without exception, superlatively good. But the theoretical claim of such dots on charts is absurd, and Jones' followers have not, to my knowledge, formalized any set of scaled parameters that might make the claim interesting. The technique in dialect fieldwork leads to practices like these: At one extreme, in the field records of the Survey of English Dialects, John T. Wright consistently transcribed [æÿ] over a wide southern area for the vowel of *cow*, *house*, etc.; listening to the records, I noted a phonetic range that included [ɛɷ], [æu], [aɷ], etc., the first element varying from lower mid front to low front retracted, and the second from higher high back rounded to higher mid back with only slight rounding. Wright was well aware of what he was doing: he was phonemicizing, but using a symbol that implied phonetic detail of a type that clearly was not intended, or that was perhaps the statistical center of the range of what he heard. I would have done the same thing, specifying the allophonic range of a normalized symbol, except that I would have used typographically more accessible symbols: Wright *knew* he was phonemicizing. Likewise, in the same survey, it is customary (among all fieldworkers, though some more than others) to write [iː] for the vowel of *clean* etc. if the vowel resembles the RP vowel of the same word, even though Jones' [iː] is a phonemicization of a quality *not* distinct from other qualities in length (certainly not length alone, and possibly not length at all). That is, at this extreme, such phoneticians are clearly not symbolizing the kind of precise phonetic information that their frame of reference claims. At the other extreme, phonic differences are often transcribed which the fieldworker knows at the time to be non-phonemic and, indeed, random. On more than one occasion in going over transcriptions made by J. Y. Mather of the Survey of Scottish Dialects at Edinburgh, I would call into question a particular notation and be told that it was "only a matter of phonetic detail" that could be ignored as nonphonemic; but concerning the same detail, in another instance, I would be told it was phonemic. Now Mather was right, in every instance that we checked by listening to his carefully taped minimal pairs: the Scots Survey is explicitly oriented toward the discovery and confirmation of phonemic contrasts in vowel systems.[5] But the same kind of variation exists also in the English survey, which is not phonemically oriented, and where it is often the case that no contrast can be found in the data. On occasion I have taken such details to the Director of the Survey, Harold Orton: like Mather, he *knows* when the details of notation are significant and when they are not. The phonemic significance or absence of it in any instance is available, therefore, in his head—not, however, in the record, and Orton is zealous to see to it that exactly what appears in the field records is what is published.[6] Kurath recently noted that "the dialectologist will . . . attach great importance to an *exact phonic record* [emphasis mine] of the speech of his informants," so that "he can observe directly how phonemic splits and mergers, whether partial or comprehensive, come about."[7] It is in my opinion a good deal less scientific, in view of the impossibility of achieving such phonetic precision on any known set of parameters, to speak of "exact phonic records" than it is to "accept an 'over-all" phonemic scheme for all varieties of American English,"[8] rejected by Kurath as unscientific. The latter at least raises an empirically decidable question; the former does not even do that.

*1APF.* That vowel variation is discrete is, in one sense, obviously false. It is not physically (articulatorily or acoustically) discrete. But the assumption means that the variation is psychologically discrete: where a naive native speaker is aware of variation, it can only be variation measurable in terms of contrastive relevance somewhere within the system either of his own speech or of a type of speech with which he is familiar. This is not as strong a constraint on a theory about the perception of variation as some might wish to place on it, at least for English: the strongest one would be that he can perceive only variants that are phonemic in his own speech. I think such a constraint is too strong, if only because few speakers of any language are mono-dialectal, and certainly few English speakers. The *extent* of familiarity with dialects other than one's own may vary a good deal, but with high geographical and social mobility, and with unremitting exposure to radio, television, and the movies these days, we all learn parts of the systems of dialects other than our own, and these are part of our store of norms to match against new phonic experience. The phonetician is in fact different only in that his store is vastly larger, and he has learned to write down, in a reasonably consistent way, a certain fraction of what he has stored.

It may be doubted that the discrete steps of perceptible variation correspond with features in the system: but I do not see what else might serve to define these limits. Chomsky and Halle distinguish between a classificatory matrix of features, and a phonetic one, the latter being the last stage in the ordered set of morphophonemic rules. The distinction appears to be one of detail (the number of features), corresponding—perhaps in a gross way—to the familiar phonemic/phonetic dichotomy. The question, then, is whether perceptible variation is limited by the phonetic matrix (a set of universal features which constitute the matrix of features for the description of human vocal noises) or by the classificatory matrix which constitutes the system of a particular language. The closest approximation to the view described in 1C above would be the former, the phonetic matrix, but I suggest that the latter, the classificatory matrix, is a closer approximation to the capacities of phonological discrimination habitually exercised by native speakers. They discriminate also other features, with detailed precision, which play no role in phonological analysis, such as voice quality, marked individually, socially, and regionally; and it is these discriminations (along with such factors as lexical and syntactic usage) rather than keener phonetic discrimination in the usual linguistic sense which seem to me to account for the ability of the average individual to sort out people to some limited extent with respect to local origins, social class, education, etc.

2C. Phonetic drift is remarkably difficult to document. Kurath[9] speaks of "phones . . . that cannot be definitely assigned to one phoneme rather than another" which are to be observed on the margin of focal dialect areas. "Such 'compromise' pronunciations (unsystematized phones)," he claims, "are a reality . . ." I can well believe that pronunciations exist about which the dialectologist with the phonological assumption of infinite gradation (1C) would be in doubt as to their phonemic assignment, particularly if his questionnaire did not seek paired items or inquire into the speaker's own reaction about the identification of these phones with others. But I cannot believe there are instances where that doubt would exist in the mind of the speaker himself; for example whether *room* had the vowel of *cut, put,* or *Luke.* Even if occasional individuals find themselves in this curious condition, I cannot believe that it is the rule among large numbers of speakers, as it would have to be to account for phonemic change through drift, i.e., through the gradual favoring of some nondistinctive variants unidirectionally, some of them becoming inter-mediate "compromise" units.

A recent highly interesting attempt by William Labov to document a specific contemporary sound change on Martha's Vineyard[10] is, I think, inconsistent with respect to both the first assumption (continuous vs. discrete variation among vowels) and the second (unconscious drift vs. selective alternation as mechanism of change). He establishes a four-degree scale of centralization from [a] to [ə] (in the diphthongs of, say, *mice* and *mouse*) which he then levels out statistically onto an index of centralization that allows any possibility from 0 to 1 (i.e., a continuous scale arbitrarily segmented for reference). He says that "the opposition [between [aɪ] and [əɪ]], though not distinctive, is clearly seen as ranging from compact to (relatively) non-compact" (288), where "ranging" suggests continuous variation, but "op-position" (which, whether distinctive in these nuclei or not, certainly *is* elsewhere in the vowel system of these dialects) suggests psychological polarity. He argues, effectively, against "the doctrine of imperceptible changes as a basic mechanism of linguistic change" (292), but he says that the "feature of centralized diphthongs [i.e., [əɪ] for [ai], etc.] is salient for the linguist, but not for most speakers; it is apparently quite immune to conscious distortion, as the native Vineyarders are not aware of it, nor are they able to control it consciously. . . . These are strictly sub-phonemic differences" (280); and later, "When a man says [rəɪt] or [həʊs], he is unconsciously establishing the fact that he belongs to the island" (304). Labov does not document the natives' unawareness or inability to control this feature, but he gives several examples which seem to me to contradict his assumption: e.g., the boy who goes away to college not sounding like an islander, but after he comes back adopting the crucial island speech characteristics so obviously that his mother remarks, "'You know, E. didn't always speak that way . . . it's only since he came back from college. I guess he wanted to be more like the men on the docks. . . .' a clear case of hypercorrection at work" (300). Indeed, with what appear to be trivial modifications in interpretation of some few details in his admirable data, Labov's article seems to me to be a documen-tation of assumption 2AP, and he would not have had to introduce the very curious and paradoxical argument about the up-islanders' (the predominant [əɪ]/[əʊ] group) "close-mouthed" articulatory style—which is said to condi-tion the relevant "allophones" even though in other words they manage to open their mouths wide enough to produce [ai] as needed (307).

H. Orton works out the assumption of drift with careful documentation of whatever intermediate stages he can from living dialects, assigning IPA symbols in an ordered sequence dependent on articulatory proximity (pre-sumably there are as many stages as there are standard symbols in the chart between the starting point and the end point on a line segment connecting the two points). Thus for the development of ME *ī* he shows the following chart (with certain symbols changed here to correspond with American usage):[11]

$$
\text{ME ī} > \text{[ɪi]}
\begin{cases}
\text{[ei]} & \ldots\ldots\ldots\ldots\ldots\ldots\ldots\ldots\ldots\ldots\text{ A} \\
\text{[ei]}\begin{cases}\text{[ɛi, ɛɪ]} & \ldots\ldots\ldots\ldots\ldots\ldots\ldots\text{ B} \\ \text{[æi]} & \ldots\ldots\ldots\ldots\ldots\ldots\text{ C}\end{cases} \\
\text{[ɛi]}\begin{cases}\text{[ai, aɪ]} & \ldots\ldots\ldots\ldots\ldots\text{ D} \\ \text{[æi]}\begin{cases}\text{[ɑi]} & \ldots\ldots\ldots\ldots\text{ E} \\ \text{[ai]} \\ \text{[ɑi]} > \text{[ā]} & \ldots\ldots\ldots\text{ F}\end{cases}\end{cases}
\end{cases}
$$

The upper member of the braced pairs is found in some contemporary dialect, symbolized by the letters to the right of the chart and listed in detail by Orton. The questions raised by such an account are many: how, for instance, does the *ī* sequence avoid intersecting with the reflexes of ME *ei, ai* (as in *they, may,* etc.)? Are the dialectal reflexes A ... F in contrast with other sources of [ei], [ɛi] today, or have they collapsed with them? If this is the history, then whence such forms as [əi]?—presumably it branches off from [ɛi], but why not assume the reverse?

Orton's work is, then, a serious attempt to document drift in English vowels by citing the phonetic shapes of intermediate stages as corresponding with such shapes where they occur in dialects today. This practice, clearly, is in accord with assumption 3C: the assumption that dialects are fundamentally conservative and preserve archaic pronunciations.

*2AP.* Few would doubt that conscious selection from a set of alternates having equal systemic (but not social) status plays a role in sound change, though at the same time few would assign it the importance I would (I think it is the major process). Labov takes Sturtevant's view as the theme for his own investigation:[12] "Before a phoneme can spread from word to word ... [I would add, from speaker to speaker.—RPS], it is necessary that one of the two rivals shall acquire some sort of prestige." This clearly suggests discrete entities in competition, and it has the virtue (pointed out by Labov[13]) of being empirically investigable in a way that imperceptible changes are not. Labov is the only scholar I know who has studied this question in this way for a homogeneous group, but one can hardly live in America without knowing southerners who, having grown up with [lɔᵘ] as their native form for *law,* have adopted the alternative [lɔ°] when they have moved north or west—and similarly throughout the system. There are inflexible individuals, of course, who steadily maintain all their original forms and increment them with alternatives in new words as they encounter them. Assumption 2AP is a slight restatement and generalization of a familiar philological view: when you can't explain a form otherwise, call it dialect mixture. 2AP suggests that dialect mixture is systemic, that dialects are not in any sense neatly distinct sets that now and then intersect. An overall pattern marking the parameters of contrast within the system of continuous intersection is one way of representing the alternatives available for selection.

*2AF.* The suggestion that the construction of simpler sets of generative rules underlies sound change is quite a recent one, virtually undocumented at the date of this writing, but interesting for many reasons.[14] It is a view which closely relates synchronic and diachronic description (i.e., to the extent that assumption 4AF is borne out, the logically simplest generative order mirrors the order of historical development and the very simplicity of the former suggests a motivation for the direction of the latter); it takes a clear and well-motivated position with respect to the question of continuous vs. discrete steps (i.e., since the rules all hinge on the presence or absence of a specified feature—$\pm$ grave, $\pm$ flat, $\pm$ compact, etc.—every rule necessarily specifies a discrete change); and it provides the first insight into how change can be both discrete and, within several generations, imperceptible—distinct rule systems can have identical output. Halle's summation of his view is imaginative:[15]

It has been suggested by Chomsky that language acquisition by a child may best be pictured as a process of constructing the simplest (optimal) grammar capable of generating the set of utterances, of which utterances heard by the child are a representative sample. The ability to master a language like a native, which children possess to an extraordinary degree, is almost completely lacking in the adult. I propose to explain this as being due to deterioration or loss in the adult of the ability to construct optimal (simplest) grammars on the basis of a restricted corpus of examples. The language of the adult—and hence also the grammar that he has internalized—need not, however, remain static: it can and does, in fact, change. I conjecture that changes in later life are restricted to the addition or elimination of a few rules in the grammar, and that a wholesale restructuring of his grammar is beyond the capabilities of the average adult. . . . Since every child constructs his own optimal grammar by induction from the utterances to which he has been exposed, it is not necessary that the child and his parents have identical grammars, for . . . a given set of utterances can be generated by more than one grammar. . . . [Halle has demonstrated how a rule system with /a/ $\neq$ /æ/ can be augmented to collapse this contrast, and how the resulting system of five rules can be replaced by one of three rules equivalent in output to the former.—RPS] I should therefore postulate that the adult, who of necessity is maximally conservative, would have a grammar [of the former type], whereas his children would have grammars with the simpler rule. It is clear that such discontinuities in the grammars of successive generations must exercise a profound influence on the further evolution of the language.[16]

*3C.* The assumption that living dialects preserve archaic pronunciation is illustrated in Orton's reconstruction of ME *i* above, about which he explicitly says: "[It] is in the main a mere enumeration of some of the sounds now representing the vowel in the dialects under consideration" (201), and that "The chief stages in the development of ME *i* to the prevailing sounds are

almost automatically suggested by its correspondences in the living dialects."
The notion of "intermediate" or "compromise" vowels was cited from
Kurath earlier in this discussion.

*3AP.* Rather than preserving the phonic shape of earlier forms, contemporary dialects may instead be assumed to preserve the *kinds* of alternatives
that existed earlier. The favoring of one of the alternatives at a given period
would lead to the suppression of others; constantly new alternatives are
available, however, such that the system is never static. Consider some of the
sets of alternatives competing in present-day America (the items chosen are
merely illustrative—in each instance the alternate vowels occur in hundreds or
thousands of items, and the syllabic nuclei either are phonemic as units or are
composed of elements that are phonemic):

*grass:* [ɛ°], [æ°], [æⁱ], [æ], [a], [a°]
    (Trager-Smith /eh, æh, æy, æ, a, ah/)

*house:* [ɨᵘ], [əᵘ], [aᵘ], [æ°], [ɛ°]
    (Trager-Smith /iw, əw, aw, æw, ew/)

*law:* [ɔᵘ], [o°], [ɔ°], [ɑ°]
    (Trager-Smith /ɔw, oh, ɔh, ah/)

*mice:* [əⁱ], [aᵉ], [a°]
    (Trager-Smith /əy, ay, ah/)

*good:* [ʊ], [ɨ]
    (Trager-Smith /u/, /i/)

*new:* [ˈʊᵘ], [ˈɨᵘ], [ʊᵘ], [ɨᵘ], [ɪᵘ]
    (Trager-Smith /yuw, yiw, uw, iw, iw/)

Certain generalizations can be made about these sets. Speaking of them in
terms of the Trager-Smith overall pattern, we observe that the alternatives
are of two types: (1) vowels alternating between horizontally or vertically
contiguous units in the 3 × 3 vowel array; and (2) semivowels (off-glides)
alternating between central and front, central and back, central and zero.
If we include English and Scots dialects, a third type is also found (which may
also exist in some southern American areas), (3) between simple vowel, vowel
plus central glide, and vowel plus length. An interesting fact about the Scots
contrasts is that the sets with contrastive length are apparently a late addition
to the system occurring not as reflexes of historical "long and short" vowels,
but as distinct reflexes of two kinds of historical "long" vowels: thus in
Berwickshire (county #27, local #6, J. Y. Mather fieldworker), these contrasts
are recorded: *beat, gate* [e] ≠ *bait, gait* [e:]; in Sutherland (county #4, locale
#1, P. Ladefoged fieldworker) these: *waste* [eˇə] ≠ *waist* [e°]; in Caithness
(county #3, locale #9, J. Y. Mather fieldworker) *leek, week, beak, speak, bake*
[ˈɨ] ≠ *leak, weak, break, ache* [ˈiː]. These contrasts are furthermore extremely
rare in the system as a whole, not occurring throughout (as is supposed for
OE and ME) but only with a fraction of the simple nuclei.

For a theory of historical vocalic change in English, the pertinence of the first two generalizations above is this: they suggest a possible constraint to be imposed on the formulation of a sound law of historical English—i.e., a generalization by which the rule which accounts for the sound change may be judged as well-formed or not: namely, that each step in the sequence of changes must conform with one of these two types of alternation (1 and 2 above). Thus for the change OE *i* to MnE [a$^{i}$], only (b) and (c) below are well-formed rules:

$$\text{(a) } [\text{ɪ}^{i}] \rightarrow [\text{ə}^{i}] \rightarrow [\text{a}^{i}]$$
$$\text{(b) } [\text{ɪ}^{i}] \rightarrow [\text{i}^{i}] \rightarrow [\text{ə}^{i}] \rightarrow [\text{a}^{i}]$$
$$\text{(c) } [\text{ɪ}^{i}] \rightarrow [\text{e}^{i}] \rightarrow [\text{æ}^{i}] \rightarrow [\text{a}^{i}]$$

(c) is well-formed but impossible because of the presumption of intersection with reflexes from other sources, as noted earlier in this discussion.

*3AF*. The only published documentation of this assumption is a Russian example of Halle's,[17] though the forthcoming Chomsky and Halle *Sound Pattern of English*[18] sets forth a convincing argument that the correct lexical representation of the American vowel [ɑ] in *pot, conic, lot*, etc., should be lax /ɔ/, and many other examples of a similar nature. I develop the argument in outline under 4AF below. If it is valid, then the difference between British and American dialects in this detail would be confined to a late phonetic rule like the following:

$$[+\text{round}] \rightarrow [-\text{round}] \text{ in the environment } [\overline{+\text{compact}}]$$

(i.e., [ɔ] → [ɑ], a rounded vowel is unrounded if compact). The rule would be required for American but not for British, and these words would be alike at the abstract level of lexical representation. I have seen also, in very preliminary form, a set of morphophonemic rules for the southern American dialect spoken by James Sledd which at the abstract level make it appear to be identical with northern and western ones, or virtually so, with all the (very obvious) surface differences accounted for in late low-level rules. This approach to phonological description has the following general form:

(1) There is a lexical entry, which may be called the canonical form of the item. To this form is supplied the least possible phonetic specification, only as much as is in no way predictable by rules stated in terms of environment (including the syntactic phrase marker). For reasons of simplicity in the form of the rules that will operate on this entry, the canonical form appears as a matrix of classificatory features, which as presently conceived correspond with binary Jakobsonian distinctive features, by and large, though this is not a necessary condition (i.e., a different set of classificatory features that could be shown to have more general properties and greater utility in the formulation of phonetic rules would surely be adopted). Thus the canonical form of a morpheme of which the second segment was a true consonant (i.e., [+ consonantal] and [− vocalic]) and of which the first segment was [s] would need to include only the feature [+ consonantal] in the first segment, since all the other features of [s] in this environment are predictable, there being no other possible consonant that can occur. A very large percentage of segments will thus be only partially specified—they will be archisegments.

(2) There is a set of ordered rules which link the canonical form to the perceived phonetic form. These are of three types: (i) redundancy rules (morpheme-structure rules, in Halle's terminology), which fill out the partially specified matrices of the canonical forms; they also serve to make the necessary discrimination between accidental gaps (phonologically permitted but nonoccurrent—i.e., forms that violate none of the redundancy rules) and systematic exclusions (phonologically impossible—i.e., forms that would violate the redundancy rules: compare, say, [skɛk with [ftɛk]); (ii) cyclic rules, such as those which assign stress, and vowel reduction[19]; and (iii), most interesting by far from the viewpoint of historical phonological studies, noncyclic rules which derive from single canonical forms such a diversity of vowels and consonants as appears in the pairs *divine/divinity, serene/serenity, sane/sanity, profound/profundity, school/scholar, cone/conic, opaque/ opacity, provide/provision*, etc.
(3) There is a phonetic representation which, like the classificatory representation of the canonical form, is in terms of features of segments, but the segments are not necessarily binary (in fact they may be continuously graded, as in stress or pitch phenomena), and they are defined as universal phonetic constants. There may be several of these features that are introduced by the rules of (2), so that their number may be greater than the number of features required for canonical specification in a particular language. Ideally these features would serve as the parameters in terms of which a suitable synthesizer could be programmed to produce satisfactory speech.

Viewed in their surface phonetic form, the dialects of English vary enormously. And yet one feels strongly that these differences are somehow reconcilable into a single phonological structure: it is too easy to catch on to the differences, when one travels about, for them to be distinct systems, or for them to be thought of as sharing only syntactic and morphological structure but having distinct phonological structures. The Trager-Smith over-all pattern was, I believe, an attempt to account for precisely this intuition. As generalized by Hill and myself,[20] where the nine vowels were viewed as no more than arbitrary symbols for the intersection of a minimal set of vocalic features, and where it was argued that the overall pattern consisted in the sharing of this particular set of features, the intention to account for this intuition was apparent and fairly explicit. The question raised by assumption 3AF, as opposed to 3AP, is whether the general form of phonological description outlined above is a more satisfying account of what is shared, of the "common core," in Hockett's terms, and of what is distinct (i.e., outside the core), than is the overall pattern concept. It appears that enormously richer kinds of generalizations are possible within the Chomsky-Halle frame of reference.

*4AF*. The notion that ontogeny recapitulates phylogeny is, in biological circles, discredited in detail (particularly for early in the development period), but it is still true that an early mutation is nearly always lethal, whereas late mutations may survive; and in a general way, this is relevant to a theory of sound change. If it is the case that the simplest grammar will represent phonological structure through a set of ordered rules, in which the depth of ordering may be very considerable, then it is apparent that a mutation early in the ordered set would be lethal to communication in that there would be so many rules operating on the output of the one early changed rule that the final output would be entirely unintelligible. This suggests that the phonological rules of modern English must contain, particularly among the earlier rules of the ordered set, a very large proportion of rules held in common with the phonological rules of earlier English. And it suggests that clues to the simplest synchronic ordering of such rules will be found in the simplest diachronic ordering of the rules of English sound change (and in general, for all languages where data is available). This gives a new high priority to the method of internal reconstruction in historical linguistics, and the simplest internal synchronic ordering becomes evidence of a high order in the methodology of historical reconstruction.

Within these terms, we might consider in particular the question, What is a phonological history a history of? It is classically a history of the phonetic representation of words—i.e., their representation in the phonetic feature matrix. This view was modified by phonemic theory in the thirties to require that it be a history of the phonemic representation of words, and much criticism of the neogrammarians depends on this distinction. But phonemic representation as then (and still) conceptualized meant a phonetic representation meeting certain minimal conditions of adequacy (all contrastive features must be represented and no non-contrastive ones can be). The further conditions that were imposed[21] assured that a phonemicization would be only a kind of emasculated phonetic transcription: what I would want to call a *principled broad transcription* (PBT), as opposed to a narrow one where no general principles could dictate the irrelevance of further detail. As generative phonological rules are presently conceptualized, a PBT has no theoretical status. One might argue that it does in fact play a special role in historical sound change, that it is that level in terms of which speakers perceive differences that cause them to modify earlier rules in the sequence, and the representation therefore appears late in the sequence, but prior to that assigned by the lowest level phonetic rules which, e.g., assign aspiration to voiceless stops in certain environments.

But considering further the question posed above, a phonological history might be viewed as having two components: a comparison of earlier and later canonical forms, and a comparison of earlier and later rules. Viewed in this way, a phonological history will look very different indeed from what we are used to. Suppose we compare the OE *grōwan* with MnE *grow*. It would be very hard to find many pairs of forms on which there is more general agreement that there has been virtually no PBT sound change (in the stressed vowel) for over a thousand years. A similar pair would be OE *weg* and MnE *way*, considered after the time when the OE final palatal spirant had lost its friction (and we get spellings like *wei*). But because Chomsky and Halle want to relate *cone/conic* and *sane/sanity* in their canonical forms, and they therefore have in MnE a general vowel shift rule which raises the low- and mid-tense vowels one notch, and drops the high-tense vowels two notches (both following a diphthongization rule) with some secondary phonetic adjustments, they must enter the canonical forms *grɔ̄* and *wǣ* in order that, by the diphthongization and vowel shift rules they may become, respectively, [grōw] and [wēy]. On the other hand, *sane* would have the canonical form *sǣn*, and *cone* the canonical form *kɔ̄n* (roughly their ME forms). Similarly, *serene*, *divine*, and the other forms cited earlier would have virtually no change in canonical form between ME and MnE. So, at least in these striking instances, a comparison of earlier with later canonical forms would show no change in those instances (like *divine*) where traditional histories show extensive change, and it would show change in a (much smaller) set of forms (like *grow*) where traditional histories show none. Then the comparison of the earlier rules with present ones would show that we have added, among others, a vowel shift rule to the noncyclic set, which accounted among other things for the phonetic difference between pairs like *divine/divinity* without disturbing our sense of underlying identity.

## II

Let us step back a few paces now and try to get a longer view of these problems—try to see them in relation to the broader objectives of linguistic inquiry and of scholarly inquiry generally. In comparison with the concrete theory, what either abstract theory does is place tighter and in some sense more difficult constraints on the kind of sound law the linguist will admit to be valid or well-formed, as if he were willing to see the data only as reflected in a mirror that had certain highly specific qualities. This is done in order to achieve the greatest possible control over the form of generalization which will correctly predict the data. It is not strange to speak of "predicting" what has already happened: we do not *know* what has already happened, only certain surface indications (like spelling change, changes in rime habits, etc.) of what has happened. We seek just that set of generalizations which will predict that the linguistic behavior encountered in these particular observations is in conformity with regular laws—i.e., governed by rule, not random. We wish to demonstrate identity, or at least close similarity, between apparently quite disparate events. It is in exactly this sense that the physicist's theory that greater heat is a manifestation of more rapid motion of molecular particles allows him to bring together under a single rule such apparently disparate data as the facts that water evaporates, that steam can be enclosed to drive a piston, and that moisture appears on colder-than-air surfaces like leaves and car windows in the mornings.

Let us take a single instance of an assumption commonly made about the history of English pronunciation and see what value it has as measured against the concrete and abstract sets of axioms: namely, the assumption that earlier English—say, from the period of the earliest documents, roughly 800 A.D.—had a pervasive contrast throughout the vowel system between long vowels and short vowels. We ask what is gained by this assumption in either theory.

1. Is the contrast functional in MnE? Certainly not in the system as a whole, though there are such scattered instances as those in Scots cited above. Halle[22] analyzes MnE as containing seven non-tense and seven tense vowels (/u, o, ɔ, a, i, e, æ/ and /ū, ō, ɔ̄, ā, ī, ē, ǣ/). It is a little difficult to comment on such a list, since it is meaningful only in conjunction with the rules which interpret these symbols phonetically. The rules will include, for example, a diphthongization rule for tense vowels (yielding ūw, ōw, ɔ̄w, īy, ēy, ǣy) and a vowel shift rule (such that ūw → ǣw, ōw → ūw, ɔ̄w → ōw, īy → āy, ēy → īy, ǣy → ēy); and there will have to be at least two more primitive units (as sources of /ɔy/ and /yuw/). Furthermore, at least one contrast suggested by this list (/a ≠ ā/) is exceedingly restricted in its dialectal distribution. So it is not clear what the relation of tense/lax is to the philological claim of long/ short contrasts. One might be tempted to argue that "long" meant "tense" and that "short" meant "lax." Such an argument is not so simple as it appears, requiring, as it does, a careful reconsideration of a number of ME contrasts (e.g., *ei/ē*, where a diphthongization rule ordered before the vowel shift rule, as at present, would collapse the contrast). I am inclined to think the resemblance between the tense/lax interpretation of MnE vowels and the long/ short interpretation of OE and ME vowels is entirely on the surface of the symbolization, though the question remains entirely open at the present time.

2. Is the contrast necessary to account for some metrical form (e.g., quantitative verse)? On the contrary, the Renaissance attempts at regularization of quantity on classical models are clear failures. At no time has English meter (including OE) been based on anything other than recurrent accentual/ prominence features (with or without syllable counting), which are partially (and perhaps totally) correlated with morphological structure (affixation), syntax (form class membership), vowel quality, and intonation.

3. Does the assumption simplify our reconstruction of English sound changes? The answer to this depends of course on how simplicity is to be measured. On other occasions[23] I have argued that simplicity in the relevant instances is to be seen in those generalizations which require fewer ad hoc hypotheses and which account for similar developments at different periods in similar ways (e.g., tenth-century lengthening and contemporary diphthongization before velars in items like *egg* are both instances where a conditioned off-glide falls in with phonetically similar glides that are unconditioned in other positions). Clearly if there is no strong counter-evidence (e.g., sound changes that are in no reasonable interpretation amenable to an analysis of vowel plus glide), then an account that manages to confine changes to *within* a single type of vocalic system is simpler than one that requires a fundamental change between earlier and later systems. This argument would apply equally, of course, to a tense/lax interpretation of both earlier and contemporary systems, if the questions raised under #1 above can be answered in such a way as to equate long/short with tense/lax.

4. Is it necessary because of such spellings in OE and ME as *ii, ee, î,* etc.? Such spellings impose the requirement that any description must posit at least two types of vowels (the "long" set and the "short" one). It is not at all obvious that the spellings in any way delimit the range of possible phonetic or phonemic interpretations of these contrasts. C. W. Barritt and I have discussed this question elsewhere[24]: we find it very hard to account for the general ready acceptance of such spellings as "evidence" for long vowels. But these spellings are evidently given great weight by those who operate from the concrete axioms, which suggests an additional axiom (4C. Alphabetic symbols in premodern orthographies are phonetically reliable). All historical linguists assume that alphabetic symbols are phonemically reliable in the sense that words which are consistently represented differentially in documents must have been phonemically distinct—and usually distinct at just those points where graphically differentiated. But the assumption of phonetic reliability is much stronger than this: I know of no explicit defense of it, even though it clearly lies behind the standard descriptions of OE and ME vowel systems. Even the assumption of phonemic reliability is subject to quite distinct interpretations, depending on the extent to which one uses "phonemic" to mean PBT, on the one hand, or "morphophonemic," on the other.

5. Is it necessary because of cognates? The question is restricted to cognates in Germanic (and perhaps Slavic), since there is little doubt that at least the classical languages, and possibly the parent IE, had a full set of long vowels in contrast with front-, back-, and (possibly) central-gliding complex nuclei. The change of the vowel system to the kind we find in MnE (and that I postulate for OE and ME) is of about the same period as the Grimm's law consonant changes, in my view. The question of cognates is difficult, therefore, in an abstract theory: surely the most difficult of these several questions for that set of axioms, yet not at all difficult for the concrete theory. This is, I suggest, an accident of what is available for historical comparison: the contemporary Germanic languages are traditionally analyzed with a long/short dichotomy in the vowel systems. I do not believe this is correct for Modern Icelandic, Modern Dutch, or most dialects of Modern German: but I am in the position, so long as I am virtually the only person claiming that the familiar analyses give a mistaken view of the phonological structure, of having to defend a contrary analysis of each language in turn, an obviously impossible position. I can only hope to make the case for English strongly and clearly enough to convince scholars in other Germanic areas that they need to look afresh at the problem.

6. Is it necessary because of the orthoepists' commentaries in the Early Modern period? On the surface the early spelling reformers and grammarians do support a short/long opposition in EMnE pronunciation, several even finding it between the reflexes of ME *î* and *i*, where it surely did not exist, except in the same sense that it still exists today. In evaluating such evidence

one must bear in mind the facts (a) that these writers were trying to make sense out of English spelling—none of them really cut loose from it, where today we count it largely irrelevant to questions of phonological structure; (b) they were trying to describe the set of vocalic oppositions, i.e., what was in contrast with what, not what the minimal components (such as distinctive features, including length) of the oppositions were; (c) they were—at best—extremely primitive phoneticians by nineteenth/twentieth-century standards (say, from Bell and Sweet to the present); and (d) they worked under the handicaps—for purely descriptive scholarship—of trying to fit English phonology to their classical training, on the one hand, and of trying to make their analyses practical for spelling reform and pedagogy, on the other.

In sum, the hypothesis that OE and ME vowels were polarized in a long/short opposition is more persuasive under axioms 1–2–3C than under 1–2–3AP, though under either set of axioms the hypothesis is hardly the granite basis for all further reconstruction of English phonological change that it has been taken to be. Without more to go on, it is impossible to judge how the whole case would stand if long/short were reinterpreted as tense/lax in a generative rule system (i.e., 1–2–3–4AF); it is not a mere terminological quibble, since the AF claimants would have to test their interpretation on a vast number of specific sound changes.

One's convictions about length in the vowel systems of earlier English are correlated with one's choice of theoretical mirrors for the reflection of relations that are inferred at many removes from citable data. It would seem to follow, therefore, that considerations appropriate to theory formation in more general terms should play a bigger role in historical English phonology: considerations such as simplicity, symmetry, elegance. Historical phonological studies of any type in fact come into existence only with numerous theory-based inferences: these mirrors should be explicitly set forth, with general recognition that historical "facts" about pronunciation (the kind that fill our historical grammars) are virtually meaningless outside an interpretation imposed upon them by a theory.[25]

## FOOTNOTES

1. See the argument that developed over this detail in S. Kuhn and R. Quirk, "Some Recent Interpretations of Old English Digraph Spellings" (*Language* 29.143–56, 1953), and R. Stockwell and C. W. Barritt, "The Old English Digraphs: Some Considerations" (Language 31.372–89, 1955).
2. E. J. Dobson, *English Pronunciation 1500–1700* (Oxford, 1956), p. 660.
3. In several studies, first in my dissertation at Virginia (1952) and most recently in the *Proceedings of the IX International Congress of Linguists* (forthcoming).
4. Loc. cit., p. 661.
5. See A. McIntosh, *Introduction to a Survey of Scottish Dialects* (Edinburgh, 1952), and J. C. Catford, "Vowel Systems of Scots Dialect" (*Transactions of the Philological Society*, 1957).

6. So far the *Introduction* and Vol. I, *Basic Material: Six Northern Counties and Man* (Leeds, 1963) have been published.

7. Hans Kurath, "Phonemics and Phonics in Historical Phonology," *American Speech* 36.93–100 (May, 1961), p. 100.

8. Ibid.

9. Ibid., p. 98.

10. "The Social Motivation of a Sound Change," *Word* 19.273–309 (Dec., 1963).

11. *Phonology of a South Durham Dialect* (London, 1933), p. 201. It may be objected that this is an older work and therefore an unfair citation alongside more recent studies; in my view, however, it is so much more detailed and explicit than recent studies that it stands comparison with any recent work and is internally far more consistent than most. My only reservation about it concerns the initial theoretical assumptions.

12. Loc. cit., p. 275.

13. Loc. cit., p. 292.

14. As far as I know, the two scholars most actively pursuing this kind of investigation are Morris Halle and S. J. Keyser, though of published views I know only Halle's "Phonology in a Generative Grammar" (*Word* 18.54–72, 1962) and Keyser's review of Kurath and McDavid's *The Pronunciation of English in the Atlantic States*, in *Language* 39.303–15 (1963).

15. Loc. cit., pp. 64–5.

16. Halle does not, in fact, take the crucial further step of demonstrating why any "sound change" in the usual sense would result from the existence of distinct sets of rules if their output were identical, as in the example that he cites.

17. Loc. cit., p. 69.

18. I have seen parts of it, for which I am pleased to be able to acknowledge the kindness of Noam Chomsky and Morris Halle. The work referred to, soon to be published by Harpers, is in my estimate sufficiently revolutionary that it will require a restudy of historical English phonology virtually from scratch. [Published 1968—Ed.]

19. N. Chomsky, M. Halle, and F. Lukoff, "On accent and juncture in English," in *For Roman Jakobson*, The Hague, 1956.

20. See A. A. Hill, *An Introduction to Linguistic Structures*, New York, 1958; and my article "Structural Dialectology: A Proposal," in *American Speech* 34.258–68, 1959.

21. See Chomsky, "The Logical Basis of Linguistic Theory," in the *Proceedings of the IX International Congress of Linguists* (forthcoming), reprinted in J. Katz and J. Fodor (Eds.), *Readings in the Philosophy of Language* (New York, 1964).

22. Loc. cit., p. 59.

23. E.g., "The Middle English 'Long Close' and 'Long Open' Mid Vowels," in the University of Texas *Studies in Literature and Language*, 2. 529–38 (1961), and "On the Utility of an Overall Pattern in Historical English Phonology," in the *Proceedings of the IX International Congress of Linguists* (forthcoming). [Both reprinted in this volume, pp. 154–163, 88–94—Ed.]

24. "Scribal Practice: Some Assumptions," *Language* 37.75–82 (1961).

[25. Since this book went to press, a number of significant papers have appeared, dealing with problems of historical change in generative terms. Aside from the treatment of the English vowel-shift and some other aspects of Early Modern phonology in *Sound Pattern of English*, the following seem to me of importance: Paul Kiparsky, "Sonorant clusters in Greek," *Lg.* 43.619–35 (1967); Joseph Voyles, "Simplicity, ordered rules, and the first sound shift," *Lg.* 43.636–60 (1967); Robert D. King, "Root vs. suffix accent in the Germanic present indicative,"

*Journal of Linguistics*, 4.247–65 (1968); Paul Kiparsky, "Linguistic universals and linguistic change," in Emmon Bach and Robert T. Harms, ed., *Universals in linguistic theory* (New York, 1968). Of interest also is Kiparsky's unpublished M.I.T. dissertation, "Phonological change" (1965). Kiparsky has also written an important review of *Sound pattern*, scheduled to appear in *Foundations of Language*. —Ed.]

# 3

## MORPHOLOGY, SYNTAX, AND LEXICON

# Introduction

Since the essentially nonphonological problems in historical linguistics are so many and so complex, I have divided the papers dealing with them, arbitrarily, into two groups: those concerned primarily with dialectology in one sense or another, and those not primarily so concerned. I find that no other hard-and-fast division, given the scope of the collection and the papers available, seems really workable. So this section will serve as an introduction to the multiplicity of problems and lines of investigation to be found in such fields as paradigmatic and semantic morphological study, syntax and its analysis, and the behavior of the lexicon in historical perspective.

In the first paper here, Samuel R. Levin challenges the traditional, historically oriented classification of the Old English strong verbs, and suggests that the seven classes of the handbooks do not represent any compelling synchronic reality; he suggests a classification based on the behavior of the paradigms in Old English, rather than on the Germanic ablaut-series that underlie them. Then J. W. R. Lindemann, in what is in part in the nature of a review article, explores the vexing question of the meaning of the Old English preverbal particle *ge-*. He shows quite conclusively that it cannot be proved in any rigorous way to be an aspect-marker, and goes on to challenge a number of other widely-held notions. He does not determine just what *ge-* actually did mean, but his article is a very valuable clearing of the ground, and lays to rest some persistent ghosts (such as that *ge-* makes a verb "perfective"), while at the same time suggesting the need for further research. In the next paper we return to the Old English strong verbs. W. P. Lehmann studies the class VII strong verbs in Old English and Old Norse with preterits in *-r-* (for example, *rǣdan*, *rēord*), and challenges the usual statement that these are reflexes of reduplicated forms. He suggests instead that they are rather the developments of special, "secondary" Indo-European preterits with laryngeal bases.

The origin of the anomalous form *she* is the subject of Robert Stevick's study, in which he attempts to trace the "natural history" of a pronoun paradigm, and the kinds of pressures that lead to the development of suppletive forms. Following this, the late C. C. Fries shows, in his paper on the development of "the structural use of word order" in English, how the language gradually came to substitute what he calls "taxemes of order" for "taxemes of selection," especially in those constructions dealing with subject-object relationships. This venture into diachronic study by one of the pioneers of the synchronic structural study of English shows the same meticulous attention to detail and avoidance of speculation that marks the best of his synchronic work. The same kind of careful study of actual items in a corpus (though from a different methodological point of view) characterizes Celia Millward's study of case-forms in Shakespearean imperatives. This paper is an important contribution to the study of the functions of the pronominal cases in Early Modern English.

The last two papers in this section, while no less meticulous in their examination of data, are much more theoretically oriented, and in the best possible sense, "speculative." While both are concerned with particular items in the history of English, both are also deeply committed to certain theoretical positions, and pay special attention to the establishment of statements of metatheory which will characterize their individual descriptions. Elizabeth Traugott, in "Diachronic syntax and generative grammar," examines some of the possibilities of generative–transformational theory as applied to diachronic study, and deals in particular with the effect of rule-changes on the English auxiliary from Old English to the present. And finally, M. L. Samuels, in "The role of functional selection in the history of English," takes up the usually neglected problem of causality in historical change, and examines the effects of such phenomena as intra-systemic pressure, homonymic clash, and phonaesthetics on various kinds of change, with examples drawn from a wide range of historical data in English.

SAMUEL R. LEVIN

# A Reclassification
# of the Old English Strong Verbs*

The traditional classification of the Old English strong verbs is crucially influenced by historical considerations. This is obvious; it is less obvious that the description is thereby distorted. It will be the purpose of this paper to show that a strictly synchronic approach results in a different analysis.

The strong verbs are traditionally presented as in the following list. Subclasses are included only so far as they bear on the discussion; the 7th class will be dealt with later. For comparison I cite the Gothic cognates.

TABLE 1 / *First six classes of Old English and Gothic strong verbs*

|      | Old English |       |        |         | Gothic |       |        |         |
| ---- | ------- | ----- | ------ | ------- | ------ | ----- | ------ | ------- |
| I    | bīdan   | bād   | bidon  | biden   | beidan | baiþ  | bidum  | bidans  |
| II   | lēogan  | lēag  | lugon  | logen   | liugan | laug  | lugum  | lugans  |
| IIIa | bindan  | band  | bundon | bunden  | bindan | band  | bundum | bundans |
| IIIb | helpan  | healp | hulpon | holpen  | hilpan | halp  | hulpum | hulpans |
| IVa  | beran   | bær   | bǣron  | boren   | bairan | bar   | bērum  | baurans |
| IVb  | cuman   | cōm   | cōmon  | cumen   | qiman  | qam   | qēmum  | qumans  |
| IVc  | niman   | nōm   | nōmon  | numen   | niman  | nam   | nēmum  | numans  |
| V    | metan   | mæt   | mǣton  | meten   | mitan  | mat   | mētum  | mitans  |
| VI   | faran   | fōr   | fōron  | faren   | faran  | fōr   | fōrum  | farans  |

Table 1 shows certain similarities between members of different classes. The preterits of classes IVb and IVc are similar in their vocalism to the preterits of class VI; the preterits of class IVa are similar to those of class V. In part, the reason for separating these similar classes is that there are differences of vowel grade in the remainder of their paradigms. Even more significant is that the different classes reflect Indo-European and Germanic root formations of different types. Three criteria enter into the traditional analysis: the particular distribution of resonants and consonants in the original root structure, the original ablaut alternation, and reduplication.[1] The function of the first two criteria is seen most clearly in the first three classes, whose root structure in Pre-Germanic is set out in Table 2.[2]

* From *Language* 40.156–61 (1964). Reprinted by permission of the author and The Linguistic Society of America.

TABLE 2 | *Pre-Germanic root structure of classes I–III*

|      | Pres.   | Pret. sg. | Pret. pl. | P. ptc. |
|------|---------|-----------|-----------|---------|
| I    | CeiC-   | CaiC-     | CiC-      | CiC-    |
| II   | CeuC-   | CauC-     | CuC-      | CuC-    |
| IIIa | CenC-   | CanC-     | C(v)nC-   | C(v)nC- |
| IIIb | CelC-   | CalC-     | C(v)lC-   | C(v)lC- |

Class I reconstructs to a root with the resonant *i* followed by a consonant; class II to a root with *u* followed by a consonant; class III to a root with a nasal or a liquid followed by a consonant.[3] With full grade, the resonants are consonantal (second members of diphthongs); with zero grade, the resonants are originally vocalic, assuming syllabic status; at a later stage, a svarabhakti vowel develops here.

Classes IV–VI have the Pre-Germanic structure shown in Table 3.

TABLE 3 | *Pre-Germanic root structure of classes IV–VI*

|        | Pres.  | Pret. sg. | Pret. pl. | P. ptc. |
|--------|--------|-----------|-----------|---------|
| IVa    | Cel-   | Cal-      | Cǣl-      | C(v)l-  |
| IVb, c | Cen-   | Can-      | Cǣn-      | C(v)n-  |
| V      | CeC-   | CaC-      | CǣC-      | C(v)C-  |
| VI     | C(v)C- | CōC-      | CōC-      | C(v)C-  |

Class IV reconstructs to a root ending in a nasal or a liquid resonant, and class V to a root ending in a consonant (stop or spirant); class VI is less determinate: the phoneme with which it ends is a stop, a spirant, a nasal, or a liquid.[4]

From the historical point of view, classes IV–VI are distinctive also in that the regular alternation $e \sim o \sim$ zero of the first three classes is not consistently carried through. The discrepancies occur in the preterit plurals of classes IV and V and throughout class VI.[5] The vowel *ǣ* in the preterit plurals of classes IV and V reflects an IE lengthened grade *ē*, as in Latin perfects of the type *vēxī* (*vehō* "I carry"). In class VI the vowel of the present stem probably reflects an old weak-grade present[6]; the vowels of the preterit go back to various sources.[7]

The historical basis for segregating the seventh class of Germanic strong verbs is that their preterits were originally formed by reduplication.[8] Of all the Germanic languages, however, only Gothic systematically retains this formation: the preterits of Gothic *haldan* "hold" are sg. *haihald*, pl. *haihaldum*; of *lētan* "let," g. *lailōt*, pl. *lailōtum*. In Old English, except for a few vestiges, the seventh class shows no reduplication.[9]

Notice, in the Gothic forms just cited, that the same vocalism is found throughout the preterit. Uniformity of preterit vocalism is true in general of the seventh class. In Old English, two major subtypes are distinguished, according as the preterit vowel is *ē* or *ēo*. In their uniform preterit vocalism, verbs of the seventh class correspond to Greek perfects of the type *léloipa* "I have left," *leloípamen* "we have left" (*leípō* "I leave").

TABLE 4 / *Seventh class of Old English strong verbs*

| | | | | | |
|---|---|---|---|---|---|
| VIIa | hātan | hēt | hēton | hāten | "call" |
| | lǣtan | lēt | lēton | lǣten | "let" |
| VIIb | blāwan | blēow | blēowon | blāwen | "blow" |
| | bēatan | bēot | bēoton | bēaten | "beat" |

Great changes have intervened between the reconstructed root structures of the Germanic strong verbs and their forms in Old English. In classes I and II the articulation of the resonants *i* and *u* with the other elements of the root has been largely obscured by subsequent sound-changes: the preterit plural and the past participle continue to show the reconstructible form, but the present and the preterit singular do not. In class III there is even less retention of the reconstructible forms: svarabhakti vowels have been developed in the preterit plural and past participle to prop up the zero-grade nasals and liquids, and the original *e* and *o* (Gmc. *a*) of the present and the preterit singular have also, in some cases, undergone sound-change.

The Old English classes IV–VI retain the original consonant structure, but show irregularities in the original ablaut alternation. Class VII shows, in addition, a drastic modification of the structure of the preterit: the original reduplication has been, for all practical (i.e., synchronic) purposes, lost.

The changes suffered by Old English in the period (more than a millennium) of its divergence from Pre-Germanic are not the main reason that the traditional classification of the Old English strong verbs is faulty. The reason, rather, is that the criteria for classification, which were perfectly appropriate for Pre-Germanic, are no longer functional in Old English. Thus, classes I–III of Old English, while still distinct, are distinct for reasons other than the original presence of different resonants in their roots. Likewise, while the seventh class of strong verbs in Old English is still distinct from the other classes, it is not because the preterit has a reduplicating syllable. In the same way, while differences of vocalism continue to distinguish some classes from others, the system of Indo-European ablaut alternation can no longer be regarded as a significant criterion of classification.

Discarding the original historical basis of the classification of Old English strong verbs, and using synchronic features as criteria, I propose the reclassification summarized in Table 5. Most of the subclasses are included; 4a belongs to IV of the traditional scheme, 4b–d belong to V; 5a–e to VI; 5f–g to IV; and all forms in 6 and 7 to VII.

TABLE 5 / *Reclassification of the Old English strong verbs*

| | | | | | | | | | |
|---|---|---|---|---|---|---|---|---|---|
| 1a | ī | ā | i | i | bīdan | bād | bidon | biden | "await" |
| b | ēo | ā | i | i | wrēon | wrāh | wrigon | wrigen | "cover" |
| 2a | ēo | ēa | u | o | bēodan | bēad | budon | boden | "command" |
| b | ū | ēa | u | o | brūcan | brēac | brucon | brocen | "use" |

| | | | | | | | | |
|---|---|---|---|---|---|---|---|---|
| 3a | i | a | u | u | bindan | band | bundon | bunden | "bind" |
| b | e | ea | u | o | helpan | healp | hulpon | holpen | "help" |
| c | eo | ea | u | o | weorpan | wearp | wurpon | worpen | "throw" |
| d | u | ea | u | o | spurnan | spearn | spurnon | spornen | "spurn" |
| e | e | æ | u | o | stregdan | strægd | strugdon | strogden | "strew" |
| | | | | | | | | | |
| 4a | e | æ | ǣ | o | beran | bær | bǣron | boren | "bear" |
| b | e | æ | ǣ | e | metan | mæt | mǣton | meten | "measure" |
| c | ēo | ea | ǣ | e | sēon | seah | sǣgon | segen | "see" |
| d | i | æ | ǣ | e | biddan | bæd | bǣdon | beden | "pray" |
| | | | | | | | | | |
| 5a | a | ō | ō | a | faran | fōr | fōron | faren | "go" |
| b | ēa | ō | ō | a | slēan | slōg | slōgon | slagen | "strike" |
| c | e | ō | ō | a | hebban | hōf | hōfon | hafen | "raise" |
| d | ie | ō | ō | ea | scieppan | scōp | scōpon | sceapen | "create" |
| e | æ | ō | ō | æ | stæppan | stōp | stōpon | stæpen | "step" |
| f | u | ō | ō | u | cuman | cōm | cōmon | cumen | "come" |
| g | i | ō | ō | u | niman | nōm | nōmon | numen | "take" |
| | | | | | | | | | |
| 6a | ā | ē | ē | ā | hātan | hēt | hēton | hāten | "call" |
| b | ǣ | ē | ē | ǣ | lǣtan | lēt | lēton | lǣten | "let" |
| c | ō | ē | ē | a | fōn | fēng | fēngon | fangen | "seize" |
| | | | | | | | | | |
| 7a | a | ēo | ēo | a | bannan | bēonn | bēonnon | bannen | "summon" |
| b | ea | ēo | ēo | ea | fealdan | fēold | fēoldon | fealden | "fold" |
| c | ā | ēo | ēo | ā | blāwan | blēow | blēowon | blāwen | "blow" |
| d | ēa | ēo | ēo | ēa | bēatan | bēot | bēoton | bēaten | "beat" |
| e | ō | ēo | ēo | ō | blōtan | blēot | blēoton | blōten | "sacrifice" |

The new arrangement, like the old, comprises seven classes. The criterion for class assignment is the vocalism of the preterit. By this criterion, the system falls into two divisions: in the first (1–4) the vowel of the preterit is different in the singular and the plural; in the second (5–7) it is the same. The vowels of the preterit, for the revised classes, are shown in Table 6. (The forms *strægd*, *strugdon* of 3e, and *seah*, *sǣgon* of 4c fall outside this scheme.)

TABLE 6 / *Vowels of preterit singular and plural*

| | | | | | |
|---|---|---|---|---|---|
| 1 | ā | i | 5 | ō | ō |
| 2 | ēa | u | 6 | ē | ē |
| 3 | a/ea | u | 7 | ēo | ēo |
| 4 | æ | ǣ | | | |

Three major changes from the traditional classification follow from the selection of preterit vocalism as the criterion of class membership: (1) classes IVb and IVc (*cuman*, *niman*, and their prefixed congeners) are combined with class VI (*faran*) to yield the new class 5; (2) class IVa (*beran*) is combined with class V (*metan*) to yield the new class 4; (3) the former subtypes of class VII are now separate classes, 6 and 7.

It is clear from Table 5 that if the principal parts of a verb are given, the class is determined. But what are the chances of uniquely classifying an individual form? If the form is a preterit of class 1 or 5–7 there is no problem.[10] The preterit singular of 3a and the preterit plurals of 4 are also distinctive. Preterit vocalism alone, however, will not distinguish between the singulars of 3b–d and 4c or of 3e and 4a, b, d, or between the plurals of 2 and 3. In these cases we make use of a subsidiary criterion, the root structure: the historical changes affecting the root structure of Old English verbs have, as it happens, preserved a difference here. Verbs of class 3 have roots ending in a nasal or liquid followed by a consonant; verbs of classes 2 and 4 do not have this structure. Thus the preterit singulars *healp, wearp, spearn* (3b–d) are distinguishable from *seah* (4c), the preterit plurals *bundon, hulpon, wurpon* (3) from the preterit plurals *budon, tugon, curon* (2).[11]

Among the past participles unique determination is possible in all but a few cases. Often the vowel is enough to show the class; thus in classes 1, 4b, 4c, 4d, 5e, 6b, 7d, and 7e. The remaining classes have the vowel *o, u, a, ea,* or *ā* in the past participle. *o* occurs in 2a, 2b, 3b, 3c, 3d, 3e, and 4a. The root structure will distinguish class-3 forms from those of classes 2 and 4. 4a contains a liquid in the root (*boren, holen*), 2 ordinarily does not. The exceptions are a few class-2 verbs whose past participles (and preterit plurals) show *r* as a result of the operation of Verner's Law, e.g., *coren* (*cēosan*), *froren* (*frēosan*). (Note that in the traditional classification it is also not possible to distinguish between *boren* and *coren*.)

The vowel *u* occurs in the past participles of 3a, 5f, and 5g. Here again root structure is decisive: *bunden* as opposed to *cumen, numen*. When the vowel is *a*, in classes 5a, 5b, 5c, 6c, and 7a, root structure is usually determinative. In the last two classes the *a* is followed by either a geminate nasal (7a) or nasal plus consonant (6c); of the verbs in class 5 only *standen* has this structure.

The vowel *ea* of class 5d is distinguished from that of 7b in that the latter is followed by a consonant cluster, the former never.[12] The vowel *ā* of 7c occurs before *w*, that of 6a does not.

Present stems of class 1a are distinctive. Whereas the *ū* of 2b is also distinctive, the *ēo* of 2a is found also in 1b and in 4c; but verbs of 1b and 4c are contract verbs, e.g., *wrēon* "cover," *tēon* "accuse" (1b), *sēon* "see," *plēon* "risk" (4c), and those of 2a are not, e.g., *bēodan* "command," *cēosan* "choose." There is no way short of listing, however, to distinguish the contract verbs of 1b from those of 4c.

In class 3, the vowel *eo* of 3c is distinctive; the *i* and *u* of 3a and 3d are distinguished from their counterparts in 5g and 5f by root-structure. (The *i* of 4d is followed by a geminate consonant, the *i* of 3a and 5g is not.) The *e* of 3b and 3e is similarly distinguished from the *e* of 4a and 4b, and from the *e* of 5c (*hebban, sceppan, swerian*) by the lack of root-final geminate or *-ri-*.

Class 5d is unique, as are 5e and 7b. Class 5a is similar to 7a in that both have *a*. In 7a the *a* is always followed by a geminate nasal or by nasal plus consonant (*spannan, blandan*), in 5a only in *standan*. The *ēa* of 5b occurs in a contract form (*slēan, flēan*, etc.) and is thus distinguished from the *ēa* of 7d (*bēatan* etc.).

The *ǣ* of 6b is distinctive. The *ā* of 7c is always followed by *w* (*cnāwan, blāwan*), that of 6a never. The *ō* of 6c occurs in contraction (*fōn, hōn*, etc.), that of 7e does not (*hrōpan, grōwan*).

If we ask how the traditional classification and the new scheme compare in making possible the unique determination of individual forms, we see that in this they are exactly alike. Neither enjoys an advantage in its ability to assign individual forms. If I nevertheless regard the reclassification as superior, it is only in part because it uses purely synchronic criteria. The use of vowel gradation as the primary criterion, with root structure a subsidiary marker, greatly simplifies the system. By modifying the role of root structure as a class index, and by abandoning reduplication altogether, we achieve classes much more uniformly differentiated. There is little motivation, aside from diachronic considerations, for separating *beran* and *metan, cuman* and *faran*, verbs with such similar vocalism in their paradigms; at this point the traditional classification is overdifferentiated. On the other hand, only their common origin as reduplicatives could justify grouping in one class verbs with such different vocalism as *hātan, hēt*, and *blōtan, blēot*; this is a clear case of underdifferentiation. The reclassification, by disregarding historical differences and focusing on synchronic evidence, presents a system of Old English strong verbs which is properly motivated; the result is neater and more adequate than the traditional scheme.

## FOOTNOTES

1. See Jacob Grimm, *Deutsche Grammatik*[2] 1.756–7 (Berlin, 1870).
2. Pre-Germanic reconstructions are chosen for convenience and effectiveness. Indo-European reconstructions would require a consideration of laryngeals or reduced-grade vowels or both; Proto-Germanic reconstructions would obscure the original ablaut alternations.

   In the tables *C* denotes a consonant or cluster, *n* a nasal, *l* a liquid. A small *v* denotes an obscure or reduced vowel which develops as Proto-Germanic *u* in the zero-grade forms of classes IIIa and IIIb. In Table 3, *v* denotes Germanic *a* (< IE *a* or *ə*) in the present of class VI, and a still more diverse vocalism in the participles of IV, V, and VI.

3. This applies to most roots in class III; but the class includes also verbs like *feohtan* "fight," *stregdan* "strew," *frignan* "ask." In the discussion that follows, some of these and other rare types will be incorporated into the analysis.
4. Class VI includes a few roots ending in more than one consonant, e.g., *wascan* "wash," *standan* "stand."

5. The *æ* for expected *a* in the preterit singular of classes IV and V is regular in Old English. The *i* of *niman* results from a Germanic sound-change; the *u* of *cuman* is that of a weak-grade present.

6. The type with reduced or zero grade is more clearly seen in presents like class I *rīpan*, III *murnan*, IV *cuman*. It is also seen, with lengthening of the original short vowel, in the rather large subclass of class II that includes *brūcan* and *lūcan*.

7. Cf., for instance, E. Prokosch, *A comparative Germanic grammar* 173–4 (Philadelphia, 1939).

8. Reduplication is one of the regular ways of forming the Indo-European perfect; the other way is exemplified in Greek *oîda* "I know," *ídmen* "we know." The latter forms lack reduplication, and retain the alternation of *o* grade in the singular and zero grade in the plural. Sanskrit reduplicating preterits reflect the same alternation: *riṇákti* "he leaves": *riréca* "he has left," *riricimá* "we have left." But the corresponding Greek formations generalize the vowel grade of the singular: *leípō* "I leave": *léloipa* "I have left," *leloípamen* "we have left."

Since Germanic shows a conflation of the Indo-European perfect and aorist, we speak instead of the preterit when dealing with Germanic verbs.

[For more detailed treatment of tense-formation and vowel-gradation in the Indo-European verb, and applications to Old English, see A. Meillet, *Introduction à l'étude comparative des langues Indo-Européennes* (University, Alabama, 1964), 153–68, 179–82, 195–251; for a very simple over all view see J. and E. M. Wright, *Old English Grammar*[3] (Oxford, 1925), 250–2.—Ed.]

9. Only traces of the original reduplication exist in Old English. A. Campbell, *Old English Grammar* 320 (Oxford, 1959), lists the following as the only sure instances: *hēht* or *hēht* from *hātan*; *leolc* from *lācan*; *ondreord* from *ondrǣdan*; *leort* from *lǣtan*; and *reord* from *rǣdan*. These forms are archaic in Old English; they occur chiefly in poetry and the old Anglian glosses.

10. When the vowel is the same as that of a present or past participle in another class, the ending will show that the form is preterit, except when the like vowels occur in a preterit singular and an imperative singular (3 *band* "he bound," 5 *far* "go"). Even then, the root structure will solve the ambiguity.

11. 3e *strēgdan* represents a small group of verbs in class III with roots that do not end in a nasal or liquid plus consonant; others are *bregdan* "brandish," *berstan* "burst," *frignan* "ask." All such verbs have roots ending in a consonant cluster, which distinguishes their preterit singular forms (*strǣgd, bǣrst, frægn*) from those of 4a, b, d (*bær, mæt, bæd*).

12. In 5d the *ea*, like the *ie* of the present stem, is conditioned by the preceding palatal consonant. The same sound-change might have occurred before a consonant cluster in the past participle, but there seem to be no verbs of this class where the change has in fact taken place.

## J. W. RICHARD LINDEMANN

# Old English Preverbal *ge-*:
# A Re-Examination of Some Current Doctrines*

Despite an occasional statement to the contrary, Anglo-Saxonists in general are agreed that the many attempts to determine the meaning and the function of the OE preverb *ge-* have been unsuccessful or, at best, badly confused. During the last century and a half there have appeared some thirty-five dissertations, monographs, and articles—to say nothing of a host of glossarial commentaries—that purport to explain this morpheme and its cognates but fail ultimately to do so. As recently as 1953 Professor Herbert Pilch of the University of Kiel, attempting to account for the disappearance of the morpheme in ME, was compelled to admit that "über ae. ȝe- herrscht noch immer weitgehende Unklarheit."[1]

Obviously there must be some reason for this frankly admitted obscurity, and the reason appears to be twofold. In the first place the preverb *ge-* has a very high degree of relative frequency. We know that in any spoken language a linguistic element with a high degree of relative frequency demands less emphasis than an element that appears more rarely and, consequently, may lose a specific denotation and acquire a very general one or several less specific and very general ones. We know that this happened with the OE preverbs *ā-*, *be-*, and *for-*, and there is no reason for assuming that this should not have happened with *ge-*.

But a more important and immediate reason for the obscurity, I believe, lies in the nature of the very doctrines that have been proposed to explain the morpheme. In too many instances these have been accepted as infallible articles of faith presumably founded on incontrovertible facts. Yet when they are subjected to close critical scrutiny they leave the impression that they are, after all, only primary assumptions not yet able to sustain themselves by means of adequate proof, or they appear to be philosophical hypotheses rather than strictly linguistic observations confined to a homogeneous language *system*. At times these doctrines reveal a very seductive cogency, but only in the light of data that have been especially selected to substantiate them; when they are more generally applied to different sets of data, they are likely to collapse. Moreover, too frequently they substitute questionable syntactic assumptions for "jene semasiologischen untersuchungen" that Hans Pollak recognized as the only proper approach to an ultimate under-

* From *JEGP* 64.65–83 (1965). Reprinted by permission of the author and the University of Illinois Press.

standing of the meaning and function of such a preverb as *ge-*.[2] But above all, these doctrines place too much reliance upon evidence produced by a comparison of a Germanic text with its Latin or Greek source alone, despite the fact that experience has taught us that translators and glossators at best follow their sources only capriciously. Not a single one of the doctrines proposed in the essays mentioned above supplements the evidence from the single source by drawing upon the equally illuminating evidence that could be derived from a comparison of one Germanic dialect with another.

Unfortunately many of the doctrines continue to thrive in the authoritative sanctity of classrooms, of grammars, and of textual notes. If they thereby perpetuate the obscurity surrounding the preverb, then they ought to be questioned, for the prominence of the preverb is such that it cries out for resolute endeavor on our part to understand it—even if our initial efforts lead us no further than understanding what it does *not* mean. With its high degree of frequency we may safely assume that the preverb *ge-* was an important thread in the whole fabric of OE, and we may also consequently assume that without a clearer understanding of it we miss many shades of meaning originally intended to be expressed in our texts, and we may even risk mistranslating those texts grossly. The fact that the doctrines apparently do not clarify the significance of the preverb suggests that these doctrines require re-examination.

It is my purpose in this paper to make such re-examination. Most of the doctrines will be discussed only briefly; the one that is now most current and that insists that *ge-* be involved in the theory of aspect will be discussed in more detail. The doctrines that purport to explain the morpheme I present below, and comment upon them in the light of whatever critical evidence is available, some of it taken from the observations of others, some from my own. Wherever I adduce evidence of my own, this is drawn from a synchronic study composed of three OE dialect versions of the *Gospel According to St. Matthew* as edited by Skeat,[3] the corpus netting some nine thousand instances of verbal usage both simplex and compound.

## I. *Ge-* Is without Meaning

This doctrine is still widely held, although it is over two hundred years old. Thomas Benson of Oxford lent it some authority when in his *Vocabularium Anglo-Saxonicum* (1701) he said, "*Ge- apud Saxones semper fere superfluum.*" In the eighteenth century Adelung's HG dictionary repeated it and doubtless gave it considerable popularity.[4] And in our own century, one relatively recent OE grammar[5] says that *ge-* "adds little or nothing," and Professor Samuels[6] of Glasgow and Miss Hollmann[6] of Jena find that in general it is "meaningless." Moreover, this doctrine has had far-reaching consequences; assuming that it was meaningless, *speculation* had somehow or other to account for its existence in the language, and on the basis of such speculations

Martens, in 1863, constructed his hypothesis implying that the function of the preverb was the same as that of the preverbs in the Slavic languages and that, having lost all lexical meaning, it served merely as a tag to indicate completed action.[8] Streitberg agreed with him.[9] The notion was pure conjecture.

The chief objection to the doctrine will be apparent at the end of this paper. For the time being, suffice it to say that this assumption overlooks the fact that all too frequently simplex and *ge*-compound have *different meanings* that cannot have developed solely out of the concept of completed action: *gan* means "to go," *gegan* may mean "to go away," "to happen," and also "to walk," and *gegan* + acc. normally means "to conquer"; *standan* means "to stand" and *gestandan* may mean "to stand up," but *gestandan* may also mean ".to stop" *and* "to *remain* standing." Moreover, it also overlooks the fact that in OE we have contrasting pairs of compounds each of which has a meaning different from that of the other: "ðonne hæbbe we begen fét *gescode* . . . ðonne bið us suiðor oðer fót *unscod.*"[10] Finally it ignores the fact that in both the Epinal and Erfurt glosses Lat. simplexes are frequently glossed by OE compounds, not OE simplexes.

## II. *Ge-* Stresses or Intensifies the Action of the Verb

As one might suspect, this doctrine is fraught with considerable ambiguity and subjectivity. For what, one may ask, is one to understand by "intensifying the action" of a verb? Is *ge-* presumed to mean the same as OE *swiðe,* "very much"? What is an "intensified" *going,* or *seeing,* or *standing*? Even Streitberg rejected such an assumption and quite rightly saw the absurdity of the multiplicity of meanings that were being attributed to *ge-*: "Was überhaupt die 'intensiv'-bedeutung von *ga-* anlangt," he says, "so ist es damit übel bestellt: überall wo man dies erklärungsmittel anwenden will, gerät man in verlegenheiten. . . . Wie ist es überhaupt möglich, daß eine einzige partikel *zugleich* so verschiedene functionen wie die genannten in sich vereinige . . . ?"[11] E. Bernhardt apparently originated this doctrine in 1870,[12] and Lorz repeated it in 1908.[13] It still prevails in some circles,[14] but the writers who apply it do not explain what they mean by it any more satisfactorily than Wackernagel did when he said that *ge-* qualifies the meaning of a verb by being "unübersetzbar leise verstärkend."[15]

## III. *Ge-* May Convert an Intransitive Verb into a Resultative Verb that is Transitive

P. Lenz, in 1886, is the first to have published this observation;[16] Lorz repeated it in 1908 (p. 14), and the doctrine has often been reiterated since. Nevertheless, to be quite exact, as we must be in these matters, the statement is not wholly true, but an inaccurate re-creating of an older syntactical system in the image of a modern one. It is true enough that such compounds as *gegan* and *gesittan* may at times be followed by accusatives, and at other times may not. But when they are followed by accusatives they are not therefore necessarily transitive; rather they can still be intransitive followed by an accusative of direction or goal;[17] e.g., *Beowulf* 2100: "*ond he hean ðonan . . . meregrund gefeoll*," "he fell on to (down to) the bottom of the lake," not "reached by falling."

## IV. *Ge-* Indicates Completion

Although this doctrine may appear to be identical with the one immediately following, which states that the preverb perfectivates, there are a few qualifications inherent in the one or the other that warrant treating them separately. Jacob Grimm was apparently one of the first to observe that the preverb had the power to indicate that the action of the simplex to which it was prefixed was accomplished.[18] Wackernagel stated simply that its function was to terminate the concept of the action, "*um den Begriff der Thätigkeit abzuschließen*" (s.v. *ge-*). But observe the astonishing exegesis of some subsequent writers intent on reconciling the idea of completion with the unwarranted assumption that *ge-* must originally have meant "with, together" and must have been the Germanic equivalent of Lat. *cum*. Dorfeld assumed that the preverb originally meant "together," and that this idea of "being together" indicated completeness, and subsequently indicated completed action.[19] Wustmann understood the evolution of completion somewhat differently: *ge-* originally meant "with": from this it went into the meaning of "fully," "entirely," and then "entirely to the end."[20] Van Swaay followed a similar kind of speculative progression: from the idea of "union" could come the idea of "collecting together," and from there on the prefix could indicate a point in the action that would be the equivalent of a "result."[21] If all of this strikes the reader as being somewhat complicated, he will simply have to accept it as a matter of record; it was typical of the semasiological gymnastics that were tried in an effort to extract from the idea of "with" an idea of completion that was not there.

Once this doctrine of completion was established it became extended to syntax, specifically to the tenses. The function of *ge-*, it said, was to indicate completed temporal action, and thereby provide verbal compounds that would compensate for those tenses, the equivalents of the Lat. perfect tenses, that never developed in the Germanic languages. Wackernagel claimed that it gave to the preterite the sense of the perfect and the sense of the pluperfect; to the present it gave the sense of the perfect, the future, and the future perfect (s.v. *ge*). Lenz believed that the prefix served to indicate the pluperfect and the future perfect,[22] and even Streitberg believed that, prefixed to a verb in the present tense, it could indicate the future.[23] The doctrine sweeps down into the twentieth century; Bloomfield and Mossé accepted it without question,[24] and Samuels applied it to the Lindisfarne Gospels as late as 1949.[25] *Ge-* thus presumably functioning to indicate the perfect tenses is known as the "perfectic *ge-*."

The doctrine of the "perfectic *ge-*" was the product of an all-too-hasty generalization. That any completeness expressed by *ge-* had to be a *lexical* completeness, a completeness per se, "*in sich selbst*," L. Tobler pointed out a century ago.[26] (For example, a verb like NE *upend* is composed of a simplex *end* and a preverb *up-*. The *up-* indicates a local goal and may therefore be regarded as locally limiting or, some would say, completing the action expressed in the simplex. But in such a statement as "He had upended the beam when we got back" the *temporal* completion is obviously not effected by the preverb *up-* but by the grammatical category of the past perfect tense.) Mourek objected to the doctrine of the "perfectic *ge-*" on the same grounds as Tobler,[27] and Behaghel showed that preterite *ge-* compounds in temporal subordinate clauses did not necessarily express a pluperfect sense, because simplexes in that position could be interpreted in the same way.[28] The data from the OE Matthew also disprove the doctrine; they reveal the following low percentages of *ge-* compounds in relation to simplexes:

*Ge-*preterites translating Lat. perfects          16%
*Ge-*preterites translating Lat. pluperfects       15%
*Ge-*present indicatives translating Lat. futures 20%[29]

## V. *Ge-* Perfectivates or Expresses Perfective Aspect

The doctrine that *ge-* perfectivates is similar to the previously mentioned doctrine except that the latter is now thrust into a verbal system analogous to that in the Slavic languages and is tricked out in terminology borrowed from Slavic grammar. Reduced to its simplest terms, the doctrine states that in the older Germanic dialects the simple form of the verb, with some very few exceptions, expressed an action in its continuity whereas the compound verb expressed an action that was cut off, or brought to an end, or completed.[30] The doctrine was first proposed by Heinrich Martens.[31]

Streitberg developed Martens' thesis in a long essay on Goth, *ga-*, an essay that was destined to become for many generations the classical *locus criticus* from which to explain the uses of preverbal *ge-* in most of the older Germanic dialects. Borrowing the term *Aktionsart* ("manner of action, character") from Delbrück to translate Slavic *vid*, a manner of *regarding* an action, Streitberg insisted that the Germanic languages made the same distinction between imperfectivity and perfectivity that the Slavic languages did. "Die *perfective* actionsart," he said, "fügt dem bedeutungsinhalt, der dem verbum innewohnt, noch den nebenbegriff des vollendet werdens hinzu. Sie bezeichnet also die handlung des verbums nicht schlechthin in ihrem fortgang . . . sondern stets im hinblick auf den moment der vollendung."[32] Then, like Martens, he insisted that the original meaning of *ga-* ("*mit*," "*zusammen*") had faded out and been *reduced to zero*; consequently, when it was prefixed to a simple verb, it "perfectivated" that verb (enabled it to indicate that the action of that verb was completed) *without modifying the meaning of the verb* (p. 103). Its function, he assumed, was the same as that of *po-* in Slavic.

This doctrine pretty well dominated the first half of the twentieth century and found a somewhat modified expression in Leonard Bloomfield's essay in 1929. From the viewpoint of explaining *ge-* this essay differs very little from Streitberg's as far as fundamental concepts are concerned. Although Bloomfield tried "to illustrate the use of *ge-*" and did so accurately enough in terms of purely descriptive syntax, his discussion was limited to only eight OE verbs —far too few to support any kind of generalization—and he failed to "explain" the prefix. Instead of *Aktionsart* he used the term *aspect* and, like Streitberg, he believed that the situation in OE was like that in Slavic: "As a matter of fact, where OE expresses aspect, it reserves the punctual (verb with prefix) for unit action and classes repeated, habitual, and generalized acts with the durative (uncompounded verb; more explicitly *beon* with present participle), exactly as does Slavic" (p. 92).

All of these doctrines are still current, but it is the last of these, V, that has assumed the most important role in practically all current grammars, textbooks, and dictionaries; for these inform us that *ge-* perfectivates, that it expresses perfective aspect, that its original function was to indicate completion, or that it makes a durative verb "punctual," i.e., causes it to indicate the beginning of an action or the end of it.[33] Despite the skill with which this doctrine is sometimes formulated, the more one works with it and tries to apply it to the older Germanic dialects, whether Old English or Gothic or Old Saxon, the more one realizes that it will not accommodate itself to linguistic facts. And it is this doctrine that demands our closest critical scrutiny.

In practice, the doctrine simply does not work. When Friedrich Weick, a disciple of Streitberg, examined the Lindisfarne Gospels, applying Streitberg's hypothesis, he discovered that the forms of the verbs in his text were different from what he believed they ought to be, and he suggested emendations in accordance with his hypothesis.[34] "Das Simplex sollte stehen," he says under *biddan* on page 3, "an Stelle des fälschlich gesetzten Kompos." On page 7, under *hyran*, we find "Das Simplex sollte stehen," "Das Kompos. sollte stehen," and on page 5 we read, "Das Simplex ist einige Male belegt, aber sonderbarerweise immer an unrechter Stelle"![35] But instead of questioning his doctrine, Weick apparently preferred to believe that the glossators of Lindisfarne were unfamiliar with their own language: "Noch deutlicher führen uns die zahlreichen Beispiele, wo geschrieben werden mußte: "das Simplex oder das Kompositum sollte stehen" vor Augen, wie sehr groß schon die Verwirrung in bezug auf die Anwendung von Simplex und Kompositum war" (p. 49).[36]

Lenz, too, had difficulties, even with the orderly prose of Alfred. Assuming that *ge-* was "syntactic," he encountered instances where the use of *ge-* failed to coincide with the provisions of his theory. Again and again we find observations like *"kein grund zu ge"* (p. 30), *"Ge ohne grund"* (p. 25, 20; p. 38, 104; p. 34, 111, 112; p. 40, 119), and *"warum ge?"*[37] (p. 39, 110; p. 45, VI). H. Hesse, too, had trouble reconciling doctrine with facts.[38] Substituting the doctrine of the *Aktionsarten* for Lenz's "syntactic *ge*" he found many passages that defied his formula, two examples of which will suffice: under *healdan* (p. 17) he says "Besser paßt jedoch das Komp.," and under *leornian* (p. 47) "... doch ist das Komp. ... wohl vorzuziehen."[39] An excellent example of how the doctrine of the *Aktionsarten* in the Streitbergian sense can seduce one into grave mistranslation occurs in Hesse's treatment of a passage on page 25, under *standan*: "*Ða ʒestod se byscop æt hire*" Hesse translates as "*trat an sie heran*" but admits that the translation is not exact because the Latin original is durative, "*adstans.*" Nevertheless, he reads "stepped over to her" because the verb is compounded with *ge-* and must, therefore, according to his doctrine, be "punctual." Thomas Miller's translation in the EETS edition is much nearer the truth: "then the bishop stood by her."

Lorz also found that Streitberg's doctrine was inadequate when applied to certain *ge-* compounds in *Beowulf*, especially when he discussed *beodan* (p. 45), *habban* (p. 54), *stæppan* (p. 65), and *þolian* (p. 68). And Streitberg himself had to admit that his hypothesis could not explain *gahausjandona* (p. 83), *gahauseiþ* (p. 80), *sitands* (p. 87), and *gahabaida* (p. 90); in order to save his doctrine, like Weick, he had to postulate textual corruption.

The whole business of depriving *ge-* of any meaning, of making it a "formal" index of perfective aspect, of "stretching the Germanic languages out on the Procrustean bed of Slavic"—Hirt's phrase—simply has not explained it. Pertinent indeed is Hans Pollak's assertion: "Vertrauener-weckender sind daher jene semasiologischen untersuchungen, die irgend eine vorsilbe als solche gelten lassen und nicht auf das wittern bestimmter actionsarten ausgehen."[40]

Despite the fact that many textbooks still acknowledge Streitberg's thesis, competent Slavicists have long ago annihilated it—as well as his assumption that aspectual situations in the Germanic languages are like those in Slavic.[41] Granted that there are similarities between early Germanic dialects and Slavic, Streitberg's critics pointed out that the verbal *systems* of the two differed greatly.

Briefly this difference is as follows. In Slavic the verbal system is composed of *two* sets of verbs, the verbs of one set being used to indicate that the action of an utterance must be viewed without reference to its completion, the verbs of the other set being used to indicate that the action must be viewed *with* reference to its completion. (This is tantamount to saying that for every Germanic verb, Slavic has two verbs.) One *or* the other of the verbs of these two sets *must* be used in order to indicate whether the action (1) is (was, will be) in a state of happen*ing* (imperfective) or (2) was (will be) in a state of happen*ed* (perfective). This contrast in the duration expressed in the utterance is what is properly called *aspect*. Aspect, then, in Slavic is determined by a *grammatical* category, is mandatory, and is *syntactic*.[42] On the other hand, there is nothing at all like this in the Germanic dialects. In these dialects a preverb may modify the action of a verb in such a manner as to indicate that the action tends towards a local goal, and even sometimes that it reaches such a goal and thereby completes the action *per se*, e.g., *overdo*, *undergo*, *bequeath*, *bypass*, or *uphold*. Such completion, however, is inherent in the semantic substance of the *word*, part of its essential meaning; completion is here not syntactic but *lexical*. What we have operating here is not aspect but "manner of action," *Aktionsart* in its true sense. *Aktionsart* is objective; aspect is subjective.[43] For an excellent exposition of the distinctions between the situations in the Slavic languages and the Germanic, one must read C. R. Goedsche, "Aspect versus Aktionsart" (*JEGP*, xxxix [1940], 189–97).

These two terms, *aspect* and *Aktionsart*, have too long been used interchangeably, the resulting confusion having seriously blurred our understanding of the functions of compound verbs. Modern linguistics insists that these two terms and what they stand for must be kept rigorously and distinctly apart.[44] They are so kept apart in the remaining portion of this discussion.

In the article mentioned above, Goedsche insisted that *ge-* could not be a formal index of perfective aspect.[45] In 1953, comparing Biblical passages in OE with identical passages in Russian, Polish, and Serbian, Pilch revealed that the old equation *simplex : ge- compound :: imp. aspect : perf. aspect* no longer holds true.[46] And in 1958, Philip Scherer, using a technique of chrones and chronemes for typical verbal sets, showed that OE *ge-* compounds as such do *not* express aspects: *hælde* and *gehælde* are both perfective and *biddað* and *gebiddað* are both imperfective; "aspectual connotation is not a function of form."[47]

However, Pilch limits his evidence to only a few Biblical passages and their Slavic parallels, and Scherer limits his to verb forms out of context. Both of them cite *only* West Saxon evidence, Scherer erroneously assuming that the West Saxon version is a "translation of the Lindisfarne Gospels." But inasmuch as it is frequently assumed that the function of preverbal *ge-* differed according to the several OE dialects, in what follows below I adduce evidence not only from "classical" OE as well as Alfredian OE but from three of the major dialects also. Moreover, I resort to a simpler and, I believe, clearer method of demonstrating aspectual connotations than those mentioned above; that is, I record complete predications, both independent and dependent, containing *ge-* verbal compounds and test them, first by showing that a certain aspect must follow *logically*, second by subjecting the predications to corollaries inherent in the aspect theory. This method will reveal that *ge-* verbal compounds are not *ipso facto* "perfective" but that they may also just as well be "imperfective" or "durative."

The quotations that follow are from the three dialect versions of Matthew mentioned above and from *King Alfred's Orosius*, ed. Henry Sweet, EETS (London, 1893). C = Corpus MS (West Saxon), R = Rushworth MS (Mercian), L = Lindisfarne MS (Northumbrian); *O* = Orosius, Wyc = Wycliffite translation, Rh = Rheims translation. The Latin is from the Lindisfarne MS. Wherever I found it pertinent, I have given a generally accepted translation of a *ge-* compound beneath the quotation. The doctrine correlating *ge-* with the aspect theory and the corollaries inherent in it are considered in the following examples.

**I.** " *When OE expresses aspect it reserves the punctual (verb with prefix* [ge-]) *for unit action* ['complexive,' 'perfective' action] *and classes repeated, habitual, and generalized acts with the durative (uncompounded verb).*"

It is true that according to the theories of aspect a perfective verb is always punctual.[48] But is a verb compounded with *ge-* punctual? The various doctrines that we have examined earlier in this paper consistently assumed that it was, but the quotations that follow, both those from Matthew and those from Orosius, when subjected to tests inherent in the theory of aspect, show that *ge-* compounds are not necessarily punctual but often durative.[49]

*1. The context may indicate the durativity:*

**Matt. 12 : 46.**
    C.  þa stod his moder 7 his gebroðra þær-úta
    L.  Heonu moder his 7 broðero stondas ł *gestodon*
        ecce mater eius et fratres stabant foris
Lenz (p. 48), *bestehen.*
Lorz (p. 36), *beistehen.*
Hesse (p. 25), *persistere.*
Wyc. "stoden without forth"
Therefore, not "stopped" but "continued to stand."

**Matt. 13 : 2.**
    C.  and eall seo mænigeo stod on þæm waroþe
    L.  and all ðreat *gestod* on wearðe
        et omnis turba stabat in litore
    Cf. MHG *gestân* in *Das Nibelungenlied* (ed. Karl Bartsch [Leipzig, 1931]), stanzas 136, 4; 460, 3; 864, 4, where it is durative and means "to remain standing" "to live." Note that the Lat. of both passages is in the imperfect tense.

**Matt. 2 : 23.**
    C.  he com þa 7 eardode on þære ceastre
    L.  cuom *gebyde* in ceastra
        ueniens habitauit in ciuitate
Not "took up his residence" or "established himself" or "settled," but "abode" there.
Hesse (p. 15), *verbleiben.*
Wuth (p. 62), *verharren, verweilen.*[50]

**Matt. 5:5.**

L. eadge biðan ða milde forðon ða agnegað eorðo

R. ... þa milde forþon þe hie *gesittaþ* eorðu

Beati mites quoniam ipsi posidebunt terram

Not "will take into their possession" but "will own" it: = NHG *besitzen*.

*O*. 276, 1. Þæt he his rise ... mid micelre unieðnesse *gehæfde*.

Not "had had" but "preserved, retained, held."

Hesse (p. 39), *bewahren*.

**II.** *A truly punctual verb cannot express the present tense; only the past, future, and future perfect.*[51] However, *ge-* verbal compounds *do* express true present tense:

**Matt. 6:2.**

C. swa liceteras doð on gesomnuncgum

L. Suæ legeres *gewyrcas* in somnungum

sicut hipocritae faciunt in synagogis

Lenz (p. 40), *ausrichten*.

This passage nicely illustrates the difference between *Aktionsart* and aspect. If Lenz is right, as I believe he is, then *gewyrcas* indicates terminative *Aktionsart* (indicating a goal), but the entire utterance, even though the action were construed as iterative, would still be imperfective. Note also that here a "repeated, habitual, and generalized" act is expressed by a *compounded* verb, *not* by an "uncompounded" one.

**Matt. 7:14.**

C. hu neara ... is ... se weg þe to life *gelædt*

R. *lædeþ*

L. *lædes*

quam angusta ... via quae ducit ad vitam

Hess (p. 37), *fortführen*.

Here again the compounded verb, *not* the uncompounded, expresses an "habitual and generalized" act: The way leads on to life now and always. Note again terminative *Aktionsart* but imperfective aspect.

**Matt. 6:7.**

C. þonne ge eow *gebiddon* · nelle ge sprecan fela

L. ðonne gie *gebiddas* nallas ge felo ... gespreca

Orantes autem nolite multum loqui

Wyc. "in preiynge nyle ȝe speke moche."

Rh. "vvhen you are praying."

**Matt. 18:26.**

C. Hlaford *gehafa* geþyld on me

R. haefe

L. haefe

patientiam habe in me

Lenz (p. 56), *festhalten*.

Clark Hall-Meritt (p. 164), *hold, preserve.*[52] Not a punctual "have," but "continue to have patience with me."

**Matt. 5:4.**

C.   Eadige synt þa þe nu wepað
L.   eadge biðon ða ðe *gemænas* nu
     Beati qui lugunt
Lenz (p. 61), *beklagen.*
Wyc. "Blessed be they that moornen."
Note that the addition of *nu* stresses the idea of the present. The weeping is *"in der erlebten Zeit als verlaufender Prozess dargestellt"*;[53] "who are in the process of mourning *now.*"


**III.** *Since a perfective (punctual) verb can have no true present, it cannot have a present participle.*[54] But verbs compounded with *ge-* appear again and again in present-participial form:

**Matt. 20:20.**

C.      com to him . . . modor mid hyre bearnum hig *ge-eadmende*
        accesit ad eum mater . . . cum filiis suis adorans
Rh.   "the mother . . . vvith her sonnes, adoring."
Wyc.                          "with her sones, onourynge."

**Matt. 26:27.**

L.    *genimende* calic ðoncunco dyde
      accipiens calicem gratias egit
Lorz (p. 77), *an sich nehmen.*
Wuth (p. 44), *annahm.*
Rh.   "And taking the chalice."

**Matt. 25:31.**

C.    þa mænegu wundredon *geseonde* . . . blinde *geseonde*
      turbae mirarentur uidentes . . . caecos uidentes
Wyc. "the puple wondride: seyinge . . . blynde men seyinge."

**Matt. 13:48.**

C.    saeton be þam strande þa gecuron hig þa godan
R.    bi waraðe *gesittende* gecuron þa gode
      secus litus sedentes elegerunt bonos
Rh.   "sitting by the shore, they chose out the good."

*O.* 110, 10: nu ic wille eac þæs maran Alexandres *gemunende beon* (i.e., "be remembering")
Lenz (p. 61), *sich errinnern.*
Lorz (p. 59), *sich errinnern.*


**IV.** *Only durative actions admit of modifiers expressing an extent of time,*[55] *punctual actions do not.* The following passages, however, reveal that OE *ge-*verbal compounds not only were modified by expressions indicating an extent of time but also that they themselves indicated a duration of time *during which* another action proceeds simultaneously:

## 1. General extent of time:

**Matt. 2:9.**
L.  heno steorra . . . fore-*geeade* hea *wið þ* . . . gestod
   . . . antecedebat eos usque . . . staret
Wyc.  "went befor hem, til it . . . stood."

**Matt. 13:30.**
L.  forletas egðer . . . *gewæxe wið to* hrípe
   sinite utraque crescere usque ad messem
Wyc.  "suffre ȝe hem bothe wexe in to repynge tyme."
   (i.e., "continue to grow.")

**Matt. 19:20.**
R.  eall ic þaes *geheold fram* iuguðe mine
C.       *geheold*
L.       *geheold*
   omnia haec custodiui
Lorz  (p. 20), *erhalten, bewahren*

Wuth  (p. 81), *erhalten*

*O.* 185, 15. siþþan he *gefor* ofer þa monegan þeod *oþ* he com to Alpis
This is the syntactic pattern which, according to Mossé, establishes his *durée limitée* for the periphrastic form. "Il exprime qu'une action a duré jusqu'à un certain point. . . . C'est donc avec *oþ, oþþæt* que l'on rencontre ce tour" (*Histoire*, 1, 86).[56]

*O.* 72, 26. Ac hine Gandes seo (ea) þaes oferfæreldes *longe gelette* ("hindered him for a long time").
Lenz  (p. 47), *verhindern.*
Wuth  (p. 88), *aufhalten.*

## 2. Specific extent of time:

**Matt. 9:20.**
L.  heonu wif ðiu blodes flouing *geðolade l gedrog tuelf uinter.*
   ecce mulier quae sanguinis fluxum patiebatur duodecim annis

**Matt. 4:2.**
L.  mið ðy *gefaeste feuortig daga*
   Cum ieiunasset quadraginta diebus
Not a *hapax legomenon*, nor, despite the Latin, is there any compulsion to translate this as "when he *had* fasted"; cf. Matt. 6:16, *middy . . . gie gefæstas* (*cum ieiunatis*) and Matt. 9:15, *gefæsdon* (*ieiunabant*).

*O.* 182, 19. Ahsige þonne eft *hu longe* sio sibbe *gestode:* þonne waes þaet *an gear*

Lorz  (p. 37), *stehen bleiben.*

Hesse (p. 25), *perstare.*

Lenz  (p. 48), *bestehen.*

*O.* 254, 6. siþþan *gestod* Romeburg XII winter . . . *þa hwile* þe Augustus þa eoðmetta wiþ God *geheold.*

*O.* 78, 32. he digellice . . . *v gear* scipa worhte and fultum *gegaderode*

Here *gegaderode* is just as durative as *worhte*; *v gear* modifies both.


*3. Time during which another action proceeds simultaneously*—"genuine durative actions . . . i.e., those where the segment of time occupied is viewed as a possible container of other acts" (Bloomfield, p. 92):

**Matt. 6:7.**

C.     þonne ge eow *gebiddon*, nelle ge sprecan fela

L.                      *gebiddas*

R.                      *gebiddandæ*

       orantes autem nollite multum loqui

Wyc. "in praying."

**Matt. 17:5.**

R.     þende he þa *gespræc* henu wolken liht oferscuade hie

       at huc eo loquente ecce nubis lucida obumbrauit eos

Wuth (p. 20), *aussprechen.*

Wyc. "ȝhit the while he spake."

Rh.   "as he was yet speaking."

**Matt. 13:25.**

L.     mið ðy uutodlice *geslepdon* . . . ða menn cuom fiond his

       cum autem dormirent homines uenit inimicus eius

Rh.   "But vvhen men vvere a sleepe, his enemy came."

       Notice, not "fell asleep" or "when they had slept" (both punctual) but "while they were sleeping."

**Matt. 27:32.**

L.     mið ðy *geeadon* . . . gemoeton monno cyriniscne

       Exeuntes . . . inuenerunt hominem cyreneum

       Not "after they went out" or "when they *had* gone out" but "as they went out."

Wyc. "and as thei ȝeden out."

Rh.   "and in going."


The passages cited above amply illustrate the proposition that *ge-* compounds do not necessarily determine perfective aspect, that they may, just as readily, determine imperfective (or durative) aspect. Jacob Grimm had observed this twofold characteristic of the compounds long ago,[57] causing one to wonder all the more why just this one morpheme, *ge-*, should have been singled out from among the whole group of inseparable prefixes—all of which *may* at times "perfectivate"—as a distinctive and exclusive marker of perfective aspect.

*Mutatis mutandis* the simplexes, too, fail to support the current doctrines. They are not necessarily durative. Here, again, *aspect depends upon context*, and, as the following passages clearly reveal, simplexes may stand in utterances that are indubitably perfective:

**Matt. 1:25.**

    C.    Heo *cende* hyre . . . sunu
    R.        gebær
    L.        gecende
            peperit

**Matt. 4:7.**

    C.    ne *costna* þu drihten
    R.      *costa*
    L.      *costa*
          temtabis

**Matt. 17:6.**

    C.    hig *feollon* on hyre ansyne
    R.      *feollan*
    L.      *gefallon*
          ceciderunt

Not "were falling on their face" but, Wyc., "feldon doun on her face"—a sudden "unit" action.

**Matt. 13:31.**

    C.    gelic senepes corne þ *seow* se man on hys æcre
    R.              *seow*
    L.              geseow
               seminauit

Again "unit action." But note the following, where the aspect is imperfective:

**Matt. 13:4.**

    C.    þa þa he *seow*. sume hig feollon wiþ weg
    R.      *seow*
    L.      *saues*
          seminat

These above two passages, with their similarity of *form* clearly reveal the extent to which aspect in OE is subjective, syntactic, and, with the exception of the "expanded form," *entirely dependent on context*.

**Matt. 28:2.**

    C.    drihtnes engel . . . awylte þone stan 7 *sæt* þær on uppan
    R.                               gesett
    L.                               gesæt

Not "was sitting on" but "seated himself." Cf. *Beow*. 490: "site nu to symle." Wyc. "turned awey the stoon, and sat thereon."

Now, if OE simplexes, as we have just seen, are capable of expressing *perfective* aspect as well as imperfective, and if *ge-* compounds are capable of expressing *imperfective* aspect as well as perfective, then *ge-* cannot be a "formal," preverbal tag indicating perfective aspect. We find for OE what Scherer[58] found for Goth. and OHG, namely, that *form*—always excepting the expanded form—does not determine aspect, but that aspect is a *connotation* inherent in specific verbal meaning *and* syntactic context. *Ge-* has no immediate bearing on aspect at all, and the doctrine is untenable.

We return for a moment to Streitberg. Streitberg, "empruntant malheureusement la terminologie des langues slaves" (Mossé, *Histoire*, II, 2), appears to have been correct in his statement about the preverb only if we accept it with the following reservations: (1) that the verbal system of the Germanic languages was not like that of Slavic; (2) that the preverb could not have been reduced to zero semantically; (3) that the compounds produced by this preverb *ge-* did not express "perfective aspect" but *might* express a terminating *Aktionsart* as we understand it today. But even this *Aktionsart* would have to be regarded as a secondary signification of *ge-*. Its primary signification would have had to be its lexical meaning, for, regardless of the time at which it became and remained a productive morpheme, a preverb expresses an *Aktionsart*, "perfectivates" if you will, only by virtue of its lexical meaning,[59] "*indem es ein bestimmtes Ziel seines Simplex scharf betonte.*"[60] That such meaning was "with, together" is most doubtful; the ideas inherent in "with, together" do not "perfectivate" or terminate.[61]

That *ge-* had lexical meaning is practically certain (Grimm, Grassmann, Pott, and Sievers all believed that it had), and it devolves upon historical linguistics to *abstract that meaning from within* the system of the Germanic dialects. "Streitberg möchte zwar perfektivierendes und lokales *ga-* durch eine unüberbrückbare Kluft trennen: die Sprachgeschichte aber verlangt ihre Vereinigung."[62]

## FOOTNOTES

1. Herbert Pilch, "Das AE. Präverb *ʒe-*," *Anglia*, LXXI (1953), 129. ["There still reigns over OE *ge-* a vast confusion."]

2. Hans W. Pollak, "Studien zum germanischen Verbum," *PBB* (*Beiträge z. Geschichte d. deutschen Sprache u. Lit.*), XLIV (1920), 380.

3. In *The Holy Gospels in Anglo-Saxon, Northumbrian, and Old Mercian Versions* . . ., ed. Walter W. Skeat (Cambridge, 1871–87).

4. J. C. Adelung, *Grammatisch-Kritisches Wörterbuch der Hochdeutschen Mundart* (Leipzig, 1796), s.v. *Ge*.

5. G. P. Krapp and A. G. Kennedy, *An Anglo-Saxon Reader* (New York, 1929), p. xci.

6. M. L. Samuels, "The *Ge-* Prefix in the Old English Gloss to the Lindisfarne Gospels," *Transactions of the Philological Society* (London, 1949), p. 66.

7. Else Hollmann, "Untersuchungen über Aspekt und Aktionsart unter besonderer Berücksichtigung des Altenglischen" (unpubl. diss., Jena, 1936), p. 102.

8. Heinrich Martens, "Die verba perfecta in der nibelungendichtung," *KZ*, XII (1863), 31–41, 321–35.

9. Wilhelm Streitberg, "Perfective und imperfective actionsart im Germanischen," *PBB*, XV (1891), 70–178.

10. *King Alfred's West-Saxon Version of Gregory's Pastoral Care*, ed. Henry Sweet, EETS (London, 1871), p. 45, 11. 12–15.

11. Streitberg, PBB, xv (1891), 91–3. ["As far as the 'intensive' meaning of *ga*- is concerned, it works badly: whenever one wishes to use this means of explanation, he falls into perplexity . . . How after all can a single particle have *at the same time* such various functions as the one in question combines in itself . . . ?"]

12. E. Bernhardt, "Die Partikel Ga als Hilfsmittel bei der Gotischen Conjugation," *ZfdP*, II (1870), 160–2.

13. Ant. Lorz, *Aktionsarten des Verbums im Beowulf* (diss., Würzburg, 1908), pp. 12–15.

14. See Bertil Weman, *Old English Semantic Analysis and Theory* (Lund, 1933), *passim*.

15. Wilhelm Wackernagel, *Altdeutsches Wörterbuch*, 5th ed. (Basel, 1878), s.v. *Ge* ["untranslatably and subtly intensifying."]

16. P. Lenz, *Der Syntactische Gebrauch der Partikel "ge" in den Werken Alfreds des Grossen* (diss., Darmstadt, 1886), p. 12.

17. B. Delbrück, *Vergleichende Syntax der Indogermanischen Sprachen*, Erster Theil (Strassburg, 1893), p. 365.

18. Jacob Grimm, *Deutsche Grammatik*, 2nd ed. as revised by Scherer (Berlin, 1878), p. 829.

19. Carl Dorfeld, *Uber die Function des Präfixes ge-* (*got. ga-*) *in der Composition mit Verben* (diss., Giessen, 1885), p. 45.

20. Rudolph Wustmann, *Verba Perfectiva Namentlich im Heliand* diss., Leipzig, 1894), pp. 18–23.

21. H. A. J. van Swaay, *Het prefix ga- gi- ge-, zijn ge schiedniss, en zijn invloed op de "actionsart," meer bijzonder in hed Oudnederfrankisch en het Oudsaksisch* (Utretcht, 1901), p. 44.

22. Lenz, *Der Syntactische Gebrauch*, p. 20.

23. Streitberg, *PBB*, xv (1891), 121–3.

24. Leonard Bloomfield, "Notes on the Preverb ge- in Alfredian English," in *Studies in English Philology: A Miscellany in Honor of Frederick Klaeber*, ed. Kemp Malone and Martin B. Ruud (Minneapolis, 1929), pp. 82, 83, 84, 87, 90, 93, 95, 97, 100, 101; F. Mossé, *Histoire de la Forme Périphrastique Être + Participe Présent en Germanique* (Paris, 1938), II, 9.

25. Samuels, "The Ge- Prefix," pp. 81–90. (But here, too, as in the rest of his paper, Samuels has the idea that the use of the prefix is determined by the "length of the Lat. verb.") See also Karl Dahm, *Der Gebrauch von gi- zur Unterscheidung perfectiver und imperfectiver Aktionsart im Tatian und in Notkers Boethius* (diss., Borna-Leipzig, 1909), pp. 18–30, and Hermann Hirt, *Handbuch des Urgermanischen* (Heidelberg, 1934), III, 126.

26. L. Tobler, "Über die bedeutung des deutschen ge- vor verben," *KZ*, XIV (1864), 124–33.

27. V. E. Mourek, reviewing a dissertation by Wustmann, in *AfdA*, XXI (1895), 195 ff.

28. O. Behaghel, *Deutsche Syntax* (Heidelberg, 1924), II, 112.

29. W. Streitberg, in *Urgermanische Grammatik* (Heidelberg, 1943), p. 280, warned against confusing perfective *Aktionsart* and the perfect tenses. Yet cf. Frank G. Banta, "Tense and Aspect in the Middle High German of Berthold von Regensburg," *JEGP*, LIX (1960), 81–3.

30. See Streitberg, *Urgermanische Gramm.*, pp. 276–81.

31. Martens, pp. 329–31.

32. Streitberg, PBB, XV (1891), 71. ["The *perfective Actionsart* adds to the innate meaning-content of the verb the subordinate idea of completed action. It thus indicates the action not merely as it goes on . . . but on the contrary always in regard to the moment of completion."]

33. See, for example, Karl Brunner, *Altenglische Grammatik nach der Angelsächsischen Grammatik von Eduard Sievers* (Halle/Saale, 1951), p. 308, n. I; Randolph Quirk and C. L. Wrenn, *An Old English Grammar* (New York, n. d. but preface dated 1957), pp. 79–80, 110–11; Fernand Mossé, *Manuel de L'Anglais du Moyen Âge*, I, Vieil Anglais (Paris, 1950), 148–50; G. L. Brook, *An Introduction to Old English* (Manchester, 1955), p. 62; Martin Lehnert, *Altenglisches Elementarbuch* (Berlin, 1959), p. 103; Henry Sweet, *Anglo-Saxon Primer*, 9th ed. (Oxford, 1957), p. 40.

34. Friedrich Weick, *Das Aussterben des Präfixes ge- im Englischen* (diss., Darmstadt, 1911).

35. Weick. ["The simplex should stand in the place of the mistakenly written compound." "The simplex should stand . . . ." "The compound should stand." "The simplex is sometimes put down, but strange to say always in an incorrect place."] See also pp. 11, 12, 15, 17, 19, 21, 22, 23, 25, 27, 29.

36. ["And further, the numerous examples where we have to write 'the simplex or the compound must stand' positively show us how very great the confusion already was in reference to the use of the simplex and the compound."]

37. ["no reason for *ge*" "*Ge* without reason" "Why *ge*?"]

38. H. Hesse, *Perfective und imperfective Aktionsart im Altenglischen* (diss., Münster, 1906).

39. ["The compound would however fit better." ". . . however . . . the compound . . . is to be given preference."]

40. Pollak, *PBB*, XLIV (1920), 380. ["The more promising semasiological investigations are those which let a prefix be considered as such, and do not proceed on the suspicion of a chosen *Aktionsart*."]

41. See especially the substantial objections expressed by the following: Carl Recha, *Zur Frage über den Ursprung der perfectivierenden Function der Verbalpräfixe* (diss., Dorpat, 1893), pp. 77–9; V. F. Mourek, *AfdA*, XXI (1895), 195 ff.; Antonin Beer, "Beiträge zur Gotischen Grammatik," *PBB*, XLIII (1918), 446–69; B. Trnka, "Some Remarks on the Perfective Aspects in Gothic," in *Donum Natalicium Schrijnen* (Nijmegen-Utrecht, n.d.), pp. 496–500.

42. A. Meillet, *Le Slav Commun* (Paris, 1924), pp. 240–4; Wenzel Vondrák, *Vergleichende Slavische Grammatik*, 2nd ed. (Göttingen, 1928), II, 373 ff.; E. Koschmieder, "Studien zum Slavischen Verbalapsekt," in *KZ*, LV (1928), 301.

43. Horst Renicke, "Die Theorie der Aspekte und Aktionsarten," *PBB*, LXXII (1950), 152–86.

44. E. Hermann, "Aspekt und Aktionsart," in *Nachrichten von der Gesellschaft der Wissenschaften zu Göttingen, Philologisch-Historische Klasse aus dem Jahre 1933* (Berlin, 1933), pp. 470–80; Josef Raith, *Untersuchungen zum englischen Aspekt: I. Teil, Grundsätzliches, Altenglisch* (München, 1951), pp. 21–32; Karl Ammer, *Einführung in die Sprachwissenschaft* (Halle, 1958), I, 167–9.

45. C. R. Goedsche, "Aspect versus Aktionsart," *JEGP*, XXXIX (1940), 196.

46. Pilch, *Anglia*, LXXI (1953), 131–33.

47. Philip Scherer, "Aspect in the Old English of the Corpus Christi MS," *Lg.*, XXXIV (1958), 251.

48. See Hirt, *Handbuch*, III, 130, and Behaghel, *Deutsche Syntax*, II, 95.

49. Van Swaay, *Het prefix ga- gi- ge-*, found nineteen *ge-* compounds in OS that were durative. His explanation of the durativity on the grounds that the meaning of a compound can undergo a shift ("*kan een verschuiving ondergaan*") is forced.

50. Alfred Wuth, *Aktionsarten der Verba bei Cynewulf* (diss., Weida i. Thür., 1915).

51. See Hirt, *Handbuch*, III, 130; Streitberg, *PBB*, XV (1891), 75, 120–4; Meillet, *Le Slav Commun*, pp. 242–4; Ammer, *Einführung*, pp. 167–9.

52. John R. Clark Hall, *A Concise Anglo-Saxon Dictionary*, 4th ed., with a supplement by Herbert D. Merritt (Cambridge, 1960), s.v. *habban*.

53. Ammer, p. 167. ["represented in the experienced time as an on-going process."]

54. Meillet, p. 242: "De même, le participe présent, qui indique d'ordinaire un procès simultané à un autre, ne se prête pas à l'aspect perfectif et il n'y a de participe présent que dans le verbe imperfectif." ["Likewise, the present participle, which ordinarily indicates a process simultaneous with another one, does not lend itself to the perfective aspect, and there is no present participle except in the imperfective verb."]

55. Hirt, *Handbuch*, III, 130; Hermann, "Aspekt und Aktionsart," p. 478.

56. ["It expresses the fact that an action has lasted up until a certain point. . . . It is accordingly with *op*, *oppæt* that one encounters this pattern."]

57. Grimm, *Grammatik*, II, 821.

58. Philip Scherer, "Aspect in Gothic," *Lg.*, XXX (1954), 223; "Aspect in the Old High German of Tatian," *Lg.*, XXXII (1956), 424, 434.

59. Behaghel, II, 96.

60. Lorz, p. 14. ["since it strictly set a fixed limit to its simplex."]

61. Behaghel, II, 97.

62. Wustmann, p. 20. ["Streitberg might of course separate a perfectivating and a localizing *ga-* by an unbridgeable chasm; but the history of the language demands their reconciliation."]

## W. P. LEHMANN

## Old English and Old Norse
## Secondary Preterits in -r-*

1. One of the fundamental changes from Proto-Indo-European to the Germanic dialects is that from a verbal system based on aspect to a system based on tense. By the time of our Germanic records the change was accomplished; aspect to be sure was still conveyed in the Germanic languages, but through morphological processes that were not consistently applied to all verbs, such as the *ga-* prefix. Tense, however, was a category marked in every verb. Moreover, unlike the PIE situation, where the imperfective (present) was sometimes marked to distinguish it from other aspects—a situation maintained in Gk. *títhēmi* "I place" beside the unmodified stem form of the aorist *éthēka* "I placed"—in Germanic only the preterit was marked, with rare exceptions like Go. *standan* beside *stōþ*, *bidjan* beside *baþ*. Accordingly the Gmc. verbal system differed from the IE system in the grammatical meaning which it characteristically expressed, and in its method of marking that meaning.

The Gmc. verb system distinguished two tenses: present and preterit. The PIE verb system had distinguished a variety of aspects: imperfective, perfective, and punctual, for which forms were made from most roots, plus other aspects that were more sporadic, such as the frequentative and the causative; these distinctions were marked by a great variety of affixes and by various types of internal change. But between Proto-Indo-European and Proto-Germanic the forms marking verbal categories, as well as the number of possible categories, were greatly reduced. Corresponding to the relatively large number of aspects in Proto-Indo-European were two PGmc. tenses; corresponding to the relatively large number of morphological processes marking aspects were three marking the preterit: one a strikingly consistent pattern of internal change, found in the so-called strong verbs (e.g., Go. *niman* : *nam*); another, reduplication, attested only Gothic (*háitan* : *haíháit*, in *saian* : *saísō*); the third, affixation, primarily of a dental suffix, found in the so-called weak verbs (Go. *nasjan*:*nasida*). Compared with the amorphous situation in Proto-Indo-European, the Gmc. verb system is neat and economical.

2. As we might expect from general linguistic observations, aberrant forms occur beside the strong and weak preterits; a widely attested OE

---

* From *Language* 30.202–10 (1954). Reprinted by permission of the author and the Linguistic Society of America.

preterit for the inf. *lætan* is *leort*; the preterit generally used for the ON inf. *sá* "sow" is *sera*. Historical linguists of the past so firmly accepted the conclusion that all Gmc. preterits are marked by one or more of the three predominant morphological processes, that they explained the aberrant forms as reflexes of older forms characterized by one of these processes. Since it was commonly assumed, until recently, that the NWGmc. 7th-class preterits were reduplicated forms somehow shortened,[1] forms like OE *leort* and OH *snera* were also explained as reduplicated, even though they contain other irregularities besides the unusual reduplication, and though no reduplicated forms are attested in North and West Germanic. In OE *leort* the root of *lætan* is considered to have been reduced to *-rt-*, and its unusual form accounted for by three statements: (1) the original root vowel was syncopated; (2) *-l-* of the stem was dissimilated to *-r-*; (3) the reduplicating vowel was diphthongized in the process known as breaking. ON *snera* is similarly explained as a reduplicated verb, modified from a hypothetical *\*se-sna* (which in turn developed from a still earlier *\*se-snow-a*) and shifted to the weak conjugation. We may wonder at the credibility of these complicated explanations, especially in the face of such clear forms as Go. *laí-lót*. I shall review briefly the list of the irregular forms in Old English and Old Norse, and explore the possibility of another origin.

3.1. The OE forms which are said to be survivals of reduplicated preterits are *heht* from *hātan* "command," *leolc* from *lācan* "leap," *leort* from *lætan* "let," *reord* from *rædan* "advise," and *ondreord* from *ondrædan* "fear." Further information on these, such as different spellings, may be found in Sievers-Brunner, *Altenglische Grammatik*[2] 336 (Halle, 1951). There too are listed other forms which some scholars have regarded as reduplicated preterits: *speoft* "spit" and *beoftun* "beat." I follow Sievers in deriving *speoft* from *\*speoftian* rather than from *spātan* "spit," for beside it there is an attested pret. ptc. *gespeoftad*; the pl. *beoftun*, rather than *beotun*, is probably a scribal error, as is the corrected *blefla*. The preterits of the five verbs listed above, on the other hand, are adequately attested. Assuming further that *ondrædan* is a compound of *rædan*, we are left with four simple verbs.

All these irregular preterit forms occur in Anglian, or in poetic texts. It is agreed that the *-eo-* vowels are reflexes of earlier *-e-*; *-e-* became *-eo-* in *leort* and *reord* by breaking; the *-eo-* of *leolc* has been ascribed to velar umlaut, but this also will be attributed to breaking (below, § 5.6). For all the OE verb forms which are supposedly reduplicated we find a general structure: CeCC, usually CerC.

3.2. The ON forms which are said to be survivals of reduplicated preterits are *bnere* from *\*bnúa* "rub," *gnera* from *gnúa* "rub," *grera* from *gróa* "grow," *rera* from *róa* "row," *sera* from *sá* "sow," *slera* from *slá* "strike," and *snera* from *snúa* "turn." For further information see A. Noreen, *Altisländische Grammatik*[4] 340–1 (Halle, 1923), and A. M. Sturtevant, *SS* 23.64–5 (1951).

The latter discusses the many difficulties created by the phonology of *gnera*, *grera*, and *snera* for those scholars who attempt to derive them from reduplicated preterits. We have no grounds for assuming a reduplication *gne-*, *gre-*, *sne-* in Germanic; and even if we do, we still have to account for the reduction of the stem to *-r-*. *Snera* presumably derives from *snúa* according to the pattern found in Go. reduplicated verbs, i.e. from *\*se-sna* or, if we wish to assume weak endings at this stage, from *\*se-snō-se-znō*, and *grera* from *\*ge-gra* (*\*ge-grō*). Just how a form like *\*se-sna* could have developed to *snera* is a difficult problem; Sturtevant assumes a metathasis of the *-n-*, after which the change of *-s-* to *-z-* to *-r-* would be credible. Yet there is little reason to assume such complex phonological changes in Old Norse, other than the supposed necessity of deriving these forms from reduplicated verbs.

The forms in question occur throughout the ON texts. Later modifications listed by Noreen, such as the forms with rounded vowels (*røra* beside *rera* etc.) are regular in Old Norse; *-e-* became *-ø-* by *u*-umlaut in the plural forms, and presumably was sometimes extended to the singular. Moreover, the *-e-* following the initial consonant is readily accounted for; it would not have been diphthongized (broken) after the *r* of *rera* and *grera*, nor in the other verbs in the 2d sg. For the ON verbs we find, then, a structure Cer-, in which C may be a cluster.

3.3. Common to all of these forms but OE *heht* and *leolc* is the element *-r-*. Furthermore, these verbs are inflected in Old Norse with weak endings *-a*, *-eR*, *-e*, rather than the strong *–*, *-t*, *–*.[2] It may be, then, that these OE and ON verbs are secondary (weak) preterits with a suffix *-r-* rather than *-d/t/þ-*. To substantiate this hypothesis we must establish the likelihood of such a weak conjugation, and suggest a plausible source for the characteristic element *-r-*.

4. It is now pretty generally accepted that the IE verb system distinguished aspect, not tense; see Meillet, *Introduction*[8] 196–7, and even such a conservative Indo-Europeanist as Hirt, *IG* 4.165. The form markers too are well explored, though no one theory of their origin is generally accepted. In the early period of IE studies, many scholars favored the views that these had developed from full words, such as auxiliary verb forms or pronouns. The preference for this type of explanation probably resulted from a lack of acquaintance with developments in other languages and from initial observations made in the Romance group, the laboratory for historical linguistic methodology. Because some Romance inflectional categories, e.g., the French future, had developed from periphrastic formations, it was assumed that this was the general method of forming new inflections. Bopp, *Über das Konjugationssystem der Sanskritsprache* (Frankfurt, 1816), found a source for many of the IE inflectional categories in periphrases of various sorts; the *s*-aorist, for example, he derived from the root *es* "to be" (18 f.), and the verbal endings from pronouns (147–51). This theory of derivation has been remarkably tenacious; Hirt still favors Bopp's suggestion for the origin of the *s*-aorist, *IG* 4.253.

It was only later that linguists came to assume that no one methodology was applicable to all languages, that one could not safely infer from one language what the course of development would be in another, that the phenomena of every language must be explained in terms of its own structure. In seeking to explain any new formation, the various substructures must be taken into account—of pertinent phonemes, of pertinent forms, of pertinent semantic relations. It no longer seems adequate to suggest, like Bopp, that the *s*-aorist was constructed by means of the verb *es-* without concerning oneself with the morphological possibilities of the language at the time of the assumed construction. We would hardly expect, say, new morphological categories of inflection arising in English to employ prefixation; for we accept the general principle that linguistic changes are limited by the structure of a language, and prefixation is not used as an inflectional marker in English.

We assume further that limitations on linguistic change continue as the structure is modified. Since modifications of structure are gradual and circumscribed in scope, it has seemed attractive to some linguists to speak of currents of linguistic development. The locus classicus is possibly Sapir's discussion in his book *Language* 157–82 (New York, 1921). Sapir introduced for such currents the term DRIFT; but in this book, which was designed for the general public as well as for linguistic students, he often uses metaphors. Others have unfortunately hypostasized drift: to a drift which has been inferred from observing one pattern of changes, further changes may be ascribed; the drift observed becomes an agent in a social convention. Prokosch supports his procedure by reference to Sapir when he states, *CGG* 34, that virtually all of the Germanic changes "follow the same 'drift'." The Germanic drift "came to a standstill," and exhibited other personal characteristics, *CGG* 34; "it exerts a stabilizing, or a modifying influence," *CGG* 36. An extreme instance of the hypostasis of drift is the so-called détresse phonologique, which according to some linguists inaugurates linguistic changes. Thus H. Lausberg, Détresse phonologique und Mehrlautphoneme, *Archiv* 187.66–70 (1950), ascribes to this factor "Notwehrmassnahmen der bedrohten Systeme." Such a view of patterns of change we reject utterly, for we view language as an element of human culture, not as a separate being or force. Yet we know that in every language there is a repertory of allophones, phonemes, morphemes, grammatical processes, and so on, and that the speakers of a language are limited to the items available in that repertory. In attempting to provide an explanation for some linguistic change, it would be unrealistic to offer one, however plausible it might be in a different language, for which there is no evidence in the language under investigation.

Oddly enough, Franz Bopp and the other early nineteenth-century linguists seem to have followed this principle, though their views on the historical setting of Proto-Indo-European, and consequently their explanations, are quite different from ours. They viewed language as a recent product of man, which had undergone remarkably great structural changes in a relatively short time: in its early stages language consisted of essentially one word per idea; a more highly developed stage combined words into complex, inflected forms; in the primitive period of Indo-European, forms like Skt. *vásmi* "I desire" had consisted of individual words—the etyma of *vás* "desire" and *mi* "I." Inflections accordingly developed from agglutinated words; composition theories harmonized well with this view of Indo-European and of man's use of language.

Today the view that Proto-Indo-European was a primitive language is virtually abandoned, along with the view that in reconstructing earlier stages of Pre-Indo-European we can work back to the infant stages of homo loquens. Yet the old notion that IE forms developed from separate words is still widely held, and is even the most prominent view set forth in our standard handbooks. Hirt, to be sure, has rejected Bopp's suggestion that the IE verbal endings are derived from personal pronouns, *IG* 4.148; but for the origin of the *s*-aorist he still finds composition with the root *es* as the most attractive theory, *IG* 4.253, on the ground that this solution corresponds to the situation that we so often find in later times. Other scholars still favor a composition theory for the origin of the IE secondary verb forms, notably the preterits.

In the nineteenth century the view was held that the secondary tenses of the IE dialects developed from compounds, of which the first element was a nominal form of some sort, the second an auxiliary. By such theories Go. *habaida*, for example, is compounded of a noun element *habai-* and a verb element *-da*; for a brief review of the various theories and references to theories on similar formations in other dialects see *Lg.* 19.19–23 (1941). Inability to identify either element gradually disturbed the credibility of such theories. Recently Paul Kretschmer has suggested an origin in periphrasis, *Objektive konjugation im Indogermanischen* (Öster. Akad. d. Wiss. Phil.-hist. Kl. Sb. 225, 2. Abh., 1947). Kretschmer seeks to explain the characteristic formant of various secondary preterits—among them the *s*-aorist, the Gmc. weak preterit, the Lat. *v*-perfect, the Gk. *k*-aorist and perfect—from incorporated pronouns: the pronominal element was added to the verb as an affixed object. As support for his theory Kretschmer adduces similar tenses in Finno-Ugric, Caucasian, Basque, and other languages. Yet the presence of such formations in a thousand languages would not be evidence for Indo-European. From the linguistic work of the past century it is clear that one could support almost any theory with individual or capricious comparisons between languages, and that such comparisons accordingly are valueless without a further check. This check we obtain from the structure of the language in question. In the IE period, for example, we expect to find ready use of possessive compounds, but relatively few adjectival compounds; in the Gmc. languages of about 1200 the situation is reversed. The compounds that we find in Finno-Ugric, Caucasian, and Basque tell us nothing about the IE situation.

Unfortunately Kretschmer's suggestion was favorably reviewed by Lane, *Lg.* 27.370–2 (1951), on the ground that Kretschmer at least provides a "uniform solution" for the origin of the diverse secondary formations in the IE dialects. But a uniform theory was proposed long ago, among others by Persson, *Beiträge* 558–9—a theory which Lane oddly labels "piecemeal partial analyses." Persson's "uniform solution" is suffixation; the formants of the secondary conjugations were suffixes which came to be restricted to a specific form category. From comparison of the various IE dialects we can posit many suffixes in Proto-Indo-European and Pre-Indo-European. In some of them a characteristic meaning became predominant, and the suffix spread throughout a set of verbal or nominal forms; the diversity of suffixes no more impairs the uniformity of Persson's suggestion than does the diversity of Kretschmer's pronominal elements. To support Persson's view, we must examine the productive types of verb formation in the late IE period, note whether we can establish examples of tense formants spreading from suffixes, and decide whether this type of spread is reasonable in the structure of Indo-European and of the early dialects.

In the early period of the IE dialects there were two productive means of distinguishing inflectional categories: internal change and suffixation. The use of both processes extended to various periods in the dialects, in those of the Gmc. group at least as late as 1200 A.D., so that we may find in them relatively late examples to clarify the early dialect situation. Compound tenses, such as *I am going, I have gone*, can be established only for the last part of this period, e.g., for Classical Sanskrit, for Latin, for the dialects after Proto-Germanic. Some means, on the other hand, were no longer productive in late Proto-Indo-European, e.g., the development of diverse endings such as *-mi, -m, -ō, -xe*, which earlier had distinguished different types of 1st singular. About the origin of the internal change there is no dispute: it was ablaut. At the time of their origin, the ablaut changes were purely phonological; only later did they come to be used to distinguish morphological categories, such as the tenses in Germanic and certain types of derivatives in Sanskrit. In this respect their history is similar to that of the umlaut vowels in German, which originally developed in particular phonetic environments, but which acquired a morphological function only after the phonological shift was completed. The umlaut vowels were associated with noun plurals, as in Ger. *Gast: Gäste*, and a similar contrast was later introduced in other nouns, such as *Acker* and *Arzt*, in which umlaut never took place. In the same way, the ablaut changes came to be so closely associated with morphological categories that they could be extended to verbs in which they had never occurred, as to OHG *scrīban*, borrowed from Lat. *scrībere*; others are probably 2nd-class verbs like Go. *lūkan, sūgan.*

A similar development may be assumed for the suffixed tense characteristics. These came to be phonologically distinctive, and were then adapted to morphological purposes in distinct inflectional categories. Again we may cite an example from Germanic. By the time of Old High German, the IE *s*-stem nouns with long root syllable had lost the final suffix in the nom.-acc. sg., but not in the nom.-acc. pl. (OHG nom.-acc. sg. *kalb*, pl. *kelbir*); the loss was purely phonological, and is ascribed to the Gmc. "laws of finals." The sg.–pl. contrast was marked in most OHG nouns by some type of suffix. Since -*ir*, by a phonological accident, was one of these suffixes, it came to be used as a plural suffix, and was then extended to many words which had not previously had an *s*-suffix, e.g., Mod. Germ. *Haupt* (cf. Lat. *caput*), *Nest* (cf. Lat. *nīdus*); for many others see H. Paul, *Deutsche Grammatik* 2.23–33. A "meaningless" suffix thus developed into a grammatical marker.

I assume a similar origin for the IE secondary verb markers. But since our records date only from the time in which such secondary forms are full-blown, I cannot prove this theory for most of the secondary conjugations. Possibly the formation whose origin is clearest is the Armenian -*c̣*-aorist, in which Kretschmer did not even try to find a pronoun. Meillet derives this from the IE *sk*-suffix; in Armenian the suffix came to be used after verbal themes ending in vowels to mark the aorist; see *Esquisse d'une grammaire comparée de l'Arménien classique* 85–6 (Vienna, 1903). In other dialects the suffix had a different meaning, or, as in Germanic, none whatever. The origin of the markers in the secondary preterits of other languages cannot be so precisely identified, but more and more scholars seem inclined to assume the spread of a suffixal element. Meyer makes such an assumption for the Latin perfect; Must and Fourquet explain the Gmc. dental preterit formant as a distinctive consonantal element that later spread.[3] Though the source suggested for this element may be unconvincing, as in Must's theory, it is worth noting that many linguists now favor this type of explanation.

Of the two productive methods of tense formation in the early IE dialects, this one was the more widespread; it probably existed in greater variety than the surviving records show. A broad survey of the dialects indicates that in Germanic a *d*-formant was the only preterit marker, in Latin a *v*-formant, and so on. But other elements may have been used as well, which were gradually eliminated; in Germanic these may have had less connection with the normal dental formant than the *s* of Go. *wissa*, the *þ* of Go. *kunþa*, or the *t* of Go. *gamostedum*.

I suggest, now, that among these diverse elements was the one that appears in the *r*-preterits of Old English and Old Norse.[4] In early Proto-Germanic, the inherited means of distinguishing the tenses, namely the difference in endings, was inadequate; and ablaut variations were confined to a relatively few verbs. On the other hand, the opposition of present vs. preterit was of great significance—as great as that of singular vs. plural was to be later in Old High German. Some means was needed to mark the tense distinction; in the verbs listed above in this paper, the means chosen was a suffix *r*. It will be of interest to determine its origin.

5.1. The OE and ON *r*-preterits are found chiefly in verbs whose roots originally ended in laryngeals or had laryngeal extensions.[5] This statement follows from Prokosch's analysis of the Gmc. 6th and 7th classes as laryngeal bases; cf. *CGG* 151, *PIEP* 69–70. We can further support it by citing, for all except the first two of these verbs (those from which the formation spread), parallel forms from other dialects which give evidence of IE laryngeals.

5.2. For OE *hātan* we have no certain extra-Gmc. cognates. WP 1.362 tentatively suggest derivation from IE *keXy-* "set in motion," as in Lat. *cieō*, *ciere*; Feist hesitates to accept this etymology.

OE *lācan* is cognate with Go. *laikan*. These are related by Fiest, *GEW* 319, 583, and WP 2.399–400, to Skt. *rejati* "makes to hop," Gk. *elelízō* "swing." None of these cognates gives evidence of laryngeal. For *lācan*, alone of the OE and ON verbs with *r*-preterits, there are no attestable forms supporting Prokosch's analysis.

OE *lǣtan* is related by WP 2.394–5 to Lith. *léidžiu* "let," Gk. *ledeĩn* "be tired," and Lat. *lētum* "destruction." The root accordingly is *leꜣ-*, which may have had a *-y-* determinative, as well as forms extended further by *-d-*; cf. PIEP 70. The expected preterit is from *leꜣyd-*.

OE *rǣdan* "advise" (*ondrǣdan* "fear") are related by Feist, *GEW* 199, and WP 1.69–76, to Skt. *rādhyati*, Lat. *rērī*. The latter is a reflex of the root with *-eꜣ-* suffix; Skt. *rādh-* and OE *rǣd-* reflect the suffixed root with *dh*-determinative, *reꜣdh-*.

5.3. In Old Norse the *r*-formation became productive. Thus, *slá* is a regular 6th-class verb with the forms *slá sló slógom sleginn*; but in the infinitive it lost its final *h*, and the resultant form *slá* came to pattern like *sá sera*. A preterit *slera* was made from it, to take its place beside the regular form *sló*. If *slera* is analogical, other *r* forms may be also. Noreen, *Altisl. Gram.* 340, considers *grera* analogical after *rera* and *gnera*, and the hapax legomenon *bnere* presumably analogical after *snera*. Heusler, *Aisl. Elementarbuch* 92, assumes that even *snera* is analogical. On the other hand, Sturtevant, *SS* 23.64–5, suggests that the attested shapes of *snera* and *gnera*, though analogical, were modified from earlier reduplicated forms. Whatever our views, we can scarcely assume that more of these *r* forms than *grera*, *rera*, *sera*, and *snera* belong to the original *r* inflection. For these we can suggest evidence of laryngeal in the root.

*Grera*, preterit of *gróa* "bud," is derived by WP 1.645–6 from the *ghrō-* which is evidenced in Lat. *grāmen* "grass." Whether or not we identify the unextended root with IE *gher-* (WP. 1606), we may assume a root for *gróa*, *gher-* with a suffix *-eX-*.

*Rera*, preterit of *róa* "row," is derived by WP 1.143–4 from the root found in Skt. *ari-tra*, Lat. *rē-mus* "oar"; these forms, like Lith. *ìrti* "row," point to a laryngeal extension. We may assume the PIE root *ꜣer-*, from which *róa* is made with the suffix *-eꜣ-*.

*Sera*, preterit of *sá* "sow," is derived by WP 2.459–63 from the root found in Lith. *séju*, *séti* "sow," Lat. *sēmen* "seed." However one may analyze the complexities of Go. *saian*, *sá* must be derived from PIE *seꜣ-*.

*Snera*, from *snúa* "turn," is less readily related to extra-Gmc. cognates. Feist sees no difficulty in connecting it with OCS *o-snovǫ* "found," but further relationships are uncertain. Feist suggests among other cognates those with which WP 2.694–5 tentatively associate it: Skt. *snāyati* "winds about," *snāvan-* "cord, sinew." For these we assume PIE *sn-eX-*, with possible further extension, or (if we admit relationship with Lat. *nēre* "spin") more precisely *sn-e³-*. *Snúa* seems to be derived from *\*snowan*, cf. OD *snēowan*; *snera* can be derived from the root unextended by *-w-*, i.e., *sne³-*.

5.4. Two of the OE *r*-preterits and four of the ON *r*-preterits are thus analyzed as indicating the presence of a laryngeal in the stem. From Prokosch's theory of the Gmc. verb, we would expect this structure; further, we would expect that the preterits of these verbs are constructed from the *e*-grade. Accordingly we assume for the OE preterits a structure similar to that of *rǣdan*, CeXC-, and for the ON preterits a structure similar to that of *róa*, CeX-. In the attested OE and ON preterits we find the patterns CerC- and Cer-. Assuming that the phonological development of *-X-* to *-r-* is plausible, we can ascribe to this origin the *-r-* which in a few verbs came to characterize a "secondary" preterit formation. In Old Norse the type spread further, but was eventually lost in favor of the dental preterit and the ablaut verbs.

5.5. The development of some PIE *-X-* to Gmc. *-r-* has been suggested in *PIEP* 58–61. It was also proposed there, 70–1, that the NWGmc. preterit stems of verbs like *lǣtan* developed from a contrast of the following type:

$$leXd- > lēd-\quad > lǣt- > lǣt-$$
$$leXyd > leXyd- > lēyt- > lē^2t-$$

We assume that the contrast present vs. preterit was marked by the difference in vocalism, as in *lēd-*: *leXyd-*. Normally this developed further to a contrast between *ǣ* and *ē*; but in some forms the laryngeal may have survived and fallen together with the *r*-phoneme, giving rise to *\*lert*, whence *leort*.

A similar contrast existed between the present and preterit of *sá* "sow." As in *láta*, OE *lǣtan*, a low front vowel was generalized in the present; since *sá*, like *láta*, is a 7th-class verb, we can assume that it had preterit forms similar to those of *lǣtan*—that is, forms with a laryngeal. Most of these were lost; in the WGmc. dialects, regular weak preterits were generalized. In Old Norse, however, *-r-* was used as preterit marker, and the weak endings were added after it.

5.6. If we make the assumption that *r* was the characteristic marker for the cited OE and ON verbs, we are left with two aberrant forms to explain, *leolc* and *heht*. The vocalism of *leolc* has long been difficult; since it is an Anglian form, it should have retained *-e-* before *-lc*, cf. Angl. *melcan*: WS *meolcan*. The aberrant *-eo-* has been explained by analogy with *reord*; see Karstien 149 for this suggestion, and for the difficulties in such an explanation. On the other hand, if *leolc* developed by assimilation from *\*leorc* < *\*lerc*, the vocalism is no longer troublesome; *e* > *eo* before *rC* here as in *leort*. It is as plausible to suggest that *-r-* became *-l-* by assimilation as to posit the opposite change; and the suggestion has the advantage of making the vocalism regular.

The -*h*- of *heht, hehtes,* etc. must be a result of analogy with the relatively numerous verbs of the pattern *weccean wehte* "wake," especially with the semantically similar *reccean* "tell": except for the 1st and 3rd sg., these forms would have rimed.

6. I have now suggested an origin for the preterit marker of the OE and ON *r* verbs; but I do not consider my statements on the source of the *r* the essential part of this study. Primarily I have been concerned to show that the *r* should not be attributed to reduplication, but rather to the type of secondary conjugation which became productive in the early IE dialects. As for the *r* itself, a more plausible origin may be suggested elsewhere. The discussion above is an effort to lay the starred reduplicated preterits that still stalk through our handbooks in treatments of the North and West Germanic strong preterit.

The data which have come down to us make it probable that reduplication was confined to East Germanic. No reduplicated forms are attested in any of the other Gmc. dialects, except the supposed reflexes discussed in this paper. Even in Gothic some preterits and the preterit-presents lack reduplication. It is possible that in the interval between Proto-Indo-European and Gothic a number of reduplicated forms were maintained, in verbs like *áukan* "increase." The type may then have been extended in Gothic because the phonological development of that language precluded a distinction between present and preterit based on the contrast of $\bar{e}^1$ vs. $\bar{e}^2$, which was so widespread in the other dialects. We can no longer assume that Gothic, with all its innovations, preserves the most archaic features of Germanic, nor that the tremendous changes from the IE to the Gmc. verb system took place in accordance with regular patterns. Numerous devices must have been in use to distinguish formal categories, and many of these must have been lost as other formations became more and more distinctive.

## FOOTNOTES

1. Of the many works on verbs of the 7th class, the following give good descriptions of the forms attested and bibliographical information: S. Feist, De sogennanten reduplicierenden Verba im Germanischen, *PBB* 32.447–516 (1907); C. Karstien, Die reduplizierten Perfekta des Nord- und Westgermanischen, *Giessener Beiträge zur deutschen Philologie* 1 (Giessen, 1921); E. Prokosch, *A comparative Germanic grammar* 176–82 (Philadelphia, 1939; abbr. *CGG*). See also Donald A. McKenzie's pertinent addition to the last in *JEGP* 39.261–3 (1940). Also useful, especially for bibliography, is J. Janko, Über germanisch *e²* und die sog. reduplizierenden Praeterita, *IF* 20.229–316 (1906–7).

2. The OE forms on the other hand have strong endings. In Old English the *r*-preterits were preserved in only one dialect, and even here in only a few verbs. Weak endings may have existed formerly in these verbs; since the *r* verbs were unproductive, strong endings may have been introduced by analogy with other 7th-class verbs. [The symbol *R* in ON -*eR* stands for a prehistoric (Runic) palatal fricative, usually derived from Gmc /z/.—Ed.]

3. Karl H. Meyer, Das lateinische Perfektum auf -*vi*, -*ui* und die slavischen Verba auf -*vati*, IF 61.29–39 (1952); Gustav Must, The origin of the Germanic dental preterit, *Lg.* 27.121–35 (1951); id., Again the origin of the Germanic dental preterit, *Lg.* 28.104–6 (1952); J. Fourquet, Anglo-Saxon *éode*, *dyde*, et la théorie du prétérit faible, *Studia neophilologica* 14.420–6 (1941–42).

4. See W. P. Lehmann, *Proto-Indo-European Phonology* 56–61 (Austin, 1952; abbr. *PIEP*) for a similar treatment of OHG *r*-preterits.

5. [Laryngeals are a class of consonants posited for PIE on the basis of Hittite forms and other evidence. There are generally assumed to have been three, symbolized *A*, ?, *X*. For bibliography and discussion see Lehmann, *PIEP* 22–35.—Ed.]

## ROBERT D. STEVICK

# The Morphemic Evolution
# of Middle English She*

To seek again for solution to the perennial puzzle of the origin of English *she*, it will be well to begin with the most certain fact in the historical context: the nominative feminine third person (singular) pronoun first appeared with a new initial consonant in the Northeast Midlands and adjacent areas, with the clearest evidence from Lincolnshire and Yorkshire. It is also certain that the pronoun did not undergo similar consonantal reshaping in other major dialect areas, and the presence of *she, sho* (and other forms) in other dialects—including the Standard dialect as it developed—is attributable to dialect borrowing. We have to do with a local development. Evidence is sufficient to indicate as well that the *she* or *sho* form was neither a reshaping of the feminine singular nominative demonstrative nor a hybrid development of the demonstrative and personal pronouns. The a priori improbability of either process is sustained especially by the continuous record of *The Peterborough Chronicle*: the *seo* form was obsolete before *scæ*, (Orm) *ʒho* and other forms occurred. Rather, the new [ʃ-] forms developed by modification of the personal pronoun form of prior stages of English. This is the position taken by most investigators since Flom's article in 1908.[1]

So far explanation of the change by which *she, sho* replaced *heo, hie* has been sought solely within the storehouse of phonological facts and processes: development of [ʃ-] forms replacing earlier [h-] forms has been accounted for by reconstructing a credible phonological sequence. Because this particular change in the pronoun occurred in an area known to have had heavy Scandinavian settlement from the latter part of the ninth century (with prominent lexical influence on English in that area), and because no other circumstance —including normal sound change of English—has been found to connect the change to, the change is attributed to influence of Scandinavian pronunciation of English. Where English had falling diphthongs, it is pointed out, Old Norse had rising diphthongs. Assuming a stress shift *héo > heó, hío > hió*, or in some instances *híe > hié*, it can be argued—with support from place-names and a few other localisms—that [hɛ́-], [hɪ́-] > [hj-] > [ç-], which was interpreted then as [ʃ-]. This "Shetland" theory implies that Scandinavians heard English *héo* as *hjó*, and the English heard Scandinavian *hjó* as [ço:], and pronounced it as [ʃo:]. But the advocate's resolution is

* From *English Studies* 45.381–8 (1964). Reprinted by permission of the author and publisher.

required to keep the argument intact, because the initial assumption about shifting of stress in diphthongs is not free from doubt.[2] Gordon,[3] for instance, places stress shift of diphthongs in Icelandic at "c. 850–1000, though in some instances considerably later. The shift took place earliest in diphthongs at the beginning of a word." (§ 48) Also, "There was not much blending of Norse and English"—within the Scandinavian-settled areas of England—"during the OE period," (§ 230) when Danish settlements were made in the East Midlands (ninth century) and Norwegian settlements followed in Yorkshire and the northwestern counties (first half of the tenth century). (§ 228) Norse phonology changed little in England, and "it is clear that the following [change] had not taken place: . . . Except initially, the stress had not been shifted in diphthongs," though *York* = OI. *Jork*, etc. (§ 220). To this uncertainty in the dialect and chronology of Scandinavian language features in England we may add the following. The phonologically credible sequence [h-´] > [hj´] > [ç´], [ʃ´] implies an unusually complex social-linguistic sequence: The English said [h--]; their Scandinavian conquerors-turned-neighbors, always keeping þ- forms for plural third-person pronouns, at some time began to give up their *h-n* feminine and masculine pronouns and used English forms; the English heard their own stress-shifted pronouns, but kept on for a while using their own pronunciation—long enough for Scandinavians to use English singular pronouns regularly; then, giving up their own pronunciation of the feminine singular nominative form, the English anglicized the Scandinavian pronunciation of their own form. This complicated sequence, though not inconceivable, is not readily credible. Throughout the period in which the two languages were in contact, English continued intact: the English dialects were never creolized. More particularly, the change took place in a word of high frequency of occurrence. That a few place-names and a few other nouns show Scandinavian [hj-] becoming English [ʃ-] is fully conceivable and probable, and there is evidence to show that change of this kind did in fact occur. But the difference between a normal one-step process, beginning with Scandinavian forms and limited to names, and the multi-step process, beginning with an English form—a pronoun—and involving only the one (nominative) form of high frequency, is so great that the parallel of phonetic change in place-names does not qualify as full warrant to postulate the same causal factor (or perhaps the same phonological sequence) for the change in the pronoun.

The reconstructed phonological sequence to account for replacement of *heo* by *she, sho, ʒho*, etc. thus remains unsatisfactory because of uncertainty of concatenating evidence. One other significant attempt to reconstruct phonological circumstances to account for development of *she* also assumes stress-shifted *hjó, hjé*, and posits sandhi occurrences of a preceding dental or alveolar.[4] Besides sharing the questionable assumption of Scandinavian-influenced stress-shift in the diphthong, the theory requires acceptance of a change occurring through a low frequency circumstance. There is no evidence, however, to suggest that the pronoun ever ceased to occur commonly after juncture or, when it occurred without preceding juncture, regularly followed dentals and alveolars. To be satisfying, an historical account of language change must offer both a sequence of linguistic circumstances and data that is credible, and evidence confirming the actual existence of those language facts and their historical relations. If that evidence can not be found either in attested patterns of phonological change within English or in potential (direct) foreign influences, perhaps it can be found in an area not yet explored for this purpose—in some structural features of those stages of English in which *she* evolved.

Besides occurring with high frequency, the feminine nominative personal pronoun was part of a closed morphological system, not an isolated lexical item like a place-name. The closed personal pronoun system was marked by prominent inflectional regularity—as it still is in modified form[5]—in the paradigmatic prefixes consisting of initial consonants: /h-/ carried the meaning "third-person singular" (and, perhaps, "third-person plural"), just as /m-/ and /θ-/ meant "first-person singular" and "second-person singular" respectively. From one point of view, then, we must regard replacement of *heo* by *she*, *sho*, etc. as quite remarkable: substitution of /š-/ for /h-/ disturbed the entire pattern of personal pronoun inflections. Feminine pronouns in case forms other than nominative did not change in this respect, retaining the third-person /h-/ inflection. Both frequency and paradigmatic factors demand therefore an historical account of this unusual change that observes the strictest conditions of unobtrusiveness for innovation.

The various spellings for the pronoun clearly indicate that prior to the [ʃ-] status of the initial consonant there was a [ç-] stage.[6] The reason commonly offered for the change, that [ç-] came to be heard as [ʃ-], is probably only partly right. At any rate, the phonological circumstances can be restated precisely in phonemic terms and must be so stated if the explanation of *heo* > *she*, *sho*, etc. is to be improved. The pronoun had an *h*-element as its inflectional prefix, and initial inflection was never in process of "decay." The allophones of /h/ could vary in position over a wide range, because there were no other phonemes both acoustically and distributionally similar: the clustering characteristics of /h/ and the spirants /f θ s/ were similar in word-initial position, for example, but /h/ did not occur in postvocalic position; /x/, with allophones having some phonetic resemblance to some /h/ allophones, occurred only in postvocalic position. Thus, under conditioning by the following vowel (or consonant), /h/ occurred as voiceless spirant articulated as glottal, velar, or palatal. (It could even overlap acoustically with palatal allophones of /x/ and remain distinct because of their different distributional features.) In short, [ç-] would not be perceived as an aberration in the /h-/ structure of third-person pronouns.

That the same conditions may have existed in other dialects without producing the same ultimate result of /š-/ is not relevant, since orthogenetic progress in language is not a concept that can be sustained by language history. But the circumstances of unique shift in the initial consonant phoneme of the pronoun suggests that still other characteristics of the speech areas of its occurrence should be examined. The consonant system in Yorkshire, Lincolnshire, and adjacent areas seems to have been much the same as in other dialect areas prior to the change in the feminine pronoun from *h--* to *sh-*. Yet, if Scandinavian speech did not materially influence the number and phonetic manifestation of individual consonants, or the formal structure of English,[7] it did contribute many lexical items to English. The clearest types are those having *sk-*, because the divergence of OE and ON is complete in this respect—OE having regularly developed *sh-* /š-/. A large number of Scandinavian words entered English between 1050 and 1150,[8] with a sufficient number beginning in *sk-* to establish, within the areas of heavy Scandinavian settlement, a type of initial consonant cluster that had disappeared when OE /sk-/ merged to produce the new /š/. Assimilation into English of the initial cluster /sk-/, through adoption of many words which were common and cognate with English words, caused significant reorganization of distributional features of spirant and palatal phonemes. Earlier /spr- str- skr-/ had developed into /spr- str-      / and /šr-/, without any change in distribution of /šr-/; likewise, earlier /sp- st- sk-/ had had its third member replaced by /š-/, which also did not change in distribution. Meanwhile the clustering patterns of other consonants did not change in general outline—Orm, for example, showing loss only of infrequent /fn- hn- gn-/ of OE and addition of only /šr-/. When, however, lexical borrowings from Scandinavian established /skr-/ and /sk-/ in English, these clusters patterned with the other three- and two-member initial clusters, with the result that /š-/ patterned with single consonants in prevocalic position—with /f θ s/—or with spirant + *r* clusters already established in the language. Postjunctural prevocalic /š/ began to be distributionally a spirant. The change in the assignment of [ç-] from /h/ to /š/ in the feminine nominative pronoun could thus occur less obtrusively than in other dialect areas or at earlier times.

This restatement of the phonological circumstances within which *heo* > *she, sho* makes it plausible to regard the replacement of the initial consonant as change by allophone rather than, say, change by borrowing or analogy. It also connects the fact that the feminine nominative pronominal [ç-] was reassigned to /š/ rather than continuing as an allophone of /h/ to regional dialect facts of date, phonology, and distinct foreign influence. It shows why the change should have occurred when and where it did. But it in no way explains why it did in fact occur.

The cause of the change may be sought in morphological aspects of the dialects of LOE and EME. The paradigmatic frame of pronouns, though it was in process of modification for case distinctions (merger of accusative with dative forms), persisted without change of gender distinctions, as well as person and number distinctions. Gender distinctions had always been functional in English as indicating either the sex of the referent or the non-significance of sex-distinction of the referent; choice of personal pronoun form was referentially determined—i.e., it was based regularly on circumstances of the physical context; by contrast, choice of members of the *se, seo, þæt* paradigm, with parallel gender forms, had been only grammatically determined. Number and person distinctions also had functional relations with the context of utterances as well as with the patterns of the utterances themselves. It is the persistence of this paradigmatic frame—the structural pattern of distinctions among personal pronoun forms—that seems to have been the ultimate cause of the evolution of Middle English *she, sho.*

It was not, however, the inconvenience or confusion of homophony of some of the feminine singular and the plural forms that led to modification of the feminine nominative pronoun, as has sometimes been suggested. The potential confusion of these forms probably did not occur nearly so often as comparison of abstracted paradigms may lead us to suppose. That *heo, hie,* etc. served in some dialects as nominative singular feminine and nominative plural would cause no difficulty so long as verb inflections showed number distinction. Dative forms were different, in -*r*(*e* and -*m*). OE genitive forms had been different, in -*e* and -*a*, and as possessive adjectives in OE and ME, physical context or antecedents would usually keep them clearly apart; *hir* and *her* (e.g., in *Sir Orfeo*) could have established the contrast; or confusion from homophony was prevented in many instances by the rapidly developing "periphrastic genitive," in which object-case pronouns *h-r* and *h-m* (after *of*) contrasted. Potential confusion of plural and feminine accusative forms, if not prevented by context, either physical or grammatical, rapidly decreased as dative and accusative forms of all pronouns leveled under dative.

That the confusion of feminine singular and of plural personal pronouns was never serious could hardly ask better evidence than both the long persistence of *h-* forms and the unrelated way in which feminine and plural pronouns diverged from *h-* forms. The fact that only the nominative form of the feminine pronoun underwent change of initial consonant, with other case forms retaining inflectional *h-*, while all plural forms eventually developed /θ-/ *þ-*, *th-* forms (i.e., allomorphs, beside /*h-*/, later ø-, allomorphs such as '*em* that persisted into NE) clearly shows that the causes of the respective changes were different. The processes were also different, in that the new plural forms were borrowed, while the feminine form was not. But whatever the process, development of new plural forms manifests the persistence of the singular-plural contrast alone. The change to /θ-/ forms was no more necessary when it occurred than it had been throughout the prior history of English; without altering the basic case (suffix) inflections /-ø -r -m/, it merely provided an expression of number distinction in the initial (inflectional) phoneme, utilizing that inflectional position for number rather than solely for person (and incidentally regularizing first, second, third person inflectional patterns in this respect). The entire change is consistent with the tendency to develop a plural morpheme in nouns and nominals in this stage of English.

On the other hand, development of feminine /š-/ manifests the persistence of gender contrast alone. The earlier pronoun {he·o} had had a number of allomorphs; in most dialects the frequent form was /he·o/ but in Mercian and Northumbrian dialects it was /hi·o hi·w hi·e/ as well as morphs without lengthened /i/.[9] The following /i·/ or /i/ would have conditioned occurrence of the [ç] allophone of /h/ dealt with above. Also, the contrast between allomorphs of masculine {he·} and feminine {he·o} was always clear. The subsequent change by which /e·o/ (or perhaps /e·w/) > /ö·/ in Anglian (and West Saxon) dialects probably maintained the conditioning under which /h/ was phonetically [ç]. The fact that during the twelfth to fourteenth centuries both {šo-} and {še·} developed in West Midland and East Midland dialects supports this inference; so does survival of modern dialectal [ʃuː].[10] But monophthongization of *ēo* left a contrast between nominative masculine and feminine forms only in /e·/ vs /ö·/, or, as was very soon the case in a few dialects, the forms were left temporarily without regular contrast. Only two means were available to distinguish these two pronouns, short of borrowing a new form: contrast in the vocalic segment or contrast in the consonantal segment. Each method of differentiation was in fact followed in one dialect or another, and in the case of *sho* both were utilized. Vocalic contrast was already operative in some dialects to distinguish masculine *he* from plural *hi*. *The Peterborough Chronicle* (Second Continuation)[11] shows masculine *he*, feminine *scæ*, plural *hi*. Elsewhere, Orm has *he, ȝho, þeȝȝ*; *Bestiary* has *he, ge, he*; *Genesis and Exodus* has *he, she / sge / ge / ghe, he*; *Havelok* has *he, she / sho, þei*; and so on. In short, once the masculine-feminine distinction by V̄ vs. Vv was obscured, the /e·/ vs. /ö·/ contrast apparently was not sufficiently dependable to distinguish the two forms, and clearly contrasting allophones of /h/ and /š/ or /e·/ and /o·/ (or in some instances both) were selected to keep communication efficient. That nominative morphs of pronouns often occur with light stress—certainly with less distinctness than citation forms—would have made potential confusion all the more likely, a circumstance under which more distinct allophones would tend to be selected.

Once the /š-/ forms were established, the analogical circumstances of nominative *he* and *þei/þeȝ* etc. and the increasing dominance of East Midland speech are sufficient to account for the displacement of *sho* by *she* wherever the two existed as allomorphs.

The empirical law of sound change occurring independently of morphological functions is in no way contradicted by the preceding hypothesis about the evolution of Middle English *she*. At the same time, the change in the English feminine nominative pronoun can not be referred to the attested regular patterns of phonological change in the language, a fact that sent philologists to Norse stress-shifts of diphthongs and models of blends or sandhi to try to account for the change. But explanations by the latter procedures, however exhaustively they are pursued, remain unsatisfactory, as we have seen. The final matter to consider, therefore, is whether the explanation developed above is superior to any offered heretofore.

The hypothesis is constructed from evidence that is unquestioned—the attested forms and the standard phonological interpretations of written records. In several ways, however, the evidence is analyzed differently. The phonemic and morphemic formulation is the first difference. A second is the extrapolation from the longer stretch of linguistic history of the kinds of change in progress in the entire system of personal pronouns (and nouns): the development of a plural (initial) inflectional morpheme, on the one hand, and the development of an acoustically distinct allomorph for the nominative feminine pronoun. A third is formulation of conditions of unobtrusiveness for the change, recognizing the frequency of the pronoun form and the initial inflectional morpheme /h-/ that conditioned the shift by allophones. Fourth, identification—or assumption—of the persisting paradigmatic frame functioning as a selective factor for phonological and morphological variants and thus ultimately causing emergence of the distinctively new pronoun forms. The concept of an active selective function of what has been called a paradigmatic frame does not serve teleological explanation of linguistic history. On the contrary, its use allows us to explain the rise of either *she* or *sho* or *ho* or any other attested form. Neither is it formulated as an hypostatization that could equally well be labeled "the will of the people" or "the Genius of the Language." In so far as its locus or substance can be described briefly, it is merely the linguistic habits of expectation and utterance of members of a speech community, the same conservative behavioral factor that accounts for continuity and coherence in any persisting language features. It is the same concept that must operate in explanation of other changes in the language, including that series of changes going on during the generations in which *she* evolved—the developments of the distinct (segmentable) plural morpheme for nouns where there had not been one in OE, as well as to the short-lived plural morpheme /-e/ for adjectives.[12] Finally, the explanation here proffered does not require reference to the dubious intermediate step of Scandinavian *hjó* or the insufficient *was-hjó* type of circumstance. In sum, this hypothesis describes a credible linguistic sequence constructed from attested data, designates a causal factor, and avoids dependence on untestable assumptions.

If the conditions assumed by the "Shetland" theory actually existed, or if sandhi conditions were influential, they may have supplied the cue, may have reinforced or modified the direction of a tendency, for the replacement of /h-/ by /š-/. But the evolution of Middle English *she* was caused and conditioned by the structure of the English dialects themselves.

# FOOTNOTES

1. G. T. Flom, "The Origin of the Pronoun 'She'," *JEGP*, VII (1908), 115–25.
2. Cf. Eugen Dieth, "*Hips*: A Geographical Contribution to the 'she' Puzzle," *English Studies*, XXXVI (1955), 209–217 (esp. p. 215).
3. E. V. Gordon, *An Introduction to Old Norse* (Oxford, 1927).
4. Cf. H. Lindqvist, "On the Origin and History of the English Pronoun *she*," *Anglia*, XLV (1921), 1–50.
5. See, for example, Archibald A. Hill, *Introduction to Linguistic Structures* (New York, 1958), pp. 145–50.
6. See Flom and Dieth, cited above, and such others as Henry Cecil Wyld, *A Short History of English*, third edition (New York, 1927), §§ 302, 303, 307.
7. Joseph Wright and Elizabeth Mary Wright, *An Elementary Middle English Grammar*, second edition (Oxford, 1928), § 162.
8. *Ibid.*, §§ 159.5, 161.
9. Cf. A. Campbell, *Old English Grammar* (Oxford, 1959), § 703.
10. Cf. Joseph Wright, *The English Dialect Grammar* (Oxford, 1905), § 406.
11. Ed. Cecily Clark (Oxford, 1958).
12. It was sufficient to differentiate demonstratives into singular and plural *this-these* and sustain the system to be filled by *that-tho/those*.

# CELIA MILLWARD

# Pronominal Case
# in Shakespearean Imperatives*

Elizabethan English in general and Shakespearean English in particular frequently uses pronouns in imperative constructions. The use of these pronouns has no correlation with the age, sex, or social status of the speaker, although Shakespeare does employ certain types of such constructions to indicate dialectal or foreign speech. The pronouns always follow the verb. In the case of constructions with periphrastic *do*, the pronoun follows *do* and precedes the main verb, although adverbial elements may come between the pronoun and the main verb.

do thou do it (H6C V.5)
Doe not thou when thou art a King, hang a Theefe (H4A I.2)
Do not you feare (Wint II.2)
Do thou but call my resolution wise (Ro IV.I)

1. Most authors have assumed that no distinction is made in Shakespearean English between the nominative and the oblique case of second-person pronouns used with imperatives. Jespersen, for example, states that "after an imperative, a nom. and an obl. case would very often be used indiscriminatively."[1] Further, he says, "It is evident that all this must have contributed very much to impair the feeling for the case-distinction."[2] Another school has asserted that *thou* and *you* are the "emphatic" forms of the pronoun and *thee* and *ye* are the "unemphatic" forms.[3]

1.1. It is certainly true that no case distinction is observed between *ye* and *you*. There are only 35 imperatives with *ye* in all of Shakespeare's plays, and these 35 examples involve only 13 verbs, ten of which are also found very frequently with *you*.[4] *You*, on the other hand, occurs over 500 times, and with 92 different verbs. In the imperative at least, *ye* seems to represent a reduced form of *you*, and *you* serves both as a nominative and as an oblique pronoun. The following table is a list of verbs that occur in Shakespeare's plays more than four times with *you* in the imperative. A second number in the parentheses indicates the number of times the verb appears with *ye*.

| | | |
|---|---|---|
| be (24, 1) | do, full verb (7) | fear (11) |
| bear (4) | do, periphrastic (15) | get (58, 2) |
| bethink (5) | fare (73, 10) | go (34) |

* From *Language* 42.10–17 (1966). Reprinted by permission of the author and *The Linguistic Society of America*.

| hark (18, 8) | mark (9, 1) | stand (6) |
| hear (14, 2) | prepare (4) | take (12, 1) |
| hie (9) | rest (9) | tell (4) |
| hold (7) | sit (7) | |
| look (73, 3) | speak (5) | |

1.2. With *thou* and *thee* the situation is different. There are over 200 occurrences of imperatives with *thou* in Shakespeare, involving 77 different verbs. Approximately the same number of imperatives with *thee* occurs, and 55 different verbs are used. Only 16 verbs appear with both *thou* and *thee*, and, as will be shown, the use of *thou* or *thee* is, in almost all instances, conditioned by other factors in the sentence.

1.3. In Shakespeare, *thou* is the subject of an imperative. Apparently, it is employed to provide a mildly emphatic tone to the imperative. In verse, it is useful for metrical purposes. Its use (as is the use of *you*) seems to be optional. There are no obvious restrictions on the types of verbs that can take *thou* in the imperative, except that it is seldom found with verbs that occur with *thee*. Three verbs are especially frequent with *thou*: *be* (34 times), periphrastic *do* (13 times), and *go* (21 times). Of the remaining 74 verbs found with *thou*, only *fear, know, lie* "recline," *say, speak*, and *tell* also appear frequently with *you*.

1.4. Verbs that take *thee* in the imperative in Shakespeare fall into three classes: (1) certain verbs of motion, (2) certain verbs of attention, and (3) verbs taking a reflexive direct or indirect object. The verbs of motion taking an oblique pronoun object in Shakespeare apparently constitute a closed class.[5] Nine verbs are involved: *aroint, come, fare, get, haste, hie, return, run*, and *speed*, of which *fare* and *get* are among the verbs occurring most often with *you*. Of these verbs, all but *aroint* and *return* could take dative objects in Old and Middle English.[6] It is noteworthy that the verb *go* (OE *gán*) never takes a case-marked object in the imperative in Shakespeare, although it frequently took the dative in Old English. On the contrary, in Shakespeare, *go* appears very frequently with *thou* and also with *we* in the imperative. The verb *fare* occurs only in the greeting formula *fare* + 2d pers. pron. + *well*[7]; perhaps it should not be classified as a verb of motion. However, because its etymology is that of a verb of motion and because there is no other suitable category in which to place it, it is listed here. The verb of motion *get* always occurs with adverbials of place; it should not be confused with the verb *get* which may take a reflexive indirect object. None of these verbs of motion ever appears with a compound reflexive of the *-self* type. A few typical examples of the class:

get thee from my sight (Cymb V.5)
get thee a-part and weepe (Caes III.1)
haste thee quick away (Meas IV.1)
High thee to Hell for shame (R3 I.3)
speed thee straight (Cor IV.5)

1.41. The so-called verbs of attention taking an oblique pronoun in the imperative also form a closed class. Only four verbs are involved: *hark, hear, look,* and *mark.* The present-day English parallel to these constructions, *mind you,* does not appear in Shakespeare. All four of these verbs occur very frequently with *you* in the imperative; none of them is ever found with *-self* forms. The construction is limited to the imperative, and the use of the pronoun is almost obligatory. Typical examples:

but hearke thee *Charmian* (Ant V.2)
and marke thee too, *Iack* (H4A II.4)
looke thee heere boy (Wint III.3)
but heare thee *Gratiano* (Merch II.2)

1.42. Verbs taking a reflexive object in the imperative in Shakespeare can be divided into those which take a reflexive indirect object and those which take a reflexive direct object. The former class is limited to five verbs: *get, make, seek, seize,* and *take.*[8] Examples:

Get thee a good husband (Alls I.1)
Make thee a Fortune from me (Ant II.5)
seek thee out some other chace (H6B V.2)
Seize thee that List (Shrew III.1)
take thee that too (Mcb II.1)

This list, of course, might be expanded if we could include items from second-person plural imperatives. But since no distinction is made between nominative and oblique cases in the second-person plural, we have no justification for calling certain occurrences of *you* indirect objects, particularly since two simple pronominal forms never occur in one imperative construction; i.e., we do not find \**Get thou thee a good husband* or \**Get thee thou a good husband.* On the other hand, *you* is obviously the subject when it co-occurs with a *-self* form as in *Do you withdraw your selfe a little while* (Oth IV.1).

Verbs taking a reflexive direct object form an open class in Shakespeare. Although only 37 different verbs were found in imperative constructions with *thee* as direct object, the semantic differences among them are so great that apparently the only restriction is that the verb be compatible with transitivity. A few examples:

Oh calme thee gentle Lord (Tit IV.1)
Do not chafe thee Cosin (Tro IV.5)
Cloyster thee in some Religious House (R2 V.1)
Hide thee, thou Bloudy hand (Lr III.2)
but hold thee still (Mcb III.2)
pall thee in the dunnest smoake (Mcb I.5)
prepare thee to cut off the flesh (Merch IV.1)
Unarme thee, goe (Tro V.3)
goe to thy cold bed, and warme thee (Shrew I.1)
yeeld thee to my hand (John II.1)

Of the 42 verbs taking a reflexive direct or indirect object, many also appear in the imperative with *thyself* or *yourself.* In general, *-self* forms are not frequent in Shakespeare, and the oblique form of the personal pronoun is often used for all persons in nonimperative as well as imperative clauses. A few examples of nonimperative uses of oblique pronouns with reflexive verbs and with verbs of motion are given below.

I will shelter mee heere (Wiv V.5)
We will haste us (Hml III.3)
was't thou faine (poore Father)/To hovell thee with Swine (Lr IV.7)
my will is even this,/That presently you hie you home to bed (Gent IV.2)
He . . . hath stolne him home to bed (Ro II.1)
the wretched Slave:/Who . . . /Gets him to rest (H5 IV.1)
there will she hide her (Ado III.1)

 1.5. It was mentioned earlier that 16 verbs appear with both *thou* and *thee* in the imperative. This does not form a large proportion of the total of 116 verbs found with either *thou* or *thee*, and, in many cases, there are only one or two occurrences of each pronominal form. Nevertheless, an attempt was made to determine the conditioning factors, if any, for the use of the different pronominal forms. Ten of the 16 exceptions are fairly easily explained. All occurrences of each form involving these ten verbs are listed here.

(1a) Beare thou my hand (Tit III.1)
(1b) beare thou this Letter (Wiv I.3)
(1c) Beare thee well in it, and leave us alone (Ado III.1)

The *thee* form in 1c is obviously the direct object of the verb; in 1a and 1b, the *thou* is the subject of the verb, which has another direct object. In examples 2 through 8 below, *thee* forms always function as either direct objects or indirect objects.

(2a) Upon the right hand I, keepe thou the left (Caes V.1)
(2b) Keepe thou the Napkin (H6C I.4)
(2c) Keep thee warm (Lr III.4)
(3a) lay thou thy basis sure (Mcb IV.3)
(3b) lay thee downe, and roare (Oth V.2)
(4a) make thou proclamation (H6C IV.7)
(4b) Make thee a Fortune from me (Ant II.5)
(4c) Go, make thee ready (Ant III.3)
(5a) Mount thou my horse (Caes V.3)
(5b) Mount thee upon his horse (R2 V.2)
(6a) Seeke thou rather to be hang'd (Oth I.3)
(6b) seek thee out some other chace (H6B V.2)
(7a) stay thou for thy good morrow (Tim I.1)
(7b) stay thou but here a while (Mid III.1)
(7c) stay thou out for earnest (Tim IV.3)
(7d) stay thou by thy Lord (Caes V.5)
(7e) But stay thee, 'tis the fruits of love I meane (H6C III.2)
(8a) Turne thou the mouth of thy Artillerie (John II.1)
(8b) Turne thee *Benvolio*, looke upon thy death (Ro. I.1)

One imperative with the verb *turn* would allow either *thou* or *thee*; *thou* appears: (8c) *turne thou no more/To seeke a living in our* Territorie (As III.1).

In example 9 below, we clearly have the distinction between a verb of attention with an oblique object, and the same verb functioning in a larger clause.

(9a) heare thou there how many fruitless pranks (Tw IV.1)
(9b) But heare thee *Gratiano,*/Thou art to wilde (Merch II.2)

The imprecation *hang thee* occurs three times in Shakespeare's plays (*hang you* also occurs). It is always directed toward living persons. However, the verb *hang* appears once with *thou*; in this case, the quotation is from a song, and the speaker is addressing a piece of paper rather than a living person.

(10a) Hang thou there upon the tombe (Ado V.3)
(10b) Hang thee Monster (Tim IV.3)
(10c) Hange thee young baggage (Ro III.5)
(10d) Marrie hang thee brocke (Tw II.5)

For two verbs, one pronominal form occurs in many examples, while the other form appears just once. The verb *take* appears 22 times with *thou* and once with *thee*. The *thee* form could be interpreted as an indirect object, but *take* does not occur with an indirect object elsewhere in Shakespeare's imperatives. The verb *fare* appears with *thou* once in the greeting formula *fare thou well*. It occurs 40 times with *thee*.

(11a) Take thou the Fee (R3 I.4)
(11b) take thou that (Tim IV.1; R3 IV.4; Tp III.2; etc.)
(11c) take thee that too (Mcb II.1)
(12a) fare thou well (Tp V.1)
(12b) fare thee well (Cymb I.5; Hml I.5; etc.)

These unique exceptions may be taken as lapses in grammaticality, as indications of the decay of the system, or simply as typographical errors.

Finally, for four verbs that occur with both *thou* and *thee* in the imperative, no obvious explanation can be offered. All examples are given.

(13a) breake thou in peeces (H6A V.4)
(13b) breake thee of (Hml I.1)
(14a) Come thou on my side (R3 I.4)
(14b) Come not thou neere me (As III.5)
(14c) Come thou neere (Ant III.3)
(14d) Come thou no more for Ransome (H5 IV.3)
(14e) Come thee on (Ant IV.7)
(15a) sit thou by my bedde (H4B IV.4)
(15b) sit thee downe (Mid IV.1; Caes V.5)
(15c) And sit thee by our side (H6C III.3)
(16a) Come, stand thou by our side (Cymb V.5)
(16b) so stand thou forth (Alls V.3; plus 3 other examples of *stand thou*)
(16c) Stand thee close then (Ado III.3)
(16d) Stand thee by Frier (Ado IV.1)

All four of these verbs are recorded with the reflexive dative in earlier stages of the English language.[9] Perhaps, therefore, the examples with *thee* are best regarded as relics of an earlier time.

2. Imperatives of the first person are of course much less frequent than those of the second person. As in present-day English, the most common way of expressing the notion of a first-person imperative in Shakespeare is by means of the construction *let* + *me/us* + uninflected verb. For example,

let me be resolv'd (Caes IV.2)
Let us sway-on, and face them in the field (H4B IV.1)

True first-person singular imperatives are so rare and so questionable in Shakespeare's plays that no real conclusions can be drawn about them. A typical example is *Broke be my sword, my Armes torne and defac'd,/And I proclaim'd a Coward through the world* (H6B IV.1). Constructions of the type *No, it will hang upon my richest Robes/ . . . attyre me how I can* (H6B II.4) are imperative in form, but quite obviously conditional in meaning.[10]

In the first-person plural imperative, *we* is almost the universal pronoun. As with the second-person pronoun, it always follows the verb. Only one clear-cut example of an imperative with *us* was found: *And pawse us, till these Rebels . . ./Come underneath the yoake* (H4B IV.4). *We* is used even with verbs that take only *thee* in the second-person singular:

Hast we for it (Ant II.2)
Prepare we for our Marriage (H5 V.2)
Retyre we to our Chamber (Mcb II.2)
returne we to the false Duke *Humfrey* (H6B III.1)

Apparently the simple reflexive pronoun was not retained in the first-person plural imperative, although it was retained in the declarative; cf. *We will haste us* (Hml. III.1).

3. As with the first-person plural imperative, the notion of the third-person imperative in Shakespeare is most frequently expressed by means of a construction with *let*.

Let not Light see my black and deepe desires (Mcb I.4)
Let him do his spight (Oth I.2)
And let the world no longer be a stage (H4B I.1)

But constructions without *let* also occur. Most of them have nouns rather than pronouns as subjects. Here the subject usually, though not invariably, precedes the verb.

And ditches grave you all (Tim IV.3)
no person be so bold,/ . . . as to touch the Listes (R2 I.3)
Every man shift for all the rest (Tp. V.1)
God comfort him in this necessity (H6A IV.3)
Walk aside the true folke, & let the traytors stay (LLL IV.3)

But when a third-person pronoun is used, it follows the verb.

Be it so (H6A I.2)
Be it knowne unto thee (H6B IV.7)
treacherous, and full of guile,/Be he unto me (R3 II.1)
Hang him, swaggering Rascall (H4B II.4)

Note that the example with the oblique form of the pronoun involves the verb *hang*, which regularly takes *thee* in the second-person singular imperative.

4. When pronouns other than the personal pronouns appear with the third-person imperative, they usually precede the verb, although usage is mixed with *some*.

one of you question yon'd man (As II.4)
each turne away his face (LLL V.2)
Some attend him (H8 I.4)
Goe some of you, and fetch a Looking-Glass (R2 IV.1)
Go some and follow him (H6B IV.8)

5. The data presented here show that a case distinction between *thou* and *thee* does exist in the imperative in Shakespearean English, but that no such distinction exists for *ye* and *you*. Three classes of verbs taking an oblique object are identified: (1) verbs of attention, (2) verbs of motion, and (3) verbs taking a reflexive direct or indirect object. Only class 3 is an open class, and only class-3 verbs appear with -*self* forms. Class-1 constructions appear only in the imperative mood, but class-2 and class-3 constructions also appear in the indicative and subjunctive moods. The pronoun is obligatory only for a few verbs, e.g., class 3 *bethink* (cf. present-day English *remind*). Although the data for first- and third-person imperatives are very limited, we may tentatively conclude that case distinction of personal pronouns is preserved in the third-person imperative, but not in the first-person imperative.[11]

## FOOTNOTES

1. O. Jespersen, *A Modern English grammar on historical principles* 7.259 (Copenhagen, 1949).
2. Jespersen 7. 261.
3. This theory has been elaborated extensively by some authors. For example, E. A. Abbott, *A Shakespearean grammar* 141 (London, 1872), explains such constructions as *look thee* and *hark thee* by assuming that *look* and *hark* are emphatic verbs, so that an un-emphatic pronoun is employed for reasons of euphony. H. Poutsma, *A grammar of late Modern English* 2.201 (Groningen, 1914), asserts that the addition of the pronoun in constructions of the type *look thee* "softens the imperiousness of the request." W. Franz, *Shakespeare-Grammatik* 100 (Halle, 1900), assumes that the use of the pronoun in such cases is an extension from true reflexives.
4. The numbers given here are based on counts made by the author from H. Kökeritz (ed.), *Shakespeare's comedies, histories & tragedies; A facsimile edition of the first folio* (New Haven, 1954). Hence figures from *Pericles* are not included. Because of the lack of act and scene divisions for many of the plays in the First Folio, divisions are listed here as in modern editions. The inevitable errors will be in the direction of smaller numbers than is actually the case. However, it is felt that none of these errors will substantially affect the conclusions reached.
5. Such constructions are included in what Curme calls the dative of interest. Cf. G. Curme, *Syntax* 107–8 (New York, 1931). I prefer to separate verbs of motion

from reflexive verbs because (1) reflexive verbs also occur with *-self* forms, while verbs of motion do not, and (2) the verbs of motion form a closed class, while reflexive verbs do not.

6. The origin of *aroint* is unknown. OE *tyrnan* occasionally took a dative object; ME *tornen* frequently did. F. Voges, "Der reflexive Dativ im Englischen," *Anglia* 6.317–74 (1883).

7. One example of *Well fare you* appears in *Timon of Athens*, I.1.

8. The example with *take* is suspect. See the discussion below of verbs that appear with both *thou* and *thee*.

9. Voges, *Anglia* 6.317–74.

10. Jespersen classifies such constructions as pseudo-imperatives.

11. This study was supported in part by a National Science Foundation Graduate Fellowship in Linguistics. I wish to thank Professor W. Nelson Francis for directing my interest toward the problem and for his suggestions. The article has been altered slightly to correct an error in the original which Professor Randolph Quirk was kind enough to bring to the author's attention.

# CHARLES C. FRIES

# On the Development of the Structural Use of Word-Order in Modern English*

[In the actor-action-goal construction and in the character-substance (or modifier-noun) construction, Old English used taxemes of selection (inflected forms) to distinguish between actor (subject) and goal (object), and to indicate the direction of modification. The development of English has been away from the use of taxemes of selection with non-distinctive and connotative word-order, toward the use of taxemes of order operating practically without the aid of other devices. The patterns of the Modern English use seem to have been established by the middle of the fifteenth century.]

"Viewed from the standpoint of economy, taxemes of order are a gain, since the forms are bound to be spoken in some succession; nevertheless few languages allow features of order to work alone; almost always they merely supplement taxemes of selection."[1] In Present-day English, however, there are two "grammatical forms" for which the taxemes of selection have been lost during the course of the historical development of English and the features of word-order do work practically alone.

The first of these is in the ACTOR-ACTION-GOAL construction, in which the substantive noun that forms the "starting-point" (the so-called subject) of the action is distinguished from the substantive noun that forms the "ending-point" (the so-called object) only by position. The difference between the sentences *The man struck the bear* and *The bear struck the man* rests solely on word-order. Such arrangements of the words as *The man the bear struck* and *Struck the man the bear* do not distinguish the starting-point from the ending-point of the action and are not the practice of Present-day English.

In Old English, however, the order of the words in such sentences has no bearing whatever upon the grammatical relationships involved. Taxemes of selection do the work, and word-order is non-distinctive and connotative. The following Old English sentences, for example, would all express the same syntactic relationships between the two substantive nouns: that the bear is the goal or end-point of the activity and the man the starting-point.

*Sē mann þone beran slōh.*
*Þone beran sē mann slōh.*
*Þone beran slōh sē mann.*
*Slōh sē mann þone beran.*

* From *Language* 16.199–208 (1940). Reprinted by permission of Mrs. Charles C. Fries and the Linguistic Society of America.

In each of the four sentences, taxemes of selection—the nominative case form for *the man*, the accusative case form for *the bear*—signal the "subject" and the "object" relationships. It is true that in most Old English nouns there is no distinction of form between the nominative and the accusative; but with these nouns are used an inflected article and an inflected adjective, and these "agreeing" words most frequently have distinct forms to separate the nominative from the accusative. As a matter of fact, in a count covering more than 2000 instances, less than ten per cent of the Old English forms which are syntactically nominative or accusative lack the distinctive case-endings. In respect to the actor-action-goal construction we are concerned with the shift from the grammatical situation in Old English, where taxemes of selection operate with only a non-distinctive and connotative word-order, to the grammatical situation in Present-day English, where distinctive features of word-order operate without taxemes of selection.

The particular historical facts of significance for our purpose are (a) the position of those words which in Old English bear the accusative inflection—the "accusative-object," and (b) the position of those words in Old English which bear the dative inflection—the "dative-object." [2] In both cases we are concerned only with those instances which do not involve the use of a preposition (function word).

(1) In Late Old English of about 1000 A.D., if the sermons of Ælfric can be taken as a fair representation of the language of that time, approximately 53% of the accusative-objects appear BEFORE THE VERB and only 47% after the verb. Typical examples are:

*ælc man . . . þe . . . ðone oðerne hyrwde* [3]
*se man ðe hine sylfne godne talað*
*and Crist on ðære hwile to helle gewende and þone deofol gewylde*
*se Ælmihtiga God ða dagas gescyrte*
*gif ðu þonne ðis lytle bebod tobrecst þu scealt deaðe sweltan*
*he ðone lyre anfealdlice gefylde*
*and ða ylcan lare eft ge-edlæhte*

(2) The change from the Old English free position of the accusative-object (either before or after the verb) to the Modern English fixed position after the verb is indicated by the following figures:

|                      | c. 1000 | c. 1200 | c. 1300 | c. 1400 | c. 1500 |
|----------------------|---------|---------|---------|---------|---------|
| Acc-obj. before verb | 52.5%   | 52.7%   | 40+ %   | 14.3%   | 1.87%   |
| Acc-obj. after verb  | 47.5%   | 46.3%   | 60− %   | 85.7%   | 98.13%  |

(3) If the sampling displayed in these figures is trustworthy, then the position following the verb had become the fixed position for the accusative-object probably by the beginning of the fifteenth century, certainly before 1500.

(4) In Old English the words with dative inflection, the so-called dative-objects, like those with the accusative inflection, are found in practically every position in the sentence. When a dative-object and an accusative-

object appear in the same sentence, the order of these words in relation to each other and to the verb may be any combination, without doing violence to the ordinary patterns of Old English. Typical examples are:

*Cartaginenses sendon fultum* [acc.] *Tarentinum* [dat.] (Or. 162.8)
*þam godan casere* [dat.] *sende theodosie ærend-gewrit* [acc.] (Æl. Saints I.536.792)
*he asende his apostlum* [dat.] *þone halgan gast* [acc.] (Wulfstan 1.230.27)
*Hi moston him* [dat.] *beran unforbodene flæsc* [acc.] (Æl. Saints II.72.91)

(5) In the materials examined for Old English (900 A.D. to 1000) we find the following distribution of 2558 instances.[4]

| | Dative-object before the verb | | Dative-object after the verb | | Dative-object before acc-obj. | | Dative-object after acc-obj. | |
|---|---|---|---|---|---|---|---|---|
| | Number | Percent | Number | Percent | Number | Percent | Number | Percent |
| Nouns | 95 | 27.6 | 249 | 72.4 | 249 | 64.0 | 140 | 36.0 |
| Pronouns | 495 | 48.7 | 518 | 51.3 | 674 | 82.8 | 141 | 17.2 |
| Both together | 587 | 43.4 | 767 | 56.6 | 923 | 76.6 | 281 | 23.3 |

In these figures three matters seem worth noting: (a) Even in Old English the dative-object usually appears before the accusative-object. This is especially true of the pronouns, with the dative-object coming first in 82.8% of the instances. (b) The position of the dative-object with respect to the verb is less certain in Old English. Of the pronouns, approximately half appear after the verb; of the nouns, nearly three-fourths appear after the verb. (c) In the case of nouns, a much larger percentage of dative-objects appears after the verb than of the accusative-objects (72.4% as against 47.5%).

(6) The materials examined for Early Middle English (c. 1200) show (a) practically the same pattern of the position of the dative-object in relation to the accusative-object as do the materials for Old English; but (b) a clear tendency to place the dative-object after the verb. The figures for (b) are as follows:

| | Dative-object before the verb | | Dative-object after the verb | |
|---|---|---|---|---|
| | Number | Percent | Number | Percent |
| Nouns | 26 | 23.0 | 88 | 77.0 |
| Pronouns | 218 | 43.0 | 288 | 57.0 |
| Both together | 244 | 39.4 | 376 | 60.6 |

(7) By Early Middle English the position of the dative-object in relation to the accusative-object seems to have become a clear pattern. In about four-fifths of the instances the dative-object precedes the accusative-object. As the accusative-object comes increasingly to be placed after the verb, the dative-object also appears after the verb but before the accusative-object.

(8) The general situation at approximately the middle of the fifteenth century seems to have been as follows.

In the actor-action-goal construction the position for words expressing the goal (the ending-point or object) has become pretty thoroughly fixed as after the verb. Accusative- and dative-objects are distinguished by the fact that the dative-object, when present, precedes the accusative-object. This positional relation of the two classes of objects had existed for several centuries. Most important is the fact that by this time no nouns functioning as accusative-objects or as dative-objects precede their verbs.[5] The position before the verb, cleared of the presence of formally distinct accusative- and dative-objects, becomes in itself the distinguishing feature of the form-class of nominative expressions. The position before the verb becomes the territory of the actor (the starting-point or subject), the position after the verb becomes the territory of the goal (the ending-point or object); both exercise the "pressure of position" upon the function of all substantives standing in each territory.

Nouns standing before the so-called impersonal verbs as dative-objects (earlier such dative-objects had clear dative-case inflectional forms) now, whenever the verb form permits, are interpreted as subjects; and nouns following these impersonal verbs—nouns which formerly had the clear inflectional characteristics of subjects—now, standing in object territory, are interpreted as objects.[6]

*The knight liked it right noght* (Tale of Gamelin 52)
*This tale nedeth noght be glosed* (Conf. Am. VII.3786)
*Whan a wolf wanteþ [h]is fode . . ., of þe erþe he et* (Alex. and Dind. 860)

The "pressure of position" can perhaps most satisfactorily account for the changes in the pronoun forms in such sentences as these:

*Me wæs gegiefen an boc = I was given a book*
*Hem nedede no help = They needed no help*

and the fifteenth-century change of verb form in an old and common expression seems also to be connected with the development of this taxeme of order as the signal for the subject:

*Habbað geleafan ic hyt eom* (OE Gospels)
*Wostow nought wel that it am I* (Chaucer)
*It is I that am here in your syth* (Coventry Mysteries)

In general, then, in the actor-action-goal construction, in respect to the distinction between actor and goal, taxemes of selection which operated in Old English without relation to word-order have been displaced by taxemes of word-order working practically alone. These taxemes of word-order seem to form a clear pattern in the fourteenth century and to be fully established by the middle of the fifteenth.[7]

The second of the grammatical forms in which taxemes of selection have been lost and features of word-order now work practically alone is the CHARACTER-SUBSTANCE (the MODIFIER-NOUN) construction.

In Old English, with taxemes of selection to show the direction of modification, modifiers appear either before or after their nouns or even separated from their nouns by other words. Some examples are the following:

*Comon þær scipu six to Wiht* (Chron. 897)
*Æþelwulfes suna twegen* (Chron. 855)
*on ænium operum mynstres þingum* (Ben. Rule 95.14)
*and ealle þara nytena frumcennedan* (Exod. 133.5)
*Ge gesawon ealle þa mæran drihtnes weorc* (Deut. 214.7)
*an lytel sæs earm* (Oros. 28.12)
*to ðæm Godes huse* (Oros. 94.18)
*þone drihtnes þægen* (Ælf. Hom. 184.249)

The progressive fixing of the word-order pattern for modification can be illustrated by the facts concerning the position of the inflected genitive modifying a noun. Adjectival in its function, the inflected adnominal genitive in Old English appears, like the adjective, either before or after the noun it modifies. Out of 2247 instances of this genitive from materials of c. 900 A.D., 1175 or 52.4% stand before the modified noun, and 1072 or 47.6% stand after it.[8]

The following figures show the developing change in this situation:[9]

|  | c. 900 | c. 1000 | c. 1100 | c. 1200 | c. 1250 |
|---|---|---|---|---|---|
| Genitive before its noun | 52.4% | 69.1% | 77.4% | 87.4% | 99.1% |
| Genitive after its noun | 47.6 | 30.9 | 22.6 | 12.6 | 0.9 |

Before the end of the thirteenth century the post-positive inflected genitive has completely disappeared. By this time the general word-order pattern to express the direction of modification has become well established: single word modifiers of the noun or adjective class preceding the nouns they modify remain in that portion, whereas single word modifiers in other positions are not so kept. As a matter of fact, in the materials examined for present-day standard English, of the 1489 single word adjective modifiers there appearing, 94.9% immediate precede the nouns they modify and only 5.1% follow their nouns.[10] For single words of these classes the position immediately before a noun has become a taxeme of order signalling an adjunct relationship. In Modern English, position alone can indicate modification, and ever since the second half of the seventeenth century[11] nouns both singular and plural in form have with increasing frequency been made into modifiers by being placed before other nouns. The nature of such modification may be of the widest variety and often extremely vague, but the direction of the modification is unmistakable.[12]

The position immediately following a noun, however, has also become a taxeme of order indicating a similar modifying relationship for word groups —phrases introduced by the function words called prepositions, and clauses introduced by relative pronouns. The development of the so-called periphrastic genitive, "the analytic genitive with *of*," is typical of this construction.

This word group rose in frequency after the post-positive genitive had practically disappeared. The following figures show the details of the progress.

|  | Post-positive genitive | "Periphrastic" genitive | Pre-positive genitive |
|---|---|---|---|
| c. 900 | 47.5% | 0.5% | 52.0% |
| c. 1000 | 30.5 | 1.0 | 68.5 |
| c. 1100 | 22.2 | 1.2 | 76.6 |
| c. 1200 | 11.8 | 6.3 | 81.9 |
| c. 1250 | 0.6 | 31.4 | 68.9 |
| c. 1300 | 0.0 | 84.5 | 15.6 |

In Present-day Standard English the pressure of position is such that all word groups tend to modify the word immediately preceding. In the material examined for Present-day English, there appear 1258 of these "prepositional phrases" as modifiers of nouns. Of these, only one (as the context proves) cannot modify the immediately preceding word:

*The undersigned was given a physical examination for promotion by a medical board* (9054)

In these same materials, of the 396 "clause" modifiers of nouns, 86% immediately follow the noun modified, and 14% have other words (invariably a "phrase" modifier of some sort) intervening. Examples of those with intervening words are the following:

*I purchased a new automobile from this company for which I paid cash* (9033)
*The family occupy a house consisting of six rooms and a bath which they own* (8303)
*The sister has made an affidavit to that effect which I am enclosing* (8234)

One other observation may be made in conclusion. Sapir distinguished between what he called the "essential or unavoidable" grammatical concepts and the "dispensable or secondary," concepts.[13] If, for example, we are to say anything about a bear and a man in connection with the action of killing, it is "essential and unavoidable" that we indicate which one did the killing and which one was killed. If the qualities "big" and "fierce" are expressed in connection with the man and the bear, it is essential to know to which of these two the qualities are to be attached: one must know the direction of the modification. On the other hand, whether the killing took place in the past, the present, or the future, whether it was instantaneous or long drawn out, whether the speaker knows of this fact of his own first-hand knowledge or only from hearsay, whether the bear or the man has been mentioned before— these matters are of the "dispensable or secondary" type and may or may not be expressed. Languages differ greatly in the extent to which their grammatical practices force the speakers to give attention to these points.

In Old English practically all the grammatical relationships to which the language gives attention—both the "essential or unavoidable" and the "dispensable or secondary" ones—can be expressed by inflections (taxemes of selection), and nearly all are so expressed. The development of English has been characterized by the loss of certain kinds of these inflections. It might almost be fair to say that the history of the English language in respect to its grammar has, in a large measure, been a movement away from the type of grammatical structure in which taxemes of selection (inflections or word forms) express both the essential and the dispensable grammatical concepts, toward a type of structure in which taxemes of selection are used only for the dispensable concepts and taxemes of order for the essential or unavoidable relationships.

## FOOTNOTES

1. Leonard Bloomfield, *Language* (1933) 198. [Bloomfield's definition of "taxeme" is as follows: "The features of grammatical arrangement appear in various combinations, but can usually be singled out and separately described. A simple feature of grammatical arrangement is a *grammatical feature* or *taxeme*. A taxeme is in grammar what a phoneme is in the lexicon—namely, the smallest unit of form." (Bloomfield, 166)—Ed.]

2. In examining the materials of Middle English and Early Modern English, where the distinctive, inflectional syllables of both adjectives and articles have been lost, only those instances were counted as accusative-objects or as dative-objects for which there were clear inflectional parallels in Old English. I am indebted to a number of my students for contributions to my collection of instances upon which these figures are based, and especially to Dr. Frederic C. Cassidy (The Backgrounds in Old English of the Modern English Substitutes for the Dative-Object in the Group Verb + Dative-Object + Accusative-Object, University of Michigan Diss., 1938), and to Dr. Russell Thomas (The Development of the Adnominal Periphrastic Genitive in English, University of Michigan Diss., 1931).

3. The practice of Old English of putting the verb at the end of subordinate clauses (similar to that of Modern German) accounts for the position of a large number of accusative-objects before the verb.

4. Figures here summarized are from those given by F. C. Cassidy, *op. cit.*

5. Pronouns with distinct case forms did occasionally appear as dative-objects or as accusative-objects before verbs.

6. The examples printed by Willem Van der Gaaf in his dissertation, The Transition from Impersonal to Personal in Middle English (1904), have been of great service. See also Otto Jespersen, A Modern English Grammar 3.11.2–35, and C. Alphonso Smith, Studies in English Syntax 66–86.

7. I have tried to describe the various aspects of the word-order pattern for the nouns of the actor-action-goal construction in the following ten statements:

(a) A single noun preceding the verb—a noun that has the full characteristics of a substantive (i.e., with possible determiners as well as inflection for number), that is not preceded by an accompanying function word, or inflected for genitive case— is the subject or the starting point of the actor-action construction.

(b) Two such nouns preceding the verb—nouns that are equivalent or refer to the same person or thing—are the subject and an appositive, the first in order being the subject.

(c) Two or more such nouns preceding the verb—nouns that do not refer to the same person or thing but which are levelled by similar accent and/or function words —constitute a compound subject (two or more subjects).

(d) If two nouns precede the verb, stand next to one another, and are not levelled by accent and/or function words, but with only one possible determiner and that before the first noun, the second noun is the subject and the first a modifier of the subject.

(e) A single noun following the verb—a noun that has the full formal characteristics of a substantive and is not preceded by an accompanying function word or inflected for genitive case—if this noun refers to the same person or thing as the subject noun, is an identifying noun—a so-called "predicate nominative."

(f) Such a single noun following the verb, if it does not refer to the same person or thing as the subject noun, is the end-point of the action or object.

(g) Two such nouns following the verb—nouns that do not refer to the same person or thing as the subject noun, but do themselves each refer to the same person or thing as the other—are a "direct" object and a "result" object, or a so-called "object complement," after such verbs as *call, make, elect, appoint, consider*. After other verbs they are "direct" object and appositive.

(h) Two or more such nouns following the verb—nouns that do not refer to the same person or thing as the subject noun and do not themselves each refer to the same person or thing as the other, but are levelled by accent and/or function words—are a compound accusative ("direct") object, i.e., several objects.

(i) Two such nouns following the verb—nouns that do not refer to the same person or thing as the subject noun, and do not themselves each refer to the same person or thing as the other, and are not levelled by accent and/or function words—are a dative-object ("indirect" object) and an accusative-object ("direct" object), the first in order being the dative or indirect object.

(j) If two nouns follow the verb, stand next to one another, and are not levelled by accent and/or function words, but with only one possible determiner and that before the first noun, the first noun is a modifier of the second and the second may be either (e) or (f) above.

8. An example from Ælfric is: *þæt he and eall Israhela folc sceoldon offrian Gode an lamb anes geares*.

9. See Russell Thomas, *op. cit.*, 65–70.

10. Typical examples of those that followed are: *of the information available; the best physical condition possible; the best information obtainable from her; at some institution not familiar to me; for the time being; for the week following; two weeks ago*.

11. I am indebted to Miss Aileen Traver for the collection of instances upon which this statement rests.

12. Some typical examples are: *a school teacher; at sea level; the examination papers; beauty culture; a summer camp; a home visit; my household effects; the newspaper clipping; at government expense; the family physician; a funeral bill; the hospital gardens; labor conditions*. The process of these noun-adjuncts seems to me to be the same as that underlying the formation of compounds. In fact it is hardly possible to draw a line bounding the compounds and separating them from these free syntactical groups. Accent and specialization of meaning set off many clear cases, but there is a wide band of borderline cases. Frequency of a particular combination often leads to the phonetic and the semantic features characteristic of a compound.

13. Edward Sapir, *Language* (1921) 99: "We are thus once more reminded of the distinction between essential or unavoidable relational concepts and the dispensable type. The former are universally expressed, the latter are but sparsely developed in some languages, elaborated with a bewildering exuberance in others."

## ELIZABETH CLOSS TRAUGOTT

# Diachronic Syntax
# and Generative Grammar*

1. *The Problem.*[1] The objectives of diachronic linguistics have always been to reconstruct the particular steps by which a language changes, and also to hypothesize about processes of language change in general. Recent discussion of the latter problem has frequently involved five closely related proposals.[2] First, language changes by means of a series of individual innovations. These innovations consist primarily in the addition of single rules to the grammar of the adult speaker. Second, these innovations usually occur at some point of break in a grammar; for example, "before the first morphophonemic rule involving immediate constituent structure of the utterance... before the phonological rules that eliminate boundary markers from the representation."[3] Third, these innovations are passed on to the next generation when the child imitates the adult. A child may internalize the adult's grammar; or, more probably, he will simplify it. This is because children have an ability, not shared by most adults, to construct by induction from the utterances to which they have been exposed, the simplest grammar capable of generating sentences. The simplification will give rise to a discontinuity in transmission from generation to generation. In the interests of preserving intelligibility, this discontinuity will be minimal. Fourth, whenever the discontinuity results in radical changes such as restructuring, a mutation occurs. Finally, these mutations, which affect the overall simplicity of the grammar, are rare.

The significance of the intelligibility criterion is summarized by Halle as follows:[4]

Linguistic change is normally subject to the constraint that it must not result in the destruction of mutual intelligibility between the innovators—i.e., the carriers of the change—and the rest of the speech community . . . This restriction clearly affects the content of the rules to be added . . . the number of rules to be added must also be restricted, for very serious effects on intelligibility can result from the simultaneous addition of even two or three otherwise innocuous rules.

It may be somewhat less obvious that the requirement to preserve intelligibility also restricts the place in the order where rules may be added. All other things being equal, a rule will affect intelligibility less if it is added at a lower point in the order than if it is added higher up.

A corollary of these various proposals is that the simplest rules in a synchronic grammar will mirror the relative chronology of those additions which

* From *Language* 41.402–15 (1965). Reprinted (with corrections) by permission of the author and the Linguistic Society of America.

do not affect the overall simplicity of the grammar. In other words, synchronic grammars reflect INNOVATIONS. They do not, however, reflect MUTATIONS.

These arguments have been presented mainly in connexion with phonological change. Ramification in all other areas of the grammar has been taken for granted, but has not been investigated in detail. Klima hints at the validity of the general claim that a synchronic syntax reflects historical change when he remarks in his article, "Relatedness between grammatical systems,"[5]

Although motivated by a purely synchronic principle of simplicity (shortness of rules), the order in which the styles are considered does, in fact, recapitulate comparable aspects in the historical development of the pronouns.

No systematic attempt has, however, been made to investigate the five hypotheses cited above in the light of syntactic change. It is the purpose of this paper to make such an attempt, and to draw some minimal conclusions which any theory of language change must include.

2. *Representative Data.* The investigation will be based on the history of the verbal auxiliary *Aux* in English. The relationship between one period of the language and another will be presented in terms of the relationships between transformational generative[6] grammars of ninth-century Old English, mid-fifteenth-century Middle English, late-sixteenth-century Early Modern English,[7] and Modern English. By *Aux* I mean the tense marker, modals, the perfect and progressive helping verbs, and a few other helping verbs which will be specified in the course of this paper.

Attempts will be made to reconstruct the intermediate steps that account for the *Aux* structures and so to account for the types of innovations that can reasonably be assumed to underlie the observed mutations.

3. *Modern English.* Consider first Modern English *Aux* constructions as a type of control, since they are well known and have been accounted for in grammars that fulfill the strongest requirements of transformational generative theory.[8]

The set of optional Modern English auxiliary verbs is established according to the following criteria: position relative to other verbs, especially in passives, negatives, emphatics, interrogatives; use in tag questions and other reduced sentences; occurrence with *n't*; and possibility of occurrence under weak stress. These verbs include (1) the subset of modals *M* (*can, may, must, shall, will*), which all require a following verb in its base form, as in *I will go, I will have gone* where *go* and *have* are base forms; (2) the nonmodal operators: *have* requiring a past participle marker *PP*, and *be* requiring a present participle marker *PrP*. Any one or more of these subsets of auxiliary verbs may occur optionally, but only in the order described: *M – have – PP – be – PrP*.

In addition to these optional formatives, every verbal construction obligatorily carries one tense marker *T*, whether the helping verbs are present or not. *T* always occurs with the first member of the construction: *He would have come,* \**He will has come,* \**He will have comes.* For this reason, *T* is generated to precede the helping verbs and *MV* and every *Aux* is said to contain at least *T*. The formants can all be generated by the following rules. Only those elements relevant to *Aux* constructions are included here.

3.1  $S \rightarrow NP - VP$

3.2  $VP \rightarrow Aux - MV$

3.3  $MV \rightarrow \begin{Bmatrix} V_t - NP \\ V_i \\ \vdots \end{Bmatrix}$

3.4  $Aux \rightarrow T$ (M) (have – PP) (be – PrP)

3.5  $M \rightarrow$ can, may, must, shall, will

A low-level affix switch rule assigns *T* to its correct position after the verbal base immediately following it.

Verbal constructions with *do* can all be accounted for by blocking the minimal auxiliary formant *T* from the main verb base in negatives, emphatics, interrogatives, tag questions, and imperatives, as in

(1)  *He does not go*
(2)  *He does go*
(3)  *Does he go?*
(4)  *What does she see?*
(5)  *She went home, did she?*
(6)  *Do be good*

In other words, *do* is automatically and obligatorily generated as a dummy carrier wherever *T* is blocked from a main verb base *MV*.

4. *Old English*.[9] The shape of the optional part of *Aux* was considerably different at other stages of the language, and this one factor to a very large extent accounts for the differences in structure of active statements, and also of passives, negatives, and interrogatives.

As at all other periods, *T* was obligatory in Old English. There is a subset of the optional helping verbs which functions very largely like the subset of modern modals, and whose members are actually their cognates: *cunn-*, *mag-*, *mot-*, *scul-*, *will-*, all requiring an infinitive marker *Inf*. These may be exemplified by

(7)  *Or.214.5: Ac þær hie hit georne ongitan cuþen* "But when they could readily understand it"

(8)  *Or.100.19: Ic mæg eac on urum agnum tidum gelic anginn þæm gesecgan* "I can also tell of a beginning similar to that in our own times"

(9)  *Or.30.33: For ðon þe hio hyre firenluste fulgan ne moste* "Because she could not satisfy her desires"

(10)  *Or.218.20: Ic sceal eac niede þara monegena gewinna geswigian þe on eastlondum gewurdon* "I shall also by necessity be silent about those many battles that took place in the East"

(11)  *Or.140.30: Þa he & þa consulas hie attellan ne mehton* "When he and the consuls could not count them"

In addition there is the cognate of the Modern English perfect helping verb, *habban* "to have" which requires *PP*, provided that *MV* is transitive ($V_t$):

(12) *Or*.172.18: *Ac him hæfdon Pene þone weg forseten* "But the Carthaginians had blocked his way"

Occasionally *MV* may be one of a small set of intransitives ($V_i$), largely a set of verbs of movement, here classified as $V_{i_{move}}$, as in

(13) *Or*.196.22: *Þa Scipia hæfde gefaren* "When Scipio had gone"

The perfect auxiliary of intransitives is regularly, however, formed by the verb *wesan* "to be" – *PP*, as in

(14) *Or*.4.17: *Hu Orosius sæde þæt he wære cumen* "How Orosius said that he had come"
(15) *Or*.236.19: *Þider hi þa mid firde gefaren wæron* "To the place where they had then marched with the army"

There are also three progressive auxiliary verbs requiring *PrP* (realized in Old English as *-ende*). They were *wesan* "to be," *beon* "to be," and *weorðan* "to become," here classified as the subset *BE*. Examples of each of these progressives are

(16) *Or*.236.29: *& him æfterfylgende wæs* "And was following him"
(17) *Or*.12.35: *Þæt seo ea bið flowende ofer eal Ægypta land* "So that this river floods all the land of Egypt"
(18) *CP*.405.25: *Ðin eagan weorðað gesionde ðinne bebiodend* "Your eyes shall see your master"

Progressive but apparently not perfect auxiliary verbs may occur with *M*. In (19), for example, we find *M* and progressive. Sentences like (20) with *M* and progressive would be possible, but not (21) with *M* and perfect auxiliary nor (22) with *M* – perfect – progressive:

(19) *Or*.110.10: *Nu ic wille eac þæs maran Alexandres gemunende beon* "Now I shall also consider Alexander the Great"
(20) *Ic sceal feohtende beon* "I shall be fighting"
(21) *\*Ic sceal gefuhten habban* "I shall have fought"
(22) *\*Ic sceal feohtende gebeon habban* "I shall have been fighting"

A further restriction is placed on the nonmodal operators: they do not occur in passive formations. Although we find (23) with the passive auxiliary formant (*BE* requiring *PP*) in the environment of *M*, (24) and (25) with passive formants in the environment of perfect and progressive auxiliary verbs respectively are ungrammatical:

(23) *Or*.128.5: *Þa Darius geseah þæt he oferwunnen beon wolde* "When Darius saw that he would be conquered"
(24) *\*Þæt he oferwunnen geworden hæfde* "That he had been overcome"
(25) *\*Þæt he oferwunnen wesende wæs* "That he was being overcome"

The examples above demonstrate that the word order is very different from that in Modern English. At the end of the ninth century the following patterns are favored, but are by no means exclusive:[10]

(a) In coordinate *and* clauses and in subordinate clauses, especially temporal clauses with time adverbs, the finite verb (*MV* carrying *T*) often occurs at the end. If there are helping verbs, *MV* will usually be followed by the nonmodal operators and *M*. The last helping verb will carry *T*. For coordinates see (16), for subordinates (7), (9), (11), (15), (23).[11]

(b) In independent clauses,[12] the finite verb occurs nonfinally except in simple intransitive sentences. If a helping verb is present, *MV* will usually be preceded by *M* or a nonmodal operator, as in (8), (10), (12), (18). When there are two helping verbs, *M* will usually precede *MV*, and the perfect or progressive will follow, as in (19).

Most linguists consider that the order subject (*SU*) – object (*O*) – main verb (*MV*) + auxiliary (*Aux*) which is typical of coordinate and dependent clauses is a "reversal" of the normal order *SU – Aux – MV – O*. In terms of simplicity of description and explanatory power, however, it is by far the simplest to set up the Old English verb phrase in the order *SU (O) MV + Aux*. This will automatically account for most coordinate and subordinate clauses. A rule will then specify that in independent clauses the last helping verb is moved to position before *MV*; in this way just one rule will account for the fact that if there is one helping verb, it precedes *MV*, but if there are two, only *M* precedes *MV*. Other orders will be accounted for by a stylistic variant rule. Independent motivation for such an analysis is provided by negative constructions formed with *ne*. If the verb is finite, *ne* precedes *MV*:

(26) *Or.*19.10: *He cwæð þæt nan man ne bude be norðan him* "He said that no man lived north of him"

If there is a helping verb in type-(a) sentences, *ne* precedes the last helping verb, as in (9), (11); in type-(b) sentences it precedes whichever helping verb precedes *MV*. The negative of (19) would therefore be

(27) *Nu ic nille eac þæs maran Alexandres gemunende beon* "Now I shall also not consider Alexander the Great"

Furthermore, this analysis obviates the necessity of an affix switch rule, a rule which has no independent motivation, especially as *T* never has to be blocked from *MV* in Old English to generate a dummy carrier.

The *Aux* will therefore be optimally generated by[13]

$$4.1 \quad S \rightarrow NP - VP$$

$$4.2 \quad VP \rightarrow MV + Aux$$

$$4.3 \quad MV \rightarrow \left\{ \begin{matrix} NP - V_t \\ V_i \\ \vdots \end{matrix} \right\}$$

$$4.4 \quad V_i \rightarrow \left\{ \begin{matrix} V_{i_{move}} \\ V_{i_x} \end{matrix} \right\}$$

$$4.5 \quad Aux \rightarrow \left( \left( \left\{ \begin{matrix} PP - habb, \text{ in env. } V_{t-}, V_{i_{move}-} \\ PP - wes, \text{ in env. } V_{i-} \\ (PrP - BE) \, (Inf - M) \end{matrix} \right\} \right) \right) T$$

$$4.6 \quad M \rightarrow cunn, mag, mot, scul, will$$

$$4.7 \quad BE \rightarrow beo, wes, weorþ$$

5. *Middle English.*[14] By the thirteenth century, the normal word order is similar to that in Modern English. That is, we find *Aux – MV (O)* favored in both independent and dependent clauses. The simplicity criterion therefore requires that this order be generated as basic for Middle English. Such analysis furthermore provides just the kind of information we need to account for the fundamental differences in verb-phrase order between Old and Middle English. Although there is not the independent motivation that *do* provides in Modern English for setting up the members of *Aux* in the order $T(M)\dots$, since no dummy carrier is generable in Middle English, this analysis is simplest, as all other orders can then be derived easily from the basic form. Other constructions can also be neatly accounted for. The negative, for example, is formed during the earlier part of the Middle English period by *ne* preceding $T$ – first base as in (28); or by *nat* following $T$ – first base as in (29); or by both *ne* and *nat* as in (30). By the fifteenth century, negatives are more generally formed by *not* ~ *nat* after $T$ – first base, as in (31), (32):

(28) Ch.*Mel.*2266: *He ne foond neuere womman good* "He never found a good woman"
(29) Ch.*Mel.*2170: *It aperteneth nat to a wys man* "It is not suitable for a wise man"
(30) Ch.*Mel.*2220: *Yet ne wolde he nat answere sodeynly* "Yet he did not want to answer immediately"
(31) *PL.*III.104.22 (1456): *And yff the maters went not to my maister entent* "And if the matters did not go according to what my master had planned"
(32) *PL.*III.87.1 (1456): *And of suche as I will not write* "And of such things as I will not write about"

As far as the shape of *Aux* is concerned, there has been considerable increase in the complexity of membership, but there is already greater environmental generalization for the perfect participle constructions. The modals are the cognates of the Old English forms and need not concern us here. As in Old English, Early Middle English modals require *Inf*, but owing to a regular late-fourteenth- and early-fifteenth-century rule, this marker is lost and is usually not overtly marked by the mid-fifteenth century. The perfect auxiliary has undergone partial reversal of context restriction: *have – PP* is used for both transitives and intransitives:

(33) *PL.*III.103.24 (1456): *Which Fenn hath promised ($V_t$) to doo* "Which Fenn has promised to do"
(34) *PL.*IV.17.10: *Wherfore the people was greved be cauce they had labored ($V_i$) so often* "For this reason the people were grieved because they had labored so often"
(35) Ch. *Mel.*3000: *For ye han entred ($V_i$) in to myn hous by violence* "For ye have entered my house by violence"

A subset of $V_i$ may also occur with *be – PP*; its members, interestingly enough, are mainly the cognates of exactly those same verbs of movement which in Old English were the only ones that could occur with *habb – PP*:

(36) *PL.*IV.68.13: *But I undrestande ther is comen an other writte to the undrescheryff* "But I understand that another writ has come to the undersheriff"
(37) Ch.*Mel.*2160: *And by wyndowes ben entred* "And have entered through the windows"

There is only one progressive formant: the verb *be* requiring *PrP*. More significant for the history of *Aux* is that the perfect occasionally follows *M* and the progressive occasionally appears after the perfect helping verb, instead of being mutually exclusive with it. When this is the case, only *have – PP*, not *be – PP*, precedes the progressive formant. Examples of this complex construction occur mainly in poetry, as in Chaucer's *Knight's Tale:*

(38) Ch.*Kt.T.*929: *We haue been waytynge al this fortenyght* "We have been waiting all this fortnight"
(39) \**We been been waytynge al this fortenyght*

Of special interest is the additional use from Early Middle English times of *do* and *gin* as auxiliaries, both requiring *Inf* at their first introduction.[15] Both were originally used only as main verbs; throughout the period homonymous verbs *do* "to cause to" and *gin* "to begin to" persist as main verbs taking infinitive complement nominalizations; another homonymous verb *do* was a member from Old English times of a small class of substitutive verbs. The auxiliary verbs in question originated in poetry; *do* spread to prose by the late fourteenth century, cf.

(40) *Appeal Usk* in *Bk.Lond.E.*26/101 (1384): *So they diden pursuwe thynges a-yeins the Franchise of london for euer* "So they pursued matters opposing the franchise of London for ever"

*Gin*, however, never became established in prose. Only *do* is generated as a formant in the mid-fifteenth-century grammar; a complete version of this grammar would generate *gin* as a deviant member of *Aux*, restricted to poetry. A grammar of Middle English prior to c.1380 would, however, specify restriction to poetry of both *do – Inf* and *gin – Inf* (*Inf* is still marked at this time).[16]

Among examples of auxiliary *do* in the *Paston Letters* are

(41) *PL.*III.2.26 (1454): *As for the prist that dede areste me* "As for the priest who arrested me"
(42) *PL.*IV.149.37 (1465) *More plainly than I may do wryte at thys tyme* "More plainly than I may write at this time"
(43) *PL.*IV.143.14 (1465) *Yf they wold do pay such dewts* "If they would pay such debts"

From (42), (43), and several other passages, it is clear that *do* may occur after *M* and *have – PP*. There is independent motivation for analysing *do* as a second position nonmodal operator mutually exclusive with *be – PrP*: both, for example, fail to occur in passive formation.

The grammar must therefore specify at least the following phrase markers:

$$5.1 \quad S \rightarrow NP - VP$$

$$5.2 \quad VP \rightarrow Aux - MV$$

$$5.3 \quad MV \rightarrow \begin{Bmatrix} V_t - NP \\ V_i \\ \vdots \end{Bmatrix}$$

$$5.4 \quad V_1 \rightarrow \left\{ \begin{matrix} V_{i_{move}} \\ V_{i_x} \end{matrix} \right\}$$

$$5.5 \quad Aux \rightarrow T \ (M) \ \left( \left\{ \begin{matrix} (have - PP) \left( \left\{ \begin{matrix} be - PrP \\ do \end{matrix} \right\} \right) \\ be - PP, \ in \ env. - V_{i_{move}} \end{matrix} \right\} \right)$$

$$5.6 \quad M \rightarrow conn, \ mow, \ moot, \ shal, \ wol$$

6. *Early Modern English.*[17] By the late sixteenth century we find further changes. The chief of these are further development of *have – PP* in the environment of $V_i$; the spread of *do* as an auxiliary verb; and the appearance of the progressive in passive constructions.

As in Middle English, *do* is not a dummy carrier, but a regular optional member of *Aux*; *do* constructions occur side by side with finite verb constructions in unemphatic assertion, negative, and interrogative sentence types. In one particular, however, the behavior of *do* differs from that of its cognate in Middle English: it invariably occurs without other helping verbs:

(44) *N.I.191.21–5: Alledging many examples . . . how studie dooth effeminate a man* "Alleging there were many examples . . . of how study makes a man effeminate"
(45) *\*Alledging many examples how study may do effeminate a man.*
(46) *N.I.158.17: Thereby I grew to consider how many base men . . . enjoyed content at will* "From this I came to consider how many base men . . . enjoyed contentment at will"
(47) *N.I.185.16: I do not doubt (Doctor Diuell) but you were present* "I do not doubt (Dr. Devil) that you were present"
(48) *N.I.208.12: That loue not to goe in greasie dublets* "That do not like to walk about in greasy doublets"
(49) *N.II.314.1: Why did I enter into anie mention of my owne misusage?* "Why did I make any mention of the way I myself was misused?"
(50) *N.II.302.5: Why iest I in such a necessarie perswasiue discourse?* "Why do I jest in such a necessary persuasive discourse?"

A few Early Modern Northern manuscripts still show use of *do* after other operators, both in prose and in poetry:

(51) *Reg.Manor Scawby Lincolnsh. (1597): That the Carrgraues shall doe execute theire office truely* "That the Cargraves shall execute their duties properly"
(52) *Scot.poems 16th C.II.189 (1578): And many other false abusion The Paip has done invent* "And the Pope has invented many other false abuses"

Since *do* as a second-position nonmodal operator is restricted to Northern dialects, we may assume that by the sixteenth century in England at least *do* had become an independent helping verb, mutually exclusive with modals, perfect and progressive auxiliaries; it is still incompatible with the passive formant.

$$6.1 \quad S \rightarrow NP - VP$$

$$6.2 \quad VP \rightarrow Aux - MV$$

$$6.3 \quad MV \rightarrow \left\{ \begin{matrix} V_t - NP \\ V_i \\ \vdots \end{matrix} \right\}$$

$$6.4 \quad V_1 \rightarrow \begin{Bmatrix} V_{i_{move}} \\ V_{i_x} \end{Bmatrix}$$

$$6.5 \quad Aux \rightarrow T \left( \left\{ \begin{matrix} (M) \left( \begin{Bmatrix} \text{(have} - \text{PP) (be PrP}-) \\ \text{be} - \text{PP, in env.} - V_{i_{move}} \end{Bmatrix} \right) \\ do \end{matrix} \right\} \right)$$

$6.6 \quad M \rightarrow$ can, may, must, shall, will

Of particular interest is the sporadic appearance of the progressive in passive formations. Unlike passive constructions with other members of *Aux*, these passives are not formed with *be – PP*. We find patterns of the kind *The man is seeing by X*, not *The man is being seen by X*.[18]

(53) Deloney, *Gentle Craft* 132.45.[19] *While meat was bringing in* "While food was being brought in"

The final stages in the development to Modern English consist in the loss of *be – PP* in the environment of most intransitive verbs, the restriction of *do* during the eighteenth and nineteenth centuries to certain explicitly determined environments, and the requirement of *be – PP* in passive constructions, whatever the membership of *Aux*. At the present stage of the language, *Aux* provides the least choices, but is also maximally generalized.

7. *Types of Change.* These then are the major mutations in the history of *Aux*. Comparison of the different grammars reveals several types of change, all of which have far-reaching effects on sentence structure. The changes may be summarized as follows:

(a) reversal of order;
(b) loss of class-context restriction;
(c) realignments of existing structures, without radical system change, as when the Old English maximal *Aux* was extended to *T* (*M*) and two successive optional nonmodal operators;
(d) addition or loss of formants, as when *do* was added, and later when *be – PP* (perfect auxiliary verb) was lost;
(e) and finally, closely related with this, really radical changes of system membership, e.g., when *do*, which was a member of the lexical system, gave rise to an operator in the syntactic system; or later when *do*, which was an optional member of *Aux*, became an obligatory, predictable element, generable as a formative in the transformational component.

8. *Innovations Accounting for Changes.* It remains to be seen how these changes came about and how they may be considered a paradigm of language change in general.

The minimal change that must be postulated to account for reversal of word order is the growing tendency to favor *SU – Aux – MV* (*O*) order in all clauses. This tendency, which is amply attested by twelfth-century data, must have developed in two stages: first, preponderence of constructions with a finite verb or one helping verb preceding *O*, as in (19); and second, attraction of a second optional member of *Aux*, if present, to pre-*O* position. The word "tendency" is used advisedly. All through Old English, both $Aux - MV$ and $MV + Aux$ patterns existed. What must be accounted for is the fact that the optimal grammar for Old English specifies $MV + Aux$ and a rule allowing for certain stylistic switches of auxiliary verbs, but no affix-switch rule. The optimal grammar for Middle English, on the other hand, specifies $Aux - MV$, a rule allowing for certain stylistic switches of auxiliary verbs, and an affix-switch rule. Any synchronic Old English grammar will mirror the two orders for auxiliary verbs. For Middle English we need a new grammar. In other words, the mutations can only be reflected by a different set of rules.[20]

The same is true of changes in context restriction of the perfect auxiliary. As OE $habb - PP$ came to predominate, it took over the function of $BE - PP$. We might postulate that since those intransitive verbs that were most frequently used (verbs of movement) could occur with both $habb - PP$ and $BE - PP$, $V_{i_{move}}$ became a model for other intransitive verbs which, although more numerous, were less frequently used. It is also noteworthy that Middle English was a time when word formation by changes of class membership or extension to new class membership was becoming particularly common; in particular, many new transitives were being formed from intransitives.[21] This meant that class-context restriction was no longer clear, and that ambiguity between the perfect auxiliary formant $be - PP$ and the homonymous passive formant could arise.[22]

A further innovation was the extension of the mutually exclusive set of perfect and progressive auxiliaries to two compatible nonmodal operators. Throughout the history of English up to the nineteenth century, and still today in the case of most sentences in which the main verb is the copula *be*, the structure "base *be* followed by base *be*" has been ungrammatical or at least deviant. Although Modern English sentences of the type *The students are being attacked* are grammatical, *The students are being hungry* is ungrammatical. Strong pressure against such structures must account for the lack of passive progressives with the passive formant in Early Modern English. It also seems to account for the lack of progressives following perfect auxiliaries of the type $be - PP$ in Middle English. Unless we are to assume that perfects followed by progressive helping verbs were possible only in transitive verb constructions, we are led to conclude that the two nonmodal operators became compatible AFTER both intransitives and transitives could take *have - PP* as the perfect auxiliary. Once the two became compatible, a mutation arose.

Although I have attempted so far to cover only those changes that took place within the *Aux* rule alone, I have had to mention far-reaching repercussions on the whole system. Change in word order requires, for simplicity of description and explanatory power, the introduction of an affix-switch rule. Behavior of progressive auxiliaries raises the question of the cooccurrence of two *be* bases. Other changes in the *Aux* further demonstrate clear cases of overall system changes. *Do*, which was a main verb requiring infinitive nominalizations, came to be reinterpreted as an auxiliary, presumably because it was followed by an unmarked infinitive. Perhaps pressure of continued association with the main verb *do* (which, as a main verb, could be preceded by auxiliary verbs) countered the tendency to use *do* in modal position; instead it came to fill the same slot as the progressive. This slot was in itself somewhat variable since it was an innovation. The very character of this third position may account for the fact that *do* came to be used more and more as an independent unit which could not tolerate other auxiliary verbs in its environment. Its failure to pattern with other members of *Aux* then further favored the eventual mutation, by Modern English, to nonmembership in the regular *Aux* construction, and to restriction to certain predictable environments.

9. *Theory of Language Change.* Given a knowledge of mutations, such as those in the development of *Aux*, and of the innovations that account for those mutations, can we say that the five proposals for a theory of language change outlined at the beginning of this paper account for syntactic change?

The proposition that language changes by means of a series of individual innovations seems to be fully supported by the history of the *Aux*, in which we can see each step develop individually. The second proposal is that the innovations usually occur at the end of some natural division of the grammar. This must give us pause. Within the syntactic component there are three main points of break: the point where the phrase structure ends and the lexicon begins; the point where the lexicon ends and the transformational subcomponent begins; and finally the point where the syntactic component ends and the morphophonemic begins.[23] Of the changes discussed, the only one that enters at such a break is the affix-switch rule, and this is the result of a mutation, not an innovation giving rise to a mutation; besides, it is largely motivated by simplicity of description rather than by actual language data when it is introduced for Middle English. Changes in context restriction of the perfect and progressive verbs occur within the high-level *Aux* rule, and do not enter at the end of the phrase structure. *Do* extends lexical membership of the category of infinitive complement taking transitives to nonlexical membership of this same high-level *Aux* rule; again, it is not possible to hypothesize that it entered as a low-level phrase-structure subcategory and was then reinterpreted as part of the *Aux*. The third proposal, that innovations are passed on to generation after generation, and the fourth, that mutations occur when the new generation reinterprets a grammar so as to effect radical changes such as restructuring, seem to be well borne out by syntactic evidence. The viability of the fifth proposal, however, that mutations are rare, is doubtful as far as syntactic change is concerned. The *Aux*, which is such a small part of the grammar, demonstrates at least six types of mutation. The four different types of pronominal usage which Klima discusses support in a totally unrelated area the observation that mutation in syntax is not rare, although it seems to be relatively infrequent in phonological change.

In view of the factors discussed above it appears that any theory of language change must include the proposals that language changes by means of the addition of single innovations to an adult's grammar, by transmission of these innovations to new generations, and by the reinterpretation of grammars such that mutations occur. Restriction of innovations to points of break seems not to be viable as a generalization for language change, nor does the statement that mutations are rare. Both these proposals must be limited to the area of phonological change.[24]

## FOOTNOTES

1. I am deeply indebted to Morris Halle and Edward S. Klima for valuable criticism of an earlier draft of this paper. My thanks are also due to Sheldon Sacks, James Sledd, and Robert P. Stockwell for many helpful suggestions.

2. For these proposals and their corollary, see especially Morris Halle, "Phonology in Generative Grammar," *Word* 18. 64–8 (1962), and the revised version in Jerry A. Fodor and Jerrold J. Katz, eds., *The structure of language: Readings in the philosophy of language* 344–9 (Englewood Cliffs, N.J., 1964).

3. *Word* 18.66, ft. 12; *Structure* 346, ft. 13.

4. *Word* 18.66; *Structure* 346.

5. *Lg.* 40.2 (1964).

6. The notion of grammar is developed by Noam Chomsky, *Syntactic structures* ('s-Gravenhage, 1957).

Questions have frequently been raised concerning the feasibility of using this notion of grammar in historical analysis, in particular concerning the appeal to intuition. A linguist theorizing about a living language ideally has as a control his own native intuition and that of the speakers around him, or at worst the native intuition of speakers of a language foreign to him. Against such intuition he can test, among other things, degrees of grammaticality and types of ambiguity. With dead languages, however, the linguist can rely only on the limited data available to him, and at best on a secondary "native intuition" which can arise only after several years of close association with the language. He can find very few, if any, syntactically minimal pairs from which to set up paradigms of grammatical versus ungrammatical sentences. Deviation and ambiguity are even more elusive. If we take in its strongest terms the requirement placed on linguistic theory that it should characterize and predict all and only the sentences of the language and also account for the native speaker's competence in producing and understanding the utterances of the language, we might ultimately conclude that a grammar can only be written by a native speaker, not a foreigner, and that grammars of dead languages cannot be written at all. The degree of accuracy will naturally vary according to the degree of acquaintance with the language. But this does not mean that all investigation of language not native to the linguist must de facto be abandoned, any more than any theory of history, whether cultural or geological, must be rejected because we cannot recapture all and only the characteristics of previous eras. We may quite legitimately put forward a theory of a dead language, in terms of a grammar which fulfills the requirements of descriptive adequacy and explanatory power. This theory will be based on all observable data, and also on unobservable data when necessary, i.e., when the logical consequences of the model would not match the observable data without this hypothesis. As in analysis of a living language, that model will be simplest which will characterize the sentences of the corpus, and so the infinite set of un-observed sentences which pattern with them. Within such a framework, deviance as well as grammaticality can tentatively be made explicit.

7. For fuller versions of these grammars, see Closs, *Syllabus for English 110, History of English* 11–6, 24–9, 34–7 (mim., University of California, Berkeley, 1964); *Deep and surface structure in Old English* (in preparation).

8. See especially Chomsky, "A transformational approach to syntax" in Archibald A. Hill, ed., *Third Texas conference on problems of linguistic analysis in English* 131–2, 144–7 (Austin, 1962); Klima; "Negation in English" in Fodor and Katz, eds., *The structure of language: Readings in the philosophy of language* 251–3 et passim; Robert B. Lees, *A grammar of English nominalizations* 19–20 et passim (Bloomington, 1960). For a discussion of the criteria by which the set of auxiliary verbs is set up, see James Sledd, *A short introduction to English grammar* 106–9 (Chicago, 1959).

9. Quotations for Old English are derived from Henry Sweet, ed., *King Alfred's Orosius*, EETS 79 (London, 1883), abbreviated *Or.*; and from Henry Sweet, ed., *King Alfred's West-Saxon version of Gregory's Pastoral Care*, EETS 45, 50 (London, 1871), abbreviated *CP*. References are to page and line numbers.

10. Recent detailed discussions of word-order problems include S. O. Andrew, *Syntax and Style in Old English* (Cambridge, 1940); Paul Bacquet, *La structure de la phrase verbale à l'époque Alfrédienne* (Paris, 1962); C. R. Barrett, *Studies in the word-order of Aelfric's Catholic Homilies and Lives of the Saints* (Cambridge, 1953); Charles R. Carlton, *Syntax of the Old English Charters* 170–256 (unpub. doctoral diss., Michigan, 1958); David P. Harris, "The development of word-order patterns in twelfth-century English" in Albert H. Marckwardt, ed., *Studies in languages and linguistics in honor of Charles C. Fries* 187–98 (University of Michigan, 1964); Bruce Mitchell, "Syntax and word-order in 'The Peterborough Chronicle'" 1122–1154," *Neuphilologische Mitteilungen* 65.113–44 (1964).

11. (13), (14), (17) are examples of deviation from this rule.

12. "Independent clauses" here include "demonstrative clauses" introduced by demonstrative adverbs *þa* "then," *þonne* "then," *þær* "there" in which the finite verb or one helping verb usually precedes the subject (cf. Andrew, *Syntax and style in Old English* 3). Both independent clauses with demonstrative adverbs and those without share the main features of verb order under discussion.

13. The rules are particularly interesting in that they are basically similar to those suggested by Emmon Bach for German, "The order of elements in a transformational grammar of German," *Lg.* 38.263–9 (1962).

$V_{i_x}$ in Rule 4.4 stands for the class of all $V_i$ that are not $V_{i_{move}}$. It includes verbs homonymous with the numbers of $V_{i_{move}}$.

14. Quotations for Middle English are taken from Hans Kurath, Sherman Kuhn, John Reidy, eds., *Middle English dictionary* (Ann Arbor, 1954–); James Gairdner, ed., *The Paston letters* 1422–1509 (London, 1904), abbreviated *PL.*, with references to volume, page, and line numbers; and Geoffrey Chaucer, *The text of the Canterbury Tales*, eds. John M. Manly and Edith Rickert (Chicago, 1940).

15. Clear loss of identity as *MV* is indicated by the occasional interchange in different MSS of *gin – Inf* and *do – Inf*; cf. *Cursor Mundi*, Göt. 2009 (c. 1400); *A neu liuelad gan he bigin* "He began a new kind of life," with MS variants *con, cun* (reduced forms of *gan*) and also *dud*. A summary and bibliography of studies on *do* and *gin* is provided in Tauno F. Mustanoja, *A Middle English syntax I: Parts of speech* 600–15 (Helsinki, 1960).

16. On some of the problems in accounting for specifically poetic deviance, cf. Samuel R. Levin, "Poetry and grammaticalness," in Horace Lunt, ed., *Proceedings of the ninth international congress of linguists* 308–15 ('s-Gravenhage, 1964).

17. Data for Early Modern English are derived from the *Oxford English dictionary*; and Ronald B. McKerrow, ed., *The works of Thomas Nashe* (Oxford, 1958), abbreviated *N.*, with references to volume, line, and page numbers.

18. The latter is a modern construction which did not come into general use until the nineteenth century. The first clear instance of a passive of this type cited by Fernand Mossé, *Histoire de la forme périphrastique être + participe présent II: Moyen-anglais et anglais moderne* par. 263 (Paris, 1938), is from a letter by Robert Southey: *A fellow whose uppermost upper grinder is being torn out by a mutton-fisted barber.* For detailed discussion of the history of the passive progressive, see Mossé, *ibid.*, pars. 231–81.

19. Thomas Deloney, *Works*, ed. Francis O. Mann (Oxford, 1912).

20. A synchronic grammar cannot account for these changes, except so far as it treats different dialects, or different reflexes of different changes. When Klima says the order in which he describes the rules for pronouns in different dialects reflects the historic order of change, he is actually referring to the order of mutations, not innovations. Each set of rules for each dialect requires different ordering of basically the same rules. Each set has its own unique relationship to the rest in the structure of the language, and cannot be collapsed under the same grammar except as a discrete subset of the grammar. It has been suggested that grammars should provide rules accounting for synchronic relatedness between grammatical systems, such that different systems may be regarded as modifications or extensions of a given basic system. This is essentially what Klima's grammar does for pronouns. In addition, it has been suggested that grammars should provide rules accounting for diachronic relatedness between grammatical systems, also such that the different systems may be regarded as modifications or extensions of a given basic system. Such grammars would reveal with great clarity the similarities and differences between stages of the language, and would provide in simpler, i.e., more compact, form the same information that separate grammars of different stages of the language provide. They cannot, however, specify actual change or provide historical perspective. A grammar of the actual changes would be a kind of algebra accounting in the simplest way possible for all relevant changes, in their chronological order.

21. See F. Th. Visser, *An historical syntax of the English language* 93–138 (Leiden, 1963).

22. Visser, *ibid.*, 131, suggests that this ambiguity was one of the factors leading to the transitivization of intransitives.

23. Further subdivisions may or may not be made according to the particular model of grammar adopted. Grammars like Lees' *Grammar of English nominalizations* allow for certain groupings in the phrase structure according to sets of subcategorizations; Charles Fillmore's study "The position of embedding transformations in a grammar," *Word* 19.208–31 (1963), specifies groupings for two-string vs. one-string transformations. In the latest models, however, such as Chomsky's blocking grammar and Klima's nonblocking grammar (cf. Klima, "Current developments in generative grammar," forthcoming in *Kybernetika* I, Prague), the phrase-structure component is minimal and cannot be subject to groupings. Context restrictions and subcategorizations are largely specified in a lexicon in which the only significant groupings are the overall categories *N*, *V*, *Adj*, etc.; only in the filter transformations do we find areas in which the concept of "point of break" is significant for syntax.

[24. For a recent large-scale treatment of some matters of syntactic change, see Robin Lakoff, *Abstract syntax and Latin complementation*, MIT Press, 1968.—Ed.]

# M. L. SAMUELS

# The Role of Functional Selection
# in the History of English*

Although even ultimate causality or teleology in studying the history
of the language has regained its former respectability in recent years, many
writers issue a caution that they are restricting themselves to *intra*-linguistic
causes of change[1] (or, if they still fight shy of the word "cause," "reasons"
or "conditioning factors"). Others have rightly pointed out that language
changes are natural, wholly to be expected, and therefore not in need of
explanation[2]; and, in that case, we are studying the "how" rather than the
"why." But, with these two provisos, the study of the subject needs no defence, and that is indeed borne out by the much profitable and suggestive
recent work[3] on it, notably by Vachek, Martinet and Malkiel. But, also
within recent years, J. L. M. Trim[4] has complained that historical linguistics
has lost its "dynamic." I cannot hope to restore this for him in a single
paper, but I can at least attempt what another scholar has called "the dis-
solution of the wall of air between functionalists and traditionalists."[5]

Much recent discussion[6] has been concerned with the problem of which
factor has priority in linguistic change—mechanical or systemic. In what
follows I shall argue that in principle, since all changes take place on both
levels, neither factor must be accorded a general priority; but that in
practice, the problem of priority can and should be measured by the total
evidence available in each individual instance of change. It is the doctrinaire
approach—the "all or nothing fallacy," as Jespersen called it[7]—that
has been the prime source of disagreement in the past, and has rendered
no service to the cause of functionalism.[8] Such dogmatism is especially
noticeable in the German school founded by Wilhelm Horn, represented
today by Lehnert[9] and Berndt,[10] who still insist that all inflectional endings
disappear for reasons of function, not of form. The approach of Professor
Martinet is quite different: he expressly emphasizes that a combination of
factors must always be reckoned with, and that functional explanations are
not the only ones possible.[11] Yet in practice and example, he usually omits
mechanical and physiological factors, and concentrates on the system.
Since, for this reason, his work has rightly been called a *tour de force*,[12]
it cannot be expected to provide a bridge for the more traditionally-
minded.

* From *Transactions of the Philological Society* (1965), 15–40. Reprinted by permission
of the author and The Philological Society.

A rapprochement, then, is needed. Both hypotheses are valid; between them, they cover the whole range of (intra-)linguistic change, and it should therefore be possible to weld them into a single, all-embracing theory of diachronic linguistics.

# I

The two levels I have mentioned may be studied through a variety of dichotomies, some of which differ considerably in their scope and applications: examples are *parole* and *langue*, "form" and "function," "structure" and "system," "etic" and "emic," "chain" and "choice," "token" and "type," "syntagmatic" and "paradigmatic." As the most suitable and explicit for my present purpose, I choose the terms "spoken chain" and "system," defined thus:

*Spoken Chain:* the total utterances made in a given speech-community over a limited period, whether fully intelligible or not.
*System:* the total of accepted and intelligible norms, established by oppositions, in the same community and period.

The relations between these two levels that have diachronic implications may be stated as follows: the spoken chain contains the whole range of potential alterations and innovations, accidental or rare variations of allophones and allomorphs, forms from neighbouring dialects, neologisms, foreign words, calques and so on (we might note especially, as features with no counterpart in the system, non-distinctive suprasegmental features of stress, intonation and juncture that provide such a fruitful source of variation).[13] These variants may

(*a*) have no effect on the system, i.e., they are rejected;
(*b*) be selected and marshalled into subsystems of oppositions, according to the current requirements of the system;
(*c*) occur in such quantity that they are *imposed on* the system, and the system may thereby be altered.[14]

Between the last two possibilities, there is a wide scope for either agreement or conflict between the two levels. A possible case of near-agreement is the eventual selection of variants in /uː/ in *poor, boor, moor* but of /ɔː/ in *floor* and *door*: in the spoken chain, there would be a greater frequency of /uː/-variants after a labial, and at the level of system, the /uː/-variants avoided homonymic clash (cf. *pour, pore, bore, more*).[15] To argue that one reason is more likely than the other (as Horn-Lehnert do[16]) is misleading: each can apply on its own level, since both levels operate in every instance.

The importance of selective variation has been stressed, in general terms, by J. Whatmough[17]; before him, Jespersen[18] and others[19] had provided isolated examples of the process. But its demonstration is far from complete, and its universal applicability as the essential link between the two levels has not been sufficiently recognized. J. L. M. Trim doubts whether we have sufficient documentation of variants from past stages of the language to show it in action,[20] but this is certainly not true of Middle English: as an example, Fig. 1

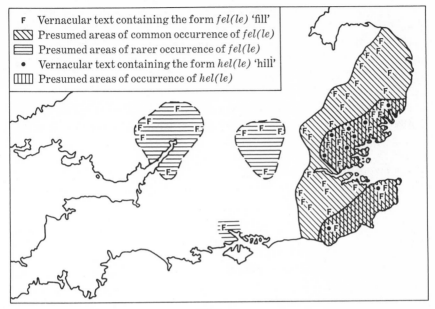

**Figure 1**

shows the avoidance of the form *hell* in the meaning "hill" in the area where it might be expected.[21] For Early Modern English, there is much orthoepist, phonetic and other evidence,[22] and dialect forms can sometimes be deduced by extrapolation from Middle or Modern English. Furthermore, Early Modern English is a suitable period for the study of selection, for the rate of both variation and selection is likely to be higher in a growing standard language than in other dialects (as shown by an opposition like *these* and *those*, the derivation of which is far from regular,[23] and which, according to Joseph Wright, did not belong in his day to any genuine English dialect other than the standard language).[24]

Other dichotomies suggested for diachronic study are obviously valid, for example "expediency" versus "expressiveness"[25] or "economy" versus "needs of communication"[26]; but I would maintain that they are vaguer and less practicable than the scheme of two levels linked by selection. Furthermore, the linking by selection is not intended as a mere compromise: its validity is amply demonstrated from the findings of linguistic geography:

(*a*) Priority of the spoken chain is demonstrated when a subsystemic opposition arises from the mere availability of two variants in a border area. As an example, Fig. 2 shows a typical westward recession of *hit* "it" in the fourteenth and fifteenth centuries. Texts in the shaded border areas show a subsystem in which *hit* occurs in initial or strongly stressed position, *it* elsewhere. When isogloss A moves westward, area *aa* will henceforth use *it* only, and the subsystem is thereby shown to have depended purely on the availability of two forms in a border area, and not on any requirements of the total system.

(*b*) Priority of the system is demonstrated when an originally rare or unusual variant in the chain spreads to fill a gap in the systems of a large area. One of several examples of this[27] is provided by the origin and spread of the form *she*. As is well known, the "regular" ME reflex of OE *heo* was *he*, so that large areas of the country were left without a formal distinction between "he" and "she," while even in the remaining areas the other surviving forms (*hy*, *heo*) were not ideal for the purpose. That a need for a new distinctive form existed probably requires no more specific proof than the graphic ambiguities apparent in many surviving texts; yet interesting indications of it occur in certain MSS.[28] where the curious variants *hei*, *hey* are

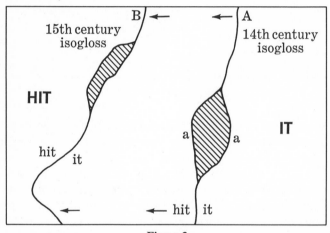

**Figure 2**

used for "he," and in one (BM. Add. 19677) *hei* "he" occurs more often in close proximity to *he* "she." Even if the spelling *hei* is not phonically significant, therefore, this MS. at least shows that its scribe wished to distinguish between the morphographs for "he" and "she."

The most probable theory hitherto advanced is that this systemic gap was filled by the selection of the originally rare stress-shifted forms /hjo/ and /hje/. As A. H. Smith[29] and E. Dieth[30] have shown, their most probable area of origin was the heavily Norse-influenced Cumberland–Yorks belt, where there are numerous parallels for the change of /hj/ to /ʃ/. The intermediate stage /ç/ would, as pointed out by Vachek,[31] survive for a time as a marginal phoneme (spelt *ʒ* or *ʒh*), but would naturally give way to /ʃ/, which was equally distinctive for the purpose of functional differentiation, yet far better integrated phonemically.

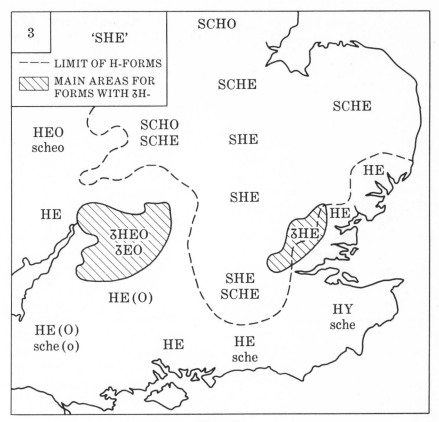

**Figure 3**

Convincing proof for this theory (as against the older derivations from OE *sēo* or ON *sjá*) is now available from study of the ME distributions of forms. The later ME distribution, schematized in Fig. 3, shows ȝ(*h*)-forms in border areas which divide the newer *s(c)he*, *s(c)ho* in the Midlands from the older *he*, *hy*, *heo* in the south. A map of the earlier ME evidence would contrast strongly, as it would show *ȝho*, *ge*, *ghe*, *yo*[32] at a number of points which later have *s(c)he* or *s(c)ho*, and *he(o)* or *hi(e)*[33] at some points of the areas that later have *ȝhe(o)*. In other words, a belt of ȝ(*h*)-forms started in the northern belt and moved southwards across the country, always followed, after what appears to have been a comparatively uniform lapse of time, by *s(c)h*-forms. Since the southward spread of *s(c)he* was thus invariably preceded by a belt of ȝ(*h*)-forms, we may justifiably conclude that the modern form *she* arose from an originally unusual phonetic variant in the spoken chain, and that it spread to large areas in which, failing such a form, the pronominal system was wholly lacking in balance.

## II

From the evidence of (*a*) and (*b*) above, it is reasonable to assume that these two types stand at opposite extremes of the whole range of diversity of linguistic change. For intermediate cases, combinations of various pressures must be assumed, and many distributions in Modern English will provide examples. One is the distribution of the reflexes of OE/y/, where the common reflex is /i/ (as in *hill* or *pit*) but where most of the so-called "exceptions" may be accounted for as follows:

(i) Conditioned phonetic variants: *blush, rush, thrush, clutch, crutch, much, merry, bury.*
(ii) Avoidance of homonymy: *left* (cf. *lift*) and perhaps *dull* (cf. *dill, dell*) and *hemlock* (cf. *him*: apart from *hymn*, there are no common words commencing with /him/).
(iii) Taboo: avoidance of /i/ in *shut, shuttle.*
(iv) Phonaesthetic reasons: *knell* (cf. *bell*), *dent* (cf. *indent*)[34]

Of the above, (i) is presumably to be regarded as mechanical in origin, the rest as systemic. But further conclusions may sometimes be drawn from a detailed knowledge of the history of individual words: the history of *much*, listed in (i), shows a long conflict between the variants *much(e)* and *mich(e)*, and we may suspect, from its collocations, that the final selection was of a vowel that would contrast with, rather than match, that of the word *little*.

The necessity of appeal to such varied influences as phonetic conditioning, homonymic clash, taboo and phonaesthetics leads to my second main point. In order to avoid the accusation of bias,[35] the scheme of study must include every possible source of evidence, i.e., not only the main subsystems (phonology, morphology, lexis) in isolation, but also the interrelations between those subsystems. If the subsystems are not completely integrated in the total system, then interrelations will include not only reciprocal influences, but conflicts, as for example between the phonemic system and phonaesthemes.[36] Whereas, therefore, chain and system can usually, for purely synchronic study, be represented in a simple diagram of parallel or crossing lines, the scheme I propose for diachronic study is more conveniently represented by circles, as in Fig. 4. Thirdly, and beyond this diagram, we must add the influence of neighbouring chains and systems of both dialect and class, and, if the evidence suggests it, the more extra-linguistic factors such as those of social pressure.[37]

Within this comprehensive scheme we proceed—as usual in empirically based science—by collecting as many significant correspondences as possible. The relationships thus established need not necessarily be causal: two related changes, one in phonology and the other in grammar, might both be symptoms of a more radical cause. But I would maintain that, whether of causes or symptoms, the detection of such correspondences still increases our knowledge.[38] They often have to be carefully weighed: an obvious example is the Great Vowel Shift. For the starting point of this change, we find no especially

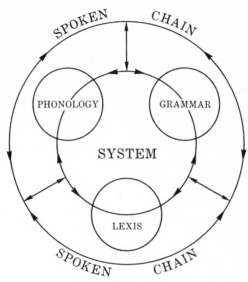

**Figure 4**

cogent systemic correspondences. The various vowel systems of Middle English were not noticeably lacking in symmetry, and, on the whole, there was a greater lack of symmetry during and after the shift than before it. The reasons given by Vachek for the start of the shift—that short /i/ and /u/ correlated with long close /ẹ/ and /ǫ/ rather than with /iː/ and /uː/, which were therefore isolated[39]—suggests hardly more than that the beginnings of the shift were not in conflict with the balance of the existing system. Professor Martinet's theory of isochrony would have more cogency if his suggested neutralization of quantitative distinctions extended to more contexts[40]; but there is clear rhyming and orthographic evidence that these distinctions survived throughout in closed monosyllables. On the other hand, there are weighty correspondences in the spoken chain: the start of the shift followed closely on the most significant prosodic change in the history of the language—the loss of final /ə/[41]—by which English became the most monosyllabic language in Western Europe: its rhythm was entirely changed, as is shown, among other things, by the drastic alterations to the existing tradition of verse-writing. Whether this change of rhythm and the beginnings of the Vowel Shift are both symptoms of some deeper prosodic cause has been debated,[42] but, in any event, the parallel yet unconnected diphthongizations and raisings in High German, Dutch and Southern English, compared with the lack of them in Scandinavian, North German, and to some extent in Scots and N. English, suggest certain long-inherited suprasegmental features of the spoken chain as the moving factor.[43] Admittedly phonemic factors, such as the addition of /aː/ to the inventory of long-vowel phonemes, would play their part;

but, as Professor Dobson suggests, this phonemicization was a direct result of the loss of final /ə/,[44] and therefore ultimately non-systemic in origin. Similarly, the remaining stages of the shift may well be due, at least in part, to push- and drag-chain processes in the system, but these will not explain the by-passing of the stage [εː], which resulted in the heavy overloading of the /eː/-phoneme around 1700, and an uneven system of three back but only two front long vowels.[45] On this evidence, we must reckon with the continued pressure of shifted variants in the spoken chain as the prior factor. Indeed, there is some slight evidence that the seventeenth-century avoidance of [εː] may have been social (i.e., extra-linguistic) in origin[46]; in that case, to insist on systemic priority for the whole shift would be tantamount to claiming that an originally systemically-motivated change had somehow "misfired."

Nevertheless, the last change, in which part of the /eː/-phoneme was redistributed to /iː/ is indeed more probably due to a process of (belated) regulation, in the system, of the state of imbalance resulting from the whole shift. An ample source of raised variants existed for ME ę̄-words only, and these were selected, in varying degrees in different dialects, to remedy the overloading of /eː/. The many homonyms in /iː/ that resulted are often regarded as an indication that this change must have been primarily *non*-systemic in character. At the same time, a more relevant fact is ignored: had the change *not* taken place, the number of homonyms in /eː/ would have been much greater, as may be judged from the following lists. The centre column of list A gives 38 forms which, as may be deduced from comparison with the two outer columns, would have become homonyms in either event (whether with /eː/ or /iː/); in B are listed 34 forms in which the selection of /iː/ avoided homonymic clash with other forms containing /eː/, while list C gives the far smaller total of 10 forms in which the selection of /iː/ actually resulted in homonymic clash.

*List A*[47]

| | | |
|---|---|---|
| been v. (p. p.) | bean n.* | bane n. |
| ⌈beer, n. | bear v.⌉ | |
| ⌊bier n. | bear n.⌋ | bare, a., v.⌋ |
| beet n. | beat v.* | ⌠bate v., n. |
| | | ⌡bait v., n. |
| cheep n. | cheap a. | chape n. |
| deer n. | dear a. | dare v. |
| feet n. pl. | feat, n., a.* | fate n. |
| flee v. | flea n. | flay v. |
| gleed n. | ⌠glead n.⌉ | glade n. |
| | ⌡glede n.⌋ | |
| Greece n. | grease n., v.* | grace n., v. |
| grieve v. | greave n.* | grave n., a. |
| heel n. | heal v.* | ⌠hale a. |
| | | ⌡hail n., v. |

List A—*continued*

| | | |
|---|---|---|
| here adv. | hear v. | { hare n. / hair n. |
| lee n. | lea n.* | lay n., a., v. |
| leed n. | lead v.* | { lade v. / laid v. (pa. t.) |
| leek n. | leak n., v. | lake n. |
| meed n. | mead n.(*) | { maid n. / made v. (pa. t.) |
| meet a., v. | { meat n.* / mete v. } | mate n., v. |
| piece n., v. | peace n. | pace n., v. |
| peel n., v. | peal n., v. | { pail n. / pale a. |
| [ peer n., v. / pier n. } | pear n. | { pare v. / pair n., v. ] |
| reel n. | real a. | rail n., v. |
| reeve n. | reave v.* | rave v. |
| see v., n. | sea n. | say v. |
| { seel v. / ceil v. } | seal n., v. | { sail n., v. / sale n. |
| seem v. | seam n. | same a. |
| seen v. (p. p.) | sean n. | sane a. |
| sheer a. | shear v.* | share v., n. |
| steel n., v. | steal v.† | stale a. |
| teem v. | team n. | tame v., a. |
| tier n. | { tear n. / tear v., n. } | tare n. |
| week n. | weak a. | wake v., n. |
| wheel n., v. / weel n. } | weal n. | { wail n., v. / whale n. |
| ween v. | wean v., a.* | { wane v. / wain n. |
| [weir n. | wear v. | ware n., a.] |

## List B

| | | | | |
|---|---|---|---|---|
| beak n., v.* | bake v. | heat n., v.* | hate n., v. |
| beast n. | baste v. | lean v., a. | { lane n. / lain v. (p. p.) |
| deal n., v.* | dale n. | | |
| { dean n. / dene n. } | { Dane n. / deign v. } | lease n., v.* | lace n., v. |
| | | leave n., v.* | lave v. |
| ear n.* | { air n. / heir n. } | meal n.* | { male n. / mail n. |
| eat v. | { eight num. / ate v. (pa. t.) } | mean v., n., a.* | { mane n. / main n., a. |
| fear v., n.* | { fare v., n. / fair a., n. } | mere n., a.* | mare n. |
| | | neal v.* | nail v., n. |
| fleam n.* | flame n. | neap n., a.* | nape n. |

## List B—*continued*

| | | |
|---|---|---|
| pea n.* . . . pay n., v. | teal n.* . . . { tail n. / tale n. } |
| peat n.* . . . pate n. | treat n., v.* . . trait n. |
| plea n.* . . . play n., v. | veal n.* . . . { vale n. / veil n. } |
| [plead v. . . . played v.] | weary a.* . . . wary a. |
| pleat n.* . . . plate n. | weave v.* . . . { wave v., n. / waive v. } |
| reap v.* . . . rape v. | wheat n.* . . . { wait v., n. / weight n. } |
| rear v., a.* . . . rare a. | |
| seat n., v.* . . . sate v. | |
| sneak n., v.*. . . snake n. | |
| spear n., v.* . . . spare v., a. | |

### List C

| | |
|---|---|
| beech n. . . . beach n.† | need v., n. . . . knead v.† |
| breech n. . . . breach n.† | peek v. . . . peak n. |
| creek n. . . . creak v. | queen n. . . . quean n.† |
| lief a. . . . leaf n. | reed n.. . . . { read v. / rede v., n.† } |
| leech n. . . . leach n., v.† | |

To judge by the criterion of form only, therefore, the conclusion is clear: the selection of /iː/ was an overall functional gain. If form-class is adopted as the more important criterion for assessing homonymy, the totals are altered somewhat, but the general conclusion to be drawn remains the same, since many forms in List A then become significant instead of merely neutral. As a rough guide, an asterisk is added in the above lists to those cases in which, on grounds of form-class, the functional yield was increased by the change (41), and a dagger to those in which it was decreased (7).

Whereas the earlier stages of the Vowel Shift are all, initially at least, examples of allophonic change, this last is a phonemic change,[48] since it involves only an alteration in the distribution between two existing phonemes. Such a change is more likely to admit of exceptions; and the controversy as to whether these are "borrowings of unshifted variants,"[49] or the untouched residue of "weak" or "sporadic" change[50] is largely one of terminology. But we shall be better able to decide on the more accurate term if we can determine whether the exceptions result from mere areal pressure in the spoken chain (i.e., a random effect of geographical position), or from systemic selection. In this case, it is quite clear that the exceptions with /eː/ were *not* selected to avoid homonymic clash, and I shall return to their explanation later.

## III

It is a commonplace of general diachronic theory that grammatical ambiguities arising from sound-change are remedied by the selection of new analogical forms.[51] It was applied in the nineteenth century to show how "regular" paradigms are restored after the "ravages of phonetic change." But much less has been done to show the close connection between threatened loss of functional distinction and the the rise of new forms. The history of the English strong verb, as presented by Long[52] and Price,[53] is a catalogue of hitherto unexplained analogical changes; yet, if the chronology of these is related to those of sound-changes, they can be shown to be selections of those variants that best preserved the vowel differentiation on which gradation depends. The process can be demonstrated from many periods, but especially the sixteenth century, for, after the middle of the fifteenth century, the loss of many distinctive verbal endings must have aggravated still further the ambiguities arising from phonetic proximity of root vowels of the past and present tenses. Verbs of Classes IV and V containing ME /ɛː/ as the root-vowel of the present (*bear, break, shear, speak, steal, tear, tread, wear, weave*) usually show a Late ME preterite in *a* (*bar(e), brak(e)*, etc.). Wright says "a new type of preterite began to be formed in the sixteenth century with ǭ from the past participle."[54] This explains the source of the /ɔː/-variants in the spoken chain, but not their selection: that must surely be due to the fact that /ɔː/ provided a better contrast to the /ɛː/ of the present than the etymologically developed /æː/ (which may well have merged with /ɛː/ in many dialects at or before this time,[55] giving, in all these verbs, the complete homonymy we today associate with *bare*, the archaic preterite of the infin. *bear*).

By this and other changes—especially that from strong to weak—the originally frequent contrast *e-a* of Classes III, IV, and V was eliminated.[56] It is significant that while *e-a* was replaced by *e-o*, the contrast *i-a* proved adequate and survived in many verbs of the types *sing-sang* (Cl. III) and *sit-sat* (Cl. V), and it even prevailed in the case of *give-gave*, in spite of the availability of the variants *geve* and *gove*. That these two contrasts, *i-a* and *e-o*, were the most important in the verb-system of EMnE is suggested by the history of the verb *get*, where we find that the contrast *get-got* was for long in competition with that of *git-gat*, and both systems are still found in modern dialects.[57]

It is only by reference to the growing importance of the *e-o* contrasts in the sixteenth century that the seemingly contradictory developments in verbs of Class I (e.g., *write, drive*) can be explained. Here, in spite of the fact that the contrast /əi/-/ɔː/, reflexes of ME /iː/-/ɔː/, was still adequate, there occur frequently, in addition to historical *wrote, drove*, the variants *wrate, drave*[58]; and these, whether pronounced with [æː] or [ɛː], would be less effective for qualitative gradation than /ɔː/. They are mysterious, as they were used for a period of about a hundred years only, and are generally supposed to be analogical creations on the model of *bare, brake*, etc., appearing at a time when these forms themselves were being ousted by the type *bore, broke*. There are, however, stylistic differences that provide a clue: *a* in Class I (*drave*, etc.) is typical of printed literature, while *o* is commoner in letters and manuscripts.[59] We may therefore reasonably surmise (i) that in Classes IV and V, the new /ɔː/ was colloquial and dialectal, and that there was a preference, in formal levels of sixteenth-century speech, for the traditional reflexes /æː/ or

/ɛ:/, and (ii) by a process of hypercorrection, this distinction was transferred to the original *o*-preterites in Class I, so that the traditional *wrote, drove* would now be less used, and replaced in formal writing by the wholly unhistorical *wrate, drave* (or, to some extent, by forms like *writ*).

Finally, when *a* was replaced by *o* in Classes IV and V, the short-lived type *wrate, drave* in Class I gave way to the original forms *wrote, drove*. As a corollary, the very existence of the type *wrate, drave* can be used as evidence that the new /ɔ:/-preterites in Classes IV and V were in fact far commoner in sixteenth-century colloquial use than literary records might lead us to suppose.

Although these details on the strong verbs of Class I do not demonstrate the principle of systemic selection, I add them here to show that when such a complex system of contrasts as the strong verb is disturbed by sound-change, the *ad hoc* selections used to restore the balance in some classes of verbs may in turn disrupt the balance in other classes. It can hardly be a coincidence that, just at this period of instability in the strong verb system, another quite unusual development was taking place: the great increase in the use of the *do*-periphrasis. Whereas all the other periphrases of the MnE verb result from an almost imperceptibly gradual growth since OE times, the *do*-periphrasis arose later, in ME, reached its peak in the sixteenth century, and after that decreased to its more restricted uses in MnE. For such a sudden rise and fall, there can only be a functional explanation. It would be unwise to assume that such a phenomenal growth was a necessary preliminary, produced by some kind of systemic "providence," for its later restricted uses. The grammars and monographs state that its sixteenth-century use was indiscriminate,[60] and that evidence alone suggests that *do, doth*, and *did* were initially simply tense-markers, systemically selected to remedy current ambiguities. Closer consideration of sixteenth-century usage confirms this view: it shows that the use of *do* is not entirely random, for, although it is already common in negative and interrogative clauses, it occurs more often (i) with certain verbs that presented ambiguities of conjugation (cf. the exclusive use of *did eat*, never *ate*, in the 1611 Gospels); (ii) with weak verbs accepted as invariable since then (*cast, put, set*).[61] Furthermore, in more literary uses it would seem to have been used purely as a signal of verbality, as it is commonly used, firstly, to "announce" the presence of neologisms from Latin like *imitate* or *illuminate*, which had not yet been fully assimilated to the grammatical system (it is notable that the termination *-ed* is avoided with verbs ending in *-ate* until after 1600), and secondly, in the long complex sentences of many Elizabethan writers, especially to denote a return to the main clause after the interruption of a subordinate clause.[62]

These examples by no means exhaust the variety of the uses of the *do*-periphrasis in the sixteenth century. The development, from this variety, of the much-needed negative and interrogative *do*-constructions is an example par excellence of systemic selection from a large field of variants originally called into use for other reasons. The situation in the seventeenth century confirms this: by the first half of the century, earlier instabilities in the verbal system had been largely remedied, and the use of the periphrasis in affirmative clauses decreased. But, as a prominent inherited feature of the spoken chain, it could not suddenly vanish, and it is therefore not surprising that seventeenth-century grammarians claim that it has an imperfect sense; that is, by virtue of mere availability it has assumed an aspectual function. Dr. Ellegård questions the grammarians' statements,[63] but analysis of the well-known *did* of Pepys' *Diary* suggests that there is some truth in them. Its further decrease, in the face of the growing expanded form (*was* + -*ing*) is natural, but this last shift of system in the late seventeenth century provides interesting confirmation of the history of its earlier functions that has been postulated here.

## IV

Interpenetration of the phonological and grammatical systems of the past can be studied only because much is already known about these systems themselves. But this is only one type of interpenetration: without the others, between lexis and phonology, lexis and grammar, the account remains incomplete. I left aside earlier those *enfants terribles* of traditional *Lautlehre*, *great, break* and *steak*, since, on grounds of functional yield only, we would certainly expect the selection of the variants /griːt, briːk, stiːk/. Walker's observations, at the end of the eighteenth century, that he found /greːt/ and/ breːk/ more expressive,[64] are often dismissed as subjective ex-post-facto judgments,[65] but those who dismiss them forget that they are, even today, open to objective verification. The eighteenth-century phonaesthetic values of /-iːk/ and /-eːk/ depended mainly on the monosyllables then current which ended in these sounds, and the words in question admit of the following semantic groupings:

1. /-iːk/:
    (*a*) Verbs denoting the making of noise, usually high-pitched: *creak, speak, squeak, shriek, screak.*
    (*b*) Verbs denoting covert action: *peek, seek, sneak* and to some extent *leak* and *reek.*
    (*c*) Nouns denoting narrow objects: *beak, creek, peak, streak, meak* "narrow tool."
    (*d*) "Derogatory" adjectives or nouns: *bleak, freak, weak, sneak, sleek, gleek* "gibe," *pique* (earlier *peek, peak*), and perhaps *meek.*
    Not classified: *eek, leek, cheek, Greek, week, teak, tweak, wreak.*
2. /-eːk/ (Mn. /-eik/):
    (*a*) Verbs denoting overt action, without any basic implication of noise: *bake, make, quake, rake, shake, slake, stake, take, wake.*
    (*b*) Nouns denoting ordinary objects or animates: *brake, cake, drake, hake, rake, snake, stake,* and perhaps *flake.*
    Not classified: *ache* v., *lake, sake, crake* (Northern), *fake* (nineteenth century).

There is strong and well-known evidence that there was, in the early eighteenth century, a choice of the two pronunciations /eː/ and /iː/ for the reflex of ME ē̞.[66] It is probable, too, that /iː/ had been accepted into London English for most of the words in the group fairly early in the century, and it is therefore reasonable to assume (as has been done above) that such words were at least beginning to contribute to the phonaesthetic values current when the variants /breːk/ and /steːk/ gained ground later. The reason why /eː/ was selected in these two words is therefore apparent: the meanings of *break* contrast strongly with 1 (*a*) and (*b*) but agree with 2 (*a*), and those of *steak*, similarly, fit 2 (*b*) better than 1 (*c*) and (*d*).

If the same procedure is applied to *great*, the following groupings result:

1. /-iːt/ in many cases suggests
   (*a*) smallness, daintiness, politeness, dexterity: *cleat, feat* (a. "dexterous"; n. "trick"), *fleet* (a. "nimble"; n. "creek"), *greet, meet* "fitting," *neat, pleat,*[67] *sweet, teat, treat,* and perhaps also *seat* n. and *meet* v.
   (*b*) natural substances or produce: *beet, gleet, peat, sleet, wheat,* and perhaps *meat*.
   Not classified: *feet, fleet* (of ships), *leet, sheet, street*; *beat, bleat, cheat, eat, heat, neat,* n.

2. /-eːt/ (/-eit/) suggests the opposite—size, expanse, tangibility, grossness: *bait, bate* "strife," *crate, eight, fate, freight, gate, grate, hate, pate, plate, prate, rate, sate, skate, slate, state, straight, weight* (and also, if expanse in time-relation is included, *late, date, wait*).
   Not classified: *strait, trait, mate*; *spate* (Northern till nineteenth century).[68]

Here again, the meanings of *great* are diametrically opposed to those predominant in 1 (*a*), but closely match those of 2. In this case it might be objected that, of the words listed above, *beat, heat* and perhaps *meat* must also have had eighteenth-century variants in /eː/, and, since their meanings approach those of 2, they might have been expected to survive in that form; but these words have already been covered by the functional explanation given above (pp. 332–334), and it is interesting to note that, when two factors are found to have conflicted thus, the various resulting forms still admit of precise explanation. *Beat, heat,* and *meat* would all have coincided, at /eː/, with other words of the same word-classes, whereas the selection of /iː/ averted such a clash in each case:

(i) beet *n.*—beat *v.*—bait *v.* and *n.*, bate *v.* and *n.*[69]
(ii) heat *n.* and *v.*—hate *n.* and *v.* (no previous /iː/-form existed).
(iii) meet *adj.* and *v.*—meat, *n.*—mate *n.* and *v.*

In these cases, therefore, the functional factor outweighed the phonaesthetic. But in the case of *great* (adj.) and *grate* (n. and v.) there was no clash at the level of word-class, and, since the phonaesthetic factor was especially strong here, it far outweighed the weaker functional one. It is in dealing with such a complex that the "all-or-nothing" fallacy appears at its most misleading: it would inhibit us from recognizing the two conflicting tendencies, from weighing their relative potencies, and from disentangling their various seams of influence.[70]

The remarks just made can only be tentative, since, apart from the magnificent alphabetical dictionaries completed and in progress, English lexis has not been studied to the same extent as phonology and grammar, and it is therefore correspondingly more difficult to examine this aspect of interpenetration. There is a need, firstly, for full and systematic phonaesthetic evaluations of different periods of English.[71] More urgent still is the need for descriptions of the lexical system itself. Even for Modern English, no full description exists, though the gap is to some extent filled by Roget's important pioneering work of 1852, especially in its latest revision (1962). For past periods, there is nothing: to extrapolate from Roget to the *OED* may be an interesting pastime, but it can tell us only the comparative age of *current* forms, and cannot include words now obsolete, or words used in different meanings in the past. We need nothing less than a comprehensive historical thesaurus, with complete dates of currency, of all the forms, past and present, ever used to express single and related ideas in English, however short-lived each form—and each sense of each form—may have been. Such a work would tell us how many and which words were available, to each writer in past periods, for the expression of a given notion (or, if you prefer, which words were either wholly or partly commutable in a given context); and it would provide the basic material necessary for detecting and solving all problems of "semantic fields" in English, notably the connections, in each field, between semantic shift, verbal obsolescence and innovation.[72] I need hardly add that it would also make a substantial contribution to literary criticism and the history of ideas. In an attempt to remedy this need, we have recently started a research project at Glasgow, but we are under no illusion regarding the size of the task.

Beyond all this, there still remains the vast problem of "favoured collocation" or "idiom." Work has been proceeding at Edinburgh on this aspect of Modern English, but, here again, we have nothing on past periods. I am open to correction, but I am not aware that any work is planned that would tell us why, for example, Sir Thomas Browne's "holds no proportion to" was replaced by other phrases like "bears no proportion to" or "is out of proportion to."

I have tried in this paper to suggest a general theory by which diachronic linguistics may repel the charges of amateurism often levelled at it. For dealing historically with the phonological and grammatical systems of English, we have inherited from our predecessors a legacy which can and should be used fruitfully, not belittled because of its terminology. In the field of lexis—apart from alphabetical dictionaries—we are comparatively poorly equipped, and the way before us is a long one.

## FOOTNOTES

1. A. Martinet, *A Functional View of Language* (1962), p. 138, and *Elements of General Linguistics*, p. 166.
2. R. Jakobson, *Selected Writings*, I, p. 651; N. C. W. Spence, *Archivum Linguisticum*, XII (1960), p. 27.

3. Especially A. Martinet in his *Économie des changements phonétiques*, Berne, 1955 (hereafter referred to as *Économie*), as well as in numerous articles. The work of Malkiel and Vachek has also appeared in the form of articles, some of the more recent of which are *Archivum Linguisticum*, XV (1963), 144 ff., *Language*, XXXVI (1960), 281–346, and *Lingua*, XI (1962), 447 ff. Fuller references to the work of Professor Vachek may be found in *Brno Studies in English*, IV (1964), p. 100.

4. "Historical, Descriptive and Dynamic Linguistics," *Language and Speech*, II (1959), p. 23.

5. C. A. Robson, *Archivum Linguisticum*, VIII (1956), p. 154, and cf. Spence, *op. cit.*, pp. 1–5.

6. In addition to works already mentioned, see N. E. Collinge, "Phonetic Shifts and Phonemic Asymmetries," *Proceedings of the Fourth International Congress of Phonetic Sciences*, Helsinki, 1961, 563 ff.

7. O. Jespersen, *Language*, p. 262, and cf. Martinet, *Word*, VIII (1952), p. 1.

8. A. G. Juilland, writing in 1953 (*Word*, IX, p. 200), suggested that the problem had already been solved by "the overcoming of the Saussurean antinomy." His further statement ("To the quasi-theological conception of a unique and indivisible cause, as we find it throughout the 19th century, diachronic phonemics opposes the conception of multiple and convergent conditions in the spirit of modern science") is certainly relevant to the present discussion, but the period since he wrote has shown that his optimism was unjustified.

9. M. Lehnert, "The Interrelation between Form and Function in the Development of the English Language," *ZAA*, V (1957), 43–56, and references there quoted.

10. R. Berndt, *Form und Funktion des Verbums im nördlichen Spätaltenglischen* (Halle, 1956).

11. *Économie*, pp. 34–6, 58–9, 98–9, 108, 114–15, 117, 169, 173–96; cf. *Word*, VIII (1952), pp. 2 and 8, and for further references, A. G. Juilland, *op. cit.*

12. H. M. Hoenigswald, *Language*, XXXIII (1957), 575 ff.

13. A. Martinet, *Word*, VIII (1952), pp. 30–1, and cf. *Économie*, p. 120 and elsewhere.

14. These ideas are ultimately Saussurean (*Cours de linguistique générale*, pp. 124–38, 142 and 237) but they have been recognized, in part or whole, by other writers since: cf. Sapir, *Language*, p. 199; Jakobson, *Principes de phonologie historique* (Appendix I to Troubetzkoy's *Principes de phonologie*, tr. Cantineau Paris, 1949), p. 335; and the works by Martinet, Juilland and Spence already quoted. Despite this recognition, however, their value for systematic diachronic study does not seem to have been realized by many of the specialists working on individual languages.

15. Since other homonymies (with *daw, flaw, maw, paw*) occurred later and are only partial, they may be omitted from consideration in the present example.

16. W. Horn and M. Lehnert, *Laut und Leben*, I, p. 495 f.

17. *Language: A Modern Synthesis*, especially pp. 168–70, 175, 179 and 203.

18. *Efficiency in Linguistic Change*, p. 49.

19. E. J. Dobson, "Early Modern Standard English," *TPS*, 1955, p. 42 [Reprinted here, pp. 419 ff.—Ed.] Many examples of the process will be found (under different titles) in the works of Gilliéron and his followers: see the references quoted in E. R. Williams, *The Conflict of Homonyms in English* (New Haven, 1944).

20. *Op. cit.*, pp. 23–5.

21. For the evidence on which this and the subsequent map are based see A. McIntosh, "A New Approach to Middle English Dialectology," *English Studies*, XLIV (1963), 1–11. [Reprinted here, pp. 392 ff.—Ed.]

22. E. J. Dobson, *TPS*, 1955, p. 35.

23. A. A. Prins, *Proceedings of the Eighth International Congress of Linguists*, p. 122; T. Heltveit, *Studies in English Demonstrative Pronouns* (Oslo, 1953).

24. *EDGr*, p. 279.

25. M. Lehnert, *op. cit.*, p. 49.

26. A. Martinet, *Word*, VIII (1952), p. 139; *Économie*, especially ch. 4; *Elements of General Linguistics*, pp. 167–70.

27. I have shown elsewhere (*English Studies*, XLIV [1963], p. 83) that the spread of *they* and *though* to areas outside the original Danelaw boundary can be explained only by the assumption of overwhelming systemic pressures. [Reprinted here, pp. 404 ff.—Ed.]

28. Cambridge University Library MS. Gg. 4.27.2, B. M. Harley 2376 (fol. 28ᵃ) and B. M. Addit. 19677.

29. *RES*, I (1925), 437–40.

30. *English Studies*, XXXVI (1955), 209–17.

31. J. Vachek, "Notes on the Phonological Development of the NE Pronoun *She*," *Sborník prací filosofické fakulty brněnské university*, III, Ser. A. (1954), 67–80; id. *Brno Studies in English*, IV (1964), 21–9.

32. In Orm, *Bestiary, Genesis and Exodus* and *De Clerico et Puella* (B. M. Addit. 23986).

33. Cf. *hie* and *he* in *Vices and Virtues*, *hie* and *heo* in the *Trinity Homilies*.

34. This leaves a residue of only *cudgel*, *fledge* and *shed*, and even these might be shown, by means of the type of phonaesthetic research exemplified later in this paper, to belong to (iv).

35. Cf., for example, C. A. Ladd, *Proceedings of the Ninth International Congress of Linguists* (Cambridge, Mass., 1962), p. 650; "... interpolation and extrapolation become arbitrary, and we have no defence against the linguist who alters the rules of the game to suit his own convenience."

36. See further on p. 338 below.

37. An inclusive approach has often been urged in the past, e.g., by Jespersen (*Language*, p. 298), Sapir (*Language*, p. 196), John Orr ("On Homonymics," *Words and Sounds in English and French*, pp. 91–133), E. Öhmann ("Über unregelmässige Lautentwicklung," *Neuphilologische Mitteilungen*, XLVII [1948], 145–64), and most recently and cogently, by Y. Malkiel (*op. cit.*, pp. 145–50, 169–73). Cf. also note 8 above. It is criticized on the grounds that it lacks rigour (C. A. Ladd, *loc. cit.*) or that it may result in a hotch-potch of unsystematized explanations (Trim, *op. cit.*, p. 19). One of the main aims of the present paper is to show that the theory is capable of systematic application, and that it therefore deserves more general acceptance.

38. Cf. the apt parallel given by Y. Malkiel, *op. cit.*, p. 150.

39. J. Vachek in *Brno Studies in English*, III, discussed by E. J. Dobson, *TPS*, 1962, p. 130.

40. *Économie*, pp. 248–56.

41. The dating of the loss of /-ə/ in the spoken language is not as uncertain as some recent writers would have us believe (e.g., J. G. Southworth in *Verses of Cadence*). The written distinction between singular and plural of the adjective (e.g., *good*/*go(o)de*) or between the strong and weak forms (e.g., *first*/ *þe firste*) is an unconscious one which *must* depend on spoken context, not scribal tradition. Yet it is consistently maintained in writing by many scribes until well into the fifteenth century, notably in the very areas (East Anglia, Warwicks., Bucks., Wilts.) which are the first to show *ey-*, *ei-* spellings for ME /iː/. The evidence from other areas is less conclusive, but certainly does not contradict the theory of a consistent chronological relationship between the two changes.

42. For a convenient summary of earlier arguments see A. A. Prins, *The Great Vowel Shift* (Groningen, 1940); A. Schmitt, *Akzent und Diphthongierung*, pp. 100 ff.

43. This possibility was supported, as a matter of general theory, by A. Martinet in 1952 (*Word*, VIII, 28–32) and again in 1962 (*A Functional View of Language*, p. 147). It seems to me to fit the evidence for the Great Vowel Shift better than his own view of 1955 (see note 40 above).

44. E. J. Dobson, "Middle English Lengthening in Open Syllables," *TPS*, 1962, p. 144.

45. A. Martinet, *Économie*, p. 99.

46. See E. J. Dobson, *English Pronunciation 1500–1700*, I, p. 145, and *TPS*, 1955, p. 41. The raised variants regarded by Gil as affected in the early seventeenth century might be expected to enter normal polite usage later in the century. For modern demonstrations of the process, see W. Bright and A. K. Ramanujan, "Sociolinguistic Variation and Language Change," *Proceedings of the Ninth International Congress of Linguists*, pp. 1107–13, with references there quoted to the works of Joos and Fischer.

47. Words of late dialect origin like *tee, raid* are omitted from these lists, as are also the four main "exceptions" (*great, break, steak, yea*: cf. pp. 337–338 below). Forms in *-r* are included, but are placed in square brackets in those cases of List A where an /ɛː/-variant was preferred to that in /iː/.

48. C. A. Ladd, "The Nature of Sound Change," *Proceedings of the Ninth International Congress of Linguists* (Ed. H. G. Lunt, 1964), pp. 650–7.

49. Bloomfield, *Language*, pp. 361–2; H. M. Hoenigswald, *Language Change and Linguistic Reconstruction*, p. 79 and footnote 11.

50. Y. Malkiel, "Paradigmatic Resistance to Sound Change," *Language*, XXXVI (1960), pp. 284–90; "Etymology and General Linguistics," *Word*, XVIII (1962), p. 213; "Weak Phonetic Change, Spontaneous Sound Shift, Lexical Contamination," *Lingua*, XI (1962), pp. 263–75; and *Archivum Linguisticum*, XV (1963), *loc. cit.*

51. Jespersen, *Language*, p. 289, and *Efficiency in Linguistic Change*, pp. 23 and 58, with reference to H. Paul there quoted; Sapir, *Language*, p. 196; Saussure, *Cours*, p. 227; Vendryes, *Le Langage*, p. 58; C. Bally, *Le langage et la vie*, pp. 26, 44, 152; E. Hermann, *Lautgesetz und Analogie*, p. 128; A. Martinet, *Word*, VIII (1952), p. 10, and *Économie*, pp. 58–9.

52. M. M. Long, *The English Strong Verb from Chaucer to Caxton*, Menasha (1944).

53. H. T. Price, *A History of Ablaut in the Strong Verbs from Caxton to the end of the Elizabethan Period* (= *Bonner Studien zur englischen Philologie*, III) (Bonn, 1910).

54. J. Wright, *Elementary Historical New English Grammar*, § 359. Cf. Price, *op. cit.*, pp. 98–104, 135, 138–41. For *o*-forms in fifteenth-century dialect texts, see M. M. Long, *op. cit.*, pp. 120, 122, 124.

55. Whether the merger took place at the stage [ɛː] or [eː] is not relevant here. See Dobson, *TPS*, 1955, pp. 43–4.

56. In Class III, the elimination of the contrast *e-a* had started even earlier:

ME delve—dalf  . . . . EMnE delve—dolve/delved
„  helpe—halp/holp  . .  „  helpe—holpe/helped
„  melte—malt  . . .  „  melte—molte(d)/melte(d)

In the verbs *bark, carve, smart, starve, warp* the change of *-er-* to *-ar-* left no alternative to a weak preterite.

The change from strong to weak conjugation is usually regarded as a natural result of analogical influence from the larger group of weak verbs, and this is no doubt true as regards the *origin* of weak variants. But it is noticeable that the rate of their *adoption* is closely related to the presence or lack of adequate vocalic contrasts in the strong verb system of a given period. This applies especially to the extensive ME change from strong to weak in Class II, where the original contrast of ę̄ and ę̆ (reflexes of OE *ēo* and *ēa*) barely survived. For OE, cf. WS *slǣpan—slēp* but Nhb. *slēpan—slēpte*.

57. From the data in Wright, *EDGr.* (Index, s.vv. *get* and *got*) it appears that the three contrasts *get-got*, *git-gat*, and *git-got* all cover appreciable areas, whereas the original *get-gat* is the rarest.

58. H. T. Price, *op. cit.*, p. 9.

59. *Ibid.*, pp. 11–35.

60. See H. Sweet, *New English Grammar*, II, p. 88; A. Ellegård, *The Auxiliary Do*, pp. 170 f.

61. O. Jespersen, *A Modern English Grammar*, V, pp. 504–6; T. Dahl, *Linguistic Studies in some Elizabethan Writers*, II, p. 88.

62. T. Dahl, *op. cit.*, especially pp. 92 f.

63. A. Ellegård, *The Auxiliary DO*, pp. 167 and 171.

64. O. Jespersen, *A Modern English Grammar*, I, pp. 338 f.

65. Cf. E. J. Dobson, *English Pronunciation 1500–1700*, II, pp. 624 and 629.

66. See, e.g., H. C. Wyld, *Studies in English Rhymes from Surrey to Pope*, p. 62; E. J. Dobson, *English Pronunciation 1500–1700*, II, p. 625.

67. The usual eighteenth-century form was *plait* (*OED*), and the phonaesthetic effect of the /iː/-variant must have been less at that period. The reassertion of /iː/ in this word provides a good example of the combined working of phonaesthetic and functional influences (cf. *plate*, n.).

68. It is not certain how far the distinction between /iːt/ and /eːt/ extends to polysyllables, since compounding may often change and even reverse the meaning of the simplex. *Complete, conceit* "fancy," "trick," *discreet, discrete, receipt* and *replete* fit their class reasonably well; *deceit* and *counterfeit* (in which the preference for /iː/ developed late) may well have joined *cheat* to form a subgroup implying misused dexterity; and a further possible connection might be traced between *repeat* and *bleat*. But there remain many others, such as *relate, delete, defeat* which seem neither to partake of, nor to contribute to, the more obvious phonaesthetic properties of their structures.

69. To judge from the OED quotations, the verb *beet* may be assumed to have become restricted to dialect well before this period.

70. The development of *yea* has been omitted from the above discussion, since the two factors involved are the same, but in this case both worked in the same direction: avoidance of the vowel of *ye*, and preservation of the established rhyme with *nay*.

71. See J. R. Firth, *Speech*, Ch. VI, and "The Use and Distribution of Certain English Sounds," *English Studies*, XVII (1935), 8–18, reprinted in *Papers in Linguistics, 1934–1951*, 34–46; G. V. Smithers, "Some English Ideophones," *Archivum Linguisticum*, VI (1954), 73–111, with references there made to the works of Wundt, Kainz, Jespersen and Entwistle. It should be emphasized, however, that we are not concerned here with absolute (i.e., "universal" or "cross-linguistic") sound-symbolism, but with the relative sound-symbolism that can be established from the phonaesthetic values applicable to a given language and period only. For the importance of this distinction see Y. Malkiel, *Word*, XVIII (1962), p. 218.

72. On "semantic fields" see S. Ullmann, *Semantics: an Introduction to the*

*Science of Meaning* (Oxford, 1962), pp. 243–58 and the numerous references there quoted. Most of the work done hitherto has been on (i) conceptual dictionaries of individual modern languages, and (ii) historical investigations of certain related notions ("fields"): of these, the former have little diachronic relevance, while the latter, though valuable, are too atomistic in approach. The need for an all-inclusive historical approach has long been recognized (Ullmann, *op. cit.*, p. 256), and the research project referred to above has been planned as an attempt to remedy that need in English.

# 4

# PROBLEMS OF DIALECT AND LANGUAGE CONTACT

# Introduction

"Linguistic history is dialectology writ large, and dialectology is the idiosyncrasies of individual speakers writ medium" (Dwight Bollinger, *Aspects of language* [New York, 1968], 135). Considering how basic the study of dialect is to many larger linguistic endeavors, it is somewhat surprising that it took so long as it did to develop a rigor comparable to that gained early, for example, in phonology. But it certainly was the last area in linguistics to be cultivated during the great flowering of the discipline in the nineteenth century. Dialect differences had been observed and commented on in the study of the classical tongues and the medieval vernaculars; there were even fairly large-scale studies of particular dialects of older languages, such as Cosijn's *Altwestsächsische Grammatik* (1883–6), but these made no use of techniques specific to dialect study. And as C. L. Wrenn pointed out in his excellent paper "Standard Old English" (1933), and as McIntosh and Samuels point out in the papers reprinted here, the techniques that many of the pioneering scholars used to establish dialect, and the criteria they relied upon, were insufficiently sophisticated and rigorous.

As in the case of phonology, it was methodology developed in the synchronic study of living languages that eventually served as the most potent source of insight in diachronic work. The anti-synchronic bias of many of the great nineteenth-century philologists (for example, Hermann Paul) was reflected in a general unwillingness to mix the two kinds of method; and even though synchronic dialect study on a principled basis had begun to develop as early as 1876 (Georg Wenker's *Deutsche Sprachatlas*), it was only in this century that the techniques developed by Wenker and his successors were applied to historical study.

The first of the papers reprinted here is not so much an attempt to use new techniques as it is a fresh look at a well-known phenomenon: the Southern English voicing of initial fricatives unvoiced in other dialects. Through a careful survey of historical evidence, W. H. Bennett suggests that [v z ð] may already have been present in the speech of the "Jutes" who settled Southern England, and may have been picked up by them during a premigration period when they lived among the Lower Franks—the remains of whose language also show this voicing.

In the next paper David DeCamp, working in the frame of reference of a synchronic dialectologist (he is a specialist in, among other things, Jamaican Creole), advances a radically new hypothesis about the genesis of the Old English dialects: "that the origins of the English dialects lie not in pre-migration tribal affiliations but in certain social, economic, and cultural developments which occurred after the migration was completed." Among other important matters he considers the cultural contact between the Frisians and the English, and sees the subsequent development of the dialects as in great part due to English-Frisian contact, especially in the southeast.

Continuing with the study of language- (and culture-) contact, Rolf Berndt in his paper challenges a number of previously accepted notions about the "eclipse" of English during the century-and-a-half following the Norman Conquest. He brings forth considerable evidence to show that English was far more widely spoken, and French far less so, and that the proportion of bilinguals among the population was nowhere near as high as has been supposed: "The tongue of the Conquerors had not 'acquired a position of dominance' and become 'widely diffused' in the country. On the contrary, the number of those people in England who had French as their mother tongue gradually decreased. . . . Those of whom it was still true at the end of this period . . . had already become a minority within the minority of those Englishmen who still had a more or less good command of the French language."

The next two papers, by Angus McIntosh and M. L. Samuels, are concerned with some striking new developments in the study of Middle English dialects, for which these two scholars are largely responsible. The results of their work have been, among other things, a radical revision of previously accepted dialect boundaries, and a new conception of the evidential value of written materials. Using a rigorous study of written sources (after the manner set forth by McIntosh in "The analysis of written Middle English" (reprinted here, pp. 35 ff.), they have developed new techniques for localization of texts, and a new conception of just what kinds of information can be used as criteria for dialect identification.

The last two papers deal with aspects of Early Modern English. In a detailed study, E. J. Dobson brings together a great deal of hitherto scattered evidence on the development and composition of "standard English" in the sixteenth century—with special reference to "an explicitly recognized standard of spoken English," a much neglected field of investigation. Dobson draws here on his intimate acquaintance with the works of the early orthoëpists such as Cooper, Gill, Robinson, and Hart, and explores the spoken standard against the background of these important commentators.

And finally, the late Helge Kökeritz provides us with a fascinating study of the survival of "ancestral" dialect traits in the works of Sir Thomas Wyatt, a poet who though he moved in the very court circles which were the exemplar of "standard" English, nonetheless allowed certain forms from his native Kentish speech to appear in his writing.

## WILLIAM H. BENNETT

# The Southern English Development
# of Germanic Initial [f s þ]*

In historical English grammar it is regularly assumed that Gmc. initial [f s þ] became voiced before voiced sounds in southern England at some time in the Old or early Middle English period. For the present purpose, Wright's description of the change[1] is sufficiently representative: "The initial voiceless spirants *f, s, þ* became the voiced spirants *v, z, ð* in late OE. or early ME. in Kentish and the southern, especially the south-western dialects, as *vader, vat, vlesch, vrend*; *zaule zǫule, zinne zenne zünne* 'sin,' *ðat ðet, ðing*. The modern dialects show that this voicing of the initial voiceless spirants must have taken place at an early period, because it is almost exclusively confined to native words, hence the change must have taken place before the great influx of Anglo-Norman words into these dialects. The use of the initial voiced for the voiceless spirants is now obsolete in Ken., Sur., Sus., and obsolescent in s. Pem., Hamp., and the I.W., but it is still in general use in east Hrf., parts of Glo., west Brks., Wil., Som., and Dev."

While there is no doubt that the voicing of initial [f s þ] occurred, the date at which it took place has proved to be a difficult problem. In the first place, the Old English spellings *f s þ/ð* are used to represent either voiced or voiceless spirants and so offer no clue whatever to the date of the change. Secondly, although the Kentish-Southern voicing of initial [f s] becomes clear with the Middle English introduction of the French spellings *v/u z* in such forms as *vrend* and *zinne*, neither the runic nor any later conventional system of English orthography has ever made a consistent distinction between [þ] and [ð], so that the voicing of [þ] can be confirmed only through Modern English evidence. It is not surprising, therefore, that attempts to date the voicing have been based on three major considerations: (1) the virtual limitation of this development to pre-Conquest words, (2) the appearance of *v*- and *z*-spellings in Middle English texts, and (3) the data provided by modern British dialects. On the basis of these considerations, accordingly, the Kentish-Southern voicing of initial [f s þ] has been assigned without exception to the late Old English or early Middle English period.

Two individual Old English spellings have some bearing on the problem, but neither appears to demand any great change in the general opinion. The oldest evidence for the voicing of initial [f] is the form *uif* = *fif* "five," which

* From *Language* 31.367–71 (1955). Reprinted (with minor corrections) by permission of the author and the Linguistic Society of America.

occurs in the Guild Statute of Bedwyn, Wiltshire, and dates from about the year 950.[2] Conversely, *v* in Lat. *versum* is rendered by *f* in WS OE *fers* "verse"; apparently this word was introduced into English after Lat. *v* had become a spirant, or the *v* would have been rendered by the Old English *w*-symbol, as in earlier loanwords, e.g., *wīn* < *vīnum* "wine," *mealwe* < *malva* "mallow."[3] But even at best, the form *uif* could show only that initial [f] had been voiced at some time before the year 950, and the form *fers* could show only that initial *f* might represent [v] in West Saxon Old English. Neither form reveals when, where, or under what circumstances the voicing took place.

If the evidence thus far considered is vague with regard to the date of the change, it is even less illuminating with regard to the possible source of the voicing process. Substratum influence arising from Cornish or Welsh appears to be out of the question, not only on phonological grounds, but also on the grounds of geographical possibility; even if Welsh and Cornish had not abounded in initial voiceless spirants, the midland area of England would have been just as susceptible to initial voicing as the southern area was. On the face of the available British evidence, then, we have no assurance whatever that the voicing of initial [f s þ] took place on English soil, as regularly assumed. The change may just as well have taken place on the Continent. On the other hand, if the voicing occurred after the Juto-Frisians and Saxons had established their settlements in southern England, the development was purely local, apparently independent of substratum influence, and in no way related to parallel changes in Continental Germanic.

Before favoring either conclusion, it may be advisable to consider the Continental Germanic aspect of the problem. Old Low Franconian, which was spoken by tribes first appearing about the lower Rhine, is barely known through a late, badly transmitted version of the Psalms. The spelling of this work, which is of uncertain date (perhaps 1000 or before), indicates the voicing of initial [f] with at least as much consistency as the average Southern Middle English text of about the same period, e.g., *vōr* "fared," *vuss* "fox," *-vallen* "fall." Middle Low Franconian provides abundant testimony for precisely the same voicing found in Kentish and Southern Middle English, even including [þ] > [ð],[4] though the spelling of course fluctuates in all three dialects:

|                     MLFr.                    |     |              Sth. or Kt. ME              |
| -------------------------------------------- | --- | --------------------------------------- |
| *vallen, varen, vat, vor, vuur*              | =   | *vallen, varen, vat, vor, vēr*          |
| *zee, zegghen, zonde, zo, zone*              | =   | *zee, ziggen, zenne, zo, zone*          |
| *daer, dat, dan, dief, dinc*                 | =   | *ðēr, ðat, ðon, ðēf, ðing*              |

In itself, however, the exact parallelism of the three voicings proves little. Unless there was a period of earlier contact between Low Franconians and the tribes that were to settle in southern England, the parallelism is only a remarkable coincidence. It is necessary, therefore, to determine whether such a period of intertribal contact occurred.

According to the *Ecclesiastical history* of the Venerable Bede, the Germanic tribes that invaded Kent were Jutes (*Iuti, Iutae*). The Old English Chronicle, in the annal for the year 449, repeats this account and refers to the invaders with the forms *Īutum, Īotum, Īutna cyn*. The same tribes are described in Anglian Old English as *Ēote, Īote, Īotan*, and in Late West Saxon as *Ȳte, Ȳtan*. In the poem Widsith occurs the form *Ȳtum*, and the Old English translation of Bede uses the phrase *Ēota* (*Ȳtena*) *lond*.[5] Though the historical evidence points to Jutland as the early "land of the Jutes," it is very unlikely that they proceeded directly from Jutland to Britain. In the Finn Episode of the poem Beowulf, for example, the two opposing tribal groups are distinguished as Frisians versus Danes. It is clear that the action of this episode takes place in the land of the Frisians, who lived along the North Sea coastline and islands between the Elbe and the Rhine. Yet in four lines (1072, 1088, 1141, 1145) Frisians are referred to as *Ēotan* "Jutes." Moreover, even if *Ēotan* in these lines is supposed not to mean the Jutes,[6] archeological studies of the Jutish settlements in England indicate a cultural connection with the lower Rhine area.[7] It is understandable, therefore, that a number of scholars[8] have concluded that the Jutes did not come directly from Jutland to England but first migrated southward along the North Sea coastline to the lower Rhine, whence their lower Rhenish cultural vestiges and their association with the Frisians.

Claudius Ptolemaeus (fl. A.D. 127–51) first locates the Saxons in an area extending from the east bank of the Elbe to the Baltic coastline, but in the early centuries of this era they spread to the south and west, forming numerous colonies near Bayeux on the northern coast of France, which accordingly came to be called the Litus Saxonicum. It was from there that the first Saxon invaders entered what are now the southwestern counties of England. In this phase of the invasion, as might be expected, each tribal group entered that part of the island which was closest and most readily accessible, the Juto-Frisians from the lower Rhine district occupying the nearby Kentish area, the Saxons of the Litus Saxonicum settling the opposing districts south and west of the Thames, and the Angles migrating westward to the corresponding northern and midland sections of the island.

There is an important geographical difference between the Anglian and the Juto-Frisian-Saxon migrations. Unlike the Angles, the Jutes migrated southward along the North Sea coast as far as the lower Rhine, and the Saxons continued even farther south to the Litus Saxonicum. In doing so, both groups entered the lower Rhenish—i.e., the Low Franconian—area. The Lower Franks had occupied this district at an early period; their recorded history begins here about A.D. 260. It was here, too, that the Juto-Frisians acquired the lower Rhenish cultural traits that they were to bring to Kent. Whether the Juto-Frisians and English Saxons also acquired the Low Franconian voicing

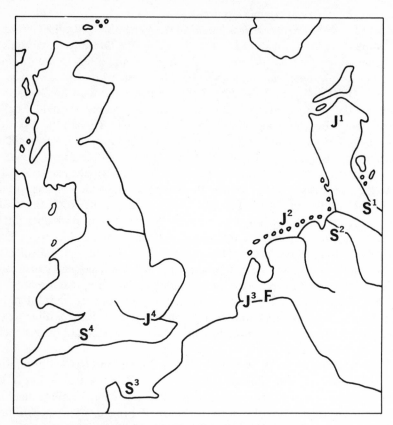

J¹ = Jutes in Jutland (Bede, Old English Chronicle)
J² = Jutes in Friesland (Beowulf 1072, 1088, 1141, 1145)
J³ = Jutes at the lower Rhine (whence the lower Rhenish culture of Jutish
        settlements in Britain)
J⁴ = Jutes in southeastern England
S¹ = Saxons between the Elbe and the Baltic coast (Claudius Ptolemaeus)
S² = Saxons in the vicinity of present-day Niedersachsen
S³ = Saxons on the Litus Saxonicum
S⁴ = Saxons in Southwestern England
F  = Lower Franks (Low Franconians)

**Figure 1**

of initial [f s þ] while still living in contact with the Lower Franks is of course
a matter for individual judgment.[9] If the exact correspondence between the
Low Franconian and the Kentish-Southern initial voicing is purely coincidental, it is at least worth noting as an interesting example of parallelism. On
the other hand, if the common voicing harks back to the time when Juto-
Frisians, Saxons, and Low Franconians occupied contiguous areas near the
mouth of the Rhine, the voicing is not a coincidence, and the speech of the

first Germanic settlers in southern England already possessed the initial voiced spirants [v z ð].[10] The latter conclusion would mean that the conventional formula for determining the initial allophones of West Saxon and Kentish Old English /f s þ/ would have to be revised.

## FOOTNOTES

1. J. and E. M. Wright, *EME gr.*[2] § 236. Cf. also R. Jordan, *Hb. d. me. Gr.*[2] (rev. Ch. Matthes) §§ 203–8, § 215; H. C. Wyld, *A short hist. of English* § 153.4; M. M. Roseborough, *An outline of ME gr.* § 33.1; J. Wright, *The English dialect gr.* § 278, § 310, § 320; and esp. E. Sievers, *Ae. Gr.* (2nd ed. rev. by K. Brunner) § 171 Anm. 3, § 192 Anm. 1, § 200 Anm., § 203 Anm. The [f/v] isophone, one of the Moore-Meech-Whitehall dialect criteria, is shown in S. Moore, *Hist. outlines of English sounds and inflections* (rev. A. H. Marckwardt) 112, and F. Mossé, *Manuel de l'anglais du moyen âge* 2.56. [In the English version, *A handbook of Middle English* (Baltimore, 1952), fig. 6, p. 38.—Ed.]

2. See M. Förster, *Sitzungsber. d. bayer. Akad. phil.-hist. Abt. 1941*, 1.790 (Munich, 1941).

3. Förster (*Anglia* 66.40 f.) would explain the *f* of *fers* as representing an Irish pronunciation.

4. J. Franck, *Mittelniederl. Gr.*[2] 9: "Das Nl. unterscheidet in der Aussprache noch heute zwei *d*, die verschiedenen Ursprungs sind, eins = germ. *d*, das zweite = germ. *th* (resp. *dh*, einem tönenden dentalen Reibelaute). . . . Da der Unterschied heute noch dauert, muss er auch im Mnl. bestanden haben." [" Dutch distinguishes in its pronunciation even today two *d*'s, of different origins, one Gmc. *d*, the second Gmc. *th* (or *dh*, a voiced dental fricative). . . . Since the distinction still continues, it must also have existed in Middle Dutch."] On the basis of Modern Dutch pronunciation, Franck suggests that MLFr. initial *v*, which fluctuates with *f* in spelling as in Kentish and Southern Middle English, may have had a voiceless onset.

5. In one passage the OE Bede uses the forms *Gēata*, *Gēatum* to refer to the Jutes, but this need not be taken to show that the Jutes and the Geats were one and the same people. See K. Malone, *MLR* 20.1 ff., 23.336 ff., *Acta philologica scand.* 4.84 and reff.; F. Klaeber, *Beowulf and the Fight at Finnsburg*[3] xlvi ff. and reff.; Prokosch, *Comp. Gc. gr.* § 5b.

6. The name occurs in the gen. as *Ēotena* (1072, 1088, 1141) and in the dat. as *Ēotenum* (1145), apparently an analogic form based on the gen. and found also in 902. As Klaeber notes (*JEGP* 14.545), attempting to explain this form as representing *eotenas* "giants" and then interpreting "giants" to mean "enemies," hence "Frisians," seems far-fetched.

7. E. T. Leeds, in *The archaeology of the Anglo-Saxon settlements* (Oxford, 1913), connects the culture of the Jutish settlements in Kent, Hampshire and the Isle of Wight with that of lower Rhenish Franks.

8. J. Hoops, *Waldbäume und Kulturpflanzen im germ. Altertum* 585; Th. Siebs, *PG*[2] 1.1158, 2a.524; Jordan, *Verhandlungen der 49. Versammlung deutscher Philologen und Schulmänner* 138 ff. (1908); E. Björkman, Studien uber die Eigennamen im Beowulf, *StEPh.* 63.21 ff., 60 f.; Klaeber, *Beowulf*[3] 232 f. and reff.

9. The possibility that the common voicing may have arisen from later cross-Channel relations between southern England and the lower Rhenish area seems extremely remote. Even with the facilities of present-day travel and communication, the Channel and the Strait of Dover are still effective barriers against the ingress of

linguistic influences. Furthermore, there is no reason for supposing that only the southern part of England was involved in relations with the lower Rhenish district; yet the English voicing of initial [f s þ] is confined to the southern and southwestern counties.

10. For a much broader treatment of the voicing process without specific reference to the problem under consideration here, see W. Steinhauser, Eintritt d. Stimmhaftigkeit bei d. westg. Reibelauten *f þ s x*, *Festschrift Max H. Jellinek* 139 ff. and reff. (Vienna and Leipzig, 1928).

DAVID DeCAMP

# The Genesis of the Old English
# Dialects: A New Hypothesis*

1. *Introduction.* The Old English dialects have traditionally been viewed as mere extensions of the dialects of the continental Germanic tribes before their migration to Britain. Following Bede's famous division of the fifth-century invaders into Jutes, Angles, and Saxons, writers have postulated three corresponding dialects: Kentish, Anglian, and Saxon. In this paper I shall develop the hypothesis that the origins of the English dialects lie not in pre-migration tribal affiliations but in certain social, economic, and cultural developments which occurred after the migration was completed. This does not imply that the continental Germanic dialects are irrelevant to the genesis of English dialects; indeed the influence of Frisian is central to my hypothesis. Only those influences, however, which were felt after the migrations were relevant to formation of the English dialects; for I believe that these dialects originated not on the continent but on the island of Britain.

The striking similarities between Frisian and the Kentish (southeastern) dialect of Old English have long been noticed. More than fifty years ago, Theodor Siebs[1] postulated a special Kentish-Frisian branch of the Anglo-Frisian limb of his Germanic family tree, insisting that Kentish was "genetically" more closely related to Frisian than were Anglian and Saxon—that Kentish speech was, in fact, merely the Frisian spoken by the fifth-century invaders of Kent. Favoring this hypothesis are the linguistic similarities, numerous Kentish-Frisian cultural affinities to be discussed later in this paper, and the sixth-century account of Procopius of Caesarea, who divided the Germanic inhabitants of Britain into *Angiloi* and *Frissones.*[2] Because the Jutes are not mentioned by Tacitus (their origin and even their existence are disputed by modern writers) and because they never·appear in Kentish place names or early written traditions, Siebs assumed that Bede had erroneously substituted Jutes for Frisians. Though no one now doubts that there were Frisians, among others, in Kent, Siebs' hypothesis can be refuted in two ways. First, the evidence summarized in § 3 of this paper indicates that all the Kentish-Frisian linguistic similarities probably did not develop until after the migrations; it is certain that some of these similarities did not appear until the eighth or ninth century. These can hardly prove a common ancestor in the fifth century.[3] Second, as will be demonstrated in § 4, modern historians have

* From *Language* 34.232–44 (1958). Reprinted by permission of the author and The Linguistic Society of America.

shown that the accounts of both Bede and Procopius were greatly over-simplified, that there were no migrations of entire tribes, rather that Kent was colonized by a mixture of continental peoples.

Siebs' argument was circular. Bede, aware in the eighth century of different political and cultural areas with rapidly developing linguistic characteristics, assumed corresponding tribal units in the fifth. Siebs then based his argument for continental origin of dialects on these same tribal names. Siebs, working strictly in the Stammbaum tradition of historical linguistics, did not accept any means for the transfer of linguistic features from one area to another except mass migration of speakers. Many linguists have been similarly bound by these Stammbaum preconceptions. Even Alois Brandl, though he recognized the importance of the church and state as additional formative influences, stated,[4] "Es ist denknotwendig, dass der Dialekt ursprünglich am Stamme hängt,"[5] and declared his first criterion for determining Old English dialect boundaries to be "Direkte Berichte über die Siedlungen der Germanenstämme in Britannien, denn auf der Verschiedenheit jener Stämme beruhte naturgemäss die ursprüngliche Verschiedenheit der Mundarten."[6] Subsequent writers have echoed Brandl's assumption, without proof but with an implied or expressed "naturgemäss."

I do not accept the continental origin hypothesis and believe that I have evidence to refute it. I propose to approach the Frisian–Old-English problem with the methods of modern linguistic geography. I assume that linguistic features can move from one area to another without mass migration of the speakers, through imitation of the speech of one area by speakers from another. Usually innovations travel from a superior to an inferior culture, following the routes of communication and trade. My plan will be (1) to establish the approximate boundaries of the dialect areas with which I will deal; (2) to present the evidence for dating the development of these dialects as post-migration; (3) to outline the political, social, and economic developments in England which conditioned the linguistic changes; and finally, (4) to describe a series of linguistic changes resulting from linguistic diffusion, changes which can account for the most basic features of the Old English dialect distribution.

2. *The Isophones.* My discussion will center on what are probably the oldest and most basic isophones of Old English. These are presented in Figure 1. North of Line A, OE $\bar{æ}$ ( < WGmc. $\bar{a}$) was raised to $\bar{e}$: *strēt/strǣt*, *dēd/dǣd*. This isophone, sometimes known as "Pogatscher's Line," was established on the basis of the distribution of place names containing the element *stret-/strat-*, e.g., *Stretford/Stratford*.[7] Line B roughly defines a southwest Midland area in which OE short *æ* was also raised to *e*: *weter/wæter*, *feder/fæder*. This *e* was still characteristic of southwest Midland speech in Middle English, and at least one Old English text in which it appears regularly, the Vespasian Psalter, can be localized with reasonable certainty.[8] Line C indicates the Kentish area, in which $\breve{æ}$ (regardless of origin) was raised to $\breve{e}$.

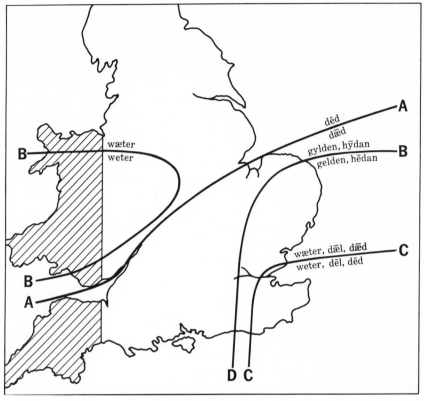

**Figure 1**

This innovation also appears regularly in Frisian. Thus we find *dēd* in the north and southwest Midland and also in Kentish-Frisian, but *dǣd* in an intervening conservative belt extending from Devonshire northeast to the old East Anglia (Norfolk and Suffolk). We find *weter* in the southwest Midland and in Kentish-Frisian, but *wǣter* in the same intervening belt and also in the North. Only in Kentish-Frisian was the long *ǣ* which resulted from umlaut of early OE *ā* (< Gmc. *ai*) raised to *ē*; thus, the Gmc. *i*-stem noun *\*dailiz* appears as *dēl* in Kentish-Frisian, but as *dǣl* elsewhere in England. The linguistic geographer will immediately recognize the peculiarity of this distribution. A well-known rule of thumb in dialectology states that lateral areas are usually conservative, central areas innovating, for changes usually spread through the center of an area, leaving isolated unchanged patches at the sides. Here, however, the central area is conservative, cutting off innovating areas to the northwest and southeast.

Line D indicates the area in which the *y̆*, resulting from umlaut of *ŭ*, was unrounded and lowered to *ĕ*: *gelden/gylden* (< *\*guldin*), *hēdan/hȳdan*

( < *hūdjan*). The ĕ forms appear in Frisian and in the southeastern counties from Kent to Suffolk. This line has been well established on the basis of place names containing such elements as *hell-/hill-* or *hull-*, and *mel-/mil-* or *mul-*.[9]

The exact location of these isophones is uncertain. Few if any Old English texts can be localized with precision and certainty. Most texts are of the ninth century or later, with very few before 800 A.D., almost none before 700. Most early texts are not originals but later copies, which may well have been altered in copying. Generally place name evidence is more reliable than textual evidence. Consequently, no comprehensive linguistic atlas, such as that provided for Middle English by Moore, Meech, and Whitehall, is possible here.[10] Our increased knowledge of Middle English aids the student of Old English dialects. Extrapolation from the linguistic geography of Middle English confirms the approximate location of the isophones in Figure 1. My lines, however, are not such precise boundaries; I do not believe the evidence warrants precision. My hypothesis depends only on the general geographical relationships of the areas to one another. It is sufficient, for example, to establish that an area of indeterminate size and boundaries existed in the southwest Midland in which early OE *æ* was raised to *e*.

3. *The Age of the Isophones.* The raising of early OE *ǽ* ( < WGmc. *ā̆*) to *ē* has traditionally been dated very early. For example, Luick writes:[11] "Offenbar liegt ein gemein-anglofriesischer Vorgang vor, dessen Anfänge mindestens in die Zeit der Nachbarschaft der beiden Stämme auf dem Kontinent fallen." Though he gives some phonological evidence, successfully refuted by Kuhn,[12] his principal reason seems to be his assumption that Anglo-Frisian similarities must either be coincidental or must prove a "gemein-anglofriesischer Vorgang" and therefore must be pre-invasion.

The best evidence for a later date is the frequent, sometimes preponderant appearance of *ǽ* (spelled *ae*, *æ*, or *ę*) beside *ē* in early texts from the *ē*-areas. In the earliest Kentish documents, *ē* for *ǽ* is relatively rare. Variants of *æðel-* as an element in personal names are regular, whereas there is only one occurrence of the *eðel-* type. For example, the name *aedilmaeri* (*Æðelmǽr*) in MS. Cott. Aug. ii.2 illustrates the seventh-century retention of both long and short *æ*.[13] These forms were long ago noticed by Chadwick and by Weightman.[14] Luick and Sievers-Brunner acknowledged them, but refused to draw from them the inference that the *ǽ* > *ē* change was still incomplete in the seventh and eighth centuries. Sievers-Brunner merely commented on these texts,[15] "doch ist deren Sprache vielleicht nicht rein kentisch." Kuhn has dealt with a similar problem in the eighth-century Mercian Corpus Gloss. In Corpus, forms with *æ* outnumber those with *e* by a ratio of five to one. Kuhn refuted the traditional interpretation of dialect mixture and demonstrated that this text illustrates a sound change not yet completed.[16] Because there is no sound evidence, other than the Frisian similarities, for a fifth-century date, we must conclude that these changes were taking place in the seventh century in Kent and perhaps as late as the early ninth century for short $\breve{æ} > \breve{e}$ in the Midland.

No one now questions the late date of the Kentish and Frisian raising to $\bar{e}$ of the long $\bar{æ}$ which resulted from umlaut, for *i*-umlaut occurred in the seventh century. Similarly the southeast Midland, Kentish, and Frisian appearance of $\breve{e}$ (as opposed to $\breve{y}$) as the umlaut of $\breve{u}$ is recognized as later than the seventh century. These two Anglo-Frisian similarities must either be discounted as coincidence or recognized as the result of post-migration influences. If we accept the latter alternative, we are denying the Stammbaum basis of the traditional argument for pre-migration dating. There would then be no reason to object to a post-migration date for the development of all the Old English dialect characteristics, even if we did not have the positive textual evidence I have outlined. If one denied the validity of all the texts, he would only be faced with two unprovable alternative assumptions and with these two unshakable precedents for Anglo-Frisian similarities developed after the migrations. And though admittedly scanty, the textual evidence cannot be ignored. We may conclude that the English dialects developed in England between the sixth and the ninth century.

Linguistic geography provides many examples of the continuing influence of one dialect upon another, even after the two have been geographically separated. Among the most striking is the loss of postvocalic retroflexion in the speech of the eastern United States. This "*r*-dropping" originated in England considerably after the establishment of the English colonies in America. The innovation was carried across the Atlantic, and its geographical distribution reflects the extent of British influence, with western New England and certain isolated localities such as Martha's Vineyard generally retaining strong retroflexion. Even an undeveloped conjecture that similar processes produced the similar features in Frisian, Kentish, and various northerly dialects would be at least as believable as the unproved assumption of continental origin. I hope to demonstrate further that historical events could have conditioned such linguistic diffusion, and to present a hypothetical but consistent sequence of developments which could have produced precisely these similarities and their approximate distribution.

4. *Frisia, Kent, and the Settlement History of England.* The myth of three Germanic tribes dividing Britain among them originates in Bede's well-known account:[17]

Now the strangers had come from three of the more mighty nations in Germany, that is, the Saxons, the Angles, and the Jutes. Of the Jutes came the people of Kent and the settlers in Wight, that is, those who hold the Isle of Wight, and those in the province of the West Saxons who are called unto this day the nation of the Jutes, directly opposite the Isle of Wight. From the Saxons, that is, those from that region which now is called the land of the Old Saxons, descended the East Saxons, the South Saxons, and the West Saxons. Further, from the Angles, that is, those from that country which is called Angeln and from that time to this is said to stand deserted between the provinces of the Jutes and the Saxons, descend the East

Angles, the Midland Angles [Mediterranei Angli], the Mercians, and all the progeny of the Northumbrians, that is, of that race which inhabits the north side of the river Humber, and the other nations of the Angles.

Until recently, this account was generally accepted by historians. It still appears, with little or no qualification, in a number of Old English grammars and histories of the English language.

In the first place, however, this paragraph is the sole authority for the tripartite division of the Germanic invaders. All other such accounts, including the entry in the Anglo-Saxon Chronicle, were clearly derived from it. Gildas, only a century after the event and two centuries earlier than Bede, called all the invaders Saxons.[18] Procopius called them Angles and Frisians.[19] Furthermore, Bede immediately abandons his classification of the invaders, never again mentions the Jutes, and seems to equate the Angles and the Saxons. He criticizes the Britons for never preaching the gospel to the "genti Saxonum sive Anglorum"—not "gentibus Saxonum et Anglorum."[20] The "Anglorum sive Saxonum gens"—not "Anglorum et Saxonum gentes"—arrive in three long ships.[21] He quotes Gregory's letter addressing Aethelbert of Kent as "regi Anglorum."[22]

Other evidence would refute Bede's classification even if he had not himself discounted it. The name *Jute* never appears in Kentish place names or personal names, and there is no evidence that the Kentish ever called themselves by that name, despite Bede's claim.[23] Archeology has indicated that migrants from Jutland were probably not even represented in the mixed group that settled in Kent.[24] Finally, the archeological evidence from Essex is similar to that from Kent and has little in common with that from Wessex.[25] Bede's assertion that Essex, Wessex, and Sussex were settled by one common race, the Saxons, simply cannot be accepted.

Modern historians agree that the conquest of Britain was not a transfer of entire continental nations, each with its own culture and language. Rather, it was a slow colonization by numerous bands representing many continental tribes, which did not themselves differ significantly from one another. Whatever tenuous tribal affiliations the invaders had had in the fifth century were soon mostly lost or confused. People migrated not as Angles, Saxons, or Frisians, but as individual adventurer-leaders, with small and heterogeneous followings.[26]

The striking variations in Kentish graves indicate that Kent especially was settled by such mixed groups. All attempts to relate the Kentish evidence to that from any one area on the continent have failed.[27] We must agree with Jerrold[28] that "The Jutish race and civilization, as described by Bede and as we know it from the graves of the late fifth and sixth centuries, was made in Kent."

During the reign of Aethelbert (c. 560–616), Kent achieved tremendous cultural and political dominance. It is no accident that Augustine's success was in Kent. In wealth and prestige, in its legal system, in learning, and in cosmopolitan outlook, Kent far surpassed anything known in England since Roman days. As Hodgkin says,[29] "Kent might seem barbarous to the Romans but to the peoples of Britain it was a center of civilization."

The fifth-century invaders may have inherited some of the culture of Roman Britain, for the principal Roman-British centers of population— Dover, Canterbury, Faversham, and Rochester—were also among the principal Germanic settlements.[30] Primarily, however, this Kentish supremacy may be attributed to Kent's unique position on the old trade route with the continent. The Kentish were the traders of England from the beginning and were exposed to all manner of continental influences. Judging from the great number of early English coins found on the sites of Frisian settlements, probably most of this overseas trade was in Frisian hands, though there may have been some trading directly with the Franks.[31] Evidence of these Frankish-Frisian influences is abundant. Augustine's mission in Kent was aided by the fact that Aethelbert had married the Christian daughter of the Frankish King Hariberht. Many sixth- and seventh-century *trientes*, small gold coins of Frankish pattern, have been found in Kent.[32] The nature of much of the magnificent ceramic work and jewelry which marks Aethelbert's day indicates that the Kentish received through the Frisians and the Franks many remnants of the dying Roman civilization in western Europe. Hodgkin has conjectured that the long-necked vases found in Kentish graves were wine vessels in which Rhenish wine was imported.[33] Aerial photography has revealed the outlines of the early fields; the open-field system in Kent and adjacent east Midland areas, as opposed to the strip cultivation practiced elsewhere in England, suggests Rhineland influence.[34] Early Kentish laws are more similar to the Frisian than to the West Saxon, in that there was no evidence of the West Saxon division of the nobility into two classes, whereas the dependent and servile classes were more elaborately classified. One of these classes, the *laet*, is clearly identical with the *litus* or *lazzus* of the Frisian, Frankish, and Old Saxon laws.[35] This evidence, though not proving a Kentish-Frisian racial identity, as once was maintained, does prove a continuing Frisian influence throughout the Anglo-Saxon period.

Aethelbert's immediate kingdom, his *regnum*, was small—little more than modern Kent and Surrey. But his *imperium* extended north to the Humber, and he probably wielded considerable influence over the independent kingdoms of Bernicia and Deira north of the Humber.[36] This prestige early extended the Kentish-Frisian trade route northward at least as far as Yorkshire. According to Bede, in 679 a Northumbrian named Imma was sold as a slave to a Frisian merchant somewhere in the neighborhood of the river Trent. The Frisian took Imma to London, possibly for shipment to the continent. However, Hlothere, king of Kent, learning that Imma was really a captured thane rather than a commoner, paid a ransom to the Frisian so that Imma could return home to Northumbria.[37] The old Deiran cemeteries have yielded archeological material strikingly similar to that from Kentish and Frisian graves.[38] The Sutton Hoo treasure, found in Suffolk in 1939, contains a purse of gold Frankish coins of the seventh century.[39] X-ray photography has recently revealed that the blade of the sword in this treasure was of the pattern-welded Rhenish type, though the jewels which decorated its sword-knot were of East Anglian workmanship.[40] The open-field system of cultivation extended northward from Kent as far as the Wash, though not west into West Saxon territory.[41] That literary traditions followed this trade route is illustrated by the Finn tale in *Beowulf*, which authorities agree originated among the Ingvaeonic peoples and was carried from Friesland both to Upper Germany and to the Mercian and Northumbrian area of England.[42] Kentish education was also imitated. Bede tells us[43] that the East Anglian King Sigbert (631–4) "set up a school in which boys should be instructed in letters, by the help of bishop Felix whom he had gotten from Kent, and who appointed them masters and teachers after the manner of the men of Kent [iuxta morem Cantuariorum]." Myres notes a tradition in *Historia Brittonum* that the first Teutonic leaders in Northumbria were a son and nephew of the Kentish Hengist; this probably represents a later attempt by the Northumbrians to connect their genealogy with that of the prestigious Kentish.[44]

We may conclude that it was along this route from the continent to Kent and then northward to Mercia and Northumbria that cultural innovations generally passed: trade goods, Christianity, education, and literature. In early years the Southwest of England remained a rather backward area, comparatively isolated from these influences.

5. *Frisian Linguistic Innovations in England.* I suggest that between the sixth and the eighth century, a series of five phonological innovations followed this route from Frisia to Kent and that the extent of their penetration to other parts of England accounts for part (not all) of the dialect pattern in the East of England. The diffusion of these innovations is illustrated in Figure 2. First is the raising of long *ǣ* ( < WGmc. *ā*) to *ē* (*dēd/dǣd*). Originating in Frisia some time in the sixth or early seventh century, this innovation soon was adopted in Kent and spread northward, eventually covering all of Germanic speaking England except the Southwest, thus producing the isophone indicated by Line E. The later reinstatement of the conservative *ǣ* in the east Midland area will be discussed below.

Not long afterward, the innovation known as *i*-umlaut, which had originated somewhere in southern Germany and had spread northward to the Frisians, was similarly carried from Frisia to Kent, and then, probably during the first half of the seventh century, spread throughout England. In the area southwest of Line E, the long *ǣ* which resulted from the umlaut of early OE *ā* (e.g., *dǣl* < *dāli*) fell in with earlier long *ǣ* (WGmc. *ā*). Hence *dǣl* and *dǣd* with the same vowel in the Southwest. Elsewhere, however, including Frisia, the older *ǣ* had already closed to *ē* and the two vowels remained phonemically distinct (*dǣl, dēd*).

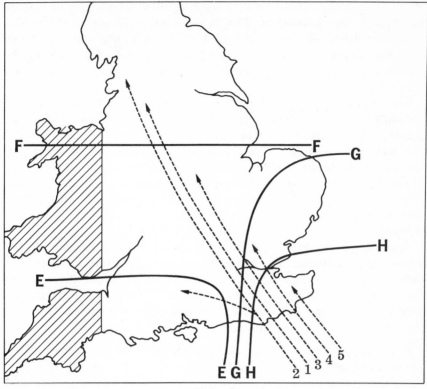

**Figure 2**

The third innovation, like the first, probably originated in Frisian: the raising of the short *ǣ* to *ě* (*weter*/*wæter*). This was carried to Kent in the late seventh century and spread northward. By this time, however, Kentish influence had diminished in the North. Kent had ceased to be a great military and political power, and had been increasingly dominated by Mercia. Kent still maintained considerable cultural prestige, but this waning influence was probably insufficient to carry the third innovation farther north than the Wash (Line F). I have already pointed out that forms containing this *ě* occasionally occur in Kentish texts as early as the late seventh century and that Kuhn found them to be comparatively rare (a ratio of about one to five) in a Mercian text of the late eighth. This indicates that the northward diffusion of *ě* must have been very slow.

Even the cultural supremacy of Kent was soon challenged. Under a succession of competent rulers in the seventh century, the northern kingdoms of Bernicia and Deira were united to form Northumbria, which became a major power, even defeating the Mercians in battle in 654. The monastery of Lindisfarne, founded in 635 by Aidan, grew in stature until the Celtic church in the North seriously rivaled the Roman church centered at Canterbury. When the apostate Mercians were reconverted to Christianity, it was by missionaries from Lindisfarne. Though the Synod of Whitby in 664 decided in favor of Rome and Canterbury, still Lindisfarne, Wearmouth, and Jarrow were the centers of learning until the Danish invasions. Consequently the northward diffusion of eighth-century Frisian innovations was increasingly restricted.

The fourth innovation illustrated in Figure 2 was the lowering and unrounding to $\check{e}$ of the $\check{\bar{y}}$ which had recently resulted from the umlaut of $\check{u}$; e.g., *gelden/gylden* ($<$ *\*guldin*), *hēdan/hȳdan* ($<$ *\*hūdjan*). This $\check{e}$ spread northward into most of East Anglia (Line G), but its appearance was probably only sporadic as far north as the Wash. The fifth Frisian innovation was the raising to $\bar{e}$ of the long $\bar{æ}$ resulting from umlaut of $\bar{a}$ ($<$ Gmc. *ai*); thus *dǣl* ($<$ Gmc. *\*dailiz*) became *dēl*, just as *dǣd* had become *dēd* more than a century before. This probably did not spread much beyond the old boundaries of Kent itself (Line H).

According to my hypothesis, eastern England in the late eighth century was a dialect transition area, as shown in Figure 2, marked by a series of east-west isoglosses indicating the northernmost extent of the Kentish-Frisian influences moving up from the Southeast. The Southwest had remained untouched by these innovations, with the exception of *i*-umlaut. Kent and Frisia had participated in all of them.

6. *The Restoration of $\check{æ}$ in the Southeast Midland.* If this pattern of isophones had remained unchanged, this explanation would certainly have been thought of long ago. Certain events in the ninth and tenth centuries, however, altered and partially obscured the pattern. Under a series of remarkably competent and successful rulers, Wessex rapidly became the leading state in England. In 825, according to the Anglo-Saxon Chronicle, the East Angles, in revolt against the domination of Beornwulf of Mercia, placed themselves under the protection of King Egbert, and the entire southeast Midland area was soon under West Saxon control. With the destruction of the northern monasteries by the Vikings, the Southwest became the dominant area in learning as well.

According to my hypothesis, the southeast Midland area had adopted many of the Kentish-Frisian innovations; but this new West Saxon influence, moving in from the Southwest, tended to reintroduce the older conservative forms, relatively uninfluenced by earlier Kentish-Frisian developments. As is indicated in Figure 3, a wedge of conservative West Saxon was driven into the dialect pattern of eastern England, separating the lateral areas of Kentish-Frisian influence in the Northwest and Southeast. Thus the dialectal principle that lateral areas are usually conservative still holds here, for the conservative $\check{æ}$ of West Saxon was really an innovation in the East, intruding into an area in which the earlier innovations had become standard.

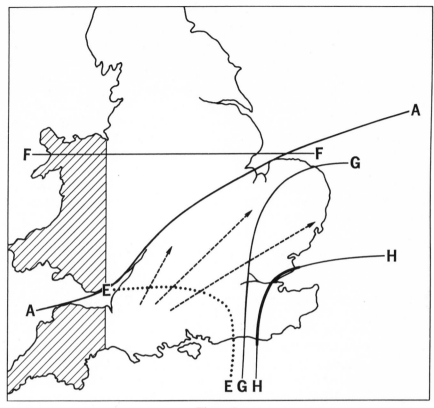

**Figure 3**

This eastward diffusion of West Saxon *ǣ* resulted from east Midland imitation of West Saxon, which by the tenth century had become recognized as the standard language of England. Wyld writes,[45]

The fact is that all O.E. documents of the later period, with very few exceptions, are written in a common form which in all essential features is W. Saxon . . . so much so that it is now commonly assumed that after Ælfred's time the prestige of Wessex in Government, Arms, and Letters, was such that the dialect of that area became a literary *koinē* in universal use in written documents.

In an article on the inconsistent use of *e* and *æ* in Farman's Mercian glosses,[46] Kuhn demonstrates the eagerness of tenth-century Mercian scribes to imitate West Saxon, even to the point of hyperurbanism. The Rushworth[1] glosses and the Worcester version of the Anglo-Saxon Chronicle, though written in areas where *ǣ* had earlier been raised to *ē*, contain relatively few *e* spellings for these words. In Rushworth[1] the West Saxon *æ* outnumbers *e* by a ratio of about twenty-five to two. Furthermore, *æ* is also substituted for *e* in more than a third of the words which etymologically represent Germanic *e* and which should have had *e* both in East Mercian and also in West Saxon, e.g., *stæfne*, ðægnum, wæg, for *stefne, ðegnum, weg*. If we accept Kuhn's hypothesis, we can see in this scribal imitation the northeastward movement of West Saxon æ actually in progress. What better evidence of linguistic imitation can we ask than hyperurbanism?

Unfortunately there is practically no direct textual evidence from the east Midland area which could verify the presence of the Kentish-Frisian forms before they were obliterated by West Saxon influence. There is only one very early East Saxon charter (MS Cott. Aug. ii.29), from the late seventh century, written in Latin but containing English personal and local names.[47] These show preponderantly *e* spellings, e.g., *hedilburge* (*Æthelburh*). Though this text is comparatively well localized, being a grant by an East Saxon to an East Saxon abbess of land for an East Saxon abbey, I agree that this is evidence too slim for conclusive verification. Yet I know of no textual evidence to refute the hypothesis.

This restoration of the conservative ǣ in the East, following the five processes illustrated in Figure 2, accounts for the dialect distribution shown in Figure 1. Line A (Pogatscher's Line) is now seen to be the northern boundary of the northeastward movement of the West Saxon ǣ. Lines C and D are essentially identical with Lines G and H respectively. The southwest Midland area bounded by Line B, characterized by the Kentish-Frisian ĕ in *weter* and *feder*, may be recognized in Figure 3 as the area between Lines F and A. Line E, no longer the boundary of West Saxon ǣ, remained the boundary of various other linguistic features which can best be considered West Saxon innovations. Some of these remained confined to the Southwest, but others later spread eastward into Kent or northward into the Mercian area.

I cannot explain why it was the ǣ and not other West Saxon features which were carried eastward in the ninth and tenth centuries. Parallels are available in modern linguistic geography: many Americans emulate the eastern New England pronunciation of *aunt, dance, calf*, and *path* with a lowered vowel (even to the point of hyperurbanisms like [hat] for *hat*) without also adopting the intrusive *r* in *law-r-and order*. We can only conclude that the ǣ became a shibboleth of the standard West Saxon dialect, and so was more widely imitated than were other West Saxon features.

A major advantage of the hypothesis presented in this paper is that it more closely parallels the formation of modern dialects as discovered by both American and European linguistic geographers. It is doubtful that the basic processes of dialect formation—innovation and diffusion—have radically changed since the fifth century. My hypothesis accounts not only for the similarities between Frisian and Kentish, but also for those between Kentish, Frisian, and various northerly dialects—similarities which have generally been ignored or dismissed as coincidental. It recognizes the evidence which led Siebs to believe, quite rightly, that Frisian was of prime importance in the formation of the Old English dialects, but avoids the inconsistencies in Siebs' theory. Finally, and perhaps most important, it is consistent with the modern conception of early English history as interpreted by the leading historians. Even the language of fifteen hundred years ago does not exist in a vacuum but is a feature of a cultural complex. Toward its historical interpretation the discovery of a sword or a purse of coins in an old burial mound can be as significant as the discovery of new texts.

# FOOTNOTES

1. Theodor Siebs, *Geschichte der friesischen Sprache* (Strassburg, 1901); *Zur Geschichte der englisch-friesischen Sprache* (Halle; 1889).
2. *De bello gotthico* iv.19.
3. This argument was used by H. Munro Chadwick, *The origin of the English nation* 67–71 (Cambridge, 1907).
4. Alois Brandl, *Zur Geographie der altenglischen Dialekte* 29 (Berlin, 1915).
5. ["It is necessary to remember that the dialect depends on the original tribe."]
6. *Ibid.* 5. ["Firsthand accounts of the settlements of the Germanic tribes in Britain; for the original variation of the dialects rests naturally on the diversity of the tribes."]
7. Alois Pogatscher, *Anglia* 23.302–9 (1901); modified by Otto Ritter, *Anglia* 37.269–75 (1913) and Brandl 31–42.
8. Sherman Kuhn, *Speculum* 18.458–83 (1943), 23.591–629 (1948).
9. Henry Cecil Wyld, *Englische Studien* 47.1–58, 145–66 (1913); modified by Brandl 42–74.
10. *Essays and studies* (Univ. of Michigan) 13.1–60 (1935).
11. Karl Luick, *Historische Grammatik der englischen Sprache* 1. § 118 (Leipzig, 1921). ["There is clearly shown a common Anglo-Frisian prototype whose beginning at least dates from the time when the two tribes were neighbors on the Continent."]
12. Kuhn, *PMLA* 54.1–19 (1939).
13. In Henry Sweet, *The oldest English texts* 427–8 (London, 1885), and in John Earle, *A hand-book to the land-charters and other Saxonic documents* 10 (Oxford, 1888). This is the only seventh-century charter of which the original is preserved.
14. Chadwick 67; Jane Weightman, *Englische Studien* 35.337–49 (1905).
15. Eduard Sievers (rev. by Karl Brunner), *Altenglische Grammatik* § 2, *Anm.* 5 (Halle, 1951). ["but their language is perhaps not pure Kentish."]
16. Kuhn, *PMLA* 54.1–19 (1939).
17. *Historia ecclesiastica* i.15.
18. *De excidio et conquestu Britanniae.*
19. *De bello gotthico* iv.19.
20. *Hist. eccl.* i.22. ["Angle or Saxon people . . . Angle and Saxon peoples."]
21. *Ibid.* i.15. ["Angle or Saxon people . . . Angle and Saxon peoples."]
22. *Ibid.* i.32. ["(to the) king of the Angles."]
23. R. G. Collingwood and J. N. L. Myres, *Roman Britain and the English settlements* 346 (Oxford, 1937).
24. R. H. Hodgkin, *A history of the Anglo-Saxons* 92 (Oxford, 1939).
25. *Ibid.* 146.
26. *Ibid.* 155; Collingwood and Myres 347–8; Peter Hunter Blair, *Anglo-Saxon England* 10–11 (Cambridge, 1956); F. M. Stenton, *Anglo-Saxon England* 6–10 (Oxford, 1947).

27. Hodgkin 92–7.
28. Douglas Jerrold, *An introduction to the history of England* 214 (Cambridge, 1952).
29. Hodgkin 262.
30. Jerrold 214.
31. Hodgkin 98–100; Stenton 219.
32. Chadwick 17.
33. Hodgkin 91.
34. Jerrold 214.
35. Hodgkin 94; Chadwick 77–8.
36. Hodgkin 261.
37. *Hist. eccl.* iv.22.
38. Collingwood and Myres 412.
39. Jerrold 223.
40. Blair 283.
41. Hodgkin 174.
42. Fr. Klaeber, ed., *Beowulf* 235 (New York, 1941).
43. *Hist. eccl.* iii.18.
44. Collingwood and Myres 412.
45. Henry Cecil Wyld, *A history of modern colloquial English* 49 (Oxford, 1936).
46. Kuhn, *PMLA* 60.631–69 (1945).
47. In Sweet 426, Earle 13. It is described in Chadwick 70. Recent scholarship has shown that this is not an original, as Chadwick and Earle thought, but a copy made at the same abbey in the late eighth century; see Dorothy Whitelock, ed., *English historical documents* 1.446–8 (London, 1955). The language could therefore be a mixture of seventh- and eighth-century forms.

ROLF BERNDT

# The Linguistic Situation
# in England from the Norman Conquest
# to the Loss of Normandy (1066–1204)*

The Conquest of England by French-speaking invaders under the leadership of William, Duke of Normandy, undoubtedly resulted in far-reaching changes not only of the social and economic conditions but also of the linguistic situation in the conquered country. English or Anglo-Saxon was no longer the mother tongue of all its inhabitants. In addition to English, French was used as a means of oral and written communication by certain sections of the population for almost three and a half centuries. But what exactly were the relations of the French and English tongues in England after the Norman Conquest? The whole question, it is true, has been assiduously discussed by generations of scholars, and works like those of Oscar Scheibner, Dietrich Behrens, Johan Vising, Percy van Dyke Shelly, M. Dominica Legge, R. M. Wilson, G. E. Woodbine, H. G. Richardson, Helen Sugget and many others have doubtless thrown much light upon the linguistic effects of the Norman Conquest. Up to the present day, however, a great many problems still remain unsolved. Moreover the ideas put forward in more recent publications are no less conflicting than those which Shelly considered as "typical of the still unsettled state of the whole question"[1] in the early twenties.

Opinions about the extent to which English and French were used in England during the three and a half centuries following the Conquest are still widely divergent, as can easily be seen from the following quotations: "With the Norman Conquest . . . French was substituted for English as the vernacular of the free classes of society."[2] "French began to oust English in the eleventh century, and was dominant during the twelfth."[3] "It was an inevitable consequence of the Conquest that both [the English nationality and the English language] were nearly destroyed. In the century following the cessation of the 'Chronicle' it appeared very possible that French and not English would be the language of England."[4]—"Search as we may, we can find no dependable evidence to show, or imply, that French superseded English, either as a written or a spoken language, during the time of the Norman kings."[5] "In the twelfth century . . . the native tongue was widely

* From *Philologica Pragensia* 8.145–63 (1965). Reprinted by permission of The Czechoslovak Academy of Sciences and the author. This paper was first printed with minor alterations from a lecture at the University of Sofia, 12 December 1964; some minor additions and corrections have been made by the author for this reprinting.

used for familiar speech."[6]—Contradictory opinions of this kind are by no means confined to characterizations of the linguistic situation in England during the first 140 years or so after the Conquest, but are more or less typical also of statements concerning the linguistic development during the thirteenth, fourteenth, and early fifteenth centuries.

It is true, of course, that direct contemporary evidence is often extremely meagre and "not always easy to harmonize."[7] Moreover it cannot be denied that, unless new material is brought to light, definite answers to a number of questions can probably never be given. Many of the statements on the diffusion of French and English in medieval England must, therefore, necessarily remain more or less hypothetical. Contradictions characteristic of the hitherto existing literature can, however, be largely eliminated by widening the scope of the investigation and studying the linguistic history in close connexion with the history of the society or community speaking the language or languages under consideration. For it is only too obvious that many scholars have been led to too sweeping generalisations or even false conclusions by taking too little account of the historical background.

This entirely new study of the linguistic situation in England from the later eleventh to the early fifteenth century is, therefore, not limited to a discussion of all the available direct contemporary evidence, but also gives fullest possible consideration to the latest results of research in the economic, social, political and cultural history of medieval England and carefully considers the linguistic evidence against the historical background.[8] Some of the results of this investigation are given in the following chapters. Lack of space unfortunately compels us, however, to confine ourselves to some very general remarks only.

a)  *Some of the most important nonlinguistic
    consequences of the Norman Conquest*

The difficult question of the extent to which English and French were used in England after the battle of Hastings can certainly not be answered without any knowledge of the effects of the Norman Conquest in general. Any study of the linguistic changes brought about by the Conquest must therefore necessarily start with a discussion of a number of other questions and try to find out as much as possible, for instance, about the numerical strength of the foreigners, the social strata to which they belonged, the pattern of their settlement, their rôle in the economic, social, and cultural life of the conquered country, the contact they kept up with their home countries, etc.

All or many of these problems are in themselves already extremely difficult to solve. Studying the available sources carefully and making full use of the results of historical research in this field does, however, enable us to draw the following important conclusions:

1. The Norman Conquest of England did not lead to a mass immigration of Normans or people from other parts of France. It was "not a national

migration." [9] The changes in the population structure were not even approximately comparable to those effected by the Conquest of Britain by the Anglo-Saxons in the fifth and the following centuries or by the Scandinavian invasions during the ninth and tenth centuries. Estimates of the strength of William's army vary between 25,000 and 5000, and many modern historians think that the most plausible number we can assume for William's army is around 5000–7000 men. How many of them actually remained in England is not definitely known. A number of them certainly returned to France after the fighting was over. On the other hand, we have to take into consideration that others of their countrymen, and almost certainly even more than had been in the army, crossed the Channel and came to settle in England in the years following the Conquest and even in the next century: merchants, craftsmen, clergymen, feudal landlords with their families, and others. Nothing definite can be said today about the exact number of these later immigrants. But there is one point on which all historians without exception do agree, namely that the Conquest of 1066 never brought about a numerical ascendancy of the foreigners. Even if we accepted the highest estimate hitherto given by Geoffrey Hill,[10] according to which the number of immigrants settling in England during the reign of William the Conqueror amounted to around 200,000, this would still mean that their number did not exceed 13% of the whole population of England at that time, generally estimated at about 1.5 million. But the number given by Hill is almost phantastically high and in no way supported by contemporary evidence. Estimates of other historians are therefore considerably lower and vary between 10,000 and 20,000. Although these later numbers may seem to be somewhat too low we may be sure that the Normans and the settlers from other parts of France always constituted a relatively small minority whose numerical strength never exceeded 10% of the whole population of England and was probably even lower—perhaps far lower—than that.

2. Least affected by changes in the population structure was undoubtedly the peasantry, which at that time and even in later centuries constituted the overwhelming majority of England, that is—if we include their wives and children—almost 85% to 90% of the total number. By far the largest part of those people actually cultivating the land and doing all the agricultural work were still men of Anglo-Saxon or Scandinavian stock as they had been in former times. "The invaders were few and could not provide a peasantry from their own ranks." [11]

This does not mean, of course, that none of the foreign followers of the Conqueror ever took to farming in later years. There is no doubt that a certain number of them—soldiers of the lower ranks, foreign mercenaries serving in the many castles built by the Conqueror, people belonging to the military retinue or to the households of great landlords or of the king, etc.— got larger or smaller strips of the conquered land for their own cultivation and so became farmers in the end. That this was so can be clearly seen from the "Domesday

Book," which here and there expressly mentions the nationality of the men living on certain lands or in certain villages. So we get entries in which some of the men are clearly designated as "francigenæ," "francigenæ homines" or "francigenæ servientes," many of whom were probably small farmers with holdings often no larger than those of villeins or cottars. But the number of men designated as foreigners is extremely small. It amounts to no more than 0.35% of the total population registered in nine mainly West Midland shires, for instance. Even if we concede that not all of the many people engaged in producing this record proceeded in the same way and made such clear distinctions between the members of the different ethnic communities, we may be sure that the actual number of foreigners among the peasantry always remained exceedingly small. Many of these foreigners lived together in small groups dispersed over the far-off manors of their feudal landlords and probably very soon lost all contact with their homes on the continent. To all appearance it did not take more than one or two generations for them to be entirely absorbed by the overwhelming majority of their English-born neighbours within the different village-communities.

3. The situation in the urban communities of the conquered land was at least not fundamentally different from that in the country. There is every reason to believe that at least part of the hundred or so communities of urban or semi-urban character in Norman England, especially the less important ones among them, remained entirely English. Others of them—geographically favoured places, protected by Norman garrisons and developing into more important centres of commerce and trade—certainly attracted larger or smaller numbers of foreigners, artisans or merchants together with their families, or even saw the establishment of "new boroughs" (novi burgi), expressly founded for the newcomers from the continent by the new Norman lords. This was certainly so in London, already then the most important trading centre of England. In the entries of the "Domesday Book," which does not give any information about London itself, we find further evidence for the presence of immigrants from Normandy or other parts of France in at least some other English towns, as for instance York, Northampton, Southampton, Nottingham, Norwich, Shrewsbury, Dunwich, or Bury St. Edmunds, whilst other sources mention the "new boroughs" of Hereford and Rhuddlan.

The figures given in these sources clearly show that the concentration of foreign settlers was at least in some English towns considerably greater than in the country. So we are told that in 1086 there lived 160 "francigenæ burgenses" (or "mercatores") in Norwich, about 65 of them in Southampton, 43 in Shrewsbury and about the same number in Northampton, or that men like these owned 145 houses in York, for instance. This undoubtedly enabled them to keep up closer contact amongst themselves or, in some cases, even with countrymen of theirs visiting English ports and markets for trading purposes.

On the other hand, however, the same and other sources equally show that the number of "French-born burgesses or merchants" among the townsfolk nowhere exceeded that of the native population. So there is no evidence whatever "that thousands and thousands of merchants, craftsmen, and trades-people of all kinds left their homes in Normandy to settle mainly in the bigger cities and trade centres on the other side of the Channel" as maintained by Dietrich Behrens at the beginning of this century.[12] On the contrary, all the evidence we have supports the assumption that the foreign immigrants among the townsfolk in the late eleventh and the twelfth century always constituted only a larger or smaller minority of the urban population of England and had to live in urban communities with a dominating native—English—element.

4. A relatively stronger Norman-French element was certainly to be found among the clergy of twelfth-century England, itself only a small group of people whose numerical strength amounted, even in the thirteenth century, to no more than about 2% of the total population. Although the lower ranks of the secular clergy, especially those living in the country parishes, to all appearances continued to be men of native extraction, the regular clergy of England soon became Frenchified to a certain extent.

Many of the older English monasteries were immediately after the Conquest or during the following decades given to foreign abbots who were soon joined by larger or smaller groups of monks mainly from Normandy, but also from other parts of France. The number of foreign monks even increased in later years, that is to say until about the middle of the twelfth century. The king and many of his barons, though rarely founding new monasteries themselves, donated considerable parts of the conquered land to continental convents like Caen, Jumièges, Fécamp, Mont St. Michel, St. Martin de Séez, St. Evroult-en-Ouche, Cluny, La Charité-sur-Loire and others. According to F. M. Stenton "it seems clear that by 1086 many of these alien properties were supporting small communities of foreign monks."[13] The same seems to hold good for the few newly founded priories and cells on English soil. The monastic revival in the early twelfth century led to a remarkable intensification of the activities of the monastic orders, which resulted in the foundation of large numbers of new monasteries, priories, and smaller cells in different parts of England.

This, of course, served to strengthen the contacts between English and continental monasteries of the same order and undoubtedly brought more French monks over to England. Where the foundations led to the establishment of a direct state of dependency the French monasteries continued to send over a certain number of monks even as late as the thirteenth or fourteenth centuries.

All this clearly indicates that monastic life in England was, especially during the first century after the Norman Conquest, strongly influenced by French-speaking foreigners. It does not mean, however, that English-born natives were entirely excluded from the regular clergy as a consequence of the

Conquest. We know for certain that even in the late eleventh and the early twelfth century a number of Englishmen were to be found among the abbots and other influential conventuals. And we may take for granted that in very many of the monasteries, priories and cells smaller or larger numbers of natives had always lived side by side with monks of French extraction. All of which is to say that most of the monasteries were, even during this early time, places in which members of both ethnic communities lived peacefully together.

The number of English-born abbots steadily increased during the latter half of the twelfth and the early thirteenth century. The same seems to be true of the lower ranks of the regular clergy, so that there is every reason to believe that things had already considerably changed at the end of this period and that people of English stock (or descendants of the early immigrants) again outnumbered the foreign monks in many of the English monasteries, amongst them such important ones as Bury St. Edmunds, for instance. In spite of changes like these, however, the monasteries of Normandy and the rest of France in many ways continued to exert a certain influence upon English monasticism even as late as the thirteenth or fourteenth centuries.

5. The Norman Conquest and the re-distribution of the conquered land naturally led to considerable changes within the lower ranks of the ruling class. By this we mean the lesser feudal landlords who held their lands by knights' service or were "tenants-in-fee-farm" or "tenants-in-farm" paying a fixed rent to the barons or ecclesiastical landlords from whom they had received their lands. This numerically strongest group within the ruling class was itself, of course, only a relatively small minority of the total population of England. Though no exact numbers can be given, the available figures lead to the conclusion that there were about 5000 knights in William's army and that the existing knights' fees at the end of the twelfth and the beginning of the thirteenth century varied between approximately 6500 and 7200 respectively. This seems to justify the assumption that the group of lesser feudal landlords in late twelfth century England probably never comprised very much more than about 10,000 or so subtenants together with their families.

But where did these men come from? To which of the two ethnic communities did they belong? There is not the smallest doubt that the Norman king and his barons as well as the ecclesiastical landlords thought first of their kinsmen and retainers from overseas when creating subtenancies. That this was so is clearly proved by the "Domesday Book" which often mentions larger or smaller numbers of "Francigenæ milites" in various places of the country and likewise gives French names amongst the "firmarii." This does not mean, however, that all of the Anglo-Saxon "thanes," forming the lower ranks of the ruling class in pre-Norman England, were driven off their lands and entirely replaced by newcomers from the continent. Though it may be true "that Norman blood was ... predominant among the lesser lords" of some English shires, as maintained by Reginald Lennard,[14] it is equally true that the lower ranks of the ruling class within the new feudal society of Anglo-Norman England did not constitute a purely Norman-French group. For the entries in the "Domesday Book" also show "that on all baronies many men were granted subtenancies who were of English descent, and some of these [the 'milites Angli' of the DB] undoubtedly held their lands by knights' service, subject to the same conditions as their Norman neighbours."[15] "English thanes survive at the time of the Domesday Survey in all parts of the country as one element of the upper military class which was to rule England during the next centuries."[16]

We are therefore fully justified in describing this greater part of the new ruling class as an ethnically mixed group comprising greater numbers of Normans and men from other parts of France as well as English-born natives. This, and the fact that such a situation almost certainly favoured inter-marriages of Normans and natives of the same class at an early stage, will have to be borne in mind when we come to a closer analysis of the linguistic situation. Historians have pointed out that "these men dealt more directly with the English people than their lords could do"[17] and that circumstances in course of time brought them into closer contact with the upper ranks of the free peasantry, almost entirely of native stock. This means that the French-born among them were from the very beginning exposed to strong influences of their predominantly English surroundings. On the other hand we must not forget, however, that the class-determined community of interests naturally demanded close relations between them and the King as well as the members of the feudal aristocracy in general.

All these are very important points, indeed. The peculiar linguistic situation within these circles can only be understood by taking all these facts into account.

6. The most far-reaching changes undoubtedly befell the most powerful group within the ruling class of England. As a consequence of the Norman Conquest, political and economic power became concentrated in the hands of a small group of great feudal landlords. This included the king himself, the greater feudal landlords among the clergy—the archbishops, bishops and the superiors of the more important convents—and the holders of lay fiefs, the vassals of the king, his "barons" or "tenants-in-chief." How great this concentration of power really was can be seen by the fact that the number of lay barons at the time of the Domesday Survey amounted to no more than about 190. And "twenty of these lay fiefs, together with a dozen of greater episcopal and monastic estates, comprised between them something like 40%, in value, of all the rural land in Domesday England."[18] The numbers remained essentially the same until the end of this period: "In 1199 there were approximately 197 lay and 39 ecclesiastical baronies in England. But many of these baronies were very small."[19]

This exceedingly small group of the most powerful territorial magnates consisted, at the time of the Domesday Survey, almost exclusively of French-born foreigners. Some of the leading Anglo-Saxon landlords, it is true, did survive the Conquest. But the vast majority of them either lost their lives or were driven off their lands or fell into insignificance, so that English chroniclers of the early twelfth century, like William of Malmesbury, complained that "today no Englishman is a duke, or a bishop, or an abbot: foreigners devour the wealth of England, and there is no hope of remedy." [20] The few surviving Anglo-Saxons amongst the tenants-in-chief, and even the greater ones amongst them, were now far less important than most of the new barons of Norman-French origin. So it was now "the rarest of exceptions for an Englishman to hold a position which entitled him to political influence or gave him military power." [21] "By 1086, indeed, almost all the important lay landlords were men of continental origin—Normans, Bretons, or Flemings, for the most part—men, or the heirs of men, who had either been the companions of the Conqueror . . . or had joined him subsequently." [22] Almost the same can be said of the great ecclesiastical landlords controlling considerable parts of the conquered land. Before ten years had passed after the battle of Hastings most of the 15 English bishoprics had already been handed over to private chaplains or other clerical friends of the new king. In order to confirm his power he also placed more and more of the older English abbacies under French-born abbots, so that by 1088 most of the thirty older monasteries were already controlled by foreign clerics. William's immediate successors pursued more or less the same policy. And although things did change somewhat in later years and Englishmen were again to be found even among the upper ranks of the clergy, it was by no means unusual, even at the end of the twelfth century, for French-born foreigners to be promoted bishops or archbishops. At the same time, that is during the second half of the twelfth century, at least part of the English abbacies, such as St. Albans, Evesham, Crowland, Coventry, Bury St. Edmunds and others, were still under foreign abbots.

The feudal aristocracy of Norman England was in fact almost entirely Norman-French in origin. "With less than half a dozen exceptions, every lay lord whose possessions entitled him to political influence was a foreigner." [23] Though exceedingly few in number, these men of the predominantly Norman-French feudal aristocracy were the true lords of the conquered country. Their numerical strength was nothing in comparison with their economic power. Their economic power, on the other hand, secured them the most influential positions in the military and civil administration of the country, so that "by 1087 Normans of the baronial class were in office in all parts of the country as keepers of royal castles and as sheriffs." [24] They replaced the Anglo-Saxons at the King's Court—the Curia Regis—at that time the most important instrument of central government. And it took more than a century before they lost most of their influence in the administration of the shires, in local government that is to say, and before the descendants of the Anglo-Saxon nobility regained access to more influential positions.

We shall certainly not go wrong in supposing that the members of the feudal aristocracy moved mainly in predominantly Norman-French circles. A good many of them probably had no permanent residence in the country but were for a long time "absentee landords," who visited their manors only occasionally. Circumstances did not really force them to get into closer contact with the rank and file of the native English population. Everything that was necessary to get maximum profits out of their demesne manors by exploiting their peasants to the utmost could be done by their stewards, baliffs, reeves, etc. It is, of course, not improbable (and even certain in some cases) that intermarriage led in course of time, in a number of cases, to the establishment of closer relations between members of the Norman-French aristocracy and Anglo-Saxon families of the same class. This in itself, however, did not make an early assimilation inevitable.

There is reason to believe that members of the baronial class even more frequently contracted continental marriages. And what is still more important is the fact that the majority of the greater barons of the late eleventh century had likewise possessions on the continent, above all in the duchy of Normandy, which was from now on and over a period of almost 150 years ruled by the King of England, who was at the same time Duke of Normandy and, as such, a vassal of the King of France. This peculiar state of affairs under which the greater lords of England were at the same time holders of fiefs in Normandy and other parts of Northern France, lasted until far into the twelfth century and even longer. So "the great men of Henry II's day [still] held lands on both sides of the Channel and frequently passed from their English to their continental possessions."[25] It is true, of course, that by this time the holders of English and Norman fiefs in some cases had already become distinct as a result of the splitting up of the estates by inheritance or escheats, so that "some of John's barons were purely English landowners with no interests at stake in France."[26]

But this did not yet apply to the uppermost circles of the feudal aristocracy. They still had personal interests on both sides of the Channel and were equally at home in England and in Northern France. Circumstances during this period in no way compelled them to adapt themselves entirely to specifically English conditions and to abandon many of the peculiarities characteristic of their own ethnic community. This did not happen until the final and irrevocable separation of the Duchy of Normandy from England, which put an end to a long period of close personal relations with their original homeland on the part of the English baronage.

b) *Linguistic communication in England from the time of the Conquest until the Loss of Normandy*

As already pointed out, the Norman Conquest and its manifold consequences made French the language of part of the population of late eleventh and of twelfth century England. England was now a country in which two languages were spoken, if we exclude Latin as an additional third language whose use was almost exclusively confined to scholarly circles. But Norman England was certainly not yet a truly bilingual country. Would it or could it ever have become one? Or was there any real likelihood of the language of the Conquerors ousting the old Anglo-Saxon idiom of the native population? Did circumstances make it possible "that French and not English would be[come] the language of England"?[27]

If things were ever to have taken such a turn, the most important changes in this direction would undoubtedly have had to take place during this first period. For never again in later centuries were England and France or parts of it so closely tied together as during these 140 years immediately following the Conquest. According to scholars like V. H. Galbraith, Johan Vising, M. Dominica Legge, R. W. Chambers, Ernst Leisi, E. A. Freeman, Hope Emily Allen and others, late eleventh and twelfth century England was indeed on the way to becoming a truly bilingual or even a French-speaking country. But even the most careful scrutiny of all the available materials will produce nothing to support assumptions like these. There is, in fact, no evidence whatever to show that "the French language acquired a position of dominance,"[28] that "French began to oust English in the eleventh century and was dominant during the twelfth."[29] The same applies to assumptions according to which "a very large part of the people of England must have habitually spoken two languages,"[30] so that "English and Normans in any class above that of serfs were . . . bilingual."[31]

The linguistic changes brought about by the Norman Conquest were obviously of quite another kind. A close investigation into these problems does, in my opinion, not admit of any other conclusions than the following:

1. The rural population of England, the free and unfree peasantry, comprising more than 80% of the total population, was undoubtedly strongly affected by the Norman Conquest so far as its living conditions were concerned. As a consequence of the acceleration of the process of feudalization and the establishment of a fully developed military feudal system, large numbers of peasants lost their former liberties and, in course of time, became villeins or serfs of the great feudal landlords. The changes actually brought about by the Conquest were, however, confined to the economic and social conditions of the peasantry. They did not concern the language of this still predominantly Anglo-Saxon part of the population.

The peasantry did not only remain essentially English in origin but also continued to use the old Anglo-Saxon language spoken by their forefathers. The Conquest itself did not create any conditions whatever to make the native peasants give up their own language and adopt the French language of the Conquerors as their new means of communication. There was not even the slightest chance of French becoming the second language of the peasantry. The foreigners amongst them were few in numbers and could scarcely expect their neighbours to learn their native French idiom. They might, of course, after some time take over a certain number of French words into their own language. But this was certainly all that could be expected.

Circumstances almost certainly compelled the small minority of peasants among the foreigners—the "French-born men or servants"—to adapt themselves as quickly as possible to their new surroundings and to acquire additional knowledge in English. It is, however, improbable that men like these remained bilingual for a long time. If they did not want to stay single they had to marry English women. Their children would be growing up in an almost entirely English environment and would probably already use English as their mother tongue. So there is every reason to believe that it took no more than one or two generations for the descendants of these foreigners to become unilingual again and speak no other language than the majority of peasants of purely Anglo-Saxon stock.

We may take for granted, therefore, that the peasantry of England had already in the early twelfth century become again an entirely and exclusively English-speaking class. None of the available information does admit of any other interpretation. All the evidence clearly shows that the "rusticanus tocius eloquii alterius quam Anglici nescius"—the peasant entirely ignorant of any language other than English—is, indeed, the typical representative of his class. Contemporary reports according to which some men of peasant origin had by supernatural inspiration acquired the gift of speaking French fluently can certainly not be drawn upon to confirm R. W. Wilson's assumption that "bilingualism was common, even to a certain extent in the lower classes." [32]

The fact, however, that the Anglo-Saxon peasantry of Norman England kept to English as their mother tongue, and that the descendants of the few foreigners amongst them gave up French at an early date, was of paramount importance for the future development of the linguistic situation in England. The numerical strength of this class alone fully guaranteed the further use of English and decisively limited the vitality of French in England, which under circumstances like these never had any real chance of ever becoming the language of the country.

2. What has been said of the peasantry seems to hold equally true for the townspeople or burgesses of later twelfth century England, or at least the majority of them. There is no doubt, of course, that during the time of the first Norman kings French was used as a mother tongue by larger or smaller groups of newly-arrived craftsmen and merchants in at least a certain number of the more important English towns. Being no more than minority groups, however, they were equally compelled to live within predominantly Anglo-Saxon communities. If they wanted to follow their trade and make a living out of it, they simply had to get into closer contact with the majority of their English-born neighbours and to try to make themselves understood to them.

Their numerical strength and importance certainly does not justify the assumption that the native majority would make serious efforts to learn the language of the foreign minority in order to facilitate communication. There is no indication, at any rate, that the English burgesses did so and that "French thus became the language of the mercantile communities."[33] It seems far more probable, indeed, that it was the foreign craftsmen and merchants who endeavoured to learn English at an early date and so eventually become bilingual.

This did not necessarily mean, however, that their children already adopted English as their mother tongue and either gave up French completely or kept it only as their second language. This may have actually been so in a number of cases, but certainly not in all. For we know for certain that at least part of the foreign craftsmen and especially traders (like Gilbert Becket, father of the later archbishop Thomas à Becket) had come over to England together with their wives or even with their families. Where they settled in larger groups or even in "new boroughs," expressly founded for them, some of their descendants of the second generation might even have had parents both of whom were of French origin.

In the long run, however, assimilation became inevitable. Living and working in a predominantly English-speaking environment and marrying English-born partners almost certainly served to anglicize them more and more and induced them to adopt the language of the majority as their new mother tongue. This, again, prepared the ground for the last step on the way towards complete Anglification. For most of them probably did not retain French for long after having adopted English as their native language, but gave up the second language entirely and so became unilingual like the majority of their neighbours. It is in no way improbable that this was true already of the third generation of descendants of the Norman-French immigrants, or at least the majority of them.

We may conclude, therefore, that almost all of the members of the urban communities of later twelfth century England did have English as their mother tongue. It is possible, however, that there were at least some townspeople who still had—and even in later times continued to have—some knowledge of French, although there is no contemporary evidence to definitely prove this. If this was so, however, it almost certainly applied only to a small group of merchants in the more important trading-centres who belonged to the most influential persons of the urban oligarchy and, as middlemen in external trade, were in close contact with French-speaking tradesmen from the continent. But the mother tongue of these burgesses, whatever their origin might be, was at this time almost certainly not different from that of the majority of their fellow-citizens whom circumstances in no way compelled to learn a second language and who could easily express all they wanted to say in their own English tongue.

The contemporary sources, it is true, do not give much direct information about the linguistic situation in the urban communities of England. What little original evidence there is, almost without any exception refers to the end of the twelfth century. The sparse information given by contemporary chroniclers, however, admits of no other conclusion than that English, and not French, was the normal means of communication of the townspeople of late twelfth century England. We may assume, therefore, that the urban population of the country (with the exception of the clergy and the members of the ruling class) had by this time—and probably even earlier—again become an entirely English-speaking population and that French was, at best, still known to a very small number of members of the merchant oligarchies in the towns.

3. The lower ranks of the secular clergy, even after the Conquest mainly of native Anglo-Saxon stock, continued to all appearances to have English as their mother tongue and remained unilingual, as a rule. The mass of the poorer priests living in the country parishes and closely connected with the English-speaking peasantry had almost certainly no—or not much—opportunity of ever learning French, even if they had wanted to. Most of these "clerici rustici" were probably very poorly educated and did not even know much Latin. For "the parish priest was often grossly illiterate with scarcely enough Latin to repeat the church services correctly."[34]

There is, indeed, no indication whatever that "there were few priests capable of preaching in English" during the latter half of the twelfth century, as maintained by Johan Vising.[35] The reverse of it seems to be true. For there is no reason to believe that the village priest described as being capable of the use of one language only and entirely ignorant of French was an exception to the rule and did not stand for the majority of his equals.

Bilingual—or even trilingual—clerics were, however, undoubtedly to be found in greater numbers amongst the upper ranks of the secular clergy of twelfth century England. We know for certain that at least part of these—private chaplains of the royal family or of members of the feudal aristocracy or the knighthood, influential diocesan officials, like archdeacons and deans, or other important persons in attendance on bishops and archbishops—either had English or French as their mother tongue and spoke Latin fluently. It is even possible that many of them were actually men of French extraction, and that some of the latter were ignorant of English, or at least did not know it well, even at the end of this period. It is certain, however, that others of them had, sooner or later, acquired some knowledge of English and were more or less bilingual or even trilingual. The same can be proved for a number of natives amongst them who had learned French and had, in course of time, become very proficient in it.

We may conclude, therefore, that French continued to be used by the upper ranks of the secular clergy either as their first or their second language and that English was equally known to most of them.

4. The changes brought about by the Norman Conquest undoubtedly made French one of the languages used in the newly founded monasteries,

cells and priories and favoured its dissemination and cultivation amongst the members of the regular clergy. This, of course, also applied to the older Benedictine monasteries of England, many of whom had been put under Norman-French abbots at an early date and had, in course of time, received larger or smaller numbers of French-born monks.

It is very probable that French remained the first language of part of the regular clergy until far into the twelfth century, because the monasteries of Normandy and other parts of France continued to send monks of theirs over to England even long after the days of the Norman kings. Their numbers were probably still increased by descendants of Norman-French families who had settled in England in the late eleventh or the early twelfth century. There is, however, no evidence to show that "there were many monastic establishments peopled entirely by Normans, where French would be the language in normal use."[36] This was certainly not true of the older monasteries and probably did not apply either to most (if to any) of the newly founded establishments. It is much more probable, indeed, that before long very many of the convents accommodated foreigners as well as natives in varying proportions and that the number of English-born monks steadily increased during the latter half of the twelfth century.

This meant, of course, that French never ousted English completely in the monasteries and that English always continued to be the mother tongue of at least part of its inmates. Monastic life in post-Conquest England, it is true, had been exposed to stronger foreign influences than many other walks of life. The Conquest and its consequences had created exceedingly favorable conditions for the cultivation of French and French culture in the cloisters of England. But it had neither made these cloisters linguistic enclaves nor places of linguistic intolerance. Opinions according to which "the Norman monks did not bother to learn English, [but] made such Englishmen as joined them to learn French,"[37] are far from the truth and can easily be refuted.

There is ample proof to show that in the monastical establishments of twelfth century England (or at least a great number of them) both languages, French and English, existed side by side and that neither of them was deprecated as an inferior language. The use of the native language by members of the religious orders is clearly evidenced by contemporary reports which likewise confirm the use of French in other cases. Much additional information can be gained from the literary output of these establishments, which does, in fact, fully support the assumption that there were, in many of the religious houses of the time, men or women capable of writing manuscripts either in Latin or in French or in English.

What cannot be gathered from the contemporary sources is, however, that "naturally the Norman monks did not bother to learn English."[37] For there is direct evidence in at least some cases that French-born clerics who had stayed in England for a few years had indeed learned English and even made use of it in preaching to the people. Nothing else would have been more natural than this. There is every reason, therefore, to assume that most of the foreigners amongst the regular clergy, in course of time, learned to understand or even speak the language of the natives amongst them, which was at the same time the first and only language of the vast majority of people living in their immediate surroundings.

Bilingualism was, however, certainly not only characteristic of French-born clerics who had come to stay in England for a longer time. For we need not search very long for evidence to show that monks or nuns, who were either of native stock or had sprung from mixed marriages, did not only know how to express their thoughts in English but were also fully conversant with French or had at least some command of it. Acquiring some knowledge of the second language must, indeed, have been quite a natural process in places where foreigners and natives were living together under the same roof. Additional facilities were provided by the convent-schools, which almost certainly no longer confined themselves to teaching Latin only but gave French a certain place in their instruction. Those striving for higher education might be given still better opportunities to improve their knowledge of French by attending the famous schools of France, like Laon, Angers, Chartres, and later the University of Paris, which at that time attracted large numbers of English scholars.

This does not necessarily mean that all of the English-born clerics in later twelfth century England had an equally good command of French and were more or less bilingual. Some might not even know a word of it, whilst others may not have been able to speak French as fluently as their mother tongue. At the end of the twelfth century there may have even been abbeys, like Bury St. Edmunds, where French had already become more of a foreign language, mastered only with difficulties by a number of its inmates. But it is very probable that the better educated natives amongst the regular clergy were still well-versed in French.

Things had undoubtedly changed in the latter half of the twelfth century. The situation in the religious houses of England at the end of this period was no longer that of the late eleventh and the early twelfth century. The number of native members of the religious orders, having English as their mother tongue, had almost certainly increased. There may have even been monastic communities consisting almost entirely of English-born monks and nuns. But even where this was so, French had not yet been completely replaced by English. For practical and conventional reasons French was, to all appearances, still retained as a second language in most of the important English monastries. It was taught in the monastery schools and continued to be used as one of the means of oral as well as of written communication by at least the better educated members of the regular clergy of early thirteenth century England.

5. The uppermost ranks of the clergy, secular as well as regular, the archbishops and bishops as well as the superiors of the most important convents,

had, during the time of the first Norman kings, doubtless formed a pre-dominantly French-speaking group. This remained essentially so in the first half of the twelfth century. Although their number decreased in later years, there were still continental-born foreigners amongst the bishops, archbishops, and abbots of late twelfth century England, whose mother tongue was un-doubtedly French. Others of the men promoted during this period were members of the Norman-French feudal aristocracy, sons or nephews of bishops, or, like Becket, descendants of immigrant merchant families, who almost certainly still had French as their mother tongue as well.

All this seems to justify the assumption that most of the archbishops and bishops and at least part of the most influential among the abbots of late twelfth and of early thirteenth century England still had French as their first language. The rest of them—men of purely English stock or of Anglo-French extraction—had almost certainly acquired French as their second language, as can be definitely proved in the case of Samson, Abbot of Bury St. Edmunds (1182–1211), and some other abbots. This is made the more probable as we know that some of them had either been church officials in Normandy or other parts of France or had spent part of their time in studying or teaching in the University of Paris or other French schools before being promoted bishops or abbots in England.

So French remained well-known in these circles and was not only spoken by those who had it as their mother tongue but also used by many (if not all) of the others whose first language was that of the overwhelming majority of the population. There is no reason, however, to assume that these were the only bilinguals among them. We do have the evidence of Nigel Wireker, it is true, according to which there were still men promoted bishops or abbots who did not know any English. And we are given the names of at least some of the continental-born clerics who, according to contemporary sources, had no—or at least only an insufficient—command of English, But this seems to have been the exception rather than the rule, even among the French-born church officials.

There is clear evidence, for instance, that Gilbert Foliot, Prior first of Cluny then of Abbeville, Abbot of Gloucester, later Bishop of Hereford (1148–63) and London (1163–88), was not only fully conversant with French and Latin but also with English. Moreover it would only seem natural that most of the French-speaking highest dignitaries of the Church at that time were at least not entirely ignorant of the native language, if they had already stayed in the country for a few years. If they took their mission seriously and did not want to be permanently dependent upon interpreters (doubtless to be found in greater numbers amongst the archdeacons, deans, chaplains, etc. in their attendance), they simply had to acquire some knowledge of English. For this alone would enable them to get into personal contact with the rank and file of churchgoers in their parishes, and was even necessary to be able to con-verse with their immediate subordinates, the members of the lower (especially secular) clergy that is to say, who, for the most part, did not know very much more than their own mother tongue.

We may conclude, therefore, that at the end of this period bilingualism was no rare accomplishment even in circles like these, and that things had, in fact, somewhat changed in the course of the twelfth century. French was certainly no longer the first language or mother tongue of all of the most important clerical landlords. But there were, even at this time, a good many of them of whom this was still true. Those to whom this did not apply had almost certainly moved with the times and adopted French as their second language.

6. The members of the lower ranks of the ruling class of late eleventh and of early twelfth century England, the lesser feudal landlords, were, as already mentioned, of different origin and consequently did speak different languages. This does, however, not seem to have lasted very long.

These feudal subtenants and lessees apparently played a much more active part in agrarian life than their liege lords (or many of them) and took a closer personal interest in the management of their estates. A good many of the Normans, Bretons, and other foreigners amongst them probably soon took up their permanent residence in the counties where they had their manors and began to take root in the country at an early date. Most of them, it would seem, had no longer any personal interests in France and, though duties in the service of their overlords may have often called them away, spent a large part of their life on their manors. This necessitated much closer relations to the predominantly English-speaking peasantry on their part than on that of their lords. Social intercourse with their equals necessarily brought them into contact with people who had English as their mother tongue. Intermarriages, evidenced as early as the late eleventh century, almost certainly served to strengthen the bonds of friendship as well as kinship between the members of both ethnic communities in this class at an early time.

Under circumstances like these it was highly probable, indeed, that the foreigners amongst the lesser lords of twelfth century England and their descendants would soon make efforts to learn the native language in order to get on in the country which they had chosen as their new homeland. Assimilation seems to have even gone further than that for, though there is no evidence to definitely prove this, we may assume that a good many (if not yet all) of the descendants of Norman or Anglo-French families of this class had even before the end of this period come to adopt English as their first language, their mother tongue. Knowledge of English is at any rate clearly evidenced in at least some cases, including men of undoubtedly Norman descent.

There is, however, at the same time evidence to show that French had by no means become unknown to men like these and to their families. Adopting English as the first language obviously did not yet mean giving up French entirely. We may conclude, therefore, that those of the lesser feudal landlords who were either of purely Norman-French stock or had sprung from mixed marriages continued to retain French, at least as their second language, until the very end of this period, and thereby remained more or less bilingual.

Knowledge of French seems also to have been characteristic of those members of the knighthood who were of English descent, or at least the majority of them. Although it is true that most of them were in closer contact with the English-speaking peasantry than their lords, it is equally true that as members of the ruling class all of them were more or less closely linked up with the King and the rest of the feudal aristocracy which was still a predominantly French-speaking group. Even for those, for whom French may not have been of much use in everyday life and in the management of their estates, there were at least social reasons for learning the language of their superiors and keeping it as a second language.

Learning French, or continuing to cultivate it, seems to have become a sort of "social obligation" in these circles, so that knowledge of French was at the same time a kind of "distinguishing sign" of their forming part of the ruling class. What little contemporary evidence there is, seems indeed to admit of no other interpretation than this. What other reasons could a certain knight of Henry II's days have had for taking on a Norman named Symon Durand for the express purpose of teaching his son French? Or what other conclusions can there be drawn from the report of a trial concerning certain lands of the Abbot of Growland (1191), which expressly mentions that one of the false witnesses "was not of the knightly class . . . [and] did not know how to speak French"?

Although it is highly probable that English had, by the end of this period, become the mother tongue of the majority of the lesser feudal landlords and their families, it can scarcely be doubted that French retained at least the position of the second language of most of them and that bilingualism prevailed amongst the lower ranks of the ruling class until the early thirteenth century and even later than that.

7. The members of the feudal aristocracy of Domesday England, the great landlords including the royal family, were almost without any exception aliens knowing and speaking no other language than French. Unlike their vassals or subtenants, unlike all the other social strata, we might even say, with the exception of the most important clerical landlords, they formed an almost exclusively French-speaking group. It was in these circles where the language of the Conquerors had, indeed, acquired a position of dominance.

This state of things almost certainly did not change very rapidly. As long as the leading magnates, the great barons of England, held lands on both sides of the Channel and spent much of their time in France, either in the service of the King or in order to see to the management of their own continental estates or to get married to French-born partners, etc., they were unlikely to take firm root in the country and come to regard England as their homeland in the fullest sense of the term. This means that radical changes in the linguistic usage of the feudal aristocracy were highly improbable until far into the twelfth or even until the early thirteenth century.

Until this time French was a most useful means of communication to them. Retaining and cultivating it was, if not absolutely necessary, at least highly desirable and advantageous. It meant, at any rate, keeping a language common to their equals in England as well as to their continental relatives, friends, and neighbours with whom they were still closely associated, and greatly helped them to look after their interests on the continent. It is beyond doubt, therefore, that the reasons they might have for maintaining French were, during this period, not yet conventional and social ones only but also, to a certain extent, truly practical ones.

Though contemporary evidence in regard to the linguistic proficiency of the members of the feudal aristocracy is extremely meagre, it can scarcely be doubted that most of them (if not all) were fully conversant with French until the very end of this period. Even if there is not much direct evidence, there is at least the great bulk of Norman-French literature produced in England during this period to prove this. A considerable part of it was undoubtedly and according to their own authors expressly written for these circles—"for the rich men who have the rents and the money"[38]—for members of the royal family as well as for earls and barons and their wives.

There is even reason to assume that most of the great feudal landlords of late twelfth century England not only knew French but did, in fact, still have it as their mother tongue or first language. This may at least be inferred from remarks of Gervase of Tilbury (1211) who, when speaking of the native language ("lingua nativa") of these circles, obviously had no other language in mind than French (or more correctly "Norman-French").

But even if we may take for granted that French was the first language not only of the baronial class of Domesday England but also of their descendants living at the end of the twelfth century, this does not necessarily any longer imply unilingualism on their part. There is, of course, nothing to prove that "the Norman overlords . . . quickly learned English for dealings with their dependents."[39] The same is true, however, of assumptions according to which English "was of little practical use to them, on account of their preoccupation with continental affairs and the lack of any necessity to use it when in England . . ., so that they made little effort to learn it."[39] What is true, is that they could more easily do without English than their bailiffs and stewards or their feudal sub-tenants and lessees. It is equally true that they moved mainly in predominantly French-speaking circles, or could do so at any rate.

But a good many of them almost certainly spent at least part of their time on their English demesne manors and must, sooner or later, have come into more or less close contact with people who did not know any other language than English. There is nothing to show that they in any way despised the native language or even refused to have anything to do with it. Even if they did not set out to learn the language systematically, it seems highly probable and natural that many of them would at least pick up some English after having stayed in the country for a longer or shorter time. This seems to have been so even in the case of a king like Henry II (1154–89), who, although not spending more than a third of his time in England, was to all appearances at least able to understand English to a certain extent, though he could not speak it fluently and therefore needed an interpreter when conversing with his English subjects.

It is not unlikely, at any rate, that a good many of his vassals, especially those who were of mixed descent or spent a greater part of their life in England and were more important English than continental landlords, had in course of time become even better conversant with English than the king. We may assume, therefore, that even the members of the feudal aristocracy of later twelfth century England (or most of them) were no longer entirely ignorant of the native language, and that a larger or smaller number of them had already become truly bilingual by adopting English as their second language. We have, however, no means of ascertaining whether there were even more far-reaching changes in at least some cases. This may have been so, but was almost certainly not yet true of the majority of the great feudal landlords of England. To them French was probably still the primary means of communication and even if they had acquired some knowledge of English, it had not yet become their mother tongue. This apparently did not happen before the thirteenth century, when the separation of Normandy from England made most of them purely English landowners with no interest at stake in France.

## Conclusions

Summing up, we may say then that the linguistic situation in England at the beginning of the thirteenth century was no longer that of the time immediately following the Norman Conquest. French, then the language of a minority in England, had neither "ousted English" nor become "dominant." There had never even been the slightest chance that "French and not English would be the language of England." The tongue of the Conquerors had not "acquired a position of dominance" and become "widely diffused" in the country. On the contrary, the number of those people in England who had French as their mother tongue gradually decreased in the course of the twelfth and early thirteenth centuries. Those of whom this was still true at the end of this period—the members of the royal family, the greater part (if not all) of the feudal aristocracy, a certain number of the higher church officials and other members of the clergy—had already become a minority within the minority of those Englishmen who still had a more or less good command of the French language.

If French had, in fact, gained some ground in England after the Conquest, it was certainly not as a mother tongue but only as a more or less foreign language of a numerically not very strong but otherwise in many ways influential part of the population of England—the lower ranks of the ruling class (or at least the majority of them), the upper ranks of the secular clergy, a greater part of the regular clergy and, at best, a very small minority within the urban oligarchy.

This, however, did not mean any decrease in the number of inhabitants to whom English was the mother tongue. If they had even in the first fifty years or so following the Conquest constituted the vast majority of the population of England, they constituted now an even greater majority. The time when all of them (or almost all of them) would again have English as their mother tongue, was, in fact, already drawing near.

French, it is true, had even now not become an entirely unimportant language in England. It was still the native language of the upper class and was maintained, cultivated, and used as a second language by those circles of society who, because of their economic and social power or their education, played an important part in the administration of the country or exerted a strong influence upon the intellectual life of the better educated classes. And although it even ceased to be the mother tongue of the English feudal aristocracy in the course of the thirteenth century, it was not before the later fourteenth or early fifteenth centuries that French lost all of its former ground in England and became a truly foreign language like any other tongue spoken outside the country. Although it became more and more of an "artificial language" in England, social custom and fashion as well as business and administrative convention promoted its continued use in the English upper circles until stronger motives, like the growth of national feeling in the fourteenth and fifteenth centuries, combined with an increasing "vernacular-consciousness," reduced their effectiveness and helped to bring about the general displacement of French by English, the "common language of all natives of England" and the only one rightly to be called the "lingua hujus nationis" ["language of this nation"].

# FOOTNOTES

1. Percy van Dyke Shelly, *English and French in England, 1066–1100* (Diss., Philadelphia, 1921), p. 9.

2. V. H. Galbraith, "The Literacy of Medieval English Kings," *Proceedings of the British Academy*, Vol. XXI (London, 1955), 227.

3. M. Dominica Legge, "Anglo-Norman and the Historian," *History*, XXVI (1941), 167.

4. R. W. Chambers, "*The Continuity of English Prose . . .*" EETS.OS.186 (1932), p. lxxxix.

5. G. E. Woodbine, "The Language of English Law," *Speculum*, XVIII (1943), 410.

6. Hope Emily Allen, *The Romanic Review*, XI (1918), 172.

7. Albert C. Baugh, *History of the English Language* (New York, 1935), p. 147.

8. Presented to the Philosophical Faculty in the University of Rostock as "Habilitationsschrift" in 1962 under the title: "Die Sprachsituation in England während der ersten dreieinhalb Jahrhunderte nach der normannischen Eroberung. Behauptung und Durchsetzung des Englischen gegenüber dem Frazösischen." Erster Teil (pp. 1–359): Sprachliche Kommunikation und gesellschaftliche Situation in England nach der normannischen Eroberung—Das Problem der Mehrsprachigkeit, ihre historischen Ursachen und Bedingungen. Zweiter Teil (pp. 1–173): Die Sprachsituation in England nach der normannischen Eroberung im Spiegel des zeitgenössichen mittelalterlichen Schrifttums (Zusammenstellung der Originalbelege, pp. 2–113, sowie Übersicht über Lehr- und Lernmaterialen im mittelalterlichen England, pp. 113–40).

9. Doris Mary Stenton, *English Society in the Early Middle Ages*[2] (Harmondsworth, 1952), p. 13.

10. Geoffrey Hill, *Some Consequences of the Norman Conquest* (London, 1904), p. 13.

11. *Cambridge Medieval History*, vol. V (Cambridge, 1926), p. 513.

12. Dietrich Behrens, "Französische Elemente in Englischen," *Pauls Grundriss der germanischen Philologie*, 2. Aufl., I.2 (Strassburg, 1901), p. 951.

13. F. M. Stenton, *Anglo-Saxon England*, Oxford History of England (reprint, Oxford, 1950), p. 666.

14. Reginald Lennard, *Rural England, 1086–1135* (Oxford, 1919), p. 68.

15. *Cambridge Medieval History*, vol. V, p. 513.

16. Paul Vinogradoff, "English Society in the Eleventh Century," *Essays in English Medieval History* (Oxford, 1908), pp. 79 and 403.

17. Doris Mary Stenton, *op. cit.*, p. 61.

18. Reginald Lennard, *op. cit.*, pp. 25 f.

19. Sidney Painter, *The Reign of King John* (Baltimore, 1949), p. 19.

20. *Willelmi Malmesbiriensis De Gestis Regum Anglorum Libri Quinque . . .*, RS. 90, Vol. I (1889), p. 278.

21. F. M. Stenton, "English Families and the Norman Conquest," *Transactions of the Royal Historical Society*, XXVI (1944), 1.

22. Reginald Lennard, *op. cit.*, p. 25.

23. F. M. Stenton, *Anglo-Saxon England*, pp. 618, 671.

24. F. M. Stenton, *ibid.*, p. 624.

25. Cambridge Medieval History, Vol. V, p. 554.

26. William Sharp McKechnie, *Magna Carta* (Glasgow, 1914), pp. 22, 68.

27. R. W. Chambers, *op. cit.*, p. lxxxix.

28. Johan Vising, *Anglo-Norman Language and Literature* (London, 1923), p. 12.

29. M. Dominica Legge, "Anglo-Norman and the Historian," p. 167.

30. E. A. Freeman, *The History of the Norman Conquest of England*, vol. V (Oxford, 1876), p. 525.

31. M. Dominica Legge, "Anglo-Norman and the Historian," p. 166.

32. R. M. Wilson, "English and French in England, 1100–1300," *History*, N.S. XXVIII (1943), 58.

33. Mildred K. Pope, *From Latin to Modern French* (Manchester, 1934), p. 420.

34. A. L. Poole, *From Domesday Book to Magna Carta, 1087–1216*, Oxford History of England (Oxford, 1955), p. 224.

35. Johan Vising, *op. cit.*, p. 14.

36. A. J. Sheard, *The Words We Use* (London, 1954), p. 227.

37. M. Dominica Legge, "Anglo-Norman and the Historian," p. 165.

38. Wace, *Roman de Rou* . . ., ed. Andresen, Vol. II, p. 36, 11. 163–5.

39. Margaret Schlauch, *English Medieval Literature and its Social Foundations* (Warsaw, 1956), p. 106.

40. A. J. Sheard, *op. cit.*, p. 202.

*ANGUS McINTOSH*

# A New Approach to
# Middle English Dialectology [1] *

## I

The work on Middle English dialectology which I propose to discuss
began in October 1952. It was the result of a period of reflection about the
relationship between the problems posed by this subject and those posed by
the dialectology of Modern Scots. In the preceding years I had been much
occupied in helping to get the Linguistic Survey of Scotland under way, and
what I had learnt from this [2] provided most of the stimulus to the attack on
Middle English which I then made. I should add that I was joined in this
work by Professor M. L. Samuels in 1953 and that what I say below owes
much to what he has contributed in our long subsequent collaboration.

I had long felt dissatisfied with the rather sketchy nature of previous studies
of this subject, and it seemed to me that their weaknesses lay far more in the
methods of approach, and in the absence of any ordered theoretical basis for
these methods, than in the limitations of the material itself. One could not
help being struck by the great contrast between the richness of detail provided about the linguistic situation in present-day Scotland (and it is relevant
to note that up to that date most of what we knew about it had been gathered
in ordinary written form from postal questionnaires), and the depressingly
small amount of information provided by the Middle English dialect maps
which Moore, Meech, and Whitehall published in 1935. [3] Despite the fact that
their work was superior to anything achieved earlier, it soon became clear that
it had several basic weaknesses. I shall try to deal with the more important of
these in turn, suggesting as I go along some of the ways in which we subsequently attempted to overcome them.

## II

I may begin by considering the treatment by Moore, Meech, and Whitehall
of what I shall call dialect criteria and what they call dialect characteristics.
First of all the number of items which they decided to record, and subsequently plot, was far too small. Those picked out were for the most part of
undoubted potential importance, but they were just a small selection, for
which no reasoned justification was offered, from the far greater number which

---

* From *English Studies* 44.1–11 (1963). Reprinted by permission of the author and
the editors of *English Studies*.

have obvious claims to be relevant. Moore, Meech, and Whitehall settled in fact on a mere eleven items in contrast with the hundreds if not thousands that are examined as a matter of course in surveys of modern spoken dialects. In a slightly earlier study[4] (1930), Dr. J. P. Oakden studied forty-five items, but even this number is not enough. Furthermore he handled his material rather cursorily, for his dialectal survey was no more than a prelude to a detailed study of alliterative poetry in Middle English, and he was therefore unable to devote more than a comparatively short period of time to what is in itself a task of enormous magnitude. I may say that I myself started with some seventy-five items and that for certain purposes we have stepped up the total to more than two hundred and sixty. As far as possible the number investigated should be controlled only by

a) the total number of items which do in fact show a variation in form between one area and any other;
b) reasonable probability of occurrence: very rare forms, such as crop up in only a few of the texts examined, are of only slight value, so that we must on this basis make a final selection from the total number judged to be eligible from the first point of view.

Secondly, the particular criteria selected for consideration were open to criticism: all too frequently, consistent dialectal contrasts were postulated in a congeries of items which were not in fact homogeneous with regard to the feature under scrutiny. Thus Moore, Meech, and Whitehall grouped together and used for one and the same purpose all words with an Old English "y" vowel, long or short. They were looking of course for the familiar /y/, /e/, /i/ variation we are taught to regard as a phonological phenomenon distinguishing (roughly speaking) the W of England, SE England, and the rest of the country in Middle English times. But in fact it is now clear, as it should already have been far earlier than 1935, that one cannot work adequately like this. Not all Old English "y" words behave alike (not even all those containing the short vowel, or all those containing the long) and their behaviour, at least to begin with, ought to have been examined separately, word by word. "Chaque mot," as Gilliéron had said long before, "a son histoire." By choosing in certain cases to ignore this, Moore, Meech, and Whitehall mishandled the evidence; some of the really telling information which must have actually been collected word by word lost its force altogether as finally presented, simply by being bundled together in meaningless or (at best) misleading generalised statements.

There is, thirdly, another way in which their handling of criteria was needlessly crude. For example (as is well known) different Middle English texts use different forms for the objective form of the third person pronoun plural, i.e., the equivalents of Modern English "them." Now Moore, Meech, and Whitehall chose to subject these to a simple binary classification; they were either listed and plotted as *h-* or not-*h-* (i.e., by implication as *h-* or *th-* etc.) forms. But analysis of any reasonable selection of texts will yield various kinds of sub-sets of these two types, many of which have a demonstrably non-random geographical distribution and are therefore themselves dialectally important. It is a commonplace, for example, that the sub-set *hom* has its own territory; nevertheless this and similar facts are not exploited by them at all.

The broad dichotomy *h-/th-* fails therefore to take into account a whole further mass of often dialectally significant information. This is not for lack of material; the information is *ipso facto* available whenever the pronoun occurs at all, because whenever it occurs it has a form, of which an initial *h-* or not-*h-* is only one characteristic. And it turns out that many other characteristics of the various forms are of dialectal relevance. Attention should certainly be paid to at least twelve of them, namely: *hem*; *hom*; *heom*; *ham*; *þem*; *þam*; *þaim*; *þeim*; *them*; *tham*; *thaim* and *theim*, and this by no means exhausts the list. The failure to exploit this kind of evidence is extremely serious: it is important to note that it is almost entirely one of method and has very little to do with the quantity or quality of the material available. Another unnecessary crudity relates to the treatment of forms for "their" as if they provided accurate evidence for forms for "them," despite the fact that Moore, Meech, and Whitehall observe that the genitive form with *h-* was more recessive than the objective form with *h-*.[5] By not treating these separately, they have wasted much valuable and easily obtainable information.

This brings me to my fourth and last point about criteria. In general, Middle English scholars are singularly unwilling to look at written texts without seeing them purely and simply as a sort of encoded form of some variety of spoken Middle English. I have tried to deal elsewhere with the theoretical background to this kind of thing.[6] My point, briefly, is that the proper way to treat written dialectal material for the purposes we are considering is to record the graphemic forms as such. Thus if there is a contrast ⟨*bane*⟩ : ⟨*bone*⟩[7] between the North and elsewhere, then for our purpose it is best treated as a contrast in graphemes irrespective of their phonemic "value," or, to speak in more mediaeval terms, as a contrast in *figurae* irrespective of the *potestas* of each.[8]

The full implications of this kind of approach are too numerous to go into in detail here, but it may be mentioned that there are clear cases of "dialectal" (or at least we may call it "regional") variation between *figurae* even when the alternative *figurae* have the same *potestas*, e.g., between *sche* and *she*, or *it* and *itt*, where the differences of spelling almost certainly have no phonic implications. Furthermore, there are many graphemic contrasts of indubitable phonic significance which, if one attemps to "convert" them into what they imply phonetically or even phonologically, are thereby transformed, from being verifiable pieces of information arrived at directly from the graphic substance, into debatable derivative conjectures. As such, they hardly constitute satisfactory material for entry on maps. Indeed, our view is that the entry on maps of written forms assessable so to speak in their own right must be carried out *before* any detailed systematic phonological or phonetic interpretation of them can be attempted.

## III

I turn now to the actual choice of textual sources made by Moore, Meech, and Whitehall, and here I offer three main criticisms. First, as to their handling of documents. They rightly saw that it was necessary to make very much greater use of localised documentary material than had hitherto been the custom, and they studied no fewer than 266 texts of this kind. Nevertheless they overlooked a great number, for I should say that at least 400 survive which require careful attention. Furthermore, a considerable number of their 266 texts were in fact, for various reasons,[9] quite without value.

The second and most serious shortcoming was in the very slight use made of literary manuscripts. Only those for which there was reasonably good external evidence for provenance were studied, the total of those so selected being 43.[10] Was it really necessary thus to pass over the enormous main body of surviving Middle English and concentrate on what cannot be more than a small fraction of one per cent of the whole? I shall discuss this question in detail later.

Thirdly, they worked with too wide a chronological spread, using thirteenth century (and even occasionally twelfth century) material side by side with texts from the fourteenth and fifteenth centuries; in this way linguistic differences due to chronological factors were confused with genuine dialectal (what I call *diatopic* as distinct from *diachronic*) differences, to the considerable confusion of the whole study. It is in fact highly important, in any work of this kind, to restrict the time-span as much as possible; if one operates beyond a range of about a century, it is necessary to handle with all due safeguards any such chronologically peripheral material as cannot for various reasons be ignored. It is not difficult to pick out the most suitable period of Middle English to focus attention on. The all-important documents in the vernacular are quite rare before 1400 and they cease to have much value after about 1450 or 1460 (in some cases considerably earlier) because they are by then becoming highly standardised. And from about 1350 onwards there is an enormous amount of dialectal literary material extant, far more than for the preceding period. The period (roughly) 1350–1450 therefore suggests itself as the span of time on which we may most profitably concentrate.[11]

Let me return now to the restrictions imposed by Moore, Meech, and Whitehall on the use of literary texts. At first sight it seems reasonable enough, perhaps even inevitable, that one should confine oneself to the study of manuscripts which are localised; otherwise where on the map is one to plot one's findings? This in fact touches the heart of the entire problem of Middle English dialectology, and clear enough hints of the need for a more ambitious sort of procedure were certainly not lacking. I should like to deal with this matter at some length.

Let us suppose that one takes the trouble to plot on maps as much as possible of the dialectal information available in localised documents which come from various parts of S Lancashire, Cheshire, SW Yorkshire, W Derbyshire, N Staffordshire and N Shropshire. If one then examines the language of *Gawain and the Green Knight*, it eventually becomes clear that this text, as it stands in MS Cotton Nero AX, can only *fit* with reasonable propriety in a very small area either in SE Cheshire or just over the border in NE Staffordshire.[12] That is to say, its dialectal characteristics *in their totality* are reconcilable with those of other (localised) texts in this and only this area. So long as the surviving text of *Gawain* is reasonably homogeneous, there is nothing surprising about this being so. But can we utilise this property of dialectally homogeneous texts?

At an early stage in the work the possibility of utilising it was tested by using the most closely similar material available in circumstances wherein such conclusions as were reached were capable of verification. Information from written responses to questionnaires relating to various lexical items in Scottish dialects was examined, the (of course known) provenance of these responses being withheld from the investigator. Attempts were then made to establish their provenance by finding where on the map the forms they contained most convincingly squared with those which had already been entered in the normal way from other questionnaires. The results, in terms of accuracy of localisation, were so startlingly successful as to suggest the advisability of applying some such procedure systematically to Middle English. This concept of reconcilability or *fit* is of fundamental importance and it will be necessary presently to say something further about it and how it can be exploited.

But first another piece of autobiography. Quite early in our investigations I happened to be examining a large chunk of the version of the *Cursor Mundi* preserved in MS Trinity College Cambridge R.3.8, because I had noticed that it was a strikingly homogeneous text with interesting West Midland characteristics.[13] I was not fully persuaded at that time of the potentialities of the *fit*-technique and I had as yet no dialect maps of my own for the West Midlands. But it so happens that the isoglosses on the relevant Moore, Meech, and Whitehall map[14] are fairly thick on the ground in that region, and it seemed to me that the text might be localised approximately by seeing with what place or area those of its dialectal characteristics which are treated on that map most neatly squared. Once the text had been analysed, it was the work of a few minutes to see that if the findings of Moore, Meech, and Whitehall, so far as they went, were more or less reliable, there was a high degree of probability that MS Trinity College Cambridge R.3.8 was written by someone who belonged within a few miles of Lichfield. At least I thought so then; I have recently worked over this problem again as it confronted me at that time, and I still think the conclusion was justified. The total evidence as it *then* was now looks thin enough, but it is certainly supported by what we have accumulated since.

It so happens that there is nothing precisely for Lichfield among the local-ised Moore, Meech, and Whitehall texts, and so I wrote to Dr. A. I. Doyle of the University Library, Durham, who throughout our researches has gen-erously put at our disposal his unrivalled knowledge of various kinds of external evidence for the provenance of late mediaeval MSS, asking him if he knew of any vernacular material, literary or documentary, known or suspected to have been written in Lichfield. He replied saying that there was reason to believe, on other than linguistic grounds, that Bodley MS Rawlinson A.389 was written there. So I obtained a microfilm of this manuscript, having previously worked (I may say) with the printed edition of Trinity College Cambridge R.3.8.[15] MS Rawlinson A.389 turned out to be in two hands, and a very short bout of analysis sufficed to show that the language of one of these two hands was quite strikingly similar, often in minute detail, to that of the scribe of the Trinity manuscript, so much so that it was difficult to believe that the two texts could be other than the work of one and the same person. The end of the story is that carefully palaeographic comparison showed beyond doubt that they *were* the work of a single scribe. The simple but un-tested process of trying to localise the language of a mediaeval English text by the fit-technique was therefore vindicated at an early stage. Subsequent examination of the characteristics of a few scraps of local (documentary) Lichfield English tended to confirm that our scribe[16] belonged there or, at the very worst, somewhere within a few miles of the town.

I now come to a consideration of the fuller exploitation of the fit-technique. As I have just said, documentary material which can be localised in Lichfield is very scanty and in fact it yields information about only a small number of items of dialectal interest. If therefore one were to use *only* such material, there could be but few entries on our dialect maps at this point. And so with all similar cases. But if we can take extra nonlocalised literary material and come to a reliable conclusion, based on the fit-technique, about its provenance, we are at once able to fill in our maps at this very point with a great mass of additional information. Similarly with *Gawain*: if its language fits only in the small area I have mentioned, then why should we not enter the forms it yields in that place on the maps, where, this time, *no* information from localised text is available at all?

Such entries must of course only be made if we are fairly sure of our hypothesis about provenance. But every time we are, we must boldly put our information on the maps, and thus gain, step by step, new knowledge about the geographical distribution of dialectal features. This will in turn facilitate the task of further similar localisations which, of course, as we proceed, will provide us with a series of maps with ever denser and denser coverage. But if we do this are we not in danger, it may be asked, of getting further and further off the right track? The answer to this is that so long as our coverage grows denser without at some stage producing an impasse where we are suddenly alarmed to find that some apparently dialectally homogeneous text will not fit *anywhere* without being seriously at variance with its nearest neighbours, we can be pretty sure that the method of proceeding is on the right lines.[17]

We must be willing to acknowledge that the *absolute* position of these texts (i.e., their grid-reference in a narrow transcription as it were) may be uncertain. But this need not disturb us so long as we are persuaded that their position relative to one another is topologically sound. We must of course be prepared to make adjustments to the positions of such texts as new evidence about further neighbouring texts becomes available. But if we do so, the continued satisfaction of the requirements of correct relative position should bring us, the denser the entries on the maps become, nearer and nearer to an absolutely correct position for each text, in favourable circumstances (where there is a good backing of localised material) perhaps even to within a few miles.[18]

One fact about MSS Rawlinson A.389 and Trinity College Cambridge R.3.8 raised a question of special interest, an interest perhaps not only for the dialectologist, but for the literary historian. For *all* the texts in these two manuscripts are of northern origin and those written by the scribe I have been speaking of were *translated* from Northern English into West Midland English. I use this term "translated" advisedly and it is used at least once in Middle English this way: MS Cambridge University Library Ii.4.9 contains as its last item the *Informacion of Richard the ermyte*, and on folio 197b this text is described as having been "translate oute of Northarn tonge into Sutherne that it schulde the bettir be vnderstondyn of men that be of the selve countre."

Such "translated" texts are normally held in great distrust by students of Middle English dialects.[19] Cold analysis shows nevertheless that such distrust is in a great number of cases entirely unjustified. If a competent scribe took on the task of turning a text from one dialect to another then he usually made a very thorough job of it, and we can use the resultant version as evidence about the dialect of the scribe himself.[20] Of course there are texts which are copied without such transformation. MS British Museum Harley 2409, for instance, contains four texts all in the hand of one scribe, yet each is in a different self-consistent dialect and obviously therefore hardly tampered with at all by him. And there are other cases where a scribe *half*-transforms his original, producing a sort of *Mischsprache* ["mixed speech"]. For example Robert Thornton can be shown to have added a Yorkshire veneer to a number of texts he copied[21] from exemplars written in various forms of Lincolnshire dialect. The most important text in this group, at any rate from the literary point of view, is the alliterative *Morte Arthure*, in which the Lincolnshire (I believe SW Lincolnshire) characteristics of the text immediately behind Thornton are clearly visible for anyone to see; deep below this there are a few other North Midland features of a different kind which the immediately underlying SW Lincolnshire scribe, himself a copyist, had not quite succeeded in obliterating.[22]

But the majority of later Middle English manuscripts which are not originals (or copies made near the place of origin) tend to be what I call translations; in any case analysis normally enables one to identify those which are not, so that we may put them to one side accordingly. We have in fact used many, indeed hundreds of, thoroughly translated texts, and by doing so have added very greatly to our information about the dialectal characteristics of areas for which there is little or no more overt and specific evidence about provenance. For instance, there are numerous Midland and Southern translations of the originally northern *Prick of Conscience*, many of which have probably never been read (since the Middle Ages) except by Samuels and myself; some of these provide quite crucial dialectal information which could be obtained from no other source.

## IV

A word may be said in conclusion about the scale, progress and aims of the work. I have already mentioned that we have used a far larger number of criteria than our predecessors. I should add that we have by now examined (with varying degrees of thoroughness) over seven hundred documentary texts and literary texts from at least two thousand manuscripts, and that we have made a fairly full analysis of something like three hundred documents and over six hundred literary texts; the resultant information has been incorporated on rough working maps. I myself have tentatively mapped what I have gleaned from well over 150 documents and more than 280 literary texts. These all belong to the North and North Midlands—the area for which I have been mainly responsible. The total amount of information available for final presentation on maps in published form is therefore very considerable and is based, one way and another, on records of certainly not less than one million observed instances of forms.

Most of the analysis has been done from microfilms or photostats; much less from originals on the one hand and printed texts on the other. I should note that the work would have been impossible in the circumstances in which it has been carried on but for our having been able to acquire a large amount of photographic material for the Library of Edinburgh University, which we could readily use whenever we had time to spare. At the present time the work is at least three-quarters completed, and we now face various difficult problems of publication. We propose to include more than a hundred maps, most of them of very considerable complexity, and the cost of bringing out the *Atlas* (including the preparation of these maps) is likely to be about £7000. It is perhaps not entirely pointless to mention here the very great difficulties which nowadays beset scholars in the field of the humanities when they try to bring out something on this scale. The effect of these difficulties has been to divert much effort and energy which might have gone into scholarly activity into exhausting, and so far not very encouraging, attempts to get financial support for publication.[23]

The results of the work are, I think, likely to be fairly revolutionary, if only because of all the new information which has been assembled and ordered. We shall be able to provide, map by map, a pretty clear and detailed account of the enormously involved and yet remarkably patterned dialectal picture in late Middle English times. The detail and density of coverage we have already been able to attain is strikingly in contrast with what has been achieved in previous approaches.

I shall merely suggest here a few of the ways in which an atlas of Middle English dialects on this scale is likely to be of value. It is a novel and exciting thing, unparalleled at present in any other language,[24] this scheme of a detailed dialect survey of the English of over half a millennium ago; the more so because it will complement that of the survey of Modern English dialects by Professor Orton and the late Professor Dieth; each survey, one may hope, will add to the value of the other. No one, incidentally, should conclude that this Middle English project will in any sense exhaust what can be done on the subject; it simply opens up new possibilities for fuller and fuller investigation.

Most maps will present the forms equivalent to a single modern English word; a map of *she*, just to name one, suggests that the history of this problematic complex of forms will have to be rewritten, and there are several others of a similar kind.[25] But such things are purely linguistic matters. Going a little beyond these, we have made a substantial beginning on the study of the distribution (from the dialectal point of view) of the surviving copies of various important texts such as *Piers Plowman* (in its different recensions), the *Cloud of Unknowing* and the *Cursor Mundi*. We have also assembled a good deal of information about the probable place of origin of various Middle English writings; I have mentioned already what we think about *Gawain*. It is worth while to add that by a sort of extrapolation which may ultimately be applied to a large number of Early Middle English texts, one is led to the conclusion that the *Ormulum* was written if not in Stamford then certainly not very far away. Finally I would say that we believe that the genesis of Standard English is a very much more complicated matter than is often thought, and that the speech habits of the South Central Midlands, exemplified very well by certain Wycliffite texts, probably play a greater part in its make-up than recent scholarship has generally recognised. Discussion of the interpretation and the application of some of the basic dialectological findings belongs however to the forthcoming paper of Professor Samuels.

## Short Bibliography

OAKDEN, J. P., *Alliterative Poetry in Middle English*, vol. i: "The Dialectal and Metrical Survey," 1930.

MOORE, S., MEECH, S. B., and WHITEHALL, H., "Middle English Dialect Characteristics and Dialect Boundaries," in *Essays and Studies in English and Comparative Literature* (University of Michigan Publications in Language and Literature XIII, 1935).

KAISER, R., *Zur Geographie des mittelenglischen Wortschatzes*, Palaestra 205, Leipzig 1937.

MOORE, S., (revised A. H. MARCKWARDT 1951), *Historical Outlines of English Sounds and Inflections*, pp. 110–26.

KURATH, H., and KUHN, SHERMAN S., *Middle English Dictionary*, *Plan and Bibliography*, 1954, pp. 8–12.

McINTOSH, A., "The Analysis of Written Middle English," *TPS*, 1956, p. 26.

FRANCIS, W. NELSON, "Graphemic Analysis of Late Middle English Manuscripts," *Speculum*, XXXVII, 1962, p. 32.

## Source material available

As of 7.11.59, the Edinburgh University Library collection of Middle English material relevant to dialectal study which had been assembled over the previous seven years amounted approximately to the following:

Microfilms, almost entirely of literary (as distinct from documentary) material, consisting, in the majority of cases, of whole manuscripts . . 530

Photostatic reproductions, usually of one to a dozen pages each, of short literary texts or of specimens of long ones . . . . . . . . . 43

Photostatic reproductions, usually of one page, of documents of various kinds . . . . . . . . . . . . . . . . . . . . 488

Total   1061

# FOOTNOTES

1. This is a revised version of a lecture delivered in the University of Edinburgh in November 1959 to the staff of the Department of English Language and General Linguistics. In substantially its present form it was made available to those attending the Fifth International Conference of the International Association of University Professors of English, Edinburgh August, 1962. On that occasion the paper was, provided to supply background information to a lecture delivered at the Conference by Professor M. L. Samuels entitled "Some Applications of Middle English Dialectology." The substance of Professor Samuels' lecture, with illustrative maps, is to appear under that same title in the next number of *English Studies*. [ES 44.81–94. It is reprinted in this collection as the next article.—Ed.]

2. Cf. A. McIntosh, *Introduction to a Survey of Scottish Dialects*, Nelson 1952 (reprinted 1961).

3. See Bibliography.

4. See Bibliography.

5. *Op. cit.*, p. 11. We may note, for instance, that MS Bodley Fairfax 14, which contains a text of the *Cursor Mundi* produced in or near Lancaster, has a quite regular paradigm *þai, þaire, ham*; there are numerous other instances of the same sort.

6. See Bibliography for reference to this and to a recent paper by W. Nelson Francis. [McIntosh's paper is reprinted here, pp. 35 ff.—Ed.]

7. The angular brackets imply graphemic renderings of forms without implications as to their phonological equivalents.

8. See David Abercrombie, *Lingua*, vol. ii (1949) pp. 58–9. For this reason it is to be regretted that Moore, Meech, and Whitehall speak of their boundary lines as "isophonic."

9. Cf. footnote 11.

10. It should be added that such evidence was not always used judiciously. For example, much is made of the fact that MS Gonville and Caius College 84/166 part 2 has flyleaves from a mid-fifteenth century account roll of Darley Abbey near Derby, and the name of T. Grovis, its abbot 1524–35, on p. 217. What is overlooked is that the manuscript is in at least four hands and that the dialect of each hand is different from that of the others. Indeed it seems to have been due solely to the accident that material contributed by the first hand (pp. 173–9) happened to be available in print that Moore, Meech, and Whitehall chose this without further ado as being characteristic of the neighborhood of Darley. In fact it is not at all clear whether the language of any of the hands belongs to this neighborhood, but this first hand almost certainly does not. A vital pivotal point on their maps is thus misplaced.

11. At least twenty-five of the two hundred and sixty-six documents considered by Moore, Meech, and Whitehall are either too early or too late (in fact, nearly all of them too late) to be of much value if we impose this condition.

12. It should be remarked that this conclusion, reached in 1954, agrees remarkably with the suggestions about the provenance of the original poem, following other lines of evidence, made by R. W. V. Elliott in "Sir Gawain in Staffordshire," *The London Times*, May 21st, 1958.

13. The whole of this version is printed in the edition by R. Morris, *EETS, OS*, 57, 59, 62, 66, 68, 99, 101.

14. It is much to be regretted that they found it necessary to cram all their material into a single map. Such conglomeration is not repeated in the new *Middle English Dictionary* (see Bibliography).

15. See footnote 13.

16. He seems to have been occupied especially with the reproduction of northern texts for use in Lichfield: Professor Samuels established in 1955 that BM MS Harley 1205 (*Prick of Conscience*) was also his work. [On the work of this scribe, see M. G. Brown and A. McIntosh, "A Dialect word in some West Midland Manuscripts of the *Prick of Conscience*," in *Edinburgh Studies in English and Scots* (forthcoming). (This is a volume of essays to be published in 1969 by Longmans). —Ed.]

It might be noted here that the linguistic characteristics of this group of texts cast grave doubt on any theory that the Vernon Manuscript belongs to Lichfield.

17. A few such texts, which did cause alarm at one stage, turned out subsequently to be of Irish provenance. The problem of the dialectology of mediaeval Anglo-Irish is one of considerable interest in itself. [See also A. McIntosh and M. L. Samuels, "Prolegomena to a study of Medieval Anglo-Irish," *Medium Ævum*, vol. xxxvii, No. 1. 1968, p. 1.—Ed.]

18. It is important to observe here that in this kind of work, maps have two distinct purposes. Their use as an end-product is obvious, but throughout our investigations maps have proved to be indispensable *Forschungsinstrumente* ["research tools"] in themselves. More elaborate plans are at present being made, in collaboration with Mr. Robert Dixon, IBM Fellow in Statistical Linguistics, Edinburgh University, to attempt the positioning of unlocalized texts by means of computer techniques.

19. Some of them, nevertheless, were used by Moore, Meech, and Whitehall, e.g., MS Bodley Fairfax 14 (for which cf. footnote 5), though with certain reservations.

20. One must naturally make some qualifications here. For instance syntax is less tampered with than lexis, morphology and orthography. And alterations which would destroy metrical features like rhyme and alliteration are very often carefully

avoided. But these habits can be assessed case by case and thereafter taken into account and allowed for.

21. In MSS Lincoln Cathedral A.5.2. and BM Additional 31042.

22. I have tried to deal with this problem in "The Textual Transmission of the Alliterative *Morte Arthure*," *English and Medieval Studies presented to J. R. R. Tolkien* (London, 1962), pp. 231–40.

23. Grateful acknowledgement is made here to the Carnegie Universities of Scotland Trust for a grant of £200 in 1958 which made possible certain preliminary experimental mapping work, and to the Leverhulme Trust for a more recent grant which has now enabled us to draw on the full-time services of a professional cartographer for one year.

24. One naturally wonders whether similar methods could not be applied successfully to at least some of the other mediaeval vernaculars.

25. A coloured map of the word *she*, based on information available at that date, was produced experimentally in the spring of 1960.

## M. L. SAMUELS

# Some Applications of
# Middle English Dialectology*

In a paper published in the February number of this journal, Professor Angus McIntosh outlined the principles and techniques that he devised in 1952 and thereafter for a new survey of Middle English dialects, and referred briefly to the work carried out on that survey since then. Its most tangible result is over a hundred maps of great complexity, which unfortunately cannot be published until the necessary resources have been mustered. In the following paper,[1] which is intended to supplement that of Professor McIntosh, I attempt to forecast some of the questions that the survey will be competent to answer. Such maps as are given here are necessarily simplified, schematic representations of the evidence;[2] and examples quoted are from texts of Southern England and the South Midlands—the area for the survey of which I was mainly responsible.

As one might expect, the survey has most relevance in two fields: for the history of the English language, and as a tool in literary research; but these are not the only ones. We should note, especially, that this is the first attempt ever made at a detailed examination of the dialects of a past stage of *any* language, and it may therefore cast light on wider problems of diachronic linguistics. Linguistic change is viewed by one school as a purely mechanical process, but by another as systemic; and the result is often conflict or stalemate. Yet the study of linguistic geography of the *past* shows clearly that these two views are not incompatible, but complementary. For example, what one school might call "loss of initial *h-* in the word 'it'" did not take place simultaneously all over the country: the boundaries for *hit* gradually receded, and, throughout the period when this was happening, texts written in the neighbourhood of a boundary show a minor system in which *hit* is used in stressed positions, *it* in unstressed. Yet slightly later, when the boundary has receded still further, texts from the same region are found to use *it* only. In such a case, it was evidently the availability of two variants that created the minor system, and not *vice versa*.

On the whole, however, it is the functional and systemic aspects of linguistic change that are most clearly illustrated; and this too is of some interest, since the remnants of the neogrammarian tradition still often

* From *English Studies* 44.81–94 (1963). Reprinted by permission of the author and the editors of *English Studies*. Several minor corrections have been supplied by the author.

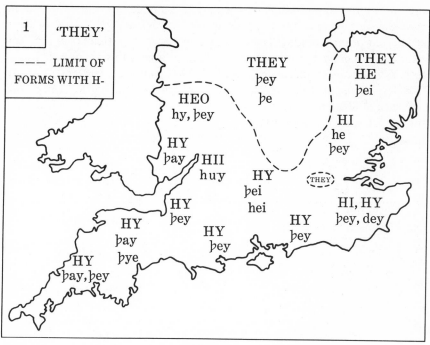

**Figure 1**

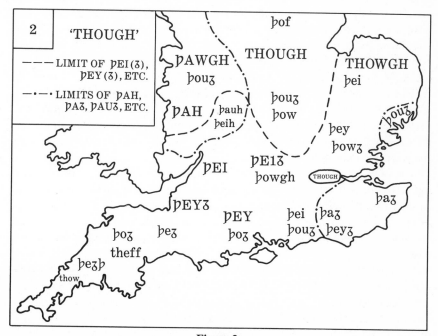

**Figure 2**

prevent a true appreciation of them. For example, we are prepared to *speculate on the possibility* that the two words *they* and *though* might have spread out of their original Danelaw area in answer to a functional need for clear communication, but we are unwilling to accept this as an established fact. Yet it can be established, if due attention is paid to the chronology of the two developments. Their spread over Southern England started before the influence of fifteenth-century London English could have had any effect; and the spread of *they* started first, closely followed by that of *though*, but never preceded by it. This can be deduced from the following diagram:

|  | *Main form for* <br> *"THEY"* | *Main form for* <br> *"THOUGH"* |
|---|---|---|
| Earlier texts <br> (mainly 14th cent.) | hy, hij, he(o) | þei(ʒ), þei(h) |
| Later texts <br> (mainly 15th cent.) | þei, they, thay | þow(ʒ), though |
| Very rare later texts | þei, þey | þei(ʒ), þey(ʒ) |

(The above diagram may be compared with maps 1 and 2, which attempt a schematization of early fifteenth-century evidence.)

In the southern area, *hy* and *though* are never combined as the main form, and since only a few rarer texts use *they* for both, we can be sure that *they* always preceded *though*, and that the interval between the adoption of the two borrowings must always have been short. In other words *they* was adopted into the southern area which already possessed that form in the meaning "though"; and, to remedy the homonymic clash caused by this, the further borrowing of *though* was made shortly after. I submit that the only conclusion that can be drawn is that the functional pressure for the adoption of *they* must have been overriding, and can only be explained at all on the grounds that the word for "they" occurs in normal speech more often than the word for "though."

It is, of course, fashionable to question the existence of homonymic clashes between words that are not of the same word-class; but fortunately the few Middle English scribes who used *they* as their normal form for both words have left us convincing evidence on this point. When they have to write the sequence "though they," they resort to archaic forms to make the distinction clear.[3]

The etymology of *they* and *though* is in any case clear enough, but in many other cases a map is essential for the interpretation of etymological evidence. The forms for "each" are typical of the problems encountered (see map 3). Each of the three forms *ech(e)*, *uch(e)*, and *euch(e)* is said to descend from a different Old English form: *ælc*, *ylc*, and *æghwilc*; but clearly ME *euch(e)* is a

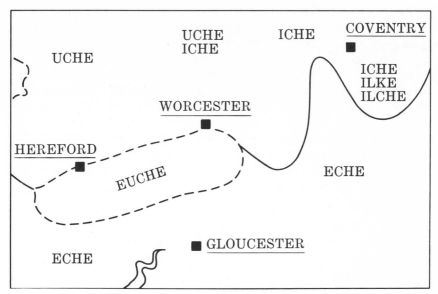

**Figure 3   Distribution of Forms for "Each" in S.W. Midlands**

border form, and, while we need not question its probable descent from OE *æghwilc*, its ME development owes as much to its geographical position as to anything else.

Similar examples could be multiplied, but perhaps the largest single contribution of this survey to the history of English is that it provides us with a frame of reference for isolating and classifying those types of language that are less obviously dialectal, and can thus cast light on the probable sources of the written standard English that appears in the fifteenth century. The relevant material falls into four main types.

The first type is one that has been recognised often enough but has proved difficult to localize: the language of the majority of Wycliffite manuscripts (though by no means limited to them), which recent scholarship, reacting against Skeat's and Dibelius' suggestions of Oxford, has tended to identify with the London dialect.[4] The most noticeable feature of this group is the sheer quantity of surviving manuscripts that belong to it, compared with other types of language from the same period.[5] Obviously this is not "Wyclif's dialect"; and it cannot even be defined as a "religious prose κοινή," in view of the secular works written in it. When reference is made to a few of its outstanding linguistic features, it becomes apparent that this is a standard literary language based on the dialects of the Central Midland counties, especially Northamptonshire, Huntingdonshire, and Bedfordshire. (As may be seen from maps 4 to 10, this view is supported by the occurrence of the following as the usual forms in this group of texts: *sich* "such," *mych* "much," *ony* "any," *silf* "self," *stide* "stead," *ȝouun* "given," *siȝ* "saw.")

The importance of this type of language should not be underestimated: we can tell from internal manuscript evidence[6] that it was copied in many outlying areas such as Somerset and Dorset; it had a wider currency than other types, and, until 1430, it is the type that has most claim to the title "literary standard." The Lollards, naturally, although they cannot be said to have invented it, were a powerful influence in spreading it, in their bibles, sermons, and tracts; once they had adopted it, they copied it faithfully, probably fanatically so. Their adoption of the type is not surprising: Lutterworth and St. Mary's Abbey, Leicester, were centres of their activity, and many of Wyclif's circle of helpers there must have been Midlanders; and, on more general grounds, we know from Higden that Midland speech was the most widely understood in the country.

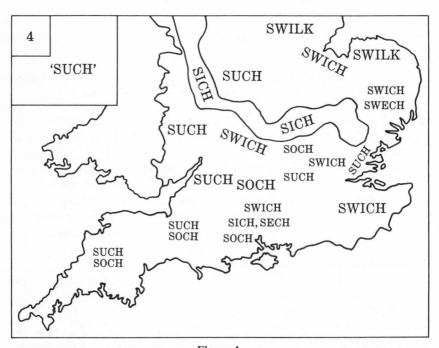

**Figure 4**

Perhaps the clearest indication that it was a well-established literary standard is that, although based on the spoken dialects of the Central Midlands, it survived in written form unchanged until the later fifteenth century: the Welshman Pecock writes it in almost exactly the same form as writers of fifty to sixty years earlier. Certainly no spoken form of English corresponding to it can have existed in Pecock's day.

I should perhaps emphasize at this point that I am referring to a written standard throughout: there is no question of a spoken standard in the

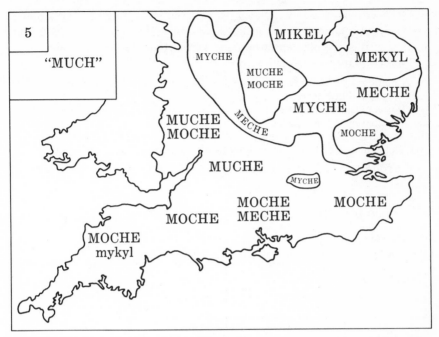

**Figure 5**

fifteenth century. We are concerned with the spoken language only in so far as any written standard must be ultimately based on it; but the evolution and spread of standard English in the fifteenth and sixteenth centuries was primarily through the agency of writing, not speech, and depended on the *quantity* written. The importance of early London written English in this evolution has been overrated: consultation of any of the large classes of documents at the Public Record Office will show clearly that, until 1430–5, English is the exception rather than the rule in the written business of administration; after that, there is a sudden change, and the proportions are reversed, from a mere trickle of English documents among thousands in Latin and French, to a spate of English documents.

What, then, of London English during this formative period? We can turn now to our three remaining types:

Type II, the earliest of the three, is found in a group of seven fourteenth-century manuscripts (the main hand in the Auchinleck MS. may be taken as typical).[7] There is no specific evidence of localization for this group, and it has been disputed hitherto: each manuscript has been assigned various provenances from Nottinghamshire to London. But on linguistic grounds there seems no doubt that they must all be from the greater London area.

There are certainly minor differences that probably indicate different parts of London or its surroundings; but they all agree in continuing features of that early Essex-type of London dialect that is seen in the English Proclamation of Henry III.[8] Some of them are dated palaeographically as late as 1360, and, in view of this, the differences between Types II and III are surprising.

Type III is represented chiefly by:

(i) A number of the documents printed in Chambers and Daunt, *London English 1385–1425*, and in Furnivall, *Early English Wills*.
(ii) The language of Chaucer, as vouched for by a consensus of the best MSS., corroborated by the evidence of (i).
(iii) The text of *Piers Plowman* in Trinity College Cambridge MS. B.15.17.
(iv) The language of Hoccleve, as established by a consensus of the MSS.

The following are some of the more obvious differences between Types II and III:

| *Type II* | *Chaucer* | *Type II* | *Chaucer* |
|---|---|---|---|
| þat ilch(e), ich(e) | thilke, that ilk(e) | þerwhile(s) (þat) | whil |
| nouȝt, no | nat | -ande, -ende -inde | -yng |
| eld(e) | old(e) | noiþer, noþer | neither |
| werld, warld | world | schuld | sholde |
| þai, hij | they | oȝain(s), aȝen | ageyns, ayeyns |
| þei(ȝ) | though | wil | wol(e), wil(le) |

The only conclusion to be drawn is that the London dialect changed suddenly and radically in the fourteenth century. The theory that two distinct dialects coexisted in fourteenth-century London, even if it were acceptable,[9] is not really relevant here, since all material of Type II is from before 1370 and all that of Type III from after that date.

But although there is a great difference between Types II and III, there is no more to support Type III as an influential literary standard than Type II. In Type III, especially, there is a heterogeneity of orthography that contrasts strikingly with the comparatively uniform spelling system of Type I. The individual usages of the court poets, Chaucer and Gower (as reliably attested by a consensus of the best manuscripts of each poet) differ considerably; yet, if both were acceptable at court, no strict norm can yet have existed. We find a similar variety both in the documents in Chambers' and Daunt's *London English* and in Furnivall's *Early English Wills*. This does not mean that these texts cannot be grouped together: if we exclude those documents and wills that, on the evidence of their dialectal forms, must have been written by immigrants into London, Type III may still be taken as representative of London

English of 1400; but any form of written standard is conspicuous by its absence. (Perhaps the nearest to it is the type of spelling that is found in both the Ellesmere MS. and in MS. Trinity Coll. Cbg. B.15.17 of the B-text of *Piers Plowman*.)

Type IV (which I shall call "Chancery Standard") consists of that flood of government documents that starts in the years following 1430. Its differences from the language of Chaucer are well known,[10] and it is this type, not its predecessors in London English, that is the basis of modern written English. Evidently, between the periods of Types III and IV, the London dialect had undergone further rapid changes; both these changes and those that preceded them are presumably to be explained on the ground that the speech of a capital city is liable to faster changes than those of the country as a whole. But it was only at the stage represented by Type IV (a stage of London English changed beyond all recognition from that of a century previous) that it was finally adopted by the government offices for regular written use; from then on, it was backed by the full weight of the administrative machine, and was certain to oust eventually (though by no means immediately) the other incipient standards.

Naturally, not all manuscripts written in something approaching standard English in the early fifteenth century belong to Types I, III, or IV. Many, especially those written in monasteries in Home Counties (such as Sion or Sheen), have a Middlesex or Surrey basis with a sprinkling of features from the main types. But this does not invalidate the classification, which can cast light on the central problem: the origin of Chancery Standard. The theory of East Midland (and particularly East Anglian) influence has been popular hitherto, but it is not borne out by an examination of either the Cambridgeshire or the Norfolk and Suffolk dialects of the time. The dialect of the Central Midlands, on the other hand, was the only one that had achieved the status of a literary standard, and this alone suggests that we should look to that region as the source of new influences on London English.

The suggestion is borne out, in a general way, by maps showing a spread of some features from the Central Midlands over the South East Midland area until London was reached.[11] But other features, notably the so-called Northern forms, *give, gave, their, them*, appear first in London as isolated enclaves. The nearest point from which they could have spread was in the north Central Midlands; there is no evidence that such forms reached London by southward shifts of isoglosses, and, if we wish for an explanation of their appearance in London, we must turn to historical and general considerations. Professor Ekwall has shown, firstly, that in the late thirteenth and early fourteenth centuries, immigration into London was highest from Norfolk, with Essex and Hertfordshire next, and then the remaining Home Counties.[12] This agrees with the Essex and generally East Anglian character of our fourteenth-century texts of Type II.[13]

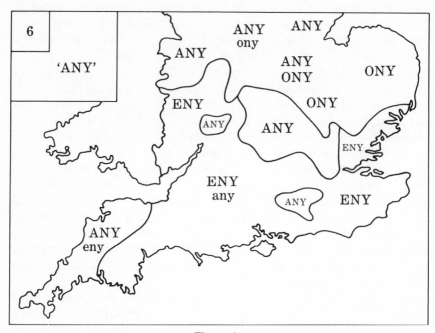

Figure 6

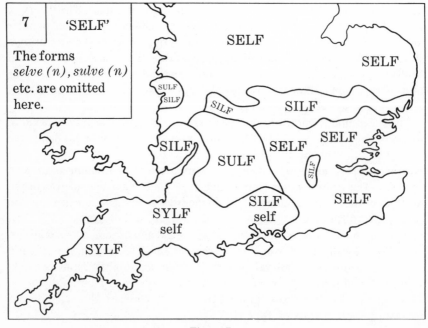

Figure 7

But Ekwall has also shown that in the fourteenth century a significant change took place: immigration from Northamptonshire and Bedfordshire increased, that from the Home Counties decreased, while that from Norfolk continued. And this is what we should expect from what little is known about medieval county populations: in Domesday Book, Norfolk and North Suffolk are the most thickly populated; but in the Poll Tax Returns for 1367, they are almost equalled by Leicestershire, Northamptonshire, and Bedfordshire.[14]

This immigration from the Central Midlands in the fourteenth century amply explains the great difference between our Types II and III; and there seems no reason to doubt that the same trend must then have continued, as it will explain the further changes from Type III to Type IV ("Chancery Standard"). There is, of course, no reason to deny a certain degree of direct Northern influence in these later changes, as several northerners held high office in this period; but there is, in written standard English, no Northern form that was not also current in at least part of the Central Midland area from 1400 onwards: only the combination of Central Midland and Northern influences could effect these changes, and, of the two, I suggest the Central Midland as the more important.

A question we have hitherto left unexplained is: why did East Anglian influence cease after the mid-fourteenth century, although immigration from there must have continued? The answer, I suggest, lies in the nature of the dialects of Norfolk and Suffolk: they were peripheral, and, as examination of any genuine fifteenth-century Norfolk text would show, unsuitable as a means of communication with either native Londoners or strangers and immigrants drawn from other parts of the country, especially the South-West. On the other hand, in the case of the Central Midlands, functional reasons would exist for the spread of linguistic features to London. In the Central Midlands, the geographical centre of the country, a standard language was developing, progressive and easily understood all over the country: nearer the periphery, in the capital and administrative centre, a need for a language of this kind existed. The fact that the two areas did not adjoin is no drawback, and we need not rely on immigration as the only explanation. Any area in the country which had a large population as well as good communications with the capital could influence its dialect, and the Central Midland counties are really the only area of which this could be said: the Gough map of fourteenth-century English roads shows that this area was served by the Great North Road and Watling Street, the most important thoroughfares in and out of London,[15] and we may therefore conclude that communications from the Central Midlands to London were better than from any other comparably distant area.

The resulting standard language naturally differed from Type I ("the Central Midland Standard"); it evolved later, from a combination of spoken London English and certain Central Midland elements, which themselves

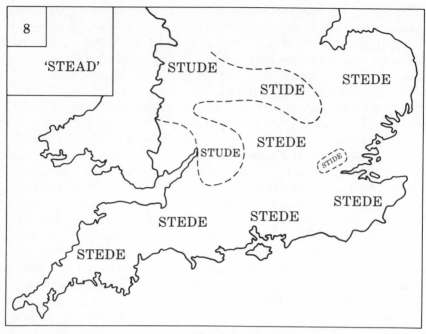

**Figure 8**

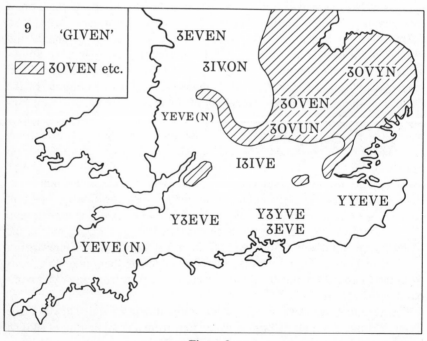

**Figure 9**

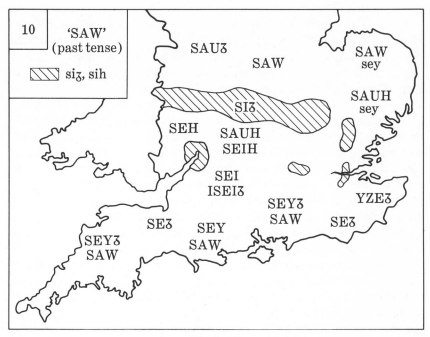

**Figure 10**

would be transmitted via the spoken, not the written language. But the result was a written, not a spoken, standard, which was to spread considerably in use by 1470. Regarding this spread, more could be learnt than hitherto from an intensive study of the *Early Chancery Proceedings* at the Public Record Office. These include a number of appeals addressed to the Chancellor that were evidently written in more remote counties, yet, apart from stray dialectal forms, they are written in some approximation to Chancery Standard. Nevertheless, its use was by no means universal: as Professor Norman Davis has shown,[16] it was more common for reasonably educated men to write some form of their own regional dialect, gradually purging it of its "grosser provincialisms," than to make a direct attempt to imitate Chancery Standard.

We have been discussing the evolution of a *written* standard, not a spoken one. The main events in the evolution of the spoken standard date from the period after 1500; and the study of them would be helped enormously if evidence existed (as it does not) to construct dialect maps for the sixteenth, seventeenth, and eighteenth centuries. But even as matters are, more use could be made of fifteenth-century evidence to cast light on the nature of the various changes than the most recent writer on the subject, Professor Dobson, is prepared to allow.[17] Naturally we have to guard against trusting overmuch in sporadic or occasional spellings, and isolated spellings may be errors. But not all ME spellings are of this kind; many have a cohesive geographical

distribution, and lend themselves to convincing phonic and phonemic interpretation. Our material for East Anglia, for example, shows an area in South
Norfolk in which ME $\bar{e}$ often appears as *y* (as in *tyth* "teeth") adjoining and
overlapping with an area in North Suffolk where ME *ī* often appears as *iy* or
*yi* (e.g., *wyis* "wise"); and this latter area adjoins and overlaps with a third,
smaller area in which the same sound occurs written *ey*. If we had met *iy*- or
*yi*- spellings alone, we might well hesitate to interpret them as the beginnings
of a diphthong, and we would probably prefer to regard them as spelling
devices for [iː]; similarly, in isolation, *y*-spellings for ME $\bar{e}$ could be attributed
to a host of phonetic explanations other than the obvious one—the raising
that we know to have been taking place in the fifteenth century. But, considering both sets in combination, it seems far more likely that the same
phonetic change is affecting the whole area, and manifesting itself orthographically in different ways in two adjoining areas; and if this was so, then
we have evidence that neither of the two changes (the raising of ME $\bar{e}$, and
the diphthongization of ME *ī*) can be given chronological priority: they both
belong to one and the same phonemic shift in East Anglia, and very probably
the same should be assumed for other areas.

I have left little space here for problems of a literary and textual kind. It
might be thought that the localization of extant copies of a work might not
tell us much about the author or his original text. Yet the usual methods
employed—a stemma of manuscripts, and perhaps localization by means of
rhymes, are often disappointing: the stemma yields a mixed dialect that can
never have been the author's, and the rhymes only a vague localization. As
an aid to these methods, a map showing the distribution of the extant copies
can often be revealing. For example, at least thirty-six of the *Piers Plowman*
texts can be localized on linguistic grounds and plotted on a map; and, even
if we bear in mind that scribes often travelled and that linguistic provenance
does not necessarily tally with actual provenance, some striking points
emerge:

(i) the C-texts circulated in Langland's own native area of the Malvern Hills;
(ii) the B-texts had a more cosmopolitan circulation, especially in the Worcester and
London areas;
(iii) the A-texts are peripheral,[18] and a most curious and surprising fact is that there
are no surviving A-texts from the more central areas in which the surviving B- and
C-texts were written.

How far these distributions are to be related either to Langland's travels, or
to the suitability of the A, B, and C versions to the area and milieu in which
they were written, are questions that I must leave to those better qualified to
judge. Similar maps can be constructed for many works that survive in a
number of copies, and often they afford less problematic conclusions.

The above paper has necessarily been restricted to a few selected examples.
There are many others, relevant not only to literary studies and textual
criticism, but also to palaeography, ethnology, and social and economic
history; but these must await exposition elsewhere.

# FOOTNOTES

1. It is substantially the same as a paper delivered to the Fifth Conference of the International Association of University Professors of English, Edinburgh, August, 1962.

2. As pointed out by Professor McIntosh on p. 4 [in this reprint pp. 394 f.— Ed.], any representation on maps of the full evidence must show the precise forms found in the manuscripts themselves. In the small diagrams that follow here, only certain selected, typical forms can be given; no claim is made to completeness, which would require far larger and more detailed maps.

3. Thus

> (i) in MS. Gonville and Caius Coll. Cambridge 386, *þi* is the usual form for both "they" and "though"; but on ff. 4b and 6a the sequence "though they" appears as *þi he*.
>
> (ii) In MS. C.C.C. Oxford 201, *þey* is the usual form for both words, but on fol. 10b "though they" appears as *þeyh3 þey*.

Similar phenomena may be observed in MSS. Bodl. Rawl. Poet. 138 and Rawl. C.35.

4. K. Brunner, *Die englische Sprache* I, p. 95.

5. The principal subjects found written in this language may be classified as follows:

> (i) A majority of the manuscripts of Wyclif's sermons and tracts, including anonymous Lollard tracts now no longer attributed to Wyclif himself.
>
> (ii) Practically all copies of the later version of the Lollard Bible, and most copies of the earlier version.
>
> (iii) Single manuscripts of many *non*-Wycliffite religious works, e.g., Laud Misc. 448 (Rolle's *Psalter*), Bodley 592 (Hilton's *Scale of Perfection*), Harley 2415 (*Pistyl of Love*).
>
> (iv) Anonymous devotional treatises, e.g., in MSS. Harley 171 and 2336, Royal 17.C.xxxiii, Bodl. Rawlinson C 69.
>
> (v) The *Lay Folk's Prayer Book*, in MSS. Cbg. Univ. Libr. Dd. XI.82 and Bodl. Ashmole 1286.
>
> (vi) Religious poems (MSS. Lambeth 853, BM. Add. 39574).
>
> (vii) Occasional manuscripts of secular works, e.g., Cbg. Univ. Libr. Ff. II.26 (Prose *Brut*), Bodl. Ashmole 1396 (Lanfranc's *Cirurgie*), BM. Royal 17.A.iii and Sloane 73 (anonymous medical treatises).

6. E.g., in MSS. B.M. Addit. 11748, Longleat 32.

7. The full list comprises:

> (i) Auchinleck MS., hands 1 and 3.
>
> (ii) The Early English Prose Psalter in BM. Add. 17376.
>
> (iii) MS. Harley 5085.
>
> (iv) Three manuscripts in the hand of a single scribe: Magd. Coll. Cambridge Pepys 2498, Bodl. Laud Misc. 622, and BM. Harley 874.
>
> (v) St. John's Coll. Cambridge MS. 256.

8. Especially noticeable in all MSS. of Type II is the comparatively rare form *þat ilche* (*iche*) "the same," corresponding to *þan ilche*, *þo ilche* in the English Proclamation of Henry III. Similarly *o3ain(s)*, a very rare form in Southern texts, may perhaps be connected with *on3enes* in the Proclamation.

9. Cf. E. J. Dobson, *TPS* 1955, pp. 34–5 [Reprinted here, pp. 419 ff.—Ed.].

10. A few of the more outstanding differences may be tabulated as follows:

| Chaucer | Type IV | Chaucer | Type IV |
|---------|---------|---------|---------|
| yaf | gaf | hir(e) | theyre, þeir(e) þair(e), her |
| nat | not | thise | thes(e) |
| bot | but | thurgh | thorough, þorow(e) |
| swich(e) | such(e) | sholde | shulde |

11. Cf. the maps for "they," "though," and "any." Other maps relevant here are those for "it," "are," "should," "from," "neither," "but" and "world"; but unfortunately considerations of space have precluded the reproduction of any further diagrams.

12. E. Ekwall, *Studies on the Population of Medieval London* (Stockholm, 1956) and *Two Early London Subsidy Rolls* (1951).

13. Forms found in Type II that suggest East Anglian influence are: *werld*, *warld* "world," *ich* "each," *þat ich(e)* "the same," *eld(e)* "old," *michel* "much," *wald* "would," *þurȝ*, *þourgh* "through."

14. H. C. Darby, *Historical Geography of England before 1800*, p. 232.

15. H. C. Darby, *op. cit.*

16. "A Paston Hand," *RES* N.S. iii (1952), pp. 209–21, and cf. *Proceedings of the British Academy* xl (1954), pp. 122–31.

17. E. J. Dobson, *English Pronunciation 1500–1700*.

18. A-texts can be assigned, on linguistic grounds, to S. Sussex, Essex, Norfolk, Durham, N. Warwickshire, N. Worcestershire, S. Shropshire.

## E. J. DOBSON

## Early Modern Standard English*

That there was a standard form of literary English in the sixteenth century is obvious and a commonplace; but the evidence that there was an explicitly recognized standard of spoken English is less well known, and the nature of this standard speech and its relation to other forms has often been obscured by the controversies of Modern English philologists. That any conception of a standard form of English, either written or spoken, was consciously held in the fourteenth century is very doubtful, despite several scraps of evidence that have been adduced[1]; the most that one can fairly say is that Chaucer's readiness to use dialect for humorous purposes in the *Reeve's Tale* shows not only a sharper awareness of dialectal differences than there is evidence of before, but also perhaps some implicit sense of the superiority of London English. But about the same date or a little later, in the Towneley *Second Shepherd's Play*, a Northern writer similarly makes fun of Southern forms, which may warn us that the mere readiness to laugh at the speech of another dialect does not imply a consciousness that one is using the destined standard language of the country. On the other hand, the Towneley instance does show that a royal official, a "yeoman of the King" as the sheep-stealer Mak is pretending to be, would be expected to use Southern English, i.e., that Southern English was, or was becoming, the recognized official language. But although a standard language undoubtedly evolved rapidly during the fifteenth century, I do not think that we come nearer to an explicit reference to the existence of such a standard until the century was over; Caxton's questionings on the best form of English to use, in the Preface to his *Eneydos*, are well known, and show that as late as 1490, when there can hardly have been the slightest doubt that the English of London would be chosen for any work of literary pretensions, its status was still imperfectly realized. It had been adopted as the norm on practical grounds, not because of any consciously held theory that it was "better" or "more correct"; only when the fact was accomplished did men begin to ask themselves, as Caxton does, whether there was one form of English which was preferable to others. But Caxton's own reference to the language of his native Weald of Kent as "rough and rude" implies a standard against which it was found wanting.

In the sixteenth century the situation changes, and the standard is explicitly recognized. In 1532 Palsgrave, in *Lesclarcissement de la Langue Francoise*, refers quite incidentally to a pronunciation of *a* "where the best englysshe is spoken." Wyld cites, from about the same date, a passage in

* From *Transactions of the Philological Society* (1955), 25–54. Reprinted by permission of the author and The Philological Society.

Elyot's *Governour* (1531) in which Elyot advises that the nurses and other women who attend a nobleman's son in infancy shall, if they cannot accustom him to speak pure and elegant Latin, "at the lest way . . . speke none englisshe but that which is cleane, polite, perfectly and articulately pronounced, omittinge no lettre or sillable, as folisshe women oftentimes do of a wantonnesse, whereby diuers noble men and gentilmennes chyldren (as I do at this daye knowe) have attained corrupte and foule pronuntiation"; and a letter by Henry Dowes, tutor of Thomas Cromwell's son, in which he says that the boy is being taught "the natural and true kynde of pronunciation."[2] From these passages it is clear that by Henry VIII's reign there was already a clear idea that there was a correct way of pronouncing English, that some form of speech had already become a criterion of good birth and education, and that it was deliberately fostered and taught. Sir Thomas Smith, in his books on the pronunciation of Greek and the spelling of English, published in 1568 but written in (or in the latter case first drafted about) 1542, alludes from time to time to dialectal pronunciations used in Derby or beyond the Trent or by Northerners or Scotsmen, but ordinarily appears to expect his readers to assume that south of the Trent there is only one type of pronunciation in use, that which he himself describes; and in a single instance when he refers to a special pronounciation in use in his native Essex, he specifically says that it is only "rustici" who use it.

So far the standard, though recognized, has been undefined; but in later sources this lack is made good. Hart, the greatest phonetician of the sixteenth century and one of the most remarkable English phoneticians of any time, is careful to define his standard both in his MS. work on orthography written in 1551 (MS. Regius 17 C vii) and in his published *Orthographie* (1569) and *Methode* (1570). It was the speech of the "learned and literate," which is the "best and moste perfite English" and "which every reasonable English man will the best he can, frame his tongue thereunto"; this he will "the nearest [he] can follow" (*Orthographie* f. 21r.). From the same passage it appears that he regarded the speech of London as conforming to this standard; and in the *Methode* he says that in the Court and London "the flower of the English tongue is vsed" (f. A [iii] v.) and elsewhere that in the Court and London "the generall flower of all Englishe countrie speaches, are chosen and used" (f. B i r–v). But he recognizes that men living far to the North and the West may speak differently, and he sees no reason why they should be ashamed to do so or be ridiculed; and he is prepared to admit their right to spell English phonetically as they themselves pronounce it. Very similar in effect is the oft-quoted passage in *The Arte of English Poesy* (1589), attributed to Puttenham, in which the author recommends as the best English "the vsual speech of the Court, and that of London and the shires lying about London within lx. miles and not much above." Puttenham, like Hart, makes a specific exception of the speech of Northerners, and indeed of all who live "beyond the riuer of Trent," and of "the far Westerne man"; of the former he says that "whether they be noble men or gentlemen or of their

best clarkes," their speech "is not so Courtly nor so current as our Southerne
English is." But Puttenham also issues a more general warning against the
prevalence of dialectalism, for in explanation of his limitation of the range of
the recommended language to sixty miles or so from London he continues,
"I say not this but that in euery shyre of England there be gentlemen and
others that speake, but especially write, as good Southerne as we of Middlesex
or Surrey do, but not the common people of euery shire, to whom the gentlemen, and also their learned clarkes, do for the most part condescend." [3] That
these were questions much in debate at the time is indicated by brief references in Edmund Coote's *English Schoolmaster* (1597), where he is willing to
allow Northerners the right to use Northern expressions in their private
correspondence, but thinks it better that they should not do so "publicly";
and for the rest speaks merely of "the barbarous speech of your country
people."

In the seventeenth century the references become even more precise. Gill,
in his *Logonomia Anglica* (1619 and 1621), in defining the type of speech on
which a reformed spelling should be based, says that "in sermone consuetudo doctorum primaria lex est. Scriptura igitur omnis accommodanda
erit, non ad illum sonum quem bubulci, quem mulierculæ, & portiores; sed
quem docti, aut culte eruditi viri exprimunt inter loquendum, & legendum." [4]
And subsequently, at the end of the fullest and most interesting account of the
English dialects in the seventeenth century that we have, he nevertheless
observes: "Quod hic de dialectis loquor, ad rusticos tantum pertinere velim
intelligas: nam mitioribus ingenijs & cultius enutritis, unus est ubique sermo
& sono, & significatu." [5] Gill's chief criterion, it will be seen, is education.
Charles Butler, in his *English Grammar* (1633), defines as his standard the
speech "of the Universities and Citties." Wallis, in the *Grammatica Linguæ
Anglicanæ* (1653), says that in describing English pronunciation he has not
bothered with the dialects of various places nor the affectations of effeminate
people or other barbarisms, nor with careless pronunciations, whether those
of the vulgar or of courtiers or affected delicate people; these he thinks are
not to be followed. His imitator Owen Price, in a passage of his *Vocal Organ*
(1665) that for once is original, says "I have not been guided by our vulgar
pronunciation, but by that of London and our Universities, where the language is purely spoken." Elisha Coles, in his *Schoolemaster* (1674), says that
he takes as his standard the language "most in use among the generality of
scholars," "the present proper pronunciation . . . in Oxford and London."
Cooper, in his *Grammatica Linguæ Anglicanæ* (1685), says that words vary in
pronunciation, for some men pronounce them according to the spelling,
others according to euphony, while others follow the dialect of their native
place; he is not therefore to be blamed if he teaches pronunciations different
from theirs. But he will say this: that he was brought up in the South, and has
spent the greater part of his working life there as headmaster of a grammar
school, and that there the purest and correct manner of speaking is the norm
("purissima & emendata loquendi consuetudo norma est"). At the end of the

century an anonymous London schoolmaster, in a spelling book of which only the second edition, published in 1704 under the title *Right Spelling*, survives, seems to regard London speech as too "fine" and "smooth" and to prefer that of the Universities; this is largely a prejudice in a man who was a bad phonetician and himself used a vulgar type of pronunciation, but it may rest on a valid sense of the superiority of educated speech over that of the ordinary Londoner such as himself.

This evidence shows that from early in the sixteenth century there was in being an idea that there was a correct way of speaking English, which might be taught; and the definitions of this form of speech, from Hart's onwards, are remarkably consistent. But the authors, in defining it, found significantly that there were various ideas to be expressed. It was in general the speech of the South of England and was not current in the North or West; it was in particular the speech of London and was in use among well-bred and well-educated people in the Home Counties. But merely to define a geographical region was not enough; hence the more precise observation that it was the language of the Court, i.e., of the highest social classes and of the administration. Again it was the language of clerks, of learned men, of scholars, and as such it was the language of the Universities, with Oxford receiving special mention—but, it must be granted, from an Oxford man. Various observers, however, find it necessary to mention and condemn not only country dialects, but also the speech of the vulgar, of effeminate and affected people, and of courtiers (by which obviously something different is meant than by the expression "the Court"); evidently there existed beside the standard language other forms which could not be described as rustic dialect, but which were not regarded as correct.

In general terms the picture presented is remarkably similar to the situation at the present time. But as soon as we begin to bring into consideration the detailed evidence of the period it becomes apparent that there are also important differences. The first and most obvious is that in the sixteenth and seventeenth centuries the standard speech was much more limited in extent; not only was its penetration of the North only incipient, and confined rather to spelling and vocabulary than to pronunciation, but also, south of the Trent, it was used by a far narrower range of people than in later times. What exactly was the position is a difficult question, and one to which scholars seem seldom to have clearly addressed their minds—on which indeed they have held views which are not only confused, but also inconsistent. Thus Wyld often cites from the documents of important country families forms which are held to demonstrate Standard English sound-changes, apparently because he assumes that as such families in later times would undoubtedly speak Standard English, so also they must have done in the seventeenth century or earlier; but in many cases the same documents contain forms that were never anything but dialectal. Yet Wyld himself assumes from Puttenham's words about the speech of Northerners that "the upper classes, and educated people generally, in the provinces, [did] not speak standard English, but their own Regional dialect," and proceeds immediately to refer to the fact that Sir Walter Raleigh is recorded to have spoken with a strong Devonshire accent[6]; and similarly Professor Kökeritz, who in general follows Wyld's views, assumes from the mere fact that Gill was born in Lincolnshire that his evidence in the *Logonomia* refers, not to Standard English, but "most likely to a modified form of his native Lincolnshire dialect,"[7] a view for which there is no internal evidence whatsoever. But this interpretation of Puttenham as meaning that provincials generally, however well-born and well-educated, used regional dialect is contrary to the rest of the evidence that I have cited, including Gill's own (which is especially clear and unqualified), that in the late sixteenth and seventeenth centuries only peasants spoke dialect; and this evidence is consistent with such a literary instance as *King Lear* IV. vi, where Edgar, wishing to conceal his identity, adopts dialectal speech—a device which would be pointless, both dramatically and in life, if the upper classes generally had used dialect. Oswald in fact immediately assumes Edgar, from his mere speech, to be a "bold peasant." As for the instance of Raleigh, it is to be observed first that he falls directly within one of the classes that both Hart and Puttenham mention as being beyond the influence of the standard language—he was a "far Western man"—and secondly that if it had been normal for a man of Raleigh's rank and distinction to use his native dialect, his use of Devonshire speech would have passed without remark; the mere fact that it is recorded shows that it seemed exceptional. But in any case Puttenham's remarks about Northerners (and by implication Westerners) are put in stronger terms than those he uses to describe the general situation; it is "the common people of euery shire" who do not use "as good Southerne as we of Middlesex and Surrey do," whereas "the gentlemen, and also their learned clarkes, do for the most part condescend" to the common people. Though Puttenham's remarks have evidently been phrased in a more carefully qualified manner than those of the other observers, they are not to be treated without regard to the latter, and in particular we must consider Gill's assertion that among "gentler and more carefully educated wits" the speech was everywhere the same both in sound and in meaning—a statement undoubtedly too far-reaching, but not made in forgetfulness of the existence of dialect. What I take Puttenham to mean— and this indeed seems an admirable statement of the position—is that the common people everywhere spoke dialect and the standard language was the possession only of the well-born and the well-educated; that in the Court and the Home Counties one might expect all well-born and well-educated people to use this standard language, but beyond those limits, though one might still find men who spoke pure standard English, the greater part of the gentry and scholars were influenced by the speech of the common people (i.e., they spoke "modified Standard"), and finally that in the far West and the North the standard did not apply at all.

If this is so, then we have no rough-and-ready means of determining which sources may be assumed to represent Standard English and which to be dialectal. The mere fact that a document originates in or near London is no guarantee that it represents standard speech, for its author may not be of the required degree of education or of the required social status; indeed two of the grammarians whose definitions I have cited, Butler and Cooper, though each was born only half the prescribed sixty miles from London and was a man of educational distinction, used pronunciations which are demonstrably influenced by dialect [8]—presumably because their social origins were undistinguished. On the other hand, a document which originates more than sixty miles from London may not be tainted by dialect. Each case must be treated on its merits, and we must be guided by internal evidence revealed by detailed and critical examination, not by *a priori* assumptions. Thus Newton, brought up in the country, still retained obvious dialectalisms when he wrote his notes on phonetics as a young man [9]; but Gill, equally born in Lincolnshire, shows none of these features—whether because he had never had them, or because education in Oxford and experience as a London schoolmaster had caused him to abandon them, it is impossible to say. Whether a man used dialectal pronunciations must have depended on factors of social rank, of family tradition, of education, and of personal experience and adaptability which we can rarely find recorded except in the barest outline. But it seems clear that the most important factor was education; the standard language was the creation, and for long remained largely the special property, of the educated professional and administrative class of London, and only gradually spread to the country gentry and to other social classes as these in their turn became better educated; and those observers who made less of the prevalence of dialect than Puttenham did probably had in mind a higher standard of education than was normally to be found among the country gentry and clergy of the time. [10]

The second feature in which the standard language of the sixteenth and seventeenth centuries differed from ours was in the much greater variety of pronunciation which it permitted. The difference is one rather of degree than of kind, for we sometimes underestimate the number of variants which exist within standard English to-day; a phonologist of two or three hundred years hence, working through Professor Daniel Jones's *English Pronouncing Dictionary* as we work through the phonetic transcriptions of the sixteenth and seventeenth centuries, might well be impressed as much with the variety as with the uniformity. But there was undoubtedly much more variety then than now. That the standard language should lack uniformity is only to be expected, in view of its origins and history; rejecting Miss Mackenzie's theory of a Middlesex–Westminster and an Essex–London dichotomy as inherently improbable and opposed to the weight of the evidence, I take the educated language of late fourteenth-century London to have been a mixed dialect, an amalgam of elements drawn from all parts of the country in which East

Midland features predominated for the reason given by Higden—that the Midland dialects were best suited as a general means of communication—and because of the geographical position of the capital. In accord with this origin, we find in sixteenth- and seventeenth-century sources much evidence of variants developed in ME or even in OE dialects, as also, in words of OF origin, of variants showing the influence on ME of differing OF dialects or sucessive stages of OF development. But there is also much evidence of variation resulting from later fourteenth- or fifteenth-century sound-changes,[11] so that it is clear that the process of admixture continued during the fifteenth and early sixteenth centuries—and of course later. Nothing is more false than to regard modern Standard English as a uniform dialect developing solely in accordance with its own sound-laws; and the misconception that it is to be so regarded has led older scholars to many errors of interpretation—the impatient rejection or neglect of perfectly genuine evidence, or the attempt to force a single interpretation on patently discrepant evidence, or (particularly in the case of Luick) to the elaboration of ingenious but improbable sound-laws to account for the development of variant ModE pronunciations from a supposed single ME source.

It was no doubt one consequence of this variety that men who had a clear conception of a standard form of speech and of how it was to be defined, and who in general conformed to this standard, could nevertheless use, in individual words or groups of words or even for individual ME sounds, pronunciations which we can detect as dialectal in origin; the less uniformity there is, the less sharply defined the limits are. And it must have been by an extension of this process that the standard language, in important cases, ended by accepting, at first as permissible variants and finally as the norm, pronunciations that had once been alien to it. It is significant that there is hardly one major grammarian of these two centuries who does not on occasion give evidence of developments different from those which he has in general accepted as his standard, and thus show not merely that he was conscious of but also that he was influenced (usually in special cases) by modes of speech which obviously he regarded as less correct.[12] But though they were capable of these inconsistencies, it seems nevertheless that educated men were in much agreement about the limits within which variety was permissible; their conception of correct pronunciation was modified with the passage of time, but providing that we allow for the changes we can trace its characteristic elements. In the course of a paper such as this one can offer only a brief, incomplete, and dogmatic sketch; but the following seem to me to be, in outline, the salient features of educated pronunciation in the sixteenth and seventeenth centuries. Of the short vowels, ME *ŭ* was retained as a rounded vowel until about 1640, as were undifferentiated pronunciations of ME *ĭ*, *ĕ*, and *ŭ* before a following *r*; in the sixteenth century ME *ă* and *ŏ* normally kept their ME values, and it was only gradually during the seventeenth century that the fronted [æ] and the lowered and partially unrounded [ɒ] came into general use, accompanied by lengthened pronunciations of ME *ă* and *ŏ* before *r* and in other cases. The ME long vowels developed slowly, and in particular ME *ę̄*, *ā*, and *ǭ* were respectively [ɛː], [æː], and open [ɔː] as a rule until 1600 and often until 1650; the newer values [eː], [ɛː], and close [oː], though occasionally found before 1600, did not become at all regular until towards or after 1650. In particular—and this is the chief criterion of the educated language at this period—ME *ę̄* was maintained as a distinct sound, identified neither with ME *ẹ̄* (which had become [iː]) nor with ME *ā*, until the very end of the seventeenth century. The ME diphthongs *ai*, *au*, and *ou* were normally still diphthongs in the sixteenth century, and though monophthongal pronunciations came into common use in the educated language during the first quarter of the seventeenth century, the old diphthongs were often still maintained; relics of them survived into the last quarter of the century. ME *ęu* was kept distinct from ME *iu*, and ME *ui* from ME *ī*, until about 1650. In unstressed syllables even the educated language used in its more everyday forms the reduced vowels and syllabic consonants typical of our own speech, but in its more formal and careful modes it preserved an extensive system of secondary stress which descended from the less popular forms of ME and which to some extent survives in modern American speech, and which had the effect of preserving clear or long vowels or the ME diphthongs in the syllables on which it fell. Educated speech resisted the loss of consonants and the simplification of consonant groups; in the sixteenth century it still preserved [ŋg] for the group *ng* in all positions, even final, and only accepted the loss of the stop in certain circumstances about and just after 1600[13]; and it was only during the course of the seventeenth century that it gradually accepted the reduction of the initial groups *wr-*, *kn-*, and *gn-*. In the sixteenth and early seventeenth centuries it retained, in its formal varieties at least, a spirantal sound in such words as *night* and *drought*; only in the second quarter of the latter century did it finally acquiesce in the present pronunciations, developed in other dialects some two centuries earlier and freely used in London English in the later sixteenth century.

This is of course an extremely conservative language; in all the features I have mentioned it retained older pronunciations after—in most cases long after—there is valid evidence that newer pronunciations had developed in other forms of speech. So conservative indeed is it that it has excited the incredulity and irritation of many scholars who, searching for evidence of new pronunciations, have been unable to believe that the old could so long continue except in dialectal holes and corners, and who have rejected the authorities on which this view is based—the English grammarians and phoneticians of the time—as unworthy of belief; their evidence is, however, far too consistent to be artificial and unreal. The strength of the conservative tendencies of the educated language seems to have varied from time to time: in the later sixteenth century it was relatively stable, but in the seventeenth century, particularly for a generation or so on either side of the middle of the century, the rate at which newer pronunciations were accepted accelerated, until another period of relative stability was reached in the eighteenth century. But throughout, in comparison with other dialects, it resisted change and was tenacious of older forms, and this surely is what we ought to expect; for an educated language is also a taught language, and the teaching of pronunciations as correct preserves them. Moreover most of the changes which were then taking place were convergent developments tending to identify hitherto distinct sounds and to increase greatly the number of homophones in the language; and to such changes an educated language, fortified by a traditional orthography, must inevitably be hostile. If we keep in mind the status and objects of the standard language, we shall not find its conservatism either unreal or unnatural. But it does nevertheless produce results disconcerting to phonologists accustomed to deal with freely-developing dialects, and especially to English phonologists accustomed to Middle English. In particular it leads to the overlapping of stages of development, even within the educated language itself; for as the latter did not exist in isolation, its users were individually apt to be influenced by more advanced forms of speech, so that more and less conservative pronunciations are found co-existing. Thus, to give a single instance, it can be proved that Smith, about or shortly after the middle of the sixteenth century, knew and apparently himself sometimes used the more advanced pronunciation of ME $\bar{e}$ as close [eː][14]; but equally it is possible to prove that Wallis, a century later, was still using the more conservative pronunciation with open [ɛː]. It may even happen that what is essentially an earlier stage of development may be preserved indefinitely in the standard language beside newer forms, especially to achieve differentiation of homophones: thus the pronunciation [muən] "mourn" is a modification of the typical sixteenth-century pronunciation [muːrn], unaffected by the lowering of the vowel which is commonly recorded in seventeenth-century educated sources and of which the final result in Southern English is [mɒːn]. In the upshot a historical phonology of Modern English must be much more complex than is commonly realized; it has to trace various levels of speech, and make allowance for periods—sometimes long periods—of overlapping development.

Considered in the context of the almost limitless variety of sixteenth-century pronunciation, the relative uniformity and stability of the educated language was clearly not a matter of chance. Men who had once formed the concept that there was a correct manner of speech, and who were resolved to teach and to learn it, must constantly have been asking themselves which of the many alternative pronunciations that they heard around them were to be preferred; the elimination and avoidance of others must inevitably, and quite properly, have been a conscious and indeed often arbitrary process. But whereas nowadays we have to exercise choice mostly between variant pronunciations of individual words, they were concerned rather with larger questions of the variant developments of the ME sounds or sound-groups;

though there is some evidence of concern with individual words, they had to be content to allow much variation in details, and especially perhaps in the quantity of vowels. The orthography to some degree influenced their choice, but not as much as is sometimes supposed; the main period of orthographical influence on pronunciation is in the eighteenth century and after, though Wallis in the mid-seventeenth century was already strongly influenced by orthographical considerations. But in the sixteenth century the spelling itself still varied greatly, and indeed the choice between variant spellings often depended on and reflected the choice between variant pronunciations; though discrepancies between spelling and pronunciation existed or soon developed, and became progressively wider, it is at least as true to say that sixteenth-century orthography reflected what was then considered the ideal pronunciation as that the ideal of pronunciation was influenced by the spelling. It is ironical that the men who are most often charged with recording archaic pronunciations merely in accord with the conventional spelling are precisely those who were loudest in their complaints that the established orthography did not adequately represent contemporary pronunciation and in their demands for its radical reform.

To what extent the schoolmasters determined or merely recorded contemporary fashions of pronunciation it is hard to say; but undoubtedly they exercised an important influence. There is even evidence that they were expected to do so, for after the first visitation of the newly-founded Merchant Taylors' School it was reported that the ushers had one fault, "that being northern men born, they had not taught the children to speak distinctly, or to pronounce their words as well as they aught."[15] In certain cases we can see the schoolmasters and teachers of language debating the choice between variants: thus Coote in 1597, and Sherwood in 1632, though admitting that *gh* in such words as *night* is often silent, come down in favour of its pronunciation as a spirant as more correct (and consequently, in Coote's case, of its being preserved in writing). But the chief instance of the jealous care of a schoolmaster for the pronunciations which he regarded as correct is Gill, in his attacks on the speech of what he called the "Mopsae" and particularly his criticism of his predecessor Hart as one who was not content, in his reformed spelling, to follow our language but instead sought to lead it, recording not "our" pronunciations but "Mopsarum fictitias." It is easy to say that Gill was intolerant and dogmatic, that he was kicking against the pricks, and that his indignation not only blinded him to Hart's merits and the extent to which his speech really conformed to Gill's own, but also made him unfair in his selection of phonetic spellings from Hart to prove his point. But analysis of his examples makes it clear that Hart's chief offence was to record monophthongal pronunciations of ME *ou* and particularly of ME *ai*.[16] Wise after the event, we know that these pronunciations, which in Gill's own time were entering the standard language, were shortly to become dominant in it, and there is a strong temptation therefore to say that Gill was an imperceptive conservative, a blind opposer of change, and failing in the true duty of a phonetician merely to record facts as they were. But Gill's duty was that of a schoolmaster, and from the point of view of his own generation he was right; to retain the diphthongs had hitherto been one of the criteria of the educated language, and Hart in using the monophthongs had undoubtedly diverged from its standards. Moreover, it is both natural and right that resistance to neologisms should be strongest and most vocal when they have already become widely current, i.e., when they are on the verge of acceptance, even if in retrospect it appears an unavailing pedantic opposition to the prevailing tendency of the language. But not all the schoolmasters' strictures were directed against pronunciations that were ultimately to be accepted. A more instructive, though less obvious, example of the processes of selection which have characterized the formation of the standard pronunciation is the history in the sixteenth and seventeenth centuries of prosthetic [j] before ME $\bar{e}$ and $\bar{ę}$ and prosthetic [w] before ME $\bar{ǫ}$ and $\bar{ǫ}$. Both developments are widespread in the modern dialects and spellings show that the [w] in particular was very common even in educated speech in the earlier sixteenth century; indeed it had royal sanction.[17] But in the last quarter of the century opinion evidently turned against them (spellings with prosthetic *y* and *w* become rare, and Coote describes them as barbarous), and though such pronunciations remained common on the fringes of educated speech and occasionally occurred within it—especially in individual words, e.g., *whole*[18]—they eventually virtually disappeared from it except in the isolated *one* and *once* (and even in this case the pronunciation with [w] was rather a late seventeenth-century readoption into the educated language to make possible a distinction between *one* and *own*).[19]

It is important to observe that in many of its characteristic features the formal educated speech described above contrasted sharply with other historically important dialects; for the failure to take account of this fact has often led to evidence that relates to these other forms of speech being cited as if it were also valid for Standard English. I am not thinking of sound-changes that were and remained dialectal, and never found place in Standard English except in the pronunciation of isolated words; the more important and misleading fact is that sound-changes which did ultimately form part of Standard English often occurred much earlier in the dialects. For the pronunciation of the Northern dialects in the sixteenth and seventeenth centuries there is a sufficient body of evidence[20] which shows that in them ME *ai* and *ou* had early been monophthongized, that the development of the ME long vowels was very advanced (ME $\bar{i}$ and $\bar{u}$ having already become [ai] and [au], against the Standard English [əi] and [ʌu], and thus equivalent to Southern pronunciations of ME *ai* and *au*, and ME $\bar{a}$ having become successively [ɛ:] and [e:]), that in consequence ME $\bar{ę}$ had lost its identity, having been replaced by the reflex of ME $\bar{e}$ or in certain words become identical with ME $\bar{a}$, and that ME *ęu* had similarly become identical with ME *iu*. For the Eastern dialects, especially those of Norfolk, Suffolk, and Essex, the evidence is sometimes less clear, for it consists chiefly of spellings[21] which, even when authenticated by the MSS., are often difficult to interpret, but it tends to show that the normal association of the East Midland dialects with those of the North holds good; in addition to the features described for the Northern dialects, there is evidence that by the sixteenth century at latest ME *ĕr*, *ĭr*, and *ŭr* were being identified, ME *ui* was becoming the same as ME *ī*, and presumably therefore ME *ŭ* had been unrounded. But the most important of these advanced dialects was one that existed in London itself; for though in one sense the standard language was that of London, in another it was only an alien artificial dialect developed in London. The native dialect of London was in origins essentially that of Essex, and though it cannot have remained a pure local speech (for immigration into London affected all classes of society) it continued to be closely related to the dialects to the East; to the resemblance in the early seventeenth century we have the explicit testimony of Gill. Evidence from various sources, including spellings and Gill's transcriptions, show that in the more advanced forms of London speech, by the later sixteenth century, ME *ai* and *ā* were identified as close [eː], ME *ou* and *au* were monophthongs, ME *ę̄* had lost its separate existence and was either replaced by [iː] or identified with ME *ā*, ME *ęu* was identified with ME *iu*, ME *ŭ* was unrounded, ME *ĕr*, *ĭr*, and *ŭr* were identified, and ME *ui* and ME *ī* had fallen together; unstressed syllables were much reduced and syncope was common; *gh* was silent or pronounced [f] (a development found early in East Anglian dialects), consonant-groups, notably initial, were freely reduced, and [ɪn] or syllabic [ŋ] could be used for final unstressed -*ing*. It is evidence that relates to this more popular London speech which in particular is often mistakenly cited as if it applied to the educated language, and in one sense justly so: for the influence of the less cultivated London speech on the standard language was profound. But nevertheless the two were always distinct, and we shall falsify and over-simplify if we do not recognize this. In Elizabethan London there were doubtless many levels of speech, or "class dialects," ranging from the purest Cockney to forms which varied only slightly from the strictest canons of formal educated language, and the future lay with the more advanced types; but their pronunciations were not yet acknowledged as correct. Some of them indeed never were accepted,[22] and others after achieving a degree of currency within the educated language were ultimately rejected again.[23] Much of the history of Modern English pronunciation is to be written in terms of the inter-play of the educated and the popular varieties of London English, but it is complex and hard to trace. Standard English as it developed was under siege from provincial and class dialects until the eighteenth century—and indeed until the nineteenth, in regard at least to the pronunciation of ME *ă* and *ŏ* before voiceless spirants; and the contrary influence of the standard language on the dialects, including Cockney, which from 1400 onwards has grown steadily stronger until it has ended by all but destroying them, is only part of the story.

For the detailed pronunciations of the standard language the best sources of evidence are the native-born English grammarians, spelling reformers, and phoneticians, whose work is pre-eminent both in range and capacity. We know much of their lives and circumstances, and above all that they were educated men—some indeed were among the leading scholars of the time. The evidence of foreign grammarians is less both in quality and quantity; often we know little of their circumstances, and rarely where or from whom they learnt their English. When they differ from native sources, it is usually in giving evidence of new pronunciations; this indeed is the chief reason why they have attracted attention. But it is unreasonable, if one's object is to discover what was the accepted educated pronunciation, to prefer the evidence of foreign to native observers; a foreigner is obviously in danger of supposing that a common pronunciation is more acceptable than it really is, and even of not realizing, because of insufficient knowledge, that the pronunciation he has learnt is not the only one. Spellings, though an important source of evidence for some purposes, are of little use in determining the educated standards of speech, for they are most significant of changes in pronunciation when they depart from the accepted orthography; but aberrant spellings necessarily come from persons who have not mastered the orthography and are therefore imperfectly educated, and who in consequence cannot be accepted, whatever their social status, as reliable witnesses to educated speech. In any case, as I have already observed, they can often be shown to have a dialectal background. Puns are of little evidential value, primarily because of the difficulty of telling whether a pun was really intended; we must rely rather on our knowledge of contemporary pronunciation to reveal to us what are possible puns, than on alleged puns to reveal to us what contemporary pronunciation was. Only in limited cases can we use puns to confirm the somewhat earlier occurrence of developments which we know from other evidence to have been in train. But even so we cannot rely on them for evidence of what were the accepted educated pronunciations, for there is no reason to suppose that an Elizabethan in punning would not take full advantage of all the variant modes of speech then current; he would not be more precise in punning than he was in rhyming, and indeed it is provable, as surely is to be expected, that the standards of punning were in fact less exact than those of rhyming.

It is rhymes which are the most interesting and difficult form of ancillary evidence. In general they show new developments earlier than the native grammarians do—as a rule some thirty or forty years earlier, but sometimes more, and in the case of the identification of ME $\bar{e}$ with ME $\bar{a}$ a full century earlier. And here is the dilemma, for either we must say, if the rhymes are reliable evidence of good contemporary speech, that the grammarians are conspiring together to describe an outmoded and archaic pronunciation, or, if the grammarians are reliable, that educated and even courtly poets used rhymes based on less correct speech. Two considerations are relevant here.

The first is that scholars who, naturally enough, have sought in rhymes chiefly for evidence of the developments known to have occurred in Standard English, have, by an unconsciously narrow selection, presented a false view of Elizabethan and seventeenth-century rhyming: there are very many rhymes which depend on pronunciations and developments which never formed part of the standard language—rhymes which rest sometimes on regional, more often perhaps on class, dialect. The chief value of the rhymes is really that they illustrate the extreme variety of pronunciation in those times, the background against which the standard language evolved; in this they resemble the lists of homophones given by seventeenth-century spelling books. But it follows that poets in their rhyming were not concerned to restrict themselves to the limitations normally imposed by the educated language. Secondly, the developments of the time, as I have already pointed out, were mostly convergent, and therefore destructive of distinctions which an educated language must seek to preserve; but for the same reason they tended greatly to increase the number of possible rhymes, so that the new pronunciations were more convenient to poets than the old.[24] There would then be a strong temptation for a poet to accept the new pronunciations for exactly the same reason that the educated language had for resisting them. It is significant that divergent developments[25] would be dated, if we relied on the evidence of rhymes, much later than they are shown by the grammarians. Moreover it is my impression that rhymes showing the convergent developments do not become really common until we approach the dates at which the grammarians also accept the new pronunciations; evidently there are factors working against rhyming expediency and restraining poets from a free exploitation of the new possibilities. One is no doubt rhyming tradition, or rather mere habits of mind—the association of one word with certain others as possible rhymes because they have been observed rhyming in earlier verse; but speech-standards must also be involved. A significant example is that some poets of about 1600 (e.g., Shakespeare) who otherwise avoid rhyming ME *ęu* with ME *iu* (though ME *ęu* words are comparatively few and limited in their rhyming possibilities) nevertheless consent to rhyme *beauty* with *duty*, for the simple and practical reason that if this rhyme was not accepted no other was possible[26]; and in general it is true that feminine and leonine rhymes, in which the technical difficulty is greater, depart more noticeably from the norms of Standard English than do monosyllabic rhymes.

But it is inaccurate to speak as if all poets rhymed in similar ways. Though as a whole they anticipate the grammarians in showing new pronunciations, some are much more apt to do so than others. Drayton, for example, is much more often cited as exemplifying new developments than is Shakespeare, though Viëtor's lists, incomplete as they are, have for half a century made Shakespeare's rhymes the most easily accessible body of such evidence. These differences between poets must often reflect their varying personal histories, but also they depend on the balance struck between the conflicting interests of rhyming convenience and conformity to prevailing standards of speech. The most striking instance is Spenser, who not only anticipates the grammarians but also his fellow-poets, at least to the extent of using freely types of rhymes which even in his younger contemporaries are noticeably rarer. A philologist judging his rhymes merely as an abstract linguistic problem can hardly avoid the conclusion that they reveal an advanced mode of pronunciation, dialectal or even vulgar; and for such a view the circumstances of Spenser's life afford much justification. He was a Londoner by birth, but his father, though described as a "gentleman," was by trade a journeyman clothmaker; moreover his parents are believed to have been migrants from Lancashire. He attended the Merchant Taylors' School, where Northern-born ushers, as we have seen, did not teach the children to pronounce as well as they ought, and went on to Cambridge, still Northern and Eastern in its affiliations; and after taking his degree he spent some time in Lancashire with his kinsmen. Thus his family connections, his merchant-class origins, and his education all make it at least plausible that he may have been influenced both by Northern dialects and by the more popular varieties of London speech; and it is precisely the advanced features of pronunciation which these two had in common that are reflected in Spenser's rhymes.[27] Yet he was a court poet, patronized by great nobles, and ambitious to excel in his art—hardly a man, one would think, to retain pronunciations which would not pass current in polished society. But even if one allows, as is probably true, that the Court's standards of pronunciation may have been less rigid than the schoolmasters', the problem remains, for there is still the contrast—less sharp, it is true—between Spenser's rhymes and those of other poets.

I doubt if it is of much significance that from 1580, when he was 28, Spenser lived almost continuously in Ireland and was therefore to some degree removed from the influence of educated London speech; nor should I stress the difficulty of the rhyme-scheme of the Spenserian stanza, though it would not encourage a self-denying purism, for his rhyming in simpler measures is no different. It is more relevant to remember that there are men who, even though highly sensitive to diction and style, are strangely unobservant of pronunciation; others who, though conscious of differences, seem unable to modify their own speech; others again who are too proud or obstinate to try. Spenser's own headmaster Mulcaster is a case in point: though born in Cumberland, he was educated at Eton and Oxford and spent his whole working life in the South; and yet it is apparent from his *Elementarie* that he retained Northern pronunciations and even, from one passage, that he had failed to observe an important Southern distinction between two sounds which was lacking in his own speech.[28] If the master, the most celebrated pedagogue of his day, could thus cling to the dialect of his boyhood, so might the pupil. But I incline to suppose that we come nearer the explanation by considering another contemporary, the spelling-reformer Bullokar. He was a man of lowly origins, and can be shown to be an example of a dialect speaker who had adopted, but not wholly consistently, a conservative form of Standard English. But when he comes to write verse, as he does not infrequently but very badly, he uses many rhymes which cannot conceivably be based on Standard English pronunciations; the stress of composition drives him back on his native dialectal forms.[29] Yet in transcribing his own verses in his phonetic script he never uses transcriptions that show the forms required to justify these dialectal rhymes; and even when the rhymes are justified by variants current in Standard English he often gives transcriptions based on other pronunciations that spoil the rhymes. He must be giving the forms which he judged to be most acceptable, and he evidently expected—we may perhaps even say desired—that his verses would be delivered in a correct and formal style, even though the basis of his rhyming was thereby destroyed. Similarly Gill, in giving phonetic transcripts of Spenser's verse (which he does often, for he greatly admired it), uses pronunciations far removed from those we should assume to have been Spenser's, and never departs from his own strict standards for the sake of the rhymes[30]; and likewise Robinson's transcripts of Barnfield's *Lady Pecunia* are not careful to preserve the phonetic basis of the rhyming. Again the passage in Puttenham in which he says, though not over-clearly, that if a poet cannot use good rhymes he may at least lessen the harm by so spelling the words as to make them eye-rhymes, in reality shows him judging purely from his own standards of speech; for the examples he cites of imperfect rhymes were probably justified by variant Elizabethan pronunciations or forms.[31] It seems that it must have been the normal practice of the time to read rhyme-words with one's own habitual pronunciation, without much regard for the poet's intentions; and if so it becomes clearer why we so seldom find any criticism of rhymes[32] and never, as far as I am aware, any condemnation of rhymes as vulgar or dialectal. Thus Gill is silent about Spenser's rhyming, though it frequently exemplifies the very pronunciations which he so strongly condemned in his contemporaries and was quick to recognize in Hart's phonetic spellings. In such circumstances a poet might well feel that there was little to be gained by conforming to strict standards of speech that made rhyming difficult; and he might rhyme, as Bullokar did, on pronunciations native to himself which he had nevertheless abandoned in public use. One reason, indeed, for the increasing laxity of Modern English rhyming may have been the spread of Standard English, leading to the delivery of poems in pronunciations different from those intended by their authors, to the belief that false rhymes had more justification by precedent than in fact was the case, and so to the increasing neglect of the rhyming by readers and subsequently by the poets themselves. I should conclude that the speech to which Spenser was born and bred was not Standard English, however he may have spoken in later life, and that he especially, and other contemporary poets in varying degrees, were prepared to base their rhymes on pronunciations with which they were familiar, whether or not they themselves used them, without asking too precisely if they were acceptable in the formal educated language; and that they did so because it was a tolerated licence, the predecessor of others more extreme, because criticism of rhymes was rare, and because standards of rhyming were becoming laxer. But if this is true, we can use rhymes only to show that pronunciations, new or old, were known, not to establish their status; to supplement, not to rebut, the evidence of the grammarians.

## FOOTNOTES

1. B. Fehr *Archiv* CXXVI 184 cites from *Rotuli Parliamentorum* II 173a (21 Edw. III (1347) 64) a complaint, in a petition against foreign clergy, that "les Provenders Aliens ne conissent n'entendent le pateys ne la lange d'Engleterre, ne la Commune d'Engleterre lour," whereby they are unable to aid or counsel their flocks by sermons, confessions, "n'en autre manere entendable," to the universal risk of the loss and damnation of Christian souls. He rejects the possibility that *la lange* refers to Anglo-Norman on the ground that a later petition of 1379–80, complaining against "gentz d'estrange lange," mentions explicitly as one of the duties of the clergy that to "enseigner le poeple"—"selbstverständlich auf englisch" ["obviously in English"], he comments. But whatever may be thought of this argument from the wording of one document to that of another, Fehr's interpretation of the phrase *le pateys ne la lange*, though accepted by Luick 35, is unconvincing, for there is no evidence that as early as 1347 there was a form of English which might be regarded as "the language" in contrast to "the dialects," still less that contemporaries recognized that there was. Mediaeval writers had an idea of "the language" as an abstract entity of which "the dialects" were particular manifestations, but not that one special form of English could be identified with "the language" in contrast to others which were "dialects." Fehr's error is to take the words *lange* and *pateys* in the modern French sense, as contrasting and mutually exclusive words; but *patois* (of which the etymology is uncertain) is not found in French in the sense "regional dialect" until the sixteenth century (cf. Dauzat *Dictionnaire Etymologique*, s.v.), and in OF it meant rather "special language"—the earliest instance, in Guillaume de Lorris' *Roman de la Rose*, 1.709, refers to the special language of birds, and is translated in the English version as *jargonyng* "warbling." The draughtsman of the parliamentary petition almost certainly intended no distinction between *pateys* and *lange*, but was merely indulging in the common legal trick of firing two shots at the same target in the hope that one would hit; in this very sentence he doubles the verb, *ne conissent n'entendent*, obviously without intending any sharp logical distinction between "knowing" and "understanding" a language, and in the same way he has doubled the object without intending the distinction which the modern meaning of the words suggests. *Le pateys d'Engleterre*, "the particular language of England" (i.e., English) is merely rather more precise than *la lange d'Engleterre*, which might possibly be taken, even if not so intended, as referring to what was still the official language, Anglo-Norman.

2. H. C. Wyld, *A History of Modern Colloquial English*, p. 103.

3. *Elizabethan Critical Essays*, ed. G. Gregory Smith, II, p. 150.

4. Ed. O. L. Jiriczek, p. 14 ["in speech the custom of the learned is the first law. Writing therefore is to be adjusted, not to that sound which herdsmen, girls, and porters use; but to that which the learned, or cultivated scholars, use in speaking and recitation."].

5. *Ibid.*, p. 34. ["As far as dialects are concerned, I would have you know that they pertain mainly to rustics: but among gentler and more carefully educated wits, speech is everywhere the same in sound and import."].

6. *Op. cit.*, p. 103.

7. H. Kökeritz, *Shakespeare's Pronunciation*, p. 9.

8. Butler had *ai* for ME *ă* before palatals, and Cooper had a pronunciation descended from *ai* in the same circumstances; Cooper also had [ɛə] < ME *ā*, the most obvious dialectalism of any of the major grammarians.

9. Cf. R. W. V. Elliot, "Isaac Newton as Phonetician," *MLR* XLIX (1954), pp. 5–12.

10. Macaulay in *The History of England*, ch. iii, observes that "many lords of manors had received an education differing little from that of their menial servants" and that "their language and pronunciation were such as we should now expect to hear only from the most ignorant clowns."

11. So the variations between *ăr* < ME *ĕr* and the unlowered *ĕr* > PresE [əː]; between sixteenth-century [ɛːər] < late ME *ę̄r* < ME *ẹ̄r*, beside [iːər] < unlowered ME *ẹ̄r* (in e.g., *hear*); between late ME *ā* < ME *au* in e.g., *chamber* and *change*, and the unaltered *au* (still common in the later sixteenth century); between [əi] < late ME *ī* < ME *īgh* and the unaltered [ɪç]. But the most obvious case is the variations in quantity resulting from fifteenth-century shortening before single final consonants. These variations rarely survive into PresE, but in some cases (e.g., ME *ĕr*) the inconsistency of PresE as between comparable words (e.g., *swerve* and *carve*) is itself a sign of dialect-mixture.

12. Thus one or two transcriptions in Gill, if not errors, show monophthongization of ME *ai* to identity with ME *ā*, which otherwise he resists; and Hodges in a single special case (the word *hair*) shows the identification of ME *ẹ̄r* (which this word has, despite its spelling with ME *ār*, though otherwise he keeps the two groups apart.

13. This is shown partly by the fact that in the earliest sources (Robinson and Gill) which distinguish [ŋ] from [ŋg] the latter is still used in many words from which it has since been lost, and also by the failure of sixteenth-century sources to distinguish [ŋ] as a separate phoneme, as they would have to do unless [ŋg] were used in all positions, in which case [ŋ] can be and would be regarded as that form of [n] which is used before [g]. It is inconceivable that so good a phonetician as Hart should have failed to recognize a distinct phoneme, especially one so easily analysable as [ŋ].

14. But he also knew open [ɛː]. Similarly he knew two pronunciations of ME *ęu*, according to the evidence of *De linguæ græcæ pronuntiatione*, though in *De linguæ anglicæ scriptione* he gives only one, the more conservative.

15. Minutes of the Court of the Merchant Taylors' Company, 16 August 1562, quoted by T. Klähr *Leben und Werke Richard Mulcasters*, p. 12. Mulcaster had been appointed the first headmaster of the school in the previous year.

16. Hart himself, in the *Methode*, gave up the representation of ME *ou* as a monophthong in favour of representing it as a diphthong. In the case of ME *ai* he not only consistently represented the sound as a monophthong, but also identified it with ME *ę̄*; Gill's objection, however, seems to be to the use of a monophthong rather than to the identification with ME *ẹ̄*—it is modern phonologists who object to the latter, because they fail to understand it.

17. Wyld, *op. cit.*, p. 307, cites *w*-spellings from the letters, etc., of Henry VIII and Elizabeth I.

18. There is evidence that in the late sixteenth century and earlier seventeenth century there was some attempt to distinguish [hoːl] as "healthy, sound" from [hwoːl] "entire," a distinction observed (though not with complete consistency) in Spenser's

variant spellings *hole* and *whole*. The distinction of sense obviously broke down, but accounts for the survival of the spelling *whole* but the pronunciation [houl].

19. Further examples of pronunciations widely current in the earlier sixteenth century which were rejected by the developing standard speech are (*a*) the raising of ME *ĕ* to *ĭ* in particular circumstances, e.g., in *git* "get," *yis* "yes," etc.; (*b*) a general tendency to lower ME *ĭ* to *ĕ*, commonly evidenced by earlier sixteenth-century spellings and by rhymes; (*c*) the corresponding tendency to raise ME *ŏ* to *ŭ* in particular circumstances, which has found acceptance in the standard language only in a few isolated words, e.g., *among*; (*d*) probably also a more general tendency, unnoticed by the phonologies but evidenced by rhymes and probably by occasional transcriptions of the spelling-reformers, to lower ME *ŭ* to *ŏ*, a development parallel to (*b*), which is recognized by the phonologies.

20. E.g., Levins's *Manipulus Vocabulorum*, Machyn's *Diary*, Mulcaster's *Elementarie*, Tonkis (MS. Regius F xviii), Hume's *Orthographie*, and comments on Northern speech made by Southern writers, e.g., Smith, Gill, and Daines.

21. In *The Paston Letters*, *The Cely Papers*, and other documents from these Eastern counties relied on by Zachrisson and Wyld.

22. The outstanding case is the typical Cockney (and generally South-Eastern) [w] < [v], which in the course of the last century has been lost from Cockney itself because of the influence of the educated language. Others were the loss of [w] in such words as *woman*, and of [j] in such as *yeast* and *yet*.

23. An obvious case is [ɪn] for unstressed [ɪŋ], which made its way into the educated language, as a variant, in the eighteenth century and still survives in the speech of restricted classes, but has never been the dominant educated form. More often a variant development of less correct London speech survives in one or two isolated words, e.g., [æ] < ME *ă* for normal ME *ŏ* in *strap* beside *strop*, [au] < late ME *ū* for normal late ME *ou* < ME *ŏ* before *l* in *prowl* < ME *prŏllen*, and [ʌ] by shortening of [uː] < ME *ǭ* for normal ME *ǭ* in *struck* p.t. and [nʌn] "none"; in each case there is evidence that the abnormal variants were formerly more widespread. In the same category, of isolated examples of tendencies once more general on the verges of StE, are to be placed [wʌn] "one," [əmən] "among" etc., and [mɒːlbərə] "Marlborough."

24. Some of these convergent developments—notably the identification of ME *ai* with ME *ā*, and somewhat later the use of [iː] < ME *ę̄* in place of ME *ẹ̄*—made it possible for large groups of words to be rhymed together which had hitherto been kept in separate but still numerous categories. But it was probably even more useful to poets, though it involved a smaller increase in the total stock of rhymes in English, when a comparatively limited group of words became rhymable with a larger group, e.g., by the development of ME *ę̄u* (which is restricted in its incidence) to identity with the much commoner ME *iu* and ME [yː] < OF [y], or by that of ME *ui* (restricted to words from OF and a few special cases) to identity with the very common ME *ī*.

25. These were the unrounding of ME *ŭ* except in labial circumstances, which produced a difference between the vowels of e.g., *cull* and *full*, and the rounding of ME *ă* after [w], which produced a difference between the vowels of e.g., *hard* and *ward*. The rhymes which these changes made invalid have been abandoned only with great reluctance by English poets, if indeed they can be said to have been renounced at all, though poets have accepted new rhymes brought about by these or associated changes, e.g., of *water* with *daughter* (found in Spenser), of *ward* with *lord*, or of *put* with *foot*.

26. Except for *lewty* "loyalty," which by 1500 had become purely a Northern word. In ME, *beauty*, being end-stressed, could be rhymed with monosyllables, but the shift of stress had made this no longer acceptable.

27. That Northern pronunciation affected Spenser's rhyming is shown by the fact that the p.tp *rode* is rhymed on the Northern form *rade* in *The Faerie Queene* VII, vii, 41 (where the rhyme-word if *maid*) and thrice elsewhere (cf. Bauermeister *Zur Sprache Spensers* § 180).

28. He says of such words as *good*, "If custom had not won this [*sc.* way of spelling, with *oo*], why not *ou*?"; and of *houl, coul,* and *skoul* (presumably *howl, cowl,* and *scowl*) "Why not as well with *oo*?" Clearly in his speech both ME *ū* and ME *ǭ* were [uː], and he had failed to realize that the traditional orthography was based on the fact that in the South the two were distinct. His error is explicable on the assumption that ME *ū* was in Southern pronunciation a rising diphthong [ʌu] with a more prominent second element; for then he might fail to observe the on-glide. But the failure, though explicable, is nonetheless remarkable.

This example of a man of high academic qualifications failing to understand the reason for the conventions of an orthography which he was at pains to defend is, I think, suggestive for. the interpretation of the "occasional spellings" of such documents as *The Paston Letters* and *The Cely Papers*. Though these contain many obviously phonetic spellings (i.e., representations of the spoken forms in terms of the conventional English letter-values), their more remarkable vagaries are often to be regarded as due to the attempt of dialect-speakers, trained to provincial ortho-graphic conventions, to imitate London spelling. Thus the uses of *ei* or *ey* in words containing ME *ī* is not due to analysis of the diphthong, which no one would doubt had developed, into a sort of *e* followed by *i* (a process intelligible in a modern phonetician or in a foreigner learning English entirely by ear, without knowledge of English spelling conventions, but not intelligible in a native accustomed to the English letter-values); it is rather an inverted spelling due to the observation that contemporary London spelling used *ei* (*ey*) in certain common words pronounced with the reflex of ME *ī*, e.g., *eye, height, deye* "die," *beye* "buy," etc. Similarly the much rarer use of *ai* for ME *ī* and of *au* for ME *ū* is hardly due to conscious phonetic analysis of the new diphthongs developed from the ME vowels, but to confusion between dialectal and London pronunciations and spellings: a man in whose speech ME *ai* and ME *au* had been monophthongized (or at least significantly altered from [ai] and [au]) would tend to identify the surviving [ai] and [au] of London English with his own diphthongs developed from ME *i* and *u*, and might occasionally, in consequence, use the spellings *ai* and *au* which corresponded in London English to the diphthongs [ai] and [au] in words in which his own diphthongs were really from ME *i* and *u*. He would do this the more easily if his own diphthongs were already [ai] and [au], though this result does not necessarily follow, for there are often in-exactitudes involved in the identification of the sounds of one dialect with those of another. In the event the significance of the *ai* and *au* spellings is much the same as if we regarded them as due to deliberate phonetic analysis, but the explanation, though more complex, is more credible; for these are documents illustrating the spread of the written forms of London English and of its spelling-conventions, in advance of the spread of its pronunciations.

29. Some of Bullokar's "rhymes" are mere jingles which cannot have been justified by any contemporary pronunciation, and in consequence one can accept others as evidence of pronunciation only with reserve; but the majority do seem to rest on his speech.

30. Yet Gill's transcriptions of verse do not give the impression that he was merely careless about the rhymes. It is chiefly when the rhymes depend on pro-nunciations that Gill did not accept as correct that his transcriptions break the rhymes (e.g., in transcriptions of Spenser, *whjl-ër—despair, qujt* "quite," vb.—*dispjt—ljht* sb.—*ljht* adj.), though in the case of *âl* "all"—*fvneral* the failure to keep the rhyme seems unnecessary (since Gill himself varies between *â* [ɒː] < late ME *au* and *a* < ME *ă* in the suffix *-al.*).

31. G. Gregory Smith, *op. cit.*, II, 85. Puttenham's chief example is the rhyme of *restore* with *doore* and *poore*, of which he says that the words are not "of like terminant, either by good orthography or in natural sound"; his objection is clearly based on his use in *restore* of [ɔː] < ME ǭ and in *door* and *poor* of [uː] < ME ǭ, but even before the lowering of [uː] to [ɔː] before *r* (which was already proceeding) *door* and *poor* had common variants in ME ǭ—in the former from OE dǒr beside dŭru, in the latter owing to the variable treatment of OF *o* in the neighborhood of labials. The rhyme of *ram* with *came*, which he also condemns, depends on the variant p.t. *cam* from the ME singular (in the sixteenth century apparently Northern); and that of *beane* with *den* (to use Puttenham's spellings) probably depends on confusion between *den* and the cognate *dean* "valley," though it might be taken as an example of a short vowel rhyming with the corresponding ME long vowel, a license commonly believed to descend from medieval times. Puttenham's examples are bad, and the whole passage confused.

32. Drummond of Hawthornden praised Daniel for his "sweetness of rhyming," which, if it was meant to refer to technical correctness, is somewhat ironic, for Daniel's rhyming shows signs of his Somerset origin, especially the frequency of rhymes between ME ŭ and ME ǒ. But Drummond no doubt had in mind merely the general artistic effect.

# HELGE KÖKERITZ

## Dialectal Traits
## in Sir Thomas Wyatt's Poetry*

Sir Thomas Wyatt's father, Henry Wyatt, was a Yorkshireman who in 1493 had acquired Allington Castle on the Medway in Kent. He had married Anne Skinner of Reigate, Sussex, and their elder son, Thomas, was born at Allington about 1503. He grew up in Kent, went to Cambridge when only twelve years old, and later held various posts of trust at court, including important missions to France and Spain; for some time, too, he was Sheriff of Kent. He escaped the fate of many an illustrious contemporary by dying prematurely of a fever in 1542 while journeying to Falmouth to meet the ambassadors of Emperor Charles V.

From a linguistic point of view, then, it appears that the general outline of Wyatt's life differed very little from that of other contemporary men of consequence. Like him they often spent their childhood and adolescence in the country before going to Oxford or Cambridge prior to entering the service of their sovereign. But unlike Wyatt most left behind no record that might provide a clue to the impact of other varieties of English on their own type of speech. Some no doubt followed the example of Raleigh later in the century who never abandoned his Devonshire dialect. Others, however, adjusted themselves to their new linguistic environment, adopting more or less successfully the characteristics of educated or courtly London speech. We can hardly be wrong in suggesting that Wyatt belonged to the latter group. Yet we can discern in his sheaf of poems the survival of certain Kenticisms, even though these would hardly be very conspicuous in the capital, where southeastern features had been part of the linguistic pattern for over two centuries. Notwithstanding a few seeming northernisms, which will be dealt with below, there is no vestige of his father's dialect. This had doubtless been neutralized by his mother's southern idiom and by his own daily contact with Kentish-speaking members of the household; we catch a glimpse of the boy listening to the songs the Allington maids used to sing "when they did sowe and spynne" (197).[1] Indeed, in the first two lines of another poem (196) Wyatt affirms his close ties with Kent, saying:

> But here I ame in Kent and Christendome
> Emong the muses where I rede and ryme.

* From Jess. B. Bessinger and Robert P. Creed, eds., *Franciplegius: Medieval and Linguistic Studies in Honor of Francis Peabody Magoun* (New York, 1965), 294–303. Reprinted by permission of the New York University Press and Allen and Unwin, Ltd.

No wonder that his muse who had "tasted the sweete and stately measure and style of the Italian Poesie" (Puttenham) and affected the cadences of Chaucer, Skelton, and the Tudor lyricists, would occasionally lapse into her native Kentish idiom.

Wyatt's Kenticisms are principally phonological. The morphological and lexical evidence is confined to the four southern past participles *yfixed* 9, *istricken* 47, *ycharged* 195, and *isene* 197, all archaic, metrical doublets ultimately derived from Chaucer; to a few instances of the southern plurals *hath* and *doth*, for example, *there selves hath bene* 102; *wee bothe . . . hathe don* 106; *the hartes of them wich . . . doth gro* 145; *some men doth say* 148;[2] and to the two words *kant* "portion" 198 and *wrislye* "shrivelled" 141. If EDD can be trusted, *cant* "portion" is now restricted to K, Ha, Sr, Sx, whereas *wrizzly* survives only in eastern So; MED cites an apparently non-dialectal instance of *cant* from c. 1460, antedating OED's first example, the Wyatt word. On closer scrutiny, a few words now labeled northern in the dictionaries, actually prove to have had a much wider distribution earlier. This is true of *kest* "cast" 71, which is regular in the Middle Kentish *Ayenbite*;[3] of *bren* "burn" (in *brent* 59, *brennyng* 181), formerly common in the south and used by Chaucer; and of *grame* "sorrow" 114, another Chaucerian echo. *Sheene* "shine" (vb) 199, found in Skelton and labeled a Scotticism (OED), has in fact been recorded also from D, Do, and So (EDD). *Girn* (in *girning* 199), a metathesized form of *grin*, is today reported from Scotland to Devon (EDD) and was earlier used by Bokenham, Skelton, Sir Thomas North, and others (OED), while a similar case of metathesis, *thrust* "thirst" 211, 229, is well evidenced from early southern texts, including Palsgrave (OED). *Narr* "nearer" 181 (< OE *nēarra*) survives in modern Ha *narre* (EDD). If *heins* in "Ffor that in heins to fle his rage so ryff" (213.16) is *hain* "enclosure" used metaphorically, it is as much a southern as a northern word; EDD reports it from So, Wi, and as a verb from Ha, Wt. The exclusively northern word *force* "waterfall" (< ON *fors*), which is listed as *forse* in Muir's Glossary (p. 285), does not occur at all in Wyatt; unglossed *forse* appears in poem 94, where it is clearly the common word "force." And the past tense forms *chase* 98, *drave* 64, *strake* 64, *wrate* pp. 248, 249, *smast* B6 (a contracted variant of *smatest*), were formerly current in the south.[4]

A phonological examination of Wyatt's rhymes and spellings will prove more fruitful. Admittedly, his rhyming sometimes appears to be as casual as his prosody often is, but such cases are so conspicuous as to cause no serious problem. For instance, he tends to rhyme only the unstressed syllables of disyllabic words as in *harbar:baner:suffre:displeasur* 4 and *reason:season: condition:fashion* 10, or a stressed and unstressed syllable as in *lif:pensif* 161, *free:sea:Thylee* 195. This practice, which may well be due to misunderstanding of Chaucer's prosody, makes most of his disyllabic rhymes phonologically unreliable. Thus *chambre:remember:daunger* 37 cannot be adduced as evidence of [ɛː] or [ẹː] in *chamber, danger,* since the three lines in question have exactly ten syllables each, the tenth being [ər], which probably alone constitutes the rhyme. But monosyllabic rhymes are phonologically useful, even though some of them may already have been traditional, for example, *love*:*prove*, *most*:*lost*.

Characteristic of the spelling is Wyatt's vacillation between conventional and unconventional forms. A word may be written in several different ways, even in the same poem, for example, *patience* 39, *paciens*, *pacience* 40, or it may change its garb for the sake of visual conformity in rhyme as in *spite*:*nyte* 39, *six*:*stix* (sticks) 101. Consonants are doubled for no apparent reason as in *rysse*:*gysse*:*devysse* 110, or in *lutte* alternating with *lute* 132. Often the suffixes -*id* and -*is* seem to have had no sounded vowel, for example, in *compellis*:*ells* 158, *kinde*:*assignid* 164, *wyld*:*begilyd* B22. Hence it is impossible to determine whether *fleith* in *fleith*:*appereth*:*fereth* 4 is monosyllabic or disyllabic; in 73, however, the meter shows it to be monosyllabic. Wyatt's *f* and *ff* denoted both [f] and occasionally [v]. The latter value is obvious in *elefn* 101, *saffry* (savory) 196, *swarfde* 41 (rhyming with *serued*:*ondeseruid*), *our sellffes* 205, *them sellfes* 207, *belovffd* 99, and probable in *profd*:*lofd*:*reprofd*:*remofd* 87, *carffd* 304.[5] In *effes* (eaves):*dises*:*ples* 209 we have instead a variant without the medial *v* (OED *ease* 6, pl. *easen*) as Shakespeare's in *ease-dropper* R3 5.3.22, whereas in *deserft* 25 and *deserftes*, rhyming with *partes* 87.2, the *f* is excrescent and pseudoetymological. French variants with *f* account for *saff* (save) 101, and so on, *natyff* 211, and *pensyf* 161, rhyming with *lif*. For *mouth* and *truth* the text has *mowgh* 207, *mowght* 201, 212, and *trowgh* 121, 199, 207, *trowght* 88, 198, 203, 213, *trowghthe* 71, spellings which reveal that *sightes* 28, *syght* 206, *sighting* 12 represent the common dialectal variant *sithe*, with [θ] or [ð], of *sigh*, found from Northumberland to the Isle of Wight and appearing as *sythyng* B1. The most significant orthographic feature, however, is Wyatt's not infrequent use of *i* or *y* mostly, but not exclusively, after historically long vowels. Thus we find *ai*/*ay* for late ME *ā* of various origin in *baigne* (bane) 206, *cayge* B38 (rhyming with *Rage*), *haist* (hast) 197, *haith* (hath) 39, 66, *tayme* B38 (rhyming with *gayne*), *taisted* 8, *chaing(e)* 132, 147, 209, *strainge* 132, *straynge* 68, which like the inverted *alith* (aileth) B3, *dalye* B50, *trators* B27, show the leveling of ME *ā* and *ai*[6]; further, and more remarkably, in *mayni'a* (many a) 101, *maynifold* 200 (EDGr reports [eː] from certain Midland counties, and a similar long vowel was used by Cooper, 1685), *laymentte* 217 (a doubtful poem), *trayvell* B29, 32, *vaylye* B43 (perhaps influenced by *vale*) and *payngys*[7] (beside *pang*) B26. ME *ẹ̄* and *ę̄* are written *ei*/*ey* in *bleyr* (blear) 105, *cheyr* (cheer) B51, *Creytour* (creature) B18, *bereyve* (bereave) B18, *feise* (fees) 198, *fley* (flee) B23, *fley* (flea) B28, rhyming with *I*, *fleith* 73, *freize* 26, *meit* (meet) 48, *steill* (steel) 31, *greiff* 5, 9, *greif(e)* 43, 51, 58, and so on, *releiff* 9, *leist* (least) 79, *theise* 199, 201, 229, *theys(e)* 114, B44, rhyming with *ways* B41 (*theise* may be a compromise between *these* and *thise*), *deiff* 58 (but *deff* 84, *deffh* 205), *weik* (weak) 93, *weyke* 201, *weyne* 129 (wean—not "ween" as glossed by Muir), *eaysyd*:

*apeaysyd* 103; this *ei/ey* may well be an analogical French spelling.[8] Note also *leynght* (length) 172, which may be a ME survival, for which see Jordan, § 103. Similarly ME *ǭ* appears as *oi/oy* in *noyns* (nonce) 198, rhyming with *bones*:*groyns* (groins), *foys* (foes) B44, and monosyllabic *goi'the*, rhyming with *trothe*:*grow'th* (p. 200); further in *soinges* (songs) 132, which may have had a long vowel, still recorded from Kent in *song*, *wrong* (EDGr § 32).[9] And OFr *ü* is spelled *uy* in *reffueys*:*acuys* 217, *truyse* 32 and *luyster* (lustre) 204, whose vowel may therefore have been long; *uy* is of course an analogical French spelling. Such forms are not uncommon in documents of the fifteenth and sixteenth centuries. They occur in the Cely Papers (Essex), the Shillingford Letters (Devon),[10] in other southern and southwestern letters,[11] and in the Diary of Henry Machyn, a London Merchant Taylor. Because of their frequency in late ME texts of northern provenance they have come to be classified as northern (Jordan §§ 19, 44, 54). Discussing the 1435 spelling *weyrs* (< OE *wera*), Kjerrström,[12] with nice understatement, characterizes Jordan's delimitation of this graphic device as "not . . . satisfactory." It would clearly be absurd to call Wyatt's usage above northern. Nearly all these spellings are either inverted or analogical forms, with the exception of *oi* for ME *ǭ* and the appearance of *i/y* after an historically short vowel. Whatever was the rationale of this use of *i* as a length mark, its occurrence in southern texts demonstrates the fallacy of taking such spellings as a criterion of northern provenance in early Modern English.[13]

Highly significant, too, is the use of *i* and *y* for ME *ę̄* and *ē* in *nydes* (needs) 197, which should be compared to *indes* 132, obviously a misreading of *nides* for *nedes* of MS. E, *nyd*, *suype* (sweep), *kype* B46, *kypes* B114, *belyve* B47, *unmyt* 198 as well as *mytt* (meet) 10, whose double *t* need not indicate a preceding short vowel (see above), *styre* (steer) B114, *Lya* (Leah) 134, *clyne* (clean) B46, rhyming with *syen* (seen), *glyne* (glean) 197, rhyming with *bene* (bean), *extryme* B114, and *unnysyd* (uneased) B35[14]; *esteme* alternates with *estime*, the original French form, in poem 196. Taken together with the rhymes to be discussed below, these *i* and *y* spellings obviously stand for [iː]. Moreover, Wyatt often writes *ie/ye*, a French spelling, for ME *ę̄*, as in *diepe* 52, 93, *hieraufter* B46, *chiere* 196, *chyer* B181, *fiever* 64, *lieper* (leper) 207, *syeke* (seek) 172, and the above *syen* B46. This *ie* rhymes with *e* as in *diepe*:*wepe* 52, and with *ei*, another French spelling, as in *myschief(e)*: *greif(e)*:*relief* 51, 58, three words which also appear as *greff*:*mescheff* B25, *greffe*:*myscheffe* B42, *greffe*:*relyeffe* B27, *gryff(e)*:*relyff* B4, B20, and in the rhyme *greffe*:*lyffe* (life) B38.

Wyatt's Kentish background reveals itself first of all in his not infrequent use of *e* for OE *y*. We find it in *bes(s)ye* B35, *besely* 37, *ded* (did) 123, 134, and so on, *kendeld* 87, *kendlid* 96, 200, *knet* 169, *merth* 216, *myrthe*:*erthe* 229, *shert* 5, rhyming with *smert*:*hert* (cf. Chaucer's *herte*:*sherte* LGW 2628–9), *sterred* (stirred) 8, 9, *sech* 214, whereas *buried* 9, though rhyming with *sterred*: *weried*, is doubtful, since it rhymes also with *greved* and hence is probably a rhyme in *-ed*. Note further *dere:ffyere* (fire) B41, a poem in perfectly regular iambic meter. Instead of *e* we sometimes find *i* or *y*, for example, in *lifft* (left) 204, *shitt* (shut), *shytt* 120, *kit*(*t*) (cut) 161 (cf. Chaucer's *shette, shitte, cut, kitte*), *bissely* 12, *kyndeled* 87, *siche* 137, 138, and *mych*(*e*) B4, 5 as well as *mitch* (6×) in Wyatt's two letters; *u* occurs in *me lusteth* 13 and normally in *such*, with the variant *soche* 152, and so on.

Equally important dialectally is the complete leveling in rhyme of ME *ẹ̄* and *ę̄* (< OE *ǣ¹, ǣ², ēa*). The following are conclusive cases: *dede* (deed): *blede* 42, 54, *dede*:*spede*:*drede* 189, *nede*:*dede*:*yede* 205, *rede*:*crede*:*wede*: *spede* 167 (a quadruple rhyme), *spede*:*rede* 227, *lede*:*glede* 24, *wene* (ween): *sene*:*mene* 36, *mene*:*sene* 192, *free*:*sea*:*Thylee* (Thule) 195, *grene*:*clene*:*kene* 64, *kene*:*medecene*:*unclene* 76, *hede* (heed):*lede* B19, *reche*:*beseche* 65, *reche*:*seche* B36, *clyne* (clean):*syen* (seen) B46, *beleve*:*preve*:*leve* (leave) 111; further *bene* (bean):*glyne* (glean):*clene* 197 and the striking *i*:*fley* (flea) B28. Their common sound was clearly [iː] as shown by the above *i* and *y* spellings, and by the inverted forms *peakes* (piques) 146, used also by Nashe in 1592 (OED), and *medecene* 76, which when trisyllabic and with a secondary stress on the final syllable must have ended in [iːn]—cf. L. *medicīna*, and modern German *Medizin*, Swedish *medicin*, both with stressed [iː] in the final syllable. The reflex of ME *ē* < OE *ě* in an open syllable is less clear: it rhymes with itself in *wreke*:*breke*, *speke*:*breke* 74, with *ǣ¹* in *heate*:*freate* 190, *hete*:*meate* B32, and with *ēa* in *frete*:*grete* 8, *eaten*:*thretyn* 8; but it is spelled *wryeke* 132 (cf. *syeke, syen* above), *meet* (meat) 197, and *brake* (break) 132, rhyming *brake*: *sake* 132, *brake*:*wreake* B24, *make the*:*betake the*:*brake the* B28. Two pro- nunciations, therefore, seem likely, one with [iː], the normal reflex of ME *ẹ̄* and *ę̄* in Kentish, the other with [ɛː] or [ęː] as in contemporary upper-class London speech.[15] The latter variant must be the basis of the rhymes *ffayne*: *mene*, *theys* (these):*ways* B41, and possibly *ffaythe*:*breathe* (breath) B34, unless both had a short vowel; [feθ] has been recorded from northwestern Devon (EDGr), corresponding to such early spellings as *feth, fethful*, which I prefer to interpret as having *ě*.[16] Before *r* ME *ę̄* and *ẹ̄* may have had both [iː] (cf. *chyer*:*cleer* B181) and [ɛː]. The best evidence of the latter vowel is the rhyming of Fr *galere* 78 with *dere* (dear), *fere* (fear), *chiere, clere*, as well as the rhymes *kare not*:*spare not*:*fere not* 151, *declare*:*bare* (bear) 181, and *ware* (were) *not*:*here* (hear) *not*, *bere* (bear) *not* 166; *ware* (were) is frequent in Wyatt.

In the treatment of ME *ī* we note first of all the remarkable use of *ay* in *th'ayes*:*layes* (eyes:lies) 35, whereas *trayed* 45 is probably the past participle of *tray* "betray," despite the E variant *tryed*. The digraph *ay* is the more noteworthy since Wyatt had doubtless leveled ME *ai* and *ā* under the latter as [ɛː] or [ęː]. Influence from *ay*(*e*) "yes" might have been reckoned with if the earliest forms of the word (from 1576 on) had not consistently been spelled *I*.[17] For *stryke* 93 MS. E has *streke*, corresponding to modern Devon *streek* (EDD) and comparable to [diːk] for *dike* in K, Sx, and Sf,[18] as well as *leek* (like) in Peele's *beleek*:*seek* (*The Arraignment of Paris* 3.4.1–2) and in Bullokar.[19] The same development is seen in *greep'the* (gripeth) 176—cf. modern Devon *greep* (EDD) and OED's anonymous sixteenth-century spelling *greep*—and in the above *sheene*, which is definitely *shine* and not, as OED suggests, a verbal use of the adjective *sheen*; in fact, Thomas Sackville, who was born in Sussex, rhymes *shyne*:*fyne*:*seene* as well as *shrike*:*beseke*, *keele*:*whyle*:*while*, *wheele*:*smyle*:*erewhile*, and *griefe*:*lief* (life),[20] identical with Wyatt's *greffe*:*lyffe*. Moreover, OE *wīc* appears as the place-name *Week(e)* in Co, Ha, So, Wt, with *e*-spellings from the fifteenth century on,[21] that is, the time when ME *ẹ̄* had become [iː]. The simplest explanation, it seems to me, is to interpret these cases as reflecting a dialectal tendency in the south to preserve ME *ī* undiphthongized. Luick (§ 485, Anm. 6) was aware of this possibility though, because of the rhyme *deke*:*eke* in *Sir Ferumbras*, he limited it to the southwest. Yet he is probably right in regarding *shriek* as a modern survival of this dialectal [iː] for ME *ī*. In *there*:*desire* 27, if a genuine rhyme, *desire* may have been pronounced with [iː] in imitation of French,[22] whereas *breers* (briars) 59 represents the original form with ME *ẹ̄*. We note further that *requyre* rhymes with both *desyre* B42 and *aper* (appear) B30—whether two pronunciations are implied or only one, with [iː], it is impossible to determine. The two rhymes *tre*:*fly* B22 and *fflee*:*lye* B36 show the confusion of the two verbs *flee* and *fly*.[23] If *bridill*:*Idell*:*mydell* 198 is a disyllabic rhyme, its first two members may have had [ɪ]; Sir Thomas Smith,[24] who was born in Essex, gives *ī* in *bridle* (which now survives only in Cumberland, EDGr), while Bullokar has one doubtful instance of *idle* in which, however, the omission of the length mark may be accidental.[25] A probably unstressed *I*, pronounced [ɪ] or restressed as [iː], rhymes with *bee* 123, *me* B1, *be*:*she* B2, and with *fley* (flea) B28. Spellings like *by* (be) B10, *my thynckith* B11, *my thynckes* B15 and *the selffe* 132 (also *thy selff*) reveal the leveling of the reflexes of shortened ME *ī* and *ẹ̄* under [ɪ].

A southern feature is the use of *o* in *bond*:*stond*:*lond* 209, *bronds*:*honds*:*fonds* 199, *lond* 212, *stond(es, -eth)* 29, 121, 212, and so on, *hande*:*withstonde* 164. Dan Michel's *Ayenbite* (1340) vacillates between *a* and *o* in *hand, land, stand*.

The leveling of ME *ọ̄* and *ou* is shown by rhymes like *ffoo*:*sloo* (slow) 8, *bestow*:*wow* 98, *troo*:*woo*:*knoo*:*goo* 167, *owne*:*mone* 65; *kno(o)* is a recurrent form. A notable inverted spelling is *owre* (oar) 28, which *Tottel's Miscellany* emended to *houre* with the result that Fowell, Hangen, and Rollins misinterpret it as "hour" despite "A ciascun *remo*" of the Italian original.[26] But *doulfull* 69, *dowlfull* 205, and *dulphulle* B8 represent the variant [duː] (now obsolete though listed as current in OED), whose ancestral OFr diphthong *ue* developed into ME *ui, ē*, and, by analogy, *ō* (Luick, § 415.3). From the rhymes *cause*:*knowes*:*clause* 166, *drawen*:*overthrowen*:*gnawen* 8, *unknowen*:*owne*:*fawne*:*sowen* B14 and the spellings *chaw* (chew) 198, *awne* (own) p. 249, we learn that ME *ou* had coalesced also with *au*, a feature characteristic not only of Kent but also of Essex, West Midland, and the southwest (Jordan, § 105, Anm.). This coalescence would therefore imply that ME $\bar{\varrho}$, too, had the antecedent vowel of modern [ɔː], now found only in *broad* and occasionally for both ME $\bar{\varrho}$ and *ou* in D, Do, So, W.[27] The same thing happened before *gh* as in *doghter:besoght her:lawghter* 198 and *frowght* (fraught) 114.

Very striking are Wyatt's rhymes between ME $\bar{\varrho}$ and $\bar{u}$ in *foode:allowdd: clowde* 199, *cowd* (could):*lowde:Roode* 197, *lowde:cowld* (could):*Shrowd* B5, *tow* (two):*now* 101, *thereto:now* 108, all of which should be compared with spellings like *howpt* (hooped) 197, *lowke* 75, *lowking* 67, *souner* 8, *prouf* 5, *reprouff:alowff* 8, *drowpith* 200, *stowpeth* 60, *howgy* (hugy) 22, and *avoo* 215 (a doubtful poem), rhyming with *how:now*. A few similar rhymes occur in Spenser.[28] They are not northern, for ME $\bar{\varrho}$ and $\bar{u}$ do not rhyme in northern English. Unfortunately we know too little about the Kentish dialect of about 1500 to determine whether it was characterized by undiphthongized ME $\bar{u}$ as a counterpart to the undiphthongized ME $\bar{\imath}$ discussed above. The Sx place name *Hove* [huːv], written *Howffe* 1531 (cf. the above Wyatt spellings), and going back to OE *hūfe* "hood, covering,"[29] appears to be a unique fossil of southern undiphthongized ME $\bar{u}$.

Wyatt's poems contain other interesting spellings and rhymes, though not so significant dialectally as to warrant a detailed treatment. Thus raising of *e* to *i* is frequent, for example, in *inimis* 141, *sildam* 31, *yett:fitt* 162, *fryndes* 170, *byn* (been) 207 (also *ben* 183, *bene:sene* 186), *thrid* 161, *stydfastly* 109. The opposite tendency, lowering of *i* to *e*, perhaps with lengthening in an open syllable, is illustrated by *ffeckell* 125, *sperit* 8, *hetherto* 13, *wedow* 198, *leve* (live) 106, and so on, *geve:leve:relieve* 199, *geven* 8, 15, *drevyn* 122; *quakynd* (quickened) 122 may be an inverted spelling showing the qualitative similarity of *e* < *i* in *quickened* and [ẹː] or [ɛː] in *quake*. Another type of lowering is the common change of *er* > *ar* in *marcye* 199, *warte* (wert):*parte* 135, *sarwyes* (service) 120, *unharde* (unheard):*reward* 157, *unfarme* (unfirm, ME *-ferme*): *harme:charme* 203. Shortening is probably indicated in *lest* (least):*request* 57, *lest:possest* 190, *sesse* (cease):*redresse* 15, and perhaps in *sayth:breth:feith: deth* 77 (a quadruple rhyme), *fete* (feet):*forgett* 155 (both words probably with [ɪ]). Yet Wyatt's erratic doubling of consonants makes it impossible to say whether the vowel was really short in, for example, *esse* (ease) 58, *knelle* (kneel) 196, *incresse:cese* 155; at times he may have rhymed a long and a short vowel of (practically) the same quality, for example, in *nekke:speke* 38 ([ẹ] and [ɛː] or [ẹː]), *hele* (hele):*well:fele* 196 ([iː] and [ɪ]), *cloke:moke* (mock):*stroke* 196 ([ɔ] and [ɔː], for which see above). Contractions of various kinds occur, for example, *En'mye* 8, *watrid* 175, *gadryng* 202, *saffry* (savory) 196, *sprites* 202, *thebrews* 202, *thevyn* (the heaven) 197, *t'assaye* 138; *ainst* (against) 184, unrecorded in OED and elsewhere, looks like an aphaeretic form of southern *a-yainst* (or possibly *to-yainst*—cf. Dan Michel's *to ayens, to yans, to yens*) with simultaneous loss of [j], though the doublet *ayenst* may have had a rhythmic variant with initial stress which made it liable to syncopation. With regard to Wyatt's consonants we notice the loss of the palatal fricative in *nyte* (night):*spite* 39 and the inverted spellings *wryght* (write) 103, *spyght* 119, *whight* (white) 86; further, the reduction of certain clusters as in *dyst* (didst) B34, *smast* (smat'st) B6, *twist, twyst* (twixt) 29, *spen my* (spend my) 104, *Granfather* p. 245, *hepe* (help) B27, *skarce* 149, rhyming with *cace:place*, *reherst:lest* (least) B33, *thou drieves* 189, *thou stondes, restes, trottes, sayse* 198, rhyming with *dayes*. Prosthetic [j] and [w] appears in *yerth* 101, *yerne* B43, *wone* B15, *won* B22, *many whon* B48, a *d* is added in *dismolde* 199 and a *t* in *deptyst* B5, clearly a variant of the shortened superlative *deppest*—it is curious that a *t* appears also in *Deptford* in Kent and Wiltshire, now pronounced without the p.[30] Only one instance of *v* for initial *f* has turned up, *vauore* B43, and only a few cases of *w* for *v*, namely *werely* B21, *dewoyd* B9, *sarwyes* 120. The recurrent *wich* (which) 153 and so on, *wens* 91, and *whete* (wet) 197 show the coalescence of *wh* and *w*. Regressive assimilation accounts for *lenthe* (length) B26 and *optayn(e)* 116, 120; but *turkylles* (turtles) B22 is an inverted spelling indicating the common colloquial change of [kl] > [tl] as in *tlean* for *clean*.

## FOOTNOTES

1. Kenneth Muir, ed., *Collected Poems of Sir Thomas Wyatt* (Cambridge, Mass., 1950), here cited by number, and the same editor's *Sir Thomas Wyatt and His Circle, Unpublished Poems* (Liverpool, 1961), referred to as *B* plus number; page references are to the two letters printed in the former volume.

2. Such forms are not unknown to Shakespeare; like him, Wyatt has also a few cases of plurals in *-s*, e.g., *suche as sekes* 124, *them . . . that thynkes* 124, *my dayes dekaes* 137 (cf. Wilhelm Franz, *Die Sprache Shakespeares*, §§ 155 f.)

3. J. K. Wallenberg, *The Vocabulary of Dan Michel's Ayenbite of Inwit* (Uppsala, 1923), p. 135.

4. See the respective Verbs in OED, where, however, *smate* "smote" is said to be only northern, clearly because Wyatt's form above was then unknown.

5. For the same scribal practice in southern documents see Max Franck, *Englische Schreibung und Aussprache im Zeitalter der Tudors und Stuarts (nach Briefen)* (Bottrop i.W., 1939), pp. 88 f. They are also typical of Henry Machyn's *Diary*, written in London between 1550 and 1553.

6. In *change, strange*, etc., *ai* appears as early as late ME (Jordan, § 224, *Anm.*). Many *ai* spellings are listed in Franck (p. 59), as well as *a* for ME *ai* (p. 70).

7. Cf. *haynge, hainge* (hang) in seventeenth-century New England documents, which have also *grain* (grand), *substainshall* (Anders Orbeck, *Early New England Pronunciation* [Ann Arbor, Mich., 1927], p. 23).

8. Surrey's *weyve*, which Tottel respelled *weaue*, is an instance of the same kind and not, as Veré Rubel (*Poetic Diction in the English Renaissance* [New York, 1941], p. 62) seems to assume, an exchange of *weave* for *waive*.

9. R. E. Zachrisson (*Pronunciation of English Vowels* [Göteborg, 1913], p. 65) reports *stroynge* and *cloys* (close) from the Shillingford Letters (Devon), and similar spellings are cited in Franck (p. 62). The now obsolete verb *groin* "grunt" (in the above rhyme *bones:noyns:groyns*) had an early monophthongal variant *grone* used, e.g., by the Londoner Palsgrave (1530): "a hogge groneth," which tended to be confused with *groan* (see OED, *groin* 1b and *groan* 2).

10. See Zachrisson, pp. 50, 64 f., Asta Kihlbom, *A Contribution to the Study of Fifteenth Century English* (Uppsala, 1926), pp. 119, 146 f., 153, 159.

11. See, e.g., Franck, pp. 36, 53, 55, 59 f., 62, 66.

12. *Studies in the Language of the London Chronicles* (Uppsala, 1946), p. 237.

13. This is unfortunately done in Axel Wijk's dissertation *The Orthography and Pronunciation of Henry Machyn, the London Diarist* (Uppsala, 1937), pp. 21 f., where Machyn's use of *i/y* as a length mark is said to be an orthographical feature "characteristic of the North generally" and hence taken as evidence of his alleged Yorkshire origin. Few, if any, of the orthographical, phonological, and grammatical criteria adduced by Wijk to substantiate his thesis are conclusively northern, not even *ees* for *eyes* (p. 28), which is reported as a Devon pronunciation in 1701 (see *Anglia*, XXIV [1901], 116, also Kihlbom, p. 37).

14. But *concyle* 124, rhyming with *whyle*:*gyle* need not be "conceal" as glossed by Muir, but should probably be identified with *concile* "reconcile," which seems to fit the context.

15. See my *Shakespeare's Pronunciation* (New Haven, Conn., 1953), pp. 194 ff. Since *a* appears in *break* (inf.) from the fifteenth century onwards, it may be analogical as suggested by Zachrisson, p. 58. [For a recent study of the problem of *ee* and *ea* spellings and their phonological significance, see Charles T. Scott, "On the dating of NE *ee* and *ea* spellings from ME *ẹ̄* and *ẹ̆*," in Irmengard Rauch and Charles T. Scott, eds., *Approaches in linguistic methodology* (Madison, Wisc., 1967), 73–9.—Ed.]

16. For these spellings see Zachrisson, (p. 68), who, however, takes them to be Anglo-Norman forms.

17. The earliest occurrence of *I* "ay(e)" is actually in Sir Thomas Smith's *De recta & emendata Linguæ Anglicæ Scriptione, Dialogus* (1568), p. 11a, where "I Latina" is said to mean "ego, aut oculus, aut etiam" ["I, or eye, or aye"] (Diebel's ed., Halle, 1913).

18. See my *Phonology of the Suffolk Dialect*, § 284, with a reference to *speke* (spike), *streek* (strike), in Edward Moor, *Suffolk Words and Phrases* (Woodbridge, 1823). Note that *drive* is [driːv] in Gl (EDGr, Index).

19. R. E. Zachrisson, *English Pronunciation . . . As taught by William Bullokar* (Uppsala, 1927), p. 48. However, I cannot subscribe to his theory that the leveling with ME *ẹ̄* may have been due to early ME shortening of *ī* with subsequent lengthening in an open syllable to *ẹ̄*. For other examples of this type see Kihlbom, pp. 36 ff., and Franck, p. 50. The 1701 list of Devon provincialisms referred to above (n. 13) gives *cheeld*, *bleend*, *neen* (nine), *kee* (cows) [< OE *cȳ*—Ed.], *ees* (eyes), which should be compared with the Devon instances cited in A. J. Ellis, *On Early English Pronunciation* (London, 1869), I, p. 191. Thomas Howell (1581) rhymes *seeke*:*leeke* twice in his "To the Reader" (*The Poems of Thomas Howell*, ed. A. B. Grosart [Manchester, 1879], pp. 171 f.).

20. In his Induction to *A Mirror for Magistrates*, 11.307–8, 314–15, 471–4, 492–5, 527–30.

21. Cf. A. H. Smith, *English Place-Name Elements* (Cambridge, 1956), II, p. 261, and my *The Place-Names of the Isle of Wight* (Uppsala, 1940), p. xcvi. My suggestion (*ibid.*) that the modern [iː] in *Week* is due to lengthening of a late ME *wick*, in early Modern English, does not seem compatible with the fresh material adduced here.

22. See Otto Jespersen, *John Hart's Pronunciation of English* (Heidelberg, 1907), pp. 28, 66.

23. This confusion is very old. In fact, it goes back to OE, where the two verbs *flēon* and *flēogan* were identical in all forms except in the infinitive, the first pers. sg. present, the pl. present, and the whole present subjunctive. The *i*-mutated forms of

the 2d and 3d pers. sg. present spread to the 1st pers. sg. and the pl., as well as the infinitive in ME, resulting in the doublets *flē(n)* and *flīe(n)* of both verbs. In Northern English *fly* became *flee*. Orr's suggestion (*Words and Sounds in English and French* [Oxford, 1953], pp. 1 ff.) that *flee* became *fly* to avoid unpleasant associations with the alleged homonym *flea*, is totally unfounded. Moreover, until the end of the seventeenth century, *flea* was pronounced [flę:] in upper-class London speech; only in southeastern dialects did it become [fli:] in the fifteenth century.

24. P. 27a and § 28.

25. Cf. Zachrisson, *Bullokar*, pp. 177, 204.

26. See further my article "Two Sets of Shakespearean Homophones," *RES*, XIX (1943), 360, n. 5.

27. EDGr, §§ 121, 123 f., 127 f., 168.

28. Arvid Gabrielson, *Rime as a Criterion of the Pronunciation of Spenser, Pope, Byron, and Swinburne* (Uppsala, 1909), pp. 77 f.

29. *The Place-Names of Sussex* (Cambridge, 1929), p. 293, and *English Place-Name Elements*, I, p. 267.

30. *The Place-Names of Wiltshire* (Cambridge, 1939), pp. 231 f., and Ekwall, *The Concise Oxford Dictionary of English Place-Names* (Oxford, 1960), p. 142.

# Appendix

## Phonetic, Phonemic, and Other Symbols Used in this Book

1. Slashes enclose /PHONEMES/; square brackets enclose [PHONES]; angle brackets enclose ⟨GRAPHEMES⟩; braces enclose {MORPHEMES}.

2. > means "becomes"; < means "is derived from."

3. *Phonetic Symbols.* There are many diverse traditions of phonetic and phonemic transcription, a number of which are used in this book. This appendix will list (a) the symbols used by the IPA (International Phonetic Association), and their most common variants; (b) the notation used by American structural linguists for phonemic transcription; and (c) the most common diacritics and special symbols of both modern practice and the "philological tradition," where spellings are supplied with diacritics. If a particular character or diacritic appears in more than one tradition with the same meaning, it will be explicated only once.

3.1 *Vowel Symbols.* In cases of alternate symbols for the same sound, the first is that of the IPA; those in ( ) are the most common alternates.

TABLE 3.1 / *Vowel symbols*

|  | Front | | Central | | Back | |
|---|---|---|---|---|---|---|
|  | *Unround* | *Round* | *Unround* | *Round* | *Unround* | *Round* |
| High | i | y (ü) | ɨ |  | ɯ | u |
|  | ɪ | ʏ (ö) | ɪ | ʉ |  | ɷ (ʊ) |
| Mid | e | ø (ö) | ə |  | ɤ | o |
|  | ɛ | œ (ö) |  |  | ʌ | ɔ |
|  |  |  | ɐ |  |  |  |
| Low | æ |  |  |  |  |  |
|  |  |  | a |  | ɑ | ɒ |
|  |  |  |  |  | ɑ |  |

3.2 *Consonant Symbols.* Items in parentheses represent variants of the IPA symbols. In pairs separated by hyphens, the articulation is the same, but the first member is voiceless and the second member is voiced. Items that are

|  | Bilabial | Labiodental | Dental | Alveolar | Prepalatal | Palatal | Velar | Glottal |
|---|---|---|---|---|---|---|---|---|
| Stops | p-b |  |  | t-d |  |  | k-g | ʔ |
| Fricatives | ɸ-β <br> vd | f-v | θ-ð | s-z | ʃ(š)-ʒ(ž) | ç j(y) <br> vl vd | x-ɣ <br> vl | h <br> vl |
| Affricates |  |  |  |  | tʃ(č)-dʒ(j) |  |  |  |
| Nasals | m <br> vd |  |  | n <br> vd |  | ɲ <br> vd | ŋ <br> vd |  |
| Laterals |  |  |  | l <br> vd |  | ʎ |  |  |
| Semivowels |  |  |  | r¹ <br> vd |  | j(y)² <br> vd | w³ <br> vd |  |

[1] A departure from IPA practice, adjusted to the needs of this book. IPA uses [r] for a "rolled" sound, and [ɹ] for the usual frictionless semivowel.
[2] [j] is used by the IPA for both the fricative and the frictionless continuant.
[3] [w] might also be placed under Bilabial, as it has a double articulation: raising of the back of the tongue and lip-rounding.

not members of pairs are marked with a subscript *vd* for voiced and *vl* for voiceless.

4. American Phonemic Transcription (after Smith and Trager, *An outline of English structure*[6] [Washington, 1957]). This is the basis for the accounts of English vowel history by Stockwell.

4.1 Simple Nuclei: /i e æ ɨ ə a u o ɔ/ as in *bit, bet, bat, just* (where in contrast with, for example, *cut*), *but, bottle* (exc. NEngl.), *book, home* (NEngl.), *caught* (where in contrast with *cot*).

4.2 Semivowels: /y w h/, that is, fronting glide, backing glide, centering glide.

4.3 Complex Nuclei (a selection, covering the most common contrasts): /iy ey ay aw ow/ as in *beet, bait, bite, bout, boat.* On all of this see Smith and Trager, esp. 27–8.

4.4 Consonants: /p t k b d g c (č) j f θ s š v ð z ž m n ŋ l r w y h/.

5. *Common Diacritics in Phonetic Transcription:*

| | |
|---|---|
| [ ̯ ] nonsyllabic | [˂] advanced |
| [ ̥ ] syllabic | [˃] retracted |
| [ː] long | [ ̈ ] fronted |
| [˄] raised | [-] centralized |
| [˅] lowered | [ ̃ ] nasalized |

6. *Common Diacritics in Transcription Using Attested Spelling:*

| | |
|---|---|
| ̨ open: ę = [ɛ] | . close: ọ = [e] |
| ¯ long: ē = [eː] | ˘ short: ĕ = [ɛ] |

˘̄ may be short or long

ȯ *o* used as a spelling for *u*: *lȯve* = [lʊv(ə)]

7. *Special Characters Used in Spelling-Transcriptions:*

ƀ voiced bilabial fricative [β]
þ voiceless interdental fricative [θ]
ǥ voiced velar fricative [ɣ]
ğ voiced prepalatal affricate [dʒ]

8. *Special Conventions Used in Specific Languages:*

(a) In ON length is marked with an acute: *drífa.*
(b) In OE length is marked with a macron: *drīfan.*
(c) In OE the so-called "long diphthongs" are marked on the first element: *ēa, ēo,* except when stress is presumed to have shifted: *eā, eō.*

9. *Symbols Used in Generative Grammars:*

A → B "A may be rewritten as B"
A — B, A + B concatenation: "A + B"
( ) Optional item
$\begin{Bmatrix} A \\ B \end{Bmatrix}$ "choose *either* A or B"

# Glossary

The definitions given here are a guide to the terminology used in the papers in this collection, whether "traditional" or "modern." The definitions are minimal operational ones, not in any sense exhaustive. For fuller treatments it may be helpful to consult one or more of the standard texts in linguistics, for example, Gleason, *Introduction to descriptive linguistics*, Bloomfield, *Language*, or some of the others listed in the Bibliography. For phonetics, G. L. Trager, *Phonetics: Glossary and tables* (SIL, OP 6 [1958]), will be useful; for general terminology see also J. Marouzeau, *Léxique de la terminologie linguistique* (Paris, 1951).

A word in a definition in CAPITALS is defined in this glossary.

**Ablative**    A CASE expressing the notion of deprivation, direction from, removal, and in Latin agency or instrument: for example, L *urbs* "city," (*ex*) *urbe* "from the city."

**Ablaut**    Internal vowel gradation, as in the principal parts of the Germanic STRONG VERBS, for example, *drive/drove/driven*. Also the specific vowel-alternations in INDO-EUROPEAN stems. See further under GRADE.

**Accusative**    A CASE expressing the notions goal of an action or motion, extent, and in L and OE the direct object of a transitive verb: for example, L *urbs* "city," (*ad*) *urbem* "to the city."

**Affricate**    A CONSONANT analyzable as a STOP with FRICATIVE release, for example, the initial [tš] in *China*. Many linguists prefer to analyze such sounds as units, for example [č].

**Allomorph**    A CONDITIONED or otherwise predictable member of a MORPHEME; any one of the MORPHS constituting a morpheme. Thus {wolf} has the allomorphs /wulf/ in the singular and /wulv/ before the plural morpheme; or the phonologically conditioned allomorphs of {-s} plural are /s/, /z/, and /iz/. See also MORPHOPHONEMIC.

**Allophone**    A conditioned or otherwise predictable member of a PHONEME; any one of the PHONES constituting a phoneme. The MnE phoneme /p/ has (among others) the allophones [pʰ] (ASPIRATED) and

[p] (unaspirated), the former initially before vowels, the latter in that position only after /s/.

**Analogy**    The tendency of the exception to conform to the rule; the process whereby aberrant forms are sporadically leveled in the direction of the statistical norm. For example, *creep* and *sleep* were originally STRONG VERBS, and would have given the MnE past forms *\*sleep* and *\*creap*, but were analogically reformed as WEAK VERBS.

**Alveolar**    Produced with the tongue against the alveolus or predental ridge, as [t d s z].

**Analytic**    Of a language that signals meaning primarily by means of word-order rather than inflectional endings, for example, MnE as opposed to Latin. The opposite of SYNTHETIC.

**Aorist**    An INDO-EUROPEAN verb category (preserved in Classical Greek) which indicated the notion of action independent of further limitation, for example, TENSE or ASPECT (Gr *a-oristos* "indefinite").

**Aphaeresis**    The loss of an initial vowel, as in *mid* < *amid.*

**Apical**    Made with the tip of the tongue: for example [t d].

**Apocope**    Loss of a final vowel, as in the change of ME /luvə/ "love" to MnE /ləv/.

**Aspect**    The expression by a verb form or verbal construction of the relation of the action to the *passage* of time. See DURATIVE, INCHOATIVE, PERFECTIVE.

**Aspiration**    Release of a puff of breath following articulation, as in initial /p/ in MnE *pit* [pʰɪt] (cf. *spit* [spɪt]).

**Assibilation**    The process by which a STOP becomes an AFFRICATE or SIBILANT: for example, L [k] > OF [ts] > MnF [s].

**Assimilation**    Approximation of one sound to a neighboring one: for example, the [k] in [ɪnkəm] "income" being a VELAR often causes the ALVEOLAR [n] to become a velar [ŋ]. See SANDHI, UMLAUT.

**Atonic**    Of a vowel bearing weak stress. (Mainly in Romance linguistics.)

**Back Formation**    A word formed on the assumption that an existing form must be derived from *it*: thus W. S. Gilbert's verb *burgle* on the assumption that *burglar* must mean "one who burgles."

**Back Vowel**    A VOWEL articulated with the back of the tongue, for example [u ʊ o ɔ ɑ].

**Bilabial**    Made with both lips as articulators, for example, [p b m].

**Biuniqueness**    The notion that "to any given phone-type in a given environment there must correspond only one possible phoneme, and to any phoneme in a given string there must correspond only one phone-type ..." (F. Householder, "On linguistic terms," in S. Saporta, ed., *Psycholinguistics* [New York, 1961], 19.)

**Breaking**     Also FRACTURE. The development of a simple vowel into a DIPHTHONG, usually by ASSIMILATION to a following consonant. For example, a front vowel before a back consonant will often develop a transitional [ə] glide, as in some Southern U.S. dialects where *self* is [sɛəlf]. In historical Germanic studies, especially a group of ON and OE sound changes, where earlier vowels are diphthongized in certain environments: PrOE *æld* > *eald*, PrN *efnaR* > *jafn*.

**Calque**     Also LOAN-TRANSLATION. Direct translation of MORPHEMES from one language to another, for example, E *skyscraper* > F *gratte-ciel*, G *Wolkenkratzer*.

**Case**     (a) The form of a noun, pronoun, or adjective, insofar as it indicates syntactic categories or relations: for example, the L ending *-em* in a third-declension noun indicates ACCUSATIVE; (b) A set of putative universal semantic relationships which often manifest themselves in affixes (cf. above), preposition + noun constructions, or selectional or sequential constraints. Cf. Charles Fillmore, "The case for case," in Emmon Bach and Robert Harms, eds., *Universals in linguistic theory* (New York: Holt, Rinehart and Winston, 1968).

**Central Vowel**     One formed near the middle of the mouth, for example, [ə i].

**Checked**     Also BLOCKED. Of a vowel in a CLOSED SYLLABLE (mainly in Romance linguistics). See FREE.

**Close Vowel**     A vowel produced with relatively great tongue height, for example, "close *e*" [e] vs. "open *e*" [ɛ].

**Closed Syllable**     A syllable ending in a consonant: for example, *far*, *nos-tril*. The opposite of OPEN SYLLABLE.

**Cognate**     Related by common ancestry. MnE *day*, G *Tag*, ON *dagr* presumably go back to common Germanic *daga-z*. Also used of languages related in the same way (L *co-gnātus* "born together").

**Commutation**     The substitution of one segment for another, as in setting up MINIMAL PAIRS in phonemic analysis.

**Compact**     Of a sound-type showing, on spectrographic analysis, a relatively great concentration of energy in a narrow central region of the spectrum. In MnE, for example, /o a/ show compact spectra, while /u i/ show the opposite, DIFFUSE. On these features and others involved in "Distinctive Feature Phonology" see Jakobson, Fant, and Halle, *Preliminaries to speech analysis*[6] (Cambridge, Mass., 1965). See also the revised feature system in Chomsky and Halle, *The sound pattern of English* (1968).

**Complementary Distribution**     A condition in which two elements in a system occur in mutually exclusive environments. Thus the ALLOMORPH /wulf/ of {wolf} appears only in the singular, and /wulv/ appears only before the plural MORPHEME {-s}. The two forms are in CD.

**Compensatory Lengthening**    Lengthening of a vowel resulting from loss of a following consonant. OE *sægde* > *sǣde* with loss of the PALATAL FRICATIVE represented by *g*.

**Complex Nucleus**    A SYLLABIC consisting of a vowel plus a SEMI-VOWEL, for example, /ay/ in *bite*.

**Constraint**    Any factor or condition operating in a language or in a theory which controls or limits a given operation. Thus in speaking English there is a *selectional* constraint which causes us to select forms of verbs that agree with their subjects, and a *sequential* constraint that causes us to put direct objects after transitive verbs. Similarly, in the writing of a grammar, certain items in the theory on which our procedure is based may act as constraints, for example, the notion of BIUNIQUENESS, or a "simplicity metric" valuing most highly RULES or sets of rules adhering to some pre-established notion of "simplicity."

**Continuant**    A consonant formed without total occlusion of the vocal tract, for example, FRICATIVES, some varieties of [l] and [r], GLIDES.

**Countertonic**    Of a vowel bearing secondary stress (mainly in Romance linguistics).

**Dative**    The CASE indicating the notions of reference or indirect object, for example, L *homo* "man," *homini* "to (the) man."

**Declension**    The inflectional PARADIGM of a noun, pronoun or adjective. Also a group of nouns, and so on, having the same kind of inflection, for example, OE "a-stem" nouns, which all have NOMINATIVE and AC-CUSATIVE plurals in *-as*, and GENITIVE singular in *-es*.

**Deep Structure**    The abstract form underlying the SURFACE structure of an utterance, before TRANSFORMATIONS have been applied. Thus "John admires himself" is a surface structure whose underlying form is on the order of "John admires John," with an obligatory transformation operating which changes the object to a reflexive pronoun. See further KERNEL, DELETION, TRANSFORMATIONAL-GENERATIVE GRAMMAR.

**Deletion**    The removal of any item from a string of items; in TRANS-FORMATIONAL-GENERATIVE GRAMMAR, a TRANSFORMATION which removes an item present in the DEEP STRUCTURE from the SUR-FACE STRUCTURE, for example, the rule which permits removal of the subject *you* from imperative sentences.

**Dental**    Produced with the tongue against the upper teeth, as [θ ð].

**Diachronic**    Literally "through time," that is, historical, as opposed to SYNCHRONIC.

**Dialect**    A variety of a language (geographical or social) that differs consistently from other varieties in phonology, morphology, syntax, lexis—or all of them.

**Diffuse**   Of a sound-type whose spectrograph shows two separate peaks of energy concentration. See COMPACT.

**Diphthong**   A sequence of two vowels of which only one is syllabic, for example, [au] in *out*.

**Dissimilation**   The change of one of two identical sounds (usually consonants) to a different one, for example, L *peregrinus* to F *pélérin*, where /r . . . r/ > /l . . . r/.

**Doublet**   An alternative form, often reflecting an identical etymology but a different development from another form, for example, *dish, disc*, both < L *discus*.

**Drift**   The movement of a language through time, conceived as having a specific direction or teleology, for example, the change of English from a SYNTHETIC to an ANALYTIC language. See E. Sapir, *Language*, ch. VII.

**Durative**   An ASPECT expressing incompleted or continuing action.

**East Germanic**   A group of languages represented by Gothic and a few later fragments commonly called "Crimean Gothic."

**Epenthesis**   The appearance within a syllable of a sound with no etymological justification, or one which was originally outside the syllable. OE spellings of *ui* for the UMLAUT of *$\bar{u}$ have been considered epenthetic, for example, *druige* for *drȳge* "dry" < Gmc *drūgi̯-*.

**Falling Diphthong**   One with stress on the first element, for example, [ai] in *bite*.

**Fortis**   Made with relatively tense musculature in the vocal tract: of consonants. In MnE (usually) voiceless consonants are fortis, and voiced ones LENIS.

**Fracture**   See BREAKING.

**Free**   Of a vowel in an OPEN SYLLABLE. See CHECKED.

**Fricative**   Also SPIRANT. A consonant formed by narrowing the space between two articulators, so that there is audible friction, for example, [f v s z].

**Front Vowel**   One articulated with the front of the tongue, for example, [i e æ].

**Gemination**   Doubling of a PHONEME. In the WEST GERMANIC gemination, consonants preceding */j/ were doubled: OE *settan* "set" < *satja-nam*, vs. ON *setja*.

**Gender**   A grammatical category often loosely equated with the "sex" of objects, or with other categories such as animate-inanimate. For example, G *Mädchen* "maiden" is neuter, so that when it is an antecedent it may take the pronoun *es* "it" (even though notionally maidens are female). Whatever the categories and their relation to "reality," gender where it exists is usually part of a formal system of agreement or concord, where, for example, a noun of gender X must be modified by an adjective of X, and so on.

**Genitive**    The CASE indicating the notions of origin, possession, material out of which something is made, for example, OE *mann* "man," *mannes* "of (the) man."

**Germanic**    A group of INDO-EUROPEAN languages, distinguished by certain innovations, notably the WEAK VERB conjugation and the set of consonant changes commonly called GRIMM'S LAW.

**Glide**    A "transitional" sound developed to facilitate passage from one sound to another: see under BREAKING; a SEMIVOWEL.

**Grade**    The position in an ABLAUT-series occupied by a given vowel. Many INDO-EUROPEAN roots were presumed to have had three grades, usually called *normal, reduced,* and *zero* or *vanishing.* Thus the IE root *\*bh-r* "carry" had the grades *\*bher-* (normal), *\*bhor-* (reduced) and *\*bhr̥* (zero) which gave rise in OE respectively to *beran* "to bear," *bær* "I carried," *byrðen* "burden." There were also lengthened grades, for example, *\*bhēr-,* which gave *bǣron* "they carried."

**Graph**    Any written sign (character, letter); any member of a GRAPHEME.

**Grapheme**    The classificatory unit of elements in written language, parallel to PHONEME, MORPHEME. The grapheme ⟨a⟩ has the allographs A, a, *A, a,* and so forth.

**Great Vowel Shift**    A late medieval sound change in English, whereby all the long vowels of Middle English changed in pronunciation, and according to the traditional accounts, the topmost vowels in the front and back series, *ī* and *ū*, "broke" to diphthongs (ultimately MnE [ay], [aw]. For a full account see any standard history of English, and for a new account, ch. 6 of *Sound Patterns of English.*

**Grimm's Law**    The name given to an important consonant shift which characterizes the Germanic languages, after one of its early formulators, Jacob Grimm. The "law" says that in Germanic the INDO-EUROPEAN voiceless STOPS became voiceless FRICATIVES (for example, IE *\*k* > Gmc *h*: L *cord-* vs. E *heart*); IE voiced stops became voiceless stops (for example, IE *\*g* > Gmc *k*: L *genus* vs. E *kin*); and IE voiced ASPIRATED stops became voiced unaspirated stops (for example, IE *\*bh-* > Gmc *b*: Skr *bhrātar* vs. E *brother*). Also called "first sound shift," *erste Lautverschiebung.*

**Hiatus**    A pause or juncture between two vowels, in which the vowels remain separate and do not coalesce into a DIPHTHONG: either external, as *I am,* or internal, as *aorta.*

**Homorganic**    Formed with the same articulators in the same position. Thus "nasal + homorganic voiced stop" = [mb] (both BILABIALS), [nd] (ALVEOLARS), [ŋg] (VELARS).

**I-Mutation**    See UMLAUT.

**Inchoative**    Also INCEPTIVE. An ASPECT expressing the notion of beginning of an action.

**Indo-European**    The large language family including Germanic, Slavic, Romance, Celtic, Indo-Iranian, Albanian, and others; the reconstructed (hypothetical) ancestor of all these language groups.

**Ingvaeonic**    Also "North Sea Germanic." Those dialects originally spoken on the shores of the North Sea, in part by those peoples Tacitus called *Ingvaeones* (OE *Ingwine?*)—that is, Old Saxon, Old Frisian, Old English. (See Campbell, *OEG* § 4 and fn. 3).

**Instrumental**    A CASE expressing the notion of means by which something is done (agency). For example, OE *sweord* "sword," *sweordum* "by means of swords."

**Inverted Spelling**    Also *back-spelling*. A kind of "overcorrection," in which a spelling that is in some cases correct is analogically transferred to cases where it is not. Thus when the *gh* in E *light* ceased to represent /x/, the graph was transferred to words with the same vowel which did not originally have /x/, for example, *delight* < F *déliter*.

**Isogloss**    In dialect geography, a line drawn from one point to another along the outer geographical limit of a given feature, usually lexical. Where a number of isoglosses for different features come together into a "bundle," we usually presume the existence of a dialect boundary.

**Isophone**    A phonological isogloss.

**Kernel**    In TRANSFORMATIONAL-GENERATIVE theory, a basic type of underlying structure from which SURFACE STRUCTURES and more complex syntactic types are derived by operations called TRANSFORMATIONS. Kernels are simple, declarative, active, and subject-verb-complement in order.

**Koiné**    A "common language," usually consisting of elements from more than one DIALECT, and spoken (or written) over a larger area than that bounding a single dialect, by speakers or writers of varying dialects, for example, Old English "poetic dialect," New Testament Greek.

**Labial**    Articulated with the lips. The class "labial" usually includes BILABIAL and LABIODENTAL consonants.

**Labialized**    With secondary labial articulation (that is, lip-rounding).

**Labiodental**    Made with the upper teeth against the lower lip, for example [f v].

**Labiovelar**    An INDO-EUROPEAN phoneme type consisting of a VELAR STOP with secondary lip-rounding, for example $*/k^w/$.

**Laryngeal**    Any sound whose articulation is in the larynx; in INDO-EUROPEAN linguistics, a class of phonemes inferred on the basis of Hittite and other evidence to have existed in PROTO-INDO-EUROPEAN and vanished in the attested dialects. See W. P. Lehmann, *Proto-Indo-European phonology* (Austin, 1955), 22–35.

**Lateral**    A consonant formed with the articulators approximated so that air is released on one or both sides of the point of articulation, for example [l].

**Lenis**    Produced with relatively lax musculature in the vocal tract. See FORTIS.

**Liquid**    A type of sound articulated without friction, and capable of being prolonged, and occasionally of serving as a SYLLABIC. The term usually refers mainly to [l] and [r].

**Loan-Blend, Loan-Shift, Loanword**    See discussion in E. Haugen, "The analysis of linguistic borrowing," reprinted in this collection on page 58 ff.

**Low-Level Rule**    A RULE appearing in a grammar at a point relatively close to the output: for example, a MORPHOPHONEMIC rule, which is low-level as compared to a PHRASE-STRUCTURE rule. That is, a rule specifying, for example, the subject-predicate relation is more general, and therefore higher-level, than one specifying, for example, the choice of noun-plural ALLOMORPHS. The higher in a grammar a rule is, the more subsequent rules will act on its output, and the greater the effect it will have on the output of the grammar as a whole.

**Metathesis**    Reversal of the order of two elements, especially sounds, for example, OE *bridd* > MnE *bird*.

**Minimal Pair**    Two forms whose meanings are distinguished by only one segment: thus a diagnostic for determining whether or not a given difference is phonemic. For example, the pair *pin*:*tin* in English establishes the phonemicity of /p/ and /t/ (their capability of signalling difference in meaning), as the other segments /-in/:/-in/ are identical.

**Morph**    Any form, considered apart from its membership in a MORPHEME; any ALLOMORPH.

**Morpheme**    A minimal unit bearing meaning, incapable of being subdivided without loss of identity, for example, {book}, {pre-}, {-ly}.

**Morphophonemic**    (1) Referring to or designating phonetic changes (selection of ALLOMORPHS) of a MORPHEME under certain specifiable conditions. The choice of the allomorph /hawz/ of {house} to precede plural {-s} is an example. A pair of forms like /haws/ ∼ /hawz/ are called *morphophonemic alternants*, as are the allomorphs /s/, /z/, /iz/ of {-s}. A pair of PHONEMES such as /s-z/, or /f-v/ (*wolf* ∼ *wolves*) which is grammatically significant is called a *morphophoneme*. See also ASSIMILATION, DISSIMILATION, SANDHI, UMLAUT. In generative phonology (see Stockwell's "Mirrors" in this volume), a general term for all processes occurring between phonological DEEP STRUCTURE and SURFACE STRUCTURE, for example, the set of ordered rules that assign pronunciation. Some writers, for example, Chomsky and Halle, *Sound Pattern*, Chapter 1, do not use the term because of its association with earlier forms of phonological theory where it was used for a unique level of representation between PHONEME and PHONE.

**Nasal**   A sound produced by lowering the VELUM so that both oral and nasal cavities serve as resonators, for example [m n ŋ].

**Nasalized**   With secondary nasal articulation, for example, F [œ̃] "un."

**Neogrammarian**   A translation of G *Junggrammatiker*, a linguistic school which arose in Germany in the later nineteenth century, and whose basic tenet was the absolute regularity of sound laws (*Ausnahmslösigkeit der Lautgesetze*). They insisted that all phonetic change follows absolutely regular laws, and that apparent "violations" of these laws can be accounted for by more rigorous formulation. See further under Verner's Law.

**Nominative**   The CASE of the subject, subject-complement, or their appositives.

**North Germanic**   The Germanic group containing the Scandinavian languages.

**Oblique**   Any CASE form other than the NOMINATIVE.

**Off-Glide**   A nonsyllabic vowel following a syllabic one, for example [i̯] in the diphthong [ai̯] as in *bite*.

**On-Glide**   A nonsyllabic vowel preceding a syllabic one, for example [i̯] in the diphthong [i̯u] in *beauty*.

**Open Syllable**   A syllable ending in a vowel, for example, *ba-* in *baker*. See CLOSED SYLLABLE.

**Open Vowel**   One produced with relatively low tongue height, for example, "open *o*" [ɔ] vs. "close *o*" [o]. See CLOSE VOWEL.

**Optative**   A verbal mood which expresses the notion of wishing.

**Oxytone**   A word bearing primary stress on its final syllable. See PAROXYTONE, PROPAROXYTONE.

**Palatal**   Pertaining to the hard palate; of vowels, relatively front and/or high, as opposed to VELAR.

**Palatal Diphthongization**   A sound change presumed to have occurred in early OE, where a preceding PALATAL consonant caused the diphthongization of a following vowel: *gǣr* "year" > *gēar*, *gefan* "give" > *giefan*. See Campbell, *Old English grammar* §§ 170–89.

**Palatalization**     The process of moving the articulation of a sound closer to the palate.

**Paradigm**     A set of related forms, usually defining a category such as "noun," "personal pronoun," and so forth; a listing of the inflectional forms of a given stem, for example, *I go, you go, he goes,* and so on.

**Parasite Vowel**     Also SVARABHAKTI vowel. One appearing as an intrusion between two consonants, for example, the *u* that appears in late OE *buruh* "fortress" < *burh*, or the [ə] in substandard MnE [fɪləm] "film." This is a form of EPENTHESIS.

**Paroxytone**     A word bearing PRIMARY STRESS on its penultimate syllable.

**Perfective**     An ASPECT expressing the notion of completed action.

**Phone**     Any sound, considered apart from membership in a PHONEME; any member of a phoneme (here used synonymously with ALLOPHONE).

**Phoneme**     A minimal unit or class of sounds, usually tied together by phonetic similarity, capable of signalling differences in meaning. See ALLOPHONE, MINIMAL PAIR, COMPLEMENTARY DISTRIBUTION. Further, Gleason, *Introduction to descriptive linguistics*, ch. 2–3, 16–21.

**Phonestheme**     A PHONEME or string of phonemes having in a given language an "esthetic" connotation as a unit: for example, /-mp/ suggesting the sound of a "heavy fall" as in *bump, slump, lump,* or /-ap/ suggesting "flaccidity" in *slop, plop, flop.* See Dwight Bollinger, "Word affinities," *Amer. Sp.* 15.62–73, reprinted in *Forms of English: Accent, morpheme, order* (Cambridge, Mass., 1965), 191 ff.

**Phrase-Structure Rule**     Those rules which determine the constituent-structure of a sentence before the operation of TRANSFORMATIONS. For example, S → NP + VP "(a) Sentence may be rewritten as Noun Phrase plus Verb Phrase." See KERNEL, DEEP STRUCTURE, SURFACE STRUCTURE, TRANSFORMATION, TRANSFORMATIONAL-GENERATIVE GRAMMAR.

**Pre-Germanic**     The hypothetical stage between Proto-INDO-EUROPEAN and the emergence of the Germanic dialects.

**Preterit(e)**     A past tense (L *praeteritum* "past").

**Preterit-Present**     A verb type that uses historical STRONG past forms as present-tense forms, and reforms its past tense according to the WEAK conjugation, for example, OE *witan, wāt* "to know, I know," where *wāt* is historically a past-tense form; the verb forms a new past tense by suffixation, *wiste*.

**Primary Stress**     The strongest degree of stress or accentuation, for example, *bláck-* in *bláckberry.*

**Productive**     Capable of being used to create or modify new forms. In MnE the only productive noun-plural MORPHEME is {-s}.

**Proparoxytone**    A word bearing PRIMARY STRESS on its antepenultimate syllable.

**Prothetic**    Of an unhistorical sound prefixed to a word, for example the [w] in MnE [wən] "one" < OE *ān*. Also *prosthetic*.

**Proto-**    A prefix indicating that a given language is a hypothetical reconstruction of an ancestral form.

**Redundancy**    In information theory, "the difference between the theoretical capacity of any code and the average amount of information conveyed" (Gleason, *Introduction to descriptive linguistics*, 379). In other words, the predictability of given items increase redundancy: in English writing, the GRAPHEME ⟨u⟩ has nearly 100% redundancy when preceded by ⟨q⟩. More generally, items whose occurrence is predictable by environment are said to be redundant from the point of view of systemic analysis, for example, the ALLOMORPH /hawz/ is redundant before {-s}. Also if, for example, in a given language all long vowels are also tense, then in describing the nature of the contrast long/short either length or tenseness will be redundant.

**Reflex**    A later form that is the descendant of an earlier one: ME /a/ is a reflex of OE /e/ and /æ/; ME *drīven* "drive" is a reflex of OE *drīfan*.

**Retroflex**    Literally "bent back." Of sounds like most varieties of MnE /r/, where the tip of the tongue is bent back toward the palate.

**Rule**    A statement expressing a general condition observed to hold in a language or a grammar, for example, OE /f/ → [v] in env. V__V "Old English /f/ is realized as [v] when between vowels," or VP → Aux + MV "Verb Phrase may be rewritten as Auxiliary plus Main Verb."

**Rising Diphthong**    One whose stress is on the second element, for example [i̯u] in *beauty*.

**Sandhi**    A form of ASSIMILATION leading to shortened or reduced forms, for example, *he's* from *he is*: also affecting consonants, as in "I'll meet you" pronounced [ail mič̌ə] where [tj] is assimilated to [č̌]. Sandhi may also be internal, as in *Sutton* < *Southdown*.

**Secondary Stress**    The second strongest degree of stress, most common in the second elements of nominal compounds, for example, *-bèrry* in *bláckbèrry*. See PRIMARY STRESS, WEAK STRESS.

**Semivowel**    A sound intermediate in quality between a vowel and a consonant; often the nonsyllabic form of a vowel, for example, [w].

**Sibilant**    A "hissing" FRICATIVE, for example, [s] or [š].

**Smoothing**    Reduction of a DIPHTHONG or TRIPHTHONG to a simple vowel, for example, the change of OE *hēah* "high" to *hēh* in some Anglian DIALECTS.

**Sonorant**    A voiced sound less sonorous than a vowel but more so than a STOP or FRICATIVE, for example, [m n r l].

**Spirant**    See FRICATIVE.

**Stammbaum**    A "family tree" showing the "genealogy" of a group of languages; the theory that assumes the possibility of rigorous demonstrations of such relationships.

**Stop**    A consonant formed by the complete occlusion of the vocal by contact of the articulators without friction; often called *plosive* because of the explosive release of air which may follow articulation: for example, [p b t d].

**Strong Noun (Adjective)**    (a) a Germanic noun or adjective whose stem ended in a vowel, for example, OE *dæg* "day" < *\*daga-z*. (b) The form of an adjective used in some Germanic languages which is marked for GENDER, CASE, and number.

**Strong Verb**    One that forms its past tense and participle by internal vowel change; see ABLAUT.

**Surface Structure**    The structure of a sentence, after TRANSFORMA-TIONS have operated on its DEEP STRUCTURE.

**Svarabhakti**    See PARASITE VOWEL.

**Syllabic**    Any sound serving as the nucleus of a syllable. In English most syllabics are vowels, but some consonants, especially [m n r l], can be syllabic, as in [bætl]] "battle."

**Synchronic**    "Descriptive" in the sense of describing the state of a language at a given point in time, without reference to history. See DIA-CHRONIC.

**Syncopation**    Loss of a medial vowel, for example, OE *sægþ* "he says" < *sægeþ*.

**Synthetic**    Of a language that communicates meaning primarily by means of inflection rather than word order. See ANALYTIC.

**Tautosyllabic**    In the same syllable as.

**Tense (n.)**    A category of verb inflection, or syntactic combination of verbs and other elements, that indicates (roughly) the relation of a verb form to the time at which an action is performed or a state occurs. In TRANS-FORMATIONAL-GENERATIVE grammars, tense is an obligatory aux-iliary to every verb.

**Tense (adj.)**    Referring to the condition of the musculature of the vocal tract, or the energy with which a sound is articulated. In a pair of vowels representing higher and lower in the same range (for example [e] and [ɛ]), the higher is usually tense and the lower lax.

**Token**    An individual instance of a type or class, for example, an individual performance of a PHONEME.

**Tonic**    Bearing chief stress.

**Transformation**    A RULE in a TRANSFORMATIONAL-GENERATIVE grammar that reorders, deletes items from, or otherwise acts on a KERNEL produced by the application of PHRASE-STRUCTURE RULES. For example, a rule which permits us to change the order in which an adverb appears in a sentence: the items on the left-hand side of the double arrow represent the kernel, and the items on the right the transform, or result of application of the rule: NP + VP + Adv ⇒ Adv + NP + VP "(a kernel having the elements) Noun Phrase plus Verb Phrase plus Adverb (in that order) may be transformed into a (nonkernel) string having the elements Adverb plus Noun Phrase plus Verb Phrase (in *that* order)."

**Transformational-Generative Grammar**     A body of linguistic theory (or the grammars produced by such a theory) that holds, among other things, that a grammar is a device which generates the sentences of a language and does not generate nonsentences, and that all grammatical processes can be depicted by means of models consisting in the application of ordered rules. For an introduction to the theory and practice of this body of linguistic thought, see Owen Thomas, *Transformational grammar and the teacher of English* (New York, 1965), and for a more advanced and general treatment, Emmon Bach, *An introduction to transformational grammars*, New York, 1965.

**Triphthong**     A sequence of three vowels of which only one is syllabic, for example, OF *ieu* [i̯ɛu̯].

**Umlaut**     A form of regressive ASSIMILATION, in which a following vowel or SEMIVOWEL affects a preceding stressed vowel. Thus in early Germanic /ō/ followed by /i/ or /j/ became /ȫ/: *\*dōm-jan* "judge" > *dȫman*, later *dēman*. The palatal caused the back-round /ō/ to shift to the corresponding front-round vowel. This particular change is called "*i*-Umlaut" or "*i*-mutation." See Campbell, *Old English grammar*, §§ 190–204.

**Velar**     Articulated with the soft palate (velum), for example [k g]. Of vowels, relatively back, as opposed to PALATAL.

**Velum**     The soft "veil" (L *velum*) of tissue at the back of the hard palate, which when lowered enables the nasal cavity to resonate in sound production. See NASAL.

**Verner's Law**     The discovery by the Danish linguist Karl Verner of the regular causes of certain irregularities in the development of the Germanic consonants which seemed in violation of GRIMM'S LAW. In terms relevant to OE, [s] > [r], [θ] > [ð], [x] > [ɣ] when the stress in PIE and early Germanic stood on the following syllable: thus *wæs/wæron* "was, were" < Gmc *\*was/\*wāsún*, and so forth.

**Vocalization**     The change of a consonant to a vowel or a SEMIVOWEL, for example, that of [l] to [u] in F *haut* "high" < L *altus*.

**Voice**     (a) The vibration of the vocal cords heard in sounds like [b d g] as opposed to voiceless [p t k]; (b) A category of verbal inflection or syntactic collocation that indicates roughly the "direction" of the action in a transitive verb sentence in relation to the subject: *I see him* (active), *I am seen by him* (passive).

**Vulgar Latin**     The spoken language of late Roman antiquity, presumably the source of the modern Romance vernaculars.

**Weak Noun (Adjective)**     A Germanic noun or adjective that had a stem ending in *-n*, for example, OE *guma* "man" < *\*gumon-*. Also the special form of the adjective in some Germanic languages used with a preceding definite article. See also STRONG NOUN.

**Weak Stress**     Also *tertiary*. The weakest degree of stress, as in *-y̆* in *bláckbèrry̆*, which illustrates three degrees. See PRIMARY STRESS, SECONDARY STRESS.

**West Germanic**     The group of Germanic languages descending from and including Old English, Old Frisian, Old High German, and Old Saxon.

# Bibliography

This is selective rather than comprehensive; it lists those books which seem to me of primary interest and importance, or are in some sense "standard." The main aim is orientation to the major works in the vast field covered by this book. For further reading on any particular subject, you may wish to consult some of the standard bibliographies, for example, A. G. Kennedy, *A bibliography of writings on the English language . . .* (New York, 1961). A very good analytical listing may be found in Harold B. Allen, *Linguistics and English linguistics* (Goldentree Bibliographies: New York, 1966), and current listings of relevant books and articles in the annual bibliography of the Modern Language Association. There are also bibliographical listings in many of the standard handbooks, for example, A. Campbell, *Old English grammar*, or K. Brunner, *Altenglische Grammatik . . .*, and F. Holthausen, *Altenglisches etymologisches Wörterbuch*.

The following classificatory symbols are used:

\* of particular importance
\*\* important but difficult
§ particularly good introductory statement

## 1. GENERAL LINGUISTICS: Surveys and Special Topics

§ Abercrombie, David. *Elements of general phonetics* (Chicago, 1967).
§ Bach, Emmon. *An introduction to transformational grammars* (New York, 1965).
\* Bloomfield, Leonard. *Language* (New York, 1933).
\*\* Chomsky, Noam A. *Syntactic structures*[3] (The Hague, 1963).
\*\* Chomsky, Noam A. *Aspects of the theory of syntax* (Cambridge, Mass., 1965).
\*\* Fodor, Jerry A. and Jerrold J. Katz. *The structure of language: Readings in the philosophy of language* (Englewood Cliffs, N.J., 1964).
§ Francis, W. Nelson. *The structure of American English* (New York, 1958).
\* Gelb, I. J. *A study of writing* (Chicago, 1952).
§ Gleason, H. A. *An introduction to descriptive linguistics*[2] (New York, 1961).
\*\* Greenberg, Joseph, ed. *Universals of language*[2] (Cambridge, Mass., 1966).
\*\* Harms, Robert T. *An introduction to phonological theory* (New York, 1968).
Hockett, Charles F. *A course in modern linguistics* (New York, 1958).
§ Jacobs, Roderick A. and Peter S. Rosenbaum. *English transformational grammar* (Waltham, Mass., 1968).
\*\* Jakobson, Roman and Morris Halle. *Fundamentals of language* (The Hague, 1956).
\*\* Jakobson, Roman, Morris Halle, and C. Gunnar M. Fant. *Preliminaries to speech analysis*[6] (Cambridge, Mass., 1965).

§ Jespersen, Otto. *Language: Its nature, development, and origin* (New York, 1964).
Koutsoudas, Andreas. *Writing transformational grammars* (New York, 1966).
Malmberg, Bertil. *Phonetics* (New York, 1963).
** Postal, Paul M. *Aspects of phonological theory* (New York, 1968).
Rauch, Irmengard and Charles T. Scott. *Approaches in linguistic methodology* (Madison, 1967).
§ Sapir, Edward. *Language* (New York, 1921).
** Saussure, Ferdinand de. *A course in general linguistics*, tr. Wade Baskin (New York, 1966).
Stern, Gustaf. *Meaning and change of meaning* (Bloomington, 1965).
§ Sturtevant, E. H. *An introduction to linguistic science* (New Haven, 1947).
§ Thomas, Owen. *Transformational grammar and the teacher of English* (New York, 1965).
Vachek, Josef, ed. *A Prague school reader in linguistics* (Bloomington, 1966).
Vachek, Josef. *The linguistic school of Prague* (Bloomington, 1966).
** Weinreich, Uriel. *Languages in contact* [4] (The Hague, 1966).
Whorf, Benjamin Lee. *Language, thought, and reality*, ed. John B. Carroll (Cambridge, Mass., 1964).

## 2. DIACHRONIC LINGUISTICS

** Hoenigswald, Henry. *Language change and linguistic reconstruction* (Chicago, 1960).
§ Lehmann, Winifred P. *Historical linguistics: An introduction* (New York, 1962).
Meillet, Antoine. *The comparative method in historical linguistics* (Paris, 1966).
Pedersen, Holger. *The discovery of language*, tr. John Webster Spargo (Bloomington, 1962).
Ross, A. S. C. *Etymology* (London, 1965).
Sturtevant, E. H. *Linguistic change* (Chicago, 1961). See also Bloomfield, *Language* Chs. 17–26, Saussure pts. III, V.

## 3. INDO-EUROPEAN LINGUISTICS

Krahe, Hans. *Indogermanische Sprachwissenschaft*, 2 vols. (Berlin, 1962–3).
** Lehmann, Winifred P. *Proto-Indo-European phonology* (Austin, 1955).
* Meillet, Antoine. *Introduction à l'étude comparative des langues Indo-Européennes* (University, Alabama, 1964).
Meillet, Antoine. *The Indo-European dialects* (University, Alabama, 1969).

## 4. GERMANIC LINGUISTICS

Hirt, Hermann. *Handbuch des Urgermanischen* (Heidelberg, 1931).
Krahe, Hans. *Germanische Sprachwissenschaft*, 2 vols. (Berlin, 1963–5).
§ Meillet, Antoine. *Caractères généraux des langues Germaniques* (Paris, 1949).
* Prokosch, Eduard. *A comparative Germanic grammar* (Philadelphia, 1939).

## 5. HISTORIES AND HISTORICAL GRAMMARS OF ENGLISH

Baugh, Albert C. *A history of the English language* [2] (New York, 1957).
§ Bloomfield, Morton W. and Leonard Newmark. *A linguistic introduction to the history of English* (New York, 1963).

Bradley, Henry. *The making of English* (London, 1904).
Brook, G. L. *A history of the English language* (London, 1958).
\* Jespersen, Otto. *A modern English grammar on historical principles*, 7 vols. (Copenhagen, 1909–49).
§ Jespersen, Otto. *The growth and structure of the English language*[9] (Garden City: Anchor Books, n.d.).
\*\* Liuck, Karl. *Historische Grammatik der englischen Sprache*, 2 vols. (Oxford, 1965).
§ Moore, Samuel and Albert L. Marckwardt. *Historical outlines of English sounds and inflections*[2] (Ann Arbor, 1964).
§ Mossé, Fernand. *Esquisse d'une histoire de la langue Anglaise*[2] (Paris, 1958).
§ Pyles, Thomas. *The origins and development of the English language* (New York, 1964).
§ Robertson, Stuart and Fred Cassidy. *The development of modern English*[2] (New York, 1954).
Schlauch, Margaret. *The English language in modern times* (Oxford, 1959).
\* Wyld, Henry Cecil. *A history of modern colloquial English*[3] (London, 1936).
\* Wyld, Henry Cecil. *A short history of English*[3] (London, 1927).

# 6. OLD ENGLISH

Andrew, S. O. *Syntax and style in Old English* (Cambridge, 1940).
\*\* Brunner, Karl. *Altenglische Grammatik (Nach der angelsächsischen Grammatik von Eduard Sievers)*[3] (Tübingen, 1965).
\*\* Campbell, A. *Old English grammar*[2] (Oxford, 1959).
Mossé, Fernand. *Manuel de l'Anglais du moyen âge*: I, *viel Anglais*, 2 vols. (Paris, 1945).
Quirk, Randolph. *The concessive relation in Old English poetry* (New Haven, 1954).
Quirk, Randolph and C. L. Wrenn. *An Old English grammar* (London, 1955).
Shannon, A. *A descriptive syntax of the Parker MS of the Anglo-Saxon Chronicle* (The Hague, 1964).
§ Wright, Joseph and E. M. *Old English grammar*[3] (Oxford, 1925).

# 7. MIDDLE ENGLISH

Brunner, Karl. *Outline of Middle English grammar* (Cambridge, Mass., 1963).
Fisiak, Jacek. *Morphemic structure of Chaucer's English* (University, Alabama, 1965).
\*\* Jordan, Richard. *Handbuch der mittelenglischen Grammatik*: I *Teil, Lautlehre* (Heidelberg, 1934).
\*§ Mossé, Fernand. *Handbook of Middle English* (Baltimore, 1958).
\* Mustanoja, Tauno F. *A Middle English syntax*. I: *Parts of speech* (Helsinki, 1960).
Swieczkowski, W. *Word order patterning in Middle English* (The Hague, 1962).
§ Wright, Joseph and E. M. *An elementary Middle English grammar*[2] (Oxford, 1928).

# 8. EARLY MODERN ENGLISH

Davies, Constance. *English pronunciation from the fifteenth to the eighteenth century* (London, 1934).

** Dobson, E. J. *English pronunciation, 1500–1700*, 2 vols. (Oxford, 1957).
Ekwall, Eilert. *Historische neuenglische Laut- und Formenlehre* (Berlin, 1956).
** Kökeritz, Helge. *Shakespeare's pronunciation* (New Haven, 1953).
Zachrisson, R. E. *The pronunciation of English vowels, 1400–1700* (Göteborg, 1913).

## 9. DICTIONARIES

Clark Hall, J. R. and Herbert D. Merritt. *A concise Anglo–Saxon dictionary*[4] (Cambridge, 1961).
Ekwall, Eilert. *The concise Oxford dictionary of English placenames*[4] (Oxford, 1960).
Holthausen, Ferdinand. *Altenglisches etymologisches Wörtebuch*[2] (Heidelberg, 1963).
Kurath, Hans and S. M. Kuhn. *Middle English dictionary* (Ann Arbor, 1954–).
* *Oxford English dictionary*, 13 vols. plus suppl. (Oxford, 1933).
*Stratmann's Middle English dictionary*, ed. H. Bradley (Oxford, 1891).
* Toller, T. Northcôte. *An Anglo-Saxon dictionary based on the ms collection of . . . Joseph Bosworth* (Oxford, 1882–98; suppl. 1908–20).

# INDEX